RHETORIC AND THE WRITING OF HISTORY, 400–1500

Manchester University Press

❦ HISTORICAL APPROACHES ❦

Series editor
Geoffrey Cubitt

The Historical Approaches series aims to make a distinctive contribution to current debate about the nature of the historical discipline, its theory and practice, and its evolving relationships to other cultural and intellectual fields. The intention of the series is to bridge the gap that sometimes exists between learned monographs on the one hand and beginners' manuals on the other, by offering works that have the clarity of argument and liveliness of style to appeal to a general and student readership, while also prompting thought and debate among practising historians and thinkers about the discipline. Titles in the series will cover a wide variety of fields, and explore them from a range of different angles, but will have in common the aspiration of raising awareness of the issues that are posed by historical studies in today's world, and of the significance of debates about history for a broader understanding of contemporary culture.

Also available:
Geoffrey Cubitt   *History and memory*

RHETORIC AND THE WRITING OF HISTORY, 400–1500

Matthew Kempshall

Manchester University Press
Manchester and New York
distributed in the United States exclusively by Palgrave Macmillan

Copyright © Matthew Kempshall 2011

The right of Matthew Kempshall to be identified as the author of this work has been asserted by him in accordance with the Copyright, Designs and Patents Act 1988.

Published by Manchester University Press
Oxford Road, Manchester M13 9NR, UK
and Room 400, 175 Fifth Avenue, New York, NY 10010, USA
www.manchesteruniversitypress.co.uk

Distributed in the United States exclusively by
Palgrave Macmillan, 175 Fifth Avenue,
New York, NY 10010, USA

Distributed in Canada exclusively by
UBC Press, University of British Columbia, 2029 West Mall,
Vancouver, BC, Canada V6T 1Z2

British Library Cataloguing-in-Publication Data is available

Library of Congress Cataloging-in-Publication Data is available

ISBN 978 0 7190 7031 0 paperback

First published by Manchester University Press in hardback 2011

First published in paperback 2012
First reprinted 2014

The publisher has no responsibility for the persistence or accuracy of URLs for any external or third-party internet websites referred to in this book, and does not guarantee that any content on such websites is, or will remain, accurate or appropriate.

Printed by Bell and Bain Ltd, Glasgow

For Helen

CONTENTS

	Acknowledgments	*page* viii
	Introduction	1
1	History and historiography	34
2	Rhetoric and history	121
3	Invention and narrative	265
4	Verisimilitude and truth	350
5	Historiography and history	428
	Conclusion	536
	Bibliography	552
	Index	601

ACKNOWLEDGMENTS

Intellectual debts and the debts of friendship are, for this book, happily hard to disentangle. This is the case for the Centre for Medieval Studies at the University of York, where a lot of the thinking, reading and talking about this volume took place, and it is especially true of Peter Biller, Natasha Glaisyer, Matthew Townend and Elizabeth Tyler, who, individually and together, offered much of its stimulation and support. More recently, at Oxford, David Leopold, Myfanwy Lloyd and Jane Garnett have sympathised and cajoled in equal measure, each of them providing a source of patience, counsel and perspective for which I will always be grateful. To Kirstin Gwyer I owe all this but also so much more – a debt which, with Zoë Elizabeth, will take at least a lifetime, I hope, to reciprocate. In addition, Marianne Ailes, Katya Andreyev, Henry Bainton, Susan Brigden, Geoff Cubitt, Cliff Davies, David d'Avray, Simon Ditchfield, Mark Edwards, Brian FitzGerald, Roy Flechner, David Ganz, Perry Gauci, György Geréby, Peter Ghosh, Matthew Grimley, Gillian Hargreaves, Kim Kempshall, Sylvia Kempshall, Jörn Leonhard, Simon Loseby, Caroline Mawson, Mark Philpott, Tom Pickles, Gervase Rosser, Lucinda Rumsey, David Rundle, John Sabapathy, Hannah Skoda, George Southcombe, Jeremy Trevett, Martin Whittingham, Mark Whittow and Lucy Wooding have all, at various stages, been kind enough to be, as well as sound, encouraging. So too has a succession of undergraduate and graduate historians at Oxford, mostly at Wadham College, for whom this book was largely written. Other debts are more straightforward and material – to the Arts and Humanities Research Council, to the Fellows of Wadham College, and to the Faculty of Modern History at Oxford, all of whom supported a year's sabbatical leave. Publication of this book, meanwhile, is due primarily to the long-suffering kindness of Emma Brennan at Manchester University Press and of Ralph Footring, freelance production editor. Its dedication to Helen Whittingham, finally, is a small token of my appreciation for the love, support and example she has unfailingly provided to a devoted brother.

Oxford
22 January 2011

INTRODUCTION

What follows has its immediate origins in a series of lectures offered to undergraduate historians at Oxford in the summer of 2004. It should therefore begin with an apology, in the strictest sense of the word, to those of my early-modern and modern colleagues within the History Faculty who thought that an undergraduate paper on the history of historiography should begin in c.1500 because that is when, and I quote, 'proper' historiography really began. Without wishing to be vague, or get into a jam, had those colleagues said that to a classicist, they would have been met with a derisory laugh; having said it to a medievalist, they got eight lectures. In that respect, at least, what follows is the product of both anger and commitment – anger that there would still seem to be stubborn vestiges of the sort of functionalist secularism which used to be claimed as historiographical orthodoxy in Oxford in the mid-1980s by 'Man and the Natural World'; commitment in that it is intended to be useful to a different generation of students who might now welcome a digest of material that can sometimes be off-putting in terms of both the nature and the quantity in which it was originally written. As such, there are, I suspect, many people for whom this book may not, in fact, be necessary – classicists, theologians, philosophers and students of medieval literature – or for whom it may simply serve as a convenient reminder of what they already know. For historians, I hope it will prove instructive and, if not entertain, then at least move them to consider the potential sophistication and complexity with which the writing of history in the Middle Ages was conducted.

To give the scepticism of my early-modern and modern colleagues its due, however, or at least the benefit of the doubt, the prospects for any systematic analysis of historiography in the medieval period might, at first sight, indeed seem poor. First of all, there is the sheer breadth with which the term 'history' appears to have been understood. Worse still, at least from a twentieth-century perspective, is the fact that the writing of history does not seem to have possessed a separate disciplinary status. For those modernists brought up on the need to assert a discrete and distinctive 'scientific' methodology for their subject, such dissolution into other disciplines presents clear problems of both integrity and classification. Finally, there is the by no means isolated impression that writing history in the Middle Ages was an activity which might need excusing, on grounds of youthful immaturity,[1] for example, or, in the case of William of Newburgh, as the result of an enforced leisure produced by illness – the ease of narrating history, William was informed, would refresh his mind without posing the difficulties presented by scrutinising elevated matters or exploring the mysteries of theology.[2] If the study of the past in the Middle Ages was 'never a field in itself, with its own programme and curriculum',[3] and if even committed medievalists have conceded that the writing of history was a 'fringe subject', an auxiliary, subsidiary or 'secondary' activity,[4] then it does at least seem reasonable to ask whether there was, in fact, such a thing as 'medieval historiography' at all.[5]

---

1 William of Malmesbury, *Commentary on Lamentations*, ed. H. Farmer, 'William of Malmesbury's Commentary on Lamentations', *Studia Monastica*, 4 (1962), p. 288; cf. Gerald of Wales, *Descriptio Cambriae*, trans. L. Thorpe, *The Journey Through Wales and the Description of Wales* (Harmondsworth, 1978), pref., pp. 212–13; Gerald of Wales, Letter 3, to William de Montibus, Chancellor of Lincoln, ed. R.B.C. Huygens, trans. B. Dawson, in Y. Lefèvre and R.B.C. Huygens (eds), *Speculum Duorum or a Mirror of Two Men* (Cardiff, 1974), pp. 170–1.
2 William of Newburgh, *The History of English Affairs*, trans. P.G. Walsh and M.J. Kennedy (Warminster 1988), Ep.ded., pp. 26–7.
3 L.B. Mortensen, 'The Glorious Past: Entertainment, Example or History? Levels of Twelfth-Century Historical Culture', *Culture and History*, 13 (1994), p. 66.
4 B. Smalley, *Historians in the Middle Ages* (London, 1974), p. 18; B. Guenée, *Histoire et Culture Historique dans l'Occident Medieval* (Paris, 1980), pp. 27, 35, 44, 45, 52, 91; J. Knape, '*Historia*, Textuality and *Episteme*', in T.M.S. Lehtonen and P. Mehtonen (eds), *Historia: The Concept and Genres in the Middle Ages* (Helsinki, 2000), p. 16.
5 B. Guenée, 'Y a-t-il une Historiographie Médiévale?', *Revue Historique*, 258 (1977), pp. 261–75, reprinted in B. Guenée, *Politique et Histoire au Moyen Age: Receuil d'Articles sur l'Histoire Politique et l'Historiographie Médiévale 1956–1981* (Paris, 1981), pp. 205–19.

It would, of course, be redundant to restate here what has been set out at greater length, and with much greater expertise and authority, in a number of existing scholarly surveys.[6] By the same token, however, it might also be helpful for students tackling such a complex and protean subject were someone to concentrate on a dimension which, it is probably fair to say, has been rather less well covered in the general secondary literature and which, as a result, is rather less widely accessible to modern historians. Of the various influences on medieval historiography, the principles of classical rhetoric constitute one of the most important but also one of the most open to misinterpretation. The chief stumbling block would seem to be a prevailing assumption, amongst some historians at least, that historiography becomes more 'properly' historical as a result of *losing* its connection with rhetoric, that is, once its 'literary' nature is discarded. In part, this process of 'derhetoricisation' is one more legacy of a 'long' eighteenth century, but its influence often still proves pervasive. Even Beryl Smalley, for example, saw fit to observe that 'the history of historiography centres on its struggle to free itself from the sister disciplines of ethics and rhetoric. Sallust welded the three subjects firmly together to the detriment of history. Medieval writers could not possibly have distinguished between moralist, rhetor and historian when they read their Sallust. The emancipation of history has meant the exorcism of his spell'.[7] Discuss and, preferably, disagree. Treating the literary and the moral as layers which have to be removed in order to uncover the 'true' history that lies beneath seems an unhelpful starting point from which to approach works of medieval history, an 'extractive, one-dimensional approach' as

---

6 R.W. Southern, 'Aspects of the European Tradition of Historical Writing I-IV', *Transactions of the Royal Historical Society*, 20-23 (1970-73), reprinted in R. Bartlett (ed.), *History and Historians: Selected Papers of R.W. Southern*, Oxford, 2004); B. Lacroix, *L'Historien au Moyen Âge* (Montreal, 1971); Smalley, *Historians in the Middle Ages*; D. Hay, *Annalists and Historians: Western Historiography from the VIIIth to the XVIIIth Century* (London, 1977), chs 1–5; Guenée, *Histoire et Culture Historique*; F.-J. Schmale, *Funktion und Formen mittelalterlicher Geschichtsschreibung: Eine Einführung* (Darmstadt, 1985). See also *La Storiografia Altomedievale* [Settimane di Studio], 17 (1970). More recently, see H.W. Goetz, *Geschichtsschreibung und Geschichtsbewusstsein im hohen Mittelalter* (Berlin, 1999); D.M. Deliyannis (ed.), *Historiography in the Middle Ages* (Leiden, 2003).
7 B. Smalley, 'Sallust in the Middle Ages', in R.R. Bolgar (ed.), *Classical Influences on European Culture AD 500–1500* (Cambridge, 1971), p. 175.

opposed to one which reconstructs and appreciates what might conveniently be termed their narrative strategies.[8]

Instead of seeking to get round, or get rid of, the role of rhetoric, a much closer and more positive understanding of the instrumental value of language is vitally important in medieval historiography, and for two basic reasons. In the first instance, the principles articulated in the discipline of rhetoric can help us understand the theory behind the writing of history in the Middle Ages, the methodology which is encapsulated in the very texts whose historiographical sophistication some early-modern and modern historians seem so keen to underestimate. If it is, in fact, no exaggeration to say of the medieval period that 'the only available theoretical rules for reconstructing the past lay in the rhetorical manuals',[9] then it would seem only reasonable to have some of these theoretical rules spelled out. Indeed, if it is this methodology, these narrative strategies, which led medieval writers to compose works of 'history' in the way in which they did, then it can also provide some idea of how their works were actually read and understood – what applies to the processes of reading and writing on the part of medieval historians can be extended to their readers and audiences too, in that there were clear expectations which an author needed to satisfy and could exploit. In the second instance, familiarity with the principles of rhetoric can help us appreciate the ways in which medieval historians could conceive of combining the classical traditions of how – and why – one should write about the past with the principles to which they were themselves conditioned through their familiarity with the Bible. Whatever the Enlightenment may

---

8 Southern, 'Aspects of the European Tradition of Historical Writing I – The Classical Tradition from Einhard to Geoffrey of Monmouth', p. 173.
9 R. Ray, 'Rhetorical Scepticism and Verisimilar Narrative in John of Salisbury's *Historia Pontificalis*', in E. Breisach (ed.), *Classical Rhetoric and Medieval Historiography* (Kalamazoo, 1985), p. 69; cf. K. Halm, *Rhetores Latini Minores* (Leipzig, 1863), pp. 588–9. Lucian's *How to Write History* was a discrete work which had been composed, in Greek, in c.166 AD, but its influence on Latin historiography began to be felt only from the mid-fifteenth century onwards (see pages 489–94): Lucian, *How to Write History*, trans. C.D.N. Costa, *Selected Dialogues* (Oxford, 2005), pp. 181–202. For the subsequent genre, and popularity, of the *ars historica* in the late fifteenth and sixteenth centuries, see E. Kessler, *Theoretiker humanistischer Geschichtsschreibung* (Munich, 1971); R. Black, 'The New Laws of History', *Renaissance Studies*, 1 (1987), pp. 126–56; and, now, A. Grafton, *What Was History? The Art of History in Early Modern Europe* (Cambridge, 2007).

have claimed (and, again, it is a long shadow that has been cast), these traditions and principles did not represent mutually exclusive patterns of thinking and writing in the Middle Ages. From Augustine onwards, techniques of classical historiography and scriptural hermeneutics were fundamentally intertwined.

These are, accordingly, the two major themes which this book is intended to introduce – the centrality of certain basic principles of rhetoric to the writing of history, and the relationship between the methodology of non-Christian and Christian historiography. In doing so, this book does not claim to be original, but, then again, as Augustine himself observed, 'it is useful to have several books by several authors, even on the same subjects, differing in style though not in faith, so that the subject-matter itself may reach as many as possible, some in this way, others in that'.[10] As a result, the aim of this book is very modest – to set out a digest of medieval historiographical rhetoric which can then serve as a guide, or even a tool-kit, that students can go away and apply to individual works of history for themselves.

History in its broadest sense was taught and studied in the Middle Ages as part and parcel of the *trivium* – that is, in the course of a basic education in grammar, rhetoric and dialectic, the first three of the seven liberal arts. Such integration meant that historiography was bound up with the very nature of speaking and writing, both at an elementary level and in the curricula of medieval schools and universities. Works of history accordingly represented one specific application of a more general, even all-inclusive, art of language.[11] This is, perhaps, the simplest point which the present study is designed to illustrate but it is also the most important one to establish and from the start. In order to

---

10 Augustine, *De Trinitate*, I.1.5, trans. E. Hill, *The Trinity* (New York, 1991), p. 68, as cited, for example, by Bede, *De Temporum Ratione*, trans. F. Wallis, *The Reckoning of Time* (Liverpool, 1999), p. 4; cf. Augustine, *De Trinitate*, XV, epil. 51, p. 436, quoting Proverbs 10:19 ('when words are many, sin is not absent').
11 J.O. Ward, 'Classical Rhetoric and the Writing of History in Medieval and Renaissance Culture', in F. McGregor and N. Wright (eds), *European History and Its Historians* (Adelaide, 1977), pp. 1–10; N. Partner, 'The New Cornificius – Medieval History and the Artifice of Words', in E. Breisach (ed.), *Classical Rhetoric and Medieval Historiography* (Kalamazoo, 1985), pp. 5–59. The classic starting point for any study of the influence of rhetoric on all forms of medieval writing remains E.R. Curtius, *European Literature and the Latin Middle Ages* (London, 1953).

understand how, and why, history was written in the Middle Ages, it is necessary to understand the principles of composition which would have been hard-wired in anyone who had been brought up with a version of classical rhetoric as the basis for their education. Whilst it would certainly be misleading to maintain that these principles offer a single or exclusive interpretative key, the present book is nonetheless intended to introduce rhetorical material which might reasonably be regarded as fundamental, taken, as it is, from the core texts which distilled that teaching and which were mediated and transmitted, in part or in their entirety, throughout the Middle Ages – first and foremost Cicero's *De Inventione* (*c*.89 BC) and the pseudo-Ciceronian *Rhetorica ad Herennium* (*c*.86–82 BC), but also Cicero's *De Oratore* (*c*.55 BC) and Quintilian's *Institutio Oratoria* (*c*.86–95 AD).[12]

So what *is* rhetoric? Perhaps the most frequently encountered response, at least amongst modernists, is the one-word answer 'style', an approach which accordingly tends to concentrate on the formal identification of tropes (defined as the deliberate change of the sense of a word or phrase from its usual signification to another) and figures of speech (defined as a change in language from its ordinary and simple form).[13] The practical effect of such

---

12 Cicero, *De Inventione*, trans. H.M. Hubbell, *On Invention* (Loeb, 1949); *Rhetorica ad Herennium*, trans. H. Caplan (Loeb, 1954); Cicero, *De Oratore*, trans. E. Sutton and H. Rackham (Loeb, 1948); Quintilian, *Institutio Oratoria*, trans. H.E. Butler (Loeb, 1920–22). For the survival and transmission of all these works, see L.D. Reynolds (ed.), *Texts and Transmission: A Survey of the Latin Classics* (Oxford, 1983), pp. 98–112, 332–4. For Quintilian, see also P.S. Boskoff, 'Quintilian in the Late Middle Ages', *Speculum*, 27 (1952), pp. 71–8; Quintilian, *Institutio Oratoria*, ed. M. Winterbottom (2 vols, Oxford, 1970), vol. I, pp. v–xv; M. Winterbottom, *Problems in Quintilian* (BICS Supplement 25, 1970), pp. 3–7; A. Mollard, 'La Diffusion de l'*Institution Oratoire* au XIIe Siècle', *Moyen Âge*, 44 (1934), pp. 161–75, and *Moyen Âge*, 45 (1935), pp. 1–9. For Cicero, *De Oratore*, see also A.S. Wilkins (ed.), *Ciceronis De Oratore Liber I* (3rd edn, Oxford, 1895), pp. 64–71.
13 *Rhetorica ad Herennium*, IV.13.18, p. 275, IV.31.42, p. 333; Quintilian, *Institutio Oratoria*, VIII.6.1–3, p. 301–3. For the distinction between trope and *figura* ('schema' in Greek), see Quintilian, *Institutio Oratoria*, IX.1.1–14, pp. 349–55; cf. John of Salisbury, *Metalogicon*, trans. D.D. McGarry, *The Metalogicon of John of Salisbury: A Twelfth-Century Defense of the Verbal and Logical Arts of the Trivium* (Berkeley, 1955), I.18 and I.19, pp. 54 and 56. For the use of tropes and figures of speech drawn from book IV of the *Rhetorica ad Herennium*, see E. Faral, *Les Arts Poétiques du XIIe et du XIIIe Siècles: Recherches et Documents sur la Technique Littéraire du Moyen Age* (Paris, 1924), pp. 52–4; for their inclusion within manuals of grammar, see, for example, Donatus, *Ars Maior*, ed. L. Holtz, *Donat et la Tradition*

an emphasis on style is that modern applications of the study of rhetoric to medieval historiography are often reduced to protracted bouts of trope-spotting. The list is as long as it is familiar: *praeteritio* or *occultatio*, that is, stating you are not going to say something, or have no knowledge of it, and yet, in the process, revealing precisely what you were ostensibly keeping hidden;[14] *synecdoche* or *intellectio*, that is, talking about a whole by means of one of its parts, or a part by means of its whole;[15] *paradyastole* or *distinctio*, that is, redescribing a virtue as a vice (or vice versa), classifying, say, a particular act as brave rather than rash, or rash rather than brave;[16] word-play or *adnominatio*, which turns on a slight change or lengthening or transposition of the letters in a word;[17] and correction or *correctio*, which retracts what has been said and replaces it with something

---

de l'Enseignement Grammatical: Étude sur l'Ars Donati et sa Diffusion (IVe–IXe Siècle) et Edition Critique (Paris, 1981), pp. 603–74; Priscian, Institutiones Grammaticarum, ed. M. Hertz, in H. Keil (ed.), Grammatici Latini (Leipzig, 1855–59), vols II, III.
14 For example, Rhetorica ad Herennium, IV.27.37, p. 321; cf. Wipo, Deeds of Conrad, trans. T.E. Mommsen and K.F. Morrison, in Imperial Lives and Letters of the Eleventh Century (New York, 1962; rev. edn 2000), VI, p. 72.
15 For example, Rhetorica ad Herennium, IV.33.44–5, p. 341; cf. Quintilian, Institutio Oratoria, VIII.6.19–22, pp. 311–13; Liutprand of Cremona, Antapodosis, trans. F.A. Wright, The Works of Liutprand of Cremona (London, 1930), I.1, p. 33, IV.11, p. 150, IV.28, p. 166, VI.8, p. 210.
16 For example, Rhetorica ad Herennium, III.3.6, pp. 167–9, IV.25.35, p. 317; cf. Quintilian, Institutio Oratoria, IX.3.65, p. 483; Vergil, Aeneid, trans. H.R. Fairclough, rev. G.P. Goold (Loeb, 2000), IV.172, p. 407; Liutprand of Cremona, Relatio de Legatione Constantinopolitana, trans. F.A. Wright (London, 1930), XXVIII, p. 251; Thietmar of Merseburg, Chronicon, trans. D.A. Warner, Ottonian Germany (Manchester, 2001), VI.52, p. 273; anon., Life of the Emperor Henry IV, trans. T.E. Mommsen and K.F. Morrison, Imperial Lives and Letters of the Eleventh Century (New York, 1962; rev. edn, 2000), pp. 125–6; William of Malmesbury, Gesta Regum Anglorum, ed. and trans. R.A.B. Mynors, R.M. Thomson and M. Winterbottom, The History of the English Kings (Oxford, 1999), IV.312, p. 555; Walter Map, De Nugis Curialium, ed. and trans. M.L.R. James, rev. C.N.L. Brooke and R.A.B. Mynors (Oxford, 1983), IV.13, p. 373. For the proximity of *constantia* and *pertinacia* see, for example, Valerius Maximus, Facta et Dicta Memorabilia, trans. D.R. Shackleton Bailey, Memorable Doings and Sayings (Loeb, 2000), III.8, p. 329; for cruelty/justice and negligence/mercy, see Moralium Dogma Philosophorum, ed. J. Holmberg, Das Moralium Dogma Philosophorum des Guillaume de Conches, lateinisch, altfranzösisch und mittelniederfränkisch (Uppsala, 1929), p. 10; for *simplicitas* and *ignavia*, see page 323, note 233; cf. Gregory the Great, Moralia in Job, trans. J. Bliss (Oxford, 1843–50), XXIII.11.19, p. 18.
17 For example, Rhetorica ad Herennium IV.21.29, p. 305; cf. Henry of Huntingdon, Historia Anglorum, ed. and trans. D. Greenway, History of the English (Oxford, 1996), VII.21, p. 447; Gerald of Wales, Expugnatio Hibernica, ed. and trans. A.B.

that seems more suitable, the change in words making the thing that is being described all the more striking by drawing attention to the fact that the original phrasing used to denote it was insufficient.[18] It would certainly be possible to go through works of classical and medieval historiography examining each one of these figures of speech in action. However, whilst rhetoric can, indeed, be approached profitably from a definition which focuses exclusively on style and ornamentation, it is also much more fundamental.

According to a second, and again commonly-encountered, definition of the term, on this occasion discussed directly by both Cicero and Quintilian, rhetoric can also be summarised as the power of persuasion (*vis persuadendi*). On this reckoning, it is the duty or function (*officium*) of an orator to speak appositely in order to persuade, and it is the goal (*finis*) of rhetoric to persuade by speech.[19] Both Cicero and Quintilian, however, are at pains to suggest that such a classification will still fall short of what is required for a complete definition of rhetoric. In their opinion, it would be much better were rhetoric to be defined as the art or science of *good* speech (*ars bene dicendi, scientia bene dicendi*), because, if grammar is the art of speaking correctly (*recte*), then rhetoric is the art of speaking well (*bene*). Translated into Latin as 'oratory' (*oratoria*), they argued, the Greek term 'rhetoric' is nothing other than eloquence which has been subjected to the rules of an art (*eloquentia artificiosa*).[20] It is the broad scope envisioned by Cicero and Quintilian which makes any exclusively stylistic modern definition of rhetoric particularly limiting. It also gives the lie to those people who want to claim that literary 'effects' simply have to be identified and then stripped away from a work of history in order to reveal a core of genuine historical 'evidence' underneath.

Defined as the art or science of speaking well, rhetoric was understood to perform three basic functions – to teach (*docere*),

---

Scott and F.X. Martin, *The Conquest of Ireland* (Dublin, 1978), II.11, p.161 (*malitia/militia; fraus/laus; eminentia/existentia; festivitas/fecunditas; verbositas/veritas*).
18   For example, *Rhetorica ad Herennium*, IV.26.36, pp. 319–21.
19   Cicero, *De Inventione*, I.5.6, p. 15; Cicero, *De Oratore* I.31.138, p. 97; Quintilian, *Institutio Oratoria*, II.15.3–6, pp. 301–3, VII.3.6, pp. 85–7; cf. Boethius, *De Topicis Differentiis*, trans. E. Stump (Ithaca, 1978), IV, p. 83; John of Salisbury, *Metalogicon*, I.24, p. 67.
20   Cicero, *De Inventione*, I.5.6, pp. 13–15; Cicero, *De Oratore*, I.18.83, p. 59; Quintilian, *Institutio Oratoria*, II.14.1–4, pp. 297–9, XI.1.11, p. 161.

to move (*movere*) and to please (*delectare*). The orator must always have these three fundamental aims in mind and different methods are necessary in order to attain each one.[21] Rhetoric teaches truths and, as such, it is connected to dialectic – it is instructive or didactic, it puts forward arguments, narrative and proofs. Rhetoric carries still greater weight, however, when it serves to move emotions rather than simply instruct the intellect and, as a result, its application was designed to prompt an audience to action, and not just to convince their faculty of reason. Indeed, it is in the handling of an audience's emotions that the power of rhetoric was thought to be displayed to its best effect – proofs might make it clear to a judge that one argument is better than another, but appeals to the emotions could make that judge actually *wish* this to be true.[22] Cicero recasts the same point in the form of a question: 'Who more passionately than the orator can encourage to virtuous conduct, or more zealously reclaim from vice? Who can more austerely censure the wicked or more gracefully praise men of worth?'[23] Rhetoric, finally, has to be pleasurable and entertaining; it must be enjoyable and appealing; the last thing it should be is dull.

It is in the light of this much fuller definition of rhetoric – as the art or science of speaking well with a threefold goal of instruction, movement and pleasure – that, according to Cicero, eloquence deals with everything which can be the subject of discussion (*disceptatio*) amongst humans.[24] In his opinion, rhetoric represents nothing less than the essence of human communication, in that it shapes the way in which *all* individuals speak and write. Rather than being a purely pragmatic or technical skill, rhetoric is therefore a profoundly philosophical and ethical discipline. Likewise, according to Quintilian, the subject-matter of rhetoric is practically

---

21 Quintilian, *Institutio Oratoria*, III.5.2, p. 397, VIII.praef.7, p. 181; cf. Cicero, *De Optimo Genere Oratorum*, trans. H.M. Hubbell (Loeb, 1949), I.3, p. 357; Boethius, *De Topicis Differentiis*, IV, pp. 83, 87.
22 Cicero, *De Oratore*, I.12.53, p. 41, I.14.60, p. 45, I.46.202, p. 143 (see also page 243); Quintilian, *Institutio Oratoria*, IV.5.6, pp. 139–41, V.praef.1, p. 155, VI.2.2–7, pp. 417–21.
23 Cicero, *De Oratore*, II.9.35, p. 223 (see also page 242); cf. Valerius Maximus, *Facta et Dicta Memorabilia*, VIII.9, p. 245.
24 Cicero, *De Oratore*, I.6.20, p. 17, II.2.5, p. 201, III.14.54, p. 43, III.16.60–19.73, pp. 49–59; cf. Boethius, *De Topicis Differentiis*, IV, p. 81.

unlimited because it deals with everything in human life which is set before it as a subject of speech. The fundamental premise of Quintilian's own treatise on the education of an orator was therefore the equivalence of the complete or perfect orator with the wise and morally virtuous individual (*vir bonus dicendi peritus*) and, as a result, Quintilian framed his analysis of the technical aspects of rhetoric with an account of the comprehensive scope of the material which the orator must master as part of an attempt to reunite the study of rhetoric with subjects which, in his opinion, had been wrongly appropriated by philosophy as its exclusive domain.[25]

It is this breadth of scope which was subsequently underlined in the handbooks of rhetoric which were produced in late antiquity by writers such as Julius Victor and Fortunatianus and which were then propagated for the Middle Ages from the fifth to the ninth centuries by Martianus Capella, Cassiodorus, Isidore, Alcuin and Hrabanus Maurus. According to Julius Victor, for example, the duty of the orator is to concern himself with 'civil affairs' (*civilia negotia*), defined as those matters on which everyone with any intellectual capacity can speak and judge. These subjects cover general opinion, laws or conduct (*mores*) – anything, in fact, which is open to accusation, defence, or simply debate over its equity and utility (*de aequo et utili*).[26] The foundation of eloquence, as indeed of everything else, is therefore wisdom (*sapientia*) and, on this basis, rhetoric can be applied to people, events or texts, and it can range all the way from universal abstract propositions to specific cases.[27] Fortunatianus makes the same point in the form of a question-and-answer dialogue. 'What is rhetoric?', he asks. 'The knowledge of speaking well', comes the reply. 'What is an orator?', he continues. 'The good man skilled in speaking. What is the function of the orator? To speak well on civil questions. To what end? In order to be persuasive, in so far as circumstances and audience allow, in civil questions. What are civil questions? Those which can fall within the common capacity of the mind, that is, those which every person can understand as an inquiry

---

25 Quintilian, *Institutio Oratoria*, II.21.4–6, pp. 357–9, II.21.20, p. 365, VII. praef.6, p. 179.
26 Julius Victor, *Ars Rhetorica*, ed. R. Giomini and M.S. Celentano (Leipzig, 1980), p. 1; cf. *ibid.*, pp. 24–5; Quintilian, *Institutio Oratoria*, V.14.28–29, pp. 312–13.
27 Julius Victor, *Ars Rhetorica*, p. 93.

into what is equitable and good'.[28] This was the inclusive definition of rhetoric which accordingly found its way into educational handbooks and thereby helped to provide the basic and essential framework for the integration of classical learning into the monastic schools of the Middle Ages. The art of rhetoric is the science of speaking well on 'civil issues', where *civiles quaestiones* are understood to refer to questions which everyone can comprehend concerning equity and goodness (*de aequo et bono*).[29] These *civiles quaestiones* are 'open to instruction' (*docti quaestiones*), in that they are questions which are capable of being grasped by everyone through the natural capacity of their minds.[30]

Rhetoric is as pervasive in medieval writing, then, as it is all-encompassing, as much a habit of mind as a defined programme of study.[31] Classical rhetoric, however, had been a notoriously difficult subject to define with reference to other linguistic disciplines.[32] Medieval rhetoric was no different. Concentrating on material drawn from Cicero and Quintilian risks giving the

---

28 Fortunatianus, *Ars Rhetorica*, trans. J.M. Miller, in J.M. Miller, M.H. Prosser and T.W. Benson (eds), *Readings in Medieval Rhetoric* (Bloomington, 1973), I, pp. 25–6.
29 Cassiodorus, *Institutiones*, trans. J.W. Halporn, *Institutions of Divine and Secular Learning* (Liverpool, 2004), II.praef., p. 173, II.2.1, pp. 178–9. The phrase *de aequo et bono* was also used by Isidore of Seville, *Etymologiae*, ed. and trans. P.K. Marshall, *Etymologies* (Paris, 1983), II.1.1, p. 22; cf. pseudo-Augustine, *De Rhetorica*, trans. J.M. Miller, in J.M. Miller, M.H. Prosser and T.W. Benson (eds), *Readings in Medieval Rhetoric* (Bloomington, 1973), pp. 9–10; Boethius, *An Overview of the Structure of Rhetoric*, trans. J.M. Miller, in J.M. Miller, M.H. Prosser and T.W. Benson (eds), *Readings in Medieval Rhetoric* (Bloomington, 1973), p. 71; Boethius, *De Topicis Differentiis*, IV, pp. 81, 87; Hrabanus Maurus, *De Clericorum Institutione*, ed. D. Zimpel (Frankfurt, 1996), III.19, p. 470; Vincent of Beauvais, *Speculum Historiale* I.55 (Douai, 1624); reprinted Graz, 1964–65), p. 22.
30 Alcuin, *Disputatio de Rhetorica et de Virtutibus*, ed. and trans. W.S. Howell, *The Rhetoric of Alcuin and Charlemagne* (Princeton, 1941), lines 57–8, p. 68; cf. Marius Victorinus, *Explanatio in Rhetoricam Ciceronis*, ed. K. Halm, *Rhetores Latini Minores* (Leipzig, 1863), p. 156: 'the orator uses full and perfect eloquence in public and private matters' (*orator est qui in causis privatis ac publicis plena et perfecta utitur eloquentia*), a definition subsequently repeated by, for example, Dominicus Gundissalinus, *De Divisione Philosophiae*, ed. A. Fidora and D. Werner, *Über die Einteilung der Philosophie* (Freiburg, 2007), p. 140.
31 R. McKeon, 'Rhetoric in the Middle Ages', *Speculum*, 17 (1942), p. 32; R. Morse, *Truth and Convention in the Middle Ages: Rhetoric, Representation and Reality* (Cambridge, 1991), p. 9; M. Camargo, 'Defining Medieval Rhetoric', in C.J. Mews, C.J. Nederman and R.M. Thomson (eds), *Rhetoric and Renewal in the Latin West 1100–1540* (Turnhout, 2003), pp. 29–31.
32 See, most recently, J. Walker, *Rhetoric and Poetics in Antiquity* (Oxford, 2000).

impression that the study of rhetoric in the Middle Ages was simply a case of the recovery and transmission of a single 'classical' mode of analysis and, as such, that rhetoric constituted a more or less static art and discipline throughout most of this period. Naturally, the picture is much more complex. Medieval rhetoric had a history all of its own.[33] The works of Cicero and Quintilian had themselves been given distinctive readings even in late antiquity, by writers such as Julius Victor and Fortunatianus, and it is as much the influence of *their* interpretations as the influence of 'classical' rhetoric which can be traced through the digests that were subsequently provided by encyclopaedists such as Martianus Capella,[34] Cassiodorus[35] and Isidore of Seville.[36] Cassiodorus, for example, pointed out that Cicero and Quintilian had translated the fundamental principles of rhetoric from Greek into Latin in such detail and with such variety that it was easier to marvel at the subject than to grasp it.

Taken as a whole, therefore, this process of deliberate and self-conscious mediation exerted a profound impact on the study and teaching of rhetoric in the Middle Ages and, as a result, often served as a prism through which many rhetorical precepts from Cicero and Quintilian were refracted. The same process is apparent in the eighth century, through the works of Bede and Alcuin,[37] and in the eleventh century, with the teaching of Byrhtferth of Ramsey, Notker Labeo, Anselm of Besate and Onulf

---

33 J.J. Murphy, *Rhetoric in the Middle Ages: A History of Rhetorical Theory from St. Augustine to the Renaissance* (Berkeley, 1974); T.M. Conley, *Rhetoric in the European Tradition* (Chicago, 1994), ch. 4; G.A. Kennedy, *Classical Rhetoric and Its Christian and Secular Tradition from Ancient to Modern Times* (2nd edn, Chapel Hill, 1999), chs 7–9.
34 Martianus Capella, *The Marriage of Philology and Mercury*, trans. W.H. Stahl, R. Johnson and E.L. Burge, *Martianus Capella and the Seven Liberal Arts* (New York 1977), V, pp. 155–214.
35 Cassiodorus, *Institutiones*, II.2, pp. 178–88.
36 Isidore, *Etymologiae*, II, pp. 22–169.
37 Bede, *De Schematibus et Tropis*, trans. G.H. Tannenhaus, *Concerning Figures and Tropes*, in J.M. Miller, M.H. Prosser and T.W. Benson (eds), *Readings in Medieval Rhetoric* (Bloomington, 1973), pp. 96–122; Alcuin, *Disputatio de Rhetorica et de Virtutibus*. For Bede, see C.V. Franklin, 'Grammar and Exegesis – Bede's *Liber de Schematibus et Tropis*', in C.D. Lanham (ed.), *Latin Grammar and Rhetoric: From Classical Theory to Medieval Practice* (London, 2002), pp. 63–91; see also, however, the reservations made in G. Knappe, 'Classical Rhetoric in Anglo-Saxon England', *Anglo Saxon England*, 27 (1998), pp. 5–29.

of Speyer.[38] This (perfectly natural and predictable) process of continuity and change becomes particularly important in the twelfth century, when a series of authors quite self-consciously set themselves the task of synthesising a 'new' rhetoric in order to reflect the shifting concerns and emphases of medieval society.[39] The results can be seen in works such as Hugh of St Victor's *Didascalicon* (*c*.1127–33),[40] John of Salisbury's *Metalogicon* (1159),[41] Matthew of Vendôme's *Ars Versificatoria* (before 1175),[42] Alan of Lille's *Anticlaudianus* (*c*.1181–84),[43] Geoffrey of Vinsauf's *Poetria Nova* (*c*.1208–13)[44] and John of Garland's *Parisiana Poetria* (*c*.1230).[45] The mid to late thirteenth century, meanwhile, saw the translation into Latin of Aristotle's *Rhetoric* and *Poetics*, texts which introduced still further challenges to the study of rhetoric and, in both cases, brought with them a body of interpretation from the Arab world in the form of commentary by Alfarabi and Averroes.[46] The thirteenth century also witnessed the translation

---

38 Byrhtferth of Ramsey, *Enchiridion*, ed. P.S. Baker and M. Lapidge (Oxford, 1995), III.2, pp. 163–9; S. Jaffe, 'Antiquity and Innovation in Notker's *Nova Rhetorica*: The Doctrine of Invention', *Rhetorica*, 3 (1985), pp. 165–81; B.S. Bennett, 'The Significance of the *Rhetorimachia* of Anselm of Besate to the History of Rhetoric', *Rhetorica*, 5 (1987), pp. 231–50; J. Linde, 'Die *Rethorici Colores* des Magisters Onulf von Speyer', *Mittellateinisches Jahrbuch*, 40 (2005), pp. 333–81.
39 See for example J. Bliese, 'The Study of Rhetoric in the Twelfth Century', *Quarterly Journal of Speech*, 63 (1977), pp. 364–83.
40 Hugh of St Victor, *Didascalicon*, trans. J. Taylor, *The Didascalicon of Hugh of St Victor: A Medieval Guide to the Arts* (New York, 1961).
41 John of Salisbury, *Metalogicon*, trans. D.D. McGarry, *The Metalogicon of John of Salisbury: A Twelfth-Century Defense of the Verbal and Logical Arts of the Trivium* (Berkeley, 1955).
42 Matthew of Vendôme, *Ars Versificatoria*, trans. R. Parr (Milwaukee, 1981).
43 Alan of Lille, *Anticlaudianus*, trans. J.J. Sheridan, *Anticlaudianus or the Good and Perfect Man* (Toronto, 1973).
44 Geoffrey of Vinsauf, *Poetria Nova*, ed. and trans. E. Gallo, *The Poetria Nova and Its Sources in Early Rhetorical Doctrine* (The Hague, 1971). For the prose version, *Documentum de Modo et Arte Dictandi et Versificandi*, see ed. E. Faral, *Les Arts Poétiques du XIIe et du XIIIe Siècles: Recherches et Documents sur la Technique Littéraire du Moyen Age* (Paris, 1924), pp. 265–320; trans. R. Parr, *Instruction in the Method and Art of Speaking and Versifying* (Milwaukee, 1968). More generally, see M. Camargo, 'Toward a Comprehensive Art of Written Discourse – Geoffrey of Vinsauf and the *Ars Dictaminis*', *Rhetorica*, 6 (1988), pp. 167–94.
45 John of Garland, *Parisiana Poetria*, ed. and trans. T. Lawler, *The Parisiana Poetria of John of Garland* (New Haven, 1974).
46 Aristotle, *On Rhetoric*, trans. G.A. Kennedy (Oxford, 1991); Aristotle, *Poetics*, trans. M.E. Hubbard, *Classical Literary Criticism* (rev. edn, Oxford, 1989), pp. 51–90.

of *De Inventione* and the *Rhetorica ad Herennium* into vernacular versions.[47] The fourteenth and fifteenth centuries, finally, saw the still broader development of a 'classical' repertoire with the rediscovery, in 1416, of a complete version of Quintilian and, in 1421, of a much improved text of *De Oratore*, together with an entirely new text, Cicero's *Brutus*.[48]

Transformations in how the principles of rhetoric were understood, taught and applied in the Middle Ages were a natural concomitant of much broader transformations in the social and political contexts in which the language of Cicero and Quintilian was being deployed. The traditional Roman contexts of speech-making, in law courts and in political assemblies, were replaced by new arenas for delivering legal and political counsel, but they were also greatly expanded and adapted, to comprise the writing of letters, the delivery of sermons and the composition of verse. Medieval rhetoric, in this sense, developed distinct forms of its own, for each of which corresponding guidelines had to be set down – respectively, the *ars dictaminis*, the *ars praedicandi* and the *ars poetriae* (or *ars versificandi*).[49] Depending on the purpose and the circumstances for which rhetoric was being deployed, moreover, or the level at which it was being taught, different aspects of the classical rhetorical tradition could be afforded greater or lesser prominence by individual writers – the logical emphasis of Aristotle's *Topics*, which was mediated through Cicero and Boethius, the poetic emphasis of Horace's *Ars Poetica*, or the basic compositional practice of schoolroom exercises

---

47 Murphy, *Rhetoric in the Middle Ages*, pp. 113–14; cf. Brunetto Latini, *Rettorica*, ed. F. Maggini (Florence, 1915); P.F. Gehl, 'Preachers, Teachers and Translators – The Social Meaning of Language Study in Trecento Tuscany', *Viator*, 25 (1994), pp. 312–20; V. Cox, 'Ciceronian Rhetoric in Italy 1260–1350', *Rhetorica*, 17 (1999), pp. 239–88; V. Cox, 'Ciceronian Rhetorical Theory in the *Volgare* – A Fourteenth-Century Text and Its Fifteenth-Century Readers', in C.J. Mews, C.J. Nederman and R.M. Thomson (eds), *Rhetoric and Renewal in the Latin West 1100–1540* (Turnhout, 2003), pp. 201–25.
48 Cicero, *Brutus*, trans. G.L. Hendrickson (Loeb, 1962).
49 J.J. Murphy (ed.), *Three Medieval Rhetorical Arts* (Berkeley, 1971); cf. M. Camargo, *Ars Dictaminis, Ars Dictandi* (Typologie des Sources 60, Turnhout, 1991); M.G. Briscoe, *Artes Praedicandi* (Typologie des Sources 61, Turnhout, 1992); D. Kelly, *The Arts of Poetry and Prose* (Typologie des Sources 59, Turnhout, 1991). See also H. Caplan, 'Classical Rhetoric and the Medieval Theory of Preaching', *Classical Philology*, 28 (1933), pp. 73–96.

(*praeexercitamina, progymnasmata*), be they moral essays (*chriae*), character descriptions (*ethologiae*) or judicial *controversiae* and deliberative *suasoriae* that were modelled on Seneca.[50] In part, this variation in substance reflected pedagogic practice, a 'grammaticisation' of rhetoric which matched its increasing application to written, rather than oral, forms of communication and which saw the formal teaching of rhetoric increasingly subsumed within the teaching of grammar.[51] In part, these changes reflected the incorporation of rhetoric into higher levels of learning where, as one of the seven liberal arts, it became the subject, not just of elementary education, but also of the academic curriculum in schools and universities and, as such, was subsumed within the teaching of dialectic.

The speculative tradition in classical rhetoric can be traced in the Middle Ages, first, in the scholarly commentaries which, from the twelfth century (and following the precedent set by Marius Victorinus in the fourth century), were written on the texts of both *De Inventione* and the *Rhetorica ad Herennium*.[52] It then continued into the thirteenth century in the form of academic disputes over the position of rhetoric within the *trivium*, that is, over its status relative to the study of both grammar and dialectic. A work

---

50 Murphy, *Rhetoric in the Middle Ages*, p. 42; cf. Seneca the Elder, *Declamationes* [*Controversiae* and *Suasoriae*], ed. and trans. M. Winterbottom and W.C. Wright (Loeb, 1974). For Seneca's distinction between declamation and historiography, see *Suasoriae*, VI.16, pp. 577–9, VI.21–22, p. 585.

51 According to Isidore, *Etymologiae*, II.1.2, p. 22, 'rhetoric is joined to the art of grammar' (*coniuncta est autem grammaticae arti rhetorica*); cf. Murphy, *Rhetoric in the Middle Ages*, pp. 138–45; M. Irvine, *The Making of Textual Culture: Grammatica and Literary Theory 350–1100* (Cambridge, 1994); C.D. Lanham (ed.), *Latin Grammar and Rhetoric: From Classical Theory to Medieval Practice* (London, 2002).

52 Marius Victorinus, *Explanatio in Rhetoricam Ciceronis*; M. Dickey, 'Some Commentaries on the *De Inventione* and *Ad Herennium* of the Eleventh and Early Twelfth Centuries', *Medieval and Renaissance Studies*, 6 (1968), pp. 1–41; J.O. Ward, 'From Antiquity to the Renaissance – Glosses and Commentaries on Cicero's *Rhetorica*', in J.J. Murphy (ed.), *Medieval Eloquence* (Berkeley, 1978), pp. 25–67; K.M. Fredborg, 'Twelfth-Century Ciceronian Rhetoric – Its Doctrinal Development and Influences', in B. Vickers (ed.), *Rhetoric Revalued* (New York, 1982), pp. 87–97; K.M. Fredborg, *The Latin Rhetorical Commentaries by Thierry of Chartres* (Toronto, 1988); J.O. Ward, *Ciceronian Rhetoric in Treatise, Scholion and Commentary* (Typologie des Sources 58, Turnhout, 1995); J.O. Ward and V. Cox (eds), *The Rhetoric of Cicero in Its Medieval and Renaissance Commentary Tradition* (Leiden, 2006).

such as John of Salisbury's *Metalogicon*, for example, reveals the very real disagreements which could arise over whether rhetoric should be regarded as one of three complementary subjects, each one of which contributed to an overarching study of language and words ('logic'), or as a discipline which needed to justify itself against the encroachments of grammar and dialectic, and even against the crude charge of redundancy.[53] The boundaries between the three subjects of the *trivium* were as permeable as they were shifting. A subsequent decline in the formal teaching of rhetoric at the university in Paris in the thirteenth century was given additional impetus by the opening sentence to Aristotle's *Rhetoric* ('rhetoric is the counterpart of dialectic'), an observation which became instant grist to the mill of those philosophers who wanted to make the subject firmly subordinate to their own discipline.[54] It was thus a very similar fight to John of Salisbury's which was taken up by Petrarch in the fourteenth century, when he argued that rhetoric needed to be reunited with philosophy, eloquence with wisdom, if truth was to be rescued from becoming an exclusively intellectual exercise in arid semantic logic.[55]

The history of 'medieval' rhetoric, in short, has a dynamic all of its own, from the eighth to the fourteenth century, in which

---

53 Cf. Henry of Andelys, *Psychomachia*, ed. and trans. L.J. Paetow, *Two Medieval Satires on the University of Paris: La Bataille des VII Ars of Henri d'Andeli and the Morale Scolarium of John of Garland* (Berkeley, 1914), pp. 37–60.
54 Aristotle, *Rhetoric*, I.1.1 p. 159. For the apparent etiolation of the teaching of Ciceronian rhetoric within the faculty of arts at Paris, see J.J. Murphy, 'The Scholastic Condemnation of Rhetoric in the Commentary of Giles of Rome on the *Rhetoric* of Aristotle', in *Arts Libéraux et Philosophie au Moyen Age* (Montreal, 1969), pp. 833–41; cf. P.O. Lewry, 'Rhetoric at Paris and Oxford in the Mid-Thirteenth Century', *Rhetorica*, 1 (1983), pp.45–63; K.M. Fredborg, 'The Scholastic Teaching of Rhetoric in the Middle Ages', *Cahiers de l'Institut du Moyen Âge Grec et Latin*, 55 (1987), pp. 85–105; M.D. Reeve, 'The Circulation of Classical Works on Rhetoric from the Twelfth to the Fourteenth Centuries', in C. Leonardi and E. Menestò (eds), *Retorica e Poetica Tra i Secoli XII e XIV* (Florence, 1988), pp. 109–24; J.O. Ward, 'Rhetoric in the Faculty of Arts (Paris and Oxford) – A Summary of the Evidence', in O. Weijers and L. Holtz (eds), *L'Enseignement des Disciplines à la Faculté des Arts, Paris et Oxford, XIIIe–XVe Siècles* (Paris, 1997), pp. 147–82.
55 For example, Petrarch, *Invectiva Contra Medicum*, ed. and trans. D. Marsh, *Against a Physician*, in Petrarch, *Invectives* (Cambridge, MA, 2003), II.82, pp. 65–7, III.147, p. 123; Petrarch, *De Sui Ipsius et Multorum Ignorantia*, ed. and trans. D. Marsh, *On His Own Ignorance and That of Many Others*, in Petrarch, *Invectives* (Cambridge, MA, 2003), II.11, p. 233, IV.92–3, pp. 303–5, VI.147, p. 351.

it moulded and adapted a tradition of classical rhetoric that was itself open to dispute and disagreement. Knowledge and study of the principles of rhetoric were thus not constant in the Middle Ages and, if there were significant developments in the teaching which was particular to the eighth, twelfth and fourteenth centuries, then it is only reasonable to assume (as does chapter 5 in what follows) that all of them had a corresponding impact on the extent to which these principles were then deployed in the writing of history. The complexity of these developments, however, and the nature of their impact on historiography, require a different kind of study to the one which is attempted here. In part, this is due to the nature of the audience for whom it is written, but it is mostly due to the fundamental point which this book is designed to make. Before analysing specific changes and developments, it is first of all necessary to clarify what might be regarded as a common language, as shared assumptions, as general principles which served as a starting-point across the board. These principles may have been discussed and applied in different ways, and with different emphases, by different authors and in different periods, but they always remained rooted in a core of classical rhetorical concepts. Rhetoric may have been more dynamic and pervasive than a single 'classical' tradition and, to that extent, for the present study to concentrate on a few texts and treatises may risk giving a misleading impression of uniformity. Nonetheless, these works, by Cicero (to whom the *Rhetorica ad Herennium* was also ascribed until the late fifteenth century) and by Quintilian (either in a complete form or, more commonly, in excerpts or as an abridgement of books I–III and X–XII of *Institutio Oratoria*),[56] can be regarded as providing a common currency, a 'discourse' even, for the writing of history in the Middle Ages.

Much the same justification also underpins the emphasis, in what follows, on the writings of Augustine, Boethius and Gregory the Great. Once again, this is not intended to suggest that the exegetical and theological traditions to which these late-antique Christian authors gave rise did not change or develop over the course of the Middle Ages. Far from it. What this concentration is designed to underline, however, is the extent to which patristic

---

56 Murphy, *Rhetoric in the Middle Ages*, p. 125.

texts such as Augustine's *On the Trinity*, *On the City of God* and *On Christian Teaching*, Boethius' *Consolation of Philosophy* and Gregory the Great's *Morals on the Book of Job*, *Pastoral Care* and *Homilies on Ezekiel* remained fundamental starting-points for all writers throughout this period. For a study which is concerned with the history of historiography, therefore, the approach taken in this book might seem wilfully transhistorical. Indeed, it might well be objected that, strictly speaking, the chronological parameters of its title should be limited to the period 400–500 rather than 400–1500. That risk, however, carries corresponding benefits. Concentration on such 'primary' material is quite deliberate and is driven by two overriding goals – in order that a survey of eleven hundred years might at least aspire to brevity and clarity, but also in order that the principles which it contains can be regarded as potentially applicable *throughout* the medieval period. If this book appears, as a result, to be a distillation, even a paraphrase, of a selection of classical and patristic sources, then this impression is not too far from one of its aims – to provide the sort of broad synthesis of Sallust, Cicero, Josephus, Quintilian, Eusebius, Orosius, Augustine, Boethius and Gregory the Great which might reflect the range of material which informed most of, if not all, the writing of history in the Middle Ages and with which modern students of medieval historiography accordingly need first to be familiar in order to make sense of the potential complexity of the texts they find in front of them. If this book also appears, in consequence, to include relatively fewer syntheses of strictly 'medieval' works of history, then this, too, is deliberate, since a second of its aims is to set out certain categories of analysis which students can then usefully apply to medieval historiography on their own.[57]

Even with such a wide brief, there remain some areas of rhetoric which, inevitably, this study is, from the outset, deliberately *not* intended to cover. Chapter 1 is designed to locate the writing of history in the Middle Ages at the confluence of three major historiographical traditions – the classical, the biblical

---

57 To that end, an attempt has been made throughout to confine references to works of history which are readily available in English translation; citations (emended where necessary) will likewise be made, wherever possible, from editions with a parallel text and translation; Latin will be quoted only when the terminology is significant or revealing.

and the chronographic. Chapter 2 is intended to introduce a fourth – rhetoric – and its contents are accordingly determined by the traditional division of rhetoric into its three fundamental categories: demonstrative or epideictic rhetoric (that is, speeches and texts which praise or blame individuals); judicial or forensic rhetoric (speeches and texts which prosecute or defend individuals in the law courts); and deliberative rhetoric (speeches and texts which argue for or against a particular course of political action in political assemblies).[58] There is variation between each of these categories in terms of both approach and emphasis but all three of these forms of rhetoric still have fundamental elements in common. In particular, all three categories divide the subject-matter of a speech or text into five constituent elements: invention or *inventio* (that is, the identification and construction of true or verisimilar arguments which will make what is being said convincing or probable); arrangement or *dispositio* (that is, the order and organisation which is given to these 'discovered' or 'invented' arguments); style or *elocutio* (that is, the choice of language and vocabulary which is appropriate to these arguments); memory or *memoria* (that is, the memorisation of the speech or text); and delivery or *pronuntiatio* (that is, the manner in which it is spoken or presented).[59] It is the first three of these five elements (*inventio*, *dispositio* and *elocutio*) which underpin the analysis of narrative that is provided in chapter 3 and which then form the basis for defining the methodology of medieval historiography in chapter 4 as a relationship between verisimilitude and truth.

Such a distribution of material is not meant to undervalue the importance of the last two elements of a speech or text, namely

---

58 Quintilian, *Institutio Oratoria*, VII.praef.6, p. 179; Cicero, *De Inventione*, I.5.7, pp. 15–17; Cicero, *Topica*, trans. H.M. Hubbell (Loeb, 1949), XXIV.91, p. 453; cf. Boethius, *De Topicis Differentiis*, IV, pp. 80, 87; Honorius of Autun, *De Animae Exsilio et Patria* (*PL* 172, cols 1241–6), III, cols 1243–4; Vincent of Beauvais, *Speculum Historiale*, I.55, p. 22.
59 Quintilian, *Institutio Oratoria*, III.3.1–15, pp. 383–91; Cicero, *De Inventione*, I.7.9, pp. 19–21; *Rhetorica ad Herennium*, I.2.3, p. 7; cf. Fortunatianus, *Ars Rhetorica*, I, p. 26; Boethius, *An Overview of the Structure of Rhetoric*, p. 75; Boethius, *De Topicis Differentiis*, IV, pp. 82, 87; Isidore, *Etymologiae*, II.3.1, p. 24; Dominicus Gundissalinus, *De Divisione Philosophiae*, p. 144; Vincent of Beauvais, *Speculum Historiale*, I.55, p. 22; M. Camille, 'Illuminating Thought – The Trivial Arts in British Library, Burney Ms.295', in P. Binski and W. Noel (eds), *New Offerings, Ancient Treasures: Studies in Medieval Art for George Henderson* (Stroud, 2001), p. 351.

memory and delivery. The entire training of an orator was held to depend on memory, since, according to Quintilian, it was only the power of remembrance which would enable the massed ranks of *exempla*, laws, rulings, sayings and deeds (*dicta et facta*) to be present to the orator in a manner that would make them immediately accessible. For Quintilian, this is why memory was rightly called the storehouse, or treasury, of eloquence (*thesaurus eloquentiae*).[60] According to Hugh of St Victor, 'the whole utility of education consists only in the memory of it for, just as having heard something does not profit one who cannot understand, likewise having understood is not valuable to one who either will not or cannot remember'.[61] As a result, the way in which memory functions was certainly understood to have an impact on the way in which a written text could be composed, not least on the basis of the principle that things to which we are well-accustomed slip easily from the memory, whereas outstanding or novel things remain for a long time in one's mind.[62] In purely formal terms, for example, this meant that mnemonic techniques of symbolic notation, which had been developed for the study of the Bible in the Middle Ages, could also be extended to works of history. In the late 1180s, for example, Ralph de Diceto was prompted to design twelve different signs or symbols for the different types of historical events he was narrating, in part to serve as a cross-referencing system, but also to act as an aid to memory. He used 'PS' for persecutions of the church, for example, a crown for the kings of England, a sword for the dukes of Normandy, a spear for the counts of Anjou and a crown on its side with two arms pulling it in different directions for the dissension between Henry II and his sons.[63] This sort of rubricated annotation was then developed

---

60 Quintilian, *Institutio Oratoria*, XI.2.1, p. 213.
61 Hugh of St Victor, *De Tribus Maximis Circumstantiis Gestorum*, trans. M. Carruthers, in M. Carruthers and J.M. Ziolkowski (eds), *The Medieval Craft of Memory* (Philadelphia, 2002), p. 39.
62 *Rhetorica ad Herennium*, III.22.35, p. 219.
63 Ralph de Diceto, *Abbreviationes Chronicorum*, ed. W. Stubbs, *The Historical Works of Master Ralph de Diceto, Dean of London* (London, 1876), pref., pp. 3–4; A. Gransden, *Historical Writing in England c.550–c.1307* (London, 1974), plate VII; cf. M. Clanchy, *From Memory to Written Record: England 1066–1307* (2nd edn., Oxford, 1993), pp. 175–6; A. Gransden, 'Prologues in the Historiography of Twelfth-Century England', in D. Williams (ed.), *England in the Twelfth Century*

still further by the elaborate marginal drawings of Matthew Paris in the thirteenth century.[64] Nonetheless, whilst it can certainly be argued that much of what is distinctive about the writing of history in the Middle Ages is encapsulated by the relationship between memory and the written word, it remains the case that, in general, when discussing memory, classical manuals of rhetoric generally limit themselves to techniques of storage and retrieval rather than engage in any analysis of the intellectual and psychological processes which these techniques might involve. As a result, although the relationship between the writing of history and the act of reminiscence as the intellectual and affective restructuring of the past is touched upon in chapter 4, a broader discussion of the relationship between the way in which the act of remembering was understood to operate in the mind and the form which this process of commemoration could then give to the act of writing about the past remains beyond the scope of the present study. To do justice to this larger issue would require a wider frame of reference than is possible, or intended, within the confines of a book whose primary focus is on the principles which are explicitly and systematically articulated in the rhetorical works of Cicero and Quintilian themselves.[65]

Similar considerations apply to the larger issues which are raised by the fifth element of a speech or text, namely *pronuntiatio*. 'Delivery' was understood to provide a significant means of moving the emotions of one's audience. Indeed, Quintilian reports the opinion of Demosthenes that *pronuntiatio* should take first, second and third place in the entire study of speaking.[66] Classical rhetorical manuals accordingly set out long lists of instructions for relating narrative in an appropriate manner – these involve a variety of appropriate hand gestures (the use of the

---

(Woodbridge, 1990), pp. 55–81, reprinted in A. Gransden, *Legends, Traditions and History in Medieval England* (London, 1992), pp. 79–80.
64 Gransden, *Historical Writing in England*, plate IX; cf. S. Lewis, *The Art of Matthew Paris in the Chronica Majora* (Aldershot, 1987).
65 See pages 456–7. For a discussion of memory, reminiscence and historiography, see, instead, M. Carruthers, *The Book of Memory: A Study of Memory in Medieval Culture* (Cambridge, 1990); J. Coleman, *Ancient and Medieval Memories: Studies in the Reconstruction of the Past* (Cambridge, 1992); and, more generally, G. Cubitt, *History and Memory* (Manchester, 2007).
66 Quintilian, *Institutio Oratoria*, XI.3.4–6, p. 245.

index finger, for example, in denunciation)[67] and even extend to dress (according to Quintilian, Cicero wore his toga in such a fashion as to conceal his varicose veins).[68] This is one reason why Quintilian thought that music was necessary to the study of rhetoric: quite apart from the need to understand poetry as *sung* verse (*carmina/canere*) and to recognise the force of music in exciting or assuaging human emotions, the delivery of both music and rhetoric required a knowledge of gesture, arrangement of words and inflection of the voice.[69] There is thus a certain way of delivering narrative, a particular intonation of the voice which is suitable for narrating what has happened and which is distinct from that used in debate (*contentio*) or in an exhortation or appeal for pity (*amplificatio*). This tone is defined as *sermo* or 'relaxed speech', and it comes closest to daily conversation.[70] This prescription has the quite practical effect that, when narrating, speakers should stay still, gently move their right hand and ensure that their facial expression shows the emotion appropriate to the opinion being expressed.[71] Orators, therefore, do not imitate the truth like players on a stage (*histriones*), but act it out in fact (*actores veritatis*).[72] It is, accordingly, a fundamental principle of rhetoric that orators should vary their voice so that they give the impression of narrating everything just as it happened, speaking rapidly when they want to show something was done vigorously and more slowly when it was done at greater leisure. The delivery of the actual words used will therefore be modified to suit their content, so that if, for example, a narrative contains any statements, demands, responses or expressions of surprise, the speaker will give careful attention to expressing with the voice the feelings and thoughts of the person being described.[73] In other words, the principles underpinning delivery are the same

---

67 Quintilian, *Institutio Oratoria*, XI.3.92–4, pp. 293–5.
68 Quintilian, *Institutio Oratoria*, XI.3.143, p. 323. cf. Macrobius, *Saturnalia*, trans. P.V. Davies (New York, 1969), II.3.5, p. 167; Sidonius Apollinaris, *Letters*, trans. W.B. Anderson (Loeb, 1965), Ep.V.5, p. 181.
69 Quintilian, *Institutio Oratoria*, I.10.9–33, pp. 165–77.
70 *Rhetorica ad Herennium*, III.13.23, p. 197.
71 *Rhetorica ad Herennium*, III.15.26, p. 203.
72 Cicero, *De Oratore*, III.56.214, p. 171; cf. J.M. Pizarro, *A Rhetoric of the Scene: Dramatic Narrative in the Early Middle Ages* (Toronto, 1989).
73 *Rhetorica ad Herennium*, III.14.24, pp. 199–201.

as those of language itself – it should be correct, lucid, ornate and appropriate.[74] *Pronuntiatio* will vary according to the nature of the case itself but also according to whether it is delivering the introduction, the narrative, the argument or the epilogue; it should conciliate, persuade and move the emotions; and last but not least, it should provide pleasure.[75]

As with memory, the practice of delivery is not without its impact on the way in which works of history were actually written in the Middle Ages, and for the very simple reason that so much medieval historiography was composed in order to be read aloud. Recitation of the deeds of outstanding individuals was, of course, nothing new – Vergil sings of arms and the man, whilst Lucan compared poets to prophets, whose praises send to a distant age the spirits of brave men killed in battle.[76] Remembering the glorious deeds of one's ancestors served as a powerful incentive to perform comparable deeds of one's own and, since commemoration of those deeds would guarantee an immortality beyond the fleeting nature of this present life, Vergil pointed out that the Muses have both memory and the power to commemorate.[77] Valerius Maximus emphasised the value of the ancient practice of dining to the sound of poems which were composed on the noble deeds of one's ancestors and recited to the flute as a means of making the young more eager to imitate them.[78] Medieval historiography followed suit. According to Einhard, Charlemagne wrote down and committed to memory 'the ancient songs in which the acts and deeds of former kings were sung', whilst 'histories and the deeds of the ancients' were read out to him as he was dining.[79] The role of poetry at Charlemagne's court was explicitly

---

74 See pages 295–6.
75 Quintilian, *Institutio Oratoria*, XI.3.30, p. 259, XI.3.151–74, pp. 327–41.
76 Vergil, *Aeneid*, I.1, p. 241, IV.14, p. 397, IX.777, p. 169; Lucan, *Pharsalia*, trans. J.D. Duff, *The Civil War* (Loeb, 1928), I.447–9, p. 37.
77 Vergil, *Aeneid*, VII.645, p. 47, IX.525–9, p. 151 (see also p. 150). For the etymology of Clio, see page 151, note 118.
78 Valerius Maximus, *Facta et Dicta Memorabilia*, II.1, p. 135.
79 Einhard, *Vita Karoli Magni*, trans. P.E. Dutton, in P.E. Dutton, *Charlemagne's Courtier: The Complete Einhard* (Ontario, 1998), XXIV, p. 31, XXIX, p. 34. For the emperor Theodosius' interest in finding out about the deeds of his ancestors, see Paul the Deacon, *Historia Romana*, ed. A. Crivelluci (Rome, 1914), XII.5, p. 166, quoted, for example, by Henry of Huntingdon, *Historia Anglorum*, I.43, p. 67.

envisaged to extol the distinguished deeds of ancient kings and to narrate for future ages what was done in the present.[80] Liutprand of Cremona stresses the importance of *fama* in battle and how the glory of such deeds is handed down to posterity.[81] 'Let a bad song not be sung about us' was a concern voiced in the *Chanson de Roland* alongside its references to deeds of bravery that were otherwise recorded in written annals.[82] Fulcher of Chartres opens his account of the First Crusade by observing that 'it is especially pleasing to the living, and it is even beneficial to the dead, when the deeds of brave men, particularly of those serving as soldiers of God, are either read from writings or soberly recounted from memory among the faithful'.[83] 'There were those', writes Rahewin, 'who publicly extolled the emperor's deeds in songs of praise'.[84] William of Tyre's *History of Deeds Done Beyond the Sea* originated in a request made by Amaury I, king of Jerusalem, who is described as preferring history to all other kinds of reading, just like his predecessor, Baldwin, who not only particularly enjoyed listening to history but 'inquired with great diligence into the deeds and habits of the noblest kings and princes of former times'.[85] Gerald of Wales, who claimed that he enjoyed a considerable reputation (*fama*) in the art of rhetoric, described the recitation of his *Topography of Ireland* to three different audiences over the course of three days at Oxford, 'a magnificent and costly achievement

---

80 'Hibernicus Exul', *In Praise of Poetry*, ed. and trans. P. Godman, *Poetry of the Carolingian Renaissance* (London 1985), lines 34–5, p. 178.
81 Liutprand, *Antapodosis*, II.14, p. 77.
82 *Song of Roland: The Oxford Text*, trans. D.D.R. Owen (London, 1972), line 1014, p. 52, line 1443, p. 62.
83 Fulcher of Chartres, *Historia Hierosolymitana*, trans. M.E. McGinty, *Chronicle of the First Crusade* (Philadelphia, 1941), I.prol., p. 9; cf. Joinville, *The Life of Saint Louis*, trans. M. Shaw, *Joinville and Villehardouin: Chronicles of the Crusades* (Harmondsworth, 1963), p. 226; Gervase of Tilbury, *Otia Imperialia*, ed. and trans. S.E. Banks and J.W. Binns, *Recreation for an Emperor* (Oxford, 2002), III.59, p. 671.
84 Rahewin, *The Deeds of Frederick Barbarossa*, trans. C.C. Mierow (New York, 1953), IV.5, p. 237; cf. Wipo, *Deeds of Conrad*, XL, p. 99; Orderic Vitalis, *Historia Ecclesiastica*, ed. and trans. M. Chibnall, *The Ecclesiastical History of Orderic Vitalis* (Oxford, 1980), VI.2, p. 217.
85 William of Tyre, *A History of Deeds Done Beyond the Sea*, trans. E.A. Babcock and A.C. Krey (New York, 1941), prol., p. 56, XVI.2, p. 138, XIX.2, p. 296; cf. *ibid.*, XX.31, p. 396, XXI.1, p. 398, and, more generally, D.W.T.C. Vesey, 'William of Tyre and the Art of Historiography', *Mediaeval Studies*, 35 (1973), pp. 435–45; P.W. Edbury and J.G. Rowe, *William of Tyre: Historian of the Latin East* (Cambridge, 1988).

since thereby the ancient and authentic times of the poets were in some manner revived'.[86]

The influence of such oral delivery on the way in which commemorative history came to be written down has left some important, if tantalising, vestiges in the historiography that has survived in textual form. Bede, for example, divided his *Ecclesiastical History of the English People* into chapters in order to delineate individual readings (*lectiones*) on the model of the Bible.[87] Agnellus of Ravenna appears to have envisaged daily readings of his history of the church of Ravenna.[88] Orderic Vitalis' prose and punctuation were designed to give his text a meaningful rhythm for individuals reciting his *Ecclesiastical History* to others or on their own.[89] Seven of the ten books of the *Deeds of the Franks* (an anonymous account of the First Crusade) end with a statement of faith, or doxology, in order to indicate the end of the reading.[90] Suger was a writer praised for his Ciceronian eloquence, but he was also noted for recounting to his monks (and late into the night) the deeds of earlier Frankish rulers, as well as for composing lessons to commemorate the anniversary of Louis VI's death as part of the liturgy at Saint Denis. Each of these performative practices can be connected to the highly episodic nature of the written text of his *Deeds of Louis* – many chapters open or close

---

86 Gerald of Wales, *De Rebus a Se Gestis*, trans. H.E. Butler, *The Autobiography of Giraldus Cambrensis* (London, 1937; reprinted Woodbridge, 2005), XVI, p. 97; cf. Gerald of Wales, *Topographia Hibernica*, trans. J.J. O'Meara, *The History and Topography of Ireland* (Harmondsworth, 1982); R. Bartlett, *Gerald of Wales, 1146–1223* (Oxford, 1982).
87 R. Ray, 'Bede, the Exegete, as Historian', in G. Bonner (ed.), *Famulus Christi: Essays in Commemoration of the Thirteenth Centenary of the Birth of the Venerable Bede* (London, 1976), p. 133; cf. anon., *Life of Gregory*, ed. and trans. B. Colgrave, *The Earliest Life of Gregory the Great* (Kansas, 1968).
88 Agnellus of Ravenna, *The Book of Pontiffs of the Church of Ravenna*, trans. D.M. Deliyannis (Washington, DC, 2004), XXXVIII, p. 144, XLV, p. 155, LIV, p. 166, LVIII, p. 172, LXII, p. 178, LXXIX, p. 193.
89 See Chibnall's 'General Introduction' to Orderic Vitalis, *Ecclesiastical History*, pp. 107–10; cf. R. Ray, 'Orderic Vitalis and His Readers', *Studia Monastica*, 14 (1972), pp. 16–33; Smalley, *Historians in the Middle Ages*, p. 12.
90 *Gesta Francorum et Aliorum Hierosolimitanorum*, ed. and trans. R. Hill (Oxford, 1962), I, p. 9, IV, p. 27, V, p. 31, VI, p. 38, VII, p. 42, IX, p. 71, X, p. 97. More than half the chapters of William of Jumièges' *Gesta Normannorum Ducum* (ed. and trans. E. van Houts, Oxford, 1992–95) have the same formulaic ending, the last chapter of each book closing with the doxology *per omnia saecula saeculorum amen*.

with general proverbial observations ('kings have long arms'),[91] most of them reveal a similar underlying moralising structure[92] and, insofar as they are given a single overarching theme, it is contained in the refrain that Louis' justice provided peace for the land and protection for widows, orphans and the poor.[93]

The connections between orality and literacy are, of course, complex and, in moving away from any idea that these two terms should be treated as polar opposites in the Middle Ages, modern historians have increasingly deployed a much richer and more nuanced conceptual apparatus ('textual community', 'social memory') with which to convey the reciprocal and interactive relationship between individual and group, the spoken and the written word.[94] The impact on how medieval historiography is now viewed has been profound – the writing of history could not just take one of many different forms but it was also only one of many different ways in which particular individuals and communities could commemorate events or actions in their past. As such, the writing of history could not, and should not, be separated from the other ways in which individuals conceived of, and talked about, the past.[95] This is as true of the Middle Ages as it is of the early-modern and modern periods.[96] Nonetheless, the relationship between written and oral forms of commemorating

---

91 Suger, *Gesta Hludowici*, trans. R.C. Cusimano and J. Moorhead, *The Deeds of Louis the Fat* (Washington, DC, 1992), XXV, p. 109, quoting Ovid, *Heroides*, XVII, line 166 – for which see Ovid, *Heroides*, trans. G. Showerman (Loeb, 1914), p. 236.
92 G.M. Spiegel, 'History as Enlightenment: Suger and the *Mos Anagogicus*', in P.L. Gerson (ed.), *Abbot Suger and Saint-Denis* (New York, 1986), pp. 151–8; reprinted in G.M. Spiegel, *The Past as Text: The Theory and Practice of Medieval Historiography* (Baltimore, 1997); L. Grant, *Abbot Suger of St-Denis: Church and State in Early Twelfth-Century France* (Harlow, 1998), pp. 8–9, 38–42.
93 For example, Suger, *Gesta Hludowici*, XIV, pp. 62–3, XV, p. 64, XVIII, p. 82, XIX, p. 86, XXIV, p. 106, XXV, p. 110, XXXIII, p. 154. For a similarly homiletic style, see Thietmar of Merseburg, *Chronicon*, I.25, p. 86, IV.73, p. 202, V.9, p. 212, VI.21, p. 251. See also page 147.
94 Clanchy, *From Memory to Written Record*; J. Fentress and C. Wickham, *Social Memory* (Oxford, 1992).
95 P.J. Geary, *Phantoms of Remembrance: Memory and Oblivion at the End of the First Millennium* (Princeton, 1994).
96 P. Nora, *Realms of Memory: Rethinking the French Past* (New York, 1996–98); P.H. Hutton, *History as an Art of Memory* (Hanover, 1993); G. Althoff, J. Fried and P.J. Geary (eds), *Medieval Concepts of the Past: Ritual, Memory, Historiography* (Cambridge, 2002).

the past and, by extension, between Latin and vernacular forms of 'historiography' (epic, saga and *chansons de geste*) lies, again, beyond the scope of the present study.[97]

The relationship between the written word and the spoken word was certainly a subject which both Cicero and Quintilian discussed at length. Indeed, according to Quintilian, the act of writing was particularly important to the orator because it constituted the sole means by which a true and deeply-rooted proficiency in rhetoric could be attained.[98] Nonetheless, delivery remains the least theorised of the five divisions of rhetoric (even less so than memory) and, as a means of communication, the concentration on an individual's modulation of voice, gesture and facial countenance involves precisely those performative, non-verbal aspects of language which are contingent upon a single occasion and which are largely invisible in the written text. In concentrating on invention, arrangement and style, therefore, rather than on memory and delivery, this study risks passing over two aspects to the writing of history in the Middle Ages which might otherwise be considered helpful in situating individual texts within a particular cultural and performative milieu.

---

[97] See, instead, G.M. Spiegel, *Romancing the Past: The Rise of Vernacular Prose Historiography in Thirteenth-Century France* (Berkeley, 1993); D. Boutet, *Formes Littéraires et Conscience Historique aux Origines de la Littérature Française 1100–1250* (Paris, 1999); A. Galloway, 'Writing History in England', in D. Wallace (ed.), *The Cambridge History of Medieval English Literature* (Cambridge, 1999), pp. 255–83; P. Damian-Grint, *The New Historians of the Twelfth-Century Renaissance: Inventing Vernacular Authority* (Woodbridge, 1999); P.F. Ainsworth, 'Contemporary and "Eyewitness" History', in D.M. Deliyannis (ed.), *Historiography in the Middle Ages* (Leiden, 2003), pp. 249–76; P.F. Ainsworth, 'Legendary History – *Historia* and *Fabula*', in D.M. Deliyannis (ed.), *Historiography in the Middle Ages* (Leiden, 2003), pp. 387–416. For the inclusion of epic and *chansons de geste* within vernacular historiography, see P.E. Bennett, 'L'Épique Dans l'Historiographie Anglo-Normande – Gaimar, Wace, Jordan Fantosme', in H. van Dijk and W. Noomen (eds), *Aspects de l'Épopée Romane: Mentalités, Idéologies, Intertextualités* (Groningen, 1995), pp. 321–30; cf. J.A.W. Bennett, 'History in Verse', in J.A.W. Bennett, *Middle English Literature* (Oxford, 1986), ch. 4; J.J. Duggan, 'Medieval Epic as Popular Historiography – Appropriation of Historical Knowledge in the Vernacular Epic', in H.U. Gumbrecht, U. Link-Heer, P.-M. Spangenberg, *et al.* (eds), *La Littérature Historiographique des Origines à 1500: Grundriss der Romanischen Literaturen des Mittelalters* (Heidelberg, 1987), vol. XI, pp. 285–311; P. Zumthor, *Essai de Poétique Médiévale* (Paris, 1972), trans. P. Bennett, *Toward a Medieval Poetics* (Minneapolis, 1992), pp. 12, 134–5.

[98] Quintilian, *Institutio Oratoria*, I.1.28, p. 35.

Once again, however, this is a choice which, in part, reflects the emphasis of the classical manuals on which this book is based and to which it is designed to serve as an introduction. It is also intended to help focus attention primarily on the methodology which informed the actual composition of the historical works that came to be produced in the light of the principles which Cicero and Quintilian had set out, rather than the way in which they were subsequently received.

As texts which were written, expounded and read as a direct result of a familiarity with classical rhetoric, works of medieval historiography are complex compositions that often need to be submitted to a process of substantial decoding. They can also be very elusive, given that it is of the essence of rhetoric for its artifice to remain concealed – it is part of the orator's skill, according to the *Rhetorica ad Herennium*, to hide their art so that it does not stand out and become visible to everyone.[99] Quintilian's ideal is for the orator to give the impression of speaking with care but without guile (*calliditas*), even if such avoidance and dissimulation themselves require the greatest artifice. This is particularly the case at the beginning of a speech or text, in the introduction or *proemium*, where all ostentation should be avoided in favour of modesty in both thought and language – the style should conceal the art, and the guile should be hidden (*calliditas occulta*), because the impression of simplicity and a lack of preparation will make one's audience much less suspicious.[100] Or, as John of Salisbury phrases it, unsophisticated and straightforward ways of putting things are very useful both to help conceal what is proposed and to help one's objective. Art should be disguised, since to show it off will always excite suspicion.[101]

---

99 *Rhetorica ad Herennium*, IV.7.10, p. 251. For the claim to rusticity as, in itself, a rhetorical strategy, see, for example, Sulpicius Severus, *Dialogues*, trans. B.M. Peebles (New York, 1949) I.27, pp. 198–9 (see also page 115) and, more generally, G. Simon, 'Untersuchungen zur Topik der Widmungsbriefe mittelalterlicher Geschichtsschreiber bis zum Ende des 12. Jahrhunderts', *Archiv für Diplomatik*, 4 (1958), pp. 99, 112, and *Archiv für Diplomatik*, 5–6 (1959–60), pp. 76–7, 82, 123–4.
100 Quintilian, *Institutio Oratoria*, II.5.7, p. 249, IV.1.55–60, pp. 37–9, IX.2.59, p. 411.
101 John of Salisbury, *Metalogicon*, III.10, p. 193; cf. Richer, *Historiae*, ed. and trans. R. Latouche (Paris, 1930–37), III.47–8, p. 56.

The resulting complexity is evident even at the level of tropes and figures of speech. In using the technique of, for example, *significatio* or 'emphasis' (that is, the figure of speech which leaves more to be suspected than has actually been asserted in words), a writer can deploy *abscisio* or 'aposiopesis', by beginning to say something but then stopping short when what has already been said is enough to leave suspicion in the minds of the audience. Alternatively, orators can invoke a comparison (*similitudo*) by bringing forward something similar but without amplifying the exact connection with their own subject-matter – this allows the audience to suspect something on which the orator has remained silent.[102] Quintilian considers this last strategy to be one of the most frequently-encountered figures of speech because, when it is not safe to speak openly or when it is not fitting to do so, comparison can be used to indicate that the real meaning is hidden. Under the rule of tyrants, he points out, or in the immediate aftermath of a civil war, it is possible to exploit such ambiguity by speaking out while also ensuring that what is being said can be understood in another sense. If there are powerful people who need to be censured, then a speaker has to proceed with circumspection.[103] William of Malmesbury's prologue to book IV of his *Deeds of the English Kings* proved Quintilian's point:

---

[102] *Rhetorica ad Herennium*, IV.53.67, pp. 401–3; cf. Macrobius, *Saturnalia*, IV.6.20, pp. 279–80; Geoffrey of Vinsauf, *Poetria Nova*, lines 1274–5, p. 79, lines 1583–4, p. 88.
[103] Quintilian, *Institutio Oratoria*, IX.2.65–69, pp. 415–17; Martianus Capella, *Marriage of Philology and Mercury*, V, pp. 177–8; cf. Tacitus, *Annals*, trans. J. Jackson (Loeb, 1937), IV.34, p. 59. According to Sidonius Apollinaris, *Letters*, Ep.IV.22, pp. 147–9, only a position of great power removed a historian from either suppressing the truth or inventing a lie (*vel supprimere verum vel concinnare mendacium*) and, whilst it is shameful to utter falsehoods, it is dangerous to tell the truth (*turpiter falsa periculose vera dicuntur*); cf. Regino of Prüm, *Chronicle*, trans. S. MacLean, *History and Politics in Late Carolingian and Ottonian Europe: The Chronicle of Regino of Prüm and Adalbert of Magdeburg* (Manchester, 2009), I pref., pp. 61–2 (see also page 446). Writing in the 1050s, William of Jumièges refused to name those who rebelled against the Duke of Normandy twenty years previously, for fear of incurring their inexorable hatred (*Gesta Normannorum Ducum*, VII.1, p. 93); in the second version of his text, produced in the early 1070s, William claimed not to have taken any pleasure in the blandishments of popularity, with its soft but pernicious allure, nor to have become entangled in the world by that snare (*Gesta Normannorum Ducum*, Ep.ded., p. 7).

Most people, I know, will think it unwise to have turned my pen to the history of the kings of my own time; they will say that in works of this character truth is often shipwrecked and falsehood given assistance, for in writing of contemporaries it is dangerous to utter bad things and good things are said to applause. Thus it is, they maintain, that with everything nowadays tending to the worse rather than the better, an author will pass by the evils which he encounters on account of fear and, as for good things, if there are none, he will make them up for the sake of applause.... Grateful as I am, therefore, for the good will of those who fear on my behalf the alternatives of lying or being hated, I will satisfy them, with Christ's help, such that I will be found to be neither a falsifier nor an object of hatred. I will summarise acts, both good and bad, in such a way that, as I navigate my ship flying unharmed between Scylla and Charybdis, even if my history [*historia*] may be found lacking in some respect, my reflection [*sententia*] will not be found wanting.... I will therefore tell in this book ... whatever there is to be told ... in such a way that the truth of things [*veritas rerum*] does not falter nor the majesty of the ruler is discoloured.[104]

William of Tyre navigates a similar route and through similar waters. Truth may be the daughter of time,[105] but it is also the mother of hatred. 'That it is an arduous task', he points out, 'fraught with many risks and perils, to write of the deeds of kings, no wise man can doubt':

> To say nothing of the toil, the never-ending application, and the constant vigilance which works of this nature always demand, a double abyss inevitably yawns before the writer of history. It is only with the greatest difficulty that he avoids one or the other, for, while he is trying to escape Charybdis, he usually falls into the clutches of Scylla.... For either he will kindle the hostility [*invidia*] of many

---

104 William of Malmesbury, *Gesta Regum Anglorum*, IV.prol., pp. 541–3; cf. William of Malmesbury, *Historia Novella*, ed. and trans. K.R. Potter (London, 1955), I.prol., p. 1; see also page 173. For William of Malmesbury's prologues, see B. Guenée, 'L'Histoire entre l'Éloquence et la Science – Quelques Remarques sur le Prologue de Guillaume de Malmesbury à ses *Gesta Regum Anglorum*', *Comptes rendus de l'Académie des Inscriptions et Belles-Lettres* (1982), pp. 357–70; Gransden, 'Prologues in the Historiography of Twelfth-Century England', pp. 136–44; see also pages 227–8.
105 Aulus Gellius, *Noctes Atticae*, trans. J.C. Rolfe, *Attic Nights* (Loeb, 1927), XII.11.7, p. 395.

persons against him while he is in pursuit of the truth of what has been done; or, in the hope of rousing less resentment, he will be silent about the course of events, wherein, obviously, he is not without fault. For to pass over the truth of things and to conceal the facts intentionally is well recognised as contrary to the duty of a historian. But to fail in one's duty is unquestionably a fault.... On the other hand, to trace out a succession of deeds without changing them or deviating from the rule of truth [*regula veritatis*] is a course which always excites wrath; for, as the old proverb states, 'deference wins friends; truth, hatred'. As a result, historians either fall short of the duty of their profession by showing undue deference [*obsequium*], or, while eagerly seeking the truth of a matter, they must needs endure hatred [*odium*], of which truth herself is the mother. Thus, all too commonly these two courses are wont to be opposed to one another and to become equally troublesome by the insistent demands which they make. In the words of our Cicero, 'truth is troublesome since verily it springs hatred which is poisonous to friendship; but deference is even more disastrous, for, by dealing leniently with a friend, it permits him to rush headlong into ruin', a sentiment which seems to reflect on the man, who, in defiance of the obligations of duty, suppresses the truth for the sake of being obliging. As for those who, in the desire to flatter [*studio adulationis*], deliberately weave lies [*mendacia*] into their record of what has been done, their conduct is looked upon as so detestable that they ought not to be regarded as belonging to the ranks of such writers. For, if to conceal the truth of deeds is wrong and falls far short of a writer's duty, it will certainly be regarded as a much more serious sin [*peccatum*] to mingle lies with truth and to hand to a trusting posterity as truth that which is deficient in truth.[106]

In his history of the conquest of Ireland, Gerald of Wales quotes the same 'proverb' from Terence, 'obsequiousness brings a man friends, but truth makes him hated'. 'I have always considered it a difficult task', he continues, 'and one involving more danger than profit, to describe in many words the man who can outlaw you by using just one. For it would win me favour (*gratia*), and yet

---

106 William of Tyre, *History of Deeds Done Beyond the Sea*, prol., pp. 53–4; cf. Cicero, *De Amicitia*, trans. W.A. Falconer (Loeb, 1923), XXIV.89, p. 197, a passage which includes the same quotation from Terence, *Andria*, trans. J. Barsby, *The Woman of Andros* (Loeb, 2001), I.1.68, p. 57: 'flattery wins friends, truth hatred'.

would be far beyond my capacity, to be able to avoid suppressing the truth in the matter of individual details and yet at no point to arouse the anger of my prince'.[107] Gerald later abandons the course of his narrative precisely on the grounds that he fears offending the great and the good: 'it is better that the truth should be suppressed and concealed for a time, even though it is in itself most useful and indeed desirable, than that it should burst forth prematurely and perilously into the light of day, thereby offending those in power'.[108]

As an introduction, the present study is intended, in sum, to operate at several different levels at one and the same time. Medieval historiography does not fit into a single genre, with its own rules, its own distinctive methodology. Precisely what made it so problematic for twentieth-century 'scientific' historians is what makes it so interesting now. It is this apparent lack of a discrete methodology which makes a study of rhetoric the best point of entry to understanding why medieval writers wrote about the past in the way, or ways, in which they did. In and of itself, this book is therefore intended to serve as a practical guide to some of the more important methodological principles which informed medieval historiography, as well as to provide a (necessarily) selective index to some of the more specialised modern commentary and scholarship. In the process, however, it may also, belatedly, prove of some value to those of my colleagues who might still want an undergraduate historiography course to be all about the 'modern' history of history-writing. Take three of the more significant twentieth-century developments in historical method: the so-called 'linguistic turn' (that is, the notion that language does not provide a neutral or transparent means of denoting or describing reality); the idea of narratology (that is, the realisation that the way in which a narrative is structured is, in itself, a mode of interpretation); and 'meaning and context' (that is, the recognition that language is conditioned, even determined,

---

107 Gerald of Wales, *Expugnatio Hibernica*, I.46, p. 127.
108 Gerald of Wales, *Expugnatio Hibernica*, III.1, p. 257; cf. Gerald of Wales, *De Eruditione Principum*, trans. J. Stevenson (London, 1858; reprinted Felinfach, 1991), II.29, p. 48.

by the circumstances in which it is used and the audience to which it is directed). It is a truth only partially acknowledged that medieval historiography, like classical historiography, might have some light to shed on all three of these subjects.[109] The modern historian does not, perhaps should not, have all the best tunes.

---

109 G.M. Spiegel, 'History, Historicism and the Social Logic of the Text in the Middle Ages', *Speculum*, 65 (1990), pp. 59–86; reprinted in G.M. Spiegel, *The Past as Text*, pp. 3–28; J.O. Ward, '"Chronicle" and "History" – The Medieval Origins of Postmodern Historiographical Practice?', *Parergon*, 14 (1997), pp. 101–28.

1

HISTORY AND HISTORIOGRAPHY

The writing of history in the Middle Ages cannot be reduced to one single formula or definition. Instead, it straddled a huge variety of genres, covering – and often combining – world chronicles, annals, histories of communities, deeds of individuals, hagiographies, biographies, autobiographies and epic poems.[1] Medieval historiography therefore does not correspond to any fixed genre, in terms of either its form or its style – it could be written in prose, in verse or sometimes as both; it could be sung as a *chanson de geste*; it could be sculpted or painted or presented in tableaux; in the case of the 'estorie' of Richard of Haldingham it could even be recorded schematically as a 'map' of the world.[2] To do justice to such heterogeneity whilst at the same time isolating

---

1 R. Ray, 'Medieval Historiography Through the Twelfth Century – Problems and Progress of Research', *Viator*, 5 (1974), pp. 35–41; B. Roest, 'Medieval Historiography – About Generic Constraints and Scholarly Constructions', in B. Roest and H. Vanstiphout (eds), *Aspects of Genre and Type in Pre-Modern Literary Cultures* (Groningen, 1999), pp. 47–61; T.M.S. Lehtonen and P. Mehtonen (eds), *Historia: The Concept and Genres in the Middle Ages* (Helsinki, 2000).
2 N.R. Kline, *Maps of Medieval Thought: The Hereford Paradigm* (Woodbridge, 2001); for the connection to Orosius, see pp. 63, 181–4. Gervase of Canterbury's *Mappa Mundi* was effectively a list of English ecclesiastical houses, arranged shire by shire, followed by a list of archiepiscopal and episcopal sees in Britain, then the rest of the world. Gervase of Canterbury, *Mappa Mundi*, ed. W. Stubbs, in *Opera Historica* (2 vols, London, 1880), vol. II, pp. 414–49; cf. V.I.J. Flint, 'Honorius Augustodunensis *Imago Mundi*', *Archives d'Histoire Doctrinale et Littéraire du Moyen Âge*, 49 (1983), pp. 7–153; V.I.J. Flint, 'World History in the Early Twelfth Century – The *Imago Mundi* of Honorius Augustodunensis', in R.H.C. Davis, *et al.* (eds), *The Writing of History in the Middle Ages* (Oxford, 1981), pp. 211–38; Gervase of Tilbury, *Otia Imperialia*, ed. and trans. S.E. Banks and J.W. Binns, *Recreation for an Emperor* (Oxford, 2002), II.1–13, 22–5, pp. 167–351, 491–529.

what might still justify the identification of such complex material as 'historiography' accordingly presents very real difficulties of classification. Of the various ways in which categorisation might be tackled, the most straightforward, perhaps, and conventional, is to identify three major determinants of historical writing in this period: the transmission and influence of classical texts; the impact of the books of the Bible; and the development of a distinctively medieval 'chronography' once the formal compilation of annals began to emerge from the calculation and composition of the liturgical calendar within the Church. Before any generalisations are made about 'classical', 'Christian' or 'ecclesiastical' traditions in the Middle Ages, it is essential to grasp exactly what, and whom, they represented and, equally importantly, just how they interrelated.

The classical tradition

The writing of history in the Middle Ages took as one of its fundamental reference points a series of works by classical historians which had survived in, or were copied from, manuscripts of the late antique period. This process of transmission means that, whereas a modern conception of a 'classical' corpus of historical works might give prominence to, say, texts by Thucydides, Polybius, Livy and Tacitus, the medieval canon of what constituted 'classical' historiography was rather different, at least until the mid-fifteenth century. First and foremost, it consisted of Sallust and the Latin translation of Josephus; after them, and with varying degrees of availability and dissemination, came Julius Caesar, Livy, Tacitus, Suetonius (including his continuation in the *Historia Augusta*) and Ammianus Marcellinus.[3] All of these works existed in eighth- and

---

3 See L.D. Reynolds (ed.), *Texts and Transmission: A Survey of the Latin Classics* (Oxford, 1983), pp. 6–8, 35–6, 205–14, 341–9, 399–404, 406–9; B. Munk Olsen, *L'Étude des Auteurs Classiques Latins au XIe et XIIe Siècles* (Paris, 1982–89); B. Munk Olsen, *I Classici nel Canone Scolastico Altomedievale* (Spoleto, 1991); B. Munk Olsen, 'La Diffusion et l'Étude des Historiens Antiques au XIIe Siècle', in A. Welkenhuysen, H. Braet and W. Verbeke (eds), *Mediaeval Antiquity* (Leuven, 1995), pp. 21–43; B. Munk Olsen, 'Chronique des Manuscripts Classiques Latins (IXe–XIIe Siècles) I–III', *Revue d'Histoire des Textes*, 21 (1991), pp. 37–76; *Revue d'Histoire des Textes*, 24 (1994), pp. 199–249; *Revue d'Histoire des Textes*, 27 (1997), pp. 29–85; cf. L.B. Mortensen, 'The Texts and Contexts of Ancient Roman History

ninth-century manuscripts (and it is, in the main, these medieval copies, not the late-antique originals, which were subsequently rediscovered by fourteenth- and fifteenth-century humanists) and, as integral texts, they exerted a profound influence on how the writing of history was understood. Just as, if not more, important, however, was the transmission of these authors in the form of excerpted texts – Livy, for example, could be read in the version distilled by Florus,[4] and Pompeius Trogus in the summary provided by Justin.[5] Likewise, digests of Roman history had been arranged schematically by Valerius Maximus in his first-century *Memorable Deeds and Sayings*,[6] and chronologically by Eutropius in his fourth-century *Abbreviation* or *Breviarium* (a work which was subsequently expanded by Paul the Deacon in the eighth century as the *Historia Romana*).[7] Valerius Maximus makes the intended value of this sort of work quite clear in the prologue to his collection: 'concerning the city of Rome and external nations I have determined to select and arrange [*digerere*] the deeds and sayings which are worthy of remembrance but which are too widely scattered in other sources to be briefly comprehended so that those who wish to take examples [*documenta*] may be spared the labour

---

in Twelfth-Century Western Scholarship', in P. Magdalino (ed.), *The Perception of the Past in Twelfth-Century Europe* (London, 1992), pp. 99–116.

4 Florus, *Epitome of Roman History*, trans. E.S. Forster (Loeb, 1929), p. 6; cf. Reynolds, *Texts and Transmission*, pp. 164–6; M.D. Reeve, 'The Transmission of Florus, *Epitoma de Tito Livo* and the *Periochae*', *Classical Quarterly*, 38 (1988), pp. 477–91.

5 Justin, *Epitome of the Philippic History of Pompeius Trogus*, trans. J.C. Yardley (Atlanta, 1994); cf. Reynolds, *Texts and Transmission*, pp. 197–9. For Pompeius Trogus as a historian who should be ranked alongside Sallust, Livy and Tacitus, see the life of Probus, in *Historia Augusta*, trans. D. Magie (Loeb, 1932), II.7, p. 339.

6 Valerius Maximus, *Facta et Dicta Memorabilia*, ed. and trans. D.R. Shackleton Bailey, *Memorable Doings and Sayings* (Loeb, 2000); cf. Reynolds, *Texts and Transmission*, pp. 428–30; G. Maslakov, 'Valerius Maximus and Roman Historiography – A Study of the *Exempla* Tradition', *Aufstieg und Niedergang der römische Welt*, II.32.1 (1984), pp. 437–96.

7 Eutropius, *Breviarium ab Urbe Condita*, trans. H.W. Bird (Liverpool, 1993); cf. L.B. Mortensen, 'The Diffusion of Roman Histories in the Middle Ages: A List of Orosius, Eutropius, Paulus Diaconus and Landolfus Sagax Manuscripts', *Filologica Mediolatina*, 6–7 (1999–2000), pp. 101–200; M.T. Kretschmer, *Rewriting Roman History in the Middle Ages – The Historia Romana and the Manuscript Bamberg, Hist.3* (Leiden, 2007).

of a lengthy search'.[8] It was the same sort of intention which lay behind William of Malmesbury's twelfth-century *Polyhistor*, his own distillation of *facta et dicta memorabilia*, and the thirteenth-century *Gesta Romanorum*, a collection of moralised historical *exempla* which was also translated into the vernacular.[9]

The primary significance of the transmission of this particular range and selection of classical historians lies in the different models of writing which they provided. Such influence could be generic – whereas Sallust wrote history as the record of recent or contemporary political and military events, Livy conceived of it as the history of a city from its foundation (*ab urbe condita*), Suetonius as the life and deeds of a single individual and Pompeius Trogus as the history of the world since Ninus, king of Assyria. Or it could be particular – Sallust's historiography directly shaped the writing of, for example, Widukind of Corvey and Richer of Rheims in the tenth century,[10] Wipo and (as Orderic Vitalis readily recognised)

---

8 Valerius Maximus, *Facta et Dicta Memorabilia*, I.praef., p. 13. For comparable claims, see Aulus Gellius, *Noctes Atticae*, trans. J.C. Rolfe, *Attic Nights* (Loeb, 1927), pref., p. xxxi; Justin, *Epitome of the Philippic History*, pref., p. 13 ('I excerpted all the most noteworthy material; I omitted what did not make pleasurable reading or serve to provide a moral, and I produced a brief anthology to refresh the memory of those who had studied history in Greek and to provide instruction for those who had not'); Macrobius, *Saturnalia*, trans. P.V. Davies (New York, 1969), I.pref.10–11, p. 28; Ivo of Chartres, prologue to the *Decretum*, trans. B.C. Brasington, in R. Somerville and B.C. Brasington (eds), *Prefaces to Canon Law Books in Latin Christianity – Selected Translations 500–1245* (New Haven, 1998), p. 133; *Moralium Dogma Philosophorum*, ed. J. Holmberg, *Das Moralium Dogma Philosophorum des Guillaume de Conches, lateinisch, altfranzösisch und mittelniederfränkisch* (Uppsala, 1929), pp. 5, 73; Gerald of Wales, *Gemma Ecclesiastica*, trans. J.J. Hagen, *The Jewel of the Church* (Leiden, 1979), pref., p. 3.

9 William of Malmesbury, *Polyhistor*, ed. H.T. Ouellette (Binghamton, 1982); *Gesta Romanorum*, trans. C. Swann, rev. W. Hooper (London, 1906); *Li Fet des Romains*, ed. L.-F. Flutre and K. Sneyders de Vogel (Paris, 1938); cf. R.M. Thomson, *William of Malmesbury* (Woodbridge, 1987), pp. 25, 66–9, 185; J. Beer, *Narrative Conventions of Truth in the Middle Ages* (Geneva, 1981), pp. 47–62.

10 Widukind, *Res Gestae Saxonicae*, ed. and trans. E. Rotter and B. Schneidmüller (rev. edn, Stuttgart, 1992); Richer, *Historiae*, ed. and trans. R. Latouche (Paris, 1930–37); cf. H. Beumann, *Widukind von Korvei: Untersuchungen zur Geschichtsschreibung Ideengeschichte des 10. Jahrhunderts* (Weimar, 1950); H. Beumann, 'Historiographische Konzeption und politische Ziele Widukinds von Korvey', *Settimane di Studio*, 17 (1970), pp. 857–94; S. Bagge, *Kings, Politics and the Right Order of the World in German Historiography c.950–1150* (Leiden, 2002), ch. 1; B. Smalley, *Historians in the Middle Ages* (London, 1974), pp. 173–4; R. Latouche,

William of Poitiers in the eleventh,[11] and Suger of Saint-Denis and William of Malmesbury in the twelfth.[12] Josephus had a comparable impact on Widukind, Rahewin and Guibert of Nogent,[13] Suetonius on Einhard and William of Malmesbury,[14] Livy on Lampert of Hersfeld.[15] Before tackling medieval historiography in terms of the criteria which it developed for itself, therefore, it is necessary to grasp what was on offer from the writings of those particular classical authors – most notably Sallust and Josephus – who proved so influential on the conception and practice of history-writing in the Middle Ages, both in and of themselves but also as part of a continuous process of transcription.

Sallust's two surviving works of history, the *Jugurthine War* and the *Catiline* (or *Catiline War*), clearly established that the historian's primary concern should be with moral judgement, motive, invented speeches, vivid battle scenes, proverbial maxims and, at the most basic level, with a subject-matter which included

---

'Un Imitateur de Salluste au Xe Siècle, l'Historien Richer', in R. Latouche, *Études Médiévales* (Paris, 1966), pp. 69–81.
11 Wipo, *Deeds of Conrad*, trans. T.E. Mommsen and K.F. Morrison, in *Imperial Lives and Letters of the Eleventh Century* (New York, 1962; rev. edn 2000), pp. 52–100; William of Poitiers, *Gesta Guillelmi*, ed. and trans. R.H.C. Davis and M. Chibnall (Oxford, 1998); cf. Orderic Vitalis, *Historia Ecclesiastica*, ed. and trans. M. Chibnall, *The Ecclesiastical History of Orderic Vitalis* (Oxford, 1980), IV, p. 259; Smalley, *Historians in the Middle Ages*, pp. 174–5; J. Schneider, *Die Vita Heinrici IV und Sallust – Studien zu Stil und Imitatio in der mittellateinischen Prosa* (Berlin, 1965).
12 Suger, *Gesta Hludowici*, trans. R.C. Cusimano and J. Moorhead, *Deeds of Louis the Fat* (Washington, DC, 1992). Compare, for example, the sleepless paranoia of Henry I in the *Gesta Hludowici* with that of Jugurtha in Sallust's *Jugurthine War*, or the riding and shooting of William Rufus in William of Malmesbury's *Gesta Regum Anglorum* with that of a young Jugurtha. See, respectively, Suger, *Gesta Hludowici*, XXVI, p. 114; Sallust, *Jugurthine War*, trans. J.C. Rolfe (Loeb, 1931), LXXII, pp. 287–9; William of Malmesbury, *Gesta Regum Anglorum*, ed. and trans. R.A.B. Mynors, R.M. Thomson and M. Winterbottom, *The History of the English Kings* (Oxford, 1999), IV.305, p. 543; Sallust, *Jugurthine War*, VI, pp. 141–3.
13 Rahewin, *The Deeds of Frederick Barbarossa*, trans. C.C. Mierow (New York, 1953), and see page 49; Guibert of Nogent, *Gesta Dei per Francos*, trans. R. Levine, *The Deeds of God Through the Franks* (Woodbridge, 1997), and see page 405.
14 G.B. Townend, 'Suetonius and His Influence', in T.A. Dorey (ed.), *Latin Biography* (London, 1967), pp. 79–111; M. Schütt, 'The Literary Form of William of Malmesbury's *Gesta Regum*', *English Historical Review*, 46 (1931), pp. 255–60.
15 G. Billanovich, *Lamperto di Hersfeld e Tito Livio* (Padua, 1945).

war and politics but geography and ethnography too.[16] Sallust's accounts of the war with Jugurtha and the conspiracy of Catiline accordingly set striking narratives of significant historical events within much wider interpretative frameworks of moral and political analysis.[17] First and foremost, this involved repeatedly denouncing the prevalence of greed and avarice in Roman public life – a corruption born of wealth, luxury and arrogance and which had so infected the conduct of nobility and populace alike that it had left everything in Rome for sale.[18] This moral critique was highlighted from the very beginning of both works.[19] The opening remarks in the *Catiline*, for example, tie the process of decline directly to the mutability of human affairs. The life of mortals, Sallust observes, was originally free from cupidity but, once the lust for power started to direct the human mind towards the conduct of war, it was found that the exercise of mental capabilities, rather than physical strength, had a particular effectiveness in military activity. In peace, by contrast, such mental capabilities were less potent, and labour was accordingly replaced by sloth, temperance by lust, and equity by arrogance. The result was instability and constant confusion, as shifts in moral conduct became mirrored by changes in fortune and rule

---

16 B. Smalley, 'Sallust in the Middle Ages', in R.R. Bolgar (ed.), *Classical Influences on European Culture AD 500–1500* (Cambridge, 1971), pp. 165–75; cf. C.S. Kraus and A.J. Woodman, *Latin Historians* (Oxford, 1997), pp.10–50; R. Syme, *Sallust* (Berkeley, 1964); D.J. Wilcox, *The Development of Florentine Humanist Historiography in the Fifteenth Century* (Cambridge, MA, 1969), pp. 130–69.
17 Sallust, *Catiline* and *Jugurthine War*, trans. J.C. Rolfe (Loeb, 1931).
18 Sallust, *Jugurthine War*, XX, p. 179. For the popularity of this final remark, see, for example, Thietmar of Merseburg, *Chronicon*, trans. D.A. Warner, *Ottonian Germany* (Manchester, 2001), III.13, pp. 137–8; William of Malmesbury, *Historia Novella*, ed. and trans. K.R. Potter (London, 1955), II.483, p. 42; cf. Vergil, *Aeneid*, trans. H.R. Fairclough, rev. G.P. Goold (Loeb, 2000), VIII.324–7, p. 83; Ralph de Diceto, *Imagines Historiarum*, ed. W. Stubbs, *The Historical Works of Master Ralph de Diceto, Dean of London* (London, 1876), p. 169.
19 Cf. Quintilian, *Institutio Oratoria*, trans. H.E. Butler (Loeb, 1920–22), III.8.9, pp. 483–5, who suggests that Sallust's prologues to the *Jugurthine War* and *Catiline* contain nothing pertinent to the history which they introduce. According to Conrad of Hirsau, Sallust's works represent two types of introduction – a prologue which introduces the subject (*ante rem*) and a prologue which is quite separate (*praeter rem*), in this case a defence against the accusations of his enemies: Conrad of Hirsau, *Dialogus Super Auctores*, ed. R.B.C. Huygens (Leiden, 1970), pp. 103–4.

(*imperium*).[20] This overarching historical process furnished Sallust with his primary reason for choosing the conspiracy of Catiline as the particular subject-matter for his writing – not just because it was, in itself, an event worthy of memory, but also because the danger which it represented was unprecedented, as it was the first manifestation of the political consequences of the moral corruption which had recently taken root in the Roman people. In his own political life, Sallust explains, he had seen shamelessness, extravagance and greed, and it was this pernicious combination of luxury and avarice – the worst of all evils – which, in his opinion, had enabled Catiline to secure support for his conspiracy.[21]

It is from the perspective of a much broader process of moral and political corruption, therefore, that Sallust constructs the background to his history – what was instituted by earlier generations as the means of conducting war and politics, how they maintained the political community, how that *res publica* had increased in size but how it had then changed from exemplifying the noblest and the best to being the worst and most vicious.[22] The turning-point for Rome, as far as Sallust was concerned, was victory in the Punic Wars.[23] With greatness secured, other peoples subjugated and Carthage destroyed, wealth and inactivity became burdensome to Rome. The love of money and the lust for power – according to Sallust, the substance of all evils – generated, in their turn, the twin vices of avarice and ambition, spreading like a plague (*labes*) and transforming Roman rule into something cruel and intolerable.[24] Such was the power of this disease (*morbum*) that Catiline was able to mount his conspiracy without being betrayed. Catiline, in short, exemplified a much deeper moral and political malaise.[25] Sallust concluded, after considerable reflection, that what had enabled the Roman people to achieve and sustain their earlier outstanding political and military feats was, not superiority of numbers or resources, nor unremitting good fortune, but

---

20 Sallust, *Catiline*, II, p. 5.
21 *Catiline*, III, pp. 7–11.
22 *Catiline*, V, p .11.
23 Cf. Livy, *Ab Urbe Condita*, trans. E.T. Sage (Loeb, 1936), XXI.1, p. 3; Valerius Maximus, *Facta et Dicta Memorabilia*, VII.2, p. 109, IX.1, p. 295.
24 Sallust, *Catiline*, X, pp. 17–19.
25 *Catiline*, XXXVI, p. 63.

the distinction of a few virtuous citizens. However, once Rome was corrupted by luxury and sloth, the *res publica* was able to overcome the vices of its rulers and magistrates only by virtue of its own greatness. This was the process that Sallust saw represented by the defeat of Catiline and this was why his narrative culminated in the artfully paired speeches, and characters, of Julius Caesar and Cato the Younger. The contrasting virtues of Caesar and Cato represented the two exceptions to the luxury, arrogance and avarice which had supplanted those very qualities of mind which had originally created and maintained the Roman *res publica*. It is Cato who delivers the devastating indictment of the degeneracy of the Roman nobility and populace, and it is his counsel to the Senate which accordingly prevails.[26]

The *Jugurthine War* picks up and develops the same broad themes as the *Catiline*. The character and conduct (*mores*) of Rome, Sallust admits, have made him sad and weary at a time when the route to public office was no longer provided by virtue but by robbery and deception. He had chosen to write about the war in north Africa not only because of its scale, its atrocity and its fluctuating successes, but also because it marked the first occasion within Rome when there was political opposition to the arrogance of the nobility – a struggle which was ultimately to reach such a peak of frenzy that it resulted in civil war and the devastation of the Italian peninsula.[27] It is thus the avarice of the Roman nobility in which Jugurtha places his hopes for success and it is the luxury, fecklessness and arrogance of the Roman nobility which provide him with great assistance throughout the course of the subsequent conflict.[28] Once again, it is the destruction of Carthage which Sallust holds responsible for the inactivity and abundance of resources which, in turn, had precipitated the growth of such corruption in Rome. On this occasion, however, Sallust gives this 'plague' of avarice a directly political manifestation, in the development of factional politics. As soon as fear of the enemy had disappeared, he writes, the *res publica* was torn in two by the effects of arrogance and licence in the nobility and the populace. Rapacity and self-interest replaced concern for the common good; unrestrained

---

26 *Catiline*, LIII–LIV, pp. 111–13; cf. Rahewin, *Deeds of Frederick*, IV.46, p. 279.
27 Sallust, *Jugurthine War*, IV–V, p. 139.
28 *Jugurthine War*, XIII, p. 155, LXXXV, p. 321.

power and avarice attacked everything until they brought about their own downfall in the 'earthquake' of civil dissension.[29] Once again, Sallust chooses to personify these failings, in this case in the form of the flawed characters of two Roman generals, Metellus and Marius, the former virtuous except for the arrogance that was characteristic of his noble rank, the latter distinguished and illustrious as a non-noble 'new man' (*novus homo*) but whose hatred had left him under the guidance of the worst of all counsellors, namely desire (*cupido*) and anger (*ira*).[30] Once again, it is left to a carefully staged speech, in this case by the tribune Memmius, to deliver a damning indictment of the venality and self-indulgence which would ultimately see the freedom enjoyed by the Roman people replaced by tyranny and slavery.[31]

If the influence of Sallust's approach to historiography was dominated by its overarching moral critique, then its impact also extended to the series of self-conscious reflections on the nature of writing history with which he chose to introduce both works. Sallust opens the *Catiline*, for example, by juxtaposing rule by the mind (*ingenium*) with rule by bodily strength or physical force (*vis*) – the former is characteristic of human beings, the latter of animals. Since life is short, Sallust continues, its remembrance (*memoria*) must be made as long as possible. Since the glory of the body or of material wealth is fleeting and fragile whereas the glory of mental virtue is shining and eternal, it is the remembrance of moral worth which should be rewarded, not with the silence that attends transient physical existence, but with a lasting reputation (*fama*).[32] This task, he concludes, is the responsibility of the historian. Even though the person who writes down what was done (*res gestae*) does not attain the same glory as the people who have performed the deeds themselves, the act of writing still constitutes a noble and beneficial contribution to the *res publica*. However, Sallust also acknowledges that this is an

---

29 *Jugurthine War*, XLI–XLII, pp. 223–7; cf. anon., *Life of the Emperor Henry IV*, trans. T.E. Mommsen and K.F. Morrison, *Imperial Lives and Letters of the Eleventh Century* (New York, 1962, rev. edn 2000), IV, p. 110.
30 *Jugurthine War*, XLV, p. 231, LXIII–LXIV, pp. 271–5, LXXXII–LXXXIII, pp. 305–7.
31 *Jugurthine War*, XXX–XXXI, pp. 197–205.
32 *Catiline*, I, p. 3.

extremely difficult task. In the first instance, this is because the words chosen by the historian must be of a quality to match the deeds done. In the second instance, it is because many people will think that, when the historian condemns wicked actions, the author is doing so simply out of ill-will and envy; conversely, when the historian commemorates the virtue and glory of good individuals, everyone will readily accept as true what they think they could easily do themselves but, if what is commemorated is anything over and above that, then they will consider the account to be false, as if it were made up (*veluti ficta pro falsis*).[33] Sallust states, therefore, that whilst his original goal in writing history was to record the deeds of the Roman people (*res gestae populi Romani*), or at least those that were worthy of being remembered, and to do so piece by piece (*carptim*), it was only because he was in political retirement that he was able to do so, since his mind was now free from hope (*spes*), fear (*metus*) and party allegiance (*partes rei publicae*).[34] In fact, he remarks, everyone who deliberates on doubtful matters will more readily perceive the truth when they are free from both hatred (*odium*) and friendship (*amicitia*), anger (*ira*) and pity (*misericordia*).[35] Sallust declares himself well aware, moreover, from the example provided by Greek historiography, that the vagaries of fortune can decide what should, or should not, be celebrated for posterity or buried in obscurity. The deeds of the Athenian people were certainly illustrious, but this was a measure, not of truth, but of the ability of the Athenian writers who had extolled them. The Greeks were not, in Sallust's opinion, as distinguished as their reputation (*fama*) made them out to be. The Roman people, by contrast, never had the benefit of such a

---

33 *Catiline*, III, p. 7, a passage subsequently quoted, and glossed, in Aulus Gellius, *Noctes Atticae*, IV.15, pp. 357–9; cf. Gregory of Tours, *Histories*, trans. L. Thorpe, *The History of the Franks* (Harmondsworth, 1974), IV.13, p. 208, VII.1, p. 388; Bernardus Silvestris, *Commentary on the First Six Books of Virgil's Aeneid*, trans. E.G. Schreiber and T.E. Maresca (Lincoln, 1979), VI, p. 51.
34 *Catiline*, IV, p.9.
35 *Catiline*, LI, p. 89, a passage subsequently quoted by, for example, the *Moralium Dogma Philosophorum*, p. 21; Cosmas of Prague, *The Chronicle of the Czechs*, trans. L. Wolverton (Washington, DC, 2009), III.7, p. 189; Rahewin, *Deeds of Frederick*, III.46, p. 219; Gervase of Tilbury, *Otia Imperialia*, III.35, p. 629; cf. Thomas Basin, *Historiae*, ed. and trans. C. Samaran, *Histoire de Charles VII* (Paris, 1933–44), prol., p. 2.

write-up because their wisest and best individuals chose to devote all their time to doing things rather than speaking or writing about them, preferring that their good deeds should be praised by other people than that they should narrate them themselves.[36] It is this imbalance which Sallust sets out to redress.

The *Jugurthine War* includes a reprise of very similar historiographical reflections to those in the *Catiline* but, on this occasion, Sallust chooses to take them one step further. He opens this new work, for example, by extending his earlier juxtaposition of mind and body to the relationship between virtue and fortune. When human life is directed by the mind, he explains, it advances to glory on the path of virtue (*via virtutis*), securing both power and reputation without any need for the intervention of fortune. It is only when people are captivated by evil desires and the pleasures of the body that the weakness of human nature is highlighted and individuals transfer their own culpability onto external events (*negotia*). The effect of sloth, luxury and physical pleasure is to make the mind torpid through neglect. Were humans to concentrate exclusively on the good, then they would rule, rather than be ruled by, events – that is, by what happens (*casus*). They would also become immortal in their glory, since it is the distinguished deeds of the mind which are eternal.[37] This is where the writing of history becomes so important. According to Sallust, the utility of commemorating what has been done (*memoria rerum gestarum*) lies in the great advantage (*commodum*) which it brings to the *res publica*. Distinguished citizens of Rome, he explains, used to say that, when they saw the images (*imagines*) of their ancestors, their minds were set ablaze towards virtue. It was not the material or the form of these images, he continues, but the remembrance of

---

36 *Catiline*, VIII, pp. 15–17; cf. Valerius Maximus, *Facta et Dicta Memorabilia*, III.2, p. 257. According to Cicero, the Romans pursued the science of living virtuously in their lives more than in their writings: Cicero, *Tusculan Disputations*, trans. J.E.King (Loeb, 1945), IV.3.5–6, p. 333. For the development of this theme, see, for example, Wipo, *Deeds of Conrad*, II, pp. 62–3, V, p. 70 (see also pages 166–7); for the dependence of virtue on the act of writing it up, see 'Probus', in *Historia Augusta*, I.1–2, p. 335; Jerome, *Life of Hilarion*, trans. W.H. Fremantle, G. Lewis and W.G. Martley (Oxford, 1893), I, p. 303 ('for the virtue of those who have done great deeds is esteemed in proportion to the ability with which it has been praised by men of genius'). See also page 493.
37 *Jugurthine War*, I–II, pp. 133–5.

the deeds which kindled this flame, a desire which could not be quenched until these citizens' own virtue equalled the reputation and glory of their ancestors.[38] Whilst emphasising the moral–didactic utility of writing history, however, Sallust also points out, characteristically, that this function is double-edged. The remembrance of glorious deeds should serve as an incentive to perform virtuous actions of one's own; the fact that it no longer seemed to be having this effect, and that his contemporaries were striving to rival their ancestors only in wealth and extravagance, was one more indication of their corruption.[39] Indeed, Sallust goes further and castigates the Roman nobility for confusing the act of reading about virtue with the actual performance of virtuous deeds. In presenting Marius, the virtuous *novus homo*, as such a contrast to the arrogance of the nobility, Sallust has him refer to his own deeds as 'images' but ones which he has made himself rather than inherited. What nobles have learned from books, Marius states, he has learned through soldiery; what nobles have merely heard and read, he has actually seen and done himself. When nobles speak in praise of their ancestors and commemorate their brave deeds, therefore, they may think that this makes them more distinguished. In fact, the reverse is true – the more glorious the life of their ancestors, the more shameful is their own sloth (*socordia*). The glory of one's ancestors is, in effect, a light (*quasi lumen*) which shines on succeeding generations, allowing neither their good nor their bad deeds to remain hidden.[40] The *memoria rerum gestarum*, in other words, serves as a castigation of vice as much as an object-lesson in virtue.

In emphasising both the importance and the difficulty of writing down virtuous deeds to be commemorated by posterity, Sallust's *Catiline* and *Jugurthine War* set out guidelines for the way in which history could serve as a moral and political critique as well as for the methods which should be deployed in order to safeguard truth from the distortions of hope, fear and partisan

---

38 *Jugurthine War*, IV, pp. 137–9.
39 *Jugurthine War*, IV, p. 139.
40 *Jugurthine War*, LXXXV, pp. 313–17; cf. Wipo, *Deeds of Conrad*, Ep.ded., pp. 52–3, prol., p. 54 (see also pages 166–7). For Marius as a model of conduct, see, for example, Gerald of Wales, *Expugnatio Hibernica*, ed. and trans. A.B. Scott and F.X. Martin, *The Conquest of Ireland* (Dublin, 1978), I.26, p. 87.

loyalty. The approach these texts exemplified provided an influential model for the writing of history – the brevity and antithesis of their epigrammatic observations or *sententiae* ('it is easy to begin a war, difficult to stop one');[41] their set-piece descriptions of battles and sieges; their ethnographic digressions on the laws, customs and language of other peoples; and their detailed depictions of the places and regions in which the events being described had occurred (*descriptiones locorum*, which, in the case of Africa, were often subsequently accompanied by maps). Both the *Catiline* and the *Jugurthine War* also include 'documents' (*documenta*), presented either as transcriptions of original letters (*exempla*) or as texts which have been explicitly summarised by Sallust himself and introduced with a phrase such as 'their import was as follows' (*earum sententia haec erat*).[42] Both works include speeches which were presented, again, either as verbatim transcriptions or as authorial versions: 'he delivered a speech of this sort' (*huiusmodi orationem habuit*); 'he spoke in this fashion' (*hoc modo disseruit*).[43] Sallust readily accepts his ignorance of some matters and the limitations to his own knowledge of what had actually happened: 'I have not discovered whether his delay was genuine or due to strategy'; 'I have learned too little'; 'it has not been uncovered' (*parum comperimus*; *parum cognovi*; *parum exploratum est*).[44] As a result, he can offer more than one causal explanation for events: 'he acted either for the sake of dissimulation in order to frighten the king or because he was blinded by desire' (*seu... seu*).[45] Sallust states that he is writing to the best of his ability (*quantum ingenium possum*) and as truthfully as he is able (*quam verissime potero*).[46] On bitterly contested issues, however, his intention is to report the opinions of others or profess to come down on neither one side nor the other: 'I will leave the matter in the middle' (*nos eam*

---

41 *Jugurthine War*, LXXXIII, p. 307.
42 *Catiline*, XXXIV, p. 59, XLIV, p. 75; *Jugurthine War*, IX, p. 147, XXIV, p. 185.
43 *Catiline*, XX, p. 35, L, p. 89; *Jugurthine War*, IX, p. 147, XXX, p. 197.
44 *Catiline*, XXII, p. 41; *Jugurthine War*, LXVII, p. 281, LXXIX, p. 301, LXXXVIII, p. 327, CXIII, p. 377; cf. Vergil, *Aeneid*, XII.320–3, p. 323.
45 *Jugurthine War*, XXXVII, p. 215, CIII, p. 361.
46 *Catiline*, IV, p. 9, XVIII, p. 31, LIII, p. 111. For the use of the second of these phrases, see, for example, William of Malmesbury, *Gesta Regum Anglorum*, II.198, p. 357 and cf. III.238, p. 445.

rem in medio relinquemus).⁴⁷ On one occasion, he simply shifts the burden of truth to his sources: 'although my account differs from the story [*fama*] which obtains for many people, I have given it as it was translated from the Punic books said to have been written by king Hiempsal and in accordance with what the inhabitants of that land themselves believe; I will relate it as briefly as possible but its trustworthiness [*fides*] rests with its authors'.⁴⁸

Sallust's influence on the writing of history in the Middle Ages was profound, reinforced, as it was, by the subsequent endorsement, not just of Martial, Aulus Gellius and Quintilian, but also of Augustine, Orosius and Jerome.⁴⁹ Not without reason, therefore, did John of Salisbury consider him to be the 'most potent' amongst Roman historians.⁵⁰ Sallust's impact, however, was, if

---

47 *Catiline*, XIX, p. 33, quoted, for example, by Sigebert of Gembloux, *Chronica* (*PL* 160, cols 57–240), col. 197; William of Malmesbury, *Gesta Regum Anglorum*, I.9, p. 29.

48 *Jugurthine War*, XVII, p. 171, quoted, for example, by William of Malmesbury, *Gesta Regum Anglorum*, I.prol., p. 17; cf. Valerius Maximus, *Facta et Dicta Memorabilia*, I.8, p. 111: 'since I am saying nothing new but recalling things handed down, let the originators prove their credibility [*fides*] and let it be my part not to shy away from items consecrated by famous literary memorials as though they were vanities'. For this disclaimer, see also Seneca, *Quaestiones Naturales*, trans. T.H. Corcoran (Loeb, 1972), IV.3.1, p. 47: 'And so I consider myself one of those witnesses with a secondhand brand of information, who say that they themselves did not actually see it. Or I may do as historians do. After they have lied to their own satisfaction about a lot of things, they are unwilling to guarantee some one point and toss out "the verification will be found among my sources" (*penes auctores fides erit*)'. This remark was repeated by Solinus, *Collectanea Rerum Memorabilium*, ed. T.E. Mommsen (Berlin, 1895), pref., p. 2; cf. G. Simon, 'Untersuchungen zur Topik der Widmungsbriefe mittelalterlicher Geschichtsschreiber bis zum Ende des 12. Jahrhunderts', *Archiv für Diplomatik*, 4 (1958), p. 91, and *Archiv für Diplomatik*, 5–6 (1959–60), p. 92.

49 Martial, *Epigrams*, trans. D.R. Shackleton Bailey (Loeb, 1993), XIV.191, p. 302; L. Holford-Strevens, *Aulus Gellius: An Antonine Scholar and His Achievement* (rev. edn, Oxford, 2003), pp. 251–3; Quintilian, *Institutio Oratoria*, IV.2.45, p. 75, X.1.32, p. 21, X.1.101–2, p. 59 (see also page 134); Augustine, *De Civitate Dei*, trans. H. Bettenson, *On the City of God Against the Pagans* (2nd edn, Harmondsworth, 1984), I.5, p. 11 (*nobilitate veritatis historicus*), III.17, p. 111; Orosius, *Seven Books of History Against the Pagans*, trans. R.J. Deferrari (Washington, DC, 1964), V.15, p. 197 (see also page 39, note 18), VI.6, p. 241; R. Mellor, *The Roman Historians* (London, 1999), p. 46; cf. Otto of Freising, *Chronicle*, trans. C.C. Mierow, *The Two Cities: A Chronicle of Universal History* (New York, 1928; reprinted 2000), II.44, p. 207.

50 John of Salisbury, *Policraticus*, trans. J.B. Pike, *The Frivolities of Courtiers and the Footprints of Philosophers* (Minneapolis, 1938), III.12, p. 192; cf. Rupert of Deutz, *De*

not equalled, then at least paralleled by that of Flavius Josephus, a writer to whom Cassiodorus referred as 'practically a second Livy' and as 'complex and many-layered' (*subtilis et multiplex*).[51] Josephus' *Jewish War* was an account, in seven books, of the events which had culminated in the destruction of Jerusalem in 70 AD. According to Josephus, this was God's judgment on a people corrupted by unprecedented impiety and riven with internal faction and dissent. It marked the inexorable and just retribution which the Zealots had brought upon a polluted city through their own manifold wickedness and which the Roman army effectively did everything possible to avoid. Even had the Romans not acted, Josephus maintains that Jerusalem, like Sodom, would still have been destroyed by an earthquake, flood or lightning – a fitting punishment on a generation whose madness had precipitated the prophesied ruin of their nation and who had themselves started the fire which burned the Temple on the very anniversary of the day on which it had first been destroyed by the Babylonians.[52] Some years later, Josephus reset this damning account within the much broader context of twenty books of *Antiquities*, a history of the Jewish people (*prosapia*) and fatherland (*patria*) over the course of some five thousand years.[53] Starting from the creation of the world, Josephus narrates the origin of the Jews, the laws through which they were first instructed in virtue by Moses, their varying fortunes, changes in their way of life, the succession of their high priests and kings, the brave deeds of their leaders and the different wars which they fought – up to, and including, their most recent conflict with the Romans. In choosing to write history on this scale, Josephus states that he wanted to inform a Greek

---

Gloria et Honore Filii Hominis Super Mattheum, ed. R. Haacke (*CCCM* 29, Turnhout, 1979), V.6, p. 153.

51 Cassiodorus, *Institutiones*, trans. J.W. Halporn, *Institutions of Divine and Secular Learning* (Liverpool, 2004), I.17.1, p. 149; cf. Otto of Freising, *Chronicle*, III.10, p. 235. For the medieval Latin manuscripts, see F. Blatt (ed.), *The Latin Josephus* (Copenhagen, 1958), vol. I, pp. 25–116.

52 Josephus, *De Bello Iudaico*, trans. G.A. Williamson, *The Jewish War* (Harmondsworth, 1970); cf. T. Rajak, *Josephus: The Historian and His Society* (London, 1983); J. Edmondson, S. Mason and J. Rives (eds), *Flavius Josephus and Flavian Rome* (Oxford, 2005).

53 Josephus, *Antiquitates*, trans. W. Whiston, *The Works of Josephus* (Peabody, 1987).

and Roman audience about the antiquity of his own people (the choice of both title and number of books was designed to mirror the *Roman Antiquities* of Dionysius of Halicarnassus). However, he was also explicitly concerned, once again, to instil the lesson that prosperity and happiness depend upon obedience to the will and the law of God; otherwise, apparent abundance and goodness would soon be turned to helplessness and calamity.[54]

Once Josephus' *Jewish War* and *Antiquities* had been translated into Latin in the course of the fourth and fifth centuries (including the version of the *Jewish War* which was subsequently circulated as 'Hegesippus'),[55] they became hugely influential as models for the writing of history. This is evident from the number and distribution of manuscripts, either of the complete texts or of excerpts, as well as in their particular impact on individual writers – on Bede, for example (an influence which extends to the autobiographical coda with which his history concludes),[56] Orderic Vitalis[57] and Rahewin (whose continuation of Otto of Freising's *Deeds of Frederick Barbarossa* is, in large part, a fusion of passages from Josephus and Sallust).[58] In the case of the *Jewish War*, Josephus' influence covers a wide range: his claims for the extraordinary nature of its subject-matter; the way in which he describes battles and sieges but also the horrors of famine and disease; his presentation of set-piece speeches before battle as well as speeches of counsel for, and against, a particular course of action; his appeals to omens, portents and prophetic dreams; his use of digressions

---

54 Josephus, *Antiquitates*, preface, pp. 27–8, XX.11.2, p. 541.
55 Cassiodorus, *Institutiones*, I.17.1, pp. 149–50; Josephus, *De Bello Iudaico*, ed. G. Squarciafico (Venice, 1486); Blatt, *The Latin Josephus*, vol. I [*Antiquitates* I–V]; *Hegisippus*, ed. V. Ussani, *Hegesippi Qui Dicitur Historiae Libri V* (Vienna, 1932); cf. H. Schreckenberg, *Die Flavius-Josephus-Tradition in Antike und Mittelalter* (Leiden, 1972). For the influence of the five-book Latin version of Josephus' *Jewish War* on Henry of Huntingdon, William of Malmesbury and Geoffrey of Monmouth, see N. Wright, 'Twelfth-Century Receptions of a Text – Anglo-Norman Historians and Hegisippus', *Anglo-Norman Studies*, 31 (2008), pp. 177–95.
56 Bede, *Historia Ecclesiastica Gentis Anglorum*, trans. B. Colgrave, rev. J. McClure and R. Collins, *The Ecclesiastical History of the English People* (Oxford, 1994), V.24, pp. 293–5; cf. Gregory of Tours, *Histories*, X.31, p. 603; Orderic Vitalis, *Historia Ecclesiastica*, V.1, pp. 7–9, XIII.45, pp. 551–7.
57 See M. Chibnall's 'General Introduction' to Orderic Vitalis, *Historia Ecclesiastica*, p. 62.
58 Otto of Freising (with continuation by Rahewin), *The Deeds of Frederick Barbarossa*, trans. C.C. Mierow (Columbia, 1953), III–IV, e.g. pp. 209–11.

(topographical depictions of Galilee and Judea, for example, but also summaries of different schools of thought, such as those of the Pharisees, Sadducees and Essenes); and his commemoration of the names of those individuals who distinguished themselves for their bravery in battle ('it is a glorious thing', Josephus writes, 'to win renown at the cost of one's life and by some splendid deed to make oneself remembered by future generations').[59] Characters of courage and virtue – Vespasian, Titus and, to some extent, Josephus himself – are accordingly set against corresponding paradigms of vicious tyranny – John of Gischala (himself modelled, in part, on Sallust's depiction of Catiline) and Simon bar Giora. King Herod, meanwhile, is put forward as a wretched juxtaposition of external prosperity and public good fortune with the private tragedy of filial and fratricidal strife.

Like Sallust, however, Josephus was also equally influential for the self-reflexive methodological prologues with which he initially justified both of his historical narratives. To commend to posterity the events of one's own time, he writes, is to provide a praiseworthy testimony (*testimonium*) and this is certainly preferable to rearranging an account of the remote past which has been written by somebody else.[60] Thus, whilst his own historiography starts with a brief outline narrative from the point at which Greek writers and Jewish prophets had left off, Josephus states that he will record in greater depth, and with as much care as he can, all the events of the war in which he had himself participated.[61] He accordingly presents his history, first and foremost, as a corrective to those accounts which had been composed by people who were not themselves present at these events but who had put together the fanciful and inconsistent things which they had heard other people narrate, writing them up 'in the manner of orators' (*oratorum more*).[62] The very first sentence of the *Antiquities* points out that those who are disposed to write history are prompted, not by one and the same concern, but by many different causes. He then makes it clear that he himself had written history not, as

---

59 Josephus, *De Bello Iudaico*, III.7.17, p. 197.
60 *De Bello Iudaico*, pref.5, pp. 22–3.
61 *De Bello Iudaico*, pref.6, p. 23.
62 *De Bello Iudaico*, pref.1, p. 21, cited by Rahewin, *Deeds of Frederick*, III.prol., p. 171.

some people did, in order to secure his own glory by displaying the ornateness (*ornatus*) of his language, nor from a desire to show favour (*gratia*)[63] to those about whom he was writing. Instead, he had been compelled by necessity because he had himself been present at the events described and because those events had been so significant that their narration would be useful to everyone (*ad communem utilitatem*).[64]

Josephus sets considerable store by the value of eyewitness testimony as a guarantee against making things up, particularly when the events themselves seem incredible – the historian's own participation in the events that are being narrated not only renders his account effective but also, he says, makes it seem morally culpable (*inhonestum*) to tell lies in front of those who know the truth.[65] As a result, Josephus explicitly differentiates his own account from that of those eyewitnesses who had broken faith (*fides*) by falsifying events, either out of obsequiousness to the Romans or from hatred of the Jews, and who had thereby written, respectively, works of praise (*laudatio*) or castigation (*accusatio*).[66] Eschewing the distortions produced by both flattery (*obsequium*) and hostility (*invidia*),[67] Josephus asserts his own intention to set out the deeds of both the Romans and the Jews 'without any lying' (*sine ullo mendacio*) and expresses his determination to honour 'the truth of history' (*veritas historiae*).[68] He has written the *Jewish War* for those who love the truth.[69] It is not flattery or 'fiction' (*figmentum*); nor is it fable (*fabula*).[70] Likewise, in the *Antiquities*, the writings of Moses (on which the truthfulness of Josephus' own account of Jewish law is said to depend) are contrasted with the baseness of fable (*turpitudo fabularum*) and the deception of what is made

---

63 For the definition of *gratia* as remembering and returning services, respect and acts of friendship, see page 286.
64 Josephus, *Antiquitates*, pref.1, p. 27.
65 *De Bello Iudaico*, pref.5, p. 22, VI.3.3, p. 341, VI.5.3, p. 349. The passage from *De Bello Iudaico*, VI.3.3, p. 341, is quoted by Eusebius, *Ecclesiastical History*, trans. G.A. Williamson (Harmondsworth, 1965), III.6, p. 115, III.10.9–11, p. 123.
66 *De Bello Iudaico*, pref.2, p. 21.
67 *De Bello Iudaico*, V.2.5, p. 283.
68 *De Bello Iudaico*, pref.4–5, pp. 22–3.
69 *De Bello Iudaico*, pref.12, p. 25.
70 *De Bello Iudaico*, pref.2, p. 21, IV.4.3, p. 243.

up (*figmenta fallaces*).⁷¹ Josephus never denies that his language will reflect his own emotions at the tragedy which has befallen his people and he requests the reader's pardon accordingly, both for the accusations which he levels against those whom he regards as culpable and for the laments which he utters for his nation's sufferings. These expressions of grief may indeed transgress what he calls the 'law of history' (*lex historiae*), but Josephus suggests to anyone who may want to pass a stricter judgment that they should ascribe the facts (*res*) to history and only the grief to the writer.⁷² In setting himself up alongside Jeremiah as the author of a bitter lament for an iniquitous people,⁷³ Josephus therefore insists that those things which grieve him must be repressed by the 'law of writing' (*lex scribendi*) – this is not the occasion for private lamentation but for setting out the facts.⁷⁴ Josephus' closing words drive the point home: 'We promised to set down this history with complete truth for the benefit of those who wished to learn how the Romans fought this war with the Jews. The quality of its exposition may be left to the judgment of the reader but, as for its truth, I do not hesitate to declare faithfully [*confidenter*] that this has been my only goal throughout what I have written'.⁷⁵

The Bible

The Bible was, of course, fundamental to how medieval writers saw the nature and purpose of the historical process, but the task of tracing the range of its influence on the actual writing of 'history' in the Middle Ages is a complex one. Much like the classical tradition, Scripture offered a varied and heterogeneous model for what historiography could, or should, entail. Within the Bible itself the preservation of a historical record was clearly envisaged to serve some very practical and immediate purposes: 'Ask the former generation and carefully investigate what the fathers remember [*memoria patrum*]. For we were born only yesterday and know nothing, and our days on earth are but a shadow. Will

---

71 *Antiquitates*, pref.3, p. 28.
72 *De Bello Iudaico*, pref.4, p. 22, cited by Rahewin, *Deeds of Frederick*, IV.14, p. 245.
73 *De Bello Iudaico*, V.9.4, p. 309.
74 *De Bello Iudaico*, V.1.3, p. 277.
75 *De Bello Iudaico*, VII.11.5, p. 395.

they not instruct you and talk to you and bring forth words from their understanding?' (Job 8:8–10); 'That night the king could not sleep, so he ordered the histories and annals of earlier times [*historiae et annales priorum temporum*] to be brought to him and read in his presence' (Esther 6:1).[76] It is this pragmatic dimension to historiography which is reflected, for example, in an eleventh-century explanation of what it means for the ancient authority of the Old Testament, 'which diligently cultivated the histories of the fathers [*historiae partum*] with fruitful labour', to 'teach in prefigurative fashion that the fruit of contemporary affairs [also] ought to be stored in the cellar of memory'. Wipo, author of the narrative which follows, lists the Old Testament material which he has in mind: 'thus we remember that Abraham freed his cousin Lot in war; thus we discover that the sons of Israel overcame various enemies; because of the ranks of these writers, we have before our eyes (*prae oculis*) the wars of king David, the counsels of Solomon, the cleverness of Gideon, the battles of the Maccabees'.[77]

From Isidore's *Etymologies* onwards, lists of historians opened with the name of Moses[78] and, at this most general of levels, the Pentateuch (that is, the first five books of the Bible – Genesis, Exodus, Leviticus, Numbers and Deuteronomy) could certainly inspire a historiography which was universal, which was concerned with the programme and economy of salvation, and which set out the direct providential significance of events ordained by God. Writing in the mid-thirteenth century, for example, Bonaventure explains the significance of tracing that history in its entirety:

> the whole world is described in a most orderly sequence by Scripture as proceeding from beginning to end, in accordance with the peculiar beauty of its well-designed song. One can view, following the sequence of time, the variety, multiplicity and symmetry, order, rectitude and beauty of the many judgments proceeding from the wisdom of God governing the world. As no one can see the beauty of a song unless his view extends over the whole verse, so no one

---

76 Cf. Otto of Freising, *Chronicle*, Ep.ded., p. 87.
77 Wipo, *Deeds of Conrad*, prol., p. 54.
78 For example, Hugh of St Victor, *Didascalicon*, trans. J. Taylor, *The Didascalicon of Hugh of St Victor: A Medieval Guide to the Arts* (New York, 1961), III.2, p. 86; Robert the Monk, *Historia Ierosolimitana*, trans. C. Sweetenham, *History of the First Crusade* (Aldershot, 2005), prol., p. 77. See page 134, note 51.

sees the beauty of the order and governance of the universe unless he beholds the whole of it. Because no man is so long-lived that he can see the whole of it with the eyes of the flesh, and because no man can foresee the future by himself, the Holy Spirit has provided man with holy Scripture, the length of which is measured by the extent of the universe.[79]

At the same time, however, great care needs to be taken in offering any generalisation about such universal history representing the 'biblical' tradition in the singular. In terms of literary models, 'the Bible' should be understood as shorthand for a heterogeneous collection of sometimes very different types of writing – hence its medieval description as 'holy books' in the plural, or as a 'holy library' (*sancta bibliotheca*).[80] It was on this basis, for example, that the entire sequence of texts in the Old Testament and the New Testament could readily be subdivided according to the different functions which each of their respective books served – whereas the Pentateuch and the four Gospels were intended to teach, and the Prophets and the Epistles to admonish, their specifically 'historical' books were designed to warn.[81] Viewed from this perspective, therefore, the most direct and practical historiographical influence of the Bible derives, in the first instance, from those canonical books which were put into this third category, namely (from the Old Testament) four books of Kings (that is, 1–2 Samuel and 1–2 Kings) and 1–2 Chronicles, and (from the New Testament) the book of Acts and Revelation. Strictly speaking, these were the eight 'historical' books which served, either separately or in conjunction, as the primary models for how to write history in the Middle Ages.

---

79 Bonaventure, *Breviloquium*, trans. E.E. Nemmers (London, 1946), prol.2.4, p. 10.
80 For example, Henry of Huntingdon, *Historia Anglorum*, ed. and trans. D. Greenway, *History of the English* (Oxford, 1996), IX.37, p. 669; Richard FitzNigel, *Dialogus de Scaccario*, ed. and trans. E. Amt (Oxford, 2007), I.8, p. 77.
81 Abelard, *Commentary on Paul's Letter to the Romans*, trans. A.J. Minnis and A.B. Scott, in A.J. Minnis and A.B. Scott (eds), *Medieval Literary Theory and Criticism c.1100–c.1375* (Oxford, 1988), prol., pp. 100–2. For a case study of commentary on 'historical' books of the Bible (in this instance, 1, 2 Samuel, 1, 2 Kings, 1, 2 Chronicles, as well as 1, 2 Maccabees, Joshua, Judith and Esther), see M. De Jong, 'The Empire as *Ecclesia* – Hrabanus Maurus and Biblical *Historia* for Rulers', in Y. Hen and M. Innes (eds), *The Uses of the Past in the Early Middle Ages* (Cambridge, 2000), pp. 191–226.

The four books of Kings provide a historical narrative of the kingship of Israel from its beginning to its end and do so according to a clear interpretative framework – both the prosperity of individual rulers and the prosperity of their kingdom are conditional upon observance of God's law and obedience to His prophets. The replacement of Saul by David, the disciplining of David, the successes and failures of Solomon, the wickedness of Jeroboam, the reformations under Hezekiah and Josiah – these are all events which exemplify the consequences of maintaining or breaking God's covenant, and in a sequence which culminates in the destruction of Jerusalem and exile into captivity in Babylon. The two books of Chronicles rework much of the same material and, although their historical narrative describes the reigns of David and Solomon without dwelling on the failings of either ruler, the cautionary import remains to the fore – the ultimate destruction suffered by the House of David, the Temple of Jerusalem and the people of Israel represented just retribution for a repeated failure to heed prophetic admonitions and to obey the laws of God.

Taken together, the books of Kings and Chronicles would seem to present a pretty straightforward model for a narrative of historical events. Although Jerome thought that the Hebrew title for Chronicles, 'Words of Days' (*verba dierum*), could be given the more meaningful title 'chronicle of the whole of sacred history' (*chronicon totius divinae historiae*),[82] these two books generally had their name transliterated from the Greek Septuagint as *Paralipomenon*. The meaning of this last term was explained by Isidore, following Jerome, as 'things that were passed over or remain', because these books contained a brief summary of those things which had not been related in full or which had been left out by earlier books of the Bible. It was this etymology which was subsequently reflected in Cassiodorus' generic definition of chronicles as 'sketches of history or very brief summaries of the past' (*imagines historiarum brevissimaeque commemorationes temporum*).[83] Read in conjunction

---

82 Jerome, *Prologue to the Books of Samuel and Kings*, trans. W.H. Fremantle (Oxford, 1893), p. 490; Isidore of Seville, *Etymologiae*, trans. S.A. Barney, W.J. Lewis, J.A. Beach and O. Berghof, *The Etymologies of Isidore of Seville* (Cambridge, 2006), VI.1.7, p. 135.
83 Isidore, *Etymologiae*, VI.2.12, p. 136; Cassiodorus, *Institutiones*, I.17.2, p. 150. Cassiodorus' definition is quoted at the very start of Ralph de Diceto's *Abbreviationes*

with other books of the Bible, however, the scriptural accounts of David and Solomon could also be read as a model of how to go on and combine a prose narrative of deeds with, respectively, poetry (the Psalms) and proverbial maxims (Proverbs, the book of Wisdom). Such a fusion of different forms was certainly evident elsewhere in the Old Testament – in the book of Ezra (which intersperses its historical narrative with the texts of official documents and with first-person autobiography) and in the book of Daniel (where a historical narrative is conjoined with predictive prophecies not only about the destiny of Israel but also about the course of world history up to the Day of Judgment). The (apocryphal) books of 1 and 2 Maccabees, meanwhile, showed how different accounts could be given of the same historical events, in this case the second-century Jewish revolt against Antiochus IV Epiphanes and his son Eupator. A military narrative, sometimes ascribed to the authorship of Josephus,[84] these two books described a succession of deeds of bravery in war which culminated in the recapture of the Temple and city of Jerusalem by Judas Maccabeus. This account was then followed by a more reflective theological commentary on the same campaigns, which dwelt more on the themes of martyrdom, of divine chastisement and punishment, as well as of divine assistance in battle. In both versions, the commemorative and didactic function of the narrative was made clear: 'this man departed from life in this way, leaving the memory of his death as an example of virtue and bravery not only to the young but also to the entire people' (2 Maccabees 6:31). It was a lesson not lost on medieval historians when they came to write narratives of martial deeds in their own times, and especially when the campaign in question culminated in the recapture of Jerusalem.[85]

Chronicorum, ed. W. Stubbs, *The Historical Works of Master Ralph de Diceto, Dean of London* (London, 1876), p. 34, and subsequently provides the basis for the title of the second part of Diceto's chronicle, *Imagines Historiarum*. See also John of Salisbury, *Historia Pontificalis*, ed. and trans. M. Chibnall (London, 1956), prol., p. 1.

84 For example, by Bede, *De Temporum Ratione*, trans. F. Wallis, *The Reckoning of Time* (Liverpool, 1999), LXVI, p. 185, and Otto of Freising, *Chronicle*, III.17, p. 244.

85 J.H. Dunbabin, 'The Maccabees as Exemplars in the Tenth and Eleventh Centuries', in K. Walsh and D. Wood (eds), *The Bible in the Medieval World* (Oxford, 1985), pp. 31–41; cf. Guibert of Nogent, *Gesta Dei per Francos*, II, p. 43, V, p. 98, VI, pp. 107, 110; William of Malmesbury, *Gesta Regum Anglorum*, IV.365, p. 639;

Just as the poetry of the Bible could be distinguished according to the various different forms in which it appeared, namely the common or mixed form of heroic epic (the 'history' of Job), the narrative of lyric (Proverbs, Ecclesiastes and the Psalms) and the dramatic or active (the Song of Songs),[86] so too could the different types of historiography which its individual books contained. In the New Testament, the apostle Luke was regarded as the master of the *stilus historicus*, the principles of which, according to Ambrose, were exemplified by the apostle Paul's instruction 'to search for the secret of truth in the simplicity of history' and embodied in his own letter to the Galatians (4:21–4).[87] This judgment applied primarily to Luke's Gospel, as its emphasis on eyewitness testimony underpinned the authority of its narrative,[88] but it was also based on the book of Acts, a narrative which, according to Eusebius at least, was likewise the product of Luke's pen.[89] The book of Acts provided a historical account of the mission of the apostles and their establishment of the Church in the aftermath of Christ's death and resurrection. These events were described with distinctive attention to the detailed circumstances of the time and the location in which they took place. Once again, both the content and the approach were picked up by medieval historians when they set out to narrate the establishment of the Church in their own times.[90] The book of Revelation, by contrast, presented a historiography of a quite different sort, namely predictive prophecy of the future course

---

William of Newburgh, *The History of English Affairs*, trans. P.G. Walsh and M.J. Kennedy (Warminster, 1988), I.21.1, p. 97. Henry of Huntingdon invokes Statius (Thebes) and Vergil (Troy) as his points of comparison for military expeditions to the east (*Historia Anglorum*, VII.6, p. 425).
86 For example, Bede, *De Arte Metrica*, ed. C.B. Kendall (*CCSL* 123A, Turnhout, 1975), I.25, pp. 139–41; cf. Jerome, *Prologue to the Book of Job*, trans. W.H. Fremantle, G. Lewis and W.G. Martley (Oxford, 1893), p. 491; Cassiodorus, *Institutiones*, I.6.2, pp. 124–5; Isidore, *Etymologiae*, I.39.9–19, pp. 65–6, VI.2.14–21, pp. 136–7.
87 Ambrose, *Expositio Evangelii secundum Lucan*, ed. C. Schenkl (Vienna, 1902), III.28, p. 119; cf. G.L. Ellspermann, *The Attitude of the Early Christian Latin Writers Toward Pagan Literature and Learning* (Washington, DC, 1949), pp. 120–2. For the relationship between the book of Acts and classical historiography, see W. van den Boer, 'Some Remarks on the Beginnings of Christian Historiography', *Studia Patristica*, 4 (Texte und Untersuchungen 79, Berlin, 1961), pp. 348–62.
88 See pages 63–4.
89 Eusebius, *Ecclesiastical History*, III.4, pp. 109–10.
90 See pages 391–2.

of events, a vision of the end of time and the Day of Judgment. Set alongside the book of Daniel, however, it too could provide an influential model for those historians to whom the signs of the last times were becoming all too evident.[91] 'I warn everyone who hears the words of this book of prophecy: if anyone adds anything to them, God will add to him the plagues described in this book. And if anyone takes words away from this book of prophecy, God will take away from him his share in ... the things which are written in this book' (Revelation 22:18–19).

If the Bible clearly provided more than one possible pattern for the writing of history, its influence was also not necessarily direct. Part of the reason for the popularity of Josephus' *Antiquities*, for example, was that books I–XI of his work effectively tidied up and refashioned the historical narrative already contained in the Old Testament. Similarly adapted versions were provided for the historical narratives of the New Testament. In the fourth century, for example, Juvencus provided a metrical version of all four Gospels 'following the sequence of historical events', whilst, in the sixth century, Julius Arator turned the book of Acts into Latin verse as 'the good deeds of the apostles'.[92] In the fifth century, meanwhile, Sedulius recounted the deeds of the King of Kings in heroic verse or, as the eleventh-century summary of Conrad of Hirsau put it, 'certain great deeds performed by God taken from the Old or New Testament and narrated to restrain and correct human wickedness'. It is the young, Conrad observed, who will benefit from a simple, literal reading of Juvencus and Sedulius, even though both their versions of Scripture are also open to more rigorous study.[93] As far as medieval writers were

---

91 See pages 84–5.
92 As related in *Accessus ad Auctores*, trans. A.J. Minnis and A.B. Scott, 'Introductions to the Authors', in A.J. Minnis and A.B. Scott (eds), *Medieval Literary Theory and Criticism c.1100–c.1375* (Oxford, 1988), pp. 18–19; Gregory of Tours, *Histories*, I.36, p. 91, quoting Jerome, *Letters*, ed. and trans. J. Labourt (Paris, 1949–63), Ep.LXX, p. 214; Paul the Deacon, *History of the Lombards*, trans. W.D. Foulke, rev. E. Peters (Philadelphia, 2003), I.25, p. 47; Otto of Freising, *Chronicle*, V.4, p. 330; cf. R.P.H. Green, *Latin Epics of the New Testament: Juvencus, Sedulius, Arator* (Oxford, 2007).
93 Conrad of Hirsau, *Dialogue on the Authors*, trans. A.J. Minnis and A.B. Scott, in A.J. Minnis and A.B. Scott (eds), *Medieval Literary Theory and Criticism c.1100–c.1375* (Oxford, 1988), p. 52; cf. *Accessus ad Auctores*, pp. 19–20; Sedulius, *Carmen Paschale*, trans. G. Sigerson, *The Easter Song* (Dublin, 1922).

concerned, therefore, the influence of specifically 'biblical' models of historiography not only reflected the variety of the original but could also be mediated through other versions of the same material. Indeed, the influence of 'the Bible' on medieval historiography could be conducted through works of history which had already applied biblical models of form and content to their own narratives of non-biblical, extra-scriptural events. Such indirect influence is evident, primarily, in the historical writings of two late-antique Christian authors, namely Eusebius and Orosius.

Eusebius of Caesarea wrote his *Ecclesiastical History* in ten books (the number, he explains, signified completion or perfection), in Greek, at some point between AD 305 and 324;[94] the first nine of these were subsequently given a (sometimes very free) Latin version by Rufinus in 402.[95] Eusebius sets out the scope of his work from the very beginning, using the preface to identify the particular subjects which the ensuing 'history' will cover. First and foremost, he establishes that his concern is to trace a line of succession from the time of the apostles to the present day. This will entail recording the nature and quality of the actions (*gesta*) which affected the state of the Church, together with the life and character of those distinguished individuals who presided over the most renowned of the churches and who taught the word of God either by writing or by preaching. Tracing this apostolic succession, it is later explained, is designed to guarantee the integrity of the faith

---

94 R.M. Grant, *Eusebius as Church Historian* (Oxford, 1980); T.D. Barnes, *Constantine and Eusebius* (Cambridge, MA, 1981), pp. 106–47; G.F. Chesnut, *The First Christian Histories – Eusebius, Socrates, Sozomen, Theodoret and Evagrius* (Macon, 1986), pp. 1–174.

95 Rufinus [of Aquileia], *Die Kirchengeschichte mit der lateinischen Übersetzung und Fortsetzung des Rufinus von Aquileja*, ed. E. Schwartz and T. Mommsen (Leipzig, 1903; reprinted Berlin, 1999). Rufinus abbreviated book X and added two further books of his own in order to bring his narrative of events up to 395. See J.E.L. Oulton, 'Rufinus' Translation of the Church History of Eusebius', *Journal of Theological Studies*, 30 (1929), pp. 150–74; F.X. Murphy, *Rufinus of Aquileia (345–411) – His Life and Works* (Washington, DC, 1945); F. Thélamon, 'L'Histoire de l'Église Comme Histoire Sainte', *Revue des Études Augustiniennes*, 25 (1979), pp. 184–91; T. Christensen, *Rufinus of Aquileia and the Historia Ecclesiastica, Lib. VIII–IX of Eusebius* (Copenhagen, 1989); P.R. Amidon, *The Church History of Rufinus of Aquileia – Books X and XI* (Oxford, 1997); D. Rohrbacher, *The Historians of Late Antiquity* (London, 2002), pp. 100–7; P. van Deun, 'The Church Historians After Eusebius', in G. Marasco (ed.), *Greek and Roman Historiography in Late Antiquity* (Brill, 2003), pp. 160–7.

which has been handed down in the teaching of the Church.[96] By the same token, however, Eusebius acknowledges that this task will also involve recording the deeds of those individuals who lapsed into error and then savaged the Christian flock by setting themselves up as teachers of a false knowledge. Likewise, the evils suffered by the Jews following their rejection of Christ (a subject for which Eusebius later explicitly records his debt to the 'reliable witness', *idoneus testis*, of Josephus)[97] provide him with his prime example of the calamitous consequences of wilful disobedience to God. Finally, Eusebius states that his history will deal with the manner and frequency of the attacks launched by non-believers against the teaching of Christ and the corresponding sufferings of those who defended it as martyrs, that is, as faithful witnesses to the truth of the word of God. Having identified these subjects as the major themes of his work, Eusebius asks to be forgiven for the fact that his resources are not equal to the task of providing a faithful and complete narrative of what was done and for having dared to tackle such an unprecedented undertaking. He then uses the remainder of the preface to explain his approach to writing down 'the deeds of Christians' (*res gestae Christianorum*), gathering them like flowers from the scattered writings of earlier authors which had been transmitted as witnesses and memorials (*indicia ac monumenta*) of the deeds of their own times. Pointing out that he has himself already produced a brief and succinct summary of the same material in chronological tables (*ex chronicis*), he explains that he now wants to expand it, ordering and sifting it into a historical narrative (*historica narratio*) so that the knowledge of these deeds will be to the advantage (*utilitas*) of those eager to read of them.[98]

The significance of both the content and the purpose of the *Ecclesiastical History* is spelled out in more detail throughout the course of the work. What Eusebius means by *res gestae Christianorum*, for example, is outlined at the beginning of book V. Other writers of history, Eusebius observes, have recounted wars through victories and triumphs – they have celebrated the

---

96 Eusebius, *Ecclesiastical History*, V.6.5, pp. 208–9; cf. Gregory of Tours, *Histories*, X.31, p. 593.
97 *Ecclesiastical History*, I.6.9, p. 52, and cf. III.9.1–10.11, pp. 121–3.
98 *Ecclesiastical History*, I.1, pp. 31–3.

brave deeds of public officials and military commanders and they have narrated the bloody deaths of citizens and enemies. His own account, by contrast, contains a narrative of what pertains to God. If it describes wars, then these are wars which have been fought for the sake of the soul; if it describes battles, then these are battles which have been waged for the heavenly fatherland; if it describes struggles, then these have been undertaken for the truth and against spiritual, not mortal, enemies, for the freedom of the spirit and not of the flesh; if it commits such conflicts to a literary memorial (*monumenta litterarum*), then these are conflicts conducted, not for earthly territory or possessions, but for the heavenly kingdom, not in a quest for the power of mortal rulers but for the sake of the glory which comes from immortal God.[99] Eusebius' concern that his history should be useful to its readers is likewise picked up in the main body of the narrative – it is not just the essential knowledge of events in which Eusebius is interested (*necessaria scientiae, scientia rerum*) but also the lessons to be drawn from them for the benefit of his readers (*instructio doctrinae, utilitas legentium*). He has therefore chosen to commemorate only those things by which his own and future generations may be edified and it is in this sense that he has described the deeds of his own day for the memory of posterity.[100] Other than gathering together the sequence of the successors to the apostles (or at least the more illustrious amongst them), Eusebius accordingly has a much sharper lesson to teach. This is brought out most strikingly in the tenth and final book, where the centrepiece is provided by his own oration on the building of the Christian Church as a new, living Temple. In juxtaposing the wicked tyranny of the emperor Licinius with the virtuous Christian rule of the emperor Constantine, Eusebius describes how the Church was first scourged through persecution as chastisement for its sins but then restored as a spiritual Temple by its bishops and pastors.[101] It was Licinius' failure to 'remember' the consequences of earlier tyranny and persecution, Eusebius points out, that brought about his own ruin; it was the Church's failure to heed divine warnings

---

99 *Ecclesiastical History*, V.pref.1–4, pp. 192–3.
100 *Ecclesiastical History*, III.24.1, p. 131, V.1.2, p. 192, VIII.pref.1, p. 327, VIII.2.3, p. 330.
101 *Ecclesiastical History*, X.4, pp. 383–401.

'in the past', its seduction by sloth and freedom, its descent into error and wrangling, which precipitated the suffering of more recent times. This was the lesson from history which Eusebius wanted to draw through the prophecies of Isaiah when recounting the events he had witnessed for himself.[102]

If the influence of the *Ecclesiastical History* on subsequent historiography lay in its definition of the substance of *res gestae Christianorum* and in the didactic purpose of setting them down in writing, then this also extended to the method of collecting them, a subject to which Eusebius refers, once again, in his preface. In gathering and distilling his material from such a wide range of earlier writers, Eusebius points out the value of incorporating oral traditions which had been handed down from the earliest authorities of the Church (*ea quae ... voce sola tradita sunt*).[103] He also repeatedly appeals to the testimony of letters and documents by citing them verbatim – often in his own translation, on one occasion with a reference to the signatures which had been appended – in order that the truth of what he was saying should be clearly evident (*ut evidens dictorum veritas fiat*).[104] Eusebius was certainly well aware of the confusion which could be caused by scribal error or by malicious tampering with the text of an original.[105] Indeed, he quotes Irenaeus' exhortation to exercise great care in transcribing texts as a necessary and useful example of diligence for all those who would be reading his own work.[106] Eusebius acknowledges where his evidence conflicts – when some people affirm that something happened and others deny it, he suggests, like Sallust, that faith in the event must be left in the middle (*nos rei fidem relinquimus in medio*).[107] The same applies where records or memorials (*monumenta*) are simply absent.[108] In reconciling the apparent conflict between the genealogies of Christ set down in the Gospels of Matthew and Luke, therefore, Eusebius

---

102 *Ecclesiastical History*, X.8–9, pp. 408–14.
103 *Ecclesiastical History*, VI.13.9, p. 251.
104 *Ecclesiastical History*, I.13.5, p. 66, and see IV.23.9, p. 184, V.19.4, p. 226, VII.1.1, p. 287. See also 1 Maccabees 8:22–32, 10:25–45.
105 *Ecclesiastical History*, II.10.10, p. 84, IV.23.12, p. 185.
106 *Ecclesiastical History*, V.20.3, p. 227; cf. Jerome, *De Viris Illustribus*, trans. T.P. Halton, *On Illustrious Men* (Washington, DC, 1999), XXXV, p. 57.
107 *Ecclesiastical History*, V.16.15, p. 220; see also page 47, note 47.
108 *Ecclesiastical History*, IV.5.1, p. 156.

uses Julianus Africanus as an object-lesson in the thoroughness with which historiographical diligence needed to be applied.[109]

In pointing up the methodological approach which he had followed in assembling his historical narrative, Eusebius established some clear historiographical guidelines for his readers. He repeats the distinction drawn by Clement of Alexandria, for example, between 'notes' (*commentarii*) that are written down for the sake of display (*ostentatio*) and those that are a means of remembering (*commemoratio*) and counteracting forgetfulness (*remedium oblivionis*).[110] The apostles, Eusebius points out, eschewed ornateness of speech (*ornatus sermonis*) and did not entrust Christ's teaching to the persuasion of human wisdom (*suasoria*) or to the plausible argument of human language (*argumentum*).[111] What particularly impresses Eusebius, however, is the value of eye-witness testimony. He is therefore always careful to appeal, where he can, to the fact that he was narrating what he had seen with his own eyes rather than what he had simply heard (*nos ... non audita sed oculis nostris inspecta narramus*).[112] Above all, Eusebius appeals to the precedent set, in this particular regard, by Luke, when he quotes the words with which the apostle had opened his narrative of events (*narratio rerum*) 'as they were handed down to us by those who, from the beginning, saw for themselves and were ministers of the word of God and whom I have followed from the outset' (Luke 1:2–3). This, Eusebius points out, is Luke's explanation for why he had written his Gospel – since many others had rashly presumed to narrate events of which the apostle himself had a much clearer knowledge, Luke, he writes, wanted to separate us from the narratives of others and establish faith (*fides*) in the truth of what he had written himself, certain in the knowledge that he had followed what had been handed down to him by Paul or the

---

109 *Ecclesiastical History*, I.7.14–15, pp. 55–6.
110 *Ecclesiastical History*, V.11.3, p. 214; cf. Isidore, *Etymologiae*, I.44.3, p. 67 (see also page 123). The prime example of such *commentarii* for the Middle Ages was Caesar's *Gallic War*, trans. H.J. Edwards (Loeb, 1917) and *Civil War*, trans. A.G. Peskett (Loeb, 1914); cf. Reynolds, *Texts and Transmission* pp.35–36. For their influence, see, for example, William of Poitiers, *Gesta Guillelmi*, I.30, pp. 47–9.
111 *Ecclesiastical History*, III.24.3–4, p. 131; cf. Cassian, *Institutes*, trans. E.C.S. Gibson (Michigan, 1964), XII.19, p. 286.
112 *Ecclesiastical History*, VIII.7.2, p. 335, and cf. VII.18.3, p. 302, VIII.2.1, p. 329.

other apostles who had seen it all from the beginning. Luke then composed the book of Acts, not from what he had heard, but from what he had seen with his eyes.[113]

Written a century or so after Eusebius, around 418 AD, Orosius' *Seven Books of History Against the Pagans* were much more polemical in intent. This was historiography which was explicitly designed to counter those pagan critics who had been claiming that the conversion of the Roman Empire to Christianity, and the consequent abandonment of the gods of their ancestors, had resulted directly in the calamities that had recently beset Rome, of which the sack of the city in 410 was but the latest, if most shocking, example.[114] Orosius' riposte was simple. As he states in the prologue, what he had done was to collect from all the available histories and annals (*fasti historiarum et annalium*) evidence for the burdens of war, the ravages of disease and the sorrows of famine, for terrible earthquakes, extraordinary floods, dreadful outbreaks of fire and cruel strokes of lightning and hailstorms, and for the suffering caused by the murder of blood-relatives and other crimes.[115] Unfolding this grim catalogue systematically (*ordinato*) but briefly (and Orosius does claim to have shown both restraint and selectivity in striking a path through such a 'dense forest' of evils),[116] his conclusion is that the disasters of the present, whilst serious, were not as bad as those which had preceded the advent of the Christian religion.

Orosius' starting-point for this history was the common opinion shared by Christians and non-Christians alike (*opinio vulgata quae nobis cum omnibus communis est*) that the world had always been governed by alternating periods of good and evil. According to

---

113 *Ecclesiastical History*, III.24, p.133, III.4, p. 110. For Eusebius' relation to the book of Acts as a historiographical model, see R.A. Markus, 'Church History and Early Church Historians', in D. Baker (ed.), *The Materials, Sources and Methods of Ecclesiastical History* (Oxford, 1975), p. 3.
114 Orosius, *Seven Books of History*; cf. H.W. Goetz, *Die Geschichtstheologie des Orosius* (Darmstadt, 1980); M.-P. Arnaud-Lindet (ed. and trans.), *Orose, Histoires (Contre les Païens)* (Paris, 1990–91), pp. ix–lxvi; Rohrbacher, *Historians of Late Antiquity*, ch. 12; G. Zecchini, 'Latin Historiography – Jerome, Orosius and the Western Chronicles', in G. Marasco (ed.), *Greek and Roman Historiography in Late Antiquity* (Brill, 2003), pp. 319–29.
115 Orosius, *Seven Books of History*, I.prol., p. 4.
116 *Seven Books of History*, I.12, p. 33, V.19, p. 215.

Orosius, these cycles have served as a providential means of disciplining humankind – because human nature constantly shifts between weakness and stubbornness, divine justice offers guidance when human beings need assistance but punishment when they abuse their freedom. The calamities of the past – chiefly wars but also famine and pestilence ('the two greatest and most detestable of all evils') – need to be seen, accordingly, either as manifest sins in themselves or as the hidden punishment for sins, be they of an entire people, of a particular ruler, or of those subjects whose tacit consent made them complicit in their ruler's crimes.[117] The practical effect of this perspective on the way in which Orosius approached his history was twofold. In the first instance, it prompted him to give his work a universalism of both time and place. Orosius chooses to start his narrative, for example, not (as he himself states) as Greek and Roman historians had done, with the origin (in the twelfth century BC) of wars and kingdoms under Ninus (that is, the king of Assyria whose lust for lordship, in Orosius' eyes, first set the pattern for pursuing cupidity at home and war abroad), but with the beginning of sin itself, that is, with the Fall of Adam.[118] Orosius accordingly starts with a geographical survey, not, as Sallust had done, of the localised region in which the narrative of his events took place, but of the entire world.[119] In the second instance, Orosius repeatedly and pointedly intersperses his history with direct comparisons between past and present. The fundamental order provided by God's providential governance of a sinful world, he argues, continued to operate after the coming of Christ. However, the subsequent spread of the Christian religion had resulted in the progressive mitigation of this suffering through a combination of intercessory prayer and divine mercy. Even though the Antichrist would ultimately bring worse tribulation, those last times were 'remote';[120] in the meantime, the nature and impact of war, famine and pestilence would gradually be reduced in their severity as the Christian faith

---

117 *Seven Books of History*, I.1, p. 6, II.1, p. 44, II.5, p. 51, VII.16, p. 310, VII.22, p. 317.
118 *Seven Books of History*, I.1, p. 5, I.4, pp. 21–2; cf. Pompeius Trogus in Justin, *Epitome of the Philippic History*, I.1, p. 14.
119 *Seven Books of History*, I.2, pp. 7–20.
120 *Seven Books of History*, I.prol., p. 5, VII.3, p. 289.

took hold. The crucial point for Orosius was that the afflictions of the present signified admonition and chastisement by God, not persecution and destruction by the Devil; the comparative tranquillity of the present was therefore due to the mercy which God was showing to His people.[121] It was only because Orosius' contemporaries had become accustomed to such relative peace and tranquillity that the moderate calamities of the present had come to seem unbearable.[122] The sack of Rome in 410 was a case in point. By comparing, in some detail, the devastation which followed the capture of the city by the Gauls in 390 BC, Orosius was able to maintain that the effects of its seizure in 410 AD were on a significantly lesser scale. They could also have been much worse – not only was the chastisement of the city held off as a last resort until after the citizens of Rome had shown no signs of repentance, but God had also chosen a Christian enemy, Alaric, as the agent of his wrath, rather than the pagan army of Radagaisus. In so far as Rome was a mixed community, God's mercy towards the piety of its Christian inhabitants had accordingly tempered his punishment of the blasphemy of the pagans.[123]

The primary goal of such a painstaking distillation of classical Roman historiography was, as far as Orosius was concerned, to demonstrate to his pagan 'detractors' that they had either forgotten, or were ignorant of, the past and were showing no concern for the future.[124] However, Orosius' synthesis of classical (which for him meant, and in order of importance, Pompeius Trogus, Livy, Eutropius, Julius Caesar, Sallust, Tacitus and Suetonius) with Old Testament historiography was also designed to ensure that his Christian audience would not make the same mistake. This represented an equally important motive for cataloguing the history of sin and its punishment in such detail. According to Orosius, whilst the Flood had represented a just retribution for the unjust licentiousness of the whole world,[125] God was also clearly capable of meting out comparable deserts to individual peoples and individual cities. Right at the start of his work, therefore, Orosius

---

121 *Seven Books of History*, IV.6, p. 134.
122 *Seven Books of History*, I.21, p. 43.
123 *Seven Books of History*, II.19, pp. 75–6, VII.3, p. 288, VII.37–40, pp. 349–55.
124 *Seven Books of History*, I.prol., p. 4.
125 *Seven Books of History*, I.3, pp. 20–1.

presents Sodom and Gomorrah (Genesis 18:20–19:28; Isaiah 1:4–31) as case-studies of how an abundance of riches produces luxury and, from this luxury, sin. If God's intention had been to make the eternal ruin of this particular region a witness (*testis*) to His judgment for future generations (Matthew 10:15), then Orosius makes sure that the admonition is addressed directly to the Romans of 410: 'I warn people of what happened to the people of Sodom and Gomorrah so that they may be able to learn and understand how God has punished sinners, how He can punish them, and how He will punish them'.[126] Orosius drives the point home by proceeding to catalogue each one of the plagues of Egypt.[127] Indeed, Orosius returns to this theme in his seventh, and final, book with an elaborate comparison between the plagues of Egypt and the calamities with which pagan Romans had been punished for their persecutions of the Christian Church. These two series of 'plagues' (*plagae*), he explains, the Egyptian and the Roman, correspond to one another in so far as a figure can be compared to a form, that is, according to the symbolic significance of each successive affliction – they represent parallel penalties for the respective oppression of the Israelites and the Christians. Such a pattern, however, in Orosius' eyes, also needs to be read into the future. These things, he comments, were done as a sign for us (*in figura nostri*). Just as the Egyptians subsequently forgot the plagues and were annihilated in the Red Sea, so this role will be transferred to the enemies of Christ in the last times prior to their eternal destruction on the Day of Judgment.[128]

Orosius' account of the travails of human history served the immediate polemical purpose of countering and correcting a non-Christian interpretation of the political and military pressures which had recently been epitomised by the sack of Rome. However, it was also designed to teach Christians what they needed to learn from the past as a means of responding to the sufferings of the present. In the first instance, this was an argument against complacency. Given that Romans in the past

---

126 *Seven Books of History*, I.5–6, pp. 23–5, VII.39, p. 353. For the castigation of contemporary society as Gomorrah see, for example, John of Salerno, *Life of Odo of Cluny*, trans. G. Sitwell (London, 1958), I.17, p. 19.
127 *Seven Books of History*, I.8–10, pp. 26–31.
128 *Seven Books of History*, VII.26–7, pp. 324–8.

had regarded the calamities with which they had been afflicted as a means of attaining the lustre of a glorious reputation (*gloria famae*), Christians should be able to endure so much more when they had been given the promise of a blessed eternity.[129] More generally, Orosius' account of both Greek and Roman history was intended to impart the same lessons drawn by Sallust from the corrupting effects of wealth and inactivity – the former producing luxury, the latter sloth – and apply them to Christians and non-Christians alike. Once again, the admonition is given a pointedly contemporary reference when Orosius comments on the sloth and licentiousness which are produced by the theatre – an 'altar of luxury' which receives the sacrifice, not of animals, but of human virtues.[130] The moral didacticism of Orosius' account of crime and punishment also extends to a series of equally Sallustian reflections on the specifically political consequences of sinful human conduct. The Athenians, for example, the wisest of all peoples, were taught by the history of their own misfortunes that prosperity came from harmony and ruin through internal discord. Their loss of liberty, Orosius remarks, leaves the *exemplum* to posterity that success in foreign war is dependent on waiving hatred and animosities at home.[131] The conquest of the Greek states by Philip of Macedon made the same point; so too did the subjugation of Numantia by Rome – harmony makes a kingdom unconquerable, discord sees it destroyed.[132] It is the history of Rome, however, which provides Orosius with the sharpest demonstration of the political consequences of such moral failings. Driven by excessive arrogance, as well as by shameless and insatiable greed, Rome's expansion was constantly checked by internal disorders. With Carthage destroyed, Rome lost the 'great whetstone' (*magna cos*) of its splendour and sharpness; it turned to sloth and luxury and was riven with a succession of bloody civil wars.[133] The providential purpose of these internal disasters may have been to check Roman

---

129 *Seven Books of History*, IV.6, p. 134, an argument originally put forward in Augustine, *De Civitate Dei*, V.18, p. 210 (see also page 101, note 246).
130 *Seven Books of History*, IV.21, p. 168.
131 *Seven Books of History*, II.17, pp. 71–3; cf. Gregory of Tours, *Histories*, V.prol., p. 254; Otto of Freising, *Chronicle*, II.19, p. 175.
132 *Seven Books of History*, III.12, p. 92, V.8, p. 188.
133 *Seven Books of History*, IV.23, p. 172.

pride but it does not lessen the horror with which Orosius recounts the nature and extent of the resulting internecine slaughter.[134] In this respect, Roman expansion appeared to present a similar pattern to the conquests of Alexander the Great. What stopped Rome suffering a similar disintegration to Alexander's empire, in Orosius' view, was the additional providential role within human history which it had now been assigned by God.

Orosius' political understanding of world history was governed by a series of universal monarchies into which it could be divided according to the four points of the compass – Babylon (Persia) to the east, Carthage to the south, Macedonia to the north and Rome to the west. This idea of a succession of empires was one which Orosius had adopted from Pompeius Trogus and then grafted onto the exegesis of Nebuchadnezzar's dream in Daniel 2 (and of Revelation 13) which he had found in Eusebius and Jerome. This transfer, or 'translation', of universal power from one people to another was the result, in Orosius' view, not of human strength (*humani vires*) or random occurrences (*incerti casus*), but of God's disposition of events.[135] Orosius proved it by tracing patterns of historical events and identifying the numerological significance with which God had invested the chronology of history.[136] The accession of Philip as the first Christian emperor in 247 AD, for example, was designed, in Orosius' view, to ensure that the one thousandth year from the foundation of Rome (753 BC) might be dedicated to Christ rather than to idols.[137] Orosius was particularly drawn to the correspondences which could be found between the history of Rome and the history of Babylon. Of the four world monarchies, Babylon and Rome were, in his opinion, like father and son – Carthage and Macedonia were simply guardians and protectors of the inheritance until Rome came of age.[138] Thus, whilst Babylon could certainly act as a more general measure

---

134 *Seven Books of History*, VI.14, pp. 257–8, VI.17, p. 266.
135 *Seven Books of History*, II.2, p. 45; cf. Otto of Freising, *Chronicle*, II.14, p. 168, III.prol., p. 221, IV.prol., p. 271.
136 *Seven Books of History*, VII.2, pp. 286–7.
137 *Seven Books of History*, VII.20, p. 315, VII.28, p. 328; cf. Bede, *De Temporum Ratione*, LXVI, pp. 206–7; Otto of Freising, *Chronicle*, III.33, p. 261.
138 *Seven Books of History*, II.1, p.44; cf. Otto of Freising, *Chronicle*, II.prol., p. 153, II.2, p. 156, II.27, p. 185.

for 'the unstable condition of all changeable things' (*mutabilium rerum instabiles status*),[139] it also offered particular parallels with the history of Rome. Orosius again demonstrates the point numerologically (both cities, he points out, were sacked around 1164 years after their foundation),[140] but also structurally and thematically. He accordingly 'interweaves' (*intertexere*) his narrative of the events of their respective histories – Babylon declined as Rome grew in strength, losing its last king at the same time as Rome gained its first. Orosius makes both the comparison and the congruence (*ordo convenientiae*) direct. Babylon and Rome, he states, had similar beginnings, similar power, similar greatness, similar times, similar good things and similar evils. What they do not share, however, is a similar decline and fall. Rome may have been sacked in 410 but it had not been deprived of its temporal power (*regnum*).[141] The reason, in Orosius' view, lay in the mercy of God and in the person of its Christian ruler, but it also lay in the particular role which Rome had come to serve as an instrument of God's providence. This significance had been revealed when the universal peace of Rome's *imperium* was ordained to coincide with the coming of Christ. This chronological conjunction of events is made characteristically precise – Octavian closed the doors of the temple of Janus (signifying universal peace) and was hailed as '*augustus*' (signifying supreme power) on the very same day that would subsequently become the feast of the Epiphany. This was faithfully commemorated, Orosius remarks, so that in every respect the empire of Caesar might be proven to have been prepared for the coming of Christ. The reign of the emperor Augustus, he argues, was the first time that the world had relinquished its wars and discord in order to obey a single law in peace and tranquillity for the common good of all nations, provinces and peoples. Not only did this universal peace facilitate the dissemination of the Christian message but its exact conjunction with the birth of Christ signified the necessity and legitimacy of a single world rule in order to suppress pride as the cause of internal dissension. Christ was born in the year in which, by God's ordinance, Caesar achieved the truest and strongest peace and,

---

139 *Seven Books of History*, II.2, p. 45, II.6, p. 54, II.10, p. 59.
140 Cf. Otto of Freising, *Chronicle*, IV.21, p. 306.
141 *Seven Books of History*, II.2–3, pp. 45–7, VII.2, pp. 285–6.

by being enrolled on the Roman census, Christ revealed his own desire to be called a Roman citizen.[142]

In charting both the calamities of human history and their comparative severity in relation to the spread of the Christian faith, Orosius set out to instruct both pagans and Christians alike about the proper significance of their past and present sufferings. For all his acknowledgment of the inscrutability of God's judgments ('all of which we cannot know nor can we explain those which we do know'),[143] Orosius was confident enough to detect a pattern of cause and effect in the 'hidden order' of things done, even when the actors themselves were unwitting agents (the destruction of Jerusalem by Vespasian and Titus, for example, by a father and a son, was a fitting punishment for those who had offended the Father and the Son).[144] In setting this universal history of sin and its concomitant punishment within the political framework of four world monarchies, Orosius also set out to demonstrate the particular providential significance of Rome, what Vergil had called, temporally and geographically, its 'limitless rule' (*imperium sine fine*).[145] Deploying an often elaborate juxtaposition of the first and the last of these 'empires', he argued that Rome would *not*, in fact, follow the same destructive cycle as Babylon or, indeed, as Carthage and Macedonia. This did not mean that Orosius underestimated the threats posed to Rome at the beginning of the fifth century. Far from it. Even in the worst-case scenario, however, what he envisaged was some future restoration (*restitutio*) of Rome under 'barbarian' rule, not its eradication.[146] That, for him, was the providential significance of the *pax Augusta*.

---

142 *Seven Books of History*, III.8, pp. 88–9, VI.1, p. 229, VI.17, p. 266, VI.20–2, pp. 274–82; cf. Otto of Freising, *Chronicle*, III.prol., p. 221. For later developments of the same argument, see, for example, Engelbert of Admont, *De Ortu, Progressu et Fine Regnorum et praecipue Regni seu Imperii Romani*, trans. T. Izbicki and C. Nederman, *Three Tracts on Empire* (Bristol, 2000); Dante, *Monarchia*, ed. and trans. P. Shaw (Cambridge, 1995); and, more generally, C.T. Davis, *Dante and the Idea of Rome* (Oxford, 1957).
143 *Seven Books of History*, VII.41, p. 359.
144 *Seven Books of History*, VII.9, pp. 302–3; cf. Wipo, *Deeds of Conrad*, XXXIII, p. 92; Otto of Freising, *Chronicle*, III.18, p. 246.
145 Vergil, *Aeneid*, I.287, p.261; see also I.236, p. 257, IV.231, p. 411, VI.781–2, p. 561, VII.98–101, p. 9.
146 *Seven Books of History*, VII.43, pp. 361–2.

Orosius' two overarching schemes – the human suffering caused by sin and its attendant punishment, and the sequence of four world monarchies which culminated in a Christianised Rome – provided the instructive core of his moral and political historiography. In the process, however, Orosius, like Eusebius, also saw fit to include frequent reflections on the particular methodology which had informed his approach to writing this sort of history. He is explicit, for example, in his appeal to indubitable material memorials (*certissima monumenta*) which he had seen for himself, be it in the physical remains of Carthaginian cities, the suggestive testimony (*indicium et coniectura*) of the fossil record left on mountains by the Flood, or the tracks left by Pharaoh's chariots deep into the Red Sea which were visible 'even today'.[147] What particularly exercised Orosius was, not unnaturally, the problem posed by having to rely on predominantly pagan historical sources. Some difficulties could be resolved with little fuss – whilst he dismisses the falsehoods of pagan oracles and soothsaying, for example, he accepts the testimony of portents and prodigies. When it comes to the evaluative nature of the terminology in which events had been recorded by his sources, Orosius is rather more guarded. Whether the age of Alexander the Great, for example, should be judged worthy of praise (because of the virtue which enabled the whole world to be seized) or whether it should instead be detested (because of the ruin with which the whole world was overturned) is a question whose answer will depend on the political allegiance and the temporal perspective of the writer. The actions themselves remain the same, Orosius observes, but they can be denoted either as 'virtue' or as 'suffering', depending on who is doing the naming – the conqueror or the conquered – and according to when the classification is taking place.[148] This principle extends also to the Goths of Orosius' own time. Both Alexander the Great and the Romans, he points out, inflicted wars upon peoples whom they later ordered under their

---

147 *Seven Books of History*, I.3, p. 21, I.10, p. 31, VI.15, p. 263, VII.2, p. 286; cf. Gregory of Tours, *Histories*, I.10, p. 75.
148 For paradyastole or *distinctio*, see page 7. For Alexander the Great in the Middle Ages, see Walter of Châtillon, *Alexandreis*, trans. D. Townsend (Philadelphia, 1996) and, more generally, G. Cary and D.J.A. Ross, *The Medieval Alexander* (Cambridge, 1956).

own laws. Who is to say, he asks, whether the Goths will not do the same (God forbid) and thereby come to be called great kings when they are currently adjudged by us to be the cruellest of enemies?[149]

What chiefly troubles Orosius about the methodology involved in writing his history is, in the first instance, the daunting scale of his undertaking. It is simply not possible, he remarks, to explicate all the things that were done or may have been done (*gesta et sicut gesta*), because of the magnitude and number of events which have been recorded at such length and by so many writers. By the same token, however, Orosius is also aware of the dangers of abbreviating this material – to indicate everything that happened in compendious brevity, but without explaining it, is to run the risk of being obscure. Nonetheless, because he is concerned with the import of events (*vis rerum*), rather than with their depiction (*imago*), this is a chance Orosius is prepared to take. Brevity may hamper the full force of understanding but this is preferable to any omitted event being thought beyond his knowledge or even not to have happened. Even a brief notice in outline, after all, can serve to refresh a reader's memory or to prompt further investigation. He therefore does his audience the service of stating where a fuller account is already well-known or can be found elsewhere.[150] In the second instance, Orosius points out the problems posed by the fact that his own motivation in writing was rather different from that of his sources. In recounting the past conflicts of this world, earlier historians had been concerned with setting out wars; Orosius, by contrast, wanted to set out the *sufferings* which had been brought about by those wars (*miseriae bellorum*).[151] Greek and Roman historians disseminated the deeds of kings and peoples for the sake of an everlasting remembrance but they were more concerned with the twin goals of bestowing praise and imparting instruction. As a result, they omitted to record large numbers of terrible events, lest they cause offence to those people for whom, or about whom, they were writing and lest the examples they drew from the past ended up frightening, rather than teaching, their audience. Freely acknowledging that he was therefore able to discover the calamities experienced by

---

149 *Seven Books of History*, III.20, p. 108.
150 *Seven Books of History*, III.prol., p. 77, III.3, p. 84.
151 *Seven Books of History*, III.prol., p. 77.

the Romans only through writers whose primary goal had been to secure favour, Orosius is prompted to speculate on just how much greater the number of calamities must have been if there are faint traces of so many miseries even in works which were devoted to praise.[152] A similar assessment is prompted by Orosius' frustration over arriving at any agreed number for Roman casualties in battle. In explicitly acknowledging that there are some inconsistencies or disagreements between the authorities on whom he is relying, Orosius attributes such variation (*varietas discordantium historicorum*) not only to their authors' primary concern with praise and flattery but also to their desire to hold up an inspiring example for present and future generations. He does not hesitate to call such deliberate distortion 'the shamelessness of lying' (*impudentia mentiendi*). What is badly set down as knowledge, he writes, amounts to the knowledge of lies (*male nota mendaciorum nota*) and, as such, those writers who are inconsistent concerning events which they have seen for themselves should be given little credence on other subjects.[153]

Faced with cataloguing 'the inextricable course of alternating evils', Orosius describes his task as a historian to be one of unfolding (*explicare*) his subject in an orderly manner (*per ordinem*).[154] In part, this order is driven by chronology – he interrupts his account of the wars of Philip of Macedon and Alexander the Great in order to describe the wars conducted by the Romans, for example, on the grounds that this is appropriate to the time at which they occurred (*pro convenientia temporum*).[155] In part, it is thematic – by moving from one part of the world to another, Orosius wanted his history to reflect the ubiquity of the evils which different peoples were suffering at the same time. The result was a deliberately 'intermingled' (*permixta*) or 'interwoven' (*intertexta*)[156] narrative of

---

152 *Seven Books of History*, IV.5, p. 129; see also I.1, p. 5; Otto of Freising, *Chronicle*, II.30, p. 187.
153 *Seven Books of History*, IV.1, p. 23, IV.20, p. 162, V.3, p. 178.
154 *Seven Books of History*, I.12, p. 33, II.3, p. 47.
155 *Seven Books of History*, III.15, p. 98.
156 The imagery of weaving or spinning was taken ultimately from the three Fates (Clotho, Lachesis, Atropos), as described, for example, by Liutprand, *Antapodosis*, trans. F.A. Wright, *The Works of Liutprand of Cremona* (London, 1930), I.11, p. 41; Walter of Châtillon, *Alexandreis*, V.162–5, p.115; Bernardus Silvestris, *Commentary on the First Six Books of Virgil's Aeneid*, VI, p .43; cf. Boethius, *Consolation*

wars, famine and pestilence throughout the entire world.[157] It is this complexity of misfortune which Orosius wished to replicate in order to demonstrate the degree to which the world had alienated and angered God.[158] Indeed, to that extent, he also suggests that it is simply not possible to arrange wars, or the hatreds and animosities which caused them, either by number (*numero*) or order (*ordine*) or reason (*ratione*). 'I have woven together an inextricable lattice-work of muddled history', Orosius writes, 'and I have henceforth entwined in words the uncertain cycles of wars which were conducted here and there with senseless fury, for the more I kept to the order of events, the more, as I see it, I wrote in a disorderly fashion'.[159] Gregory of Tours was later to make the same point – the muddled and confused order of his narrative reflects the disorder of the events which he is describing.[160]

Orosius' favoured image for the historian's perspective on such tumultuous confusion is that of a watchtower (*specula*, *spectaculum*) placed above the fires and smoke of innumerable wars on the plain below – fires which have been kindled by the torch of cupidity and which have blazed forth with evils throughout the world.[161]

---

of Philosophy, trans. S.J. Tester (Loeb, 1973), IV.6, p. 357, and, more generally, A. Demandt, *Metaphern für Geschichte: Sprachbilder und Gleichnisse im historisch-politischen Denken* (Munich, 1978) pp. 311–15. For William of Malmesbury's figure of hammering out or minting coin, see *Gesta Pontificum Anglorum*, ed. and trans. M. Winterbottom and R.M. Thomson, *The History of the English Bishops* (Oxford, 2007), II.75.11, p. 253, and *Gesta Regum Anglorum*, I.62, p. 95, II.149, p. 243.
157 *Seven Books of History*, II.12, p. 61, V.4, p. 181; cf. Otto of Freising, *Chronicle*, II.17, p. 172.
158 *Seven Books of History*, II.18, p. 74.
159 *Seven Books of History*, III.2, p. 83; cf. Boethius, *Consolation of Philosophy*, III.12, p. 305: 'weaving an inextricable labyrinth with arguments' (*inextricabilem labyrinthum rationibus texens*).
160 Gregory of Tours, *Histories*, II.prol., p. 103; cf. Gerald of Wales, *Expugnatio Hibernica*, II.prol., p. 135: 'so the reader must not expect an ordered narrative or elegance of style in this part of my book; for, of necessity, to meet the demands of the short time available, the individual events described appear in a jumbled sequence [*turbate*], thus reflecting the very disturbed times themselves [*turbatissima*]'. What follows, according to Gerald, may therefore seem to posterity a brief sample of the material (*materiae delibatio*), rather than a full historical narrative (*historiae narratio*).
161 *Seven Books of History*, I.1, p. 7, II.18, p. 74, III.23, p. 112. For the eyes as watchmen (*speculatores*) whose high position enables them to fulfil their function by giving them a vantage point, see Cicero, *De Natura Deorum*, trans. H. Rackham (Loeb, 1933), II.56.140, p. 259.

It is from this vantage-point that Orosius is able to 'measure' (*permetior*) the quality of one period of time against another. First and foremost, this means comparing (*conferre, comparare*) the suffering of the past with the suffering of the present, but Orosius also extends the technique to cover a wide range of more specific, often very precise, examples. He compares Babylon with Rome, for instance, Alexander the Great with Augustus, Christian Rome with pagan Rome, and Goths with Gauls, but also Sicily past and present, the first and last queens of Carthage, and the invasions of Britain by Julius Caesar and Claudius. So fundamental to his narrative is this comparative approach that Orosius is able to emphasise the horrors of the civil wars in the first century BC by pointing out that they *lack* a point of comparison, even a loose one (*comparatio ambigua*), such was their enormity and confusion.[162]

As an approach to the writing of history, Orosius' concern to recount the sufferings of the past in all their complexity and to compare particular periods and events with one another is intended to serve two purposes. In the first instance, Orosius is adamant that historiography should not be relegated to the realm of a literary exercise. Although he is certainly prepared to season his own narrative with a series of citations from Vergil, selectively deployed in order to heighten the impact of what he is saying at any given moment, Orosius is also careful to contrast the truths (*vera*) that he is uncovering and the trustworthiness (*fides*) of his own account with the fables (*fabulae*) of poets and the falsehoods (*falsa*) and lies (*mendacia*) of writers who have been motivated by the desire to praise and instruct.[163] The very real suffering of the past should not be lessened by the passing of time. Nor should it be reduced to the level of an intellectual exercise and the entertainment of fable (*exercitia ingeniorum et oblectamenta fabularum*).[164] Orosius points out that this is how the bloody conquests of Philip of Macedon, for example, have become simply pleasant stories (*dulces fabulae*), held up as praiseworthy deeds of bravery rather than as the most bitter of calamities.[165] Instead, Orosius wants his audience to understand the reality of the suffering and

---

162 *Seven Books of History*, V.22, p. 219, V.24, p. 225.
163 *Seven Books of History*, VI.17, p. 266, VII.26, p. 324.
164 *Seven Books of History*, II.18, p. 74.
165 *Seven Books of History*, III.14, p. 98.

wickedness which he is recording. He describes himself weeping and grieving as he relates the recurring evils and misfortunes of previous ages: 'as I turned these things over in my mind, did I not make the miseries of my ancestors my own, viewing them as the common condition of living?'. Orosius accordingly grieves in silence for those who are not moved to tears by such suffering, people whose insensibility makes them disbelieve anything which they have not experienced for themselves.[166]

In the second instance, by combining descriptions of the sufferings of the past with such frequent points of comparison, Orosius intends to reinforce what he regards, perhaps, as the most important function served by historiography. History not only serves as a means of correction and instruction for the present but it also provides a source of consolation. This principle had originally been highlighted by Seneca: 'a man will therefore find the greatest solace [*maximum solacium*] in the thought that what has happened to himself was suffered by all who were before him and will be suffered by all who come after him. For that reason, it seems to me that it is the nature of things to have made general what is made hardest to bear so that this equality might serve as consolation [*consoleretur*] for the cruelty of fate'.[167] Rufinus stated that he had been asked to translate Eusebius for the sake of consolation as well as edification,[168] whilst Macrobius presented history explicitly as an antidote to sorrow.[169] For Orosius, it is Vergil's *Aeneid* which provides the occasion for an extended meditation on the importance of the passing of time for an understanding of the significance of the suffering of the present. According to Vergil, Orosius writes, Aeneas sought to bring solace to those

---

166 *Seven Books of History*, III.20, p. 107.
167 Seneca, *On Consolation to Polybius*, trans. J.W. Basore (Loeb, 1932), I.4, p. 359. Compare this with Abelard's 'letter of consolation' or 'history of calamities', a work which combines confession (of pride and lust) and apologetic (against a series of calumnies, not least the accusation that he fled his monastery of St Gildas) and where consolation is provided in the final paragraph by the Holy Spirit or 'Comforter' ('paraclete' or *consolator*): Abelard, *Historia Calamitatum*, trans. B. Radice, *The Letters of Abelard and Heloise* (Harmondsworth, 1974), pp. 57–106. More generally, see P. von Moos, *Consolatio – Studien zur mittellateinischen Trostliteratur über den Tod und zum Problem der christlichen Trauer* (Munich, 1971–72).
168 Rufinus [of Aquileia], 'Preface to Books X–XI of Eusebius' *Ecclesiastical History*', trans. W.H. Fremantle (Oxford, 1892), p. 565.
169 Macrobius, *Saturnalia*, VII.1.18–19, pp. 443–4.

of his companions who had survived dangers and shipwreck by saying 'perhaps it will help one day to remember even these things'.[170] This reflection (*sententia*), Orosius comments, may have been made up to suit one single occasion (*semel apte ficta*) but, in his view, it has a more general significance according to its threefold aspect of past, present and future. First of all, he explains, the greater the difficulty of the deeds which have been done in the past, the more pleasure they give when they are subsequently related in words; second, deeds in the future are made more desirable by aversion to the present and are always believed to be better; and, third, no just comparison can be made at the time for the sufferings of the present because, however insignificant the latter may be, they will always be a much greater source of vexation than those of greater magnitude which have occurred in the past or that will subsequently occur in the future. These three temporal considerations provide Orosius with the rationale for his own account of the sufferings of the past. Only a comparison of events across time (*comparatio rerum*) will produce a correct judgment on the relative degree of present suffering.[171] In the case of his contemporaries, therefore, Orosius suggests that, faced with the troubles of external pressures, Italy should be 'consoled' by the remembrance of those wars of the past by which it had been torn apart with incomparably greater cruelty (*incomparabiliter crudelius*). Orosius saw his own history of the suffering brought by war, pestilence and famine in this light: it provided consolation for the sufferings of the present (*ad consolationem miseriae recentis*).[172]

It is difficult to overestimate the importance and influence of Eusebius and Orosius as models of Christian historiography in the Middle Ages.[173] Gregory of Tours in the sixth century,

---

170 Vergil, *Aeneid*, I.203, p. 255, VI.377, p. 533; cf. Macrobius, *Saturnalia*, V.11.5, p. 324, VII.2.9–10, pp. 447–8; William of Malmesbury, *Gesta Regum Anglorum*, II.121, p. 183; Richard of Devizes, *Chronicle*, ed. and trans. J.T. Appleby (London, 1963), pp. 63–4. For Servius' fourth-century commentary on this line, see *In Vergilii Carmina Commentarii*, ed. G. Thilo and H. Hagen (Leipzig, 1878–1902), vol. I, p. 79.
171 Orosius, *Seven Books of History*, IV.prol., pp. 121–2.
172 *Seven Books of History*, V.24, p. 227, VII.22, p. 317.
173 For the *Historia Ecclesiastica Tripartita*, a Latin compilation of extracts from Socrates, Sozomen and Theodoret which was made by Cassiodorus in order

for example, and Bede in the eighth readily adopted both the approach and the substance of a large number of the same themes. Even without his subsequent endorsement and recommendation by pope Gelasius I in 494, it is not difficult to see why the influence of Orosius in particular should have been so prevalent – a universal pattern of crime and punishment, the providential world empire of a (restored) Christianised Rome, the complexity of 'interwoven' events, the consolation provided by a comparison of past, present and future. The popularity revealed by the sheer number of manuscripts of his *Seven Books of History* extends to translations into the vernacular and for the same reason. When it was adapted and translated into Old English in the course of the ninth century, for example, the resonance of key aspects of Orosius' message became very clear to Alfred of Wessex: an explicit preference for single rule amongst a number of competing kingdoms ('if there are diverse kingdoms, how much better is it if one kingdom is the greatest to which the entire power of the other kingdoms is subject?'); the presentation of the emperor Theodosius as a paradigm of virtuous Christian governance, a ruler whose victories against 'barbarian' and internal enemies depended, not just on his own strength, but on the assistance provided by God, on prayer, fasting and the singing of psalms by day and by night.[174]

Orosius, above all, made a natural historiographical companion to Boethius, who had likewise set out to provide consolation for those suffering in the face of adversity, evil and, in his own case, imminent death. The *Consolation of Philosophy* (c.524 AD) did so, in the first instance, by exposing the transience of worldly goods and prosperity but also by means of an extended reflection on 'the singleness of providence, the course of fate, the

---

to serve as a continuation of Eusebius, see M.L.W. Laistner, 'The Value and Influence of Cassiodorus' *Ecclesiastical History*', *Harvard Theological Review*, 41 (1948), pp. 51–67; reprinted in M.L.W. Laistner, *The Intellectual Heritage of the Early Middle Ages: Selected Essays* (Ithaca, 1957), pp. 22–39; cf. H. Leppin, 'The Church Historians – Socrates, Sozomenus and Theodoretus', in G. Marasco (ed.), *Greek and Roman Historiography in Late Antiquity: Fourth to Sixth Century AD* (Brill, 2003), pp. 219–54. More generally, see G.W. Trompf, *Early Christian Historiography: Narratives of Retribution* (London, 2000).
174 *Seven Books of History*, II.1, p. 44, VII.34–6, pp. 341–7. For Alfred and Orosius, see J. Bately (ed.), *The Old English Orosius* (Oxford, 1980).

suddenness of chance, the knowledge and predestination of God, and the freedom of the will'.[175] Meditating on the vagaries of fortune and fame should open people's eyes not only to the identity and location of true worth and lasting goodness – love of wisdom, knowledge of self – but also to the underlying principles of order by which the universe is divinely governed. This conception of providential harmony (as much Stoic and Neoplatonic as it was Christian) should, in Boethius' opinion, be regarded as compatible both with the presence of evil in the world (including the apparent 'success' of wicked people, and especially of tyrannical rulers) and with the freedom of individual human will and action.[176] By instilling the lesson that material well-being and worldly success did not, in themselves, constitute true happiness and by offering the reassurance that events in this life were the result neither of random chance nor of ineluctable necessity, Boethius' reconciliation of fortune, providence and freedom of the will established a particularly influential model for those writers struggling to explain the mutability and precariousness of human achievements, be they personal, public or political. In this sense, any specifically historical narrative could, and should, prompt similar mediation and consolation, if not at a metaphysical level, then at least as a moral expression and resolution of very real anxieties over the apparent injustice of what seemed to happen to good (and evil) people in this life: 'ancient times are full, and the present times are full too, of examples of kings whose happiness changed to misfortune'; 'whatever you see here happen contrary to your expectation is indeed right order in fact, although in your opinion it is perverse confusion'.[177]

The Bible presented medieval writers of history with a very wide range of, sometimes contrasting, models for both the form and the content of their historiography, extending all the way from the universalism of world history to the commemoration of particular deeds. In the hands of Eusebius, the patterns provided by both

---

175 Boethius, *Consolation of Philosophy*, IV.6, p. 357.
176 For commentary, see H. Chadwick, *Boethius: The Consolations of Music, Logic, Theology and Philosophy* (Oxford, 1981), ch. 5; for Boethius' subsequent impact, see M.T. Gibson (ed.), *Boethius: His Life, Thought and Influence* (Oxford, 1981).
177 Boethius, *Consolation of Philosophy*, III.5, p. 251, IV.6, pp. 365–7; see also page 275.

Old and New Testaments were used to create a hugely influential model for ecclesiastical history but also for the methodological analysis of the sources on which that narrative was based. In the hands of Orosius, these principles were applied to produce a particularly complex combination of Christian and non-Christian historical narratives which, as an explicitly comparative analysis of discipline and punishment, simultaneously embodied instruction, admonition and consolation. Combined with the more abstract reflections of Boethius, their impact was profound. In the tenth century, for example, Liutprand of Cremona opened his *Antapodosis* with 'wise Boethius' and proceeded to model much of his subsequent narrative on the *Consolation of Philosophy*.[178] In the twelfth century, Eadmer invoked 'consolation' as a goal of his *History of Recent Events*,[179] whilst Henry of Huntingdon not only set up his *History of the English* to provide 'consolation from grief' (*solamen doloris*), but organised it according to a pattern of divine scourging, in this case the series of five *plagae* with which the English people had been afflicted – Romans, Picts, Saxons, Danes and Normans – as punishment both for their own sins and for those of their rulers.[180]

Chronography

Whilst the 'classical' and 'biblical' traditions provided, in themselves, a wide range of models for the form and content of historiography, medieval writers were also able to draw on a tradition of chronography, which underpinned them both – that is, on the type of history-writing which was concerned primarily

---

178 Liutprand, *Antapodosis*, I.1, p. 31, VI.1, p. 205.
179 Eadmer, *Historia Novorum in Anglia*, trans. G. Bosanquet, *Eadmer's History of Recent Events in England* (London, 1964), prol., p. 1; cf. Thietmar of Merseburg, *Chronicon*, I.prol., p. 67, VIII.27, p. 379; Richard of Devizes, *Chronicle*, prol., p. 2.
180 Henry of Huntingdon, *Historia Anglorum*, prol., p. 3, I.4, p. 15, I.47, pp. 75–7, II.35, p. 123, IV.25, p. 255, IV.30, p. 265, V.praef., pp. 273–5; cf. William of Malmesbury, *Gesta Regum Anglorum*, I.54, p. 83, I.70, p. 105, quoting Alcuin, *Epistolae*, ed. E. Dümmler (Berlin, 1895), *Ep*.17, p. 47, who is himself citing Gildas; Orderic Vitalis, *Historia Ecclesiastica*, VIII.15, p. 229; Gervase of Canterbury, *Mappa Mundi*, proem., p. 416. For the general moral and spiritual signification of the ten plagues, see, for example, Honorius of Autun, *De Decem Plagis Aegypti* (PL 172, cols 265–70).

with recording what actually happened in any given year. The distinctiveness of this third tradition in the Middle Ages was, in part, a continuation of a longstanding classical differentiation between 'annals' and 'history', but it was also given its own particular direction by the subsequent association of the calculation of the calendar with the liturgical year of the Christian Church.

According to Cicero, the writing of history in Rome had its origins in nothing more elevated than a series of annals which were put together each year by the chief priest and posted up so that there would be a public remembrance of events (*memoria publica*). Many people then followed this manner of writing, leaving simple memorials (*monumenta*) of dates, people, places and deeds, without any rhetorical 'ornamentation'; they simply narrated things with the aim of brevity and intelligibility and did not elaborate in the manner of Herodotus or Thucydides. In Cicero's opinion, however, it was now high time that Roman historians finally followed their Greek forebears and expanded upon events rather than merely narrating them, becoming *exornatores rerum* rather than simply *narratores*.[181] Writing in the second century, Aulus Gellius reinforced both the distinction and the value-judgment which Cicero had placed upon it. Some people, he states, are of the opinion that history differs from annals on the grounds that, whilst both types of writing narrate what has been done, history is a narrative of those things which the narrator has experienced in person. Others, he continues, argue that annals are the same as history but that history is not the same as annals on the basis that, whereas history is an exposition or demonstration of *res gestae*, annals simply provide an annual compilation of *res gestae*, maintaining the order of each year. For his own part, Aulus Gellius is in no doubt that history is superior to annals – whereas annals merely set out what was done and in what year it was done, history also sets out the reason (*ratio*) and the deliberation (*consilium*) behind it. As a result, he concludes, annals are absolutely incapable of inspiring people to defend the *res publica* or make them reluctant to do something wrong; simply to record the names of those people in whose period of office war

---

181 Cicero, *De Oratore*, trans. E. Sutton and H. Rackham (Loeb, 1948), II.12.52–13.56, pp. 237–9; cf. Cicero, *Epistulae ad Familiares*, trans. D.R. Shackleton Bailey, *Letters to Friends* (Loeb, 2001), V.12, p. 161; Macrobius, *Saturnalia*, III.2.17, p. 195.

was begun and ended without also stating what was done in the war, which laws and decrees were issued and with what deliberation (*consilia*) all this was carried out is not to write history but to narrate fables to children.[182]

Despite the exhortations of both Cicero and Aulus Gellius for writers of history to move beyond mere compilation, an annalistic tradition of historiography proved very resilient in the Middle Ages. In part, this owed its inspiration, once again, to Eusebius, whose two major works, the *Ecclesiastical History* and the *Chronological Tables*, embodied precisely this distinction between history and chronography but also a relationship between them.[183] Eusebius' *Chronici Canones* (subsequently translated and continued by Jerome) set out to integrate the chronology of Scripture with the historical events of Greece and Rome; he painstakingly wrote down events in parallel columns so that the history described in the Old and New Testaments could be correlated and synchronised with the history which was already familiar from classical historiography.[184] The influence of Eusebius' chronographic work can be traced on Orosius, who used the *ab urbe condita* dates given by his Roman sources but who was also precise about dating his own work from Creation, the *annus mundi*.[185] When Isidore of Seville inserted a world chronicle into book V of his *Etymologies*, replacing Eusebius' parallel columns with a single chronological sequence (*series temporum*), the die was cast.[186] As a result, when Gregory of Tours wrote his *Histories* he began with Adam and then established a sequence of time which was explicitly tied to

---

182 Aulus Gellius, *Noctes Atticae*, V.18, pp. 433–5; cf. L. Holford-Strevens, *Aulus Gellius: An Antonine Scholar and His Achievement* (rev. edn, Oxford, 2003), pp. 241–59, and, more generally, T.P. Wiseman, *Clio's Cosmetics: Three Studies in Greco-Roman Literature* (Leicester, 1979), pp. 9–26.
183 See page 442.
184 Eusebius, *Chronicon*, ed. R. Helm, *Die Chronik des Hieronymus* (3rd edn, Berlin, 1984); cf. A. Mosshammer, *The Chronicle of Eusebius and Greek Chronographic Tradition* (Lewisburg, 1979); R.W. Burgess, 'The Dates and Editions of Eusebius' *Chronici Canones* and *Historia Ecclesiastica*', *Journal of Theological Studies*, 48 (1997), pp. 471–504; B. Croke, 'The Origins of the Christian World Chronicle', in B. Croke and A.M. Emmett (eds), *History and Historians in Late Antiquity* (Sydney, 1983), pp. 116–31.
185 Orosius, *Seven Books of History*, VII.43, p. 363. He dated his own work to 5,618 years since the beginning of the world, that is, to 418 AD.
186 Isidore, *Etymologiae*, V.39.2–42, pp. 130–3.

Eusebius, Jerome and Orosius up to, and including, the exact calculation of years with which the work concluded.[187]

Alongside the influence of these classical and Christian traditions from late antiquity, however, an even more decisive impetus behind the continuation of an annalistic form of writing was provided by the liturgy of the early medieval Church. Not only did the computation of the calendar (*computus*) act as a stimulus to the accurate calculation of the cycle of the years but the compilation of Easter tables (as well as of martyrologies, necrologies and lists of ecclesiastical feasts and saints' days) served as a formal, physical location in which (as had been the practice of the priests of pagan Rome) the significant events of each year could be recorded.[188] The potential historiographical significance of such calculations becomes evident in the eighth century, above all in the works of Bede. Like Eusebius, Bede wrote history which covered both 'historical' and 'annalistic' genres. In 731, he wrote his *Ecclesiastical History of the English People*, a work in five books which applied Eusebian themes to the Anglo-Saxon Church and peoples.[189] In 714, however, Bede had already written *On the Reckoning of Time*, a text in which, after a demonstration of how to calculate the lunar calendar and the dates of Easter, he had set out a chronicle of the significant events of world history, with dates calculated in a single chronological sequence of years numbered from Creation.[190] The immediate purpose behind Bede's calculations had been to correct unwarranted and potentially dangerous eschatological speculation. Despite long-established official denunciations of the presumption involved in calculating the end of time (according to Matthew 24:36, Mark 13:32–3, Luke 12:35–6, and 1 Thessalonians

---

187 Gregory of Tours, *Histories*, pref., p. 63, I.prol., p. 69, IV.51, p. 249, V.prol., p. 253, X.31, p. 603; cf. W. Goffart, *The Narrators of Barbarian History* (Princeton, 1988), ch. 3; M. Heinzelmann, *Gregory of Tours – History and Society in the Sixth Century* (Cambridge, 2001), pp. 104–6.

188 R.L. Poole, *Chronicles and Annals: A Brief Outline of Their Origin and Growth* (Oxford, 1926); C.W. Jones, *Saints' Lives and Chronicles in Early England* (Ithaca, 1947); cf. K. Harrison, *The Framework of History to AD 900* (Cambridge, 1976); H.E. Barnes, *A History of Historical Writing* (New York, 1963); J.W. Thompson, *A History of Historical Writing* (New York, 1942); D. Dumville, 'What Is a Chronicle?', in E. Kooper (ed.), *The Medieval Chronicle II* (Amsterdam, 2002), pp. 1–27.

189 For Bede's own annalistic summary of his material, see *Historia Ecclesiastica Gentis Anglorum*, V.24, pp. 290–3.

190 Bede, *De Temporum Ratione*, trans. F. Wallis (Liverpool, 1999).

5:2, it would come 'like a thief in the night'),[191] a reading of Eusebius' chronology perhaps inevitably invited a calculation of when exactly the end of the sixth age would be nigh.[192] Eusebius had dated the age of the world to 5,198 years at Christ's birth (5,199 according to Jerome's revision); there were six days in Creation and, according to Psalm 90:4 and 2 Peter 3:8, 'one day is like a thousand years'; hence the world would end in 802 AD, that is, when it was 6,000 years old. Mindful of the dangers created when the tribulations catalogued by Orosius were equated with the list of eschatological signs provided by the book of Revelation, Bede followed his mathematical computation of a coordinated lunar–solar calendar with a chronicle of the world which revised Eusebius' original figure for the age of the world at Christ's birth radically downwards, to 3,952 years. Henceforth it would now be doubly erroneous to believe that the world would end in 802 AD or even, according to Bede's own revised chronology, in 2048 AD. To reinforce the point, Bede provided Easter tables for the next three hundred years, up to and including 1064 AD.

The tension between chronography and eschatology was to reappear at various points throughout the Middle Ages,[193] but the purely formal consequences of a computational annalistic tradition for the writing of history were profound. It is this tradition, represented by Bede's *Chronica Maiora*, which was continued in the tenth century, for example by chroniclers such as Marianus Scotus, and which then flourished well into the eleventh and twelfth centuries, with writers such as Sigebert of Gembloux (who began his own universal *Chronicle* in 381, the year at which Eusebius had stopped).[194] The writing of history and the compilation of annals may therefore have served different purposes

---

191 See, for example, Augustine, *De Civitate Dei*, XXII.30, p. 1091.
192 For the 'six ages', see page 102.
193 B. McGinn, *Visions of the End: Apocalyptic Traditions in the Middle Ages* (rev. edn, New York, 1998).
194 P. Classen, '*Res Gestae*, Universal History, Apocalypse – Visions of Past and Future', in R.L. Benson and G. Constable (eds), *Renaissance and Renewal in the Twelfth Century* (Oxford, 1982), pp. 387–417; A.-D. von den Brincken, *Studien zur Lateinischen Weltchronistik bis in die Zeitalter Ottos von Freising* (Düsseldorf, 1957); K.H. Krüger, *Die Universalchroniken* (Typologie des Sources 16, Turnhout, 1976); M.I. Allen, 'Universal History 300–1100: Origins and Western Developments', in D.M. Deliyannis (ed.), *Historiography in the Middle Ages* (Leiden, 2003), pp. 17–42.

in theory, but they were also, in many ways, complementary – Eusebius and Bede between them provided a precedent for those writers, such as Orderic Vitalis, who wanted to do both. Indeed, the fact that a terminological distinction between historiography and chronography was never consistently applied reflects the way in which, in practice, the two approaches could be combined. It was thus familiarity with Eusebius' *Chronici Canones* which underpinned Hugh of St Victor's decision in *c*.1130 to produce a series of lists and tables (chronological and geographical, of kingdoms, popes, emperors and rulers, as well as of historiographers) which his students could memorise as the foundation for the literal 'historical' sense of their exposition of the Bible.[195] According to Hugh, there were three matters on which the knowledge of past actions especially depends – the persons who performed the deeds, the places in which they were performed and the time at which they were performed.[196] These three 'circumstances' provided the core of Hugh's tables, which he presented as a brief summary of the otherwise nearly infinite events of history and which, when memorised, were to serve as the foundation of a foundation, a 'first foundation', of all knowledge.[197] The actual writing of history, meanwhile, consisted of a narrative of actions which was expressed in the basic, literal meaning of the words. As such, when Hugh came to discuss the place of written history within the educational curriculum in his *Didascalicon*, he added to his triad of person, time and place a fourth category, one which required a narrative, rather than tabular, arrangement. This fourth element was denoted by the term 'actions' (*negotium*).[198]

---

195 Hugh of St Victor, *De Tribus Maximis Circumstantiis Gestorum*, trans. M. Carruthers, in M. Carruthers and J.M. Ziolkowski (eds), *The Medieval Craft of Memory* (Philadelphia, 2002), pp. 33–40; cf. G.R. Evans, 'Hugh of St Victor on History and the Meaning of Things', *Studia Monastica*, 25 (1983), pp. 223–34; L.B. Mortensen, 'Hugh of St Victor on Secular History – A Preliminary Edition of Chapters from his *Chronica*', *Cahiers de l'Institut du Moyen-Age Grec et Latin*, 62 (1992), pp. 3–30. For Otto of Freising's lists of kings, emperors and popes, see his *Chronicle*, VII, pp. 449–50; for Richard FitzNigel's tricolumnar 'history', see his *Dialogus de Scaccario*, I.5, p. 41.
196 Hugh of St Victor, *De Tribus Maximis Circumstantiis Gestorum*, pp. 36, 39.
197 *De Tribus Maximis Circumstantiis Gestorum*, p. 39.
198 W.M. Green, 'De Tribus Maximis Circumstantiis Gestorum', *Speculum*, 18 (1943), p. 485 n. 2; cf. Hugh of St Victor, *Didascalicon*, VI.3, p. 136.

Far from simply acceding to the ranking expressed by Cicero and Aulus Gellius, the 'historical' works of Eusebius and Bede ensured that a more equitable distinction between history-writing and chronography was perpetuated throughout the Middle Ages. Given a choice between the two, neither Cicero nor Aulus Gellius had thought there was much of an alternative – history provided pleasure, or rather a combination of pleasure with utility.[199] Others were not so sure. According to Justin's epitome of Pompeius Trogus, both Livy and Sallust had gone beyond the limits of history when they included within their narrative direct speeches which had been composed in their own style.[200] Even the author of the *Historia Augusta* claimed to have put deeds above eloquence and, as a result, rather than imitate Sallust, Livy or Tacitus, had chosen those writers who had committed lives and events to the memory of posterity, not so much through stylistic distinction, as through truth.[201] The chronographic and annalistic tradition of Eusebius and Bede added a self-authenticating element to the expression of such reservations and concern. According to Hugh of Fleury, for example, whose *Ecclesiastical History* of c.1110 encompassed historical events up to 855, it was annalistic dating which distinguished history from 'old-wives' tales' (*aniles fabulae*). Deeds which are committed to writing without the certainty of a king-list or other chronology, he argued, could not be accepted as *historia* but must be classed instead as *aniles fabulae*.[202] This dismissive comment was repeated in the 1180s by Ralph de Diceto, a writer who noted that Bede had written both *historia* and *chronica* and whose own historical works (*Abbreviationes Chronicorum, Imagines Historiarum*) were strongly influenced by the chronographic lists

---

199 Cicero, *De Finibus*, trans. H. Rackham, *On Ends* (2nd edn, Loeb, 1931), V.19.51, p. 453.
200 Justin, *Epitome of the Philippic History of Pompeius Trogus*, XXXVIII.3.11, p. 238.
201 'Probus', in *Historia Augusta*, I.6, p. 337, II.6–7, p. 339.
202 Hugh of Fleury, *Historia Ecclesiastica* (PL 163, cols 821–54), III prol., col. 833. For the phrase *aniles fabulae*, see also John of Salisbury, *Metalogicon*, trans. D.D. McGarry (Berkeley, 1955), I.24, p. 71; cf. Quintilian, *Institutio Oratoria*, I.8.19, p. 155.

of Hugh of St Victor.[203] The comment was also cited approvingly in c.1260 by Vincent of Beauvais in the prologue to his encyclopaedic *Speculum Maius*.[204]

Conversely, when William of Malmesbury came to write his *Deeds of the English Kings* he was clearly keen to distinguish history from annals and very much in favour of the former. His own work, he writes, would fulfil the desire for a 'somewhat grander narrative' (*grandiuscula narratio*) and, unlike the *Anglo-Saxon Chronicle*, it was a *full* account of the deeds of kings (*plena gesta regum*), a *full* history (*plena historia*), which would do more than just provide a series of names and years.[205] In emulating Bede, that 'ecclesiastical orator',[206] William announced that he would season with Roman salt what had become, since Bede, a 'barbarian' narrative, aspiring to 'polish' and 'elegance' by including the 'flowers of rhetoric' which were absent from a chronicle such as that of Marianus Scotus.[207] In the first instance, this meant combining utility with pleasure and, as a result, proffering both Cicero and Vergil as potential guides for his work.[208] In the second instance, it meant imposing some sense of order and causality on what he was writing – a year-by-year account, after all, could be confusing, and writers of annals were duty-bound to commit to writing, not what they themselves wanted, but what the times provided for them.[209] Like Orosius, William was certainly under no illusions as to the difficulties that writing this sort of history would present ('it is not my purpose to unravel one by one the inextricable labyrinths of his labours'), but, like Cicero, he remained convinced that his

---

203 Ralph de Diceto, *Abbreviationes Chronicorum*, p. 15; cf. G.A. Zinn, 'The Influence of Hugh of St Victor's *Chronicon* on the *Abbreviationes Chronicorum* by Ralph of Diceto', *Speculum*, 52 (1977), pp. 38–61.
204 Vincent of Beauvais, *Speculum Maius* (Douai, 1624; reprinted Graz, 1964–65), prol. V, col. 4.
205 William of Malmesbury, *Gesta Regum Anglorum*, Ep.ded., p. 9, I.prol., p. 15, II.213, p. 393.
206 *Gesta Regum Anglorum*, I.59, p. 91.
207 *Gesta Regum Anglorum*, I.prol., p. 15, I.59, p. 89, II.149, p. 241; William of Malmesbury, *Gesta Pontificum Anglorum*, IV.164, p. 459.
208 *Gesta Regum Anglorum*, II.prol., p. 151, V.prol., p. 709; William of Malmesbury, *Historia Novella*, I.prol., p. 1.
209 Cf. William of Tyre, *History of Deeds Done Beyond the Sea*, trans. E.A. Babcock and A.C. Krey (New York, 1941), XXIII.pref., p. 506.

work should be concerned, not just with deeds (*gesta*), but with what was deliberately intended (*consilia*).[210]

Given the differences of opinion which could clearly exist over where exactly the boundary should be drawn between history and chronography and, just as importantly, over the relative priority which should be accorded each type of writing, it is perhaps not surprising to find at least one twelfth-century writer making the distinction between history and annals ('which are called chronicles by another name') the subject of an extended discussion right at the start of his 'historical' work.[211] Writing more or less contemporaneously with Ralph de Diceto, Gervase of Canterbury was well aware of the disagreements between chroniclers themselves over the exact calculation of years, both in terms of when exactly they should begin, and end, and in terms of the computational discrepancy which had arisen between the Gospels and the chronology of Dionysius and which had already been noted in the *Chronicle* of Marianus Scotus. With different people writing different things, Gervase concludes, with everyone attempting to come on their own to the treasury of truth by the correct path, many false things are written about the deeds and words (*facta et dicta*) of kings and rulers.[212] Gervase did not himself want to write down everything that was capable of remembrance, only what should be remembered, that is, those things which seemed to be worthy of remembrance. This combination of accuracy and selectivity provides Gervase with what he hopes will be the hallmark of his own *Chronica*. It is with the difference between histories and chronicles, however, that Gervase chooses to open the prologue to his work. Historians and chroniclers, he states, in one sense have a single intention and subject-matter (in that both of them aim at the truth and include examples of living well, by means of

---

210 *Gesta Regum Anglorum*, II.121, p. 181, V.prol., p. 709.
211 Gervase of Canterbury, *Chronica*, ed. W. Stubbs, *Opera Historica* (London, 1879), prol., pp. 87–91; cf. V.H. Galbraith, *Historical Research in Medieval England* (London, 1951), pp. 1–3; A. Gransden, 'Prologues in the Historiography of Twelfth-Century England', in D. Williams (ed.), *England in the Twelfth Century* (Woodbridge, 1990); reprinted in A. Gransden, *Legends, Traditions and History in Medieval England* (London, 1992), pp.125–51; C. Given-Wilson, *Chronicles: The Writing of History in Medieval England* (London, 2004), pp. xix, 1, 21, 61, 126.
212 Gervase of Canterbury, *Chronica*, prol., p. 89. For Gervase's own *Gesta Regum*, see ed. W. Stubbs, *Opera Historica*, II, pp. 3–106.

which humans can be instructed in order to profit in the good) but, in doing so, they also have a different manner of handling their material and a different form of writing. The historian's approach is diffuse and elegant, whereas the chronicler proceeds with simplicity and brevity.[213] To drive this point home, Gervase appeals to some ornate imagery of his own, drawn from Horace and from Vergil. The historian, he writes, 'throws out his bombast and sesquipedalian words', whereas the chronicler 'meditates upon the woodland muse with a slender reed-pipe'; the historian sits 'amongst those who sow magnificent and grandiloquent words', whereas the chronicler 'pauses at the hut of Amyclas lest there should be a fight over his poor roof'.[214] Gervase warms to the contrast. 'It is germane to the historian to aim at the truth', he writes, 'to delight his listeners or readers with his sweet and elegant discourse, to set out truthfully the actions [*actus*], conduct [*mores*] and life [*vita*] of the person being described, and to seek to comprehend nothing other than what seems to be the rationale of history [*ratio historiae*]. The chronicler, on the other hand, computes the years of the Lord's incarnation and the months and days of those years, and also briefly sets out the actions of kings and rulers which occurred in these times and commemorates the events and portents or wonders [*miracula*]'.[215] In drawing such a clear distinction, however, Gervase is also only too well aware of the ease with which these boundaries can be crossed. 'There are many', he concludes, 'who, when writing chronicles or annals, exceed their boundaries, for they take pleasure in extending their threads and glorifying their fringes [Matthew 23:5]'.[216]

---

213 *Chronica*, prol., p. 87. Compare William of Jumièges, who explicitly places his own work in the library of chronicles (*cronicorum bibliotheca*) because it is not ornamented in the elegant and weighty style of rhetoricians (*non rethorum venusta exornatum gravitate*) nor with the venal wit and splendour of polished utterance, but conducted in an unelaborated style and simple language that is clear for every reader: William of Jumièges, *Gesta Normannorum Ducum*, ed. and trans. E.M.C. van Houts (Oxford, 1992), Ep.ded., p. 5.
214 *Chronica*, prol., p. 87; cf. Horace, *Ars Poetica*, trans. H.R. Fairclough (Loeb, 1929), 98, p. 459; Vergil, *Eclogues*, trans. H.R. Fairclough, rev. G.P. Goold (Loeb, 2000), I.2, p. 3; Lucan, *Pharsalia*, trans. J.D. Duff, *The Civil War* (Loeb, 1928), V.516–31, pp. 277–9.
215 *Chronica*, prol., p. 87.
216 *Chronica*, prol., pp. 87–8; cf. Walter Map, *De Nugis Curialium*, ed. and trans. M.L.R. James, rev. C.N.L. Brooke and R.A.B. Mynors (Oxford, 1983), I.25, p. 89.

Whilst such transgressors may desire to compile a chronicle (and Gervase states that he will himself 'compile' rather than 'write' his own work),[217] 'they proceed in a historical manner, and what they ought to have stated briefly, and in a style of writing that is humble discourse, they attempt instead to make weighty by the use of bombastic words'.[218]

Classical, biblical and chronographic traditions combined

Put side by side, classical, biblical and chronographic traditions in the writing of history provided a very varied and complex set of models on which medieval authors could draw. Sallust and Josephus may have served as the predominant classical paradigms but they were far from being the only ones available – Florus' version of Livy, Justin's digest of Pompeius Trogus, Suetonius' *Lives* and the *Historia Romana* could each exercise a greater attraction at a particular time or for a particular purpose. Chronicles and the book of Acts may have provided the most influential models drawn from within the Bible but the books of Daniel, Revelation and the Maccabees could be tailored to suit more immediate prophetic or martial goals. It is the *range* of alternatives, the variation in historiographical practice, which needs underlining here. Nowhere is this more evident than in assessing what the legacy of late-antique Christian or 'patristic' historiography might have entailed for the Middle Ages.

For all the authority exercised by Eusebius and Orosius, these two historians were far from exerting an exclusive influence on the subsequent course of explicitly Christian historiography. Orosius, for example, set great store by aligning his work with Augustine's *City of God*, the first ten books of which he had read by the time he was writing his own work. Indeed, Orosius begins and ends his history by attributing the inception of the work to Augustine's invitation and its survival to Augustine's approval. Augustine's own reaction to Orosius was much cooler than this self-declared endorsement would suggest. When he completed

---

217 *Chronica*, prol., p. 89. For the shifting connotations of this particular term, see N. Hathaway, 'Compilator – From Plagiarism to Compiling', *Viator*, 20 (1989), pp. 19–44.
218 *Chronica*, prol., p. 88.

the *City of God* in *c*.427, Augustine took care to recommend Jerome's account of the four world monarchies, rather than the analysis provided by Orosius, and he actually described Orosius' account of the plagues of Egypt as ingenious but speculative and mistaken.[219] Augustine was also much more cautious than Orosius in detecting signs of God's favour or disfavour in His governance of the universe. He was likewise much more wary of treating the history of the world from the neatly triumphalist perspective which had been read out of Eusebius. God could actively intervene, for sure, but His providence could also be permissive; He could let Nature, and humankind, take its course. Rome was not, in Augustine's view, the fourth and last world monarchy; like any other human institution, it, too, would rise and fall. Such differences of opinion were far from insignificant. Indeed, Augustine's disagreement with the historical conclusions put forward by both Eusebius and Orosius should serve as one more qualification on any temptation to generalise about a single tradition of 'universal' Christian historiography.

The example of Augustine is still more important as an illustration of the way in which classical, biblical and chronographic traditions of historiography were not necessarily mutually exclusive but could, instead, be juxtaposed, if not combined. For someone who had such a profound impact on the conception and practice of historiography in the Middle Ages, it is striking that Augustine did not himself produce anything which offered itself as a work of 'history'.[220] This did not mean, however, that Augustine refrained from commenting on, and analysing, the significance of this particular form of writing. Augustine's understanding of historiography derived from his engagement with early Christian historians, most notably Eusebius and Jerome, but it was rooted, first and foremost, in the Bible. This is brought out most strongly in *De Doctrina Christiana*, where Augustine initially

---

219 Orosius, *Seven Books of History*, VII.43.20, pp. 363–4; Augustine, *De Civitate Dei*, XVIII.52, p. 836, XX.23, p. 945; cf. T.E. Mommsen, 'Orosius and Augustine', in T.E. Mommsen, *Medieval and Renaissance Studies* (Ithaca, 1959), pp. 325–48; H.I. Marrou, 'Saint Augustin, Orose et l'Augustinisme Historique', *Settimane di Studio*, 17 (1970), pp. 59–87; W.H.C. Frend, 'Augustine and Orosius on the End of the Ancient World', *Augustinian Studies*, 20 (1989), pp. 1–38.
220 Smalley, *Historians in the Middle Ages*, p. 44: 'Augustine's book [*City of God*] represents a vision of history, not a blueprint for historiography'.

confines his discussion to the nature of history-writing as chronography. 'Whatever is revealed about the order of past times by that which is termed history [*historia*]', he writes, 'is of the greatest assistance in understanding the holy books, even if it has been learned outside the Church as part of childhood education'.[221] As an illustration of this principle, Augustine cites the knowledge of consular names for particular years, information which could be used to date the life and ministry of Christ. Thus, whilst the number of years that Christ lived after his baptism can certainly be worked out from the Gospel of Luke, in order to prevent any doubts arising, it is established with greater clarity and certainty by cross-comparison with secular history (*historia gentium*).[222] It is by means of similar chronological study that a temporal relationship can be established between Greek philosophy and the Old Testament and the conclusion drawn that, if there is any intellectual debt owed by one to the other, then it is by Plato to Jeremiah and not the other way around.[223]

In the *City of God*, Augustine proceeds to add to the need to establish an accurate chronology two further criteria for historiography – the value of eyewitness testimony and the importance of textual criticism. As an example of the latter, writing of his 'duty to defend the historical truth of the scriptural account', in this case the accuracy of the long life spans given by Genesis to Adam's descendants before the Flood, Augustine defends the idea of antediluvian longevity in two stages. First, he appeals to the archaeological evidence which he has seen for himself, namely the discovery of extraordinarily large bones. Second, he establishes the ground-rules for sorting out any textual discrepancy between the Hebrew version of the Old Testament and the Latin translation of the Greek Septuagint. 'Where it is impossible for two texts simultaneously to provide a true record of historical fact', he writes, then due to the possibility of error in scribal transcription and transmission, 'greater reliance should be placed on the

---

221 Augustine, *De Doctrina Christiana*, ed. and trans. R.P.H. Green, *On Christian Teaching* (Oxford, 1995), II.28.105, p. 105.
222 *De Doctrina Christiana*, II.28.106, p. 105.
223 *De Civitate Dei*, VIII.11, pp. 313–14.

original language from which it was translated'.[224] Augustine then proceeds to integrate the history of Old Testament Israel with corresponding events in the history of Assyria and of Rome, a task for which he uses the universal chronology which had been composed by Eusebius and then translated (and extended) by Jerome.[225]

In the first place, therefore, Augustine's view of the usefulness of history (*utilitas historiae*) comprises the order, or sequence, of events in time, material for which Augustine consistently refers his readers to the chronology (*historia temporum*) written by Eusebius, 'because of the questions in the divine books which require its use'.[226] The scope of authorial intervention which is allowed in this type of historical writing is accordingly given very strict parameters. Augustine points out, for example, that the historian does not himself compose the order of time (*ordo temporum*) which he narrates.[227] Although 'historical narrative' (*historica narratio*) recounts things which have been instituted by human beings, 'history itself' (*historia ipsa*) should not be numbered amongst human constructions, in that what has happened in the past cannot be undone. Instead, it must be considered as part of the order of time, whose creator and controller is God. In Augustine's view, this also reflects a distinction between narrating what has been done (*facta narrare*) and teaching what should be done (*facienda docere*). It marks the difference between the history which narrates deeds in a faithful and useful way (*fideliter atque utiliter*) and the sort of writing which aims to teach what should be done with the rash advice of a soothsayer rather than with the trustworthiness of an witness (*fide indicis*).[228]

By restricting his definition of history-writing in De Doctrina Christiana essentially to matters of chronography, Augustine's initial approach to the subject formed part of a much broader argument about the nature of human understanding. If the connection between history and biblical exegesis depended on

---

224 *De Doctrina Christiana*, II.28.105–8, pp. 104–7; *De Civitate Dei*, XV.9–14, pp. 609–20, quoted, for example, by Bede, *De Temporum Ratione*, LXVI, p. 162.
225 *De Civitate Dei*, XVIII.1–46, pp. 761–828.
226 *De Doctrina Christiana*, II.39.141, pp. 123; cf. Hugh of St Victor, *De Tribus Maximis Circumstantiis Gestorum* (see page 86).
227 *De Doctrina Christiana*, II.32.121, pp. 113.
228 *De Doctrina Christiana*, II.28.109, p. 107 (see page 280).

establishing a true chronology, then, as far as Augustine was concerned, such a demonstration formed only the first part of a process, because establishing the temporal order or sequence of events was different from understanding their significance. A narrative of what has happened, or what has been done, is conceptually distinct from explaining the cause of those events, the reason *why* something was said or done.[229] History, in this strict sense, was different from explanation or aetiology – it was simply a statement of the order of things, without any other meaning than what is conveyed by the words themselves.

In common with other early Christian writers, Augustine's basic theological approach to the Bible was to distinguish between the letter and the spirit, between the literal truth of the biblical narrative and its spiritual truth, between the word itself and what it meant, between the event and what it signified. As a theologian, however, Augustine was also acutely aware of the limits of, and limitations on, human understanding and, by extension, people's ability to perceive the true meaning and significance of the world around them. The dislocation of the relationship between Creation and Creator which had been brought about by human sin, by the fall of Adam and Eve, had necessarily resulted in the disruption of humankind's capacity to acquire, and enjoy, a direct knowledge of God. In consequence, humans were necessarily thrown back on indirect knowledge, on signs and symbols, the interpretation of which was dependent on the assistance provided by God's grace. The form which this divine assistance took was revelation and this occurred either in the sacred history which had been set out in the Bible or in the day-to-day guidance which was offered by the Holy Spirit. Even in the case of sacred history, however, the limitations

---

[229] Augustine, *De Utilitate Credendi*, trans. R. Kearney, *The Advantage of Believing*, in Augustine, *On Christian Belief* (New York, 2005), III, pp. 119–23; Augustine, *De Genesi ad Litteram Imperfectus Liber*, trans. R.J. Teske, *On the Literal Interpretation of Genesis: An Unfinished Book*, in Augustine, *On Genesis* (Washington, DC, 1991), II, p. 147: 'it is a matter of history when deeds done – whether by men or by God – are reported...; it is a matter of aetiology when the causes of what is said or done are reported'; cf. Aquinas, *Summa Theologiae*, ed. and trans. T. Gilby, *et al.* (Blackfriars edn, London, 1964–80), Ia.1.10 in/ad 2, pp. 37–9: 'history is, as Augustine himself explains, when something is simply put forward; aetiology when its cause is indicated' (*historia est, ut ipse Augustinus exponit, cum simpliciter aliquid proponitur; aetiologia vero cum causa dicti assignatur*).

on sinful human understanding remained all too evident. The Bible contained the record of God's communication with humankind by means of words and events but these were, in Augustine's phrase, 'veiled secrets' (*opaca secreta*).[230] For Augustine, therefore, words and events in biblical history were signs and, as such, they possessed a meaning which went beyond their literal, their strictly 'historical', truth. This was the task in which the theologian was accordingly engaged with scriptural exegesis, with the exposition of the Bible, to which the study of chronology was such a useful adjunct. It was also the task to which the approach to Christian teaching outlined in *De Doctrina Christiana* was devoted. It was a task, however, which Augustine considered endless, and for one simple reason. The truth, he writes, will 'increase and multiply'.[231]

When applied to the study of the Bible, therefore, Augustine's approach to historical events depended on a distinction between the literal and the spiritual truth of a particular event and involved a necessarily unending struggle to be free from the effects of imperfect human understanding. Viewed from the perspective of historiography, this naturally raised the question of whether the same approach could apply to the writing of non-biblical history, to historiography which was not contained in the Old Testament or the New, especially if the definition of history (*historia*) comprised both something that was written or had happened (*quid scriptum aut quid gestum sit*) and something that had not happened but was only written as if it had happened (*quid non gestum sed tantummodo scriptum quasi gestum sit*).[232] Augustine was even more aware of the limitations on human understanding when it came to history outside the canon of Scripture than he was for the history it contained. This is why, in *De Doctrina Christiana* at least, Augustine sees the utility of historiography lying within such tight chronographic parameters. In part, this was due to his view of the way in which God ordered and controlled the universe in a constantly changing harmony. For Augustine, divine providence came in two forms: active providence, when God intervenes directly in Creation, and permissive providence, when God allows Nature, and events, to take their own course. Active providence

---

230 Augustine, *Confessions*, trans. H. Chadwick (Oxford, 1991), XI.2.3, p. 222.
231 *Confessions*, XIII.24.37, p. 296.
232 *De Utilitate Credendi*, III, p. 120.

covers only those events which form part of God's revelation of the means by which humankind will ultimately be saved, a revelation which comes through the words of the prophets and the destiny of Israel. Permissive providence, meanwhile, governs all those events which are not directly ordered by active providence. It is permissive providence, therefore, which accounts for the presence of evil in the universe and the worldly success of wicked rulers (Augustine gives the examples of the emperors Nero and Julian the Apostate, both of whom were 'allowed' to reign by God). Whether a particular historical event is actively ordained by God, however, or is simply permitted to happen in a sinful world, the action of divine providence is inscrutable to human understanding. 'Let us believe', Augustine writes, 'although we cannot grasp it, that He who made the whole creation, both spiritual and corporeal, ordered all things in number and weight and measure [Wisdom 11:21]'. 'But', Augustine adds, 'God's judgments are inscrutable, and His ways are past searching out [Romans 11:33]'.[233]

Augustine's awareness of the limitations on human understanding extended to the capacity of the intellect to perceive what is inside the human mind. One of the most painful images of the sinful human condition described in the *City of God* occurs when the human judge is forced to condemn an innocent man to torture because of an inability to perceive the inner workings of his conscience.[234] Indeed, when the inadequacy of human understanding is put next to the inscrutability of divine providence in non-biblical history, it is perhaps not surprising that Augustine should have been so careful to restrict the trustworthiness (*fides*) of 'history' to studies of chronology. In the *City of God*, Augustine eschews a narrative of the calamities which resulted from the second Punic War with the observation that, were he to enumerate them all, he would become 'nothing but a writer of history'

---

[233] Augustine, *De Diversis Quaestionibus ad Simplicianum*, trans. B. Ramsey, *Miscellany of Questions in Response to Simplician*, in Augustine, *Responses to Miscellaneous Questions* (New York, 2008), I.2.22, p. 207; cf. *De Civitate Dei*, XX.2, pp. 896–8; *De Genesi ad Litteram Libri Duodecim*, trans. J.H. Taylor, *The Literal Meaning of Genesis* (New York, 1982), IV.3–6, pp. 107–11; Augustine, *Enchiridion de Fide et Spe et Caritate*, trans. B. Harbert, in Augustine, *On Christian Belief* (New York, 2005), XXIV.95–6, p. 328, XXVI.100, p. 331.
[234] *De Civitate Dei*, XIX.6, pp. 859–61.

(*nihil aliud quam scriptores etiam nos erimus historiae*).[235] It is also striking that when Augustine does tackle a broader conception of historical narrative, it comes in the form of *Confessions* – a record of his own providential guidance by God, of his understanding of the inner workings of the one human mind of which he might have more certain knowledge. However, although the *Confessions* concerns events of which the author *was* able to claim a greater degree of knowledge and certainty, both in terms of God's overall plan and in terms of the facts themselves, the term 'history' is never used.[236] This is why it is also integral to his account that it should culminate in such an extensive meditation on the problematic nature of memory and of time, the former as a means of intellectual comprehension, the latter as a subjectively experienced phenomenon in which past, present and future could all be present in one individual's mind.[237]

Augustine's approach to non-biblical history, however, also has a more positive side than his insistence on the limits of human understanding might suggest. In *On True Religion*, Augustine refers to seven stages in human spiritual development and understanding, and he identifies the first of these as 'history'. On this occasion, Augustine defines the utility of history in more expansive terms than in *De Doctrina Christiana*. History is useful, he now states, in that it nurtures by means of examples (*utilis historia quae nutrit exemplis*).[238] A distinction between a narrative of deeds (*narratio rerum factarum*) and the faithfulness of that account to what actually happened (*fides rerum gestarum*) was familiar from Augustine's understanding of the figurative, rather than literal, interpretation of events in the past.[239] It was therefore important to him that the definition of historical narrative should be, not just

---

235   *De Civitate Dei*, III.18, p. 116.
236   Cf. C. Müller, 'Historia', in C. Mayer (ed.), *Augustinus-Lexikon* (Basel, 1986), cols 366–77; Augustine, *Confessions*, ed. J.J. O'Donnell (Oxford, 1992).
237   *Confessions*, X–XI, pp. 179–245. See also chapter 4.
238   Augustine, *De Vera Religione*, trans. E. Hill, *True Religion*, in Augustine, *On Christian Belief* (New York, 2005), XXVI.49, p. 61.
239   For example, *De Genesi ad Litteram*, I.1, p. 19, and IX.12.22, p. 85: 'in this treatise I have not attempted to examine prophetic mysteries but to entrust the faithfulness of what happened to the defining quality of history' (*neque hoc opere suscepimus prophetica aenigmata perscrutari sed rerum gestarum fidem ad proprietatem historiae commendare*).

true (*historiae quae res veraciter gestas continent*),[240] but trustworthy and useful (*historia facta narrat fideliter atque utiliter*). Otherwise, it would simply be curiosity or childish erudition.[241] Augustine's point of reference here is not so much biblical exegesis or chronography as the classical tradition of historiography with which he had been familiar before his conversion to Christianity, when he was a teacher of rhetoric at Milan – history is useful because it persuades people of what is good, and persuades them to put it into practice by means of *exempla*. In the *Confessions*, it is true, Augustine takes great care to distance himself from his former profession as a teacher of rhetoric – when he had practised oratory in Milan, he writes, he was nothing but a peddler of words (*venditor verborum*) and, when he recalls that he wrote an *encomium* for the emperor Valentinian II, these 'lies' and this 'mendacity' were a matter for profound regret.[242] Nevertheless, even if it was something which had to be handled with care, rhetoric remained a vitally important instrument at Augustine's disposal, no more so than in his appreciation of the role of historiography. Within the *Confessions*, after all, Augustine was self-consciously writing an account of his own life in order that it might serve as a useful example to others, as an *exemplum* of repentance and conversion for his audience to imitate.

Augustine's understanding of what form the utility of exemplary history might take is epitomised by the *City of God*. The role of history in this work is, in part, determined by the two audiences which Augustine was addressing. In comparison with Augustine's other works, the *City of God* displays an atypical wealth of classical learning, ranging from Vergil and Cicero to Varro and Porphyry, and this wide frame of reference extends to works of classical history. The presence of Vergil, the most revered poet

---

240 *De Civitate Dei*, XVIII.13, p. 777.
241 *De Doctrina Christiana*, II.28.109, p. 107; cf. *De Civitate Dei*, XVIII.40, p. 815. For the vice of curiosity, see, for example, *Moralium Dogma Philosophorum*, p. 11, quoting Cicero, *De Officiis*, trans. M.T. Griffin and E.M. Atkins, *On Duties* (Cambridge, 1991), I.8–19, p. 8, and Seneca, *De Beneficiis*, trans. J.W. Basore (Loeb, 1935), VII.1.3–7, pp. 455–9; Hugh of St Victor, *Didascalicon*, V.10, p. 134; Bernardus Silvestris, *Commentary on the First Six Books of Virgil's Aeneid*, VI, pp. 102–3; cf. Ecclesiasticus (Sirach) 3:22.
242 *Confessions*, VI.6.9, p. 97; cf. IX.2.4, p. 157: 'that seat of mendacity' (*cathedra mendacii*).

of the foundation and destiny of Rome, and of Varro, the most significant antiquarian of its religion and history, was of critical importance to his argument because, in many respects, it was the *history* of Rome which constituted the language and currency of contemporary paganism. Reading Livy in the 390s amounted to an act of religious devotion, a cultivation of what the educated pagans to whom Augustine was directing his work would term 'the custom of our ancestors' (*mos maiorum*) or simply 'antiquity' (*vetustas*). In producing a revisionist account of Roman history in the *City of God*, therefore, Augustine was launching an attack on a key tenet of pagan *religious* belief, using the same authorities and arguments as his opponents but turning them back upon themselves with the rhetorical technique of *retortio*.[243]

The details of Augustine's dismantling of an idealised history of the Roman republic are well known.[244] In essence, Augustine picked up the Roman historian who was most sympathetic to a denunciation of Roman corruption and luxury, namely Sallust, and used his account of 'empty glory' (*vana gloria*) and 'lust for power' (*libido dominandi*) in order to explain how the rise and success of the Roman *res publica* had been due, not (as Livy had argued) to a love of virtue and liberty, but to greed for the praise of their fellow citizens and to a craving for dominance over other humans. Augustine took a similar approach to Cicero's definition of what entitles any political community to be termed a *res publica*, again turning a classical pagan authority against classical pagan history. Rome, he concludes, had not, in fact, fulfilled the requirements of Cicero's definition (a multitude of people whose association has been produced by a common sense of what is just and by a shared advantage). Instead, Augustine produces an alternative definition of his own (a multitude of people whose association is produced by a harmonious sharing in the objects of its love) which *would* fit, but on the basis of which Rome must be classified in the same group of organisations which comprises gangs of thieves and robbers and the eastern empires of Assyria and Persia. Rome had been no better than the very kingdoms

---

243 G. O'Daly, *Augustine's City of God – A Reader's Guide* (Oxford, 1999), pp. 49, 78–9, 105 n.5.
244 For what follows, see P. Brown, *Augustine of Hippo: A Biography* (London, 1967), chs 23–7.

whose tyranny and luxury had been the antithesis of everything it had ever claimed to stand for; indeed, it had been no better than a group of criminals, united only by a common interest in which their plunder was divided according to an agreed convention. Augustine's third, and final, body-blow to his pagan audience concerned the gods of the Roman pantheon. By examining ancient Roman history and, more importantly, the Roman historians themselves, Augustine reduced Roman deities, one by one, to a mythical status, either by placing them in a firmly literary context or by explaining the social and political function which caused them to be made up in the first place.

The cumulative effect of Augustine's historical revisionism in the *City of God* was devastating, and it is not without justification that he has been called 'the great secularizer of the pagan Roman past'.[245] Augustine's pagan audience was certainly left in no doubt as to the lesson which Augustine wanted them to learn from the *exempla* of their own history: the history of Rome was nothing more than a catalogue of vanity, greed and power; it was little short of the history of the crimes and follies of humankind. The 'useful examples' of the *City of God*, however, were also directed at another audience – Roman Christians. As a work of apologetic and polemic, Augustine's use of history was designed to provide Christians with arguments to use against their pagan opponents but it was also designed to force them to take a good look at themselves. If pagan Romans had been capable of performing such extraordinary deeds when they were motivated by vanity and greed, Christians should be capable of doing far more when their motivation was true glory and true virtue. Roman history, in other words, was useful as a corrective to Christian complacency and Christian pride.[246] Even if Augustine agreed that Roman heroes had been replaced by Christian martyrs and Christian saints as *the* exemplary figures to be imitated, he still believed that pagan history could provide an important moral lesson. The moral–didactic historiography of classical Rome, in other words, the examples of 'useful history', could still serve a specifically Christian purpose.

---

245 Brown, *Augustine*, p. 266.
246 Augustine, *De Civitate Dei*, V.18, p. 210; cf. Orosius, *Seven Books of History*, IV.6, p. 134 (see page 68); Henry of Huntingdon, *Historia Anglorum*, I.14, p. 37.

Augustine's concern with history-writing in the *City of God*, finally, was not limited to the chronological studies of Eusebius and the exemplary history (and historiography) of pagan Rome. Most important of all, perhaps, was his analysis of what was *meant* by the ordered sequence of time, a view which is sometimes given the rather misleading term 'progress'. Augustine was concerned to establish a linear view of history, in the first instance as a response to the sort of cyclical or repeating theories which were present in much classical philosophy but also in the work of some early Christian writers, most notably Origen. As a result, at the very end of the *City of God*, he produced a comprehensive historical sequence which covered the history of the universe from Creation to the Day of Judgment. This universal history had six stages: the first epoch (which corresponds to infancy) stretched from Adam to the Flood; the second (childhood) stretched from the Flood to Abraham; the third (adolescence) stretched from Abraham to David; the fourth (young adulthood) stretched from David to the Babylonian Captivity; the fifth (mature adulthood) stretched from the Babylonian Captivity to Jesus Christ; the sixth (old age) stretched from the Crucifixion to the Second Coming. According to this framework, human history since the first century AD had entered into its sixth and final phase – old age – and was demonstrating all the characteristics of that period in life – pain, illness and infirmity. Once God's revelation to humankind had been made complete, therefore, with the advent of Christ and with the completion of the Bible, Augustine considered the course of history to be a process of the interior spiritual renewal of individual souls. In exterior terms, history merely revealed a process of bodily infirmity and material decay.[247] It is from this

---

[247] *De Civitate Dei*, X.14, p. 392, XVI.24, p. 683, XVI.43, p. 710, XXII.30, p. 1091; Augustine, *De Genesi Contra Manicheos*, trans. R.J. Teske, *Two Books on Genesis Against the Manichees*, in Augustine, *On Genesis* (Washington, DC, 1991), I.23.35–41, pp. 83–8. For Augustine's view of the 'six ages' as part of a basic education in the rudiments of Christianity, see *De Catechizandis Rudibus*, trans. C.L. Cornish, *Of the Catechizing of the Unlearned* (in Augustine, *Seventeen Short Treatises*, Oxford, 1847), XXII.39, pp. 228–9; for its influence, see, for example, Isidore, *Etymologiae*, V.38.1–5, p. 130; Bede, *De Temporum Ratione*, LXVI, pp. 157–8; Bede, *De Temporibus*, ed. C.W. Jones (*CCSL* 123C, Turnhout, 1980), XVI, pp. 600–1; Nennius, *Historia Brittonum*, ed. and trans. J. Morris (London, 1980), p. 18; Hugh of St Victor, *De Sacramentis Christianae Fidei*, trans. R.J. Deferrari, *On the*

perspective of old age, therefore, 'progress' of a quite specific kind, that Augustine's view of Christian Rome was formed.

In his earlier writings, Augustine seems to have shared Eusebius' view of a Christianised Rome as the goal of the historical process, even as the culmination of the four world empires prophesied in the book of Daniel. By the time he was writing the *City of God*, however, it was a very different story and Augustine pointedly turned his back on this more triumphalist tradition of Christian historiography. It has always proved a temptation to treat this shift in Augustine's views as the product of his reaction to the sack of the city of Rome in 410, because Augustine's denial of any correlation between Christianisation and earthly prosperity would then read as *both* a consolation for Christians *and* a defence against pagans in the immediate aftermath of 410. However, as soon as the *City of God* is placed in the context of Augustine's other writings, and in particular in the context of his view that human history had already entered the period of old age, the neat historical coincidence between the composition of this text and the events of 410 has to be put rather less forcefully. The sack of Rome was, for him, one timely reminder amongst many that Christians should concern themselves with interior renewal, that they should store treasure for themselves in heaven, not concern themselves with any earthly prosperity. Augustine himself reserved judgment on whether 410 would indeed ultimately mark the end of Rome. What he is quite clear about is that this could happen sooner or later.[248] It is in this sense that,

---

Sacraments of the Christian Faith (Cambridge, MA, 1951), I.1.28, p. 26; Gervase of Tilbury, *Otia Imperialia*, II.26, pp. 529–47; Bonaventure, *Breviloquium*, prol., pp. 8–10. For the scheme of the 'five ages', based on the parable of the labourers in the vineyard (Matthew 20:1–19), see Gregory of Tours, *Histories*, X.31, p. 604; cf. Orderic Vitalis, *Historia Ecclesiastica*, I.1, p. 134, III, p. 5, XIII.45, p. 555. More generally, see W.M. Green, *Augustine on the Teaching of History* (Berkeley, 1944); P. Archambault, 'The Ages of Man and the Ages of the World – A Study of Two Traditions', *Revue des Etudes Augustiniennes*, 12 (1966), pp. 193–228; J.A. Burrow, *The Ages of Man: A Study in Medieval Writing and Thought* (Oxford, 1986), pp. 79–92.
248 T.E. Mommsen, 'St. Augustine and the Christian Idea of Progress –The Background of the City of God', *Journal of the History of Ideas*, 12 (1951), pp. 346–74; F.E. Cranz, 'The Development of Augustine's Ideas on Society Before the Donatist Controversy', *Harvard Theological Review*, 47 (1954), pp. 255–316; reprinted in R.A. Markus (ed.), *Augustine – A Collection of Critical Essays* (New York, 1972); F.E. Cranz, '*De Civitate Dei* XV.2 and Augustine's Idea of the Christian Society',

if Augustine was the great seculariser of the Roman pagan past, then he was also the seculariser of the Roman Christian present.

Augustine's account of the historical significance of the sixth age and of Christian Rome also depended on a still wider theological context than his view of linear time. Augustine believed that the whole of human history could be organised, not only according to the six ages of man, but also according to the single, transhistorical, idea of a division between two human communities. This scheme is, perhaps, the most striking example of the way in which Augustine thought that particular historical truths could be understood as 'signs' of a universal spiritual truth. In this instance, the actual historical cities of Babylon and Jerusalem served to signify two spiritual paradigms of human association which occur in every period in history. Thus, Babylon symbolised the earthly city – a human association which represents love of self to the exclusion of God, and which is characterised by pride, greed and confusion. Jerusalem, on the other hand, symbolised the city of God – a human association which represents love of God to the exclusion of self, and which is characterised by humility, charity and harmony. The key point for Augustine was that, although these two communities could always be distinguished in theory, it was only on the Day of Judgment that they could, and would, be distinguished from one another in practice. The city of God and the earthly city, in other words, were separable only eschatalogically; whilst they remained within the confines of earthly history and earthly time, members of the city of God and members of the earthly city would mingle with one another, combining to form a 'mixed' community.[249] The net effect of such a fusion was that, in Augustine's view, the most that could ever be hoped for in any age was, not for one community to triumph over the other, but for a combination of the two communities to achieve a limited degree of peace, an agreement to secure the material necessities of life, a security which preserved them from the worst consequences of their own sinful conduct.[250]

Speculum, 25 (1950), pp. 215–25; reprinted in R.A. Markus (ed.), *Augustine – A Collection of Critical Essays* (New York, 1972).
249 See page 107.
250 Augustine, *De Civitate Dei*, XIX.17, pp. 877–9, and, more generally, R.A. Markus, *Saeculum – History and Society in the Theology of Augustine* (Cambridge,

To maintain that the course of human history is governed in theory by two ideal communities, two paradigms of moral conduct, which in practice are combined to form an imperfect and sinful mixture, has important consequences for Augustine's views on the writing of history. Its immediate polemical use was to counter Porphyry's accusation that Christianity was of purely parochial significance, important only to Palestine. With his division of the whole of human history into two universal communities, Augustine could now respond that biblical history had a significance for the whole of humankind. Its literary consequences were also far-reaching. Prior to Augustine, forms of Christian historiography tended to be provided either directly by the Old Testament (as a line of prophetic words and events which foreshadowed the coming of Christ) or indirectly by Eusebius (as the preservation of a doctrinal tradition within the Church in the face of heresy and persecution). Augustine's two cities moved beyond these alternatives and invited a universal history, one which included non-Jewish and non-Christian sources, the history of Babylon as well as the history of Jerusalem.[251] If human history is the history of a 'mixed' community, of combinations of good and evil people, then it is necessarily a history of human sinfulness. Selfishness, pride, vanity and the lust for power were not the sole preserve of a pagan Rome, nor of a decadent Assyria; they were constant features of every community, including a Christianised Roman Empire and including a Christian Church. This had critical consequences for Augustine's view of 'Christian society'. Augustine's influential description of the emperor Theodosius, for example, is revealed in this light to be, not some sort of *encomium*, as his own version of Eusebius' idealisation of a (Christian) ruler along the lines laid down by Psalm 72, as some shoddy piece of political flattery. It is, instead, a cautionary

---

1970); cf. R. Williams, 'Politics and the Soul – A Reading of the *City of God*', *Milltown Studies*, 19–20 (1987), pp. 55–72; O. O'Donovan, 'Augustine's *City of God* XIX and Western Political Thought', *Dionysius*, 11 (1987), pp. 89–110; G. Bonner, '*Quid imperatori cum ecclesia?* St. Augustine on History and Society', *Augustinian Studies*, 2 (1971), pp. 231–51.
251 A. Momigliano, 'Pagan and Christian Historiography in the Fourth Century AD', in A. Momigliano (ed.), *The Conflict between Paganism and Christianity in the Fourth Century* (Oxford, 1963), pp. 79–99; reprinted in A. Momigliano, *Essays in Ancient and Modern Historiography* (Oxford, 1977).

tale. Peace, security and prosperity, Augustine was saying, are all achievements which have been shared by pagan emperors and wicked rulers; they are not unique to Christian rule. What distinguishes Christian rule are humility and justice – these are the achievements which should be a Christian emperor's constant aims.[252] Likewise, Augustine takes great care to make his definition of political authority in human society sufficiently comprehensive to cover bishops and not just temporal rulers. According to Augustine, the Church must be just as wary as the Empire in the face of vainglory and the lust for power.

Augustine, in short, saw the writing of history operating on three complementary levels. First and foremost, the study of chronology furnished a useful instrument of biblical exegesis. Second, the study of instructive *exempla* provided important moral and political lessons, be they from Christian or non-Christian history. Even allowing for the inscrutability of providence, and even allowing for the limitations on human understanding, history could still fulfil the functions it had been given by classical historians. Christian saints may have taken over as the *exempla* to be imitated by his audience but such moral–didactic history could still extend to learning from those people who were not such paragons of virtue. Even if his audience reflected on sinful history, in other words, these pilgrims or resident aliens (*peregrini*) could still be led back to their true homeland, the city of God. Third, the writing of history, both within the Bible and outside it, could be used to demonstrate the *significance* of events rather than just their chronological occurrence, above all in the universal presence of two paradigmatic forms of human association, the two 'cities'.

As a theologian, Augustine saw a world full of misery, suffering, disease, accidents, natural disaster and sin, a world which, like the book of Job, offered no automatic connection between personal merit and prosperity. Augustine's approach to history in the *City of God*, therefore, is as much a response to the Christian triumphalism represented by Eusebius as it is an attack on the idealisation of a pagan Roman past by Livy. Augustine accepted a notion of progress only in terms of an unfolding revelation which

---

252 *De Civitate Dei*, V.24–6, pp. 219–24. Contrast this with, for example, Eusebius' *Laus Constantini*, trans. H.A. Drake, *In Praise of Constantine: A Historical Study and New Translation of Eusebius' Tricennial Orations* (Berkeley, 1976), pp. 83–102.

culminated in Scripture; otherwise, the linearity of history was stamped with an indelible pattern of two cities – Babylon and Jerusalem, the earthly city and the city of God – which could not, and would not, be separated from each other until the Day of Judgment. At its most positive, Augustine saw the resulting mixture of the two cities as a guarantee of a degree of peace and harmony; at its most neutral, it was a providential remedy for the worst aspects of sinful human conduct. At its most negative, however, he saw it, in one of his most vivid images, as an olive press. The world, he explains, is a means by which the pure olive oil of the human spirit may be extracted from a mixed pulp of good and bad fruit. Politics, for Augustine, was indeed a matter of pressing the flesh. 'What does it matter', he asks, 'under whose rule a dying man lives?'[253] History revealed the mutability of human affairs (*mutabilitas rerum humanarum*); it represented a sequence of calamity (*series calamitatis*).[254] The logic of recording simply *what* happened, rather than the aetiology of *why*, was to reveal the fluctuation of suffering and thereby to concentrate attention on the next life. The sombre realism of this vision, in other words, was matched only by a corresponding hope in the promise of an eternal life of peace in the heavenly city.

The importance of appreciating the variety and complexity of the different traditions on which medieval authors could draw from within classical and patristic historiography should, in itself, be an uncontentious starting-point from which to consider the writing of history in the Middle Ages. Its consequences can be traced in a series of works, each one of which presented its own distinctive combination according to the nature and purpose of the 'history' it was recording. The potential significance of such variation is best illustrated, perhaps, by Otto of Freising, the twelfth-century writer whose *Chronicle* is often held up (and, to some extent, misleadingly) as somehow representative of medieval historiography. When Otto set himself the task of composing a universal history, it is difficult to ascertain whether the original conception owed more to Eusebius or to Orosius or, as his alternative choice of title – *On*

---

253 *De Civitate Dei*, V.17, p. 205; Augustine, *Sermones*, trans. E. Hill (New York, 1990–95), XIX.6, pp. 383–4.
254 *De Civitate Dei*, XVII.13, pp. 743–4, XIII.14, p. 523.

the Two Cities – might suggest, to Augustine.[255] Indeed, what makes Otto of Freising so fascinating is the way in which he strives to combine the approaches of the three patristic authors who, in many respects, offered strikingly discordant accounts of what the writing of Christian history could, or should, represent.[256]

Otto of Freising states explicitly in his prologue that the two most important sources on which he had drawn were Augustine and Orosius. He characterises the former as having produced a very sharp and eloquent treatise (*disputatio*) on the origin, progress, goal and membership of the city of God, whilst the latter had written a very useful history (*historia*) of the manifold suffering which humans had experienced through the disasters of war and through changes of kingdoms.[257] In formal terms, Otto of Freising's material debt to Orosius is perhaps the more readily apparent, above all in the overarching scheme of four world empires from the book of Daniel and the principle of their successive transference, or translation, from east to west (*translatio imperii*).[258] Otto introduces some modifications to this model (both learning and religion have followed the same trajectory) and some improvement (the lapse of time has revealed the Roman Empire to be neither eternal, as pagans had thought, nor divine, as even Christians had thought), but he points out that such clarifications are simply in accordance with the 'increase in knowledge' which had been prophesied in Daniel 12:4.[259] Otherwise, Otto of Freising's history closely follows the pattern set by Orosius, 'interweaving' a chronological narrative of events in Rome and in Babylon and using their conjunction to draw out a series of significant comparisons and parallels, not least between the people of Rome and the people of Israel.[260]

The result is an account of the sufferings (*miseriae*) experienced in a changeable world of unstable political power, where even the supreme achievements of Cyrus, of Alexander the Great and

---

255 Otto of Freising, *Chronicle*, VIII.prol., p. 453.
256 Cf. Classen, '*Res Gestae*, Universal history, Apocalypse', pp. 400–3; von den Brincken, *Studien zur Lateinischen Weltchronistik*.
257 Otto of Freising, *Chronicle*, prol., pp. 95–6.
258 *Chronicle*, Ep.ded., p. 91, II.12–13, pp. 166–7, V.35, p. 358.
259 *Chronicle*, prol., p. 95, V.prol., pp. 322–3, VII.35, p. 448.
260 For example, *Chronicle*, II.9, p. 163, II.42, p. 204, III.6, p. 229, VI.22, p. 383.

ultimately of Rome itself were all brought to nothing.[261] Calamities and persecutions are put forward by Otto as part of a providential order to discipline and punish. Numerical sequences of *plagae* represent God's sentence on a sinful humanity,[262] the product, not of predetermined outcomes or accidental events (*fatalis eventus, fortuiti casus*), but of the profound and righteous judgment of God.[263] However hard it might be for human minds to fathom, it remains the case that no evil is permitted to happen in the world which does not serve some further purpose.[264] The combination of instability and suffering which provides the core of Otto of Freising's history thereby serves a similar consolatory function to its role in Orosius: 'when we remember the calamities of past times there is a sense in which we also forget the pressure of the present'.[265] Indeed, when Otto subsequently came to send his *Chronicle* to the emperor's chancellor, Rainald of Dassel, he opened his dedicatory letter with an appeal to the 'solace' (*solamen*) which had been invoked by Boethius' *Consolation of Philosophy*, a work which Otto later defines as 'a particularly useful philosophical work on contempt for the world [*de contemptu mundi*]'.[266] Rather than comprising an account of the deeds of the ancients (*gesta priorum*), therefore, Otto's history, like that of Orosius, is primarily concerned with charting suffering and the changeability of transient events. In fact, Otto goes one step further in his choice of terminology – the discerning reader of his work, he observes, will find a sequence of, not so much histories (*historiae*), as pitiful tragedies (*tragediae*).[267]

---

261 *Chronicle*, II.14, p. 168, II.25, p. 183, IV.31, pp. 317–18.
262 *Chronicle*, III.45, p. 270.
263 *Chronicle*, II.14, p. 168, III.prol., p. 221, IV.prol., p. 271.
264 *Chronicle*, VII.prol., p. 403.
265 *Chronicle*, II.prol., p. 153. The same sentiment appears in Rufinus' 'Preface' to Eusebius' *Ecclesiastical History*, p. 565; cf. Valerius Maximus, *Facta et Dicta Memorabilia*, VII.2, p. 117 (*consolatio*), IV.4, p. 395 (*solacia, recreatio*).
266 *Chronicle*, Ep.ded., p. 90, V.1, p. 325; cf. Boethius, *Consolation of Philosophy*, III.1, p. 229 (*solamen*). For a similar conjunction of historiography and contempt for worldly matters, see Henry of Huntingdon, *Historia Anglorum*, book VIII (*De Contemptu Mundi*), pp. 585–619, according to whom (XI.23, p. 799) everything will eventually end up as dung (*finis/fimus*). Richard of Devizes likewise offers his *Chronicle* as a solace (*solatio*), as he sets out the instability of the things of this world as a means of proving their worthlessness (p. 2); cf. N. Partner, *Serious Entertainments: The Writing of History in Twelfth-Century England* (Chicago, 1977).
267 *Chronicle*, prol., pp. 93–4; cf. T.M.S. Lehtonen, 'History, Tragedy and Fortune in Twelfth-Century Historiography with Special Reference to Otto of Freising's

Evidence for Otto of Freising's debt to Augustine, whilst formally not as extensive as the evidence for his text being a digest of Orosius, can nonetheless be traced throughout the course of his work. He uses the *City of God*, for example, for its analogy of life on earth to a pilgrimage (*peregrinatio*), its citation of Regulus as an exemplary model of virtue which should put Christians to shame, and its concern that the Church should be just as wary as temporal rulers of the influence of worldly power and property.[268] The real significance of Augustine's work for Otto, however, lies less in the substance of what is borrowed than in the qualifications which it causes him to place on some of the more confident conclusions which had been forwarded by Orosius. Rather than adopt Orosius' comparative method to produce a favourable juxtaposition of the past with the present, for example, Otto uses it to underline Augustine's point that the world has entered its period of old age (*senectus mundi*) – it is not just mutable but frail and is, as it were, drawing its last breath.[269] Rather than compose a history of two cities, Otto points out that he has written virtually about only one – the 'mixed' community of the Church, which contains the elect and the reprobate, as the grain is combined with the chaff.[270] Otto's history is therefore as much about the decay of worldly things (*defectus*) as it is about their transience.[271] Past, present and future all point to the same conclusion. 'We are so oppressed by the memory of disasters in the past', he writes, 'their onset in the present, and fear of them in the future, that "we receive the sentence of death in ourselves and despair even of

---

Chronica', in T.M.S. Lehtonen and P. Mehtonen (eds), *Historia: The Concept and Genres in the Middle Ages* (Helsinki, 2000), pp. 29–49; H.A. Kelly, *Ideas and Forms of Tragedy from Aristotle to the Middle Ages* (Cambridge, 1993). For the classical association of history with tragedy, see G. Giovannini, 'The Connection Between Tragedy and History in Ancient Criticism', *Philological Quarterly*, 22 (1943), pp. 308–14; F. Walbank, 'History and Tragedy', *Historia – Zeitschrift für Altegeschichte*, 9 (1960), pp. 216–34; cf. Paschasius Radbertus, *Epitaphium Arsenii*, trans. A. Cabaniss, *Charlemagne's Cousins – Contemporary Lives of Adalard and Wala* (Syracuse, 1967), II.8, p. 163; *Gesta Stephani*, ed. and trans. K.R. Potter, rev. R.H.C. Davis (Oxford, 1976), II.78, p.155.
268 *Chronicle*, prol., pp. 93, 95, II.34, pp. 192–4, IV.prol., p. 274.
269 *Chronicle*, V.prol., pp. 322–3.
270 *Chronicle*, V.prol., p. 324, VII.prol., p. 404.
271 *Chronicle*, prol., p. 95.

life" [2 Corinthians 1:8–9]'.[272] Likewise, when Otto adds Boethius to Orosius in order to reinforce the role of historiography as consolation, he also integrates Boethius' conception of how fortune operates within an Augustinian conception of God's providential order. Having opened his prologue with a Sallustian account of how the wise individual escapes the cyclical motion of temporal affairs only through exercising the faculty of reason,[273] Otto cites the instability of such rotation (*volubilitas*) as part and parcel of God's permissive providence.[274] These are changes which God 'weaves' in this world.[275] According to philosophers, Otto remarks, changes in worldly power form the wretched sport of fortune's wheel but, in truth, the uncertain state of affairs represents the means by which God prompts humans to abandon the suffering of this world and to seek true life in the next.[276]

When Otto of Freising wrote of the consolation of history, therefore, he found it by contemplating the next life, rather than in the Orosian observation that suffering has been worse in the past. Otto charts the mutability of kingdoms in this world primarily so that it can be contrasted with the immutability of the kingdom of heaven. His imagery is taken from the Psalms (104:25–6): like the sea, the world will destroy with its storms those who entrust themselves to its waves, rather than hold fast to the wood of the cross as a ship in which they will reach the safe haven of the heavenly kingdom.[277] This is the reflection with which Otto accordingly closes each one of his books – the mutability of things in this life prompts consolation from the life to come; contempt for this world produces contemplation, and love, of God.[278] Otto in fact adds an eighth, and final, book to Orosius' total of seven, so that he could conclude his own work, as Augustine had done, with

---

272 *Chronicle*, VII.34, p. 445.
273 *Chronicle*, prol., p. 93; cf. page 44.
274 *Chronicle*, V.35, p. 357.
275 *Chronicle*, III.prol., p. 222.
276 *Chronicle*, VI.9, p. 370; cf. Boethius, *Consolation of Philosophy*, II.2, p.183 (see pages 281–2).
277 *Chronicle*, VI.prol., p. 360. For the *saeculum* as the sea, see, for example, Boethius, *Consolation of Philosophy*, I.3, p. 143, I.4, p. 145, I.5, p. 161; Bede, *De Temporum Ratione*, LXX, p. 245, LXXI, p. 249 (see page 283).
278 For example, *Chronicle*, II.43, p. 205, II.51, p. 216, IV.33, p. 321, V.36, p. 359, VI.17, p. 377, VII.24, p. 433.

an account of the heavenly Jerusalem.[279] Otto concedes that the resulting juxtaposition of a historical narrative of worldly calamities with the profound mysteries of Scripture might be criticised by some people, but he defends the arrangement on the grounds that his intention was to 'imitate' the *exemplum* set by the conclusion to Augustine's *City of God* (i.e. books XX–XXII). Indeed, Otto points out that the Bible, too, was made up of books which combined an account of the evils and suffering of this world with the secrets of divine mystery. Daniel, for example, begins with a historical narrative (*historica narratio*) and concludes with a most profound vision, whilst the miracle placed at the end of John's Gospel (John 21) makes the preceding narrative of truth (*narratio veritatis*) practically an introduction (*tamquam proemium*) to this one prefigurement of the heavenly life.[280]

For all Otto of Freising's commitment to Orosius' account of the order of divine judgment in history, moreover, he is also keen to stress its inscrutability. As it had done for Augustine, Romans 11:33 prompted Otto to reflect that humans cannot comprehend the secret counsels of God. And yet, Otto remarks, humans are frequently obliged to attempt to give an account of, or even to explain, the reasons behind them (*reddere rationem*). 'Are we then to attempt an explanation of things we are unable to understand?', he asks. 'We can certainly provide human reasons [*rationes humanae*]', he concludes, 'even though we may still be unable to comprehend the divine [*rationes divinae*]'.[281] Having warned against the dangers of relying on human reasoning to uncover the causes of things,[282] Otto is therefore naturally drawn to Augustine's sad paradigm of the inability of the human judge to perceive the hearts of men,[283] and, above all, to Augustine's

---

279 For the symbolism of the number eight as perpetual beatitude, see, for example, Isidore of Seville, *Liber Numerorum* (*PL* 83, cols 179–200), IX, col. 189; Byrhtferth of Ramsey, *Enchiridion*, ed. P.S. Baker and M. Lapidge (Oxford, 1995), IV, pp. 211–13; Henry of Huntingdon, *Historia Anglorum*, XII.praef., p. 805; and, more generally, H. Meyer and R. Suntrup, *Lexikon der mittelalterlichen Zahlenbedeutungen* (Munich, 1987), cols 565–80.
280 *Chronicle*, VIII.prol., pp. 455–6.
281 *Chronicle*, III.prol., p. 218, cf. IV.18, p. 299.
282 *Chronicle*, VIII.4, p. 460.
283 *Chronicle*, VIII.19, p. 478; cf. Augustine, *De Civitate Dei*, XIX.6, pp. 859–61 (see page 97).

confession of epistemological uncertainty, which Otto quotes: 'I do not wish everything that I have set down to be rashly believed because some things are not so fully believed by me as though there were no doubt about them in my mind'.[284] Otto accordingly concludes his own history by quoting and glossing the same observation: 'for, as I have said above of Augustine, some matters are set down in his writings, not as assertion [*assertio*], but only on the basis of opinion and investigation [*opinio et investigatio*], and the scrutiny of a definitive judgment [*examen finitivae sententiae*] has been left to those who are wiser'.[285]

Otto of Freising's approach to calamity and consolation reveals the complex way in which an Orosian and Augustinian view of human history could be combined within a single work of medieval historiography. In explicitly writing a chronicle, however, Otto was also well aware of the debt which he owed to the Christian chronographic tradition that had been initiated by Eusebius. The transition in his narrative to more contemporary history, for example, is marked by the observation that 'thus far we have set down extracts from the books of Orosius, Eusebius and those who wrote after them, even to our own time'.[286] Methodologically, this debt to Eusebius extends to the recognition of conflicting testimony and the verbatim citation of documents,[287] but it was expressed, first and foremost, in Otto's concern to establish an accurate chronological framework and, where necessary, to synchronise alternative systems of dating and acknowledge discrepancies between different calculations.[288] The most straightforward function served by Otto's *Chronicle* was therefore to set out what he termed 'the sequence of history' (*series historiae*), and it was epitomised in his numerical listing of series of emperors, kings and popes.[289] Otto accordingly draws attention to the two levels on which his work will operate by explicitly addressing two

---

284 *Chronicle*, VIII.34, p. 511; cf. Augustine, *De Civitate Dei*, XXI.7, p. 978.
285 *Chronicle*, VIII.35, pp. 513–14.
286 *Chronicle*, VII.11, p. 417.
287 For example, *Chronicle*, I.8, p. 133, IV.2, p. 278, VI.18, p. 378; cf. Otto of Freising, *Deeds of Frederick*, I.49, p. 84, II.8, p. 120; Widukind, *Res Gestae Saxonicae*, III.70, pp. 224–6.
288 For example, *Chronicle*, I.5, p. 129, III.6, pp. 230–1, V.31, p. 353, VII.34, p. 445; cf. Gervase of Canterbury, *Chronica*, prol., pp. 87–90.
289 *Chronicle*, IV.4, p. 283, IV.19, p. 304, V.13, p. 341, VII.35, pp. 449–52.

different audiences in his prologue – whereas the devout listener (*religiosus auditor*) will observe what is to be avoided by reason of the countless miseries which are wrought by the unstable character of worldly affairs, the diligent or curious student (*studiosus seu curiosus indagator*) will find the sequence of past events set out in a manner which is free from confusion (*non confusa*).[290]

Otto of Freising's concern to establish the ordered sequence of historical events is expressed as a commitment to truth – just as grammar and logic select only what is useful, so the function of chronographers (*facultas chronographarum*) is to choose the truth and to avoid lies.[291] Otto's commitment to chronography, however, is still more revealing for the sort of history which it prompts Otto to describe himself as having deliberately chosen *not* to write. In establishing the *series rerum gestarum*, for example, Otto claims that his intention is to write down what has been done (*res gestas scribere*), and not to justify or render an account of the reason *why* it was done (*non rerum gestarum rationem reddere*).[292] The immediate context for this disclaimer is the question of whether or not it was legitimate for the emperor Otto I to depose pope John XII in 963, a historical precedent whose significance had been bitterly contested in the Investiture Conflict in the eleventh century and one which was to prove just as resonant for Frederick Barbarossa and pope Alexander III in the twelfth.[293] Otto of Freising expresses a similar reluctance when he comes to describe the excommunication and deposition of the emperor Henry IV: 'whether all these things were done lawfully or otherwise, we do not venture to determine [*nos non discernimus*]'; to judge or discuss (*iudicare vel discutere*) the providential significance of this clash between the temporal and spiritual powers lies beyond the author's powers (*vires*).[294] Likewise, it is not, in Otto's view, the purpose of his present work to settle the legitimacy of the Donation of Constantine.[295] Otto was also well aware of how

---

290 *Chronicle*, prol., p. 96; cf. II.25, p. 183.
291 *Chronicle*, Ep.ded., p. 90.
292 *Chronicle*, VI.23, p. 384.
293 Cf. page 196.
294 *Chronicle*, VII.prol., p. 404, VII.11, p. 416; cf. Otto of Freising, *Deeds of Frederick*, I.61, p. 101.
295 *Chronicle*, IV.3, p. 280.

national allegiances could produce differences of interpretation in historical writing. He notes, for example, that the division of the Frankish Empire had split people's loyalties and individual writers would accordingly praise their own particular *res publica* as far as their talents allowed. For his own part, Otto states that he will attempt to keep to the middle path suggested by Numbers 21:22, turning neither to the left nor to the right, but trying to the best of his ability to hold to the order of truth (*series veritatis*).[296] These expressions of restraint and reluctance, however, go beyond political sensitivity to contemporary conflicts or personal loyalty to his own (and Frederick Barbarossa's) grandfather, Henry IV. They also rest upon a particular view of the relationship between historiography and rhetoric.

Otto of Freising was well aware of the need to acknowledge the errors and lies (*erroris mendacia*) contained in pagan historiography and to distinguish classical 'history' from the more fanciful of their fables (*fabulae*).[297] When he discusses the pivotal moment in the history of Rome when Aeneas defeated Turnus, he praises Vergil's poetic account for the beauty of its verse but leaves open the question of whether the event had thereby been described truthfully (*veraciter*) or deceptively (*fallaciter*) and with the cosmetic paint of praise (*fuco adulationis*).[298] Otto's equivocation is worth noting. This is the same language he uses when, having alerted Rainald of Dassel to the fact that some things he has written in his own work of history might count against Frederick Barbarossa's predecessors or ancestors, he repeats that his primary allegiance is to the truth. 'It is better to fall into the hands of men', he explains, 'than to abandon the duty of a writer by painting over a monster's face with cosmetic colour [*fucatum colorem*]'.[299] The imagery is from Wisdom 13:14 but, once again, the connotation of cosmetics was exact – Otto

---

296 *Chronicle*, VI.18, p. 378.
297 *Chronicle*, I.18, p. 139, I.21, p. 141, I.26, p. 146.
298 *Chronicle*, I.26, p. 145. For *fuco/fucatus*, see Sulpicius Severus, *Dialogues*, trans. B.M. Peebles (New York, 1949), I.27, pp. 198–9 (see page 28), where such artificial colouring is contrasted with rustic speech; cf. Astronomer, *Life of Louis*, trans. A. Cabaniss, *Son of Charlemagne – A Contemporary Life of Louis the Pious* (Syracuse, 1961), prol., p. 30 (*fuco adulationis*); and, more generally, T. Janson, *Latin Prose Prefaces – Studies in Literary Conventions* (Stockholm, 1964), p. 140.
299 *Chronicle*, Ep.ded., p. 91; cf. Boethius, *Consolation of Philosophy*, I.5, p. 161.

would rather give offence to the powerful than use the 'colours' of rhetoric to disguise the truth.

Otto of Freising repeatedly expresses his admiration for those writers in the past, including Augustine, who combined their wisdom with the practice of eloquence. Even in the writing of the saints, he observes, secular learning (*secularis scientia*) is known to accompany divine wisdom, thereby assisting in its ornamentation rather than obeying any need.[300] Conversely, Otto was also keen to point out that the human judge is prevented from perceiving the truth, not only – as Augustine had argued – by his inability to perceive the inner workings of the human heart, but also by all the double-speak and casuistry (*tergiversationes et cavillationes*) which characterise the process of accusation, defence and testimony in a human court of law. Babylon has its gold, its 'wisdom', by means of which it allures whoever is simple and foolish with astute casuistries and sharp sophistical argumentation.[301] For his part, Otto is careful to contrast his own lack of skill and learning (*imperitus, indoctus*) with the wisdom and eloquence (*sapientia ac eloquentia*) of those authors whose works he had distilled into his compendium.[302] Otto makes a point of rejecting the criticism that his own, more straightforward, approach reflects the fact that everyone is a historian these days, or rather, as Otto chooses to put it, 'everyone, educated or uneducated, is these days a writer of poems'.[303] He is not writing out of rashness (*temeritas*) or frivolity (*levitas*), but out of love (*caritas*) and, if his work is to be pleasing (*delectare*), then it is to be pleasing to God.[304] His style may be uncultivated (*incultus*) but this is not to be scorned because, as the apostolic simplicity (*apostolica simplicitas*) of some of his sources demonstrates, sharp subtlety (*arguta subtilitas*) will sometimes (*nonnumquam*) kindle error, whereas holy rusticity (*sancta rusticitas*) is *always* the friend of truth.[305]

---

300 *Chronicle*, VIII.33, p. 511; cf. III.27, p. 256, III.35, p. 262, IV.8, p. 287.
301 *Chronicle*, VIII.19, p. 478, VIII.20, p. 482.
302 *Chronicle*, prol., p. 96. Rahewin discusses Otto of Freising's learning, which includes rhetorical tropes: Rahewin, *Deeds of Frederick*, IV.14, pp. 246, 249.
303 *Chronicle*, prol., p. 96, quoting Horace, *Epistles*, trans. H.R. Fairclough (Loeb, 1929), II.1.117, p. 407.
304 *Chronicle*, prol., pp. 96–7.
305 *Chronicle*, prol., pp. 96–7. For rusticity, see page 28; for the style which is suitable for the writing of history, see pages 135–6, 297–8, 365; Simon, 'Untersuchungen

By deliberately eschewing rhetorical sophistication, Otto positions his work firmly within the annalistic tradition of historiography championed by Hugh of Fleury, but this does not mean he is unaware of the didactic purpose which writing history in this vein can still serve. However, whilst acknowledging that history commemorates deeds which are worthy of record and of being handed down to posterity, or which can serve as a warning and reproof,[306] Otto remains adamant that his work is not intended to provide *exempla* that will inspire its readers to exploits in war. Nor was he writing simply for the sake of curiosity (*curiositas*).[307] Instead, his work was designed to set out calamities, suffering and the changeability of events in this world. As a result, Otto expressly cautions against any expectation that his history will contain maxims (*sententiae*) and moral reflections (*moralitates*). His intention is simply to interweave the sufferings of the earthly city with the progress of the citizens of Christ through (and beyond) those sufferings and to do so, not in the manner of a treatise or disputation (*more disputantis*), but simply following a logical or explanatory order (*ordine disserentis*).[308]

By repeatedly pointing out what sort of history he was *not* writing in his *Chronicle*, Otto of Freising reveals the much wider terms of reference within which he clearly considered historiography might otherwise be expected to function by his audience – eloquence, ornamentation, poetry, subtlety, curiosity, pleasure, explanation, bellicose *exempla*, legal precedent and political justification. In the event, Otto finds it hard to toe such a strict line as consistently as he might have wished, particularly when it comes to including maxims and moral reflections,[309] or indeed rhetorical tropes[310] and lines of verse.[311] Nonetheless, given the range of

---

zur Topik der Widmungsbriefe mittelalterlicher Geschichtsschreiber', pp. 79–80, 89–94.
306 *Chronicle*, V.prol., p. 324, V.9, p. 338.
307 *Chronicle*, II.32, p. 191.
308 *Chronicle*, II.prol., p. 154.
309 For example, *Chronicle*, II.36, p. 197, III.15, p. 241, III.20, p. 249, VI.prol., p. 360.
310 For example, synecdoche (*Chronicle*, prol., p. 94, II.32, pp. 190–1), word-play (*Chronicle*, III.25, p. 255, VI.13, p. 373, VII.9, p. 414, VII.14, p. 421), praeteritio (*Chronicle*, I.8, p. 133, I.19, p. 140), metonymy (*Chronicle*, VIII.17, p. 476).
311 For example, *Chronicle*, VI.31–2, pp. 393–4.

qualities which Otto does generally succeed in excluding from his 'sequence' of events, it is perhaps hardly surprising that he should have felt such unease when presenting his *Chronicle* to Frederick Barbarossa some ten years after its original composition. He wrote his history, he explains, in the bitterness of spirit caused by the turbulent times which had preceded Frederick's accession. It was because of this that he had not so much written down a sequence of deeds (*series rerum gestarum*) as woven together this suffering in the manner of a tragedy.[312] The didactic value of the work for the emperor was accordingly expressed in rather different terms than those used for Rainald of Dassel. A knowledge of such history would still, in Otto's view, be both morally worthy and advantageous for Frederick. By considering not just the deeds of brave men but also the strength and power of a God who alternates kingdoms, gives them to whomsoever He wants and allows changeability in all things, the emperor will fear God and thereby rule in prosperity for many years to come.[313] It is equally unsurprising, however, that Otto then concluded his dedicatory letter by accepting the offer to write something else – the deeds (*res gestae*) of Frederick himself. For this new work of 'history', his rationale would be very different.

If Frederick Barbarossa's own response to Otto of Freising's *Chronicle* was to claim that he had derived both pleasure and instruction in virtue from reading of the glorious deeds of emperors,[314] then Otto of Freising was not slow to pick up the hint. The theme of mutability was certainly still present in his *Deeds of Frederick*, but this time Otto states explicitly that he is writing pleasurable history (*iocunda historia*), not tragedy.[315] The opening lines of Otto's prologue to his new work underline their straightforwardly classical didactic purpose: 'the intention of all those who have written down *res gestae* before us has been to extol the shining deeds of brave men in order to move the minds of humans to virtue and either to suppress with silence the dark deeds of the wicked or, if they are brought into the light, to set

---

312 *Chronicle*, Ep.ded., p .89; cf. page 109.
313 *Chronicle*, Ep.ded., pp. 88–9.
314 'Letter of Frederick Barbarossa to Otto of Freising', trans. Mierow, in Otto of Freising, *Deeds of Frederick*, p. 17.
315 Otto of Freising, *Deeds of Frederick*, I.47, p. 79.

them down as a source of terror'.[316] Moreover, Otto was also quick to pick up on Frederick's invitation, not to 'compile' events as he had done in his *Chronicle*, but to 'amplify and augment' them (*dilatanda ac multiplicanda*).[317] This was Otto's cue to include vivid descriptions of battles and sieges, maxims and set-piece speeches, as well as lengthy digressions on the nature of God, on the Trinitarian controversy surrounding Abelard and Gilbert of Poitiers, and on the justification for the Second Crusade. Otto draws attention to these new characteristics, once again, in his prologue: 'nor will it be regarded as inconsistent with a work of this sort if the language [*oratio*] is exalted when the opportunity for a digression presents itself and the simple diction of history [*plana historica dictio*] will change to loftier, that is philosophical, heights'.[318] For this work, Otto is happy to appeal to classical precedents, starting with poetry and fable. 'This practice', he writes, 'is not at variance with the prerogative of the Roman Empire, namely to intersperse simpler with loftier affairs. Lucan and Vergil and all the other writers of this city frequently elevated their style of expression so as to touch certain ultimate secrets of philosophy, in recording not only deeds [*res gestae*], but also fables [*res fabulosae*], whether modestly in the manner of shepherds or peasants or in the more exalted style of princes and lords of the earth'.[319] Once again, Otto has two audiences in mind, but this time he seeks justification for his approach in terms of both pleasure and subtlety: 'this is how, not only those whose pleasure [*voluptas*] consists in hearing the sequence of deeds [*series rerum gestarum*], but also those to whom the height of subtle reasoning [*sublimitas subtilitatis*] affords greater delight, are attracted to read and study such a work'.[320]

Otto of Freising's sensitivity to the range of expectations which a work of 'history' might encounter from his audience, his capacity to adapt the differing emphases of Eusebius, Augustine and

---

316 *Deeds of Frederick*, prol., p. 24. For the immediate political context, see Bagge, *Kings, Politics and the Right Order of the World*, ch. 6, esp. p. 381. See also S. Bagge, 'Ideas and Narrative in Otto of Freising's *Gesta Frederici*', *Journal of Medieval History*, 22 (1996), pp. 345–77.
317 'Letter of Frederick Barbarossa', pp. 17, 20.
318 Otto of Freising, *Deeds of Frederick*, prol., p. 28.
319 *Deeds of Frederick*, prol., p. 28.
320 *Deeds of Frederick*, prol., p. 28.

Orosius to suit his own particular didactic purposes, and his willingness to change his methodological approach according to whether the 'history' he was writing comprised consolatory 'chronicles' or inspirational 'deeds', all point to the complexity of what 'historiography' might denote, or rather connote, in the Middle Ages. In part, this was the natural result of interweaving the different traditions – classical, biblical and chronographic – which were transmitted from late antiquity. In part, this was due to the consequences of another tradition, and one which Otto explicitly acknowledges in his references to eloquence, ornamentation and poetry. This fourth tradition for the writing of history was provided by classical rhetoric.

2

RHETORIC AND HISTORY

In seeking to establish exactly how the writing of history was conceptualised and practised in the Middle Ages, a sensible starting point is to identify where historiography fitted into a programme of study, that is, where medieval authors would themselves have encountered the writing of history as a body of material and as part and parcel of their education.[1] What becomes immediately apparent is that, initially at least, it would have been as an integral component of the study of grammar and rhetoric – in grammar, as excerpts from classical historians and, in rhetoric, as the theory and practice of narrating events from the past. Self-conscious reflections on what the writing of history actually involved were therefore intimately bound up, from the outset, with the teaching of these two disciplines. As a result, if 'it has ... become indisputable that the subordinate rank of history in the schema of the liberal arts is no index to its actual importance',[2] then this disjunction needs to be explored, and illustrated, by setting out just how much historical and historiographical content the teaching of grammar and rhetoric actually contained.

---

[1] For the teaching of grammar and rhetoric, see S. Reynolds, *Medieval Reading: Grammar, Rhetoric and the Classical Text* (Cambridge, 1996); V. Law, *Grammar and Grammarians in the Early Middle Ages* (London, 1997); C.D. Lanham (ed.), *Latin Grammar and Rhetoric: From Classical Theory to Medieval Practice* (London, 2002); R. Black, *Humanism and Education in Medieval and Renaissance Italy: Tradition and Innovation in Latin Schools from the Twelfth to the Fifteenth Century* (Cambridge, 2001).
[2] R. Ray, 'Medieval Historiography Through the Twelfth Century – Problems and Progress of Research', *Viator*, 5 (1974), p. 51.

Grammar

The all-encompassing scope of grammar was a well-established principle in classical and late-antique discussions of learning. Martianus Capella, for example, whose fifth-century treatise *Marriage of Philology and Mercury* was one of the most influential texts transmitting the liberal arts to the Middle Ages, described how grammar overlapped with the study of poetry, rhetoric, philosophy, history, mathematics and music, all of which could be deployed in order to construct or expound the meaning of a written text.[3] Within this overarching inclusivity, other writers picked out history as a particular example of a discipline which, on this basis, had been absorbed by the teaching of grammar. The fundamental nature of their connection was highlighted, not least, by Augustine, alongside some rather sharp observations on the difficulties which this association could then raise. The inclusion of the study of history within the discipline of grammar, he suggested, ended up causing more trouble to the grammarians than to the historians themselves ('it is filled more with cares than with pleasure or with truth'), because it had led to questions being asked about the truth-content of fable and the historical accuracy of poetry. Nonetheless, with this caveat, the general point remained – because whatever is worthy of remembrance is entrusted to writing and, as such, becomes part of the discipline of letters (*litteratura*), history has been added to the discipline of grammar, 'for its name is one but its subject-matter is limitless and many-sided' (*infinita multiplex*).[4]

Augustine's comments on the relationship between grammar and history were echoed and extended in the sixth century in the course of an even more influential summary which was provided by Isidore of Seville. In his *Etymologies*, a work which, like Martianus Capella's, had a fundamental impact on both the content and the categorisation of medieval learning, Isidore classifies history under the heading of grammar and then proceeds to

---

3 Martianus Capella, *The Marriage of Philology and Mercury*, trans. W.H. Stahl, R. Johnson and E.L. Burge, *Martianus Capella and the Seven Liberal Arts* (New York, 1977), III, pp. 64–105.
4 Augustine, *De Ordine*, trans. R.P. Russell, in *Divine Providence and the Problem of Evil* (New York, 1948), II.12.37, pp. 314–15; cf. K. Pollmann and M. Vessey (eds), *Augustine and the Disciplines: From Cassiciacum to Confessions* (Oxford, 2005).

outline a 'many-sided' definition of the subject which covered, not one, but a multitude of possibilities. He writes:

> History is the narrative of deeds [*narratio rei gestae*] by means of which those things that have been done in the past are known. History is so-called from the Greek 'historein', that is, from [the verb] to see or to know. For amongst the ancients, no one used to write history except the person who had lived among, and seen, those things which were to be written down, since it is better that we ascertain what has happened with our eyes than to assemble it from what we have heard, because things which have been seen can be put forward without lying. This discipline pertains to grammar because it commits to letters whatever is worthy of memory. For that reason histories are called 'memorials' [*monumenta*] because they provide the memory of deeds.[5]

Isidore continues:

> There are three types of history. The deeds of a single day are called 'ephemera', which are termed by us a diary [*diarium*], for what the Latins call 'daily' [*diurnus*] the Greeks call 'ephemeral'. Deeds done over the course of individual months are called 'calendars'; 'annals' are the deeds of individual years. Whatever is worthy of memory in domestic and military matters, at sea and on land, is set out year-by-year in brief 'notes' [*commentarii*]; they are termed 'annals' from the fact that they are yearly deeds; the history of many years or times results from these annual annotations being diligently set down in books. The difference between history and annals is this – history concerns the times which we have seen, whereas annals concern those years which our own age does not know. As a result, Sallust wrote history, whereas Livy, Eusebius and Jerome wrote both annals and history. There is also a difference between history, argument and fable, for histories are true things which have been done, whereas arguments are those things which, even if they were not done, could nonetheless have happened, whilst fables are things which were neither done nor could have happened because they are contrary to nature.[6]

---

5 Isidore, *Etymologiae*, trans. S.A. Barney, W.J. Lewis, J.A. Beach and O. Berghof, *The Etymologies of Isidore of Seville* (Cambridge, 2006), I.41.1–2, p. 67; cf. Dominicus Gundissalinus, *De Divisione Philosophiae*, ed. A. Fidora and D. Werner, *Über die Einteilung der Philosophie* (Freiburg, 2007), p. 126.
6 Isidore, *Etymologiae*, I.44.1–5, p. 67; cf. Hugh of St Victor, *De Scripturis et Scriptoribus Sacris* (PL 175, cols 9–28), III, col. 12; John of Garland, *Parisiana Poetria*, ed. and trans. T. Lawler (New Haven, 1974), V.303–72, pp. 99–103;

For history to be conceived of in this way, as an integral part of grammar, had far-reaching consequences for the subject. According to Quintilian, the teaching of grammar comprised two elements – on the one hand, a methodical instruction in the principles of speech and, on the other, an exposition of historical and poetic authors (*enarratio auctorum*).[7] Grammar should therefore combine the discipline of speaking or writing correctly (*scientia recte loquendi*) with what Quintilian calls the *enarratio historiarum* (or *lectio historiae*) and the *enarratio poetarum*.[8] The defining activities of the grammarian were thus to discuss the nature of speaking, to explain issues or questions, to expound histories and to talk through – literally 'narrate out' (*enarrare*) – poems.[9] This twofold aspect to grammar – not just the principles of writing and speaking correctly but also the 'science' of interpreting poets and historians – was echoed by Marius Victorinus and propagated from at least the early ninth century by writers such as Hrabanus Maurus.[10] As a result, by the early twelfth century, Hugh of St Victor could classify history as a part of grammar alongside prose, metre and fable.[11] At the most basic level, this categorisation meant that excerpts from classical historians were studied and learned alongside excerpts from classical poets as prime examples of particular points of grammar. The practical results of this pedagogic scheme can be gauged, for instance, from the fact that a work such as Sallust's *Histories* was transmitted in the Middle Ages, not as an entire text (like his *Jugurthine War* and *Catiline*), but as a series of some five hundred fragments, all of

---

Vincent of Beauvais, *Speculum Doctrinale* (Douai, 1624; reprinted Graz, 1964–65), III.127, col. 297.
7 Quintilian, *Institutio Oratoria*, trans. H.E. Butler (Loeb, 1920–22), I.9.1, p. 157.
8 *Institutio Oratoria*, I.4.4, p. 63, I.8.18, p. 155, II.5.1, p. 247.
9 *Institutio Oratoria*, I.2.14, p. 47.
10 Marius Victorinus, *Explanatio in Rhetoricam Ciceronis*, ed. K. Halm, *Rhetores Latini Minores* (Leipzig, 1863), p. 202; Hrabanus Maurus, *De Clericorum Institutione*, ed. D. Zimpel (Frankfurt, 1996), III.18, p. 468; cf. M. Dickey, 'Some Commentaries on the *De Inventione* and *Ad Herennium* of the Eleventh and Early Twelfth Centuries', *Medieval and Renaissance Studies*, 6 (1968), pp. 38–39. See also Seneca, *Letters*, trans. R.M. Gummere (Loeb, 1920), Ep.88, p. 351, quoted, for example, by John of Salisbury, *Metalogicon*, trans. D.D. McGarry (Berkeley, 1955), I.22, p. 63.
11 Hugh of St Victor, *Didascalicon*, trans. J. Taylor (New York, 1961), II.29, p. 80; cf. III.4, p. 88; Isidore, *Etymologiae*, I.5.4, p. 42.

which were embedded in the contents of treatises on grammar.[12] Still more significant, however, were the consequences of pairing history with poetry so closely within the actual process of teaching.

The study of grammar was not just a question of speaking and writing correctly but also a course of moral instruction and, as such, both the *enarratio historiarum* and the *enarratio poetarum* were regarded as serving a profoundly ethical purpose.[13] A text such as Horace's *Epistles*, for example, was therefore regarded primarily as a means of instruction in virtue and good conduct, as well as in the correction of vice;[14] likewise Horace's *Satires*, alongside those of Juvenal. In the 1180s, Alexander Neckham accordingly coupled satire with history-writing as means of moral instruction and recommended that this material be read so that students would 'learn, even at a young age, to flee from vice and desire to imitate the noble deeds of heroes'. Neckham then provided a recommended reading-list: the poetry of Statius, Vergil, Lucan, Juvenal, Horace and Ovid, followed by the prose of Sallust and Cicero (including *De Oratore* and *De Officiis*), and then Solinus, Sidonius Apollinaris, Suetonius, Quintus Curtius, Pompeius Trogus and Livy.[15] In proffering this curriculum, Neckham was expressing a thoroughly classical ideal. In Quintilian's opinion, for example, inculcating sound moral principles at an early stage of an individual's education could be readily effected through the use of excerpted observations or *sententiae*, since these provided a means of combining learning with pleasure. This was best achieved by memorising the sayings of distinguished men (*dicta*

---

12 B. Smalley, *Historians in the Middle Ages* (London, 1974), p. 1; L.D. Reynolds (ed.), *Texts and Transmission: A Survey of the Latin Classics* (Oxford, 1983), pp. 347–9. These fragments included the letter of Mithridates with its bitter castigation of Roman imperialism: see Sallust, 'Letter of Mithridates', trans. J.C. Rolfe, *Sallust* (Loeb, 1931), pp. 432–41.
13 P. Delhaye, 'Grammatica et Ethica au XIIe Siècle', *Recherches de Théologie Ancienne et Médiévale*, 25 (1958), pp. 59–110.
14 *Accessus ad Auctores*, trans. A.J. Minnis and A.B. Scott, 'Introductions to the Authors', in A.J. Minnis and A.B. Scott (eds), *Medieval Literary Theory and Criticism c.1100–c.1375* (Oxford, 1988), p. 35.
15 Alexander Neckham, *Sacerdos ad Altare Accessurus*, ed. C.H. Haskins, *Studies in the History of Medieval Science* (Cambridge, MA, 1927), prol., pp. 372–3. For the study of rhetoric, Neckham recommended *De Inventione*, the *Rhetorica ad Herennium*, *De Oratore* and Quintilian's *Institutio Oratoria* (p. 374); cf. Reynolds, *Medieval Reading*, pp. 7–16.

clarorum virorum) and, above all, through selections from the poets, because poetry is more pleasing to the young.[16] It is on the basis of this combination that the relationship between history and poetry could be described by Quintilian as very close; in fact, he concludes, there is a sense in which history is actually a 'prose song' (*est enim proxima poetis et quodam modo carmen solutum*).[17]

The effects of pairing history with poetry on the way in which classical texts were deployed in the teaching of grammar were far-reaching. Reviewing his own experience of grammatical education in the schools of Paris, for example, John of Salisbury described how, in expounding the orators and the poets, Bernard of Chartres would admonish his students to give a thorough reading to histories and poems.[18] The extent to which an explicitly historical awareness was central to the way in which standard school texts were studied can be traced in the collections of schoolroom 'approaches' or introductions to individual authors, the so-called *accessus ad auctores*. One such list of twenty-one authors, put together in the eleventh century by Conrad of Hirsau, includes many classical poets but, like Neckham's, it also includes both Sallust and Cicero, as well as a definition of history as eyewitness testimony which was taken directly from Isidore of Seville.[19] The idea behind such introductions was to teach students to approach a particular text by identifying its author, its title, its subject-matter, the purpose for which it had been written, the type of writing to which it belonged, the way in which the author had handled the material, the life of the author, and the intention with which it had been written.[20] Such an approach originally took its

---

16 Quintilian, *Institutio Oratoria*, I.1.36, pp. 37–9; cf. Bernardus Silvestris, *Commentary on the First Six Books of Virgil's Aeneid*, trans. E.G. Schreiber and T.E. Maresca (Lincoln, 1979), VI, p. 38: 'Those who enter Apollo's temple see the pictures of history and fable on the outside. The temple of Apollo is the philosophic arts; those entering should first understand pictures before writing so that they may pay attention to stories and fables, and this is the reason why in the portico pictorial history and fable are displayed'.
17 *Institutio Oratoria*, X.1.31, p. 21; see also page 360.
18 John of Salisbury, *Metalogicon*, I.24, p. 69.
19 Conrad of Hirsau, *Dialogue on the Authors*, trans. A.J. Minnis and A.B. Scott, in A.J. Minnis and A.B. Scott (eds), *Medieval Literary Theory and Criticism c.1100–c.1375* (Oxford, 1988), p. 43.
20 A.J. Minnis and A.B. Scott (eds), *Medieval Literary Theory and Criticism c.1100–c.1375* (Oxford, 1988), ch.2; cf. E.A. Quain, 'The Medieval *Accessus ad Auctores*',

cue from Boethius' translation of, and commentary on, Porphyry's 'Introduction' or *Isagoge*,[21] but by the eleventh and twelfth centuries this had developed into a systematic method of assessment which would analyse a text's title, method of procedure, subject-matter, arrangement, purpose, utility and the branch of knowledge to which it belonged. In the thirteenth century, these categories were then overlaid by an Aristotelian schema of four causes, whereby a text would be approached by means of its material cause (subject), efficient cause (author), formal cause (style and structure) and final cause (goal or objective).

When applied to Scripture, such an evaluation of genre, historical context and authorial intention provided a writer such as Abelard with the means of harmonising apparently discordant authorities in patristic commentary on the Bible.[22] Still more significantly, when applied to texts outside Scripture, the questions 'who', 'what', 'why', 'in what manner', 'where', 'when' and 'how' furnished a method which was drilled into medieval writers as the normal way of approaching *any* text, be it prose or verse, history or poetry.[23] Deployed in the twelfth century in the nascent study of canon law, for example, it provided a decisive impetus towards reconciling and, as a consequence, systematising the otherwise contradictory rulings and opinions of Church councils and individual popes from the past: 'different regions established many things because of places, persons and the times, but which, when necessity does not require them, can be changed if utility urges'.[24] Boethius had already pointed out that 'the customs and conventions of different peoples vary so much that what is praised in one may be judged deserving of

---

Traditio, 3 (1945), pp. 215–64; A.J. Minnis, *Medieval Theory of Authorship: Scholastic Literary Attitudes in the Later Middle Ages* (2nd edn, Aldershot, 1988), ch.1, especially pp. 18–28.
21 Porphyry, *Introduction*, ed. L. Minio-Paluello, *Porphyrii Isagoge Translatio Boethii* (*Aristoteles Latinus* I.6–7, Bruges, 1966); and trans. J. Barnes (Oxford, 2003).
22 See also pages 410–13.
23 Cf. Aristotle's *Categories*, trans. J.L. Ackrill (Princeton, 1984), 1b25–2a4, p. 4; and see Marius Victorinus, *Explanatio in Rhetoricam Ciceronis*, pp. 206–7.
24 R. Somerville and B.C. Brasington, *Prefaces to Canon Law Books in Latin Christianity: Selected Translations 500–1245* (New Haven, 1998), p. 165; cf. N.M. Häring, 'The Interaction Between Canon Law and Sacramental Theology in the Twelfth Century', in S. Kuttner (ed.), *Proceedings of the Fourth International Congress of Medieval Canon Law* (Rome, 1976), pp. 483–93.

punishment in another',[25] and this soon became a fundamental principle of both interpreting and applying the law: 'canonical precepts should be adapted to different persons, events and times by varying procedure and varying application'.[26]

Given that the study and practice of eloquence were acknowledged to depend on its frequent exercise in writing,[27] it is a very short step to see in this methodical line of questioning a pattern which came to influence the approach of medieval writers, not only in composing introductions to their own works of history, but also to the personal and historical 'circumstances' which would explain the meaning of the sources on which they were basing their own accounts.[28] Otto of Freising provides an explicit illustration of this principle in action in the 1140s when he discusses the interpretation of Ambrose's views on baptism. 'They do not consider with proper care under what circumstances authors speak', Otto observes, 'what it is they say merely by way of opinion, what by way of assertion, what by way of consoling themselves in the extremity of their grief'.[29] In writing his own *Chronicle* in the early 1190s, Richard of Devizes lists the various categories (why, how, when, how much, what sort of, who, at what times, how many, with what result) which occupy the attention of those historians who have written on a larger scale than he has himself done.[30]

The fact that, taken together, history and poetry were bread and butter to the teaching of grammar has several important consequences for the way in which history came to be written in the Middle Ages. In the first instance, it means that a work such as Horace's *Art of Poetry* (*Ars Poetica*) can shed as much light on historiography as a work such as Cicero's *De Oratore*.[31] History

---

25 Boethius, *Consolation of Philosophy*, trans. S.J. Tester (Loeb, 1973), II.7, p. 219.
26 Somerville and Brasington, *Prefaces to Canon Law Books*, p. 166, and cf. pp. 189, 199.
27 Quintilian, *Institutio Oratoria*, X.1.2, p. 3; Cicero, *De Oratore*, trans. E. Sutton and H. Rackham (Loeb, 1948), I.33.150–3, pp. 103–5 (*optimus et praestantissimus dicendi effector ac magister*), I.60.257, p. 189 (*perfector dicendi ac magister*).
28 Ray, 'Medieval Historiography Through the Twelfth Century', p. 52; R.M. Thomson, *William of Malmesbury* (Woodbridge, 1987), p. 34; B. Lacroix, *L'Historien au Moyen Âge* (Montreal, 1971), pp. 69–84, 243–6.
29 Otto of Freising, *Chronicle*, trans. C.C. Mierow (New York, 1928; reprinted 2000), IV.18, p. 299.
30 Richard of Devizes, *Chronicle*, ed. and trans. J.T. Appleby (London, 1963), p. 3.
31 See page 359.

and poetry stood side by side as types of narrative whose function was to bring benefit as well as pleasure.[32] In the case of poetry, this resulted in an ethical function which directly paralleled that of history – satire, for instance, attacks vices and thereby promotes virtue, whilst tragedy encourages patience in the face of suffering and thereby inspires contempt for fortune.[33] As a consequence, whilst Gerald of Wales regarded both poetry and historiography to be under threat from the study of logic in the 1180s, as well as from the lucrative 'sciences' of law and medicine, he nonetheless clearly considered the two subjects to be on a par in terms of both their ethical goals and their linguistic brilliance. 'Who now in his writings', he asks, 'be they poetry or history, can hope to add lustre to the art of letters? Who in our time, I ask, is building up a system of ethics, or, held firm for ever in the works he writes, recording for eternity deeds which are nobly done?'[34] In the second instance, it means that the list of classical 'historians' with which medieval writers were conversant needs to be extended from writers of prose, such as Sallust, Josephus and Livy, to authors such as Homer, Vergil, Dares Phrygius, Lucan and Statius, all of whom wrote in verse.[35] Vergil was heralded by

---

32 For the pairing of utility with pleasure, see, for example, Orderic Vitalis, *Historia Ecclesiastica*, ed. and trans. M. Chibnall, *The Ecclesiastical History of Orderic Vitalis* (Oxford, 1980), prol., p. 131; Richard FitzNigel, *Dialogus de Scaccario*, ed. and trans. E. Amt (Oxford, 2007), I.5, p. 41; see also page 359, note 35, and page 361.
33 P. Mehtonen, *Old Concepts and New Poetics: Historia, Argumentum and Fabula in the Twelfth- and Thirteenth-Century Latin Poetics of Fiction* (Helsinki, 1996), pp. 84–5.
34 Gerald of Wales, *Itinerarium Cambriae*, pref., p. 64; cf. Gerald of Wales, *Descriptio Cambriae*, pref., p. 216: 'there is no respect paid any more to writers, whether they are historians or poets'; both sources trans. L. Thorpe, *The Journey Through Wales and The Description of Wales* (Harmondsworth, 1978). See also Gerald of Wales, *Expugnatio Hibernica*, ed. and trans. A.B. Scott and F.X. Martin, *The Conquest of Ireland* (Dublin, 1978), pref., p. 9. For the comparability of a 'good historiographer' (*bonus historiographus*), philosopher and poet, see, for example, *Liber Eliensis*, trans. J. Fairweather (Woodbridge, 2005), prol., p. 1.
35 For Homer, see *Ilias Latina*, ed. M. Scaffai (2nd edn, Bologna, 1997); Reynolds, *Texts and Transmission*, pp. 191–4; *Accessus ad Auctores*, pp. 16–17; Conrad of Hirsau, *Dialogue on the Authors*, p. 60. For Vergil, see D. Comparetti, *Virgil in the Middle Ages*, trans. E.F.M. Benecke (Princeton, 1997); B. Munk Olsen, 'Virgile et la Renaissance du XIIe Siècle', in J.-Y. Tilliette (ed.), *Lectures Médiévale de Virgile: Actes du Colloque Organisé par l'Ecole Française de Rome* (Rome, 1985), pp. 31–48; C. Baswell, *Virgil in Medieval England: Figuring the Aeneid from the Twelfth Century to Chaucer* (Cambridge, 1995); J.M. Ziolkowski and M.C.J. Putnam, *The Virgilian Tradition: The First Fifteen Hundred Years* (New Haven, 2008). For Dares Phyrgius,

Macrobius as the master of every branch of knowledge, a writer who combined wisdom with eloquence and whose use of rhetorical figures revealed him to be no less eminent as an orator than as a poet.[36] He was also a writer who, like a historian, explicitly set out to bring to mind the causes of the events he was narrating (*Musa, mihi causas memora...*), as well as to describe the order of things (*ordo rerum*), namely 'who were the kings, what were the times, [and] what was the state of affairs' (*qui reges ... quae tempora ... quis status rerum*).[37] It is the presence of Lucan on the list of 'historians', however, which proved just as, if not more, influential on the practice of medieval historiography.

According to Servius, Lucan did not, in fact, deserve to be reckoned amongst the poets, on the grounds that he seemed to have written a history rather than a poem, a judgment which was echoed by Quintilian, who thought Lucan a better model for orators to imitate than poets.[38] Like Sallust, Lucan had provided a damning political commentary on the last years of the Roman republic. Written as ten books of narrative epic in hexameter verse, Lucan described the civil wars between Pompey the Great and Julius Caesar as a savage struggle in which command of the entire world had been at stake and which had culminated in one,

---

see page 183; for Lucan, see pages 130–3; for Statius' *Thebaid* and *Achilleid*, see Reynolds, *Texts and Transmission*, pp. 394–7; Statius, *Achilleid*, trans. D.R. Shackleton Bailey (Loeb, 2003); Statius, *Thebaid*, trans. D.R. Shackleton Bailey (Loeb, 2003). According to Giovanni Villani, Vergil and Lucan were, alongside Sallust, Livy, Valerius Maximus and Orosius, '*maestri d'istorie*': see Giovanni Villani, *Chronicle*, trans. R.E. Selfe and P.H. Wicksteed, *Villani's Chronicle: Selections from the First Nine Books of the Croniche Fiorentine of Giovanni Villani* (London, 1906), VIII.36, p. 321.
36 Macrobius, *Saturnalia*, trans. P.V. Davies (New York, 1969), I.16.12, p. 107, III.11.9, p. 155, V.1, p. 282, and, more generally, IV.1–6, pp. 254–81; cf. Conrad of Hirsau, *Dialogue on the Authors*, p. 62; Bernardus Silvestris, *Commentary on the First Six Books of Virgil's Aeneid*, pref., p. 1: 'We hold that, in the *Aeneid*, Virgil has "the observance of twofold teaching", as indeed Macrobius says: "he taught the truth of philosophy and he did not neglect poetic fiction".' Although Macrobius discussed the verse epics of Homer and Vergil as narratives of past events, he suggested that Homer deliberately avoided writing as a historian by eschewing a linear chronological account (*Saturnalia*, V.14.11, p. 346; see also page 300).
37 Vergil, *Aeneid*, trans. H.R. Fairclough, rev. G.P. Goold (Loeb, 2000), I.8, p. 241, VII.37–8, 44, p. 5.
38 Quintilian, *Institutio Oratoria*, X.1.90, p. 51; cf. P. von Moos, 'Poeta und Historicus im Mittelalter – zum Mimesis-Problem am Beispiel einiger Urteile über Lucan', *Beiträge zur Geschichte der deutschen Sprache und Literatur*, 98 (1976), pp. 93–130.

supreme, funereal day (*summa dies, funesta dies*) at the battle of Pharsalia in 48 BC.[39] This struggle, in Lucan's view, was a frenzy of madness (*furor*), worse than civil war,[40] a rabid conflict in which violent force and unspeakable crime had been given the names of virtue and justice, in which a hitherto powerful and victorious people had single-handedly turned to disembowel itself, brother against brother, father against son. For Lucan, it was also nothing less than a conflict between liberty (*libertas*) and monarchical rule (*regnum*). As a result, his *Pharsalia* carefully juxtaposed the savage and bellicose tyranny of Caesar, not just with Pompey (as the flawed champion of the senate), but with the 'holy' Cato (*sanctus Cato*), the rigid embodiment of moral and political virtue, an unyielding defender of laws and liberty who ultimately chose to escape slavery through suicide.[41]

In lamenting the self-inflicted wounds which had such long-lasting consequences for Rome and the entire world, Lucan stated his intent to explain the 'causes' of the momentous events which he was describing (*causae tantarum rerum*). He found them in the jealousy of Fortune (that is, as he defines it, in the principle that greatness and success will always collapse under its own weight),

---

39 Lucan, *Pharsalia*, trans. J.D. Duff, *The Civil War* (Loeb, 1928), VII.195, p. 383, VII.427, p. 401. For the definitive battle between Aeneas and Turnus as 'the day of the fates' (*dies parcarum*), see Vergil, *Aeneid*, XII.150, p. 311; cf. William of Malmesbury, *Gesta Regum Anglorum*, ed. and trans. R.A.B. Mynors, R.M. Thomson and M. Winterbottom, *The History of the English Kings* (Oxford, 1998–99), III.245, p. 457, where the Battle of Hastings is described as *dies fatalis*. More generally, see J.G. Haahr, 'William of Malmesbury's Roman Models: Suetonius and Lucan', in A.S. Bernardo and S. Levin (eds), *The Classics in the Middle Ages* (New York, 1990), pp. 165–73; N.Wright, 'William of Malmesbury and Latin Poetry – Further Evidence for a Benedictine's Reading', *Revue Bénédictine*, 101(1991), pp. 122–53; N.Wright, '*Industriae Testimonium* – William of Malmesbury and Latin Poetry Revisited', *Revue Bénédictine*, 103 (1993), pp. 482–531.
40 Lucan, *Pharsalia*, I.1, p. 3. For the popularity of this line, see, for example, Paschasius Radbertus, *Epitaphium Arsenii*, trans. A. Cabaniss, *Charlemagne's Cousins: Contemporary Lives of Adalard and Wala* (Syracuse, 1967), II.7, p. 158; Widukind, *Res Gestae Saxonicae*, ed. and trans. E. Rotter and B. Schneidmüller (rev. edn, Stuttgart, 1992), III.18, p. 176; Conrad of Hirsau, *Dialogue on the Authors*, p. 111; Cosmas of Prague, *Chronicle of the Czechs*, trans. L. Wolverton (Washington, DC, 2009), II.45, p. 173, II.47, p. 176, III.36, p. 226; William of Malmesbury, *Gesta Regum Anglorum*, II.199, p. 359; John of Salisbury, *Metalogicon*, IV.42, p. 275; Gerald of Wales, *Expugnatio Hibernica*, I.7, p. 45, I.45, p. 121, I.46, p. 127, II.15, p. 169, II.31, p. 221.
41 M. Leigh, *Lucan: Spectacle and Engagement* (Oxford, 1997).

in the inability of leaders to share their power with rivals, and (again like Sallust) in the ruin which is always wrought on powerful peoples by the corrupting effects of peace, wealth and luxury. This aetiological approach to verse historiography took several forms. Lucan's poetry is shot through, for example, with Stoic reflections on whether the course of events (*series rerum*) follows a harmonious series of fixed and unchanging causes, whether it results from the will of higher powers, or simply reflects the uncertainties of chance (*fors*) and blind accident (*casus*) which can be personified as Fortune (*fortuna*) and the Fates.[42] His verse narrative of events also includes numerous conventionally 'historiographical' features: physical descriptions of places; set-piece battle scenes; moving speeches by the chief protagonists; omens, prophecies and portents (including a comet, which signifies changes in the rule of earthly kingdoms); mythical explanations (*fabulae*) of the origins of rivers and cities; and a number of digressions – on the stars, on the poisonous snakes of north Africa and on the source of the Nile. Above all, the *Pharsalia* is peppered with a series of epigrammatic observations (*sententiae*) – on the nature of reputation (*fama*), on the difference between true liberty and its empty shadow, on the dangers of living under a ruler who has reigned for a long time, on the instability of power and the rapidity with which things can turn to disaster (*vertigo rerum*), and on the evil example (*exemplum*) set by Alexander the Great when he made the whole world his prey.

In composing his work in this manner, Lucan himself drew attention to what he saw as his primary responsibility to later generations. He explicitly anticipates the effects of what he has written, moving his audience to hope and fear as if the events he was describing were about to happen rather than having already taken place. As a prophetic poet (*vates*) of such great evils, he presents himself as a writer who has been charged with the sacred task of immortalising particular individuals for posterity. Indeed, he reflects on a point in the future when the Roman name will itself be a *fabula*, not as a result of the erosion of time, but through the guilt of a civil war which destroyed the memorials of what Rome had achieved (*monumenta rerum*).[43] This lesson was not lost

---

42 See pages 271–2.
43 Lucan, *Pharsalia*, I.447–9, p. 37, VII.207–13, p. 385, VII.397, p. 399, VII.552–4, p. 411, IX.980–6, p. 579.

on his medieval audience. Whilst Orosius described Lucan as the greatest poet (*optimus poeta*),[44] Isidore chose to echo Servius in suggesting that Lucan should not, in fact, be numbered amongst the poets, because he seemed to have composed a history rather than a poem.[45] In the eleventh century, Arnulf of Orleans put the two authorities together in a line-by-line commentary on the *Pharsalia*. Lucan, he wrote, was not just a poet, but a poet and a historian combined, who clearly distinguished the fabulous and the fictive elements in his verse from the truth of his historical narrative. If Lucan had thereby sought to join together pleasure with utility, then the latter consisted of his poem acting as a deterrent to any similar civil war in the future. For Arnulf, the *Pharsalia* was, in short, an ethical work, not because it delivered moral precepts as such, but because it encouraged its audience to practise the four cardinal virtues through its portrayal of individual characters such as Cato.[46]

Rhetoric

The study of works of history was as integral to the teaching of rhetoric in the Middle Ages as it was to an education in the principles of grammar. Honorius of Autun, for example, identified 'histories' (*historiae*) as the first of the four categories of writing (the other three were fables, oratory and ethics) which made rhetoric one of the liberal arts that could lead a soul back from its exile in ignorance and towards its true home in wisdom.[47] Later in the twelfth century, Peter of Blois classified five types of prose-writing or *dictamen* – the first, and most important, was the

---

44 Orosius, *Seven Books of History Against the Pagans*, trans. R.J. Deferrari (Washington, DC, 1964), VI.1, p. 232; Otto of Freising, *Chronicle*, II.50, p. 215.
45 Isidore, *Etymologiae*, VIII.7.10, p. 181; Servius, *In Vergilii Carmina Commentarii*, ed. G. Thilo and H. Hagen (Leipzig, 1878–1902), I.382, p. 129.
46 Arnulf of Orleans, *Glosule Super Lucanum*, trans. A.J. Minnis and A.B. Scott, in A.J. Minnis and A.B. Scott (eds), *Medieval Literary Theory and Criticism c.1100–c.1375* (Oxford, 1988), prol., pp. 155–6; cf. Arnulf of Orleans, *Glosule Super Lucanum*, ed. B.M. Marti (Rome, 1958), II.410, p. 128; *Accessus ad Auctores*, pp. 42–3; Conrad of Hirsau, *Dialogue on the Authors*, pp. 110–11.
47 Honorius of Autun, *De Animae Exsilio et Patria* (PL 172, cols 1241–6), III, col. 1244; cf. V.I.J. Flint, 'The Place and Purpose of the Works of Honorius Augustodunensis', *Revue Bénédictine*, 87 (1977), pp. 97–127.

epistle or letter, but the second was history (*historia*); then came wills (*testamentum*), polemic (*invectiva*) and exposition (*expositio*).[48] At the most basic level, familiarity with history was regarded simply as a particularly useful part of the rhetorician's armoury. Quintilian warned against the superfluous labour of pursuing absolutely everything that has ever been written and pointed out that it is sufficient for the *enarratio historiarum* to expound what is generally received or what has been remembered on the basis of authors who were acknowledged to be distinguished.[49] This is why Cicero thought it necessary to give a list of these historians in the sort of overview provided by *De Legibus*.[50] Quintilian gave a similar summary of both Greek and Roman historiography, recommending Thucydides and Herodotus, Livy and Sallust (even though Sallust was the greater *auctor historiae*, Quintilian remarks, Livy offers fewer pitfalls as a basic model for rhetorical training).[51] Passages from these historians should, in Quintilian's

---

48 Peter of Blois, *De Arte Dictandi Rethorice*, cited in J.J. Murphy, *Rhetoric in the Middle Ages: A History of Rhetorical Theory from St. Augustine to the Renaissance* (Berkeley, 1974), pp. 229–30.
49 Quintilian, *Institutio Oratoria*, I.8.18, p. 155.
50 Cicero, *De Legibus*, trans. J.E.G. Zetzel (Cambridge, 1999), I.6–7, p. 107.
51 Quintilian, *Institutio Oratoria*, IV.2.5, p. 75, X.1.32, p. 21, X.1.101–2, p. 59; cf. Martianus Capella, *Marriage of Philology and Mercury*, V, p. 207. Comparable lists are given by, for example, Sigebert of Gembloux, *Liber de Scriptoribus Ecclesiasticis* (*PL* 160, cols 547–88), col. 588C; Orderic Vitalis, *Historia Ecclesiastica*, prol., p. 131; Hugh of St Victor, *De Tribus Maximis Circumstantiis Gestorum*, ed. G. Waitz, *Archiv der Gesellschaft für ältere deutsche Geschichtskunde*, 11 (1858), pp. 307–8, who names thirty-two; Peter of Blois, *Letters* (*PL* 207, cols 311–14), Ep.101, col. 314, who states that he benefited from 'frequent' consultation of Pompeius Trogus, Josephus, Suetonius, Hegesippus, Quintus Curtius, Tacitus and Livy; John of Salisbury, *Historia Pontificalis*, ed. and trans. M. Chibnall (London, 1956), prol., pp. 1–2; John of Salisbury, *Policraticus*, trans. J. Dickinson, *The Statesman's Book of John of Salisbury* (New York, 1927), VIII.18, p. 356; Ralph de Diceto, *Abbreviationes Chronicorum*, ed. W. Stubbs, *The Historical Works of Master Ralph de Diceto, Dean of London* (London, 1876), prol., pp. 20–4, who lists no fewer than forty-one. See A. Gransden, 'Prologues in the Historiography of Twelfth-Century England', in D. Williams, *England in the Twelfth Century* (Woodbridge, 1990); reprinted in A. Gransden, *Legends, Traditions and History in Medieval England* (London, 1992), p. 69. Salimbene's *Chronicle*, trans. J.L. Baird, G. Baglivi and J.R. Kane (Binghamton, 1986), p. 177, lists ten different writers of history and classifies them on stylistic grounds according to whether they are sweet and mellifluous (e.g. Job, Ecclesiasticus, Gregory the Great, Bernard of Clairvaux) or heavy, difficult and obscure (e.g. Livy, Orosius, Ambrose, Hosea and the Gospel of Mark); cf. P. Mehtonen, 'Scriptural Difficulty and the Obscurity of *Historia*', in T.M.S.

view, be learned off by heart, since rhetoricians generally aim to secure authority for what they are saying from historians, and not just from other orators. Indeed, in his opinion, the act of writing histories alongside speeches was therefore rightly (*merito*) counted as part of oratory. The richness of history, he concluded, should form part of an orator's written training because it will nourish the orator like a succulent and pleasing fruit-juice.[52]

This is not to say that history-writing was thought to be identical to oratory. Cicero listed a number of differentiating features. Historiography certainly provides an ornate narrative, and its descriptions of regions and battles are interspersed with debates and speeches of exhortation. However, it adopts a smooth and flowing style, rather than the sharp and contorted diction of the orator.[53] Quintilian followed suit. History is written in order to narrate rather than to prove; its entire concern is with the remembrance of posterity and reputation, not with conflict over something in the present.[54] History is what orators write in their retirement, as a memorial (*monumenta rerum*) for the benefit of posterity.[55] For Cicero, the historian's treatment of words and the type of language used (*oratio*) should therefore be broad and expansive, flowing steadily with a certain smoothness.[56] For Quintilian, history has a style all of its own. Like poetry, it has a greater licence than oratory in its choice of vocabulary and in its use of figures of speech. It should flow gently, as exemplified by the work of Herodotus – since its contents should be carried along, they are less suited to being stopped with separate clauses and pauses for breath. The writing of history accordingly requires a certain roundness (*quaedam orbs*), a quality of being woven together (*contextus*), such that its individual parts remain connected as it flows in various directions, like people who join

---

Lehtonen and P. Mehtonen (eds), *Historia: The Concept and Genres in the Middle Ages* (Helsinki, 2000), pp. 60–2.
52 Quintilian, *Institutio Oratoria*, I.6.2, p. 113, I.6.11, p. 117, X.1.31, p. 19.
53 Cicero, *Orator*, trans. H.M. Hubbell (Loeb, 1962), XX.66, p. 355.
54 Quintilian, *Institutio Oratoria*, X.1.31–4, p. 21.
55 *Institutio Oratoria*, XII.11.4, p. 497; cf. Sallust, *Catiline*, trans. J.C. Rolfe (Loeb, 1931), IV, p. 9; Sallust, *Jugurthine War*, trans. J.C. Rolfe (Loeb, 1931), IV, pp. 137–9 (see also page 43).
56 Cicero, *De Oratore*, II.15.62, p. 245.

hands in order to walk steadily, holding and being held by each other in turn.[57]

Nonetheless, even if Quintilian thought that at least some of the historian's virtues should be avoided by the orator (the fullness of Livy's expository style, he suggests, might not be a good model if a writer's goal is to inculcate belief or credibility), he remained convinced that it was permissible, and desirable, for orators to draw on works of history, particularly in digressions and as a storehouse or treasury (*thesaurus*) of examples. Indeed, the greatest utility of history was, in his opinion, that it gave the orator a knowledge of what has happened and of *exempla*. This means that orators will be able to draw testimony from antiquity (*vetustas*), rather than simply from their clients, a form of evidence which will prove all the more effective because it alone is free from the charge of being motivated by hatred (*odium*) or favour (*gratia*).[58] Likewise, it is in the context of their similarities, rather than their differences, that Cicero chose to express his surprise that, despite the priority of *historia* within the study and practice of oratory (it was, he suggested, a task particularly pertinent to orators),[59] the discipline of rhetoric had not provided the writing of history with its own set of rules. In *De Oratore*, he accordingly set out to remedy the omission by outlining what he regarded to be some self-evident truths. 'Do you see how great a task history is for the orator?', he asks.

> It may in fact be the greatest task in terms of fluency and variety of language [*oratio*]. And still I do not find that the rhetoricians have anywhere furnished it with rules of its own – for its rules are obvious. Everybody knows that the first law of history is not to dare saying anything false [*falsum*]; that the second is to dare saying everything that is true [*verum*]; that there should be no suggestion of partiality [*gratia*], none of animosity [*simultas*], when you write. These foundations are, of course, familiar to everyone. The actual superstructure is a matter of substance and words [*res et verba*]. The treatment of the content demands chronological arrangement [*ordo temporum*]

---

57 Quintilian, *Institutio Oratoria*, IX.4.18, p. 515, IX.4.129, pp. 579–80, X.1.31, p. 21.
58 *Institutio Oratoria*, II.5.19, p. 255, II.7.2–4, p. 263, II.18.5, p. 347, X.1.31–4, pp. 19–23, X.1.73, p. 43, X.1.101–4, pp. 59–61, X.5.15, pp. 121–3; see also page 183.
59 Cicero, *De Legibus*, I.5, p. 107.

and the description of regions. Also, since readers, in the case of great events which are worthy of memory, first expect deliberations [*consilia*], then actions [*acta*] and, after that, the outcome [*eventus*], it requires the author to indicate what he thinks was good about the deliberations, to show in his treatment of the things done [*res gestae*] not only *what* was done or said but also *how*, and, in speaking about the outcome, to give an account of all its causes, whether they were the product of circumstance [*casus*], of wisdom or of rashness. And he must describe not merely the deeds of the people involved but, for all those of an outstanding reputation [*fama*] and name [*nomen*], also their lives and nature.[60]

Cicero's understanding of both the foundation and the superstructure of the writing of history provided a check-list of those elements which he, at least, regarded as essential to the recording of deeds which are worthy of remembrance: truth, impartiality, chronology, topography, deliberation, action, consequence, causality, circumstance, life, character and reputation. Moreover, in underlining the importance of the connection between subject-matter (*res*) and the language in which it is expressed (*verba*, *oratio*), Cicero's summary also highlighted the centrality of the connection between history and rhetoric on which each of these elements depends. As a result, whilst the study of history may subsequently have become bound up with the teaching of grammar, the writing of history was also understood to draw on the full range of linguistic strategies to which the teaching of rhetoric was devoted. To this end, historiography developed an intimate connection with each of the three basic categories into which rhetoric had been traditionally divided according to those areas of public life which it was designed to service: demonstrative or epideictic rhetoric (speeches and texts which praise or blame individuals); legal or judicial rhetoric (speeches and texts which prosecute or defend individuals in the law courts); and deliberative rhetoric (speeches and texts which argue for or against a particular course of political action in political assemblies).[61] These three categories

---

60 Cicero, *De Oratore*, II.15.62, pp. 243–5.
61 See page 19; cf. Fortunatianus, *Ars Rhetorica*, trans. J.M. Miller, in J.M. Miller, M.H. Prosser and T.W. Benson (eds), *Readings in Medieval Rhetoric* (Bloomington, 1973), I, p. 26; Isidore, *Etymologiae*, ed. and trans. P.K. Marshall (Paris, 1983), II.4.1–8, pp. 26–30; Boethius, *De Topicis Differentiis*, trans. E. Stump (Ithaca, 1978), IV, pp. 80–2.

of rhetoric proved to be much more than just functional instruments tied to particular social and political institutions within the classical world. What is so striking about the subsequent study and teaching of rhetoric is that it survived the decline of those legal and political institutions which rhetoric had originally been created to serve. Even without the law courts and the senate, in other words, this threefold categorisation of rhetoric remained central to the way in which language was considered to regulate relations between individuals and groups throughout the Middle Ages. As a result, demonstrative, judicial and deliberative rhetoric continue to provide the most convenient means of analysing the various ways in which rhetoric conditioned the writing of history between c.400 and c.1500.

Demonstrative rhetoric

Demonstrative or epideictic rhetoric is, in many ways, the most straightforward of the three types of classical rhetoric to analyse. Viewed from the perspective of medieval historiography, it is also, perhaps, the most familiar, given that it involves 'setting out' (*demonstrare*) the life of an individual. Demonstrative rhetoric is defined by its aims, namely praise (in which case it is classified as an *encomium*, that is, as panegyric or *laudatio*) or censure and blame (in which case it is classified as castigation or *vituperatio*).[62] A speech or text which is delivered in order to praise or to blame an individual has two essential functions. The first of these is the maintenance of an individual's reputation (*fama*), both in the present and, subsequently, in the remembrance of posterity (*memoria posteritatis*). It produces a commemoration of moral worth (*honesta commemoratio*), in the sense that what is praiseworthy has its source in what is morally worthy or virtuous (*honestum*). As a result, demonstrative rhetoric is based, first and foremost, upon an understanding of moral virtue. Although Cicero insists that virtue is not pursued for the sake of praise alone, he does concede that the prospect of praise will double an individual's incentive to pursue a virtuous

---

62 *Rhetorica ad Herennium*, trans. H. Caplan (Loeb, 1954), I.2.2, p. 5; Quintilian, *Institutio Oratoria*, III.4.12–13, p. 395; cf. Priscian, *Praeexercitamina*, trans. J.M. Miller, in J.M. Miller, M.H. Prosser and T.W. Benson (eds), *Readings in Medieval Rhetoric* (Bloomington, 1973), VII, pp. 61–3.

life. The goal of demonstrative rhetoric is, in consequence, to set out someone's life in terms of what is morally worthy (*honestum* or *honestas*), that is, in relation to goods which are sought wholly for their own sake. Each of these goods – virtue, knowledge and truth – possesses a force and a character which are, in themselves, enough to make them goals in their own right rather than ones which are sought for any additional benefit or advantage.[63] Virtue, in this context, is defined by Cicero as a disposition of the mind in harmony with reason and nature; it is synonymous with *honestas* and it comprises the cardinal elements of wisdom (or prudence), justice, temperance and fortitude.[64] As a result, in every circumstance in which human character is studied, these four virtues and their opposites will provide the template for the way in which an individual's character will be described.[65]

The first point to make about demonstrative rhetoric, therefore, is that it presupposes knowledge of the intimate connection between the praise which is due to an individual and the presence or absence of virtue. This can be positive, namely when a speaker or writer runs through the four cardinal virtues and their subcategories, applying each of them in turn to the individual who is being praised. Or it can be negative – self-evidently, perhaps, when the castigation of the wicked involves the condemnation of vice and, as such, entails running through all those vices which serve as the counterparts to virtue. According to Quintilian, the praise and blame of demonstrative rhetoric depend, as a result, upon a handling of what is right and what is wicked, upon being able to distinguish things that are morally worthy (*honesta*) from those that are morally reprehensible (*turpia*).[66] So too for Cicero – a knowledge of all the virtues is indispensable for the construction of an *encomium*; without a knowledge of virtues and vices, it is impossible either to praise a good man appropriately and fully, or to brand and blame the wicked.[67] Everything in a panegyric is related

---

63 *Rhetorica ad Herennium*, III.4.7, p. 169; Cicero, *De Inventione*, trans. H.M. Hubbell (Loeb, 1949), II.4.12, p. 177, II.51–2, 156–7, p. 325; Cicero, *Topica*, trans. H. M. Hubbell (Loeb, 1949), XXIV.91, p. 453.
64 Cicero, *De Inventione*, II.53.159, p. 327.
65 *Rhetorica ad Herennium*, III.8.15, p. 183.
66 Quintilian, *Institutio Oratoria*, II.20.8, p. 353, XII.2.16–17, p. 391.
67 Cicero, *De Oratore*, II.85.348, p. 463.

to the moral standing (*dignitas*) of the individual in question.[68] This is why manuals of rhetoric such as Cicero's *De Inventione* contain such handy summaries of all the virtues and their corresponding vices; it is also why this particular part of Cicero's work was transmitted in the Middle Ages so frequently on its own.[69]

So what effect does a concern with virtue and praise, or indeed with vice and castigation, have upon the actual content of what is said, or written, in demonstrative rhetoric? In the first instance, the connection between praise and virtue results in this theme forming the central part of the introduction or *exordium* with which a speech or text of demonstrative rhetoric will open. This is clearly set out in the *Rhetorica ad Herennium*, for example, in the course of describing how an *exordium* or introduction can be drawn from four possible sources: from the person of the speaker or writer; from the person who is being spoken or written about; from the person of the audience; and, finally, from the subject-matter itself. In an introduction based on the person of the speaker or writer themselves, a speaker or writer should say that their praise of an individual has been prompted by a sense of duty and necessity. Alternatively, they should say that they are doing so from positive commitment (*studium*), because such is the virtue of the person being praised that everyone should wish to commemorate it, or because it is only right to set out, from the praise given to this person by others, what sort of character they are. Conversely, if the speaker is castigating someone, then they should say that they are doing this because this person deserves it, or from positive commitment, because they think it useful that such singular wickedness should be brought to everyone's attention, or because it is pleasing to be shown what meets general approval from the castigation of others. If the speaker is basing their introduction on the person about whom they are speaking, then, when they praise someone, they should say that they fear their own inability

---

[68] Cicero, *De Oratore*, I.31.141, p. 99.
[69] Cicero, *De Inventione*, II.53.159–54.165, pp. 327–33. See, for example, Augustine, *De Diversis Quaestionibus LXXXIII* trans. B. Ramsey, *Miscellany of Eighty-Three Questions*, in Augustine, *Responses to Miscellaneous Questions* (New York, 2008), 31, pp. 45–7; Augustine, *Retractationes*, trans. M.I. Bogan, *Retractions* (Washington, DC, 1968), I.25, p. 108; Alcuin, *De Virtutibus et Vitiis* (*PL* 101, cols 613–38), XXXIV–V, col. 637; and, more generally, S. Mähl, *Quadriga Virtutum: Die Kardinaltugenden in der Geistesgeschichte der Karolingerzeit* (Cologne, 1969), pp. 97–101.

to match their subject's deeds with words; that everyone ought to proclaim (*praedicare*) the virtues of this individual; that the deeds themselves transcend the eloquence of all those who praise them.[70] If the speaker is basing their introduction on the person of their audience, then, when they praise an individual, they should say that, since they are praising someone who is not unknown to the audience, they will say only a few words in order to serve as a reminder of that individual; or, if the individual is unknown to the audience, the speaker should seek to make the audience want to know this individual; since the people before whom the individual is being praised have the same concern for virtue as the person who is being praised, the speaker or writer will hope to secure a ready approval of that individual's deeds from those whose approval is desired. Conversely, if someone is being castigated, the speaker or writer should either say a few words about that person's wickedness if they are well known or, if the individual is not known, they should seek to make them known in order that their audience may disapprove of, and avoid, their wickedness. If the speaker bases their introduction on the subject-matter, finally, then they should say that they are uncertain as to what they would most rather praise, or express the fear lest, although they are saying a lot, they will pass over even more.[71]

Having shaped the way in which the introduction or *exordium* is written, the form which the connection between praise and virtue will subsequently give to the main body of the work is a narrative of the actions performed, the 'deeds done' (*res gestae*), by a virtuous individual. According to the *Rhetorica ad Herennium*, the speaker or writer should first set out the things they intend to praise or censure, then recount, and in order, what was done and

---

70 Cf. Einhard, *Vita Karoli*, trans. P.E. Dutton, in P.E. Dutton, *Charlemagne's Courtier: The Complete Einhard* (Ontario, 1998), pref., pp. 15–16 (see also page 158); Widukind, *Res Gestae Saxonicae*, III.74, pp. 228–30; John of Salerno, *Life of Odo of Cluny*, trans. G. Sitwell (London, 1958), prol., p. 4; Odo of Cluny, *Life of Gerald of Aurillac*, trans. G. Sitwell (London, 1958), III.8, p. 169; and, more generally, G. Simon, 'Untersuchungen zur Topik der Widmungsbriefe mittelalterlicher Geschichtsschreiber bis zum Ende des 12. Jahrhunderts', *Archiv für Diplomatik*, 4 (1958), pp. 55–62, 99, 106.
71 *Rhetorica ad Herennium*, III.6.11–12, pp. 175–9; cf. Valerius Maximus, *Facta et Dicta Memorabilia*, trans. D.R. Shackleton Bailey, *Memorable Doings and Sayings* (Loeb, 2000), II.7, p. 183.

at what time it was done, so that the audience may understand exactly what the person under discussion has done and how they did it. Before this narrative is embarked upon, however, it will be necessary to set out the virtues or vices of this individual, and then to demonstrate how physical advantages (or disadvantages) and favourable (or unfavourable) circumstances have been handled by an individual with this sort of character.[72] It is a particular combination of narrative action and moral virtue which thereby provides the core of a work of demonstrative rhetoric. At its heart is the depiction of character (*ethologia*), according to which a speaker or writer enumerates an individual's virtues in so far as they are revealed through their actions and in conjunction with their physical advantages and external circumstances. The *Rhetorica ad Herennium* establishes a clear arrangement for setting out a 'life' (*vita*) in this way.[73] First come the external circumstances of an individual's youth: this involves factors such as descent (that is, their ancestors) and education (that is, how the individual has been well trained in virtue and moral worth throughout their childhood). Second come physical advantages: this involves praising factors such as the bearing and form which that individual possesses by nature, the strength and speed which they have acquired through exercise, and the good health which they have attained through diligent control over their passions. Third come the external circumstances of that individual's maturity and the way in which their virtues and vices have been revealed by wealth, power, glory, friendships, enmities and (last but not least)[74] the sort of death with which their life ended and the sorts of event which happened afterwards.

If the combination of a narrative of an individual's life and deeds with a description of their character forms the basis of an *encomium* in demonstrative rhetoric, then, according to both Cicero and Quintilian, this combination is one which, of all areas of philosophy, an orator should know the most thoroughly.[75] At

---

72 *Rhetorica ad Herennium*, III.7.13, p. 179.
73 *Rhetorica ad Herennium*, III.7.13–14, pp. 181–3; cf. Cicero, *De Oratore*, II.11.45–6, pp. 231–33; Priscian, *Praeexercitamina*, VII, p. 61.
74 Quintilian, *Institutio Oratoria*, VII.praef.8, p. 181.
75 Cicero, *De Oratore*, I.15.69, p. 51; Quintilian, *Institutio Oratoria*, II.4.21, p. 235; cf. Boethius, *Consolation of Philosophy*, I.4, p. 147: '*mores... totiusque vitae rationem*'.

the same time, this combination of *vita, gesta* and *mores* is open to considerable nuance and sophistication. Self-evidently, not everything is going to be praised. Sometimes it will not be necessary to cover *all* of the categories of physical advantage and external circumstance, given that some of them will simply not be applicable.[76] In fact, Cicero suggests that the author of an *encomium* should select only those actions which are praiseworthy because they are of outstanding importance, or unprecedented, or unparalleled in their character. Nor is it simply a case of concentrating on only one individual – the person being praised can be compared with other outstanding individuals, even to the extent of demonstrating who is better and who is worse. It is not just the nature of the vices and the virtues which is under discussion, after all, but also the question of their degree.[77] Nor is there only one way of doing it. According to Quintilian, praise of human beings involves a great variety of considerations. The time preceding the birth of the individual will be taken up with a discussion of their country, their parents and their ancestors, together with oracles and omens which promised that individual's future distinction. Praise of the individual should be based on character, physical form and chance external circumstances, of which the last two are less important than the first. Praise of character, however, can be given in one of two ways: sometimes it is better to follow the order of events and *res gestae* at each particular stage in an individual's life, praising them in their childhood and schooling and afterwards in the weaving together (*contextus*) of their acts and words; at other times, it is possible to divide praise of an individual according to specific virtues, dealing with each of them separately and assigning to the virtues of wisdom, justice, temperance and fortitude those deeds which the individual has performed under the influence of each. Which of the two approaches is chosen as the more advantageous will depend on the nature of the subject-matter, but Quintilian maintains that the author should always bear in mind that what pleases an audience the most (in other words, what fulfils the third function of rhetoric)[78] is an account of deeds which that individual was the first (or only, or one of few) to

---

[76] *Rhetorica ad Herennium*, III.8.15, p. 183.
[77] Cicero, *De Oratore*, II.85.347, p. 463.
[78] See pages 8–9.

perform, or deeds which surpassed hope or expectation, or deeds which were done for the sake of others rather than self-interest.[79]

Different things, moreover, are owed differing amounts of praise.[80] According to Cicero, the external gifts of fortune (that is, descent, physique and wealth), whilst desirable in themselves, do not constitute any true ground for praise on their own, since praise should be given to virtue alone. Strictly speaking, it is the way in which these goods of fortune and nature have been used and controlled by an individual that reveals the presence or absence of virtue. These external goods may be praised, therefore, but only in so far as they have provided the capability and material for virtuous action.[81] Likewise, virtue, whilst being praiseworthy in itself, and a necessary element in anything that can be praised, can be differentiated according to the degree of praise which is appropriate for its different aspects. In particular, there is a distinction to be drawn between those virtues which are manifested as qualities of conduct or behaviour towards other people and those virtues which consist of an intellectual ability or an internal quality of mind. Of the two categories, it is the former which Cicero suggests should be more prominent in an *encomium*. Even though virtues such as wisdom, magnanimity and intellectual strength should be the object of admiration (*mirabilia*), praise should concentrate primarily on virtues such as clemency, justice, kindness, good faith and bravery, since these virtues bear fruit, not so much for the individual who possesses them, as for humankind in general. Individual virtues, moreover, have distinct functions and each virtue has an appropriate form of praise – justice, for example, involves reciting what has been done in good faith and with equity. Particular praise, however, is bestowed on actions which are performed by brave individuals without personal profit or reward. Great praise and admiration are thus generally given to an individual who bears adverse circumstances wisely and is not crushed by fortune. Those actions which also involve effort and personal danger provide, in Cicero's opinion, particularly fruitful material for an *encomium*, because they can be related in a most eloquent style and will readily receive

---

79 Quintilian, *Institutio Oratoria*, III.7.10–16, pp. 469–73.
80 Cicero, *De Oratore*, II.84.342–7, pp. 459–61.
81 Cf. Quintilian, *Institutio Oratoria*, III.7.13–14, p. 471.

an audience. It is those virtues, in short, which are of benefit to others and are either difficult or dangerous which mark out an individual of outstanding virtue.

Even from this brief outline it will be clear just how much influence was exerted on the practice of medieval historiography by classical principles of demonstrative rhetoric. 'Even if I were to combine eloquence, knowledge and memory', wrote Thietmar of Merseburg, 'they would still not suffice to express Caesar's praise'.[82] Such influence operates at a variety of different levels and in a number of different genres, but it is particularly evident in the writing of 'lives' (*vitae*) and 'deeds' (*res gestae*), be they of saints (that is, hagiographies),[83] popes, bishops and abbots,[84] or of emperors, kings, dukes and counts. Within a Christian biblical tradition, commemoration of an individual's life and deeds and their commendation to the remembrance of posterity was recognised, in and of itself, to serve a fundamental function: 'the just man will be in eternal memory' (Psalm 112:6). The book of Maccabees, the model for so many 'histories' of crusading deeds, expressed it in the simple phrase 'remembrance in this world is a blessing' (*et in saeculum memoria eius in benedictione*).[85] Guibert of Nogent's account of the First Crusade, for example, takes this responsibility very seriously and explicitly passes over in silence those knights whose reputation for martial ferocity was not matched by their actual

---

82 Thietmar of Merseburg, *Chronicon*, trans. D.A. Warner, *Ottonian Germany* (Manchester, 2001), II.44, p. 124, referring to the emperor Otto I.
83 For hagiography, see T.J. Heffernan, 'Christian Biography – Foundation and Maturity', in D.M. Deliyannis (ed.), *Historiography in the Middle Ages* (Leiden, 2003), pp. 115–54; M. Goodich, 'Biography 1000–1350', in D.M. Deliyannis (ed.), *Historiography in the Middle Ages* (Leiden, 2003), pp. 353–85; cf. T. Head (ed.), *Medieval Hagiography: An Anthology* (London, 2001). For the rewriting of saints' lives, see M. Goullet, *Ecriture et Réécriture Hagiographiques. Essai sur les Réécritures de Vies des Saints dans l'Occident Latin Medieval VIII–XIIIe Siècle* (Turnhout, 2005).
84 M. Sot, *Gesta Episcoporum, Gesta Abbatum* (Typologie des Sources 37, Turnhout, 1981); R. Kaiser, 'Die *Gesta Episcoporum* als Genus der Geschichtsschreibung', in A. Scharer and G. Scheibelreiter (eds), *Historiographie im frühen Mittelalter* (Vienna, 1994), pp. 459–80; M. Sot, 'Local and Institutional History 300–1000', in D.M. Deliyannis (ed.), *Historiography in the Middle Ages* (Leiden, 2003), pp. 100–14.
85 1 Maccabees 3:7; cf. Proverbs 10:7: 'the memory of the righteous is blessed and the name of the wicked will rot' (*memoria iusti cum laudibus et nomen impiorum putrescet*); Ecclesiasticus (Sirach) 44:1,14: 'Let us now praise famous men, and our fathers that begot us.... Their bodies are buried in peace, but their name lives for evermore'; Cosmas of Prague, *Chronicle of the Czechs*, I.34, p. 87.

deeds and who therefore possessed, in Lucan's phrase, merely the shadow of a great name.[86] Likewise, with those people whose *fama* was subsequently sullied: 'I would insert their names on this page were I not aware of the fact that they returned to criminal acts.... My silence is not unjust'.[87] Henry of Huntingdon reflected on both the immortal *fama* and the everlasting opprobrium which could be bestowed by the writer of verse and of history,[88] using 2 Samuel 7:9 to set up David as the prime example of the importance of a great name (*magnum nomen*) in contrast to the oblivion of silence.[89] Indeed, it is sensitivity to the transitory nature of human memory which makes Henry so committed to historiography and prompts him to speculate on whether his work would be read into the third millennium. Like Boethius, Henry reflected on the fragility of both memory and the written record: 'how many men famous in their own time are now completely forgotten for want of written record, although what is the value of such records themselves when they and their writers are lost in the obscurity of long ages?'[90]

Liturgically, this principle of commemoration was reflected in the account which was given of an individual's deeds either on their death or on the anniversary of their death. This practice had its origins in the martyrologies and necrologies which were compiled and circulated by individual monastic communities. 'Histories', in this liturgical sense, originated in the brief accounts of saints' lives which were written in order to be read out in church on their feast day. John of Salerno, for example,

---

86 Guibert of Nogent, *Gesta Dei per Francos*, trans. R. Levine, *The Deeds of God Through the Franks* (Woodbridge, 1997), IV, p. 79, VII, p. 155; cf. Lucan, *Pharsalia*, I.135, p. 13.
87 *Gesta Dei per Francos*, VII, p. 130.
88 Henry of Huntingdon, *Historia Anglorum*, ed. and trans. D. Greenway, *History of the English* (Oxford, 1996), V.17, p. 309, VI.6, p. 349, VII.34, p. 471, VII.44, p. 491, VIII.3, p. 497, XI.11, p. 791; cf. Gerald of Wales, *Expugnatio Hibernica*, I.9, p. 49, II.15, p. 171, II.17, p. 179.
89 *Historia Anglorum*, VIII (*De Contemptu Mundi*), p. 601; cf. Suger, *Gesta Hludowici*, trans. R.C. Cusimano and J. Moorhead, *The Deeds of Louis the Fat* (Washington, DC, 1992), IX, p. 43; William of Malmesbury, *Historia Novella*, ed. and trans. K.R. Potter (London, 1955), I.457, p. 13.
90 *Historia Anglorum*, VIII (*De Contemptu Mundi*), p. 617; cf. Boethius, *Consolation of Philosophy*, I.4, p. 153: 'in order that the order and truth of the matter should not lie hidden for later generations, I have written it down to be remembered'; II.7, p. 219.

justifies his 'life' of Odo of Cluny by opening his narrative with an appeal to Ecclesiasticus (Sirach) 44:15 ('the people will tell of their wisdom and the Church will show forth their praise'), whilst works such as the *Golden Legend* provided a collection of such lives arranged according to the ecclesiastical calendar.[91] However, this practice could be extended to other individuals too. Widukind, for example, records the collective commemoration of Otto I's past deeds immediately prior to his funeral.[92] Sometimes such commemoration was given physical form: 'his deeds were recorded on lead tablets', Otto of Freising writes, 'and buried by his side'.[93] Its historiographical consequences are exemplified by the work of Thietmar of Merseburg, who assembled the necrology for his own church and whose *Chronicle* is accordingly characterised by its obituary notices of named individuals and, on occasion, the date of their death on which they were to be commemorated.[94] The result is a historical narrative which is punctuated with a series of intercessory prayers, for Otto I, Otto II and Otto III,[95] but also for Merseburg,[96] Lotharingia,[97] sinners[98] and, last but not least,

---

91 John of Salerno, *Life of Odo*, prol., p. 3; Jacobus de Voragine, *The Golden Legend*, trans. W.G. Ryan (Princeton, 1993); cf. Eadmer, *Life of Anselm*, ed. and trans. R.W. Southern (Oxford, 1972), I.30, p. 54, and, more generally, L. Arbusow, *Liturgie und Geschichtsschreibung im Mittelalter* (Bonn, 1951); R. Jonsson, *Historia: Études sur la Genèse des Offices Versifiés* (Stockholm, 1968); C. Hannick, 'Liturgie und Geschichtsschreibung', in A. Scharer and G. Scheibelreiter (eds), *Historiographie im frühen Mittelalter* (Vienna, 1994), pp. 179–85.
92 Widukind, *Res Gestae Saxonicae*, III.75, p. 234.
93 Otto of Freising, *Chronicon*, VII.20, p. 428. Compare, for example, the epitaph carved into the tombstone of Isarn, abbot of Saint-Victor, in Marseille (*La France Romane au Temps des Premiers Capétiens 987–1152*, exhibition catalogue, Éditions Musée du Louvre, Paris, 2005, p. 240).
94 For example, Thietmar, *Chronicon*, II.34, p. 117, IV.75, p. 203, VI.39, p. 264, VI.63, p. 281; cf. Liutprand of Cremona, *Antapodosis*, trans. F.A. Wright, *The Works of Liutprand of Cremona* (London, 1930), III.3, p. 111. For Thietmar's own date of birth, see *Chronicon*, III.6, p. 131.
95 Thietmar, *Chronicon*, II.45, pp. 124–5, III.25, p. 147, IV.49, p. 187, IV.53, p. 190; cf. Suger, *Gesta Hludowici*, prol., pp. 23–4; Galbert of Bruges, *The Murder of Charles the Good*, trans. J.B. Ross (New York, 1959), XIV, p. 117; William of Malmesbury, *Gesta Regum Anglorum*, I.56, p. 87.
96 *Chronicon*, VI.prol., p. 235, VI.21, p. 252.
97 *Chronicon*, IV.14, p. 161.
98 *Chronicon*, VI.41, p. 266, VII.21, p. 321.

for Thietmar himself.[99] This practice was also enshrined in the *Liber Pontificalis* or 'Book of Pontiffs', a collection of short notices of individual popes, which, in its emphasis on the recovery and defence of ecclesiastical rights, lands and privileges, proved an important literary model for works such as Paul the Deacon's *History of the Bishops of Metz* and Suger's *De Administratione*.[100]

Commemoration of an individual's name and actions in a written text had a still more profound scriptural resonance in the 'Book of Life' – an individual's deeds were 'written' in their remembrance by God and they would be recited on the Day of Judgment: 'and I saw the dead, small and great, stand before God; and the books were opened; and another book was opened, which is the Book of Life; and the dead were judged out of those things which were written in the books, according to their works' (Revelation 20:12). According to Odo of Cluny, Gerald of Aurillac had his life-story recited from a book prior to being granted entry into heaven.[101] According to Henry of Huntingdon, a book of good deeds and a book of bad deeds form the basis of heavenly judgment; according to Guibert of Nogent, the testimony of good deeds is what is weighed in the scales of that judgment.[102] 'Rendering an account' (*reddere rationem*) was thus applied both literally and figuratively by Richard FitzNigel in his *Dialogue of the Exchequer* 'when the books of all are opened and the doors shut'.[103] Thietmar's *Chronicle* again serves as a prime example

---

99 *Chronicon*, I.prol., p. 67, IV.61, p. 195, IV.75, pp. 203–4, V.1, p. 206, VI.43, p. 267, VI.72, p. 286, VIII.12, p. 369, VIII.16, p. 372; cf. *Encomium Emmae Reginae*, ed. and trans. A. Campbell (Cambridge, 1949), II.21, p. 37, II.24, p. 39 (for Cnut); Henry of Huntingdon, *Historia Anglorum*, VII.27, p. 459 (for his father), VIII, p. 497 (for himself); William of Tyre, *History of Deeds Done Beyond the Sea*, trans. E.A. Babcock and A.C. Krey (New York, 1941), prol., p. 59.

100 *Liber Pontificalis*, trans. R. Davis, *The Book of Pontiffs* (2nd edn, Liverpool, 2000); *The Lives of the Eighth-Century Popes*, trans. R. Davis (Liverpool, 1992); *The Lives of the Ninth-Century Popes*, trans. R. Davis (Liverpool, 1995); cf. R.H. Bautier, 'L'Historiographie en France aux Xe et XIe Siècles', *Settimane di Studio*, 17 (1970), pp. 809–15; Sot, 'Local and Institutional History', pp. 96–100.

101 Odo of Cluny, *Life of Gerald of Aurillac*, IV.5, p. 175.

102 Henry of Huntingdon, *Historia Anglorum*, IX.47, p. 683; Guibert of Nogent, *Monodiae*, trans. J.F. Benton, *Self and Society in Medieval France* (Toronto, 1984), III.19, p. 220; cf. Athanasius, *Life of Antony*, trans. C. White, in *Early Christian Lives* (Harmondsworth, 1998), LV, pp. 43–4, LXV, p. 49.

103 Richard FitzNigel, *Dialogus de Scaccario*, I.5, p. 39; cf. Paschasius Radbertus, *Epitaphium Arsenii*, I.21, p. 132.

of the correlation with historiography. 'Many deeds of our king and emperor', he writes of Henry I, 'are worthy enough to be remembered for ever but, because I cannot describe them as they occurred, sadly I must omit them.... I have written a small book concerning his great deeds but hope that his memory will be inscribed in the Book of Life'.[104] In heaven, Thietmar points out, the deeds of a righteous man 'have been inscribed upon a silver tablet',[105] but demons, too, are described as holding books in their hands, 'from which they gravely read out the deeds of a wicked man which have been inscribed there'.[106] Thietmar's own task in writing history is therefore analogous: 'with Christ, the blessed live on through their virtues but, in this world, they survive through writing. Hence it would not be good to remain silent regarding the excellent life of such a father; rather it should be described in the light of truth [*lux veritatis*] to the advantage of all'.[107] Otto of Freising stages an extensive discussion of this principle in action.[108] Conversely, names could, according to Psalm 69:28 and Revelation 3:5, be blotted from the Book of Life. Odo of Deuil goes as far as refusing to refer to Manuel Comnenus by name explicitly because 'his name is not written in the Book of Life'.[109]

Specifically Christian principles of commemoration had their secular equivalent within the classical historiographical tradition. Vergil describes how Minos, judge in the underworld, calls a court of the silent and learns of men's lives and misdeeds whilst, in the groves of the fortunate, Aeneas is shown the shades of those whose deeds have made them worthy of remembrance.[110] Liturgical commemoration, moreover, had its ceremonial roots in the *fasti*

---

104 Thietmar, *Chronicon*, I.28, p. 87.
105 *Chronicon*, VI.76, p. 288.
106 *Chronicon*, IV.72, p. 201.
107 *Chronicon*, VI.64, p. 281.
108 Otto of Freising, *Chronicle*, VIII.16, p. 475; cf. Liutprand, *Antapodosis*, III.22, p. 118: 'a man well worthy of praise and remembrance'.
109 Odo of Deuil, *De Profectione Ludovici VII in Orientem*, ed. and trans. V. Berry (New York, 1948), I, p. 11; cf. Paschasius Radbertus, *Vita Adalhardi*, trans. A. Cabaniss, in *Charlemagne's Cousins: Contemporary Lives of Adalard and Wala* (Syracuse, 1967), LIX, p. 61.
110 Vergil, *Aeneid*, VI.432–3, p. 537, VI.664, p. 553; cf. Walter Map, *De Nugis Curialium*, ed. and trans. M.L.R. James, rev. C.N.L. Brooke and R.A.B. Mynors (Oxford, 1983), V.7, pp. 507–9.

of ancient Rome – these provided a means of leaving to posterity an example of upright living and served as an encouragement to pursue eternal renown.[111] Pliny the Elder records how honours (*honores*) were inscribed underneath commemorative public statues so that an individual's achievements should be read not only on their tombs, whilst Valerius Maximus records how the Athenian council made a formal inquiry into what had been done by individual citizens 'so that men would follow moral worth memorious of the fact that they had to render an account [*reddere rationem*] of their lives'.[112] The corresponding legal penalty of *damnatio memoriae* was quoted, for example, by Rahewin as the punishment in Roman law for those who conspire against the emperor – not only would these individuals lose their lives but they would also have their memory branded with infamy.[113] The historiographical corollary was clear. Given the brevity of human life, Vergil considered it the function of virtue to extend fame by deeds (*sed famam extendere factis, hoc virtutis opus*), for which Turnus was a case in point – his *fama* was such that he would remain alive on the lips of men.[114] For his own part, therefore, Vergil appeals to the Muses, who have both memory and the power to commemorate.[115] It seemed to Tacitus, meanwhile, that 'a historian's foremost duty is to ensure that merit is recorded, and to confront evil deeds and words with the fear of posterity's denunciation'.[116] Or, as Valerius Maximus put it, 'a great and good part of the

---

111 *Accessus ad Auctores*, p. 29; cf. Polybius, *Histories*, trans. I. Scott-Kilvert (Harmondsworth, 1979), VI.53, pp. 346–7 (see also pages 510–11).
112 Pliny the Elder, *Natural History*, trans. H. Rackham, W. H. S. Jones and D. E. Eicholz (Loeb, 1938–63), XXXIV.9, pp. 139–41; Lucan, *Pharsalia*, VIII.806–7, p. 497; Valerius Maximus, *Facta et Dicta Memorabilia*, II.6, p. 167; cf. *Itinerarium Peregrinorum et Gesta Regis Ricardi*, trans. H.J. Nicholson, *The Chronicle of the Third Crusade* (Aldershot, 1997), prol., p. 21.
113 Rahewin, *The Deeds of Frederick Barbarossa*, trans. C.C. Mierow (New York, 1953), IV.43, p. 276, quoting Justinian, *Institutes*, ed. P. Krüger, trans. P. Birks and G. McLeod (London, 1987), IV.18.3, p. 145.
114 Vergil, *Aeneid*, X.468–9, p. 205, XII.235, p. 317.
115 *Aeneid*, VII.645, p. 47, IX.525–9, p. 151.
116 Tacitus, *Annals*, trans. J. Jackson (Loeb, 1931), III.65, p. 625; cf. T.J. Luce, 'Tacitus on "History's Highest Function" – *Praecipuum Munus Annalium*', *Aufstieg und Niedergang der römischen Welt*, II.33.4 (1991), pp. 2904–27; A.J. Woodman, '*Praecipuum Munus Annalium* – The Construction, Convention and Context of Tacitus, *Annals*, III.65.1', *Museum Helveticum*, 52 (1995), pp. 111–26; reprinted in A.J. Woodman, *Tacitus Reviewed* (Oxford, 1998), pp. 86–103.

glory of famous men is claimed by their impressive sayings or deeds which stubborn remembrance [*pertinax memoria*] includes in her immortal power'.[117]

It is a combination of biblical and classical imperatives, therefore, whose influence can be traced throughout the Middle Ages, from the lives 'Of Illustrious Men' (*De Viris Illustribus*) by Jerome and Gennadius in the fourth and fifth centuries all the way to works of the same title by Petrarch and Salutati in the fourteenth.[118] What this tradition also reveals, however, is the significance of the second essential function of demonstrative rhetoric: the purpose of an *encomium* is more than just praise, more than just honourable remembrance and commendation to the memory of posterity; it is also the inculcation of virtue in one's audience through their imitation of a good example. A corresponding purpose is served by the castigation of a wicked individual – as 'a memory of everlasting shamefulness',[119] but also an *exemplum* of vice to be avoided. An individual's character is formed or shaped by contemplation of what is good and what is wicked and it is therefore the aim of the orator to emend people's vices and correct their *mores*.[120] This is where the second function of demonstrative rhetoric comes into its own – it is designed to *move* rather than just to teach and to please. Vergil describes Turnus' concern to be worthy of his ancestors and how he inspires his men accordingly by instructing them to remember the great deeds of their ancestors for which they had been praised; Vergil also recounts how Pallas prevents his men from fleeing by invoking the brave deeds they have performed, the wars they have won and the hope of emulating his own praiseworthy father; and how Aeneas instructs his son

---

117 Valerius Maximus, *Facta et Dicta Memorabilia*, VI.4, p. 43.
118 Jerome (with continuation by Gennadius), *De Viris Illustribus*, trans. E.C. Richardson (Oxford, 1892), pp. 359–402; B.G. Kohl, 'Petrarch's Prefaces to *De Viris Illustribus*', *History and Theory*, 13 (1974), pp. 132–44; Coluccio Salutati, *Letters*, ed. F. Novati (Rome, 1891–1911), Ep.VII.11, pp. 289–302 (see also pages 482–6). For Clio as the embodiment of the connection between fame and the act of writing history ('cleos' translates as *gloria* in Latin), see Fulgentius, *Mythologies*, trans. L.G. Whitbread, in *Fulgentius the Mythographer* (Colombus, 1971), I.15, p. 56; Coluccio Salutati, *De Laboribus Herculis*, ed. B.L. Ullman (Zurich, 1951), I.9.10, p. 43, I.10.20, p. 52; cf. Bernardus Silvestris, *Commentary on the First Six Books of Virgil's Aeneid*, VI, pp. 37, 56.
119 Paschasius Radbertus, *Epitaphium Arsenii*, II.9, p. 164.
120 Quintilian, *Institutio Oratoria*, II.4.20, p. 235, XII.7.2, pp. 419–21.

to remember (*sis memor*) and to ensure that, in later years, as he recalls the *exempla* of his kinsmen, they will rouse his spirit.[121]

When viewed in terms of the effect which words will have on an audience, an example (*exemplum*) was generally acknowledged to constitute a better means of instruction than a precept. Sallust recorded this observation in the context of the didactic function served by wax images of one's ancestors, Valerius Maximus made it the underlying principle of his entire collection of *facta et dicta*, whilst Gregory the Great endorsed it at the opening of his *Dialogues* and, indeed, throughout the *Moralia in Job*: the lives of predecessors serve as a model for those who come afterwards.[122] By the twelfth century, the principle had become proverbial: 'people are better taught by example than by words' (*exemplo melius quam verbo quisque docetur*).[123] Abelard opened the 'consolatory' history of his own calamities with the observation that, when it comes to arousing or assuaging the emotions, *exempla* often have a greater capacity than words.[124] William of Malmesbury observed that *exempla* are better than words in his *Gesta Regum* and, when pairing precepts with examples in his *Life of Wulfstan*, he pointed out that 'nature has formed some people that, though they know both to be necessary, they are more inclined to listen to *exempla* than to exhortations'.[125] John of Salisbury stressed the utility of

---

121 Vergil, *Aeneid*, X.281–2, p. 192, X.369–71, p. 199, XII.649, p. 347, XII.439–40, p. 331; Walter of Châtillon, *Alexandreis*, trans. D. Townsend (Philadelphia, 1996), VI.413–21, p. 138.
122 Sallust, *Jugurthine War*, IV, pp. 137–9 (see also pages 44–5); Valerius Maximus, *Facta et Dicta Memorabilia*, IV.4, p. 387, V.6, p. 513; Gregory the Great, *Dialogues*, trans. O.J. Zimmerman (Washington, DC, 1959), I.1, p. 6; Gregory the Great, *XL Homiliae in Evangelia*, trans. D. Hurst, *Forty Gospel Homilies* (Kalamazoo, 1990), II.38, p. 351; Gregory the Great, *Moralia in Job*, trans. J. Bliss (Oxford, 1843–50), pref.2.4, pp. 16–17, XXIII.19.34, p. 29, XXV.7.15, pp. 104–5, XXV.7.17, pp. 106–7.
123 *Proverbia Sententiaeque Latinitatis Medii Aevi*, ed. H. Walther (Göttingen, 1963–67), I, p. 1067; cf. G. Simon, 'Untersuchungen zur Topik der Widmungsbriefe mittelalterlicher Geschichtsschreiber bis zum Ende des 12. Jahrhunderts', *Archiv für Diplomatik*, 5–6 (1959–60), pp. 103–5.
124 Abelard, *Historia Calamitatum*, trans. B. Radice, in *The Letters of Abelard and Heloise* (Harmondsworth, 1974), prol., p. 57; cf. C.S. Jaeger, 'The Prologue to the *Historia Calamitatum* and the "Authenticity Question"', *Euphorion*, 74 (1980), pp. 1–15; reprinted in C.S. Jaeger, *Scholars and Courtiers: Intellectuals and Society in the Medieval West* (Aldershot, 2002), pp. 2–5.
125 William of Malmesbury, *Gesta Regum Anglorum*, I.36, p. 55; William of Malmesbury, *Vita Wulfstani*, ed. and trans. M. Winterbottom and R.M. Thomson (Oxford, 2002), I.prol., p. 11.

his examples right from the start of the *Policraticus*, his didactic treatise on moral and immoral conduct in political and ecclesiastical office.[126] Indeed, when Gerald of Wales completed his book *On the Instruction of Rulers*, he made the logical step of dividing it into two discrete sections – book I took the form of a collection of moral precepts 'established by the testimonies of Christian and pagan writers', whereas books II and III taught the same principles but by means of the *exempla* presented by Henry II and his sons.[127] In his narrative of the conquest of Ireland, moreover, Gerald pointed out the utility of describing an *un*successful precedent: 'although it cannot be a remedy [*medela*] for what has happened in the past, it may still serve as a warning [*cautela*] for the future'.[128] It is expedient, Gerald continues, to understand what should be avoided by looking at others' evils, since the castigation which earlier *exempla* offer by way of instruction does not actually harm us in person.[129] Gervase of Canterbury drove the point home. Of the three categories into which moral instruction was conventionally divided – prohibition, precept and example – *exempla* are effective on people whose moral weakness has left them unmoved by either precept or prohibition. 'There are many people', he writes, 'whose minds are more easily inclined to

---

126 John of Salisbury, *Policraticus*, trans. J.B. Pike, *The Frivolities of Courtiers and the Footprints of Philosophers* (Minneapolis, 1938), prol., pp. 6–7; cf. Macrobius, *Saturnalia*, VII.1.21, p. 444.
127 Gerald of Wales, *De Eruditione Principum*, trans. J. Stevenson (London, 1858; reprinted Felinfach, 1991), I.pref., p. 8; cf. Hugh of St Victor, *Didascalicon*, V.7, p. 128. Compare Gerald's opening remarks in his *Gemma Ecclesiastica*, trans. J.J. Hagen, *The Jewel of the Church* (Leiden, 1979), pref., p. 3: 'This instruction has two approaches, one of precept, the other of example. As Jerome tells us, "long is the road that leads by precept, short and convenient is that which leads by example".... I have inserted examples at apposite places in the course of the doctrinal instruction in order that in reading you may gain learning from the latter and from the former derive consolation and inspiration to imitate a praiseworthy life'; cf. R. Bartlett, *Gerald of Wales, 1146–1223* (Oxford, 1982), pp. 69–100; F. Lachaud, 'Le *Liber de Principis Instructione* de Giraud de Barry', in F. Lachaud and L. Scordia (eds), *Le Prince au Miroir de la Literature Politique de l'Antiquité aux Lumières* (Rouen, 2006), pp. 113–42.
128 Gerald of Wales, *Expugnatio Hibernica*, II.35, pp. 235–7.
129 *Expugnatio Hibernica*, II.39, p. 251. Gerald quotes for good measure: 'the ruin of predecessors instructs their successors, and a mistake made in former times serves as a perpetual warning'. See Ennodius, *Vita Epiphani*, ed. W. Hartel (Vienna, 1882), p. 364; cf. Gerald of Wales, *Descriptio Cambriae*, II.9, p. 272; Walter Map, *De Nugis Curialium*, IV.3, p. 299.

avoiding evil, or doing good, by examples rather than by prohibitions or precepts'.[130] The same conclusion continued to be drawn in the thirteenth century, by Bonaventure and by Aquinas,[131] and in particular with regard to the intellectual capacity of the laity: 'reasoning by example avails much with lay people who are pleased with examples'.[132]

As a means of moral instruction that was better suited to the needs and capabilities of weaker, or less committed, audiences, the narrative of deeds served a vital didactic function. The consequences for the relationship of rhetoric to the writing of history were clear. According to Quintilian, *exempla* are more effective than what is taught by particular disciplines because, whereas a teacher issues commands, an orator simply sets something out and an audience is able to understand it without direct guidance.[133] This is why

---

130 Gervase of Canterbury, *Chronica*, ed. W. Stubbs, in *Opera Historica* (London 1879), ingressus ad prol., pp. 84–7; cf. Gransden, 'Prologues', pp. 65–6. For this tripartite categorisation, see, for example, Abelard, *Commentary on Paul's Letter to the Romans*, trans. A.J. Minnis and A.B. Scott, in A.J. Minnis and A.B. Scott (eds), *Medieval Literary Theory and Criticism c.1100–c.1375* (Oxford, 1988), pp. 100–1.
131 Aquinas, *Summa Theologiae*, ed. and trans. T. Gilby, *et al.* (Blackfriars edn, London, 1964–80), IaIIae 34.1, p. 67: 'in matters of human activity and passion, where experience counts for so much, example carries more weight than words' (*magis movent exempla quam verba*); Bonaventure, *Breviloquium*, trans. E.E. Nemmers (London, 1946), prol., pp. 7, 15.
132 Robert of Basevorn, *Forma Praedicandi*, trans. L. Kruhl, *The Form of Preaching*, in J.J. Murphy (ed.), *Three Medieval Rhetorical Arts* (Berkeley, 1971), XXXIX, pp. 182, XLIX, p. 205. For *exempla* in general, see C. Bremond, J. Le Goff and J.-C. Schmitt, *L'Exemplum* (2nd edn, Typologie des Sources 40, Turnhout, 1996); A. Vitale-Brovarone, 'Persuasione e Narrazione – L'*Exemplum* Tra Due Retoriche (VI–XII Sec.)', *Rhétorique et Histoire: L'Exemplum et le Modèle de Comportement dans le Discourse Antique et Médiéval. Mélanges de l'École Française de Rome*, 92 (1980), pp. 87–112; J. Berlioz and M. Polo de Beaulieu (eds), *Les Exempla Médiévaux: Nouvelles Perspectives* (Paris, 1998); cf. K. Stierle, 'L'Histoire Comme Exemple, l'Exemple Comme Histoire', *Poétique*, 10 (1972), pp. 176–98; P. von Moos, *Geschichte als Topik – das rhetorische Exemplum von der Antike zur Neuzeit und die historiae im Policraticus Johanns von Salisbury* (Hildesheim, 1988); P. von Moos, 'Das argumentative Exemplum und die "wächserne Nase" der Autorität im Mittelalter', in W.J. Aerts and M. Gosman (eds), *Exemplum et Similitudo: Alexander the Great and Other Heroes as Points of Reference in Medieval Literature* (Groningen, 1988), pp. 55–84.
133 Quintilian, *Institutio Oratoria*, X.1.15, p. 11; cf. Salutati, *Letters*, Ep.VII.11, p. 292 (see also page 485), who gives the example of Frontinus – rather than relying on precepts and rules, he placed what he was teaching before the eyes of his readers by means of infinite examples or 'strategemata', thereby confirming it as if with the strongest reasoning.

Quintilian concludes that, even if orators should be learned in all branches of knowledge, even if they should know all about dialectic, ethics and natural philosophy, it is also, and perhaps still more, important for them to know and constantly reflect upon the distinguished sayings and deeds (*dicta ac facta*) which have been handed down from antiquity. And nowhere, he points out, is there a greater number or quality of *exempla* for these 'sayings and deeds' than in the memorials (*monumenta*) of Rome. The Greeks may prevail in terms of their precepts (*praecepta*), but the Romans are superior in terms of their *exempla* and it is the latter which, in Quintilian's eyes, mark the greater achievement. Wisdom, justice, temperance and fortitude, he concludes, are all best taught, not by precept, but by the historical examples of Fabricius, Curius, Regulus, Decius and many others.[134] The *Disticha Catonis* (a late-antique manual of moral advice, in verse, erroneously attributed to Cato the Elder) put the point more pithily still: 'the lives of others are our teachers' (*aliena vita est nobis magistra*).[135] This is the maxim which was quoted, for example, by John of Salisbury in the prologue to his *Historia Pontificalis*, where it is followed up with an even more trenchant observation. 'Whoever is ignorant of the past', John writes, 'rushes blindly into the future.... Nothing after the grace and law of God teaches the living more correctly and more forcefully than if they learn from the deeds of the dead'.[136] The twelfth-century digest entitled the *Moralium Dogma Philosophorum* quoted Seneca to make the same point: 'we should follow in the footsteps of our ancestors,

---

134 *Institutio Oratoria*, XII.2.29–30, p. 399; cf. Sallust, *Catiline*, VIII, pp. 15–17 (see page 44); Valerius Maximus, *Facta et Dicta Memorabilia*, IV.3, p. 373, IV.3, p. 371, VI.3, pp. 35–7, I.1, pp. 27–29, IV.4, pp. 389–91, V.6, p. 517; Otto of Freising, *Chronicle*, II.19, p. 175.
135 *Disticha Catonis*, ed. M. Boas, rev. H.J. Botschuyver (Amsterdam, 1952), III.13, pp. 168–9: *multorum disce exemplo quae facta sequaris, quae fugias, vita est nobis aliena magistra*; cf. Terence, *Adelphoe*, trans. J. Sargeaunt, *The Brothers* (Loeb, 1912), lines 414–16, p. 261: *denique inspicere tamquam in speculum in vitas omnium iubeo atque ex aliis sumere exemplum sibi*; Horace, *Satires*, trans. H.R. Fairclough (Loeb, 1929), I.4 lines 105–21, pp. 57–9; cf. Bernardus Silvestris, *Commentary on the First Six Books of Virgil's Aeneid*, VI, pp. 79–80. For dissemination of the *Disticha Catonis*, see Boas, pp. vii–lxxxiv; T. Hunt, *Teaching and Learning Latin in Thirteenth-Century England* (Cambridge, 1991), vol. I, pp. 66–79.
136 John of Salisbury, *Historia Pontificalis*, prol., p. 3; cf. P. von Moos, 'The Use of *Exempla* in the *Policraticus* of John of Salisbury', in M. Wilks (ed.), *The World of John of Salisbury* (Oxford, 1984), pp. 207–61.

choosing the morally virtuous individual and having him constantly before our eyes [*ante oculos*] so that everything that we do is done, as it were, in his sight'.[137]

Two functions, in short, lie at the heart of demonstrative rhetoric. First, there is praise of virtue, which is established through a depiction of character and a narrative of deeds – these provide the means by which a remembrance of moral worth will be handed down to posterity. In doing so, however, a second goal is created – to stimulate the imitation of this virtue, or of these virtuous actions, on the part of one's readership or audience. The two functions are not mutually exclusive. On the contrary, the nature of their interdependence is underlined in the prologues to many medieval *vitae* and *gesta*. Take, for example, Sulpicius Severus' *Life of Martin of Tours*, a fifth-century work which became one of the most influential accounts of a saint's life in the Middle Ages. Sulpicius opens his hagiography by expressing his profound reservations over the concern shown by classical writers with the immortality of fame, contrasting it with a Christian's concentration on the immortality of a blessed and eternal life, for which such concern is irrelevant. 'Many mortals', he writes, 'vainly devoted to study and worldly acclaim, have sought to immortalise their reputation, or so they believed, by using their pen to give an account of the lives of famous men'.[138] By the same token, however, Sulpicius also acknowledges that this practice did have some benefits: 'although this did not bring them everlasting fame, the hope they had conceived did, however, bear some small fruit because they prolonged their memory, although in vain, and by presenting the examples of great men they stimulated in their readers a considerable desire to emulate these people'.[139] He also accepts that such a practice might be too well-entrenched to be ignored altogether: 'this human error, handed down through literature, has become so prevalent that it has clearly found many

---

137 *Moralium Dogma Philosophorum*, ed. J. Holmberg, *Das Moralium Dogma Philosophorum des Guillaume de Conches, lateinisch, altfranzösisch und mittelniederfränkisch* (Uppsala, 1939), pp. 26–7; Seneca, *Letters*, Ep.11.8, pp. 63–5.
138 Cf. Boethius, *Consolation of Philosophy*, II.7, p. 223: 'what little fame is left to them, just their empty name in writing. And if we read and learn their glorious names, do we then know the dead?'
139 Sulpicius Severus, *Life of Martin of Tours*, trans. C. White, in *Early Christian Lives* (Harmondsworth, 1998), praef.I.1–2, p. 135.

who wish to emulate this vain philosophy or this foolish heroism. For these reasons, I think it would be useful if I were to write a detailed record of the life of this most saintly man as an example to others in the future. It would serve to rouse the enthusiasm of its readers for true wisdom, for heavenly service and for divine heroism. In doing so, we will also be pursuing our own advantage in such a way that we may expect, not empty renown from our fellow men, but an everlasting reward from God. For even if we ourselves have not lived in such a way as to be an example to others, we have at least made an effort to prevent a man who deserves to be imitated from remaining unknown. I shall therefore undertake to write the life of St Martin'.[140]

Sulpicius Severus' *Life of Martin*, and the preface with which it was introduced, served as a model for many subsequent *vitae*. It was well known in the ninth century, for example, when, in an account of the 'transfer' of the relics of two saints from Rome to Francia, Einhard provided a cogent summary of Sulpicius' preface, including a clarification of the precise nature of authorial motivation. 'Those who have set down in writing and recorded the lives and deeds of the just', Einhard writes, 'and of people living according to divine commands, seem to me to have wanted to accomplish nothing other than to inspire by means of examples of this sort the spirits of all people to emend their evil ways and to sing the praises of God's omnipotence.... Since their praiseworthy intention was so obviously to accomplish nothing other than those I described, I do not see why it should not be imitated by many others'.[141] More significant still was Einhard's subsequent decision to use this principle as the basis for setting out the *vita*, not of a saint, but of a temporal ruler. The result was his 'life' of Charlemagne, a work which has been called 'the first secular biography of the middle ages'.[142] In an elaborate prologue to this work, Einhard sets out exactly why he thought he should write it and, in the process, offers a subtle adaptation of Sulpicius

---

140 *Life of Martin*, praef.I.5–7, pp. 135–6.
141 Einhard, *Translatio et Miracula Marcellini et Petri*, trans. P.E. Dutton, in *Charlemagne's Courtier* (Ontario, 1998), pref., p. 69.
142 J.M. Wallace-Hadrill, 'The Franks and the English in the Ninth Century – Some Common Historical Interests', in J.M. Wallace-Hadrill, *Early Medieval History* (Oxford, 1975), p. 204.

Severus' preface for the purposes of recording the life of a king. His justification is worth citing at length:

> After I decided to describe the life and character, and many of the accomplishments, of my lord and foster father, Charles, that most outstanding and deservedly famous king, and seeing how immense this work was, I have expressed it in as concise a form as I could manage. But I have attempted not to omit any of the facts that have come to my attention, and not to irritate those who are excessively critical by supplying a long-winded account of everything new. Perhaps, in this way, it will be possible to avoid angering with a new book those who criticise the old masterpieces composed by the most learned and eloquent of men. And yet I am quite sure that there are many people devoted to contemplation and learning who do not believe that the circumstances of the present age should be neglected or that virtually everything that happens these days is not worth remembering and should be condemned to utter silence and oblivion. Some people are so seduced by their love of the distant past that they would rather insert the famous deeds of other peoples in their various compositions than deny posterity any notion of their own names by writing nothing. Still, I did not see why I should refuse to take up a composition of this sort since I was aware that no one could write about these things more truthfully than me, since I myself was present and personally witnessed them, as they say, with the trustworthiness of sight. I was, moreover, not sure that these things would be recorded by anyone else. I thought it would be better to write these things down, along with other widely known details, for the sake of posterity than to allow the splendid life of this most excellent king, the greatest of all the men in his time, and his remarkable deeds, which people now alive can scarcely imitate, to be swallowed up by the shadows of forgetfulness.... Could I keep silent about the splendid and exceedingly brilliant deeds of a man who had been so kind to me, and could I allow his life to remain without record and due praise as if he had never lived? But to write an account what was required was Ciceronian eloquence, not my feeble talent which is poor and small, indeed almost non-existent.[143]

---

143 Einhard, *Vita Karoli*, trans. P.E. Dutton, *Charlemagne's Courtier* (Ontario, 1998), praef., pp. 15–16; cf. H. Beumann, 'Topos und Gedankengefüge bei Einhard', *Archiv für Kulturgeschichte*, 33 (1951), pp. 337–50; H. Beumann, *Ideengeschichtliche Studien zu Einhard und anderen Geschichtsschreibern des früheren Mittelalters* (Darmstadt, 1962), pp. 1–14; D. Ganz, 'The Preface to Einhard's *Vita Karoli*', in H. Schefers (ed.), *Einhard: Studien zu Leben und Werk* (Darmstadt, 1997), pp. 299–310; D. Ganz, 'Einhard's Charlemagne – The Characterization of

The influence of Einhard's *Vita Karoli* on subsequent medieval historiography can be gauged from the remarkable number of surviving manuscripts. Its impact can be traced in the eleventh century, for example, on Wipo's *Deeds of Conrad*, not least in the recapitulation of many of the key components from its prologue – the fear of forgetfulness, the incitement to imitate virtue, the importance of fame and glory, and the need to commemorate moral virtue for the benefit of posterity.[144] Addressing his work to Conrad's son, the emperor Henry III, at some time between 1039 and 1047, Wipo includes a dedicatory letter which spells out his motives for writing. Wipo's other works, the *Proverbia* and *Tetralogus*, both of them written in verse, were intended to instruct Henry III and the *Deeds of Conrad* are clearly designed to follow suit: 'I have thought it fitting, Lord Emperor, to write the illustrious life and the glorious deeds of the Emperor Conrad, your father, lest the light hide under a bushel, lest the ray of the sun be hidden in a cloud, lest memorable valour be overcast by the rust of oblivion.... To you, most exalted Emperor, I dedicate this work, to you I represent the deeds of your father, so that as often as you consider doing very distinguished things, you will picture to yourself first, as in a mirror [*in speculo*], the valorous deeds of your father'.[145] Wipo expands his didactic purpose still further in the prologue proper:

> Because a more useful example is wont to render the spirit of one who imitates it the more ready and strong in action, I have thought it apt and fitting to connect with chains of letters the fleeting memory of passing affairs, in particular not to pass over the merits of the Christian Empire in sluggish silence, not only so that from this a certain glory may endure through the perpetuation of their memory for those who administered the Empire well in this life, but also so that a design of right living may be at hand for coming

---

Greatness', in J. Story (ed.), *Charlemagne: Empire and Society* (Manchester, 2005), pp. 38–51.
144 Wipo, *Deeds of Conrad*, trans. T.E. Mommsen and K.F. Morrison, in *Imperial Lives and Letters of the Eleventh Century* (New York, 1962; rev. edn 2000); cf. S. Bagge, *Kings, Politics and the Right Order of the World in German Historiography c.950–1150* (Leiden, 2002), ch. 3. For the direct comparison to Charlemagne, see *Deeds of Conrad*, III, p. 66, VI, p. 72.
145 *Deeds of Conrad*, Ep.ded., pp. 52–3; cf. Gerald of Wales, *Expugnatio Hibernica*, prol., p. 23. For the image of the mirror, see page 168.

generations if they wish to emulate their forebears.... For thus the good are incited to virtue, but the evil are set aright through a censure which commands respect. This, then, is the end of writing, which no religion forbids and intent commands, and which will benefit the country; and something said well is of advantage to posterity. What passes is manifest; whatever is to come, however, is not known beforehand. Led on by this motive and by this hope, I have wished to write for the common use of readers something which would be pleasing to hearers. For if something deserving of respect be transmitted here, the reader will be able to imitate it openly.... These things I have set forth by way of preface; now I shall come to the deeds of the Emperor.[146]

The twin principles of commemoration and instruction which informed the writing of the life, character and deeds of one particular individual could also be applied to the writing of histories with a still broader scope. Perhaps the most famous and, again, one of the most influential was Bede's *Ecclesiastical History of the English People*, completed in 731 and a work whose prologue, once again, explains the didactic purpose behind its composition. Dedicating his work to Ceolwulf, king of Northumbria, Bede writes as follows:

> I gladly acknowledge the unfeigned enthusiasm with which, not content merely to lend an attentive ear to hear the words of Holy Scripture, you devote yourself to learn the deeds and sayings [*gestis sive dictis*] of the men of old, and more especially the famous men of our own race. For if history relates good things of good men, the solicitous listener is spurred on to imitate the good; and if it records evil things of wicked men, the devout and pious listener or reader is nonetheless kindled, by avoiding what is harmful and perverse, to pursue with greater solicitude himself those things which he has learned are good and worthy in the sight of God. This you perceive, clear-sighted as you are; and therefore, in your zeal for the spiritual well-being of us all, you wish to see my history more widely known, for the instruction of yourself and those over whom divine authority has appointed you to rule.[147]

---

146 *Deeds of Conrad*, prol., pp. 53–6.
147 Bede, *Historia Ecclesiastica Gentis Anglorum*, trans. B. Colgrave, rev. J. McClure and R. Collins, *The Ecclesiastical History of the English People* (Oxford, 1994), pref., p. 3; cf. Ralph de Diceto, *Abbreviationes Chronicorum*, p. 29.

This was the same approach summarised by William of Malmesbury, some five centuries later, in the dedicatory letter to his own *Deeds of the English Kings*: 'in the past, books of this kind were written for kings or queens in order to provide them with an *exemplum* for their lives so that they could be instructed to follow successes, avoid miseries, imitate wisdom and despise stupidity'.[148] For outstanding individuals (William's dedicatee, in this instance, was Robert of Gloucester, illegitimate son of Henry I), such a work will serve 'as a mirror' (*quasi e speculo*).[149] The writing of history, in short, was an aspect of ethical writing tailored to the life of virtue (*ad bene vivendum*); because of the pleasure it brings (by 'seasoning' moral conduct with a pleasing knowledge of deeds), it stimulates its readers, by means of *exempla*, to pursue good things and be wary of the bad.[150]

The same principles could also work in reverse. *The Ruin of Britain* was composed by Gildas in *c*.540 in accordance with the principles of demonstrative rhetoric but, in this case, the form followed was a castigation of vice, as the sins of British rulers are blamed for the calamities which were befalling their respective kingdoms.[151] Gildas opens his prologue, as Josephus had done, by stating that he is weeping rather than declaiming: 'In this letter I shall deplore rather than denounce; my style may be worthless but my intentions are kindly. What I deplore with mournful complaint is a general loss of good, a heaping-up of bad'.[152] However, although his work will therefore be a 'tearful history' (*flebilis historia*), it will also be, not a discussion (*disceptatio*),

---

148 William of Malmesbury, *Gesta Regum Anglorum*, Ep.ded., pp. 7–9.
149 *Gesta Regum Anglorum*, Ep.ded., p. 11; cf. William of Malmesbury, *Vita Wulfstani*, I.prol., p. 11.
150 *Gesta Regum Anglorum*, II.prol., p. 151.
151 Gildas, *De Excidio Britanniae*, ed. and trans. M. Winterbottom, *The Ruin of Britain* (Chichester, 1978). For the rhetorical sophistication of both the language and the structure of this work, see M. Lapidge, 'Gildas's Education and the Latin Culture of Sub-Roman Britain', in M. Lapidge and D. Dumville (eds), *Gildas: New Approaches* (Woodbridge, 1984), pp. 27–50, especially pp. 43–6. More generally, see B. Croke, 'Latin Historiography and the Barbarian Kingdoms', in G. Marasco (ed.), *Greek and Roman Historiography in Late Antiquity* (Brill, 2003), pp. 375–81.
152 *De Excidio Britanniae*, pref., p. 13; cf. Ralph de Diceto, *Abbreviationes Chronicorum*, p. 22: *Gilda Britonum gesta flebili sermone descripsit*. For tearful lamentation, see Boethius, *Consolation of Philosophy*, I.1, pp. 131–2. See also pages 198, 215.

but a rebuke (*increpatio*).[153] Indeed, Gildas questions the utility of tears which merely anoint a wound when what the enemies of God really require is cauterisation and public fire.[154] His work, he states, will be a denunciation in the manner of an Old Testament prophet – like Isaiah and, above all, Jeremiah – inveighing against a foolish people and their stiff-necked kings.[155] For Gildas, the Old Testament is, in this respect, a mirror. Britain is a modern-day Israel, wandering sinful in the trackless desert, and it is his responsibility to denounce the sins and crimes of the House of Jacob.[156] Gildas accordingly describes how he had reflected on the book of Lamentations in the Old Testament and on the wailing and gnashing of teeth in the New, but, by 'stoning the clergy with his accusations', he points out that this catalogue of evils is not only a complaint (*querula*) but also an admonition and a warning.[157] He writes:

> This and much more besides that I have decided to leave out in the interests of brevity, I frequently pondered, my mind bewildered, my heart remorseful. For when they strayed from the right track, the Lord did not spare a people that was peculiarly His own among all nations, a royal stock, a holy race, to whom He had said 'Israel is my first-born son' [Exodus 4:22], or its priests, prophets and kings, over so many centuries the apostle, minister and members of that primitive church. What then will He do with this great black blot on our generation? It has heinous and appalling sins in common with all the wicked ones of the world, but, over and above that, it has, as though inborn in it, a load of ignorance and folly that cannot be erased or avoided.[158]

The bulk of Gildas' 'history' is thus an extended citation of prophetic passages from the Old Testament which spell out the dire consequences of sinful and tyrannical conduct on the part of temporal rulers, as well as by those 'false prophets' in authority

---

153 *De Excidio Britanniae*, pref, p. 13, XXVI, p. 29, XXXVII, p. 36. For the comparison with Cicero, *Pro Sestio*, trans. R. Gardner (Loeb, 1958), see Lapidge, 'Gildas's Education', pp. 42–4.
154 *De Excidio Britanniae*, CVIII, p. 77.
155 *De Excidio Britanniae*, XLIII–XLVI, pp. 40–2, XLVII–L, pp. 42–5.
156 *De Excidio Britanniae*, XXI, p. 25, XXVI, p. 28.
157 *De Excidio Britanniae*, pref., p. 13, XXXVII, p. 36, XLVII–XLIX, p. 43, LV, p. 47, LXIV–LXV, pp. 51–2.
158 *De Excidio Britanniae*, pref., p. 15.

within the Church who fail to observe the New Testament injunctions which were laid upon them at their ordination.[159] Gildas accordingly enumerates the sins both of those who held temporal power and of those who exercised authority within the Church – in each case, those given the responsibility of office have betrayed the trust invested in them. In doing so, Gildas' purpose is also to remind his audience of the punishments which will attend the catalogue of sins and sinful actions which he has listed. This is the explicit didactic function of his work. It was when the remembrance (*memoria*) of earlier chastisement by God was replaced by ignorance, he points out, that truth and justice were overthrown, leaving no trace (*vestigium*), not even a memorial (*monumentum*), in the minds of kings and clergy, with the exception of a very few.[160] This remembrance was the remedy which had been lacking and which his own work was needed to supply.

If praise of virtue and castigation of vice provided the core of demonstrative rhetoric, their impact on the writing of history could appear separately or in tandem. In the sixth century, Gregory of Tours clearly felt it necessary to justify the particular combination of good and evil which was contained in his *Histories* and he did so on the grounds that mixing calamities and wicked deeds with the lives of the saints had a precedent in both Eusebius and indeed in Scripture itself.[161] Bede made the same sort of combination germane to his entire conception of the didactic function of what he was writing.[162] By the early eleventh century, Thietmar of Merseburg seemingly took the juxtaposition for granted – his own historiography would provide commemorative praise of the dead for the instruction and edification of the living, but it would also serve as 'a terrifying admonition to the pious'.[163] Thietmar, like Gildas, saw invasion and 'rule by foreigners', prefigured by the Old Testament, as a scourge (*plaga*) which could be inflicted by God on a sinful people. It was therefore a punishment

---

159 For false prophets in Gregory of Tours, see his *Histories*, trans. L. Thorpe, *The History of the Franks* (Harmondsworth, 1974), IX.6, pp. 486–7, X.25, pp. 584–6.
160 Gildas, *De Excidio Britanniae*, XXVI, p. 28.
161 Gregory of Tours, *Histories*, II.prol., p. 103 (see also page 75).
162 See page 160.
163 Thietmar, *Chronicon*, I.24, p. 85, VI.9, p. 244, VI.17, p. 249. For the age of gold, see *Chronicon*, II.45, p. 124, quoting Horace, *Epodes*, trans. N.Rudd (Loeb, 2004), XVI.63–66, p. 311; *Chronicon*, III.14, p. 138, quoting Lamentations 4:1.

explicitly invoked in the prologue to his *Chronicon*: 'Christ, glory of kings and moderator of governments, grant to your kingdom and those subject to it that the glory of praise may be to you and not to us, and that your flock may never fall under foreign rule. O you Christians, pray now with the voice of your hearts. May the majesty of the Lord mercifully grant that evil not bind and distress us as we much deserve'.[164] Thietmar's, too, was a sinful generation which had been corrupted from an age of gold and which therefore stood under the imminent threat of chastisement. It took a work of history, however, to spell it out: 'the anger of heaven is revealed but it takes a watchful eye to detect it'.[165]

By the twelfth century, the demonstrative combination of commemoration and instruction but also denunciation and admonition had become a staple feature of medieval historiography. According to Henry of Huntingdon, it was a 'true law of history' (*vera lex historiae*) to follow Moses' example and write of vices as well as virtues.[166] Henry used the very first paragraph of the prologue to his *History of the English* (a work which drew explicitly upon both Bede and Gildas) to emphasise the superiority of history to philosophy as a vehicle for such moral teaching and, in particular, for instruction in the four cardinal virtues and their corresponding vices. 'Homer', he writes, 'showed as clearly as in a mirror [*speculum*] the prudence of Ulysses, the fortitude of Agamemnon, the temperance of Nestor, the justice of Menelaus, and on the other hand, the imprudence of Ajax, the feebleness of Priam, the intemperateness of Achilles, the injustice of Paris, and in his narrative he discussed what is right and proper, and their contraries, more clearly and more agreeably than the philosophers'.[167]

Tracing the influence of demonstrative rhetoric on medieval historiography would therefore seem to present, on this reckoning, a pretty straightforward picture of commemoration and moral didacticism. The purpose of *encomia* and *castigationes* (or

---

[164] *Chronicon*, I.prol., pp. 66–7; cf. Bagge, *Kings, Politics and the Right Order of the World*, ch. 2. For Thietmar's correspondingly negative portrayals of Boleslav Chobry and Vladimir of Kiev, see *Chronicon*, V.23, p. 221, VI.12, p. 245, VII.72, pp. 357–8, VIII.2, p. 362.
[165] *Chronicon*, VIII.29, p. 382.
[166] Henry of Huntingdon, *Historia Anglorum*, VII.36, p. 473. For this phrase, see also pages 289–90.
[167] *Historia Anglorum*, prol., p. 3.

vituperationes) was to allocate praise and blame respectively; they combine a description of character and a narrative of deeds in order to reveal virtues and vices. In the first instance, this combination is designed to ensure that remembrance (*memoria*) or reputation (*fama*) can be handed down to posterity and, in the second instance, to provide an example (*exemplum*) of good and bad conduct which can be imitated or avoided by their audience. There is more to the influence of demonstrative rhetoric, however, than this summary of its two basic functions might suggest. Both the rhetoric and, by extension, the historiography it produces are more complex and, as a result, more interesting than they might, at first sight, appear.

Praise should not, for example, be fantastical. Snorri Sturluson pointed out that 'it is the habit of poets to give the highest praise to those princes in whose presence they are, but no one would have dared to tell them to their faces about deeds which everyone who listened, as well as the prince himself, knew were only falsehoods and fabrications – that would have been mockery, not praise'.[168] Nor did praise mean unalloyed flattery. There is criticism built into demonstrative rhetoric, not least for the sake of variety. According to Cicero, even the greatest praise and admiration has to possess some shadow or relief in order to make what is highlighted stand out all the more prominently.[169] Bede makes the same point, for instance, with reference to Aidan, the bishop of Lindisfarne whose preaching and pastoral care made him a model of episcopal virtue but whose computistical error over the 'Irish' dating of Easter left him open to criticism. 'I have written these things about the character and work of Aidan', Bede states, 'not by any means commending or praising his lack of knowledge in the matter of the observance of Easter ... but, as a truthful historian [*verax historicus*], I have described in a straightforward manner those things which were done by him or through him, praising such of his qualities as are worthy of praise and preserving their memory for the benefit of my readers'.[170] Einhard

---

168 Snorri Sturluson, *Heimskringla*, trans. L.M.Hollander (Austin, 1964), pref., p. 4.
169 Cicero, *De Oratore*, III.25–26.100–1, p. 81.
170 Bede, *Historia Ecclesiastica*, III.17, p. 137. For Bede's account of Aidan and Cuthbert as part of his wider agenda of pastoral reform in the Church,

includes comparable 'shadows' in his account of Charlemagne – he reports criticism of the king's indiscriminate hospitality towards strangers (complaints, he remarks, which were 'not unmerited') and describes a physique which certainly fell short of the ideal (Charlemagne's voice did not correspond to his robust physique, his neck was short and thick, his stomach a little round).[171]

Praise involves comparison but this can be implicit rather than explicit. Indeed, according to the *Rhetorica ad Herennium*, it is actually a fault in making a comparison to think it necessary to castigate one thing when praising another.[172] This was a point which was made expertly, if obliquely, by Einhard. In commemorating the deeds of Charlemagne during the reign of his son, Einhard was inviting his audience to draw a comparison with Louis the Pious – there is thus a barb to his observation that Charlemagne's actions were 'scarcely capable of imitation' (*vix imitabiles actus*).[173] Paschasius Radbertus, too, was well aware of the potential consequences of such comparison but, in his case, he makes the point explicit: 'because ... people think they are disparaged when they hear others praised, there now exists no place to speak about good men'; 'if therefore we praise [Wala], they think that they are themselves reproved'.[174] Wipo appeals to the same principle in addressing his *Deeds of Conrad* to the emperor's son when, having already pointed out that Henry III should look at the deeds of his father 'as in a mirror', he follows it with a sharp Sallustian observation. 'It often comes to pass,' he writes, 'that shamefacedness and perturbation of the mind on the part of descendants is borne easily from praise of their ancestors if, although they have praised their deeds with repute as their teacher, they have not at least equalled them; for just as valour ennobles many common men, so nobility without valiant deeds degrades many from their

---

see A. Thacker, 'Bede's Ideal of Reform', in P. Wormald, D. Bullough and R. Collins (eds), *Ideal and Reality in Frankish and Anglo-Saxon Society* (Oxford, 1983), pp. 130–53.
171 Einhard, *Vita Karoli*, XXI–XXII, p. 30.
172 *Rhetorica ad Herennium*, II.28.45, p. 139; cf. Geoffrey of Vinsauf, *Poetria Nova*, ed. and trans. E. Gallo, *The Poetria Nova and Its Sources in Early Rhetorical Doctrine* (The Hague, 1971), lines 241–63, pp. 27–9.
173 Einhard, *Vita Karoli*, praef., p. 15 (see also page 250).
174 Paschasius Radbertus, *Epitaphium Arsenii*, I.21, pp. 131, 134.

noble estate'.[175] Wipo makes the point twice more in the main body of his text, on both occasions with words put into the mouth of Conrad himself: 'it ill behoves us to extol with empty words..., our ancestors preferred to advance their glory with deeds rather than with pronouncements'; 'it seems to me more upright to do what I ought, rather than hear from another what should be done ... I remember you have said often that, not the hearers of the law, but the doers are made just [Romans 2:13]'.[176] The result, in Wipo's case, is a tightly constructed history with a very specific didactic purpose, passing rapidly over a condensed narrative of events in order to concentrate on a small number of what Wipo himself states are carefully selected episodes (most notably Conrad II's election and coronation) and a series of set-piece speeches setting out the principles of Christian rulership. Conrad is accordingly presented as a supreme judge and legislator but the primary lesson for his son, Henry III, is that this was a ruler who actually carried out in practice the principles expressed at his consecration and, as a result, produced justice, peace and order in his kingdom. Suger exploits a very similar technique in his *Deeds of Louis VI*, a work which may have been started whilst its subject was still alive but whose finished version was completed under Louis VII. Suger's selective account of Louis VI's deeds includes explicit criticism of the indolence of the king's own father, Philip I, whose neglect of the royal ministry not only stood in contrast to the activity of his son but also made his own actions no longer worthy of the memory of posterity.[177] Given that Suger's narrative of Louis VI's *gesta* stops in *c*.1130, rather than with the king's death in 1145, this lesson would surely not have been lost, in turn, on Louis' own son, Louis VII.

The inclusion of instructive criticism within an *encomium*, be it implicit or explicit, was an important feature of demonstrative rhetoric and had, from late antiquity onwards, enabled panegyric to serve a function which went well beyond straightforward

---

175 Wipo, *Deeds of Conrad*, prol., p. 54; cf. Sallust, *Jugurthine War*, IV.5–6, pp. 137–9; Thietmar, *Chronicon*, IV.39, p. 179 ('misdeeds dishonour good birth'), quoting Horace, *Odes*, trans. N. Rudd (Loeb, 2004), IV.4.35–6, p. 229.
176 *Deeds of Conrad*, II, pp. 62–3, V, p. 70; cf. Sallust, *Catiline*, VIII, pp. 15–17 (see also pages 43–4).
177 Suger, *Gesta Hludowici*, XIII, p. 61.

praise.[178] Combining advice to a ruler with flattery was a prescription familiar from Seneca the Elder.[179] The same principle applied to the type of historical writing which Wipo's imagery of a mirror directly invokes. Holding up an ideal invited comparison with its reflection in reality: 'anyone who listens to the word but does not do what it says is like a man who looks at his face in a mirror and, after looking at himself, goes away and immediately forgets what he looks like' (James 1:23–4). For the compiler of the *Moralium Dogma Philosophorum*, it was the responsibility of the young, in particular, to look at other people's lives as if in a mirror (*tamquam in speculo*) and to take from them their example; indeed, the more distinguished the lives of one's ancestors, the more disgraceful is the inactivity of their descendants.[180] In *c*.829, Freculf of Lisieux explained he had written his *Histories* so that the young Charles the Bald, son of Louis the Pious and the empress Judith, 'can inspect as if it were in a mirror ... what should be done and what should be avoided'.[181] From that point on, the use of such imagery inspired the inclusion of history-writing within a long tradition of so-called 'mirror-for-princes' literature (*speculum principis*).[182]

The particular examples of Einhard and Wipo suggest that the key to any such critical reading of 'lives' and 'deeds' is often provided by their prologues. Viewed in this light, it becomes instructive to return to the guidelines which had been set out for

---

178 See, for example, Venantius Fortunatus, *Poems*, trans. J. George (Liverpool, 1995) and Sidonius Apollinaris, *Carmina* trans. W.B. Anderson (Loeb, 1936), II, pp. 5–57, V, pp. 61–113. More generally, see S.G. MacCormack, 'Latin Prose Panegyrics', in T.A. Dorey (ed.), *Empire and Aftermath: Silver Latin II* (London, 1975), pp. 143–205; S.G. MacCormack, 'Latin Prose Panegyrics – Tradition and Discontinuity in the Later Roman Empire', *Revue des Etudes Augustiniennes*, 22 (1976), pp. 29–77; S.G. MacCormack, *Art and Ceremony in Late Antiquity* (Berkeley, 1981).
179 Seneca, *Declamationes* [*Suasoriae*], ed. and trans. M. Winterbottom and W.C. Wright (Loeb, 1974), I.5–7, pp. 491–7.
180 *Moralium Dogma Philosophorum*, pp. 45, 54, quoting Sallust, *Jugurthine War*, LXXXV, pp. 315–17; cf. Thomas Basin, *Historiae*, ed. and trans. C. Samaran, *Histoire de Charles VII* (Paris, 1933–44), pref., p. 2: *veluti speculum quoddam morum*.
181 Freculf, *Historiae*, ed. M.I. Allen (*CCCM* 169A, Turnhout, 2002), II prol., p. 436.
182 cf. Augustine, *Letters*, trans. R. Teske (New York, 2005), Ep.211, p. 28; Gregory the Great, *Moralia in Job*, II.1, p. 67; Alcuin, *De Virtutibus et Vitiis*, V, col. 616. For the mirror-for-princes genre, see, most recently, F. Lachaud and L. Scordia (eds), *Le Prince au Miroir de la Literature Politique de l'Antiquité aux Lumières* (Rouen, 2006).

the writing of the introduction or *exordium* in classical manuals of rhetoric. It is all too easy to dismiss prologues as collections of commonplaces. Protestations of personal inadequacy, expressions of debt and gratitude, and an insistence that the author is writing only at the request of others, or under compulsion, are, after all, standard features of this part of a text. Whilst all these elements certainly serve an important function, however, they are far from providing the whole picture.[183] This is hardly surprising, perhaps, given that an emphasis on the centrality of the *exordium* (including the relationship between a dedicatory letter and the introduction proper) was a marked feature of the way in which prose composition was taught as part of the medieval *ars dictaminis*.[184] What becomes readily apparent, in fact, is that there was a general understanding that there was, not one, but two basic types of *exordium* or introduction – on the one hand, the *principium* or *proemium* and, on the other, the *insinuatio* or *ephodos*. The purpose of both types was to render the audience attentive, teachable and benevolent.[185] However, whereas a *principium* or *proemium* achieves these goals openly and immediately, by a process of transparent reasoning, an *insinuatio* seeks the same ends but indirectly and unobtrusively, in a hidden fashion, by dissimulation and circumlocution.[186]

The purpose behind drawing the distinction between a *proemium* and an *insinuatio* was to accommodate the fact that the choice of

---

183 See T. Janson, *Latin Prose Prefaces: Studies in Literary Conventions* (Stockholm, 1964), especially pp. 64–83; G. Simon, 'Untersuchungen zur Topik der Widmungsbriefe', pp. 55–69, 99–117.
184 Murphy, *Rhetoric in the Middle Ages*, pp. 203–10; cf. Alberic of Monte Cassino, *Flores Rhetorici*, trans. J.M. Miller, *Flowers of Rhetoric*, in J.M. Miller, M.H. Prosser and T.W. Benson (eds), *Readings in Medieval Rhetoric* (Bloomington, 1973), II.1–5, pp. 133–6; *Rationes Dictandi*, trans. J.J.Murphy, *The Principles of Letter Writing*, in J.J. Murphy, *Three Medieval Rhetorical Arts* (Berkeley, 1971), pp. 16–18. For the preface in the form of a letter (Ep.ded.), see Seneca, *Declamationes [Controversiae]*, trans. M. Winterbottom and W.C. Wright (Loeb, 1974), I.pref., pp. 3–25; for the combination of an epistolary preface with an *exordium* more generally, see Simon, 'Untersuchungen zur Topik der Widmungsbriefe'.
185 See pages 190–1; cf. William of Malmesbury, *Vita Wulfstani*, I.prol.4, p. 13: 'now those who have a rhetorical training to rely on start what they have to say by making their hearers first well disposed, secondly attentive, and thirdly to learn. And this manner of speaking I too follow when the subject demands it'.
186 *Rhetorica ad Herennium*, I.7.11, p. 21; Cicero, *De Inventione*, I.15.20, p. 43; cf. Quintilian, *Institutio Oratoria*, IV.1.42, p. 29; *Rationes Dictandi*, p. 17.

content for an introduction is determined by the nature of what it is introducing. If it is simply a case of describing a self-evident truth, a prologue is unnecessary and the narrative can begin immediately. In these instances, and with good judges, an *exordium* is not needed at all.[187] What makes an introduction necessary is when an audience needs to be persuaded or instructed in an area, or on a subject, of which it is unsure, when a speech or text describes both virtue and vice, or, in the most extreme case, when a sceptical or hostile audience needs to be convinced that the truth is other than what it currently believes. It is in this last scenario that recourse will be made to the subtleties of an 'indirect' introduction or *insinuatio*.

According to Cicero, Quintilian and the *Rhetorica ad Herennium*, the subject-matter of a speech or text can possess one of five characteristics: something which is morally worthy (*honestum*); something which is subject to doubt (*dubium* or *anceps*), in the sense that it involves both virtue and vice; something which is lowly or unimportant (*humile*); something which is the precise opposite of moral worth, namely what is shameful (*turpe*) or surprising to defend (*admirabile*); and something which is obscure (*obscurum*), because of either the slowness of the audience or the difficulty of the subject. As a result, if the subject-matter of a speech or text is moral worth, then an introduction can be used to show either why the case is morally worthy or simply what it is that is going to be discussed. Alternatively, given that the favour of the audience has already been secured (because of the subject-matter itself), an *exordium* can be dispensed with altogether and the text will begin straightaway – with the narrative, with a law, with a written document or with something which strongly supports the case. If the subject-matter is open to doubt, on the other hand, then a *proemium* will be deployed which is designed to secure the goodwill of the audience in order to circumvent the effects of what is disgraceful. If the subject-matter is lowly or unimportant, then a *proemium* will be constructed in order to make the audience attentive. If the material of a speech or text is disgraceful or surprising to defend, finally, when the subject-matter itself has already alienated or angered the audience, then use should be made of an

---

187 Quintilian, *Institutio Oratoria*, IV.1.72, pp. 45–7, quoting Aristotle, *On Rhetoric*, trans. G.A. Kennedy (Oxford, 1991), III.14, pp. 262–3.

insinuatio, unless, that is, goodwill can first be secured by attacking one's adversaries.[188] Subject-matter which is open to doubt, which is contentious, or which is anathema to an audience will, in each case, affect the exact way in which a prologue is written, and indeed read. However, it will also, and just as significantly, shape the subsequent narrative of deeds done (*res gestae*). It is the last of these three categories which also marks the transition from demonstrative rhetoric to legal or judicial rhetoric, that is, the rhetoric which is concerned with accusation and defence, when the speaker or writer may need to convince a sceptical judge or a hostile jury of the truthfulness of their account of events.

Judicial rhetoric

Legal or judicial rhetoric is distinguished from demonstrative rhetoric, in the first instance, by its goal. Whereas the goal of demonstrative rhetoric is moral worth (*honestum*), the goal of judicial rhetoric is defined by what is equitable (*aequum*), that is, by what is right or just (*ius*).[189] Judicial rhetoric deals with the accusation of an individual on a particular charge, or with the defence of an individual against a particular charge; it involves petitioning a judge or audience for a judgment in the speaker's favour; and, as such, its subject-matter is, by definition, open to doubt, to disagreement, to conflicting versions of events, literally 'controversy' (*controversia*).[190] Judicial rhetoric, however, also shares considerable common ground with demonstrative rhetoric – the act of accusing or defending an individual on a charge of having done something, after all, necessarily involves combining a description of character with an account of what has (or has not) been done and, in these terms, presupposes familiarity with many of the same principles which define *ethologia* and *narratio rei gestae*.

---

188 *Rhetorica ad Herennium*, I.3.5–6, pp. 11–13; Cicero, *De Inventione*, I.15.20, pp. 41–3; Quintilian, *Institutio Oratoria*, IV.1.40, p. 27; cf. pseudo-Augustine, *De Rhetorica*, trans. J.M. Miller, *On Rhetoric*, in J.M. Miller, M.H. Prosser and T.W. Benson (eds), *Readings in Medieval Rhetoric* (Bloomington, 1973), pp. 21–3; Fortunatianus, *Ars Rhetorica*, V, p. 30; M. Camille, 'Illuminating Thought – The Trivial Arts in British Library, Burney Ms.295', in P. Binski and W. Noel (eds), *New Offerings, Ancient Treasures: Studies in Medieval Art for George Henderson* (Stroud, 2001), p. 351.
189 Cicero, *De Inventione*, II.4.12, p. 177; Cicero, *Topica*, XXIII.91, p. 453.
190 *Rhetorica ad Herennium*, I.2.2, p. 5.

Extensive parts of judicial rhetoric are thus frequently devoted to either praising or castigating individuals and accordingly depend on the rules already set out for demonstrative rhetoric.[191]

Nonetheless, despite such common ground, it remains the case that classical manuals of rhetoric are much more interested in discussing judicial rhetoric than demonstrative. Occasions for demonstrative rhetoric arise less frequently, according to the *Rhetorica ad Herennium*, and they are therefore rarely handled on their own.[192] According to Quintilian, although panegyrics concern themselves with some truth (*aliqua veritas*), such *laudationes*, in common with the whole of demonstrative rhetoric, are permitted to exhibit more rhetorical ornamentation because they are designed to give pleasure to the populace. In judicial rhetoric, by contrast, the art of the orator should usually remain concealed.[193] Panegyrics received similarly short shrift from Cicero. They are less weighty, he suggests, and more restricted than other kinds of oratory. The Greeks wrote them more for the purpose of reading and entertainment, or for personal adornment, than as something useful for public life. Roman panegyrics, on the other hand, did serve a public purpose, either when they were delivered as a brief and simple testimony or when they were written as a funeral speech. Unlike Quintilian, however, Cicero still maintained that such *testimonia* and *funebres laudationes* were unsuitable for rhetorical elaboration.[194] As a result, Cicero devotes the bulk of his writing on the rules of rhetoric to analysing the legal or judicial type.[195] It is judicial rhetoric, for example, which occupies most of the argument of *De Inventione*.

Cicero's emphasis on judicial rhetoric was due, in part, to the fact that it was acknowledged to be by far the most difficult of the three types of rhetoric.[196] Whatever the precise rationale, this

---

191 *Rhetorica ad Herennium*, III.8.15, pp. 183–5; Quintilian, *Institutio Oratoria*, II.1.10–11, p. 209; cf. page 262.
192 *Rhetorica ad Herennium*, III.8.15, p. 183.
193 Quintilian, *Institutio Oratoria*, II.10.11, p. 277.
194 Cicero, *De Oratore*, II.84.341, p. 457; cf. Quintilian, *Institutio Oratoria*, III.7.1–6, pp. 465–7.
195 Cf. Cicero, *Orator*, XIII.42, p. 339 (a part of the text not known until 1421), where Cicero concedes that demonstrative rhetoric nurtures or nourishes eloquence and is, in this sense, the 'nursery' of the orator.
196 *Rhetorica ad Herennium*, II.1.1, p. 59.

concentration remains significant because judicial rhetoric was also acknowledged to be the category of rhetoric which was most closely allied to the writing of history – this at least was the opinion of Marius Victorinus, who made a point of drawing this connection in his fourth-century commentary on *De Inventione*.[197] It was an opinion seemingly shared by Quintilian, on the grounds that the narrative of what has been done by an individual in the past is the section of a forensic speech to which a judge will always pay the closest attention.[198] Most significant of all, however, is the way in which this affinity was subsequently picked up by medieval writers. William of Malmesbury, for example, explicitly identified the two goals of his *Historia Novella* as moral worth (*honestas*) and equity (*aequitas*), the former consisting of exemplary deeds, the latter of God's just distribution of punishment and favour.[199] The affinity is equally prominent in his *Gesta Regum*, where William argues that his narrative of the deeds of kings is not to be confused with cosmetic colouring (*fuco*).[200] In criticising an account of the emperor Henry V's expedition to Rome on the grounds that it displays more favour (*gratia*) to the ruler than is fitting, William points out that the author in question was writing panegyric rather than history.[201] In his *Historia Novella*, William therefore draws a clear contrast with his own work: 'nothing will be provided by me out of favour [*gratia*], but only the truth of history ... without the cosmetic colouring of lies'.[202] It is from this perspective that William suggests, in the *Gesta Pontificum Anglorum*, that Aldhelm

---

197 Marius Victorinus, *Explanatio in Rhetoricam Ciceronis*, p. 203.
198 Quintilian, *Institutio Oratoria*, II.1.10, p. 209, IV.2.116–19, pp. 113–15; cf. Martianus Capella, *Marriage of Mercury and Philology*, V, pp. 207–8.
199 William of Malmesbury, *Historia Novella*, I.prol., p. 1.
200 See page 227. Cf. William of Malmesbury, *Gesta Regum Anglorum*, III.285, p. 519; Valerius Maximus, *Facta et Dicta Memorabilia*, IV.1, p. 349: 'the principle of my undertaking has been to take it all as material to be recorded, not praised' (*non laudanda ... sed recordanda*).
201 *Gesta Regum Anglorum*, V.420, p. 765, V.426, p. 771; cf. B. Weiler, 'Royal Justice and Royal Virtue in William of Malmesbury's *Historia Novella* and Walter Map's *De Nugis Curialium*', in I. Bejczy and R. Newhauser (eds), *Virtue and Ethics in the Twelfth Century* (Leiden, 2005), pp. 318–28 . For William of Jumièges' criticism of Dudo, see page 365, note 62.
202 William of Malmesbury, *Historia Novella*, III.503, pp. 64–5; cf. John of Salisbury, *Historia Pontificalis*, I, p. 4; Gervase of Tilbury, *Otia Imperialia*, ed. and trans. S.E. Banks and J.W. Binns, *Recreation for an Emperor* (Oxford, 2002), II.21, p. 489.

'has no need of being championed with lies', since, in this instance, 'a simple belief in the truth is greater than eloquently-expressed and fine-sounding lies'.[203] And yet, as William himself accepts, the account of Aldhelm which he did then produce was an assemblage of knowledge (*congeries scientiae*), rather than a display of eloquence (*ostentatio eloquentiae*), and, as such, was not so much a description of the life of the saint as testimony which provides the documentary means for a knowledge of that life (*vitae ipsius testimonium, cognitionis instrumentum*).[204] In order to provide a narrative of an individual's life and deeds which steered between these two extremes, in other words, avoiding both cosmetic colouring and the mere collection of evidence and information, William needed a middle way. He found it in the language of judicial rhetoric.

So what are the principles of judicial rhetoric, and why are they so important as a method by which the writing of history in the Middle Ages might be approached? In strictly legal terms, classical forensic guidelines were necessarily varied since, in Roman law, there was no fixed measure, or type, of judicial proof. Instead, it would vary according to the case in question – sometimes, but not always, the truth could be found within public records; sometimes proof could be provided by the number of witnesses brought forward, sometimes by their dignity and authority, but sometimes it lay simply in shared opinion (*consentiens fama*). According to the *Corpus Iuris Civilis*, there were no firm rules for evaluating the testimony of witnesses, nor indeed of any other form of evidence, and as a result their credibility or faithfulness (*fides, credulitas*) would always need to be subjected to careful examination. The testimony of a single witness was generally thought insufficient (*vox unius vox nullius*),[205] and no one was considered to be a proper witness in their own case; otherwise, two witnesses were usually deemed sufficient. What remained decisive, however, was, not the number of witnesses, but the sincerity and reliability of testimony by which the light of truth (*lex veritatis*) was strengthened. This involved a preference for autopsy (that is, in its literal sense, of eyewitness

---

203 William of Malmesbury, *Gesta Pontificum Anglorum*, ed. and trans. M. Winterbottom and R.M. Thomson, *The History of the English Bishops* (Oxford, 2007), V.230, p. 577, V.273, pp. 653–5.
204 *Gesta Pontificum Anglorum*, V.187, p. 501; cf. V.246, p. 595.
205 Huguccio of Pisa, *Derivationes*, ed. E. Cecchini, *et al.* (Florence, 2004), p. 1216.

observation) and for testimony given in person and under oath, but it also meant investigating the social standing of witnesses, their moral probity and whether they were likely to be swayed by enmity, favour or profit.[206] This was where the principles of judicial rhetoric came into play. For the sake of convenience, they can be analysed under four headings: the defendant (that is, the individual who is accused or defended); the charge (that is, the action or deed of which that individual is accused of having done or from which they are being defended); extrinsic testimony (that is, authority to which appeal can be made in support of either the accusation or the defence, be it in the form of individual human witnesses to the act or of written, documentary evidence); and, finally, the individual doing the accusing or defending (that is, the speaker or author themselves).

The description of character, of a person's attributes, virtues and vices, serves two purposes in judicial rhetoric – it provides a means of establishing *whether* an individual did the thing which they are charged with doing (that is, it serves a question of fact) and a means of establishing *why* that individual might have done, or not done, the act of which they stand accused (that is, a question of motive). Both questions are issues of conjecture (*coniectura*) and such speculation concerns either fact (*de re*) or character

---

206 For witnesses in Roman law, see Justinian, *Digest*, ed. T. Mommsen and P. Krüger, trans. A. Watson (Philadelphia, 1985), XX.5.1–25, pp. 650–53; Justinian, *Codex*, ed. P. Krüger (Berlin 1884), IV.20.1–20, pp. 158–60; for different types of proof (*probationes*), see *Codex*, IV.19.1–25, pp. 156–7; for the credibility of written documentation (*fides instrumentorum*), see *Codex*, IV.21.1–22, pp. 160–3; for oaths, see *Digest*, XII.2.1–42, pp. 364–72. For canon law, see Gratian, *Decretum*, ed. E. Friedberg, *Corpus Iuris Canonici* (Leipzig, 1879–81), II.3.9.15–17, cols 532–3; for English 'common law', see [Glanvill], *Tractatus de Legibus et Consuetudinibus Regni Anglie Que Glanvilla Vocatur*, ed. and trans. G. D. G. Hall, *The Treatise on the Laws and Customs of England Commonly Called Glanvill* (London, 1965), II.17, pp. 34–5: 'Each juror summoned for this purpose must swear that he will not state falsehood nor knowingly be silent about the truth. The knowledge required from the jurors is that they shall know about the matter from what they have personally seen and heard, or from statements which their fathers made to them in such a way that they are bound to believe them as if they had seen and heard for themselves'. Cf. W. Ullmann, 'Medieval Principles of Evidence', *Law Quarterly Review*, 62 (1946), pp. 77–87; R. Bartlett, *Trial by Fire and Water: The Medieval Judicial Ordeal* (Oxford, 1986); P. Geary, 'Oblivion Between Orality and Textuality in the Tenth Century', in G. Althoff, J. Fried and P.J. Geary (eds), *Medieval Concepts of the Past: Ritual, Memory, Historiography* (Cambridge, 2002), pp. 111–22.

(*de animo*).[207] According to Quintilian, such conjecture is based on things that happened in the past, be it the person who did them, the causes which brought them about, or the deliberation (*consilium*) with which they were performed. As a result, the task of judicial rhetoric is to ask, first, what did a person want to do, second, what were they able to do and, third, what they actually did. The fundamental question underpinning all three, however, is to ask what sort of individual is the person under discussion (*qualis est*).[208] The premise here is quite explicit. It is provable or probable (*probabile*) that individuals with certain characters will tend to perform certain acts because past actions and words generally form the basis of a present assessment. In other words, judicial process is all about establishing a pattern of behaviour.[209] An act or deed has to be consonant with the person charged with having done it and therefore any accusation or defence of an individual must involve a description of their past life (*vita acta*) – in other words, an account of their moral character and their past deeds. Either an individual can be discredited on the basis of their past actions (that is, by castigating them) or an individual can be defended (that is, by showing their life to have been hitherto morally upright). In seeking pardon for an individual, therefore, their good deeds will be recounted, particularly those which were done out of duty towards the *res publica*, to their parents and to others. Or they can be coupled with the good deeds of their ancestors and thereby shown to be greater than any present errors – the result will be that the individual in question will seem to have done more good than bad. Judgment, it can then be claimed, should be reached on the basis of an individual's past life since, unlike a false accusation, this cannot be made up for the occasion (*fingere, confingere*), or altered in any way.[210]

---

207 Quintilian, *Institutio Oratoria*, VII.2.1, p. 45.
208 *Institutio Oratoria*, VII.2.27, p. 63. Compare, for example, William of Poitiers' observation that Harold was the sort of man (*qualis*) whom poems say is Hector or Turnus, whereas William is like Achilles or Aeneas: William of Poitiers, *Gesta Guillelmi*, ed. and trans. R.H.C. Davis and M. Chibnall (Oxford, 1998), II.22, pp. 135–7.
209 Quintilian, *Institutio Oratoria*, V.10.28, p. 217, V.10.64, pp. 235–7; Cicero, *De Inventione*, II.29.90, p. 257.
210 Cicero, *De Inventione*, II.10.32–11.37, pp. 193–9, II.35.106, p. 273; *Rhetorica ad Herennium*, II.2.3–3.5, pp. 63–7, II.17.25, p. 103.

Given the centrality of the question 'what sort of person?' (*qualis est*), Cicero makes it an important part of his analysis of judicial rhetoric to provide a detailed list of all the headings under which the character of any individual can be described – what he terms the 'attributes given to persons' (*attributa personis*).[211] The most important of these are as follows: name (*nomen*); nature (*natura*), which, in turn, comprises sex, race (*natio*), fatherland, ancestors, kin, age, temperament and physical condition; way of life (*victus*), which comprises upbringing, education, friends, occupation and domestic life; and fortune (*fortuna*), which comprises status, wealth, power, reputation, children and manner of death. The list also extends to *habitus* (a constant disposition of mind or body); *affectio* (a temporary disposition, such as an emotion or illness); *studium* (committed mental activity, such as philosophy or poetry); *consilium* (a deliberate reason for doing or not doing something – in other words, purpose or intent); deeds (*facta*); circumstances (*casus*); and what has been said (*orationes*). Whereas Quintilian thought that judicial rhetoric should start with a description of character, Cicero argued that the first step should be to establish motive or intent. The cause of an action, he states, is either unreflective impulse or ratiocination and, as such, it will have been prompted either by some emotion (such as love or anger) or by careful and considered reflection on whether to do something, or not to do it, generally for the sake of some advantage such as glory, power, wealth or friendship. Establishing motive or intent is fundamental because nothing can be proved to have been done unless some reason can be shown *why* it was done; indeed, in this regard, for the individual in question to *think* there is advantage or disadvantage in their action is more significant as a cause than whether any advantage or disadvantage actually resulted. It is the intention with which the deed is done which is important – what an individual wanted to do and what they had the ability to do – rather than what they actually did and the success with

---

211 *De Inventione*, I.24.35–25.36, pp. 71–5, II.9.28–31, pp. 189–93, II.13.42, p. 203–5; cf. Quintilian, *Institutio Oratoria*, V.10.23–31, pp. 213–19; Boethius, *De Topicis Differentiis*, IV, p. 89; *Accessus ad Auctores*, p. 43 (where Lucan's descriptions of Pompey and Caesar are understood in terms of the attributes of person, especially *factum, casus* and *oratio*); Matthew of Vendôme, *Ars Versificatoria*, trans. R. Parr (Milwaukee, 1981), I.38–95, pp. 27–51.

which it was carried out; hence the need to show cause or will or power or ability on the part of the individual.[212] As far as Cicero is concerned, it is the particular combination of character with intent, therefore, which lies at the heart of how, and why, judicial rhetoric should set out to narrate what has been done in the past.

Describing an action which is the subject of conflicting versions, of controversy, also involves what Cicero calls the 'attributes given to events' (*attributa negotiis*).[213] These enable a speaker or writer to describe the entire chain of causation for a given action (*ratio faciendi*) – not only why, for what purpose, an act was done, but also where, when, how and by what means.[214] These attributes presuppose relating what happened before the act, what was actually done in the course of the act and then what happened afterwards, either as a direct result of the action itself (*eventus*) or simply what followed in a chronological sequence (*consecutio*). Once again, Cicero provides a long list of the topics that should be covered. What was actually done by an individual involves a description of place, time, occasion (*occasio*), the manner in which it was done and an individual's ability to do it – in other words, the opportunity to do something, the time it took to do it, the circumstances in which it was done, the mentality (*animus*) with which it was performed and the means which made it possible. Each one of these attributes is then broken down by Cicero and revealed to be governed by certain criteria. 'Opportunity' (*opportunitas*), for example, is a physical property of place which concerns the size of the location in which an action was done, its distance from other places, its own character and the nature of its surrounding region. 'Time' (*tempus*), meanwhile, concerns preceding events, including those which happened in the distant past and which

---

212 Cicero, *De Inventione*, II.5.17–7.24, pp. 181–7; cf. Quintilian, *Institutio Oratoria*, VII.2.39–40, p. 71. Compare Thietmar, *Chronicon*, VI.85, p. 294: 'if one performs the deed with devotion ... it makes no difference that it is of no use to the intended beneficiary'; cf. Augustine, *Enarrationes in Psalmos*, trans. M. Boulding, *Expositions of the Psalms* (New York, 2000–04), XXXI.2.4, p. 365. For the 'ethic of intention' in the twelfth century, see Abelard, *Ethics*, ed. and trans. D.E. Luscombe (Oxford, 1971), pp. 45–7; J. Marenbon, *The Philosophy of Peter Abelard* (Cambridge, 1997), ch. 11.
213 *De Inventione*, I.26.37–28.43, pp. 75–83, II.12.38–14.46, pp. 201–9.
214 Quintilian, *Institutio Oratoria*, V.10.32–52, pp. 219–29; Boethius, *De Topicis Differentiis*, IV, pp. 89–92.

now seem so far beyond belief (*incredibilia*) that they are counted as fables (*fabula*). There are also events which, although they too occurred a long time ago and are remote from memory, still inspire the belief (*fides*) that they have been truthfully handed down because definite memorials of them (*monumenta*) have been written down and are extant. 'Time' also includes those things which have been done more recently and which are common knowledge. It extends to cover those things which are still going on, and those things which will follow as a consequence of the action in question, a category for which it is necessary to consider what usually happens and, as a result, what has happened in the past. 'Manner' (*modus*), finally, concerns the state of mind in which an act was done, that is, whether it was done secretly or openly, under compulsion or by persuasion, through ignorance, accident or necessity, and with what particular emotions.

Attributes of person and attributes of action are closely connected and, taken together, provide Cicero with a straightforward formula for the way in which the narrative of a deed should be approached in judicial rhetoric. The narrative of what was done, he argues, will follow the sequence of relating, first, why and with what intent it was done; second, why it was done in this way rather than another; and, third, whether it was done intentionally or followed as a consequence of external factors.[215] Thus, as far as the act or deed itself is concerned, the approach required by judicial rhetoric amounts to asking three fundamental questions – whether something has been done, what it is that has been done, and what the significance is of what has been done. In all matters of controversy or contention, therefore, Cicero states that it is necessary to ask these three questions: whether something happened (*an sit*), what it was that happened (*quid sit*), and what was the quality of what happened (*quale sit*).[216] Quintilian repeats both the approach and the terminology, citing Cicero as his authority. Everything which can form the subject of controversy or disagreement, he declares, is covered by the questions 'is it?', 'what is it?' and 'what value does it have?'[217] One or more of these

---

215 Cicero, *De Inventione*, II.14.45, p. 207.
216 Cicero, *Orator*, XIV.45, p. 339; cf. Augustine, *De Diversis Quaestionibus LXXXIII*, 18, p. 37.
217 Quintilian, *Institutio Oratoria*, III.6.44, pp. 431–3, V.10.53, p. 229.

questions is asked in every demonstrative, judicial or deliberative case, but it is the conjunction of all three which is central to judicial rhetoric – whether a thing has been done, what it is that has been done and whether it was done rightly.[218]

Each one of the three questions of judicial rhetoric (*an sit, quid sit, quale sit*) requires the speaker or writer to take a particular approach.[219] Whether something was done (that is, whether it happened, what was its origin, what was its cause) is resolved by means of signs and conjecture. What that something is, meanwhile, is resolved by means of definition, an approach which can include etymology, designation and description (for example, if there is a doubt over whether Nero was an emperor or a tyrant, then the statement is made that he was a tyrant because he was cruel and debauched – that is, because he demonstrated the characteristics which *define* the tyrant, as opposed to the moderation and piety which *define* a king).[220] The qualitative judgment which should be placed upon the action depends, finally, on a discussion of what is good or bad, just or unjust, morally worthy or shameful, equitable or inequitable. Every subject which involves controversy contains these three basic questions of fact, definition and quality. Various permutations result. First and foremost, the controversy can be about whether something happened at all. Alternatively, controversy can be about what exactly it was that happened – when, for example, there is agreement that something happened but disagreement over the name or term which it should be given. Something which has been done, after all, can appear differently to different people and, for that reason, different people will call it by different names – in which case, the act in question needs to be defined in words and briefly described. Sallust's account of Cato's indictment of the *mores* of contemporary Rome, for example, contained a prime instance of such redescription with its observation that 'in truth we have long since lost the true names for things; squandering the goods of others is now called liberality, rashness in wicked kings is called bravery'.[221] Tacitus made the same point

---

218 Quintilian, *Institutio Oratoria*, III.11.2, p. 523, VII.praef.8, p. 181; Boethius, *De Topicis Differentiis*, IV, p. 84.
219 Cicero, *Topica*, XXI.82–XXII.85, pp. 445–9; Cicero, *Orator*, XIV.45, p. 339.
220 Boethius, *In Ciceronis Topica*, trans. E. Stump (Ithaca, 1988), III, p. 95.
221 Sallust, *Catiline*, LII, p. 103; see also page 323.

with Roman 'peace' and 'liberty', Orosius with the achievements of Alexander the Great.[222] Controversy, finally, can be about the significance of what has been done – when, for example, there is agreement that something occurred, when there is agreement on what it was that occurred, but disagreement over whether this was just or unjust, advantageous or disadvantageous.[223] Put all this together and the result is a series of detailed guidelines for how an individual should be accused of, or defended from, having performed a particular act or deed.

According to the principles of judicial rhetoric, in short, narrating what has been done (*narratio rei gestae*) presupposes a total of four fundamental questions – the original issue of character (what sort of person or individual has done it, as a means of explaining why it has been done), plus the three judicial questions (whether it has been done, what it is that has been done and what value should be placed on what has been done). Faced with a particular accusation or charge, Cicero accordingly deploys these four questions to create various strategies of defence. When there is agreement that an act took place, for example, but disagreement over whether it was just or unjust, the strongest defence is simply to prove that a particular action is, in absolute terms, morally worthy. Failing that, a number of options present themselves, each of which involves the introduction of external considerations. In arguing that a deed should be judged, not by the name or definition which is attached to it, but by the deliberation (*consilium*) exercised by the person who performed it, by its cause and by the time at which it was done, it is possible to accept that the act took place but claim that it was motivated by a good intention (in that it was to the advantage of the *res publica* or of many people) or that it prevented a worse evil from taking place. Alternatively, responsibility can be rejected, intention denied and the charge (and sometimes the act itself) removed to some other person or some other thing (*remotio criminis*),[224] or the action can simply be compared with the other courses of action which were available. This type of defence (*purgatio*), when it is the individual's

---

222 Tacitus, *Agricola*, trans. M. Hutton, rev. R.M. Ogilvie (Loeb, 1970), XXX, p. 81; Orosius, *Seven Books of History*, III.20, p. 108; see also page 72.
223 Cicero, *De Inventione*, I.8.11–9.12, pp. 23–5.
224 See page 218, note 372.

intention which is defended rather than the act, can also deny any intent to perform the action in question, attributing responsibility either to ignorance or lack of knowledge, to accident or fortune, to necessity, or to external circumstance. If the plea is necessity, for example, then this can involve expanding upon the power of fortune and the weakness of humankind, both of which can serve to counteract an individual's originally good intention.[225] This extends to what Cicero terms the changeability of things (*commutatio rerum*), which comes about as a result of time, events or human concern (in the sense that some things will not be considered by people in the same way as they used to be). Certain matters, in other words, need to be considered with reference to both the time at which and the deliberation (*consilium*) with which they were performed, not just according to their intrinsic nature. In all such matters, an assessment will depend on what was required by the times, on what was worthy of the people concerned – in other words, not on what was done, but with what intention it was done and in what particular context.[226]

Like demonstrative rhetoric, judicial rhetoric involves combining a narrative of what has been done (*narratio rei gestae*) with a depiction of character (*ethologia*). Unlike demonstrative rhetoric, it also involves an appeal to extrinsic testimony. Legal witness (*testimonium*) can be established by various means, but the basic distinction lies, according to both Cicero and Quintilian, between human and documentary sources. Human witnesses are, of course, always open to doubt. They can be attacked for the moral turpitude of their lives, for the self-contradictory nature of their testimony, or simply on the grounds that what they claim to have happened either could not have happened or did not happen or could not have been known by them or that their words and arguments have been motivated by cupidity. According to the *Rhetorica ad Herennium*, it is possible to argue that signs and arguments therefore deserve more credence than witnesses, because signs and arguments can be used to set out how something was truly done (*quomodo re vera sint gesta*) whereas witnesses

---

225 Cicero, *De Inventione*, II.28.83–29.90, pp. 249–53, II.31.94–33.102, pp. 261–9; *Rhetorica ad Herennium*, I.14.24–15.25, pp. 43–9; Quintilian, *Institutio Oratoria*, VII.4.3–15, pp. 107–13; Boethius, *De Topicis Differentiis*, IV, p. 85.
226 *De Inventione*, II.58.176, p. 343.

can be corrupted by bribery, partiality (*gratia*), fear or animosity (*simultas*). Quintilian makes the same point with regard to the use of history – testimony drawn from the events and *exempla* of antiquity is more effective because it alone is free from the accusation of having been motivated by either hatred or favour.[227]

By the same token, however, the testimony of witnesses can also be supported, on the grounds of their authority, their virtuous life and the consistency of their evidence.[228] This more positive evaluation of extrinsic human testimony is particularly important as far as the writing of history is concerned because of its emphasis on the way in which human witnesses rely on what is perceived by one of their five senses (sight, hearing, touch, smell or taste),[229] of which sight was consistently regarded as the most important. The superiority of eyewitness testimony for the historian was emphasised by Josephus, Eusebius and Isidore of Seville.[230] This was why Dares Phrygius' account of Troy was preferred to those given by Homer and Vergil – because the author was thought to have been an eyewitness and was therefore a more credible *testis* to the truth of what he was describing (*veritas historiae*) than the fictions of the two poets.[231] In making use of Isidore's *Etymologies*, Otto of Freising produces his own gloss on the significance of autopsy for the writing of history:

> Let it suffice to have narrated these incidents of the progress and success of that expedition – a few out of many. For not all the brave

---

227   Quintilian, *Institutio Oratoria*, X.1.34, p. 23 (see page 136). For the definition of *gratia* see pages 286–7.
228   *Rhetorica ad Herennium*, II.6.9–7.11, pp. 75–9.
229   *Rhetorica ad Herennium*, II.5.8, p. 71.
230   See pages 51, 63, 123; cf. Macrobius, *Saturnalia*, I.8.4, p. 64: 'history is seen by our eyes and heard by our ears'.
231   For example, *Itinerarium Peregrinorum et Gesta Regis Ricardi*, prol., p. 22; Joseph of Exeter, *De Bello Troiano*, ed. and trans. A.K. Bate, *Trojan War* (Warminster, 1986), I, p. 31; cf. Bernardus Silvestris, *Commentary on the First Six Books of Virgil's Aeneid*, pref., p. 1 ('Virgil does not write ... the true version of the story, as does Dares Phrygius'), II, p. 16 ('And since speech is sometimes true and sometimes false, the mixture of the truth of history and the falsity of fables in the narration follows this same pattern. The Greek destruction of Troy is history but Aeneas' honesty is fiction, for Dares Phyrgius narrates that Aeneas betrayed his city'), VI, p. 37. For Dares himself, see Dares Phrygius, *De Excidio Troiae Historia*, trans. R.M. Frazer, *The Trojan War: The Chronicles of Dictys of Crete and Dares the Phrygian* (Bloomington, 1966); cf. Vergil, *Aeneid*, V.368–85, p. 471; Isidore, *Etymologiae*, I.42.1, p. 67.

deeds there accomplished could be related by us in completeness of sequence and charm of style as if we had seen them with our own eyes. For it is understood to have been a custom of the ancients that those who had perceived with their senses the actual events as they took place should be the ones to write about them. Whence also it is customarily called 'history' from *hysteron* which, in Greek, signifies 'to see'. For everyone will be competent to speak more fully of the things which he has seen and heard. Being in need of no man's favour [*gratia*], he is not carried hither and thither in search of the truth, doubtingly anxious and anxiously doubting. Indeed, it is hard for a writer's mind to depend on another's judgment as though incapable of making an investigation of its own.[232]

Taking his cue from Eusebius, Bede had found the scriptural authority for his association of history and eyewitness testimony in the opening verses of Luke's Gospel.[233] Guibert of Nogent similarly quoted both John 3:32 ('He testifies to what he has seen and heard, but no one accepts his testimony') and John 19:35 ('The man who saw it has given testimony, and his testimony is true. He knows that he tells the truth, and he testifies so that you also may believe').[234] Guibert accordingly presents his own account as true testimony (*verax testimonium*), rather than something which has been made up (*confinxisse*).[235] Gerald of Wales quotes John 3:11: 'we speak of what we know, we bear witness to what we have seen' (*quod scimus loquimur, quod vidimus testamur*).[236] The source

---

232 Otto of Freising, *Deeds of Frederick Barbarossa*, trans. C.C. Mierow (New York, 1953), II.41, p. 159; cf. Otto of Freising, *Chronicle*, IV.27, p. 313, V.18, p. 345, VII.29, p. 439, VII.32, p. 441; Gerald of Wales, *Topographia Hibernica*, trans. J.J. O'Meara, *The History and Topography of Ireland* (Harmondsworth, 1982), I.2, p. 35. More generally, see J. Beer, *Narrative Conventions of Truth in the Middle Ages* (Geneva, 1981), pp. 23–34.
233 Eusebius, *Ecclesiastical History*, trans. G.A. Williamson (Harmondsworth, 1965), III.4, p. 110, III.24, p. 133 (see also pages 63–4); Bede, *In Lucae Evangelium Expositio*, ed. D. Hurst, *Commentary on Luke* (*CCSL* 120, Turnhout, 1960), I.1.1–4, pp. 19–21.
234 Guibert of Nogent, *Gesta Dei per Francos*, IV.prol., p. 73; Guibert of Nogent, *Monodiae*, III.4, p. 154; cf. Deuteronomy 19:15 ('in the mouth of two or three will stand all testimony'), quoted, for example, by Thietmar, *Chronicon*, I.13, p. 77; Wipo, *Deeds of Conrad*, Ep.ded., p. 53; Eadmer, *Historia Novorum in Anglia*, trans. G. Bosanquet, *Eadmer's History of Recent Events in England* (London, 1964), IV.194, p. 207.
235 Guibert of Nogent, *Monodiae*, II.4, p. 134.
236 Gerald of Wales, *Expugnatio Hibernica*, II.36, p. 239.

of such prioritisation, however, was also found in Roman law. The preference for autopsy over second-hand reporting received its most influential formulation, for example, from Justinian's *Institutes*: 'truth is imprinted more by the trustworthiness of sight than through the ears' (*cum magis veritas oculata fide quam per aures animis hominum infigitur*).[237] It is this legal emphasis on eyewitness veracity which subsequently became an important part of a medieval historian's claim to accuracy and authority.[238] The phrase 'trustworthiness of sight' (*oculata fides*) occurs in several prologues to works of history, in John of Biclaro, for instance, and, most influentially, in Einhard: 'I was aware that no one could write about these things more truthfully than me, since I myself was present and personally witnessed them, as they say, with the trustworthiness of sight'.[239] Liutprand of Cremona explicitly distinguishes what he has heard from reliable witnesses from what he has seen for himself.[240] If anyone doubts the facts, Odo of Cluny remarks, they can put them to the test with their own eyes and so gain credence of the past.[241] 'I will describe my own experience', Thietmar of Merseburg writes, 'I will not lie'.[242]

Failing the evidence provided by one's own eyesight, then testimony will certainly have to come from other people but, once again, medieval historians are keen to state that the eyewitnesses they drew upon were of a certain calibre. In his *Res Gestae Ælfredi* of 893, Asser repeatedly attests that he had seen something for himself, 'with my very own eyes' (*quam nos ipsi nostris propriis oculis*

---

237 Justinian, *Institutes*, III.3.6, p. 99.
238 For example, Paschasius Radbertus, *Vita Adalhardi*, II, p. 26; Paschasius Radbertus, *Epitaphium Arsenii*, I.prol., p. 83, I.14, p. 120; Henry of Huntingdon, *Historia Anglorum*, VIII (*De Contemptu Mundi*), p. 585; *Itinerarium Peregrinorum et Gesta Regis Ricardi*, prol., p. 22.
239 John of Biclaro, *Chronicle*, trans. K.B. Wolf, in *Conquerors and Chroniclers of Early Medieval Spain* (2nd edn, Liverpool, 1999), prol., p. 57; Einhard, *Vita Karoli*, praef., p. 15 (see also page 158); cf. Suger, *Gesta Hludowici*, XIX, pp. 87, 91, XXI, p. 102, XXIV, p. 107.
240 Liutprand, *Antapodosis*, IV.1, p. 143. For the superiority of eyewitness to doubtful rumour, see I.1, p. 31.
241 Odo of Cluny, *Life of Gerald*, IV.7, p. 176; cf. II.6, p. 138; John of Salerno, *Life of Odo*, II.5, p. 47.
242 Thietmar, *Chronicon*, VI.78, p. 289; cf. VIII.9, p. 367.

vidimus);²⁴³ otherwise, his witnesses are described as 'truthtelling' (*veredici*), a term with a specifically judicial connotation ('verdict'): 'as we have heard from those who saw it and truthfully related it' (*sicut ab his qui viderunt veredicis referentibus audivimus*).²⁴⁴ In the tenth century, John of Salerno reports that many things were said about Odo of Cluny, narrated 'on oath' as testimony of the events to which the narrators had themselves been witnesses.²⁴⁵ Odo himself warns that the amazing things he will record about the life of Gerald of Aurillac would be practically unbelievable were they not asserted on such good testimony.²⁴⁶ 'What I am going to relate is remarkable', he writes, 'and it may seem incredible, but I believe the two witnesses who assert it'.²⁴⁷ Indeed, although Odo is aware of other things that were being said about Gerald which deserved to be both related and admired, he states that he would rather keep silent about them because they rested on common report and not on the four witnesses named in his prologue, whose testimony he has carefully investigated and on whose authority he has otherwise been relying for his narrative.²⁴⁸ In the eleventh century, the author of the *Encomium Emmae Reginae* records what he has seen with his own eyes explicitly in order to

---

243 Asser, *Res Gestae Ælfredi*, trans. S. Keynes and M. Lapidge, *Alfred the Great* (Harmondsworth, 1983), XXII, p. 75, XXXIX, p. 79, XCIV, p. 103; cf. 1 John 1:1–2: 'that which ... we have seen with our eyes, which we have looked at...; we have seen and we testify' (*quod vidimus oculis nostris, quod perspeximus ... et vidimus et testamur*).
244 *Res Gestae Ælfredi*, XIII, p. 71, XV, p. 72, XXXVII, p. 79, XCVII, pp. 104–5; cf. Fulcher of Chartres, *Historia Hierosolymitana*, trans. F.R. Ryan, *A History of the Expedition to Jerusalem 1095–1127* (Knoxville, 1969), II.34, p. 189: 'just as I saw with my eyes or learned carefully from truthtelling narrators' (*prout oculis vidi vel a relatoribus veridicis perscrutans diligenter didici*). According to Quintilian, phrases such as 'I saw it with my eyes' or 'I saw it myself before my eyes' are good examples of using superfluous words ('pleonasm') *unless* this is done for the sake of emphasis: Quintilian, *Institutio Oratoria*, VIII.3.53–4, p. 241, IX.3.46, p. 473; cf. Vergil, *Aeneid*, XII.638, p. 345: *vidi oculos ante ipse meos*.
245 John of Salerno, *Life of Odo*, prol., p. 4; cf.III.8, p. 79.
246 Odo of Cluny, *Life of Gerald*, I.39, p. 128; cf.I.42, p. 131.
247 *Life of Gerald*, II.21, p. 149. For the importance of two or more witnesses, see Deuteronomy 19:15 (see also page 184, note 234), Matthew 18:16, 2 Corinthians 13:1 (see also page 202, note 316); cf. Thietmar, *Chronicon*, I.13, p. 77; Rahewin, *Deeds of Frederick*, III.28, p. 202.
248 *Life of Gerald*, II.33, p. 159; cf. pref., p. 91.

make his assertions more credible.[249] Issuing a diclaimer against flattery, lying and meddling, Turgot opens his *Life of Margaret* with a firm affidavit ('as God is my witness and judge, I swear that I have added nothing to the facts') and explicitly eschews any literary embellishment with a reference to Aesop's *Fables* ('I have been silent on many things so that they will not seem incredible or, like the saying of the orator, I shall be said to adorn the crow with the colours of the swan').[250] 'Let us first present the case', writes Thietmar, 'and then judge...'.[251] 'This story does not come from scattered references in untrustworthy writers', declares William of Malmesbury, 'but from eyewitnesses of mature years and the greatest reliability and learning'.[252]

The citation of written documentation was naturally regarded by Cicero and Quintilian as a particularly important form of extrinsic testimony when a text itself – a law, for example, or a last will and testament – formed the subject of controversy. In these circumstances, Quintilian suggested it would often be necessary to speak against the testimony of documents (*tabulae*), either by rebutting or by attacking them.[253] Disputes over the nature of something that had been written were generally understood to take one of five forms: when the words themselves are at variance with the intention of the writer; when there is a discrepancy between two or more laws; when what is written signifies two or more things; when something is discovered from the written text which has not actually been written; and when the meaning or definition of an individual word is in doubt.[254] For all five cases, judicial rhetoric provided a series of rules for evaluating the

---

249 *Encomium Emmae Reginae*, III.20, p. 36: *ut credibiliora fiant quae assero ... dicam pro exemplo, quod etiam oculis meis me vidisse recordor*.
250 Turgot, *Life of Margaret of Scotland*, trans. L.L. Huneycutt (Woodbridge, 2003), prol., p. 163; cf. L.L. Huneycutt, 'The Idea of the Perfect Princess – The *Life of St Margaret* in the Reign of Matilda II (1100–1118)', *Anglo-Norman Studies*, 12 (1990), pp. 81–98.
251 Thietmar, *Chronicon*, VI.96, p. 301; cf. I.12, p. 76, I.13, p. 77, IV.37, p. 178, VI.22, p. 252, VI.79, p. 290, VII.32, pp. 329–30.
252 William of Malmesbury, *Gesta Pontificum Anglorum*, V.263, p. 629. For sworn testimony, see, for example, William of Malmesbury, *Gesta Regum Anglorum*, II.204, p. 377.
253 Quintilian, *Institutio Oratoria*, V.5.1, p. 165.
254 Cicero, *De Inventione*, I.13.17, pp. 35–7; *Rhetorica ad Herennium*, I.11.19–13.23, pp. 35–43; Cicero, *De Oratore*, II.26.110–12, pp. 279–81; Cicero, *Topica*,

weight which should be placed upon the testimony of written documentation. In the case of ambiguity, for example, when what is written has more than one meaning, Cicero suggests two approaches can be adopted. In the first instance, it should be shown that there is, in fact, no ambiguity provided that the word or words under discussion are used according to their customary meaning. In the second instance, if the ambiguity has arisen from words being considered separately and by themselves, then the meaning should be clarified by what precedes the words in question or what follows them – in other words, by considering the entirety of what has been written in the text. What writers mean can then be estimated from their other writings, from their actions, their words, their character and, indeed, from their whole life. It thereby becomes a straightforward process of estimating what it is likely (*veri simile*) that a writer intended to say, by considering the whole document in which the ambiguous words occur, by examining the character of the writer and by analysing those things which are attributed to people who possess the same sort of character as the writer. Having concentrated on the vocabulary used, and having asked at what time it was written, it should then be possible to understand what the author was likely (*veri simile*) to have meant to write at such a time, and what was the more advantageous and morally worthy outcome for him to intend.[255]

If the controversy turns on the difference between the exact words that are written and what the writer intended, between the letter and the spirit, then a number of possible approaches are listed. In order to prove that the considered opinion (*sententia*) behind what is written should be given greater weight than the actual words (*verba*) themselves, it is necessary to demonstrate either that the writer always had the same end in view and sought the same result or that, in this precise instance, the writer's purpose was adapted to suit a particular occasion because of some particular act or event. Intent, in other words, is a matter of showing either that the writer always desired one result or desired a particular result on a particular subject and at a particular time, including when nothing was actually written down. Defending the

---

XXV.96–XXVI.96, p. 457; cf. Quintilian, *Institutio Oratoria*, VII.5.6, p. 135; Boethius, *De Topicis Differentiis*, IV, p. 84.
255   Cicero, *De Inventione*, II.40.116–41.121, pp. 285–9.

literal meaning of what has been written (*scriptum*), on the other hand (that is, against the claim of a different intention), takes the form of praising the writer, insisting that consideration be given to nothing except what has been written, and putting forward the text itself. To this end, it can be argued that it is possible to get much closer to a writer's intention (*voluntas*) if it is extrapolated from their own written work, that is, from the written document which has been left as an image, as it were, of their will (*imago voluntatis*).[256] When the intention of the writer seems at variance with what is written, the following approach is suitable: first, narrate what the individual has done, praise the writer and recite the written text; second, question one's opponents, ascertain the writer's meaning, and put forward the reason why they intended to write what they wrote; third, demonstrate that this was written clearly, concisely, appositely, fully and with a definite rationale; conclude, finally, by pointing out the dangers of departing from the letter of the text.[257]

The prime example which is given by Cicero for controversies which arise over the meaning of a written text is that of disputes over a last will and testament.[258] The revocation or establishment of wills, in fact, is regarded as typical subject-matter for judicial rhetoric.[259] For Quintilian, therefore, the classic case of a legal question is a disputed will, particularly when it involves arguments over the intention (*voluntas*) of the testator as opposed to the letter of the law (*scriptum*). Wills, he states, are a particular focus of disputes which concern the ambiguity of a written text. They turn on such questions as which is the most natural interpretation of the text, which is the most equitable, and what was the intention of the person who wrote, or uttered, the words under debate.[260]

Last, but not least, comes the establishment of the credibility of a case through the trustworthiness of the person who is actually doing the speaking or the writing. In basing an argument on

---

[256] Cicero, *De Inventione*, II.42.121–44.128, pp. 291–7; cf. Quintilian, *Institutio Oratoria*, VII.6.1–12, pp. 135–43.
[257] *Rhetorica ad Herennium*, II.9.13, p. 81.
[258] Cicero, *De Inventione*, II.40.116, p. 285; Cicero, *De Oratore*, I.57.241–2, p. 175.
[259] For example, *De Oratore*, I.38.175–39.180, pp. 121–5.
[260] Quintilian, *Institutio Oratoria*, III.6.95–103, pp. 459–63, VII.9.3, p. 155, VII.9.15, p. 161.

character and conduct (*mores*), on how individuals should (and should not) act, the speaker or writer must themselves be a good individual, in the sense that they should actually possess (or be believed to possess) the virtues that are advocated and not just be arguing for them on the part of their client. Such goodness creates faith or trustworthiness (*fides*).[261] Once again, this *fides* is secured primarily by means of the introduction with which an individual opens a speech or text. The *exordium* should be serious and should contain everything which pertains to moral worth. Because the best and most eloquent orators approach speaking with some trepidation (on account of the difficulty of speaking, the different possible outcomes of their speech, and the expectations of their audience),[262] the most useful attributes to display are gentleness of voice, a facial expression signifying modesty, smoothness of language, a claim to good faith, and the appearance of dealing unwillingly and under compulsion with something which, in fact, the speaker or writer is anxious to pursue. As a rule, the less artifice shown the better, since an impression of brilliance, liveliness and polish will weaken both the trustworthiness of the speech and the authority of the speaker.[263]

As was the case with demonstrative rhetoric, therefore, the purpose of an introduction in judicial rhetoric is to render an audience benevolent (*benivolus*), attentive (*attentus*) and teachable (*docilis*).[264] Benevolence, or goodwill, is secured from an audience if the speaker or writer is thought to be defending what is advantageous to the audience or to be working on behalf of good people (or at least on behalf of people who seem good and advantageous to the audience), thereby supporting moral worth and advantage (*dignitas et utilitas*) rather than their own personal gain.[265] It is better for the speaker or writer to present themselves

---

261 Quintilian, *Institutio Oratoria*, VI.2.18, p. 427.
262 Cicero, *De Oratore*, I.26.120, p. 85.
263 *De Oratore*, II.43.182, pp. 327–9, 335; Cicero, *De Inventione*, I.18.25, pp. 51–3; Quintilian, *Institutio Oratoria*, IV.1.54–60, pp. 37–9; cf. Martianus Capella, *Marriage of Mercury and Philology*, V, pp. 206–7; see pages 172, 337.
264 Cicero, *De Inventione*, I.15.20, p. 41; Quintilian, *Institutio Oratoria*, IV.1.5, p. 9 (see also page 169); Cicero, *Topica*, XXVI.97, p. 457; cf. Isidore, *Etymologiae*, II.7.2, p. 38; Conrad of Hirsau, *Dialogue on the Authors*, p. 43; Bernardus Silvestris, *Commentary on the First Six Books of Virgil's Aeneid*, pref., pp. 4–5.
265 Cicero, *De Oratore*, II.51.206–7, pp. 349–51.

as a faithful witness than as a zealous advocate, as someone who is acting out of duty to a friend or a relative, or for the sake of the *res publica*, and to stress the moral worth of the person they are defending.[266] Goodwill is secured, accordingly, from four main sources. In the first instance, it can be derived from the speaker's own person, that is, by dwelling on their own deeds and duties, on the difficulties they have with the task, or by making a humble supplication through presenting themselves as weak and unprepared. Goodwill, in this context, must be secured for the speaker or writer, and not just for the individual being accused or defended, but the same principles apply: describe one's own virtues, achievements and reputable life; praise one's own services (but without arrogance) by revealing one's conduct towards the *res publica*, to one's friends and towards the audience, at the same time as setting out one's own inadequacy, need, loneliness and misfortune. Goodwill can be secured, in the second instance, from the person of one's opponents, by making them hated, unpopular or contemptible, not least by accusing them of laziness and sloth; in the third instance, from the person of the judge or audience, by praising their deeds and the esteem in which they are held; and, finally, from the nature of the case itself. Attentiveness is likewise secured by using the *exordium* to emphasise a number of key points: whether the subject is important, new, unprecedented, or stretches belief; whether it concerns everyone, or the audience, or the gods, or the highest interest of the *res publica*; whether the speaker or writer promises brevity; and whether the matter at issue is set out. Teachability, similarly, is secured by explaining the point on which the controversy turns, the essence of the case, but by doing so clearly and briefly.[267]

In using an *exordium* to establish credibility through the trustworthiness of the speaker, judicial rhetoric draws on the principles set out for a *proemium*, that is, on the type of introduction which appeals directly to the goodwill and attentiveness of the judge or audience. The alternative is to deploy an *insinuatio*, the type of introduction which achieves the same ends indirectly, by stealth

---

266 Quintilian, *Institutio Oratoria*, IV.1.6–13, pp. 9–13.
267 Cicero, *De Inventione*, I.16.22–23, pp. 45–7; *Rhetorica ad Herennium*, I.4.7–8, pp. 15–17.

and circumlocution.[268] An *insinuatio* will be necessary, for example, when the mind of an audience is already violently opposed to the case which is being made, when the individual or the subject-matter has already alienated a judge or audience. Such hostility can have any one of three causes: the moral turpitude of the case itself; the persuasive impact of an earlier speaker or writer; and simple fatigue (a factor which, in Cicero's opinion at least, should not be underestimated). In any one of these instances, either goodwill can be secured by a direct attack on one's opponents or the *exordium* has to be made much more subtle. If it is the turpitude of the case which causes offence, for instance, then the individual who is causing that offence should be replaced by another individual who *is* loved or favoured, or the thing which is causing the offence should be replaced by something (or someone) which *is* approved. The result is that the mind of the audience will be transferred from what it hates to what it loves. The speaker or writer should start, therefore, by dissimulating or concealing the fact that they are about to defend a particular position. That defence will gradually be embarked upon only when the audience has begun to be mollified, not least by the speaker stating that they agree with what their opponents regard as scandalous. The speaker can deny any intention to discuss the opposing view which the audience favours and yet, by a hidden form of words, do precisely that. The speaker can also appeal to a judgment made by others in an analogous case, be it of equal, lesser or greater importance. If it is a simple case of fatigue, finally, then the speaker should promise to speak briefly, or should open with something which prompts laughter, with a defence, with a plausible fable (*fabula veri simili*), with something ironically inverted or ambiguous or unexpected

---

268 *Rhetorica ad Herennium*, I.6.9–10, pp. 17–21 (see also pages 169–71); cf. Fortunatianus, *Ars Rhetorica*, V–VI, pp. 30–2; Eadmer, *Historia Novorum in Anglia*, I.18, p. 18. For *insinuatio* in Chrétien de Troyes' *Yvain*, see T. Hunt, 'The Rhetorical Background to the Arthurian Prologue – Tradition and the Old French Vernacular Prologues', *Forum for Modern Language Studies*, 6 (1970), pp. 1–23; T. Hunt, 'Tradition and Originality in the Prologues of Chrestien de Troyes', *Forum for Modern Language Studies*, 8 (1972), pp. 328–32. For vernacular prologues in general, see J. Wogan-Browne, N. Watson, A. Taylor and R. Evans (eds), *The Idea of the Vernacular: An Anthology of Middle English Literary Theory 1280–1520* (Exeter, 1999).

or new, with a novelty, or with some 'history' (*historia*) or verse. To make a hostile judge attentive, a speaker will promise to argue otherwise than as prepared, not to imitate their opponents, nor to talk as others usually do.[269] The goal of an *insinuatio* remains the same as that of a *proemium*, but it depends throughout on concealment and dissimulation.

If the nature of a rhetorical *exordium* is determined by which of the four types of subject-matter it is introducing – something that is intrinsically morally worthy; something that is subject to doubt in that it involves both virtue and vice; something that is lowly or unimportant; or something that is shameful – then it is the second and fourth of these categories which form the essence of judicial rhetoric and which, as a result, will require an *insinuatio* rather than a *proemium*. The consequence for medieval historiography, once again, is that introductions or prologues to works of history are often much more subtle, much more complex, than they might seem, or than they are explicitly claiming, to be.

Liutprand of Cremona's *Antapodosis* provides a case in point. That Liutprand himself knew all about the expectations of a *proemium* is clear from the words he gives to Otto I in commanding one particular messenger to cut to the chase: 'Come tell us what you were sent for at once and invert the usual order by giving us the facts first. Banish this company's fears and fill their hearts with joy; then you may bring out your compliments to myself and indulge in the long preliminaries of a rhetorical *proemium*. It is what you have to say, not how you say it, that we are this moment expecting. We would rather be made to rejoice by rustic simplicity than left on thorns by Ciceronian wit [*Tulliana facetia*]'.[270] What Liutprand says in the introduction to his own work is therefore revealing as much for what it does not say as for what it does. He has written this work, he states, in response to a

---

269 *De Inventione*, I.17.23–5, pp. 47–51; *Rhetorica ad Herennium*, I.6.10, pp. 19–21. For the avoidance of *fastidium* see, for example, Sulpicius Severus, *Life of Martin*, pref., p. 136; Einhard, *Vita Karoli*, praef., p. 15; Widukind, *Res Gestae Saxonicae*, pref., p. 16; Eadmer, *Life of Anselm*, I.35, p. 62; and, more generally, Simon, 'Untersuchungen zur Topik der Widmungsbriefe', pp. 87–8; Janson, *Latin Prose Prefaces*, p. 154.
270 Liutprand, *Antapodosis*, IV.30, pp. 169–70; cf. Otto of Freising, *Deeds of Frederick*, I.51, p. 88.

request from a Christian bishop in the Umayyad caliphate 'to set down the deeds of the emperors and kings of all Europe'.[271] The fact that he had delayed complying for two years was due to what he calls his 'complete lack of eloquence' and to the hostility and jealousy of his critics, namely those proud and slothful people who think too much has already been written and, in any case, that nothing is said which has not already been said before.[272] Liutprand's rejoinder is to claim that his work will provide not only more knowledge (something true lovers of wisdom should always be seeking) but also pleasure and refreshment for those who are tired by the difficulties of Cicero's wit (*perplexa faceti Tullii lectione*).[273] Such recreation is necessary if the mind is not to be weakened and it takes the form of being distracted by the useful humour of comedy or by the pleasurable history of illustrious men (*heroum delectabili historia*).[274] It is only after this profession of personal inadequacy, diffusion of hostility and a promise of useful entertainment that Liutprand finally indicates the actual contents of his work: God is always just; He therefore overwhelms the wicked as repayment of their crimes and exalts the virtuous as repayment for their good deeds; this is happening now, every day, as God fights against our enemies and adversaries. Liutprand then begins his narrative with a straightforward synecdoche ('one example out of very many'), drawn from the Saracen colony at Fraxinetum.[275] The vividness and humour of Liutprand's subsequent narrative, however, do not completely conceal the seriousness of the point he wanted to communicate to the bishop of Elvira – accommodation and alliance with heathens,

---

271 Liutprand, *Antapodosis*, I.1, p. 31.
272 Cf. Terence, *The Eunuch*, trans. J. Barsby (Loeb, 2001), prol.41, p. 319.
273 *Antapodosis*, I.1, pp. 31–2. For Liutprand's acknowledgment of the vices, as well as the virtues, of rhetoric, see, for example, II.22, p. 81, II.41, p. 89, III.40, p. 129; for his appreciation of the trope of irony, see II.59, p. 97, V.23, p. 193.
274 *Antapodosis*, I.1, p. 32; cf. III.52, p. 138. For history, comedy and tragedy, see Orderic Vitalis, *Historia Ecclesiastica*, VII.16, p. 107 (see also page 403); Otto of Freising, *Chronicle*, Ep.ded., p. 89; Otto of Freising, *Deeds of Frederick*, I.47, p. 79 (see also page 118); and, more generally, T.M.S. Lehtonen, 'History, Tragedy and Fortune in Twelfth-Century Historiography with Special Reference to Otto of Freising's *Chronica*', in T.M.S. Lehtonen and P. Mehtonen (eds), *Historia: The Concept and Genres in the Middle Ages* (Helsinki, 2000), pp. 29–49.
275 *Antapodosis*, I.1, pp. 32–3; cf. I.4, p. 34, I.14, p. 47.

be they Saracens or Magyars, will always incur a just retribution from God.[276]

Quintilian accepts the very real difficulties which can arise when individuals fear offending those people against whom they are speaking or writing. In such circumstances, he suggests, they should follow the strategy of Cicero and, when they want to disparage someone and yet keep their favour intact, concede everything else to their opponents whilst pointing out that it is only in this one respect that the person being described falls short, and they should add, if possible, a reason why this should be the case (it may have resulted from stubbornness, for example, or from anger or the influence of others). The general remedy for such a difficulty is for the speaker to make it seem throughout what is being said that their attitude to their opponent is not only one of respect but even of love, whilst what they are saying is in support of a just cause and is being expressed not only in moderation but also out of necessity.[277] This strategy is likewise central to the argument of the *Rhetorica ad Herennium* when it lists 'parrhesia' or licence (*licentia*) as the figure of speech which should be employed when speaking before people who ought to be either respected or feared whilst at the same time reprehending them (or those close to them) for some error. In claiming the right to speak freely, there are various techniques and degrees of dissimulation by which the speaker can soften or mitigate any acrimony or anger that is thereby created – for example, by framing their criticism with praise, or by appealing to a model of friendship where it is possible to be loyal *both* to a friend *and* to the truth.[278]

The extent to which all these principles of judicial rhetoric left an imprint on medieval historiography can be gauged, in the first instance, from its prevailing concern with accusation and defence. It should not be assumed that all medieval descriptions of character and narratives of 'deeds done' were written simply as *encomia* along the lines laid down by demonstrative rhetoric. In the course of the preface to his 'life' of Gerald of Aurillac, Odo of Cluny explains that his goal is to commemorate his subject as an *exemplum* to be imitated

---

276 See pages 328–9.
277 Quintilian, *Institutio Oratoria*, XI.1.68–72, pp. 195–7; cf. Liutprand, *Antapodosis*, III.19, p. 117; Thietmar, *Chronicon*, V.7, p. 210.
278 *Rhetorica ad Herennium*, IV.36.48–37.50, pp. 349–55.

and as an admonition to be heeded, but the first reason he cites is the desire to set the record straight, not just for those who doubt and disbelieve but also for those who seek to justify their own sinful approach to wealth and power by appealing to an erroneous and self-serving account of Gerald's life.[279] Many individual *vitae* and *res gestae* were clearly written specifically as a defence of their subject against certain accusations. Liutprand of Cremona composed his *Deeds of Otto* in 964–65 in order to justify the emperor's actions in deposing a pope – he accordingly summons witnesses, cites original documentation and states that the 'justice' of Otto I's actions is being recorded for posterity.[280] Gerald of Wales writes his *Conquest of Ireland* in order both to defend the rightful claims of the kings of Britain (for which he cites papal privileges verbatim) and to justify and commemorate the role played by his own kin-group, the FitzGeralds (defending them, in turn, against their detractors).[281] The authors of such works might not necessarily reveal as much in the introductions to their texts but, read in the light of the fundamental distinction between *proemium* and *insinuatio*, this is often a quite deliberate strategy. Three prime examples are provided by Paschasius Radbertus' 'life' of Wala, the anonymous 'life' of Emma and the anonymous life of Henry IV.

As a monk at Corbie from 812, Paschasius Radbertus was the beneficiary of the extensive collection of Ciceronian texts which had been assembled by Hadoard, himself a pupil of Alcuin.[282] Paschasius had first written a life of Wala's brother, Adalhard (Hadoard's successor as abbot). In this, he goes out of his way to indicate his familiarity with the author he calls 'the king of Latin eloquence' (*rex eloquentiae latinae*).[283] Paschasius takes the opportunity presented by praise of Adalhard's appearance, for example, to observe that 'according to rhetoricians, a perfect individual's

---

279   Odo of Cluny, *Life of Gerald*, pref., p. 91; cf. III.12, p. 171.
280   Liutprand, *Gesta Ottonis*, trans. F.A. Wright, in *The Works of Liutprand of Cremona* (London, 1930), IV, p. 217, IX, pp. 221–2, XI, p. 224, XX, p. 231. For Thietmar's criticism of the same action, see his *Chronicon*, II.28, pp. 112–13, II.35, p. 118; cf. Otto of Freising, *Chronicle*, VI.23, p. 384.
281   Gerald of Wales, *Expugnatio Hibernica*, II.5–6, pp. 143–9, II.15, pp. 169–71, II.33, p. 231.
282   D. Ganz, *Corbie in the Carolingian Renaissance* (Sigmaringen, 1990), especially ch. 5.
283   Paschasius Radbertus, *Vita Adalhardi*, XX, p. 37.

quality [*qualitas*] is considered in terms of their name, fatherland (*patria*), lineage, status, fortune, body, education, conduct [*mores*], way of life, whether they administer things well and what household custom they maintain, their disposition of mind, art, situation, dress, countenance, gait, speech, and emotions'.[284] Not only does Paschasius proceed to use the framework provided by 'attributes of person' to describe, point by point, what sort of individual (*qualis*) Adalhard was,[285] but he also compares the task to Cicero's account of the painter Zeuxis 'in the second book of *On Invention in the Art of Rhetoric*'. Like Zeuxis, Paschasius, too, would be producing a likeness (*imago*) 'which will endure through the ages as a marvellous work', but he will have to do so by drawing from the several different models which Adalhard himself combined, 'because Nature has not finished anything in a single example which is perfect in all its parts'.[286] Paschasius' approach to historical narrative was similarly informed by 'attributes of events', and so he describes 'who, what, why, where, when, how and by what means, something was done'.[287] He was clearly well aware of both the techniques and the goals of classical rhetoric. In praising Adalhard's own eloquence, for example, Paschasius points out that 'his narrative was always particularly clear, brief, and lucid, the kind of speech which orators extol with highest praise, leaving nothing obscure or doubtful in meaning.... It was indeed most suitable for persuading or dissuading. He always moved his hearers to more avid attention, to a desire warmer than fire; he shattered torpor and aroused the indolent'. 'If such eloquence were granted to me', Paschasius concludes, 'I might more satisfactorily fulfil what I have attempted'.[288] This was rhetoric, however, which he knew needed to have a particular relation to the truth.

---

284 *Vita Adalhardi*, LV, p. 58; see also page 177.
285 *Vita Adalhardi*, LVI–LXIV, pp. 59–63; cf. Eadmer, *Life of Anselm*, I.21, p. 36: 'it seems to me impossible to obtain a full knowledge of the basis of his life if only his actions [*actus*] are described and nothing is said about who or what sort of person he was [*quis vel qualis*] in his speech'.
286 *Vita Adalhardi*, XX, pp. 37–8; cf. *De Inventione*, II.1.3, p. 169.
287 Paschasius Radbertus, *Expositio in Matheo Libri XII*, ed. B. Paul (*CCCM* 56, Turnhout, 1984), II, p. 146; cf. pseudo-Augustine, *De Rhetorica*, VII, p. 12; Alcuin, *Disputatio de Rhetorica et de Virtutibus*, ed. and trans.W.S. Howell, *The Rhetoric of Alcuin and Charlemagne* (Princeton, 1941), lines 105–11, p. 73.
288 Paschasius Radbertus, *Vita Adalhardi*, LXIII, p. 63; see also page 317.

As a result, when Paschasius came to summarise, at the very end of his work, just how he had ensured that remembrance and praise of Adalhard would be preserved forever in posterity, he declares that he has woven 'a cloak of letters' (*pallas litterarum*) but, in doing so, has not used 'the eloquence of cosmetic art' but has laboured to wrap it in 'a clean winding-sheet of purity' (*neque enim fucatae artis eloquentia texo sed sindone munda puritatis opere illud involvo*).[289]

Composed soon after Adalhard's death in 826, Paschasius Radbertus presents his 'life' as a funeral lament delivered over the abbot's grave (literally, an *epitaphium*) and, as such, its praise of character and deeds served a quite specific function.[290] Although Paschasius states that it is for posterity that examples of virtues (*exempla virtutum*) are committed to writing (in this case so that the *fama* of Adalhard's most holy life will be proclaimed for ever),[291] he also invokes the 'eloquent' models of Ambrose and Jerome for the more immediate juxtaposition of tears with consolation – as Ambrose had observed, whilst the grief of writing may increase the sorrow, the memory of the person who is lost and lamented is generally a source of peace, since that person seems to live again in speech.[292] However, when Paschasius came, some ten years later, to start a 'life' of Adalhard's brother, Wala, his task was far from being so straightforward.[293] Like Adalhard, Wala had fallen foul of Louis the Pious upon the latter's accession in 814: 'the devil's envy acted in [Louis] and truth suffered violence in the usual trickeries of wicked men'.[294] Whereas Adalhard was sent into exile, Wala was effectively forced to enter his brother's monastery

---

289 *Vita Adalhardi*, LXXXV, p. 76. The clean linen cloth is a reference to Matthew 27:59; for cosmetic colouring, see page 115, note 298.
290 See page 215.
291 *Vita Adalhardi*, I, p. 25, LXXXIII, p. 74.
292 *Vita Adalhardi*, I–II, pp. 25–6, quoting the opening words of Ambrose, *De Obitu Valentiniani Consolatio* (*PL* 16, cols 1357–84), col. 1357; cf. *Vita Adalhardi*, LXXIII, p. 68, and, more generally, P. von Moos, *Consolatio: Studien zur mittellateinischen Trostliteratur über den Tod und zum Problem der christlichen Trauer* (Munich, 1971–2), vol. I, pp. 137–46.
293 Paschasius Radbertus, *Epitaphium Arsenii*, trans. A.Cabaniss; cf. D. Ganz, 'The *Epitaphium Arsenii* and Opposition to Louis the Pious', in P. Godman and R. Collins (eds), *Charlemagne's Heir: New Perspectives on the Reign of Louis the Pious* (Oxford, 1990), pp. 537–50; M. De Jong, *The Penitential State: Authority and Atonement in the Age of Louis the Pious* (Cambridge, 2009), pp. 102–11.
294 Paschasius Radbertus, *Vita Adalhardi*, XXX, p. 43.

at Corbie. Following the brothers' rehabilitation in 822, however, Wala then played a leading role in supporting Louis' son, Lothar, first in governing Italy and then (after succeeding Adalhard as abbot in 826) in opposing Louis' division of the Frankish empire. Wala's involvement in the crisis of 828–30 resulted in a further period of exile in 831 and, after his attempts to act as mediator in the renewed conflict of 833 left him once more at the mercy of the emperor, in 834 he had little option but to flee to Italy, to the monastery at Bobbio, where he died in 836. Wala's life and deeds were thus a subject of some political sensitivity, and the nature of Paschasius' composition was accordingly fraught with considerable difficulties, if not danger.

Paschasius himself was clearly well aware of the problems presented by the situation in which he found himself writing ('we must now think over beforehand what, to whom, and when we may speak'), particularly when acknowledging that 'it would be useful to many people to dissimulate what should be set forth and to declare what should be kept silent'.[295] As he points out, 'it is not now the time to proclaim anything praiseworthy about [Wala]'.[296] Indeed, he explicitly concedes that 'whilst various situations are happening, the pen is confused in communication, the order of speech is not maintained, and a richer supply of tears is not drawn from its source in the heart'.[297] Keeping some things hidden (*secreta*), Paschasius can therefore only look forward to the day when he can break his prudent silence, 'when it will be permissible for me to state openly what [Wala] did and to unfold more clearly the more important things about him'.[298] This is one reason why, as Paschasius himself accepts, he has written so enigmatically and allusively,[299] as well as in a style which is not simple but mixed (*modesto stilo*).[300] It may also be why he chose to give his account the form of a fictive dialogue between pseudonymous interlocutors and refers to Wala throughout by the name of 'Arsenius' (that is, the tutor who had been chosen by the emperor

---

295 Paschasius Radbertus, *Epitaphium*, I.8, p. 106, I.9, p. 108.
296 *Epitaphium*, I.10, p. 111.
297 *Epitaphium*, I.9, p. 107.
298 *Epitaphium*, I.11, p. 115.
299 *Epitaphium*, I.11, p. 115.
300 *Epitaphium*, I.prol., p. 85; see also pages 295–6.

Theodosius to educate his son but who subsequently rejected such worldly honour in favour of the desert). Only when the 'torches of enmity have been laid to rest', Paschasius concludes, will he be able to set everything out openly (*palam*) to those people who want to hear it.[301] The result, on Paschasius' own account, is a text written in two discrete stages – book I at some point following Wala's death in 836 and seemingly circumscribed by fear of the consequences of writing too freely, and book II begun only when circumstances made it possible for him to do what ought to be done and set down what he had previously omitted.[302] It is therefore this second book which deals in detail with the events of 828–30 and 833–34, in which he vehemently denounces the actions of empress Judith and Bernard of Septimania and quotes verbatim from the full and frank castigation of sins which Wala had personally delivered before Louis the Pious in December 828, as well as the accusations exchanged between the emperor and his sons in 833 on the 'Field of Lies'.[303] The final version of Paschasius' text that emerges is a work of considerable despair, completed in the aftermath of 843, perhaps as late as the 850s, following his retirement as abbot of Corbie, but in either case at a point when he had witnessed the division of an empire whose unity had, in his eyes, hitherto provided a bastion against the vice, discord and calamity he associated with the sixth, and final, age of the world.[304]

Ostensibly, Paschasius' 'life' of Wala belongs to the same genre of lament and consolation as his earlier 'life' of Adalhard. This much is made clear right at the start of the text, where Paschasius effectively summarises the principles which had also informed his earlier work – this will serve as a memorial for ages to come, a likeness of its subject's character (*imago morum*) painted

---

301 *Epitaphium*, I.21, p. 130.
302 *Epitaphium*, II.prol., p. 147.
303 *Epitaphium*, II.1–3, pp. 149–55, II.17, pp. 186–90. For the appellation 'field of lies' (*campus mendacii, campus mentitus*), see Thegan, *Life of Louis*, trans. J.R. Ginsburg and D.L. Boutelle, rev. P.E. Dutton, in P.E. Dutton (ed.), *Carolingian Civilization: A Reader* (Ontario, 1993), XLII, p. 150; Astronomer, *Life of Louis*, trans. A.Cabaniss, *Son of Charlemagne: A Contemporary Life of Louis the Pious* (Syracuse, 1961), III.48, p. 96.
304 *Epitaphium*, II.10, p. 172, II.19, p. 193, II.20, p. 195. For the ages of the world, see page 102.

in the manner of Zeuxis 'because in his actions [he] displayed the probity of many illustrious men'.[305] In demonstrating not only what sort, but also how great, an individual he was (*qualis quantusve*),[306] it will constitute a 'funeral oration in the manner of the ancients' (*epitaphium ... more priorum*).[307] Grief is therefore once again combined with consolation: 'weeping and tears are alleviations of desire, and desire is the happy recollection of the lost', bittersweet, as Seneca put it, like apples.[308] Wala, Paschasius insists, is an example to be imitated in every respect: 'recollection itself ... will renew our grief, but such memory is pleasure for the mind and an incitement to virtue'.[309] Indeed, by truly imitating his virtues, Paschasius and his audience will ensure that Wala remains in their presence for ever.[310] The first part of Paschasius' prologue to his work accordingly proceeds along lines which his audience might have expected from any such introduction that was informed by demonstrative rhetoric. The author is writing in response to a request and with a profound sense of his own unworthiness for the task. So much so, in fact, that Paschasius states (quoting Terence) that he has been 'unable to find any suitable beginning for these matters' and, as a result, will simply 'begin to narrate those things which in part I have observed with these eyes, in part heard with these ears' and, he adds (now using words of his own), 'which I have understood more fully with my mind'.[311] The second part of the introduction, however, elaborates at some length on the offence which Paschasius fears his account will now cause because of the hostility Wala himself attracted: 'woe to me, my mother, why did you give birth to me, a man of contention, a man of discord in the whole earth?' (Jeremiah 15:10).[312] As far as he was concerned, Paschasius claims he had no desire for 'the

---

305 *Epitaphium*, I.prol., pp. 83–5.
306 *Epitaphium*, I.7, p. 101, I.9, p. 107, I.11, p. 113, I.26, p. 138; cf. *Vita Adalhardi*, XXV, p. 40 (*tantus ac talis*).
307 *Epitaphium*, I.prol., pp. 84–5.
308 *Epitaphium*, I.5, p. 96, quoting Seneca, *Letters*, Ep.63, pp. 431–3; cf. *Epitaphium*, I.8, p. 105, I.15, p. 121, I.29, p. 145, II.23, p. 200.
309 *Epitaphium*, I.15, pp. 120–1, I.16, p. 125, I.17, pp. 125–6.
310 *Epitaphium*, I.17, p. 126.
311 *Epitaphium*, I.prol., p. 83; cf. Terence, *Hecyra*, trans. J. Barsby, *The Mother-in-Law* (Loeb, 2001), III.3 lines 361–3, p. 185.
312 *Epitaphium*, I.prol., p. 84, I.1, p. 89.

devastation of fire to be kindled from ashes after disputes and discord have been lain to rest', 'striving to beat with a stick everything which is already burned out to see if it would blaze up once again'.[313] Indeed, he raises the possibility that hardly anyone, or only the occasional individual, will actually believe his portrait of Wala's character.[314] Nonetheless, having expressed such anxieties over the potentially incendiary and unbelievable nature of his material, Paschasius uses the rest of the prologue to set about justifying the approach and the content of his work against both of these criticisms.

What is so striking about the second half of Paschasius' prologue to his *epitaphium* is the judicial language to which he appeals. His defence of the truth (*veritas*) and credibility (*fides*) of his account, for example, opens with a guarantee adapted from Seneca: 'who ever required sworn compurgators [*iuratores*] of a historian? Yet, if it should be necessary, there are a great many honest men [*probi viri*] who will set their right hands in oath to the statements you enter [*assertiones*]'.[315] Paschasius is certainly prepared to appeal to such testimony in the same way that he had done in his life of Adalhard, citing 'suitable witnesses' (*testes idonei*) throughout his account, including the 'proof' of Adalhard's own life (*testis est vita eius*).[316] However, he also acknowledges that to secure credibility for his account of Wala will not be an easy task. Truth is frequently trampled upon, he remarks, and even if the proof of his narrative were to be attested (*adtestatus*) by the sun itself, 'which gazes on everything', it will rarely be listened to. Indeed, such is the hostility (*invidia*) of Wala's enemies that his opponents will themselves 'swear with outstretched arms', particularly when they recognise

---

313 *Epitaphium*, I.prol., p. 85.
314 *Epitaphium*, I.prol., p. 86; cf. I.9, p. 108 (*vix talia creduntur*).
315 *Epitaphium*, I.prol., p. 86, quoting Seneca, *Ludus de Morte Claudii* [*Apocolocyntosis*], ed. and trans. P.T. Eden (Cambridge, 1984), I.proem., p. 29. For knowledge of this text in the Middle Ages, including by William of Malmesbury, see Reynolds, *Texts and Transmission*, pp. 361–2.
316 Paschasius Radbertus, *Vita Adalhardi*, XVI, p. 36, XVIII, p. 37, XXII, p. 39, XL, p. 51, LVIII, p. 60, LIX, p. 61, LXIII, p. 63, LXXVIII, p. 71; cf. *Epitaphium*, I.4, p. 95, I.6, pp. 98–9, I.9, p. 109, I.20, p. 130, I.21, p. 131, II.prol., p. 148 ('truth will be better commended by three witnesses' [2 Corinthians 13:1]), II.8, p. 162 ('these matters were reported by the most serious and most truthful men such that there could be no doubt about them').

the source of what follows. Nonetheless, Paschasius remains adamant that it would be morally unworthy (*indignus*) to remain silent about the truth through fear, just as, in his life of Adalhard, he recognised that the 'laws of truth' (*iura veritatis*) should not be renounced out of torpor and sloth.[317]

Even without a clear narrative sequence (*ordo et status narrationis*),[318] Paschasius continues his portrait of Wala's character amounts to a history of what was done (*quasi rei gestae historiam*) and, as such, it is explicitly identified as a narrative which will represent truth (*veritas*) as distinct from fable (*fabula*). There will always be people, he observes, for whom truth is only ever a fable and a game (*ludus*); it is also unreasonable to imagine that *any* account will be equally pleasing and believable to everyone. Indeed, given that some people do not even believe the truth of Christ, despite the quantity and the quality of the witnesses (*testes*) available there, Paschasius accepts that he has no real grounds for complaining.[319] He is left, therefore, with a clear goal. According to the *Disticha Catonis*, belief (*fides*) is rare when many people say many different things. Paschasius thinks he would therefore be wrong, on this basis, to believe everything readily, or rashly, and to be so impressed with the belief of the masses, or indeed of any individual, that he is incapable of accepting a better point of view. Paschasius wants to prove his likeness of Wala with such clarity that, once it has been set out, no further judgment will be necessary, since he will thereby also have proved its credibility (*probanda est igitur imago ... probanda et fides*).[320] A truthful account of Wala will make this possible since 'it is not good and honest men who attack and defame him but harmful and malignant men, or the ignorant deceived by rumours, who pursue him with hatred'. Instead, Paschasius concludes, 'the most worthy and splendid deeds commend him everywhere and his life itself serves as a witness [*protestatur*]; those who therefore seek to drag his life down and diminish his praise are actually arraigning themselves [*seipsos accusant*]'.[321]

---

317 *Vita Adalhardi*, IV, p. 27, XXX, p. 44.
318 *Epitaphium*, I.29, p. 145.
319 *Epitaphium*, I.prol., pp. 87–8.
320 *Epitaphium*, I.7, p. 103; cf. *Disticha Catonis*, I.13, p. 46, II.20.2, p. 122.
321 *Epitaphium*, II.10, p. 172.

In the event, it is unclear just how wide or public an audience Paschasius' judicial defence of Wala was given. The manuscript evidence suggests that circulation of his *Epitaphium* may have been restricted simply to the monks of Corbie. Indeed, an allusion to Seneca's *Apocolocyntosis* in the prologue may indicate that this was always intended to be a 'private' text: 'if you ask him, he will relate it to one person only, for I believe that he will never speak a single word in the presence of many.... Whatever he saw, he affirmed that he would tell no one in expressed words'.[322] Not that a detailed defence of Wala would have been a redundant exercise within the confines of his own monastery. Paschasius is clearly concerned to defend Wala as an embodiment of Benedictine ideals ('it seemed to me ... that he bore the person of father Benedict'),[323] often against a series of quite specific charges. 'Many', he reports, 'cried out that he pillaged all the goods of our monastery', 'many strive to reproach him for leaving [by fleeing to Bobbio] the place where he was professed and elected'.[324] Paschasius wonders why 'sometimes people insist that he was austere or harsh', why 'they say that he did not conform his actions sufficiently [to the model of Christ's love] and was himself less loved in return and less visited by many'.[325] 'Certain people amongst us', Paschasius observes, 'did not at the time understand that ... these things were not offered to him as gifts, but to be transmitted through him to us'.[326] Above all, Paschasius was clearly concerned to refute the charge that Wala's involvement in politics was inconsistent with the prescriptions of the Rule of Benedict. 'Many people', he records, 'make this false accusation [about Wala's attempts to mediate in the events of 833], as if he ought not to have had any further care for these things nor to involve himself in such matters', whereas, in

---

322 *Epitaphium*, I.prol., p. 87; cf. Seneca, *Apocolocyntosis*, I.proem., p. 29. For the 'private' circulation of an ostensibly 'public' work of history, see J. Nelson, 'Public Histories and Private History in the Work of Nithard', *Speculum*, 60 (1985), pp. 251–93; reprinted in J. Nelson, *Politics and Ritual in Early Medieval Europe* (London, 1986); cf. J. Nelson, 'History-Writing at the Courts of Louis the Pious and Charles the Bald', in A.Scharer and G. Scheibelreiter (eds), *Historiographie im frühen Mittelalter* (Vienna, 1994), pp. 439–40.
323 *Epitaphium*, I.prol., p. 85; cf.I.prol., p. 86, I.21, pp. 131–3.
324 *Epitaphium*, I.14, p. 120, II.21, p. 196.
325 *Epitaphium*, I.23, p. 135, I.25, p. 137.
326 *Epitaphium*, I.29, p. 145.

Paschasius' account, the justification was clear – Wala was acting on behalf of the Christian faith, the emperor, the emperor's sons, the empire, the well-being of the people and the *patria*, justice and laws, stability and unity, peaceful concord, and the eradication of vice.[327] This was the force, and the value, of arguing that, like Zeuxis' portrait, Wala's perfection consisted of more than just the one ideal provided by Benedict.

Paschasius' central contention throughout his *Epitaphium* is that Wala bore the image, not only of Benedict, but also of a second Jeremiah, advising, admonishing, correcting and, where necessary, bitterly castigating the sins of his people through invective (*invectio*).[328] His was a generation, after all, which was experiencing a justifiable scourging from God,[329] and, like Jeremiah, Wala could see that the Augustinian conflict between the mingled cities of Jerusalem and Babylon[330] would once more result in a figurative 'captivity' to the tyranny of pride and self-love. Paschasius wrote his own commentary on Jeremiah's book of Lamentations in the mid-840s and the prophetic conjunction of truth with justice runs right through his characterisation of both Adalhard and Wala as advocates of 'justice and truth' (*iustitia ac veritas*).[331] It is a model which Paschasius will follow in his own work 'even though pursued by threats and wounded by defamation'. 'Lest anyone say that such things should not be heaped up nor unfolded in a lamentation [*in threnis*], let them know that there is no more appropriate place, especially when such evils are increasing, when truth is attacked by hatred, when justice is vanquished. So it was that Jeremiah the prophet, after rebukes, persecutions and assaults, turned to lamentation and wept most bitterly over everything that had happened because of transgressions'.[332]

---

327 *Epitaphium*, II.11, p. 175, II.15, pp. 180–1; cf. H. Mayr-Harting, 'Two Abbots in Politics – Wala of Corbie and Bernard of Clairvaux", *Transactions of the Royal Historical Society*, 40 (1990), pp. 218–27.
328 *Epitaphium*, I.prol., p. 84, I.prol., p. 86, I.1, p. 89, I.2, pp. 90–1, I.4, p. 95, I.21, p. 131, I.23, p. 135, II.2, p. 151, II.5, p. 156.
329 *Epitaphium*, II.1, p. 149.
330 *Vita Adalhardi*, XLIII, p. 52.
331 *Epitaphium*, I.3, p. 94, I.8, p. 104, I.26, p. 138, I.27, p. 142, II.1, p. 149, II.24, p. 204; cf. *Vita Adalhardi*, VII, p. 29, XXX, p. 44, XXXI, p. 45.
332 *Epitaphium*, II.8, p. 164.

Paschasius' own defence of truth and justice takes the form of a point-by-point refutation of the charges levelled against Wala, in his lifetime and against his posthumous reputation. Paschasius himself makes the case with an apposite piece of *praeteritio*: 'although we have the capacity to plead at length [*facultas perorandi*], we cannot respond to individual charges with what is said to each one of them; let us therefore beg the grace of piety rather than pour forth complaints and refutations [*querelae reprehensionum*]; let us offer the sorrow of our hearts rather than take up the part of our noble friend for his defence [*ad defensionem eius*]'.[333] Adalhard, too, after all, had fallen victim to 'the deceit of false accusers' (*fraus calumniantium*), to 'the blind and stupid cunning of perverse men' who planned 'to besmirch and stain good men's reputation for virtue [*fama virtutis*]' and who 'lied in order to befoul [their] honour and happiness'.[334] However, whereas Adalhard himself had given thanks that he would be found worthy to suffer abuse (*contumelia*) for the sake of the truth (Acts 5:41),[335] Paschasius clearly though it necessary to set the record straight. Wala's *fama* stood in even greater need of someone who would act, like Adalhard, as an advocate of the truth (*assertor veritatis*) and a pleader of legal cases (*quaerimoniam iura causidicus*),[336] since, as things stood, if anyone related anything publicly about Wala, people seemed to take greater pleasure from what was false, empty or made up (*falsum aut vanum vel fictum*).[337] Paschasius accordingly defends Wala against slander and calumny, against rumour and ignorance, against lies, hatred and spite, against people who disparaged him and charged him with the faults of others, who said that good is evil and evil good, and who continued to do so right up to the present: 'this is what I still hear today that some people falsely accuse him...; this is in no way the case, as you erroneously suppose and as at that time many people thought'.[338] From the outset, Paschasius presents

---

333 *Epitaphium*, II.8, p. 163. For *praeteritio*, see page 7.
334 *Vita Adalhardi*, XXX, p. 44, XXXI, pp. 45–6.
335 *Vita Adalhardi*, XXXVI, p. 49.
336 *Vita Adalhardi*, XXXVIII, p. 50, LI, p. 57.
337 *Epitaphium*, I.21, p. 130.
338 *Epitaphium*, II.4, p. 155; cf. I.5, p. 96, I.7, p. 102, I.8, pp. 104–5, I.9, p. 108, I.10, p. 111, I.11, p. 115, I.21, pp. 130–1, I.26, p. 140, I.26, p. 142, I.29, p. 146, II.1, p. 149, II.8, p. 163, II.9, p. 165.

himself facing a disbelieving public who are charging Wala with 'what they call guile [*versutia*] and faithlessness [*infidelitas*]'.[339] It is Paschasius' intention to prove that neither accusation stands up to forensic scrutiny. Wala, he writes, 'sought, not his own advantage in anything, but Christ's [Philippians 2:21]. He errs, therefore, who judges that [Wala] was summoned to face the danger of exile or death because he knowingly or wilfully neglected something in those affairs; or that he injured the *patria*, violated the majesty of empire, dishonoured the emperor and his sons, broke faith, and disrupted the peace. He was not accused by good and prudent men of disdaining ecclesiastical laws or hating the king's glory or the fullness of the empire.... As a result, in all these matters, he was deservedly cited as not guilty [*non reus*] of malevolence but guilty [*reus*] of virtue, for blessed are the ones who suffer persecution for the sake of justice [Matthew 5:10]'.[340]

Wala's accusers provide a constant point of reference throughout Paschasius' text, right up to the bitter end, when a disbelieving slanderer (*sichofanta incredulus*) is summoned to claim that an individual who had been exposed to such great trials and cast down by the pressures of such adversity did not merit the attention that he was being given.[341] If Paschasius' funeral remembrance starts by characterising itself as an outpouring of grief, then his formal expressions of lamentation and consolation are subsequently combined, quite deliberately, with a specifically judicial pursuit of the truth of the past. Paschasius, by his own account, has not attributed to Wala more than he should have done or more than is true.[342] He has, instead, narrated for posterity the full truth about him (*ad plenum veritatem de illo ... narrare*)[343] and has revealed things more clearly so that Wala should appear free of accusation (*excusabilis*).[344] Paschasius' final summary therefore explicitly pairs the terminology of lament with the historiographical language of judicial cause and effect,

---
339 *Epitaphium*, I.2, p. 91, I.3, p. 92.
340 *Epitaphium*, II.10, p. 171; cf.II.8, p. 160, II.9, p. 166, II.10, pp. 168–9, 171–2, II.11, pp. 174–5.
341 *Epitaphium*, II.24, p. 204.
342 *Epitaphium*, I.16, p. 123.
343 *Epitaphium*, II.1, p. 149.
344 *Epitaphium*, II.9, p. 167.

of what happened, and why. 'We have now ... grieved', he writes, 'over what has been done in the past [*quae gesta sunt*], over what has happened [*quae contigerunt*]; we have wept over critical moments and diverse outcomes [*discrimina rerum et varios eventus*]; we have reckoned the trials; with lamentation we have enumerated the diverse substance of the causes [*varia causarum negotia enumeravimus*]'.[345] As a result, Paschasius concludes, 'although we have rightfully lamented, although we have bemoaned the various attacks on him and enumerated his manifold trials, we have also expounded what occurred [*casus exposuimus*]'.[346]

The *Encomium Emmae Reginae* (the title is not original), like the *Epitaphium Arsenii*, presented its author (an anonymous monk from Saint-Bertin in Saint-Omer in Flanders) with a whole host of practical and political difficulties. The text was written in 1041–42, ostensibly in praise of a Norman queen, but this was a queen who had been married, successively, to two kings of the English (the West Saxon Æthelred II and the Danish Cnut), who was therefore mother to two claimants to the English throne (Harthacnut and Edward [the Confessor]), and who was suspected of complicity in the events which had led to the capture, blinding and subsequent death of a third son, Edward's younger brother Alfred, in 1036–37. To celebrate the history of Emma's 'life and deeds' was therefore far from being a straightforward task. The immediate political context within which the text was written, moreover, and to which it seems to have been intended as a direct contribution, was both complex and highly charged. Emma and Harthacnut were trying to establish their rule in England following the death of Harald Harefoot in 1040, that is, after three years of exile for Emma in Flanders and, in Harthacnut's case, as many as seventeen years in Denmark. More specifically, the author seems to have been addressing a court audience made up of English, Danes and Normans at a point in 1041–42 when Edward was being associated in a form of co-rule with his half-brother. This, at least, is the clear implication of the concluding paragraph of the *Encomium*, which uses an allusion to Lucan (*Pharsalia* I.92) to argue that this 'triumvirate' had brought an end to internecine strife, but also to warn of

---

345 *Epitaphium*, II.22, p. 197.
346 *Epitaphium*, II.23, p. 200.

the destructive discord that would descend were such a trinitarian harmony to be broken. In the event, Harthacnut's untimely death in June 1042 meant that this vision was soon superseded and a new codicil had to be appended to the text but, as originally conceived, the author seems to have intended the *Encomium* to serve as an assertion of Emma's central political role in a live discussion of dynastic legitimacy and continuity. This is a 'historical' work, therefore, with a political reputation to defend and a dynastic agenda to articulate, but which was also anticipating, and on both counts, a potentially hostile reaction from its audience.[347]

The *Encomium Emmae* is a work of considerable literary sophistication and draws on a specific range of classical and Christian sources (Sallust, Lucan, Sulpicius Severus and, above all, Vergil); it also reveals at least a passing familiarity with the norms of Scandinavian praise-poetry.[348] The chief difficulty with its interpretation lies in the relationship between the main body of the text and its two introductions (a dedicatory letter addressed directly to Emma herself, followed by a prologue addressed to a wider readership and audience). In trying to establish the intention and purpose behind the work it has thus proved particularly problematic to explain how an initial acknowledgment that history-writing should be free from both rhetorical ornamentation and falsehood can be followed by a narrative which includes such fabulous, fictive and tendentious contents, and how a commission to write to the praise and glory of Emma produces a text two-thirds of which is devoted to celebrating the deeds of Svein and his son Cnut.[349]

---

[347] For the political context, see the supplementary 'Introduction' to the reissue of Campbell's edition of the *Encomium Emmae Reginae* by S. Keynes (Cambridge, 1998). See also F. Lifshitz, 'The *Encomium Emmae Reginae* – A "Political Pamphlet" of the Eleventh Century?', *Haskins Society Journal*, 1 (1989), pp. 39–50; E. John, 'The *Encomium Emmae Reginae* – A Riddle and a Solution', *Bulletin of the John Rylands Library*, 63 (1980), pp. 58–94; P. Stafford, *Queen Emma and Queen Edith: Queenship and Women's Power in Eleventh-Century England* (Oxford, 1997), pp. 28–40.
[348] See Campbell's introduction to his translation of *Encomium Emmae Reginae*, pp. xxix–xxxiv, and Keynes' 'Introduction', pp. cxi–cxvi; cf. A. Orchard, 'The Literary Background to the *Encomium Emmae Reginae*', *Journal of Medieval Latin*, 11 (2001), pp. 156–83; E.M. Tyler, 'Fictions of Family – The *Encomium Emmae Reginae* and Vergil's *Aeneid*', *Viator*, 36 (2005), pp. 149–79.
[349] Cf. Smalley, *Historians in the Middle Ages*, p. 76: 'Emma herself disappears behind a cloud of rhetorical borrowings'; Keynes, 'Introduction', p. lxxi: 'the *Encomium* represents the triumph of literary artifice over historical truth; and

Despite the author's claim to be composing a true narrative (*vera lectio*) and *not* to be making up falsehoods (*falsa fingendo*) because of any personal partiality (*gratia*),[350] the *Encomium* ends up presenting a very particular reading of historical events – it omits some inconvenient truths (Æthelred II is never mentioned by name, nor as Emma's first husband), glosses over others (Edward and Alfred appear simply as 'noble sons', their exact parentage deliberately obscured) and sticks resolutely to Emma's interpretation of what had happened (Harald Harefoot had been a tyrant and a usurper and he was not even Cnut's biological offspring). Given the sensitivity of the issues which had to be negotiated by the author, such economy may be perfectly understandable, but given that his audience would itself have had a very clear sense of what was, and was not, 'true', such dissimulation sits a little awkwardly with what is said about falsehood in the introduction. Unless, that is, this prefatory material is read in the light of the guidelines for composing an *insinuatio*.

Close reading of both the dedicatory letter and the prologue suggests that the author is trying hard, not only to secure the goodwill of his audience (protesting his own unworthiness, lamenting the inability of words to do justice to the excellence of his subject-matter, promising brevity, insisting that he is writing on command), but also to anticipate and deflect the criticism that both his subject-matter and his treatment of it may attract. In the dedicatory letter, therefore, the author explicitly sympathises with the anxiety that some people in his audience may have that, once one falsehood is introduced into a historical narrative, this will invalidate the entire account.[351] Indeed, the reason the author adduces for doubting that his abilities are up to the Sallustian task of committing to posterity a remembrance of Emma's deeds (*memoria rerum gestarum*) is that such a *historia* would demand that he must not stray from the straight path of truth. If someone is writing the deeds of an individual, he explains, and introduces anything false into the truth, be it through error or, as is often the

---

while truth is still there, it is a truth which lies hidden in the artifice'; A. Gransden, *Historical Writing in England c.550–c.1307* (London, 1974), p. 58: 'the rhetorical element detracts from the value of the *Encomium* as a historical source'.
350 *Encomium Emmae Reginae*, I.1, p. 11, II.9, p. 25.
351 Cf. page 381.

case, for the sake of ornamentation, then as soon as the introduction even of one lie (*mendacium*) has been discovered, the audience will consider that the deeds described have not, in fact, been done (*facta velut infecta*). This is why the author considers historians should be wary lest, by making certain interpolations and juxtaposing falsehood with what is true, they lose the very name which they seem to possess from their official position: 'the actual event makes the [written] truth believable, but the [written] truth also gives credence to the event [*res enim veritati, veritas quoque fidem facit rei*]'. Having expressed doubts over his own ability on this particular score, the author then generalises the observation – he is acutely ashamed of how badly people tend to conduct themselves in this regard. He therefore describes himself as caught in a jam (*angustia*). Either he can indulge in words in order to express the truth of what has happened but, as a result, be bitterly criticised for empty verbiage (*vana loquacitas*), or he can, as he has just said, avoid saying anything false by being more restrained in his narrative but, as a result, be criticised for having hidden what was open when he ought to have uncovered what lay concealed. Faced with the prospect of writing history without elegance of language (that is, as a simple, unadorned and potentially obscure narrative), he is afraid that he will then be called verbose (*loquax*) if he proceeds to employ what he terms a 'complex narrative' (*multiplex narratio*). Since he is unable to avoid writing altogether, the author clearly has to choose – either subject himself to these varying judgments from other people or, by being silent, ignore what his queen has commanded. After due consideration, the author states that he would prefer to be criticised by some people for verbiage than to conceal from everyone the truth of a particularly memorable subject. This is therefore the path he has selected and, now that he has set to one side his own mitigating circumstances (*excusabiles ... occasiones*), he will start to weave together his narrative.[352]

The dedicatory letter to the *Encomium* is clearly drawing attention to, and seeking the audience's pardon for, a deliberately chosen feature of the narrative which follows. It will be *multiplex*, that is, it will use rhetorical ornamentation and, as such, risk mixing falsehood with truth in the interests of revealing what

---

352 *Encomium Emmae Reginae*, prol. (Ep.ded.), p. 5.

should not be hidden. The connotations evoked by the author's precise use of language here drive the point home. In particular, the phrases *facta velut infecta* and *multiplex narratio* set up a direct parallel with Vergil's account of the capacity of *fama* (that is, rumour, opinion or reputation) to mix fact with falsehood, what is done with what was not done (*facta atque infecta*), what actually happened with what is said or believed to have happened. This is the 'complex register' (*multiplex sermo*) which Vergil describes being enjoyed by *fama*, 'holding fast to what is made up [*ficta*] and wrong, as much as it announces what is true [*verum*]'.[353] Right at the start of his narrative, in other words, the author of the *Encomium* alludes to Vergil's point in order to alert his audience to the fact that his work may indeed include a combination of what is true with things that have been made up. By evoking Vergil, rather than simply Sallust or Sulpicius Severus, and by subsequently referring to Vergil's account of Anchises' anniversary boat race as an 'ancient fable',[354] the author is aligning his own text with the well-established characterisation of the *Aeneid* as a work which combined both truth and fiction (*vera cum fictis*) within the same narrative.[355]

If the dedicatory letter alerts the audience to one aspect of the ensuing *res gestae* which might otherwise prove problematic, then

---

[353] Vergil, *Aeneid*, IV.188–90, p. 409. See Tyler, 'Fictions of Family', pp. 163–7, for the further suggestion that the author's choice of terminology deliberately evokes Vergil's account of Sinon (the 'lying' Greek warrior who combined true things with false in order to make the Trojans accept the wooden horse), as well as Macrobius' view of fable that 'weaves together' a foundation of truth with a 'made-up' covering and Horace's poetic mixture of true things with false. Cf. Macrobius, *Commentary on the Dream of Scipio*, trans. W.H. Stahl (New York, 1952), I.2, p. 85; Horace, *Ars Poetica*, trans. H.R. Fairclough (Loeb, 1929), 151–2, p. 463. Compare Cosmas of Prague, *Chronicle of the Czechs*, III.19, pp. 203–4.
[354] *Encomium Emmae Reginae*, I.4, p. 13.
[355] Servius, *In Vergilii Carmina Commentarii*, pref., p. 4; cf. Bernardus Silvestris, *Commentary on the First Six Books of Virgil's Aeneid*, pref., p. 5: 'Let us now consider these matters with regard to philosophical truth. To the extent that he writes about the nature of human life, Virgil is a philosopher. His procedure is to describe allegorically by means of an integument what the human spirit does and endures while temporarily placed in the human body.... The integument is a type of exposition which wraps the apprehension of truth in a fictional narrative, and thus it is also called an *involucrum*, a cover. One grasps the utility of this work, which is self-knowledge; it is very useful for man to know himself, as Macrobius says "from the sky comes *nothis elitos*", that is, know yourself'. See page 383.

the prologue, addressed directly to the reader, raises a second. Once again the author anticipates a hostile reaction, this time to his apparent error or lack of expertise in not making Emma herself central to his work. The deeds he had been commissioned to write up are immediately qualified as deeds that pertain to the honour of Emma and her family (*rerum inquam tuo tuorum honori attinentium*), that is, the deeds of Svein, Cnut and Harthacnut. Again it is Vergil to whom the author appeals in order to extenuate or justify the fact that, even though he may open with the praiseworthy deeds of Svein, his work is nonetheless consistently dedicated to the praise and glory of Emma. This time, the comparison is made explicit. The *Aeneid*, he writes, is devoted to the praises of Octavian (Augustus), even though practically no mention of him by name, or clearly very little, is actually introduced by Vergil into the text itself. If this precedent is not, in itself, convincing, then the reader simply has to look at the structure of the *Encomium*, where they will find that praise of Emma circumscribes the entire text, appearing at the beginning (the dedicatory letter), in the middle (her marriage to Cnut) and at the end (her piety in Bruges and her rule with Harthacnut).[356] The *Aeneid* is a potentially delicate text to be invoked here as a comparison (*a similibus*) given that, if Svein and Cnut subsequently appear as the equivalents of Anchises and Aeneas, this could come dangerously close to making Emma the equivalent of Lavinia, that is, Aeneas' second wife ('the cause of all this woe is again an alien bride, again a foreign marriage').[357] As a result, the author goes out of his way to demonstrate how Emma's marriage to Cnut was, in fact, a unifying instrument of peace and reconciliation between warring peoples.[358] Otherwise, reference to Vergil provides him with the requisite authority for putting into practice one further guideline for an *insinuatio* – start by replacing a source of potential hostility (Emma) with something or someone (a *fabula* or *historia*) which is loved or approved by its audience (the magnificent invasion fleet of Svein and the deeds of Cnut).

Having used books I and II to remind his audience of what an Anglo-Danish elite in 1041–42 should have in common – the

---

356 *Encomium Emmae Reginae*, prol., pp. 7–9.
357 Vergil, *Aeneid*, VI.93–4, p. 513, XI.479–80, p. 269.
358 *Encomium Emmae Reginae*, II.16, p. 33.

deeds of their predecessors which they would themselves now do well to imitate – the author is able to bring in gradually the real substance of his political agenda in book III. Emma had to demonstrate the virtue of her actions and the legitimacy of her rule. She needed an account of the years 1035–40 which would justify what she had done in the eyes of the erstwhile supporters of Harald Harefoot, which would clear her of any suspicion of complicity in the murder of Alfred, and which would bolster support for Harthacnut (not least with respect to Edward, whose summons in 1041 may have been as much a judicious bid for security as it was a necessary and visible means of support). The *Encomium* fulfils each of these three functions in turn. First and foremost, the author produces an account which exculpates Emma from any complicity in the death of her younger son, citing verbatim the text of a letter which, it is claimed, had been forged in order to trick Alfred into coming over to England.[359] Indeed, in reminding his audience of a mother's pain and sorrow at both the fact and the manner of Alfred's 'martyrdom', the author does not shy away from narrating the emotive details of his death. It is Harthacnut, not Edward, who is then credited with sentiments of grief and revenge for his (half-)brother's fate; it is Harthacnut's familial resemblance to Emma's dead son which provides the queen with her one shred of consolation; it is Harthacnut, not Edward, who helps his mother recover the legitimate inheritance of the kingdom in 1040.

Throughout the *Encomium*, clear concerns are expressed over the dangers which await a kingdom that is divided against itself (Mark 3:24) or between brothers.[360] The death of Eadric Streona, summarily executed for his guile and deception, is made a cautionary tale of disloyalty, 'in order that soldiers may learn from this example to be faithful, not faithless, to their kings'.[361] In highlighting such issues, the *Encomium* betrays the delicacy of the situation. Despite the reassurance of its very last paragraph, the emended quotation from Lucan with which it closes conveys real anxiety over the consequences of renewed discord. Emma's deeds had to be presented favourably in order to secure her political position

---

[359] For discussion of the authenticity of this letter, see Keynes, 'Introduction', pp. xxxiii–iv, lxiii–v.
[360] *Encomium Emmae Reginae*, II.2, pp. 17–19, II.12–14, pp. 29–31.
[361] *Encomium Emmae Reginae*, II.15, pp. 31–3.

and she had to be defended against specific charges – why, for example, had she considered it expedient (*utile*) to go into exile in 1037 rather than risk sharing the fate of her younger son?[362] In both instances, the author of the *Encomium* faced real difficulties in defusing a potentially hostile reception from his audience and in supplementing truth with ornamentation. In each case, however, the author uses the prologue to acknowledge his dilemma and thereby seek the goodwill of his audience, both for the case he was pleading and for the manner in which he was doing so.

The anonymous *Life* of Henry IV was written some time after the eponymous emperor's death in 1106. Like the *Epitaphium Arsenii*, it takes the form of a funeral lament and, as was the case for Paschasius Radbertus, this is the author's overt pretext for discussing the life and deeds of its subject: 'it is the custom of those who grieve when they lament a dead friend to recount his whole life and habits to the increase of their grief'.[363] It does not take long, however, before a more pointed sub-text emerges. This was a work, after all, which was being written during the lifetime of Henry's successor, that is, the very son whose faithless rebellion against his father would occupy the last third of the work. It is perhaps hardly surprising, then, that the anonymous author should have used the prologue to draw attention to the potential hostility which his work might attract: 'But you may protest at my unrestrained grief and advise me to hold back my weeping lest perhaps it become known to those who rejoice at the emperor's

---

362 *Encomium Emmae Reginae*, III.7, p. 47.
363 *Life of the Emperor Henry IV*, trans. T.E. Mommsen and K.F. Morrison, in *Imperial Lives and Letters of the Eleventh Century* (New York, 1962), I, p. 102, XIII, p. 137. For tearful lamentation, see Jeremiah 9:1; Boethius, *Consolation of Philosophy*, I.1, pp. 131–2 (see page 161). For the possibility of a liturgical connection associated with the provisions made by Henry IV for feeding the poor on the anniversary of his coronation and death and as part of a commemoration of himself and his family, see I.S. Robinson, *Henry IV of Germany 1056–1106* (Cambridge, 1999), p. 312; for the close relationship between the guidelines set down in *Rhetorica ad Herennium*, III.6–8, pp. 173–85, see R.M. Stein, 'Signs and Things – The *Vita Heinrici IV Imperatoris* and the Crisis of Interpretation in Twelfth-Century History', *Traditio*, 43 (1987), pp. 105–19; for the genre of lament or *planctus*, see C. Thiry, *La Plainte Funèbre* (Typologie des Sources 30, Turnhout, 1978); cf. Odilo of Cluny, *Epitaph of Adelheid*, trans. S. Gilsdorf, *Queenship and Sanctity: The Lives of Mathilda and the Epitaph of Adelheid* (Washington, DC, 2004), pp. 128–43.

death. You counsel me rightly, I confess. But I cannot command myself not to grieve, I cannot contain myself from mourning. Although they may whet their fury upon me, although they may long to tear me limb from limb, grief knows no fear, grief feels no pains inflicted'.[364] This is a work which has been written out of a sense of duty, because Henry IV's death had marked the loss of peace, justice and fidelity.[365] The author dramatises his dilemma with allusions to both Horace and Vergil: 'here I would break off my pen; for we have come to factions, to deceptions, and to crimes, of which to write true things is a danger, to write false, a crime. "Here the wolf threatens, there the hound". What therefore shall I do? "Shall I speak or be silent?" My hand begins and falters, writes and rejects, notes and erases, so much that I almost do not know what I will'.[366] The same equivocation is evident in the main body of the text when the author chooses to duck the issue of whether he himself believed the charges which Henry IV had levelled against pope Gregory VII but lists them all the same (and quotes Sallust as his justification for doing so): 'And so the king sought reasons and opportunities to cast him [Gregory VII] out. And it was found that he had occupied the Roman see which he had rejected once before and which, therefore, he should have rejected since he had wilfully aspired to it while he was archdeacon and his lord was still living. Whether these things are true or false can be discovered with too little accuracy. Some averred it; others said that it was a fabrication [*figmentum*].... As for me, however, the matter must be left unsettled, since I cannot defend, nor do I dare to affirm, uncertain things'.[367] It is hardly surprising, therefore, that the author wants ultimately to remain anonymous: 'But it is foul to leave mutilated something begun and to have painted the head without the members. I shall persevere, therefore, as I began, steadfast and secure in the fact that as your trustworthiness has been completely proven to me, so

---

364 *Life of the Emperor Henry*, I, p. 102; cf. Smalley, *Historians in the Middle Ages*, pp. 73–4.
365 *Life of the Emperor Henry*, I, p. 102.
366 *Life of the Emperor Henry*, I, p. 105; cf. Horace, *Satires*, II.2.64, p. 141; Vergil, *Aeneid*, III.39, p. 351.
367 *Life of the Emperor Henry*, VI, pp. 114–15; cf. Sallust, *Catiline*, XIX, p. 33 (see also pages 46–7); Smalley, *Historians in the Middle Ages*, p. 2.

you will reveal these writings to no one; or if, perhaps, they go abroad, that you will not reveal the author'.[368]

In the course of his narrative of the emperor's life, the anonymous author lists the accusations which had been levelled against Henry IV, not once, but twice – on the occasions of his deposition and excommunication by pope Gregory VII.[369] Concerning the events of 1076, for example, he points out that 'in order to extenuate his resources they fabricated and wrote up criminal charges [*crimina*] against him, mixing true things with false – the worst and most foul which hate and spiteful malice could devise and which, if I were to put them down, would make me ill in writing and you in reading them. Thus they accused him before the Roman pontiff, Gregory, saying that it was not seemly that so profligate a man, known more by crime than by title, should rule, most of all since Rome had not conferred the regal dignity upon him; that it was necessary that her right in setting up kings be returned to Rome and that the pope and Rome, according to the counsel of the princes, should provide a king whose life and wisdom would be congruent with so great an honour...'.[370] Concerning the events of 1080, the author recounts how, when Henry's enemies 'saw that they had no success, either in arms or in the election of kings, they armed themselves again with calumnies [*convitia*] and charged him [*criminati sunt*] before the pope, besides other things, with many and impious deeds. They asserted that often he had been exiled from the royal office because of his crime; that he had slain the most Christian kings whom they themselves had created, not without the authority of the pope; that he had usurped the royal office through bloodshed; that he had laid everything waste with fire, pillage and the sword; and that he had exercised his tyranny against the Church and the kingdom in every way'.[371] The account of Henry IV which is given in the anonymous *Life*, the narrative of his character and deeds, is, to a significant extent,

---

368 *Life of the Emperor Henry*, I, p. 105. For the possible identity of the author, see Bagge, *Kings, Politics and the Right Order of the World*, p. 314; for anonymity produced by fear, see, for example, *Rationes Dictandi*, X, p. 20; for anonymity more generally, see Simon, 'Untersuchungen zur Topik der Widmungsbriefe', pp. 118–19.
369 Robinson, *Henry IV*, pp. 113–14, 195–6, 345–57.
370 *Life of the Emperor Henry*, III, p. 108.
371 *Life of the Emperor Henry*, VI, p. 114; cf. Lucan, *Pharsalia*, VIII.52, p. 441.

the author's point-by-point rebuttal of each one of these criminal charges, calumnies and 'dark rumours' (*sinister rumor*).[372] The emperor was not this sort of person (*qualis est*) and these events either did not happen or were motivated by a different intention. The vicissitudes he encountered were neither the consequence of his sins nor punishment for his acts of injustice, but the wrongs suffered by a righteous father at the hands of his own son.

If the first point to be made about the influence of judicial rhetoric on the writing of history is the centrality of accusation and defence, the second concerns the importance of extrinsic testimony. Gildas' castigation of the sins of kings and clergy, for example, is described as a charge-sheet (*adstipulatio convitiarum*) and the supporting *exempla* which he cites from the Old Testament as an irrefutable accusation (*invictus adstipulator*). Those accused are addressed directly with an 'apostrophe', 'as if they are present' (*quasi praesens*), witnesses are summoned, and the judgment of God is anticipated. Tyrants and negligent churchmen, in other words, are being put on trial by Gildas for their failure to implement the terms of the book of Wisdom and the Davidic covenant.[373] With regard to human testimony, the impact of judicial rhetoric on medieval historiography is revealed by the legal language (*testis*, *testimonium*, *veredicus*) which is such a marked feature of its vocabulary – in the *oculata fides* of Einhard, for example, or in the combination of eyewitness testimony with the truthtelling evidence of others in Asser.[374] For writers to have seen events with their own eyes remained, as Isidore had suggested, the best guarantee of forensic historical truth. Otherwise, it became a case of emphasising the reliability of those who related what they had themselves seen, or of simply shifting the responsibility to the witnesses themselves. This last strategy was used, for example, by Snorri Sturluson when incorporating oral tradition into his *Heimskringla*: 'although we do not know for

---

372 *Life of the Emperor Henry*, VIII, p. 121. For *remotio criminis* (page 181), see, for example, *Life of the Emperor Henry*, VI, p. 114, VIII, p. 121, IX, p. 123; for the hostile accounts set down by Lampert of Hersfeld and Bruno of Merseburg, see page 255.
373 Gildas, *De Excidio Britanniae*, XXVII, p. 29, XXXIX, p. 37, XLIII, p. 40; cf. Lapidge, 'Gildas's Education', p. 47.
374 See pages 185–6; cf. *Encomium Emmae Reginae*, I.1, p. 9 (*veredica relatio*).

certain whether these accounts are true, yet we do know that old and learned men consider them to be so'.[375]

The historian's judicial appeal to extrinsic testimony extends to the verbatim citation of written documentation, a technique which was already a feature of historical narratives in Sallust and Eusebius and, following them, in Gregory of Tours and Bede.[376] In the eighth century, for example, Paul the Deacon appeals both to the truth-content of eyewitness testimony and to the principle that the citation of documentary evidence can provide a guarantee against lying: 'if anyone may think that this is a lie and not the truth of the matter, let him read over the prologue of the edict which King Rothari composed of the laws of the Lombards and he will find this written in almost all the manuscripts as we have inserted it in this little history'.[377] In the twelfth century, Rahewin's continuation of Otto of Freising's *Deeds of Frederick Barbarossa* uses this strategy to profess a studied (if ultimately unconvincing) neutrality on at least four occasions.[378] 'Copies of this and other letters which passed back and forth in this time of confusion', Rahewin writes, 'I have taken pains to insert in this work so that any reader who may wish to judge, attracted and summoned, not by my own words or assertions, but by the actual writings of the parties themselves, may choose freely the side to which he desires to lend his favour [*favor*]'.[379] Rahewin then expands on the principles which are at stake:

> Now, being about to speak of this commotion, we desire, as we said above, that the reader shall not depend on our words but that, as we place on record the letters sent back and forth, he may decide from them what side he should defend or to whom he wishes to remain

---

375 Snorri Sturluson, *Heimskringla*, pref., p. 3.
376 See pages 46, 62; Gregory of Tours, *Histories*, IX.20, pp. 503–7, IX.39, pp. 527–9, X.16, pp. 571–5; Bede, *Historia Ecclesiastica*, I.24, p. 38, I.28–32, pp. 54–60, II.4, pp. 76–7, II.8, pp. 83–4, II.10–11, pp. 87–91, II.17–19, pp. 101–5, III.29, pp. 165–6, IV.17, pp. 199–200, V.7, p. 245, V.16–17, pp. 263–6, V.19, p. 274, V.21, pp. 276–85.
377 Paul the Deacon, *History of the Lombards*, trans. W.D. Foulke, rev. E. Peters (Philadelphia, 2003), I.21, pp. 39–40; cf. IV.29, p. 172, IV.47, p. 201.
378 Cf. Eusebius, *Chronicon*, ed. R. Helm, *Die Chronik des Hieronymus* (Berlin, 1984), praef., p. 9.
379 Rahewin, *Deeds of Frederick*, III.8, p. 181; cf. Somerville and Brasington, *Prefaces to Canon Law Books*, p. 160.

loyal. But we seek indulgence for ourselves, who venerate with due respect both persons, namely the priestly and the royal, too much to venture to make a rash judgment [*iudicare*] concerning one of them. And so the following is a copy of a letter sent by the supreme pontiff to the archbishops and bishops concerning these matters.[380]

In the following book, Rahewin again disclaims any favour towards either party and invites his audience to assess the justice of the case for themselves:

> We would again remind the reader that he should not assess the truth of this matter [*veritas huius rei*] from what we say or write, but come to his own judgment [*proprium iudicium*], after comparing all that was written on both sides, as to which party was the more correct or – so to speak – 'who bore arms with greater justice' [Lucan, *Pharsalia* I.126]. For if we were either to extol or to extenuate the case of either side, we would be departing from our purpose. And assuredly, the rest of the body of our history would not be sound were we to show the disease of personal favour [*domestici favoris morbus*] in this important part of it.[381]

And finally:

> But we would remind the reader repeatedly that in this matter he is not to consult our account in order to discover the truth of this matter [*rerum veritas*], but to rely on the letters and documents which have come into our hands and have seemed to deserve inclusion in this work, subjecting them to his own judgment [*arbitrium*], since what was done seems to give its own sufficiently faithful account of this controversy [*controversia*], the outcome of the struggle [*litis decisio*], and the judgment of the council [*concilii iudicium*].[382]

Viewed from the perspective of extrinsic testimony, judicial rhetoric could clearly influence the particular form which was given to a 'historical' work. Einhard's life of Charlemagne, for example, is striking for the fact that it concludes with the verbatim citation of the emperor's will, including its ratifying list of signatories. Charlemagne, according to Einhard, 'decided to draw up a will so that he might make his daughters and illegitimate children heirs to some part of his estate. But the will was

---

380 *Deeds of Frederick*, III.16, p. 190.
381 *Deeds of Frederick*, IV.59, pp. 287–8.
382 *Deeds of Frederick*, IV.75, pp. 308–9.

left too late and could not be completed. Nevertheless, three years before he died, he divided up his precious possessions, money, clothes, and other moveable goods in the presence of his friends and officials. He called on them to ensure that, with their support, the division he had made would remain fixed and in force after his death. He described in a charter what he wanted done with the goods he had divided. The terms and text of this are as follows...'.[383] This is the part of Einhard's text which is often neglected by modern commentary, or which is used to suggest that Einhard was simply imitating the summary of Augustus' will that Suetonius had provided as a conclusion to his own life of an emperor. Yet the appropriation of ecclesiastical property by laymen was a particular grievance at the time Einhard was writing, not least in the series of four church synods in 829 at which bishops not only appealed to Louis' piety and devotion in order to restore this property but also to 'the custom of his father'. Given that these synods explicitly professed themselves ever mindful (*semper memores*) of the way in which Charlemagne had shown such concern to carry out similar works of piety, his testamentary ecclesiastical benefactions of 811 and 814 were live legal issues. For Einhard to have recorded the deliberation, documentation and process in which they originated was accordingly a contribution to a critical debate – in the circumstances of the late 820s, the intention, terms and implementation of Charlemagne's will formed a bone of bitter political contention.[384]

An even more direct, and explicit, connection with judicial procedure is provided by Galbert of Bruges, a legal notary who wrote down a narrative of the murder of Charles 'the Good', count of Flanders. In describing the count's death (he was killed in church in 1127 by his own vassals whilst at prayer during Lent) and the violent upheavals which ensued, Galbert presents himself as an eyewitness, producing his summary of events in Bruges between 1127 and 1128 amidst the most turbulent and dangerous of circumstances and forcing himself practically against his own will to set down both what had been done and the reasons for it.[385] For

---

383 Einhard, *Vita Karoli*, XXXIII, p. 37.
384 M.S. Kempshall, 'Some Ciceronian Models for Einhard's "Life" of Charlemagne', *Viator*, 26 (1995), pp. 26–7.
385 Galbert of Bruges, *Murder of Charles*, XXXV, p. 164.

all its apparent straightforwardness, this self-professed attempt simply to understand what was happening,[386] for the sake of truth and for the memory of posterity,[387] went through several stages of composition – from a contemporaneous record made on wax tablets (chapters 15–67, 72–85), through their elaboration into a description of the count's martyrdom or 'passion' (*passio*) (chapters 1–14, 68–71, 86–92), to an explanation of the subsequent conflict between Charles' successor, William Clito, and Thierry of Alsace, which ended only with the former's death in July 1128 (chapters 93–121).[388] At the heart of this shifting historical narrative, moreover, lies a fundamental concern with justice and judicial process. At one level, Galbert locates this in the judgment of God, from whom 'there is nothing hidden which will not be revealed' (Matthew 10:26).[389] Divine vengeance is thus visited upon particular individuals, on generations and on Flanders itself, as God justly punishes even the apparently virtuous Charles because of the sins of the fathers (Exodus 20:5, 34:7; Deuteronomy 5:9) – in his case, Robert the Frisian.[390] Viewed in this light, Galbert's explanatory framework for understanding exactly why such calamities should have befallen his own community was, to all intents and purposes, no different from that of Orosius. What remains distinctive about Galbert's account is that, as befits a legal notary, this record of events also took its cue from the action (and inaction) of human justice and, in particular, from the sworn inquest (*inquisitio*) which was set up by William Clito in September 1127 explicitly in order to establish who had done what, when and where, in the course of the events surrounding Charles' murder earlier that year.

Galbert describes the terms of this comital inquiry in some detail: 'to declare by true assertion the names of those who had killed Charles and who had plundered his property, as well as

---

386   *Murder of Charles*, CXIV, p. 299.
387   *Murder of Charles*, prol., p. 80.
388   J. Rider, *God's Scribe: The Historiographical Art of Galbert of Bruges* (Washington, DC, 2001); J. Rider and A.V. Murray (eds), *Galbert of Bruges and the Historiography of Medieval Flanders* (Washington, DC, 2009); cf. Smalley, *Historians in the Middle Ages*, p. 109: 'his observation was unclouded by learning'.
389   *Murder of Charles*, LVII, p. 208.
390   *Murder of Charles*, LXIX–LXX, p. 237.

those who had subsequently given them aid and protection'.[391] William Clito's handling of this inquest, however, clearly left many people unsure as to whether justice had, in fact, been secured and Galbert goes on to report those instances in which punishment accordingly devolved to God. Galbert himself was certainly only too well aware of the difficulties involved in establishing what had actually happened, when lies could be so cleverly and deceitfully presented as the truth.[392] 'Although this was false', he comments, 'the lie seemed credible' as it was spread abroad.[393] In Galbert's account, Bertulf, provost of Bruges (Galbert's superior, and arch-traitor against Charles), 'seemed to prove his innocence by crafty and cunning arguments' (*calliditatis et astutiae ... argumentis*).[394] In July 1128, Galbert concludes, 'many lies were circulating in Bruges' about what had actually happened.[395] When he opens his own account of Charles' murder, therefore, Galbert's conventional disclaimer about eloquence and the truth assumes a particularly sharp resonance. 'When I set out to describe the death of such a great prince', he states, 'I did not seek to embellish it with eloquence or to display the modes of different colours, but I related only the truth of things [*veritas rerum*], and even if my style is dry, by writing I still commend to the memory of the faithful the strange outcome [*peregrinus eventus*] of his death'.[396]

From the very start of his narrative, Galbert makes it clear that he was thoroughly familiar with the role played by rhetoric in the service of pleading cases in a court of justice. Having used his introduction to outline the theme of subjection to the powers ordained by God (1 Peter 2:13), as well as the instability caused by the treacherous machinations of the Devil, Galbert proceeds with a brief statement of the peace and justice which had been instituted by the rule of Charles. He concludes his opening chapter, however, with a pointed observation on the double-edged nature of the use of rhetoric in law. In governing themselves according to law and justice, he writes, 'people devised, by skill and study,

---

391 *Murder of Charles*, LXXXVII, pp. 258–9.
392 *Murder of Charles*, XXXIV, p. 162.
393 *Murder of Charles*, XLIX, p. 190.
394 *Murder of Charles*, LVII, p. 208.
395 *Murder of Charles*, CXVIII, p. 305.
396 *Murder of Charles*, prol., pp. 79–80.

every kind of argument for use in the courts, so that when anyone was attacked they could defend themselves by the strength and eloquence of rhetoric or when they were attacking they might ensnare their enemy who would be deceived by the wealth of their oratory'. Such rhetoric, he remarks, was not the exclusive preserve of those educated and trained in the art of oratory – Galbert echoes Cicero's observation that the gift of eloquence, together with its rational methods of inference and argument, could equally well be endowed by Nature. It is the deception wrought by such rhetoric, however, which, Galbert concludes, God set out to discipline by punishing the misuse of this natural gift.[397] By making his own judicial record of events, Galbert was acutely aware of the dangers involved: 'it should be noted certainly that no intelligent men among us at Bruges dared to speak the truth about the calamity and misfortune', for fear, that is, of being defamed – and silenced – as a traitor.[398] Nonetheless, it is an explicitly judicial framework which Galbert has in mind when he produces his own *narratio rei gestae*. This is why Galbert takes such care to establish the precise chronology of events, noting the month or the week or sometimes even the time of day at which something was done, as well as to include written documentation. Setting the record straight, in his eyes, served an immediate judicial, not just historiographical, purpose.

The extrinsic testimony of judicial documentation could form an integral part of a historical narrative for communities as well as for individuals. Gregory of Tours pointed out that legal restitution of property depended on providing a history of the case,[399] and this is one reason why so many land grants made by charter include a brief narrative of what had happened to that land in the past. There could be a close overlap between these charters and the writing of an actual 'history'. Thietmar of Merseburg, for example, identifies two overarching themes in the prologue to his *Chronicon* – on the one hand, the deeds of the Saxon kings and, on the other, the rise, fall and restoration of the see of Merseburg. It is one of the key arguments of his history that there is a salutary connection between the two – the afflictions experienced by the

---

397 *Murder of Charles*, I, p. 84.
398 *Murder of Charles*, CXVI, p. 303, CXVIII, p. 305.
399 Gregory of Tours, *Histories*, X.8, p. 554.

former are punishment for their despoliation of the latter.[400] Central to Thietmar's narrative is therefore the suppression of the see of Merseburg under Otto II in 981 until its restoration under Henry II in 1004, a date which is picked out for especial commemoration. This moral–didactic narrative, however, is also designed to be instrumental – Thietmar's prologue also directly charges his successor as bishop of Merseburg with the responsibility of collecting and maintaining what had been dispersed over the course of more than twenty years.[401] As a result, Thietmar uses his *Chronicon* to describe in some detail both the lands and the rights which needed defending, listing the properties granted by charter, for example, sometimes including the names of witnesses, in order to replace those legal texts which had been destroyed or deliberately corrupted.[402]

Thietmar of Merseburg's judicial concerns were not untypical. Indeed, it remains a striking feature of much of the writing of history in monasteries in the twelfth century that this historiography made extensive use of, and may indeed have developed directly from, the historical components of charters which described the circumstances of particular bequests of land. The connection between a collection of charters (or cartulary) and a historical narrative for the foundation of a monastery could certainly be very direct.[403] In England, for example, much monastic historiography after 1066 seems to have been inspired by a pressing need to prove title to property, to justify the possession of lands and rights which were coming under serious legal (and illegal) pressure in the aftermath of the Norman Conquest.[404] Eadmer, for instance, laments the absence of a written record of

---

400 Thietmar, *Chronicon*, III.prol., p. 126; cf. VI.prol., p. 235.
401 *Chronicon*, I.prol., p. 67; cf. III.16, p. 140.
402 *Chronicon*, III.1, p. 128, III.16, p. 140, VI.36, p. 262, VI.81, p. 291, VII.24, p. 323, VIII.13, p. 371.
403 Gransden, *Historical Writing in England*, pp. 88–91, 271–86; cf. E. Freeman, *Narratives of a New Order: Cistercian Historical Writing in England 1150–1220* (Turnhout, 2002); A. Jotischky, *The Carmelites and Antiquity: Mendicants and their Pasts in the Middle Ages* (Oxford, 2002). For the later mendicant orders, see B. Roest, 'Later Medieval Institutional History', in D.M. Deliyannis (ed.), *Historiography in the Middle Ages* (Leiden, 2003), pp. 288–307.
404 R.W. Southern, 'Aspects of the European Tradition of Historical Writing IV – The Sense of the Past', *Transactions of the Royal Historical Society*, 23 (1973), pp. 246–56.

events in the past and expresses the hope that his own documentation of Anselm's dispute with the king over the rights of the church at Canterbury may prove helpful to any future scholar searching for a precedent, not least through its verbatim citation of the relevant letters and documents.[405] Even without the stimulus of such immediate judicial and political concerns, in the course of the twelfth century there was an increasing need for documentation of legal proof to land, as opposed to simply oral tradition and custom, which could also lead to the production of forgeries.[406] As John of Salisbury recognised, 'information in chronicles is valuable in establishing or abolishing customs and for strengthening or weakening privileges'.[407] Orderic Vitalis' *Ecclesiastical History*, for all the universalism of the chronographic form which it was given in c.1136–37, seems to have at least originated as a more localised history of the monastery at Saint Evroult, which had been inspired by the need to collect the requisite material evidence of its lands and rights for Henry I's visit in 1113.[408] William of Malmesbury's *Deeds of the English Kings* and his *Deeds of the English Bishops* likewise interweave a narrative

---

405 Eadmer, *Historia Novorum in Anglia*, pref., p. 1, III.136, p. 143, IV.175, p. 187, IV.215, p. 230. Eadmer subsequently records Anselm's life and conduct (*vita et conversatio*) as a complementary narrative which will reinforce his defence of the archbishop's actions in the *Historia Novorum* (*Life of Anselm*, pref., p. 2: 'readers of the former work cannot fully understand Anselm's actions without the help of this work, nor can readers of this work do so without the help of the other'). For the accusations, see *Historia Novorum in Anglia*, I.61, p. 63, II.75, p. 79, III.121, p. 127, IV.159–60, p. 170, IV.171, p. 183, IV.213, p. 228; cf. Gransden, *Historical Writing in England*, pp. 128–35; R.W. Southern, *St Anselm and His Biographer* (Cambridge, 1963).
406 E.A.R. Brown, '*Falsitas Pia sive Reprehensibilis* – Medieval Forgers and their Intentions', in *Fälschungen im Mittelalter* (Hanover, 1988–90), vol. I, pp. 101–19; F.-J. Schmale, 'Fälschungen in der Geschichtsschreibung', *Fälschungen im Mittelalter*, vol. I, pp. 121–32; M. Chibnall, 'Forgery in Narrative Charters', *Fälschungen im Mittelalter*, vol. IV, pp. 331–46; G. Spiegel, 'Forging the Past – The Language of Historical Truth in the Middle Ages', *History Teacher*, 17 (1984), pp. 267–83; G. Constable, 'Forgery and Plagiarism in the Middle Ages', *Archiv für Diplomatik*, 29 (1983), pp. 1–41; M. Clanchy, 'Remembering the Past and the Good Old Law', *History*, 55 (1970), pp. 165–76. For the 'renewal' or 'restoration' of evidence, see M. Clanchy, *From Memory to Written Record: England 1066–1307* (2nd edn, Oxford, 1993), pp. 148–9, 318–27.
407 John of Salisbury, *Historia Pontificalis*, prol., p. 3.
408 Orderic Vitalis, *Historia Ecclesiastica*, XI.43, pp. 175–7; cf. Chibnall, 'General Introduction' to Orderic Vitalis' *Historia Ecclesiastica*, p. 32.

of *gesta* with a series of charters – some genuine, some forged, but all of them detailing benefactions of rights and property which had been made to the monastery of Malmesbury and whose alienation or expropriation, by Norman nobles or by the bishop of Salisbury, William regarded as anathema.[409]

It is William of Malmesbury, in fact, who underscores the third, and last, point which needs to be made about the influence of judicial rhetoric on medieval historiography, namely the importance of establishing credibility for the speaker or writer with a judge or jury and the care with which their introductions or prologues should therefore be constructed. Goodwill can be secured from an audience by concentrating on the dispassionate qualities possessed by the author.[410] Take William's preface to book III of his *Deeds of the English Kings*, an *exordium* in which the author goes out of his way to distance his narrative from the extremes of praise and castigation that would be found in demonstrative rhetoric.[411] William retains both a moral–didactic purpose and the pleasure principle as his twin motives for writing, but he also asserts his own personal qualifications – he is a moderate and dispassionate witness, praising good deeds but also mitigating wicked actions in so far as the passing of such judgments can be made consonant with the truth. The result, he hopes, will be an audience which is neither antagonistic nor fatigued but attentive, teachable and benevolent. As he explains:

> King William [the Conqueror] has been taken as their subject, under the spur of differing motives, by authors both Norman and English. The Normans in their enthusiasm have overpraised him, and his good and bad deeds alike have been lauded to the sky; the English, inspired by the enmities of their people, have savaged their lord with foul calumnies [*convitia*]. For my part, having the blood of both peoples in my veins, I propose to maintain the following moderation in relating: good deeds, so far as they have come within my knowledge, I will publish without cosmetic colouring [*sine fuco*]; misdeeds I will touch on lightly and as it were in passing, so far as is

---

409 For example, William of Malmesbury, *Gesta Pontificum Anglorum*, V.220, p. 555; cf. J.S. Barrow, 'William of Malmesbury's Use of Charters', in R. Balzaretti and E.M. Tyler (eds), *Narrative and History in the Early Medieval West* (Turnhout, 2006), pp. 67–85.
410 See pages 190–1.
411 Cf. page 30.

needed to make them known. Thus my history will not be accused of lying, nor shall I be branding with a censor's judgment [*nota inuram censoria*] a man whose actions, even when they do not merit praise, at least almost always admit of excuse [*excusari*]. Willingly, therefore, and with due care, I will recount such incidents in his life as may provide a stimulus for the indolent or an example for the active, useful for our own day and of pleasure to later generations. I shall not, however, waste much time in telling of things of no practical value, which are indeed tedious to the reader and make the writer hated. There are quite enough people already to tear the deeds of good men to pieces with the tooth of envy. My chosen province is to extenuate faults so far as I can without sacrificing the truth, and to praise good actions without undue verbiage. True judges [*veri arbitri*], I believe, will acquit me both of cowardice and of inelegance in showing such moderation. The same principle shall be observed not only for William but also for his two sons: nothing to excess, nothing which is not said truly. The first of the sons [William Rufus] did little worthy of praise, save in the first days of his reign; all his life long he despoiled his subjects to buy the favour of his knights. The second son [Henry I], who in character resembled his father rather than his brother, maintained an invincible spirit in bad times and in good. If one looks at his campaigns, it would be hard to say whether caution or audacity predominated; if one considers the outcome, one wonders whether he was more fortunate or unsuccessful. But the time will come when the reader may judge [*arbitretur*] these things. Now, about to begin my third book, I think I have said enough to make him attentive and teachable, and he will kindly persuade himself to be well-disposed.[412]

At least two drafts of William of Malmesbury's *Gesta Regum* were written, one of them at some point in the period before 1126 and then a revised version in 1135, and, like the *Gesta Pontificum*, the second version was designed to moderate, as often as not, the criticism contained in the first. Even in 1135, William's equivocal assessment of Henry I was, in the circumstances, no

---

412 William of Malmesbury, *Gesta Regum Anglorum*, III.praef., p. 425. For Rufus, see T. Callahan, 'The Making of a Monster – The Historical Image of William Rufus', *Journal of Medieval History*, 7 (1981), pp. 175–85. More generally, see J.G. Haahr, 'The Concept of Kingship in William of Malmesbury's *Gesta Regum* and *Historia Novella*', *Medieval Studies*, 38 (1976), pp. 351–71; B. Weiler, 'William of Malmesbury on Kingship', *History*, 90 (2005), pp. 3–22.

doubt judicious,[413] but the judgments he delivered on the deeds of Henry's father and elder brother would have carried no less political weight. William's preface can therefore be read at face value or it can be read between the lines. To do the latter, however, it needs to be put back into the particular political context of the turbulent last ten years of the reign of Henry I and, as such, to be read in the light, not so much of judicial rhetoric, as of deliberative rhetoric, that is, the rhetoric which was used in arguing for, or against, a particular course of political action.

Deliberative rhetoric

The connection drawn by classical writers between the art of rhetoric and participation in public or political life was a particularly close one, from the actual institutions of the law court and the senate to the theoretical scope of *civilia negotia* and *civiles quaestiones*.[414] Cicero opens his *De Inventione*, for example, with an analysis of the great benefits derived by the political community, the *res publica*, when its rulers combine wisdom with eloquence. Eloquence, he argues, makes life safe and secure; it also renders life morally worthy, distinguished and pleasurable; it produces praise, honour and moral standing. As a result, in Cicero's opinion, the principles of rhetoric should be classified as an important part of political thought (*civilis scientia*).[415]

Deliberative rhetoric – speaking for, or against, a particular course of action in a public assembly – was the specific category of rhetoric which was most immediately concerned with directly political subjects. The act of deliberation is defined accordingly

---

413 For the similar instance of Henry of Huntingdon's rewritten eulogy of Henry I after his death, and his own acknowledgment of the disparity between the two accounts, see his *Historia Anglorum*, VIII, pp. 607–9, X.1, pp. 699–701; for Orderic Vitalis, see *Historia Ecclesiastica*, X.16, pp. 295–7, XIII.19, pp. 451–3; cf. R. Ray, 'Orderic Vitalis on Henry I – Theocratic Ideology and Didactic Narrative', in G.H. Shriver (ed.), *Contemporary Reflections on the Medieval Christian Tradition* (Durham, 1974), pp. 119–34; A. Cooper, '"The Feet of those that Bark shall be Cut Off" – Timorous Historians on the Personality of Henry I', *Anglo-Norman Studies*, 23 (2001), pp. 47–67; see also page 252.
414 See pages 10–11.
415 Cicero, *De Inventione*, I.4.5–5.6, pp. 13–15; cf. Quintilian, *Institutio Oratoria*, II.15.33, p. 315. For the same point expressed pictorially, see Camille, 'Illuminating Thought', p. 349.

by the *Rhetorica ad Herennium* as a choice between two or more courses of action, either in the present or in the future, where the primary goal of the speaker or writer is to advise what is useful or advantageous (*utilitas*).[416] The goal of deliberative rhetoric, in this respect, is therefore persuasion or dissuasion concerning something which is subject to counsel (*consultatio, consilium*) or open to debate (*contio*); it involves the expression of a considered opinion (*sententia*) in the course of a political discussion (*civilis disceptatio*).[417] There is a distinction here, however, between counsel and judgment: whereas judgment (*iudicium*) is exercised in things which have been set out (*ostendere*), counsel deals with things which are hidden, which are in doubt, or which have simply not yet been revealed. Persuasive speeches accordingly depend on conjecture, in the sense that what is deliberated is whether something can or will happen in the future. As a result, whereas judgment is very often a matter of certainty, *consilium* is a form of deeply-considered reasoning which weighs things up, compares them, and relies on its own discovery and assessment of arguments.[418]

Although deliberative rhetoric was normally defined by the goal of identifying and securing utility or advantage, the exact form which this *utilitas* should take remained open to debate. According to the *Rhetorica ad Herennium*, for example, the utility involved in political deliberation (*civilis consultatio*) could take one of two forms – either it was moral worth (*honestas*) or it was security and protection (*tuta*). 'Moral worth', by this reckoning, includes the advantage which derives from doing something that is right and praiseworthy – 'right' in the sense that it is done in accordance with virtue and duty and is thereby performed in accordance with the four cardinal virtues; 'praiseworthy' in the sense that it produces a remembrance of moral worth (*commemoratio honestatis*), both at the time and in the future. 'Security and protection', meanwhile, consist of the advantage that derives from avoiding, by whatever means, a present or imminent danger. This second type of *utilitas*

---

416 *Rhetorica ad Herennium*, III.2.2, p. 157, III.2.3, p. 161.
417 Quintilian, *Institutio Oratoria*, III.4.1, p. 391; Cicero, *De Inventione*, I.5.7, p. 17; Boethius, *De Topicis Differentiis*, IV, p. 81.
418 Quintilian, *Institutio Oratoria*, VI.4.3, pp. 515–17, VII.praef.9, p. 181; cf. Vergil, *Aeneid*, XI.445–6, p. 267.

has, in turn, two elements which can be considered, the *Rhetorica ad Herennium* suggests, either separately or together: 'force' (*vis*), that is, the physical or military strength of armies, fleets and weapons; and 'strategy' (*dolus*), that is, the 'craft' which is involved when deploying money and promises but also dissimulation, lies and other techniques. Both force and strategy are thus categories of advantage which are intrinsic to the discussion of war and the governance of the *res publica*.[419] According to the *Rhetorica ad Herennium*, nothing is more advantageous, in these contexts, than security (*incolumitas*), because it is a prerequisite for the exercise of virtue. As such, nothing should really be considered morally worthy which does not provide physical safety (*salus*).[420]

Whereas the *Rhetorica ad Herennium* subsumes moral worth and virtue, protective force and strategy, within a single category of 'advantage', Cicero is much more concerned to distinguish between these two sets of goals. *De Inventione*, for example, argues that deliberative rhetoric has the objective of establishing which of several possible courses of action is the one that is not only morally worthy (*honestum*) but also advantageous (*utile*). Although Cicero explicitly acknowledges that some people (he is thinking of Aristotle) believe that the goal of deliberative rhetoric is to secure advantage alone,[421] it is the combination of advantage with moral worth in which he is primarily interested. It is this conjunction, for example, which provides him with one way of distinguishing deliberative rhetoric from demonstrative rhetoric, since he regards the goal of the latter to be moral worth on its own.[422] More significantly, it is the relationship between utility and moral worth which directly connects Cicero's analysis of deliberative rhetoric to his *De Officiis*, a treatise which was devoted to demonstrating that any conflict between what is morally worthy and what is advantageous is more apparent than real, and therefore that any course of action which is morally worthy is, by definition, advantageous.[423] Indeed, for Valerius Maximus, Cicero's argument

---

419 *Rhetorica ad Herennium*, III.2.3–4.7, pp. 161–9.
420 *Rhetorica ad Herennium*, III.5.8, p. 171.
421 Cf.Aristotle, *On Rhetoric*, I.3, p. 49 (see pages 468–9).
422 Cicero, *De Inventione*, II.4.12, p. 177, II.51.156, p. 325.
423 Cicero, *De Officiis*, trans. M.T. Griffin and E.M. Atkins, *On Duties* (Cambridge, 1991); cf. M.L. Colish, *The Stoic Tradition from Antiquity to the Early Middle Ages* (Leiden, 1990), vol. I, pp. 143–52.

subsequently provided the very definition both of justice and of Rome, 'where nothing is judged expedient which could seem less than morally worthy'.[424]

In *De Inventione*, Cicero gives a number of examples of what he means by the particular combination of advantage with moral worth which, in his opinion, should be the defining goal of deliberative rhetoric. There are, he states, three categories of things which are sought after: goods such as virtue, knowledge and truth, all of which are sought in their own right, for their intrinsic worth (*dignitas*); goods such as wealth, which are sought because of some benefit or advantage that they bring; and, finally, goods such as friendship, which are sought both because they have an intrinsic worth (the act of doing good for the sake of another person) and because they bring some advantage in return. When goods in this third and last category are referred to simply as 'morally worthy' (*honesta*), this is because it can be assumed that advantage is included within them, since they possess both intrinsic worth (*dignitas*) and utility (*utilitas*).[425] In addition to friendship, Cicero gives further illustrations of this third category as glory (*fama cum laude*, that is, a praiseworthy reputation), status or dignity, and plenty (*amplitudo*, that is, a great abundance of power, standing and resources).[426] What actually constitutes advantage in this final case comprises the same two elements described by the *Rhetorica ad Herennium*, that is, security or safety (now defined as maintaining a position of physical well-being, or *salus*, intact) and power or potential (defined as the capability to deploy whatever is suitable in order to preserve one's own position and weaken someone else's). Cicero then spells out the broader consequences of these definitions for the course of a particular political argument since, if the 'civil' subject-matter which forms the basis of deliberative rhetoric is to be governed by general considerations of *honestum*

---

424 Valerius Maximus, *Facta et Dicta Memorabilia*, VI.5, p. 53. Likewise, when the Athenians were informed that Themistocles was planning something advantageous but far from just, the entire assembly cried out that what did not seem equitable was not expedient either (Valerius Maximus, *Facta et Dicta Memorabilia*, VI.5, pp. 63–5).
425 Cicero, *De Inventione*, II.52.157–8, pp. 325–7.
426 *De Inventione*, II.55.166–7, pp. 333–5.

and *utile*, then these, in turn, will have to be related to more immediate considerations of necessity and circumstance.[427]

The greatest necessity, according to Cicero, lies in doing what is morally worthy; then comes security; finally there is what is practicable or serviceable (*commodum*). It is often essential, Cicero suggests, for deliberative rhetoric to compare these three categories of necessity with one another – although moral worth is intrinsically superior to security, there may still be deliberation over which of them should be counselled as the preferred course of action, given that security may provide the immediate means by which moral worth can be attained at some point in the future.[428] Practicability can never be a match for either moral worth or security but what is possible or feasible remains an important consideration in the 'advantage' which is aimed at by deliberative rhetoric. This last aspect of necessity stands in a very close relationship to Cicero's appreciation of the circumstances produced by the changes which are wrought through time, events or human action. Whereas necessity is considered in terms of force (*vis*), however, circumstance or condition (*affectio*) is considered in terms of the act itself and the person doing it; it is defined accordingly by what is demanded by the particular time and occasion at which the act in question is being done, or counselled, and the intention with which it is performed. What Cicero terms the changeability of things (*commutatio rerum*) is the product of time, events or commitment (*studium*), such that there will be periods and occasions when some things will not be considered in the same way as they used to be. Certain matters, in other words, need to be considered with reference to the exact time at which they were performed and the

---

427 *De Inventione*, II.25.76, p. 241, II.56.169–57.170, p. 337; cf. Isidore, *Etymologiae*, II.4.4, p. 26. For the prevalence of this tripartite distinction, see, for example, Suger's account of his building work at Saint-Denis, a task he would not have attempted 'had not so great, so necessary, so useful and worthy an occasion demanded it' (*si tanta, tam necessaria, tam utilis et honesta non exigeret opportunitas*). Suger, *Libellus Alter de Consecratione Ecclesiae Sancti Dionysii* [*De Consecratione*], II, p. 89; cf. Suger, *De Rebus in Sua Administratione Gestis* [*De Administratione*], I, p. 42 (*honestum et utile*), XXXIV, p. 80 (*honestum et utile*); both sources ed. and trans. E. Panofsky, *Abbot Suger on the Abbey Church of St.-Denis and Its Art Treasures* (2nd edn, Princeton, 1979). See also Hugh of St Victor, *De Archa Noe*, in *Selected Spiritual Writings* (New York, 1962), II.8, p. 91.
428 *De Inventione*, II.58.173–4, p. 341.

intent or deliberation (*consilium*) which informed them, not just according to the intrinsic nature of the actions themselves. In all such matters, any qualitative assessment of value will depend on what was required by the times and on what was worthy of the people concerned – in other words, not on what was done *per se*, but with what intention it was done and at what time.[429]

Very similar considerations to those articulated in *De Inventione* are put forward by Quintilian. Since all deliberation concerns matters which are in doubt, he argues, deliberative rhetoric will always deal with *three* categories rather than two – with what is morally worthy and with what is advantageous, but also with what is possible (*possible, conducibile*). Consideration of advantage will therefore involve questions of time ('it is expedient but not now'), place ('it is expedient but not here'), person ('it is expedient but not for us or against these particular people'), type of action ('it is expedient but not in this way') and degree ('it is expedient but not to this extent').[430] It is on the same basis that Valerius Maximus concedes that there may be occasions on which noble spirits will yield to expediency (*utilitas*) and bow to the power of fortune, since there are cases where counsels of greater safety are chosen in preference to those of 'grander show', which would lead to collapse.[431] Vergil likewise describes how Dido was forced to act in certain ways by the harshness of her circumstances (*res dura*) and the newness of her kingdom.[432] It was this tradition of sensitivity to circumstance, in short, which was transmitted to medieval writers and, by extension, to medieval historians. Many things which seem to be morally worthy by nature can be transformed into the opposite by time and circumstance; categories of moral worth (*honestum*) and advantage (*utile*) always need to be associated with what is necessary, possible and suited to both time and place.[433]

Whether the 'advantage' defined by necessity and circumstance extends, as the *Rhetorica ad Herennium* had argued, to the use of

---

429 Cicero, *De Inventione*, II.52.158, p. 327, II.58.176, p. 343 (see page 182); cf. *Rhetorica ad Herennium*, II.17.26, p. 105 (*fortuna, commutatio rerum*).
430 Quintilian, *Institutio Oratoria*, III.8.22–25, 35, pp. 491–3, 497; cf. *Rhetorica ad Herennium*, II.14.21, p. 97 (*honestum, facile, conducibile*).
431 Valerius Maximus, *Facta et Dicta Memorabilia*, VII.6, p. 165.
432 Vergil, *Aeneid*, I.563, p. 281.
433 *Moralium Dogma Philosophorum*, pp. 24–5, quoting Cicero, *De Officiis*, III.25.95, p. 137; Rahewin, *Deeds of Frederick*, IV.4, p. 235.

dissimulation and lies (*mentitio*) is not spelled out in *De Inventione*. What Cicero does say is that an individual will sometimes have to debate whether it is moral worth or security which should be given the greater consideration. In such situations, he observes, nothing is more desirable in deliberative rhetoric than to argue in favour of moral worth (*dignitas*), since there is nobody who does not think that this should be the highest objective. At the same time, however, Cicero is enough of a realist to recognise that advantage can nonetheless often assume a prior claim. This is particularly the case when people are afraid lest, were considerations of expediency to be neglected, it would simply become impossible to practise moral worth. At the very heart of deliberative rhetoric, Cicero concludes, lies a difference of opinion (*controversia*), either over which of two (or more) alternatives represents the most advantageous course of action or, if there is agreement on that score, whether the chief consideration should, indeed, be moral worth (*honestum*) rather than simply what is expedient (*utile*).[434] In *De Oratore*, Cicero accordingly provides guidelines for how a comparison of these two considerations should be handled. When the two criteria appear to be in conflict, the defender of expediency will enumerate the advantages (*commoda*) of peace, wealth, power, revenue, military strength and everything else by which advantage is measured. The proponent of moral worth, on the other hand, will collect examples of ancestral achievements which have been glorious, even though they may have involved danger, and will magnify the value of an immortal remembrance in posterity – such glory, by itself, will produce advantage and is always connected with moral worth. On both sides, however, Cicero is careful to emphasise that it is still important to establish what it is possible, and impossible, to achieve. After all, he points out, every act of deliberation will terminate as soon as it is understood that a course of action is impossible, or if it is simply shown to be necessary.[435]

Whilst moral worth and advantage, *honestum* and *utile*, are therefore the two categories according to which deliberative rhetoric should evaluate a particular course of action within the political community, quite how the relationship between them could be

---

434 Cf. Boethius, *De Topicis Differentiis*, IV, p. 81.
435 Cicero, *De Oratore*, II.82.333–6, pp. 451–3.

defined and construed was clearly open to further debate, not least in terms of their relation to what was practicable or possible, either for a particular person or at a particular time or place. Discussing what is morally worthy (*honestum*) and morally reprehensible (*turpe*), the advantages (*commoda*) and the disadvantages (*incommoda*) of mind, body and external circumstances, and placing *honesta* before *utilia* are, as a result, all listed as typical arguments when comparing one thing with another in Cicero's *Topica*.[436] Such flexibility and sensitivity to circumstance could also extend to consideration of the particular nature of an audience. Quintilian, for example, accepts Cicero's argument that deliberative rhetoric is primarily concerned with moral worth (*dignitas*), together with the assumption that nothing is advantageous which is not morally worthy. However, Quintilian also points out that, because such opinions are frequently delivered before the uneducated (*imperiti*), and especially before the populace, of whom a majority is generally understood not to be learned (*indocti*), it is necessary to distinguish explicitly between *honestum* and *utile* and to adapt what is being said to the general understanding (*communes intellectus*).[437] For Quintilian, therefore, at least in these circumstances, deliberative rhetoric becomes a matter of deciding whether to prefer moral worth over advantage, or vice versa (that is, *despite* the opinion of those people, such as Cicero, who, Quintilian accepts, thought that nothing can be advantageous which is not morally worthy), and deciding between two or more courses of action which are advantageous.[438] Viewed from the perspective of debate or counsel which is being delivered before a popular or less learned audience, therefore it is the very fact that deliberative rhetoric requires consideration and discussion of criteria that stretch all the way from moral virtue to security to physical force to strategy, dissimulation and even deceit, which becomes significant, not just the relative value which a speaker or writer might then themselves place on each of these particular types of advantage. Moral worth on its own cannot be taken for granted, in short, either as the goal of political counsel or as the motivation for individual action.

---

436 Cicero, *Topica*, XVIII.69, p. 435, XXIII.89, p. 451; cf. Aristotle, *On Rhetoric*, I.5–7, pp. 57–74.
437 Quintilian, *Institutio Oratoria*, III.8.1–2, pp. 479–81.
438 *Institutio Oratoria*, III.8.26–37, pp. 493–9.

Cicero himself clearly thought that considerations of advantage were inseparable from those of moral worth – this much is clear from *De Officiis*. The author of the *Rhetorica ad Herennium* was, equally clearly, not so sure – advantage can take the form of moral worth, but it can also take the form of deceit. Since the goal of deliberative rhetoric is to secure *utilitas*, if a speaker or writer is able to show that both security and moral worth will result from a particular course of action, then they should promise to demonstrate the presence of both types of benefit, but, if only one of these will result, then they will indicate which of the two it is.[439] This is the first point that needs to be made about the influence of deliberative rhetoric on medieval historiography: if the twin criteria of *honestum* and *utile* are central to the discussion and analysis of any public or political action, then the relationship between these two evaluative terms is not stable. Moral virtue was acknowledged to require security in order to be practicable, for example, and it was recognised that it should therefore respond to the demands of both time and occasion. For writers such as Gregory of Tours, Liutprand of Cremona and Thietmar of Merseburg, a concern with practicability is accordingly a striking feature of their respective accounts of how political rulers act in reality – by *vis* and *dolus*, by force and strategy – and these are not always pejorative terms.[440] According to the *Rhetorica ad Herennium*, after all, a more acceptable term for 'strategy' is, in fact, not *dolus*, but counsel or *consilium*.[441] Sallust regards 'strategy' to be characteristic of the treachery (*perfidia*) shown by Jugurtha and the Numidians, but he also credits none other than Cicero with both *astutia* (shrewdness) and *dolus*.[442] Likewise, Josephus describes his own actions as showing bravery and intelligence but also strategy and

---

439 *Rhetorica ad Herennium*, III.4.8, pp. 169–71; cf. Vergil, *Aeneid*, XI.704, p. 285. According to the *Encomium Emmae Reginae*, III.8, p. 24, Eadric Streona was outstanding in counsel but treacherous in guile; cf. Cosmas of Prague, *Chronicle of the Czechs*, III.53, p. 240.
440 For example, Sallust, *Jugurthine War*, XXV.9, p. 189; Gregory of Tours, *Histories*, II.42, p. 158, III.31, p. 188, IV.16, p. 212, IV.29, p. 223; *Encomium Emmae Reginae*, I.13, p. 13. For Liutprand and Thietmar, see page 328, note 448.
441 *Rhetorica ad Herennium*, III.4.8, p. 171.
442 Sallust, *Jugurthine War*, XLVI, p. 235, LIII, p. 249; Sallust, *Catiline*, XXVI, p. 45.

cunning.[443] Valerius Maximus could oppose Roman prudence to Punic cunning but, in castigating the tricks, treachery and deceit of the Carthaginians (*dolis et insidiis et fallacia*), he also points out the proximity of craftiness to wisdom, not least when practised by the elder Scipio.[444] Whereas, for Cicero, knowledge which is deployed without justice should be called shrewdness (*calliditas*) rather than wisdom (*sapientia*),[445] for Valerius Maximus, strategies formed a distinguished part of *calliditas* which was far removed from censure (even though, because such actions can hardly be expressed suitably by a Latin word, he suggests they remain denoted by their Greek transliteration, 'strategemata').[446] In short, whilst it is certainly the case that, for many medieval writers, *dolus* remains a term of condemnation (it is the *modus operandi* of the Greek emperor Alexius in the First Crusade, for example),[447] this vocabulary could be used in a more neutral and pragmatic vein.[448]

---

443 Josephus, *De Bello Iudaico*, trans. G.A. Williamson, *Jewish War* (Harmondsworth, 1970), II.21.3–5, pp. 174–5.
444 Valerius Maximus, *Facta et Dicta Memorabilia*, I.8, p. 123, VII.3, pp. 127–9, VII.4, pp. 153, 157, IX.6, p. 343.
445 Cicero, *De Officiis*, I.19.63, p. 26, quoted in *Moralium Dogma Philosophorum*, p. 30.
446 Valerius Maximus, *Facta et Dicta Memorabilia*, VII.4, p. 147; cf. Frontinus, *Strategemata*, trans. C.E. Bennett (Loeb, 1925).
447 For example, *Gesta Francorum et Aliorum Hierosolimitanorum*, ed. and trans. R. Hill (Oxford, 1962), I, p. 6, II, pp. 10–12, II, p. 17. For Greek cunning and trickery, a characterisation based ultimately on Vergil (*Aeneid*, I.754, p. 293, II.36, p. 297, II.309–10, p. 315) and epitomised by the figure of Sinon (*Aeneid*, II.65–66, p. 299: 'hear now the treachery of the Greeks and from one crime learn them all'; II.152, p. 305; II.195, p. 307), see, for example, Valerius Maximus, *Facta et Dicta Memorabilia*, IV.7, p. 419 ('the monstrous falsehoods of a nation prone to make things up'); Liutprand of Cremona, *Relatio de Legatione Constantinopolitana*, trans. F.A. Wright, in *The Works of Liutprand of Cremona* (London, 1930), XXX, p. 252; Widukind, *Res Gestae Saxonicae*, III.71, pp. 226–8; Cosmas of Prague, *Chronicle of the Czechs*, III.19, pp. 203–4; Rahewin, *Deeds of Frederick*, III.20, p. 197; Henry of Huntingdon, *Historia Anglorum*, VIII, p. 511. For the cunning and deceit of Ligurians, see Vergil, *Aeneid*, XI.715–17, p. 285; for the cunning of the Normans (and not just the eponymous Robert 'Guiscard'), see Henry of Huntingdon, *Historia Anglorum*, VI.20, p. 373, VI.27, p. 385, VI.30, p. 393; for the cunning, falsehood and deceptive fictions of the Irish, see Gerald of Wales, *Expugnatio Hibernica*, I.25, p. 85, II.11, pp. 159–61, II.20, pp. 187–9, II.39, p. 251; for *Danaii* as Danes, see Walter Map, *De Nugis Curialium*, V.4, p. 435.
448 For example, Widukind, *Res Gestae Saxonicae*, I.30, p. 72, II.16, p. 126, II.21, p. 134; Liutprand, *Antapodosis*, I.4, p. 34, I.32, p. 54, II.33, p. 86, II.41, p. 89, II.55, p. 96, II.62, p. 98, III.9, p. 113, VI.3, p. 206, compared with III.19, p. 117, III.26, p. 122, III.41, p. 130; Thietmar, *Chronicon*, VII.21, p. 320 (*dolosus*) and

Lucan's *Pharsalia* had already demonstrated the extremes to which these criteria, and this debate, might be taken in deliberative rhetoric when he described the *consilium* that was put forward in order to persuade Ptolemy to kill Pompey in Egypt: what is advantageous (*utile*), it was argued, differs as much from what is right (*rectum*) as the stars are distant from the sea; political power will therefore be completely destroyed if it only weighs up what is just (*iusta*) and morally worthy (*honestum*), since in reality virtue and the highest power do not go together.[449] In a similar vein, Josephus recorded the argument of Vespasian's counsellors that considerations of expediency should always be preferred to moral worth whenever the two are in conflict; Josephus also observed that John of Gischala executed anyone who advocated courses of action which were both *honestum* and *utile*.[450] Even as a theoretical possibility put into the mouths of others, the priority afforded to utility over moral worth was clearly a perspective which political counsel had to take on board. This much was evident from classical manuals of rhetoric and from classical historians, but it was also clear from the twelfth-century synthesis of Cicero and Seneca, the *Moralium Dogma Philosophorum*, a work which was structured around a discussion of moral worth (that is, the four cardinal virtues and their sub-divisions) and utility (that is, goods of the soul, goods of the body and external goods) and concludes with an analysis of the relationship between them. The main body of this text opens with the explicit statement that deliberative counsel has three aspects – moral worth, utility, and the potential conflict between them – and proceeds to set out in some detail how different moral goods and advantageous goods can be compared between themselves and with one another.[451]

VII.72, p. 358 (*fraudulenta calliditas*), compared with I.9, p. 74 (*callide viriliterque*) and IV.9, p. 157 (*vi et arte*). For Anselm's *dolus* and 'holy guile' (*sancta calliditas*), see Eadmer, *Life of Anselm*, I.9–10, p. 16.
449 Lucan, *Pharsalia*, VIII.487–95, pp. 472–3; cf. Arnulf of Orleans, *Glosule Super Lucanum*, p. 415; *Scholia in Lucani Bellum Civile*, ed. H. Usener (Leipzig, 1869), p. 275; *Adnotationes Super Lucanum*, ed. J. Endt (Leipzig, 1909), p. 322.
450 Josephus, *De Bello Iudaico*, III.10, p. 222, VII.8, p. 381; cf. Orosius, *Seven Books of History*, VII.31, p. 335.
451 *Moralium Dogma Philosophorum*, pp. 6–7. For the issue of authorship, see J.R. Williams, 'The Quest for the Author of the *Moralium Dogma Philosophorum*', *Speculum*, 32 (1957), pp. 736–47.

Its discussion of the apparent conflict between moral worth and utility, and its digest of Cicero's conclusion that moral worth is, in fact, intrinsically advantageous, is prefaced, however, with a verbatim quotation of the expedient advice offered to Ptolemy in Lucan's *Pharsalia*.[452]

Given that considerations of circumstantial necessity or utility became standard criteria for judging whether dispensation could be made from the normal prescriptions of the law (Ivo of Chartres, for example, made the 'necessity of the moment, ... the necessity or utility of the times' a key diagnostic for assessing whether an action should be tolerated rather than condemned),[453] it is perhaps not surprising that discussion of the relationship *between* moral worth and advantage, *between* virtue and practicability, should have proved a major political and public concern of medieval historiography.[454] Wipo's *Deeds of Conrad* ties the provision of political counsel directly to the categories of *honestum* and *utile*, and includes a set-piece example of deliberation over a doubtful matter, namely who ought to rule the kingdom.[455] Bad counsel, according to the anonymous *Life of the Emperor Henry IV*, is motivated by selfish advantage, whereas it should be always governed by what is *honestum et utile*.[456] Henry of Huntingdon, in

---

452 *Moralium Dogma Philosophorum*, pp. 68–72.
453 Ivo of Chartres, prologue to the *Decretum* and *Panormia*, trans. B.C. Brasington, in R. Somerville and B.C. Brasington, *Prefaces to Canon Law Books in Latin Christianity: Selected Translations 500–1245* (New Haven, 1998), pp. 141–2, 145–6, 150, 153, 156. Ralph de Diceto includes a digest of Ivo's prologue, alongside those of historians such as Justin, Bede, Robert of Torigni and Hugh of St Victor, at the start of his *Abbreviationes Chronicorum*, pp. 24–33. Cf. *Decrees of the Fourth Lateran Council*, ed. and trans. N.P. Tanner, *Decrees of the Ecumenical Councils* (London, 1990), canon 50, p. 257: 'it should not be judged reprehensible if human decrees are sometimes changed according to changing circumstances [*secundum varietatem temporum*], especially when urgent necessity or evident advantage demands it'.
454 For example, Gregory of Tours, *Histories*, IV.13, p. 207 (*consilium bonum utilemque*); William of Malmesbury, *De Laudibus et Miraculis Sanctae Mariae*, ed. J.M. Canal (2nd edn, Rome, 1968), prol., p. 50; Walter of Châtillon, *Alexandreis*, V.378, p. 120; William of Newburgh, *The History of English Affairs*, trans. P.G. Walsh and M.J. Kennedy (Warminster, 1988), I.11, p. 67, I.30, p. 127.
455 Wipo, *Deeds of Conrad*, I, p. 58, II, p. 62.
456 *Life of the Emperor Henry*, II, p. 106; cf. Horace, *Epistles*, trans. H.R. Fairclough (Loeb, 1929), I.2.3–4, p. 263; Paschasius Radbertus, *Vita Adalhardi*, XVI, p. 36, XXXVIII, p. 50; Astronomer, *Life of Louis*, VII, p. 39 (*honestum et utile*), 43, p. 87 (*necessitates et ... utilitates*), 56, p. 111 (*utilitates necessarii*).

fact, makes the distinction central to his claim that historiography provides a better means of teaching ethics than philosophy:

> Where does the magnificence of brave men shine more brightly, or the wisdom of the prudent, or the judgments of the just, or the moderation of the temperate, than in the context of *res gestae*? Indeed, we have heard what Horace said, in praise of Homeric history, that it 'defines what is noble [*pulchrum*] and what is infamous [*turpe*], what is advantageous [*utile*] and what is not, more fully and better than Chrysippus and Crantor' [Horace, *Epistles*, I.2]. Whereas C[r]antor and Chrysippus sweated to produce many volumes of moral philosophy, Homer ... in writing history ... discussed what is morally worthy and advantageous [*honestum et utile*], and their contraries, more clearly and more pleasurably than the philosophers.[457]

Right at the start of his history, in other words, Henry advertises the moral–didactic purpose of his work (it is all about the four cardinal virtues), but he also highlights the *deliberative* value of what he is writing – it is about deciding what is *honestum* and *utile*.[458] Otto of Freising juxtaposes the same two criteria,[459] and treats Widukind's famous story of Hatto's guile as a case-study in whether such low cunning could, in fact, be justified by its utility to the kingdom.[460] Gerald of Wales quotes Vergil's disclaimer for Aeneas' strategic use of deception (*insidiae*) in battle ('who asks of an enemy whether he employs guile or virtue?'),[461] and observes that most people are concerned with what is expedient rather than what is honourable.[462] Even though Gerald immediately

---

457 Henry of Huntingdon, *Historia Anglorum*, prol., p. 3 (see also page 164); Bernardus Silvestris, *Commentary on the First Six Books of Virgil's Aeneid*, IV, p. 26.
458 Cf. Henry of Huntingdon, *Historia Anglorum*, V.17, p. 309.
459 Otto of Freising, *Chronicle*, II.19, pp. 174–5; Otto of Freising, *Deeds of Frederick*, I.19, p. 49, I.20, p. 51, I.65, pp. 104–6; cf. Widukind, *Res Gestae Saxonicae*, III.75, p. 232; Suger, *Gesta Hludowici*, XIX, pp. 92–3. For Otto of Freising's views on cunning, see his *Chronicle*, II.24, p. 179, II.25, p. 181, II.29, p. 186, II.34, p. 192, IV.10, p. 288, IV.26, p. 311; and his *Deeds of Frederick*, I.11, p. 44.
460 Otto of Freising, *Chronicle*, VI.15, p. 375; cf. Liutprand, *Antapodosis*, II.6, pp. 71–2; Widukind, *Res Gestae Saxonicae*, I.22, pp. 58–62; Thietmar, *Chronicon*, I.7, pp. 71–2.
461 Vergil, *Aeneid*, II.390, p. 321: *dolus an virtus, quis in hoste requirat*; cf. Macrobius, *Saturnalia*, V.16.7, p. 355; *Moralium Dogma Philosophorum*, p. 38; Cosmas of Prague, *Chronicle of the Czechs*, III.19, p. 203.
462 Gerald of Wales, *Topographia Hibernica*, III.99, p. 107, III.101, p. 109; cf. Gerald of Wales, *De Eruditione Principum*, II.3, p. 14, III.2, p. 56.

adds the Ciceronian safeguard that only what is honourable can be said to be entirely expedient, the frankness of his original concession remains.

The second point that needs to be made about the relationship between deliberative rhetoric and the writing of history concerns the particular prominence which is given by this type of rhetoric to an understanding of the events of the past. For Cicero, the incitement and restraint which are central to providing advice or counsel (*consilium*), as a means of persuading people to act, serve a vital social and political function. In both cases, success is closely tied to the use of history. 'Who can exhort people to virtue more passionately than the orator', he asks, 'and who can call them back from vice more sharply? Who can castigate the wicked more bitterly and who can praise the good more eloquently? Who can break cupidity more forcibly by their accusation? Who can alleviate grief more gently by their consolation? As for history [*historia*], the witness of the ages [*testis temporum*], the light of truth [*lux veritatis*], the life of remembrance [*vita memoriae*], the teacher of life [*magistra vitae*], the messenger of antiquity [*nuntia vetustatis*], what other voice than that of the orator can entrust it to immortality?'[463] Cicero makes the same connection in *De Legibus*, giving it, if anything, an even broader scope: '[the orator] must use not just [a] refined type of argument but also a more expansive style of speaking through which to guide peoples, to establish laws, to chastise the wicked and protect the good, to praise famous men and to issue instructions for safety and glory suited to persuading his fellow citizens, to exhort people to honour, to call them back from crime, to be able to comfort the afflicted, to enshrine in eternal memorials the deeds and opinions of brave and wise men together with the disgrace of the wicked'.[464]

---

463 Cicero, *De Oratore*, II.9.35–6, pp. 223–5 (see page 9); cf. Quintilian, *Institutio Oratoria*, XII.11.30, p. 513. For the popularity of this passage, see, for example, Gerald of Wales, *Descriptio Cambriae*, pref., p. 217; Gerald of Wales, Letter 3, to William de Montibus, Chancellor of Lincoln, ed. R.B.C. Huygens, trans. B. Dawson, in Y. Lefèvre and R.B.C. Huygens (eds), *Speculum Duorum or a Mirror of Two Men* (Cardiff, 1974), p. 171; Vincent of Beauvais, *Speculum Doctrinale*, III.127, col. 297; Vincent of Beauvais, *Speculum Historiale* (Douai, 1624; reprinted Graz, 1964–65), VI.18, p. 180; Henry Knighton, *Chronicon*, ed. J.R. Lumby (London, 1889), pref., p. 2.
464 Cicero, *De Legibus*, I.62, p. 127.

According to Cicero, an orator therefore needs to be familiar with everything which concerns the interests and organisation of the political community – this means public laws but it also includes the remembrance of deeds done in the past and the examples of antiquity (*monumenta rerum gestarum et vetustatis exempla*). It is this combination of subject-matter, therefore, the remembrance of antiquity (*memoria antiquitatis*) with the authority of public laws and the principles of ruling the *res publica*, which needs to be at their disposal when orators are engaged in the task of inspiring a languid people to pursue what is fitting, leading their audience away from error, rousing them against the wicked, or assuaging their hostility to the good.[465] Orators should be familiar with laws, in short, but also with history – they should know the order of *res gestae* and the remembrance of things past (*vetus memoria*), particularly of Rome but also of other commanding peoples and of illustrious kings. The commemoration of antiquity (*commemoratio antiquitatis*) and the putting forward of examples (*prolatio exemplorum*) bring to a speech both trustworthiness and authority, as well as the greatest pleasure. In any case, Cicero suggests, not to know what happened before you were born is to remain forever a child. What is the age of human beings, he asks, unless it is woven together (*contexitur*) with the age of one's predecessors by means of the remembrance of ancient matters (*memoria rerum veterum*)?[466]

It is on this basis that Cicero, Quintilian and the author of the *Rhetorica ad Herennium* all actively encourage the reading of works of history. The orator requires knowledge, not just of public law, but also of history (*historia*), the course of antiquity (*iter antiquitatis*) and a mass of individual *exempla*.[467] Urging the path of moral virtue in deliberative rhetoric accordingly involves collecting the glorious examples of one's ancestors (*exempla maiorum*) and extolling the immortal remembrance of posterity.[468] To recommend a course of action when the speaker has a remembrance of it having been done, either through being present themselves or through having heard about it from someone else, is to exercise the virtue

---

465 Cicero, *De Oratore*, I.46.201–2, pp. 141–3.
466 Cicero, *Orator*, XXXIV.120, p. 395.
467 Cicero, *De Oratore*, I.60.256, p. 189; cf. *De Oratore*, I.5.18, p. 15 (*omnis antiquitas, exemplorum vis*); Quintilian, *Institutio Oratoria*, XII.11.17, p. 505.
468 *De Oratore*, II.82.335, p. 453.

of prudence. This will make it easy to persuade people to adopt a similar course of action by putting it forward as an *exemplum* to be imitated.[469] Those who know what has happened to others will readily foresee (*providere*) from these events what lies ahead for their own concerns, whereas those who lack such knowledge (*imperiti*) are more easily deceived by their lack of prudence, because they will be unable to find *exempla* in the *res gestae* of the past.[470] When giving counsel in deliberative rhetoric, in short, *exempla* are of the greatest value because what has been experienced in the past constitutes the easiest method of securing agreement amongst humans – depending, of course, on the authority of the example cited and on the nature of the audience being addressed.[471]

Such theory was matched in practice. When Josephus' frank advice to surrender was ignored by the defenders of Jerusalem, for example, he describes himself turning to the precedent of past history.[472] Liutprand has Henry I of Saxony appeal explicitly to the deeds of former kings (*priscorum facta regum*) and the writings of the holy fathers.[473] Likewise, Wipo describes Conrad II invoking 'ancestral histories' (*historiae patrum*) at a public assembly of his nobles.[474] The claims made by deliberative rhetoric for the utility of the past, however, go beyond treating history simply as a storehouse of examples (*thesaurus exemplorum*). The author of the *Rhetorica ad Herennium* is rather cautious in equating the citation of examples with the force of testimony or witness, 'proving' what a precept has merely admonished. Such *exempla* are put forward to demonstrate, he argues, not in order to confirm or to testify – the difference lies in the fact that an example is used to point out the nature of what is being said, whereas testimony confirms that what

---

469 *Rhetorica ad Herennium*, III.3.4, p. 165.
470 *Rhetorica ad Herennium*, IV.9.13, p. 261. For John of Garland, the manner in which history indicated the future corresponded to the rhetorical trope of *transitio*, 'a figure whereby the mind of the listener, with the aid of the preceding narration, understands what is to come': John of Garland, *Parisiana Poetria*, V.321–6, p. 101; see also Mehtonen, *Old Concepts and New Poetics*, p. 155.
471 Quintilian, *Institutio Oratoria*, III.8.36, p. 497.
472 Josephus, *De Bello Iudaico*, V.9, p. 307.
473 Liutprand, *Antapodosis*, II.27, p. 84.
474 Wipo, *Deeds of Conrad*, XX, p. 82.

is being said is actually the case.[475] Quintilian, by contrast, has no such concerns. There is, he maintains, no subject to which the use of *exempla* is more suited than deliberative rhetoric because, generally speaking, the future seems to respond to what has happened in the past and experience (*experimentum*) is, as it were, the testimony of reason (*velut quoddam rationis testimonium*).[476] In Quintilian's eyes, therefore, an appeal to the past amounts to an argument from similarity (*similitudo*) and an appeal to similar events in the past is a particularly useful approach to take when speaking of what will happen in the future. An *exemplum* is remembrance of something done in the past, or thought to have been done in the past, and is used to persuade an audience of a particular point (*commemoratio rei gestae aut ut gestae utilis ad persuadendum*). Such deeds can be recounted either in their entirety or in part, depending on how well-known they already are to an audience or on which particular aspect is useful to persuade that audience of the particular action which is being counselled. As far as Quintilian is concerned, citation of a historical example is an especially persuasive form of argument, since it is readily believable that what generally occurs in one or more cases (that is, in cases other than the one under discussion) is also appropriate in the case in question. Comparison with similar things, he argues, is a type of extrinsic proof (*probatio*), especially when it concerns those *exempla* which shine with the authority of *res gestae*, what the Greeks call 'paradigms'. Hence, unlike Cicero, who separates parallel (*collatio*) from example (*exemplum*),[477] Quintilian argues that they are part and parcel of the same type of proof. Citation of historical *exempla*, he argues, comparison with similar events, can extend to poetic fables and parables, as well as to maxims or sayings, but all of these possess less force as proof than the remembrance of something done, or thought to have been done in the past.[478] The narrative of what has been done in the past, in short, the citation of historical precedent, and comparison with similar events, are all crucial features of deliberative rhetoric, of counselling for or against a particular course of action, of predicting *and proving* what will

---

475 *Rhetorica ad Herennium*, IV.1.2, p. 231, IV.3.5, pp. 237–9.
476 Quintilian, *Institutio Oratoria*, III.8.66, pp. 511–13.
477 Cicero, *De Inventione*, I.30.49, pp. 89–91 (see page 326).
478 Quintilian, *Institutio Oratoria*, V.11.1–8, pp. 271–5, V.11.15–21, pp. 281–3.

occur as a consequence of that action in the future. Or, as William of Malmesbury has Anselm say, 'I can tell what will happen in the future from what has happened in the past'.[479]

So where did a consideration of deliberative rhetoric leave historiography in the Middle Ages? In Quintilian's view, what carries the greatest weight in counselling for or against a particular course of political action is the authority of the speaker or writer themselves. If an individual wants everyone to believe their judgment as to what is *honestum* and *utile*, then that individual ought to possess, or be thought to possess, the highest wisdom and virtue.[480] Cicero makes the same point: to speak persuasively for or against a given course of action is a task which only someone of the greatest weight of character can undertake, since to give counsel on matters of the utmost importance requires wisdom, moral worth and eloquence – to see into the future, to put forward authoritative proofs and to be persuasive.[481] As a result, the importance of establishing such personal credibility and trustworthiness places a particular burden, once again, on that part of the text in which the authority and character of the speaker or writer is established, namely the *exordium* or introduction.[482] Writers of history in the Middle Ages, from Einhard to Wipo to Henry of Huntingdon, were not slow to act on the advice.[483] As for the contents of the history that followed, deliberative rhetoric provided, first and foremost, a set of guidelines for the way in which political debate, political controversy, could take the form of an appeal to historical precedent, either as material which could be introduced into the course of a particular public argument (Edward I, for example, famously ordered chronicles to be searched in order to justify his own claim to arbitrate in the matter of Scotland)[484] or in the form of a work of history *tout court*. Second, deliberative rhetoric showed how an appeal to historical

---

479 William of Malmesbury, *Gesta Pontificum Anglorum*, I.49, p. 139.
480 Quintilian, *Institutio Oratoria*, III.8.12–13, p. 485.
481 Cicero, *De Oratore*, II.81.333, p. 451.
482 See pages 140–1, 168–71.
483 See pages 158–60, 164, 241.
484 E.L.G. Stones and G.G. Simpson, *Edward I and the Throne of Scotland 1290–1296: An Edition of the Record Sources for the Great Cause* (Oxford, 1978), vol. I, pp. 137–62, 222–4. Cf. C. Given-Wilson, *Chronicles: The Writing of History in Medieval England* (London, 2004), pp. 65–9.

precedent, the calling to mind, the commemoration of the deeds of one's ancestors, could become a vitally important part of public life, of personal and political legitimation. Each of these characteristics can be shown to have a particular affinity with the writing of history in the Middle Ages.[485]

Like Gildas, Gregory of Tours had to wipe away the tears as he wrote his history and, like Gildas, Gregory's concern with the remembrance of posterity (*memoria posteritatis*) was tied directly to the perils of forgetting what had happened in the past.[486] Gregory's clear didactic purpose in writing his history is that the Franks ought to have learned from the past – they should have been warned by the fate of their predecessors and, in particular, by the fact that inattentiveness to the terms of the Old Testament covenant would produce chastisement, and ultimately punishment, from God.[487] Observance of God's laws and commandments was the precondition for success in this life; failure to do so would result directly in the dominance of foreign peoples.[488] Such a lesson could also be couched in explicitly political terms. In an impassioned apostrophe, or direct address, to the Frankish king, for example, Gregory presents a vivid picture of the consequences of dissension and echoes Orosius' judgment on Numantia – concord preserves a kingdom, discord destroys it.[489] More significantly, however, this is also a lesson which he wants to convey to all those who are charged with ministry within the Church – 'let this be a warning to the clergy'.[490] This advice lies at the heart of Gregory's profound sense of his own episcopal

---

485 Cf. Nelson, 'History-Writing at the Courts of Louis the Pious and Charles the Bald', p. 437: 'what distinguished history's teaching function was not just its purveying of private morals and exemplary conduct, but its direct reference to politics – to public life.... History was produced and consumed as a means of critique and contestation'. See also G. Spiegel, 'Political Utility in Medieval Historiography – A Sketch', *History and Theory*, 14 (1975), pp. 314–25.
486 Gregory of Tours, *Histories*, pref., p. 63, V.34, p. 296.
487 *Histories*, V.pref., pp. 253–4; cf. I.4, p. 70, II.4–6, pp. 114–16, VI.6, p. 333, VI.45–6, p. 379.
488 *Histories*, I.12, p. 77; cf. Thietmar, *Chronicon*, I.prol., p. 66, I.19, p. 81, II.7, pp. 96–7, III.14–17, pp. 139–42, VI.48, p. 271, VII.36–45, pp. 332–9, VIII.30, p. 382.
489 *Histories*, V.prol., p. 254; see page 68; cf. Paul the Deacon, *History of the Lombards*, VI.24, p. 270.
490 *Histories*, VIII.19, p. 451.

responsibility in offering counsel to kings by writing his *Histories*, and it underpins the sharpness of the contrast which he then draws between those Frankish rulers who listened to their bishops in the past and those who now persecuted them in the present.[491]

Wipo's account of the deeds of Conrad II makes the author's concern with delivering political advice quite explicit. Wipo defined counsel prior to action (Ecclesiasticus [Sirach] 37:16) as the seed of the following fruit – it is the part of foresight (*providentia*) to prepare within for that which is needed without.[492] At the same time, he was well aware from his own reading of Macrobius that there were several methods of offering that counsel to the political community or *res publica* – credible dreams and fabulous narratives, he explains, can both serve as a means of persuading rulers to be just and to avoid the besetting Sallustian sins of sloth and pride. For Wipo, however, it was, first and foremost, the writing of history, and in the manner of the Old Testament, which provided the most effective method of all. Christians should, in this respect, emulate their pagan predecessors. 'The ancients', he explains, 'erected statues and the biggest memorials possible to victorious rulers ... and thought that their deeds should be inscribed so that, after they had died, honour might be made manifest to the perpetual memory of posterity'. This practice was imperative to the survival of the political community, since they 'judged that the actions of the *res publica* would die simultaneously with its rulers unless what happened were noted down, and that a very great disaster would ensue from slothful silence if what any man now dead pursued during his lifetime should not be apparent from surviving writings'. Historical writing for Christian rulers, in Wipo's opinion, should now go one step further. Those who make manifest in their writings those things which are done well by Christian rulers, that is, when they describe them upholding the law and peace of Christ, are doing nothing other than preaching the gospel.[493]

The historiographical component of political counsel did not always aspire to the moral heights expounded by Gregory of

---

491 *Histories*, IV.47–8, p. 244, V.18, pp. 276–7, VIII.30, pp. 460–2.
492 Wipo, *Deeds of Conrad*, I, p. 60; cf. Ecclesiasticus (Sirach) 32:24 ('do nothing without counsel and when they are done you will not repent'), quoted, for example, by Eadmer, *Life of Anselm*, I.6, p. 10.
493 *Deeds of Conrad*, prol., pp. 54–6.

Tours or by Wipo. It could also be much more pragmatic and instrumental. A *narratio rei gestae* might constitute demonstrative praise for the sake of posterity, or it might represent a judicial defence against a charge of wrongdoing, but it could also provide deliberative counsel for the sake of present political action, and all the more effectively if such a narrative *exemplum* was generally acknowledged to be a better means of instruction than a precept. According to Gerald of Wales, Henry II of England 'could never forget anything he had heard and which was worth remembering, so he had at his command a knowledge of almost every history [*historiarum omnium fere promptam notitiam*] and [therefore] had to hand an experience of almost all situations'.[494] When it was a case of citing historical *exempla*, there was a particularly strong affinity between demonstrative rhetoric and deliberative rhetoric. Quintilian points out, for example, that *encomia* or panegyrics can bear similarity to political advice, in as much as what is usually put forward for praise in demonstrative rhetoric is generally the same as what is advised as a course of action in deliberative rhetoric.[495] Writing in praise of an individual, holding up an individual's deeds in the past as an example to be imitated in the present, could therefore carry a sharp political edge. This is why the historical content of the *speculum principis* genre was thought to be such an effective means of offering political education and advice.[496] Gregory the Great's gerundive encapsulated perhaps the pithiest, and most influential, formulation of this principle in action, as an extension of the moral or tropological sense of Scripture: deeds done, he writes, are deeds which *should* be done (*res gestae, res gerendae*).[497] Or, as Hugh of St Victor was to recast it, 'what is said to have been done signifies that something ought to be done' (*per id quod factum dicitur aliquid faciendum esse significatur*).[498]

---

[494] Gerald of Wales, *Expugnatio Hibernica*, I.46, p. 133.
[495] Quintilian, *Institutio Oratoria*, III.7.28, p. 479.
[496] See page 168.
[497] Gregory the Great, *XL Homiliae in Evangelia*, II.21, p. 158 (*res gesta aliquid ... signat gerendum*); Gregory the Great, *Moralia in Job*, XIX.20.29, p. 421 (*quod sic est veraciter factum ut significaret aliquid veraciter faciendum*); Gregory the Great, *Dialogues*, IV.40, p. 244; cf. pages 397–8.
[498] Hugh of St Victor, *De Sacramentis Christianae Fidei*, trans. R.J. Deferrari, *On the Sacraments of the Christian Faith* (Cambridge, MA, 1951), prol.4, p. 5; cf. Hugh of St Victor, *Didascalicon*, VI.5, p. 145 (*fecerit / faciendum*); Bonaventure, *Breviloquium*,

Given such a close connection between historical *exempla* and deliberative rhetoric, the immediate political context can often provide important indications as to why a work of history should have been written at a particular time and why its author may have chosen to highlight some events rather than others. Einhard's account of the life, deeds and character of Charlemagne offers a good example of this principle in practice. In the midst of the political crisis of 828/29, Louis the Pious summoned a series of public, political assemblies in order to set out the reforms which were necessary at every level of society, starting with the king himself. In these particular political circumstances, the *memoria* of Charlemagne clearly became a highly charged issue and any comparison of father and son, implicit or explicit, carried a sharp political edge: Charlemagne's familial concord as a contrast to Louis' fractious and rebellious relations with his sons; the cruelty of Charlemagne's wife, Fastrada, as a mirror to that of Louis the Pious' wife, Judith; Charlemagne's devotion to Frankish songs as the obverse of Louis' unsmiling piety; a roll call of success in war as a pointed reminder of Louis' lack of martial virtue; and, most striking of all, perhaps, an opening to a 'life' of Charlemagne setting out a justification for the deposition of the Merovingians as a cautionary tale for any ruler who lacked utility (a lesson which may have been reinforced by a deliberate confusion of Zechariah with Stephen as the pope who deposed Childeric III).[499]

Asser's *Deeds* of Alfred of Wessex illustrates the same point – given that this text is rare for the fact that it is self-dated, it naturally invites the question of why Asser should have chosen to write it in 893, when the king was still alive. This was a year in which the Vikings had resumed their raiding of mainland Britain after a fifteen-year interlude – as such, Asser's text may thus have been written, and read, as a timely reminder of the need to show loyalty, and as a timely condemnation of what he refers to as the stubborn laziness of those of Alfred's subjects who had not complied with their ruler's earlier commands. The year 893, however, also places the composition of the text in the immediate aftermath of Alfred's

---

prol.4.1, p. 12: *per id quod factum est, datur intelligi aliud quod faciendum est*; Henry of Huntingdon, *Historia Anglorum*, VIII, p. 503.
499 Einhard, *Vita Karoli*, I, pp. 8–10, XV, pp. 42–4, XIX, pp. 58–62, XX, p. 64, XXIX, p. 82.

alliance with a number of Welsh kings – as such, Asser's *res gestae* can also be read as a demonstration of Alfred's wealth and generosity, making available an account of the king's deeds in Latin for an audience who knew no Old English (the compilation of the *Anglo-Saxon Chronicle* had begun in 891/92) in order to persuade these Welsh kings of the superiority of West Saxon, as opposed to Hiberno-Norse, overlordship. In 893, moreover, Alfred was getting old, and the whole issue of an open succession was becoming a bone of contention between his son (Edward the Elder) and nephew (Æethelwold). Read in this light, there are certain features of the text which assume considerable contemporary political resonance within the West Saxon court – most notably the emphasis on the perils of filial rebellion, on the legitimacy of a father's testamentary disposition and on Alfred as a designated heir (*secundarius*).[500]

The instrumental value of certain works of historiography – *narratio rei gestae* which is proffered as political advice – is a feature of the writing of history in the Middle Ages that should not be underestimated. Not all agenda are as implicit as those of Einhard or Asser. Liutprand's 'ephemeral' account of his legation to Constantinople, for example, takes the form of a letter to Otto I, Otto II and the empress Adelheid, and its self-confessed purpose is to counsel direct political action in the present, namely to summon the patriarch of Constantinople and the emperor Nicephoras to account for their actions and on pain of war.[501] The second life of Mathilda, wife of Henry I of Saxony and mother of the emperor Otto I, was written in order to justify and legitimate the succession of her great-grandson, Henry II, in 1002.[502] Thietmar's admonitory chronicle was written a decade later, at a time (1012–18) when the author wanted to warn his audience of the potential political crisis which would be caused by Henry II's childlessness.[503]

---

500 Asser, *Res Gestae Ælfredi*, XII–XIII, pp. 70–1, XVI–XVIII, pp. 72–3, XXIX, p. 77, XXXVIII, p. 79, XLII, p. 80; cf. J. Nelson, 'Reconstructing a Royal Family – Reflections on Alfred, from Asser Chapter 2', in I. Wood and N. Lund (eds), *People and Places in Northern Europe 500–1600* (Woodbridge, 1991), pp. 47–66.
501 Liutprand, *Legatio*, LXII, p. 274; cf. H. Mayr-Harting, 'Liudprand of Cremona's Account of His Legation to Constantinople (968) and Ottonian Imperial Strategy', *English Historical Review*, 116 (2001), pp. 539–56.
502 Odilo of Cluny, *Epitaph of Adelheid*, pp. 88–127.
503 Thietmar, *Chronicon*, I.19, p. 81, VI.48, p. 271, and, more generally, Bagge, *Kings, Politics and the Right Order of the World*, p. 107. For Thietmar's description

Some historians were clearly able to articulate the political advice they wanted to deliver; others chose, or were forced, to be more circumspect. Like William of Malmesbury,[504] Henry of Huntingdon used the prologue to his *History of the English* in order to draw explicit attention to the political significance of the context in which it was being written. Having invoked the four cardinal virtues and the distinction between *honestum* and *utile*, Henry appeals to the particular didactic function which he wants his history to serve: 'In the recorded deeds of all peoples and nations which are the very judgments of God, [*exempla* of] clemency, generosity, honesty, caution and the like, and their opposites, not only provoke men of the spirit to what is good and deter them from evil, but even encourage worldly men to good deeds and reduce their wickedness. History therefore brings the past into view as though it were present and allows judgment of the future by representing the past'.[505] If Henry of Huntingdon readily acknowledges that it was Bede who had provided him with his template for rulers serving either as *exempla* to be imitated or as warnings (*cautela*) to be avoided,[506] he also makes a point of spelling out just how Ceowulf of Northumbria should have read the history which Bede had dedicated to him.[507] The message for Henry's own work was clear and he addresses king Henry I accordingly with a direct apostrophe, inviting him to look at, and learn from, the examples now set before him.[508]

Henry of Huntingdon's *History of the English* ultimately comprised a total of ten books but they were written over a period of some thirty years, between 1123 and 1154. There were thus at least six versions of his work, each of them produced as part of a process of constant revision and, for the years after 1135, during a time when the Anglo-Norman realm was riven by the disputed succession between Stephen and Matilda. The first eight books are all about good and bad rulership and the punishments

---

of deliberation and counsel in action, see, for example, *Chronicon*, VI.33, p. 260, VI.62, p. 280.
504 See pages 29–30, 161, 227–8.
505 Henry of Huntingdon, *Historia Anglorum*, prol., p. 5.
506 *Historia Anglorum*, IV.10, p. 229, VI.38, p. 405, VI.39, p. 407; cf. Orderic Vitalis, *Historia Ecclesiastica*, prol., p. 131.
507 *Historia Anglorum*, IV.16, p. 237.
508 *Historia Anglorum*, VIII (Letter to Henry I), pp. 503, 543, 557.

(*plagae*) which have been visited by God upon a sinful people.[509] Book IX describes its contents as *De viris illustribus Anglorum* and takes many of its moral–didactic *exempla* from Bede, not least for the details of the eight kings who gave up their kingdoms to become saints. The tenth, and last, book deals with strictly contemporary history and the civil wars of Stephen's reign. The final event described is thus the coronation of Henry of Anjou as king Henry II and its closing words are: 'and now a new book must be devoted to a new king'.[510] No such book was written. Either this simply reflects the nature of the *Historia Anglorum* as a work in progress or, as Henry of Huntingdon's prologue suggests, it continues an open invitation for rulers to learn the lessons from the past. Writing some twenty years later, John of Salisbury was rather less subtle. His particular cautionary moral–didactic *exempla* for the instruction of rulers, he states, were excerpted from his own larger work entitled *On the Death of Tyrants*.[511] Gerald of Wales spelled it out more bluntly still: 'such therefore and so bloody are the deaths of tyrants, as very many examples show from ancient times.... No king of the Norman race, even to our own days, has ended his life in a praiseworthy death when he has passed over six or seven years'.[512]

Whilst historiography served as a means of proffering political counsel, it could clearly become highly charged. Forgetting the past was, in this respect, just as instrumental as its remembrance. Valerius Maximus made the point neatly with his account of how Thrasybulus issued a decree which forbade any mention of the divisive events of the recent past. 'This oblivion', he comments, 'which the Athenians call "amnesty"' recalled the shaken and tottering state of the community to its former condition'.[513] In the absence of such official amnesia, the past could become bitterly contested.[514] A striking example was provided in the thirteenth

---

509 See page 81.
510 *Historia Anglorum*, X.40, p. 777.
511 John of Salisbury, *Policraticus*, trans. Dickinson, VIII.20, p. 367.
512 Gerald of Wales, *De Eruditione Principum*, III.31, p. 114.
513 Valerius Maximus, *Facta et Dicta Memorabilia*, IV.1, p. 357.
514 For the difficulties involved in making Florentines 'forget' politically divisive events of the recent past, see, for example, Leonardo Bruni, *History of the Florentine People*, ed. and trans. J. Hankins (Cambridge, MA, 2001–07), III.28, pp. 265–7, III.54, p. 289.

century by the political use which was made of the character and deeds of Louis IX. Philip IV of France made repeated appeals to his grandfather as an important part of his claim to legitimate political action but, in doing so, history proved to be a double-edged sword. Joinville may have started his 'life' of Louis IX in the 1270s as an account of the Seventh Crusade but its final form was a response to a request from Philip IV's queen, Jeanne, following Louis' canonisation in 1297. The work now became a didactic text and the pairing of the exemplary with the cautionary is made explicit. The king's canonisation, Joinville writes, 'has brought great honour to those of the good king's line who are like him in doing well and equal dishonour to those descendants of his who will not follow him in good works. Great dishonour, I repeat, to those of his line who choose to do evil; for men will point a finger at them and say that the saintly king from whom they have sprung would have shrunk from acting so badly'.[515] When it was completed in c.1309, after Jeanne's death, Joinville's comments on justice, on good government, on rapacious avarice, on the perils of Crusade, on ambitious brothers, on the malpractice of Templars, on the Treaty of Paris, and on the inappropriate expression of grief at the death of a queen, all provided contemporary political commentary on the perceived failings of Louis IX's grandson, Philip IV.[516]

The deliberative component of medieval historiography embraced a political culture which, like judicial rhetoric, went well beyond the deeds of kings. Within the Church, for example, the production and circulation of the polemical literature which accompanied the Investiture Conflict may have been driven primarily by issues of ecclesiological principle but one of its most striking rhetorical features was the invocation of legal and historical

---

515 Joinville, *Life of Saint Louis*, trans. M. Shaw, *Joinville and Villehardouin: Chronicles of the Crusades* (Harmondsworth, 1963), p. 351; cf. pp. 172, 328. More generally, see P. Archambault, 'Joinville – History as Chivalric Code', in P. Archambault, *Seven French Chroniclers: Witnesses to History* (New York, 1974), pp. 41–57; M. Kauffmann, 'The Image of St Louis', in A.J. Duggan (ed.), *Kings and Kingship in Medieval Europe* (London, 1993), pp. 265–86.
516 Joinville, *Life of Saint Louis*, pp. 176, 267, 315–16, 334, 336, 345–6, 347–9.

precedent.[517] Lampert of Hersfeld, for example, combined a universal chronicle with a more detailed history of the years 1073–77 in order to explain how, and why, the Saxons had rebelled against the unjust tyranny of Henry IV to defend liberty, the *res publica* and the customs of their ancestors. Bruno of Merseburg's *On the Saxon War*, meanwhile, assembled arguments, as well as documentation, as part of the political and legal process to depose Henry IV.[518] In twelfth- and thirteenth-century France, the production of Latin and vernacular historiography for ducal and comital audiences expressed more than just a 'literary' agenda – the response of those dukes and counts whose independence was being eroded by the Capetians was to commission works of history which argued for their political autonomy and moral worth.[519] In twelfth- and thirteenth-century Italy, Genoa and Padua produced publicly approved and authorised histories of their respective communities.[520] Perhaps the most striking generic example of the

---

517 Cf. I.S. Robinson, *Authority and Resistance in the Investiture Contest: The Polemical Literature of the Late Eleventh Century* (Manchester, 1978), pp. 60–7; R. Knox, 'Finding the Law – Developments in Canon Law During the Gregorian Reform', *Studi Gregoriani*, 9 (1972), pp. 419–66.
518 Lampert of Hersfeld, *Annales*, ed. O. Holder-Egger (Hanover 1894), pp. 140–304; Bruno of Merseburg, *De Bello Saxonico*, ed. W. Wattenbach (Hanover, 1880). See also Otto of Freising, *Chronicle*, V.22, p. 347, VI.35, p. 400; cf. Bagge, *Kings, Politics and the Right Order of the World*, ch. 4, and p. 261; H.-W. Goetz, 'Geschichte als Argument – Historische Beweisführung und Geschichtsbewusstsein in den Streitschriften des Investiturstreits', *Historische Zeitschrift*, 245 (1987), pp. 31–69; H.-W. Goetz, 'Fälschung und Verfälschung der Vergangenheit – zum Geschichtsbild der Streitschriften des Investiturstreits', in *Fälschungen im Mittelalter* (Hanover, 1988–90), vol. I, pp. 165–88; Robinson, *Authority and Resistance*, pp. 128–9, 133.
519 G.M. Spiegel, *Romancing the Past: The Rise of Vernacular Prose Historiography in Thirteenth-Century France* (Berkeley, 1993); P. Magdalino (ed.), *The Perception of the Past in Twelfth-Century Europe* (London, 1992); L. Shopkow, 'Dynastic History', in D.M. Deliyannis (ed.), *Historiography in the Middle Ages* (Leiden, 2003), pp. 217–48; cf. Gilbert of Mons, *Chronicle of Hainaut*, trans. L. Napran (Woodbridge, 2005); Lambert of Ardres, *The History of the Counts of Guines and Lords of Ardres*, trans. L. Shopkow (Philadelphia, 2007).
520 B. Guenée, *Histoire et Culture Historique dans l'Occident Medieval* (Paris, 1980), p. 136; A. Vasina, 'Medieval Urban Historiography in Western Europe 1100–1500', in D.M. Deliyannis (ed.), *Historiography in the Middle Ages* (Leiden, 2003), pp. 327–41; J. Dotson, 'The Genoese Civic Annals – Caffaro and His Continuators', in S. Dale, A.W. Lewin and D.J. Osheim (eds), *Chronicling History: Chroniclers and Historians in Medieval and Renaissance Italy* (University Park, 2007), pp. 55–85.

influence of a broader political agenda, however, was provided by the Crusades. The exceptional nature of the First Crusade made it a natural subject for inclusion as a historiographical digression, not least because of the opportunities it presented for favourable comparison with ancient and classical military campaigns to the eastern Mediterranean – by Agamemnon, Alexander the Great, Vespasian and Titus. The First Crusade produced a series of contemporary narrative accounts (notably the *Gesta Francorum*, together with works by Fulcher of Chartres, Raymond of Aguilers and Peter Tudebode), but these were soon being rewritten by Guibert of Nogent, Robert the Monk, William of Malmesbury and Baudry of Bourgeuil.[521] By the time William of Tyre was writing his own narrative of the Crusades in 1170–84, he was doing so in order to analyse the cause of their recent failure and thereby provide a demonstration of the need for political unity in western Christendom and an argument for full financial support.[522]

Perhaps the most familiar dimension of historiography as a form of deliberative rhetoric is the function it served as a means of political legitimation, providing a narrative of the past, not for individuals, but for groups or communities. In the first instance, this found expression in the close connection between the writing of history and the foundation or re-foundation of monasteries.[523]

---

521 J.O. Ward, 'Some Principles of Rhetorical Historiography in the Twelfth Century', in E. Breisach (ed.), *Classical Rhetoric and Medieval Historiography* (Kalamazoo, 1985), pp. 103–65; L.B. Mortensen, 'Change of Style and Content as an Aspect of the Copying Process – a Recent Trend in the Study of Medieval Latin Historiography', in J. Hamesse (ed.), *Bilan et Perspectives des Études Médiévales en Europe* (Louvain-la-Neuve, 1995), pp. 274–5.
522 Smalley, *Historians in the Middle Ages*, p. 9; cf. P.W. Edbury and J.G. Rowe, *William of Tyre: Historian of the Latin East* (Cambridge, 1988).
523 M. Chibnall, 'Charter and Chronicle – The Use of Archive Sources by Norman Historians', in C.N.L. Brooke, D.E. Luscombe, G.H. Martin and D. Owen (eds), *Church and Government in the Middle Ages* (Cambridge, 1976), pp. 1–17; cf. A.G. Remensnyder, *Remembering Kings Past: Monastic Foundation Legends in Medieval Southern France* (Ithaca, 1995); A.G. Remensnyder, 'Topographies of Memory – Center and Periphery in High Medieval France', and B. Schneidmüller, 'Constructing the Past by Means of the Present – Historiographical Foundations of Medieval Institutions, Dynasties, Peoples and Communities', two chapters in G. Althoff, F. Fried and P.A. Geary (eds), *Medieval Concepts of the Past: Ritual, Memory, Historiography* (Cambridge, 2002), pp. 193–214, 167–92; Roest, 'Later Medieval Institutional History', pp. 278–84; J.O. Ward, 'The Monastic Historiographical

At a more inclusive level, the recording of 'history' became an integral part of ethnogenesis, that is, a process whereby the identification of a *gens* or people, rather than being precipitated by large-scale tribal invasions on the part of racially and linguistically discrete groups, was deliberately shaped in order to reflect a new social and political reality.[524] This has led to many works of medieval historiography being regarded as active constructions of ethnic identity by means of a narrated past, the imposition on, and acceptance by, a 'people' of the history of their dominant group or dynasty. Such histories can therefore take the form, for example, of an account of the fusion of different peoples in the past (as had been the case with Vergil's *Aeneid*),[525] or a structured forgetting (amnesia) of the separate traditions of subject or rival peoples. This sort of history-writing served as the equivalent of a written genealogy for an entire political community – texts which legitimised a newly-established dynasty or a new political entity by means of an origin myth (*origo gentis*), as often as not tying it to Troy, or in the case of Scotland to an Egyptian princess called Scota.[526]

Whilst it remains a moot point whether early medieval authors *themselves* thought that this is what they were doing when they originally composed their histories, it certainly seems to be how they subsequently came to be read by later generations.[527] Jordanes, it is argued, did this for 'the Goths' with his *Getica* of *c*.550 (following Cassiodorus' earlier work of *c*.525), Gregory of Tours for 'the Franks' in *c*.590, Bede for 'the English' in 731, and

---

Impulse c.1000–1260: A Reassessment', in T.M.S. Lehtonen and P. Mehtonen (eds), *Historia: The Concept and Genres in the Middle Ages* (Helsinki, 2000), pp. 71–100.
524 H. Wolfram, 'Le Genre de l'*Origo Gentis*', *Revue Belge de Philologie et d'Histoire*, 68 (1990), pp. 789–801; P.J. Geary, *The Myth of Nations: The Medieval Origins of Europe* (Princeton, 2002).
525 Vergil, *Aeneid*, XII.834–8, p. 359; cf. IV.112, p. 403.
526 S. Reynolds, 'Medieval *Origines Gentium* and the Community of the Realm', *History*, 68 (1983), pp. 375–90; cf. N. Kersken, 'High and Late Medieval National Historiography', in D.M. Deliyannis (ed.), *Historiography in the Middle Ages* (Leiden, 2003), pp. 181–215.
527 For the way in which a series of historical texts could be put together in the same manuscript in order to make a broader political point, see, for example, R. McKitterick, 'Political Ideology in Carolingian Historiography', in Y. Hen and M. Innes (eds), *The Uses of the Past in the Early Middle Ages* (Cambridge, 2000), pp. 162–74.

Paul the Deacon for 'the Lombards' in c.790.[528] There are much more clear-cut instances of this type of historiography later in the Middle Ages. It is a familiar feature from the ninth century, for example, when the Carolingians produced the *Gesta Regum Francorum* and the West Saxons the *Anglo-Saxon Chronicle*, but also in the tenth century when the Ottonians were furnished with Widukind's *Res Gestae Saxonicae*.[529] In the 990s, Aimoin of Fleury composed the *Deeds of the Franks* in order to connect the new Capetian dynasty with the Merovingians, but it was the monastery of Saint-Denis which provided the decisive impetus for such historiography from the early twelfth century onwards, culminating in the thirteenth-century vernacular *Grandes Chroniques*.[530] Further afield, Cosmas of Prague (Bohemia),[531] Saxo Grammaticus (Denmark), Theodoricus Monachus (Norway),[532] Gallus Anonymous (Poland), and Amatus of Montecassino, William of Apulia and Geoffrey Malaterra (Norman Sicily),[533] all set out to explain and justify the legitimacy of newly-established temporal power by means of a historical narrative of the past.[534] Saxo, in particular, gives a concise explanation, in the prologue to his *Gesta Danorum*, of why, given the pattern established by Bede, it was necessary for the Danes to have a national history in Latin.[535]

---

528 W. Goffart, *The Narrators of Barbarian History* (Princeton, 1988); cf. J.M. Pizarro, 'Ethnic and National History c.500–1000', in D.M. Deliyannis (ed.), *Historiography in the Middle Ages* (Leiden, 2003), pp. 43–87; B. Croke, 'Latin Historiography and the Barbarian Kingdoms', pp. 363–75, 381–87.
529 R. McKitterick, *History and Memory in the Carolingian World* (Cambridge, 2004).
530 Spiegel, *Romancing the Past*.
531 Cosmas of Prague, *The Chronicle of the Czechs*, trans. Wolverton.
532 S. Bagge, 'Theodoricus Monachus – Clerical Historiography in Twelfth-Century Norway', *Scandinavian Journal of History*, 14 (1989), pp. 113–33.
533 K.B. Wolf, *Making History: The Normans and Their Historians in Eleventh-Century Italy* (Philadelphia, 1995) chs 4–6; cf. Hugo Falcandus, *Historia*, ed. and trans. G.A. Loud and T. Wiedemann, *The History of the Tyrants of Sicily by 'Hugo Falcandus' 1154–69* (Manchester, 1998); G.A. Loud, 'History Writing in the Twelfth-Century Kingdom of Sicily', in S. Dale, A.W. Lewin and D.J. Osheim (eds), *Chronicling History: Chroniclers and Historians in Medieval and Renaissance Italy* (University Park, 2007), pp. 29–54.
534 L.B. Mortensen, 'Working with Ancient Roman History – A Comparison of Carolingian and Twelfth-Century Scholarly Endeavours', in C.Leonardi (ed.), *Gli Umanesimi Medievali* (Florence, 1998), p. 419. For the Iberian peninsula, see P. Linehan, *History and the Historians of Medieval Spain* (Oxford, 1993).
535 Saxo Grammaticus, *The History of the Danes, Books I–IX*, trans. P. Fisher (Woodbridge, 1979–80), pref., pp. 4–9.

Perhaps the best-documented example, however, is provided by the Normans, initially within late tenth-century Normandy, with the work of Dudo of Saint-Quentin, but then subsequently in the historiography which flourished after William's conquest of England in 1066, with the works of William of Poitiers and William of Jumièges in the 1070s, and then in the continuation of the *Deeds of the Norman Dukes* by Orderic Vitalis and Robert of Torigni throughout the course of the twelfth century.[536]

Dudo of Saint Quentin's *History of the Normans* (or, as he describes it himself, the *mores* and *acta* of the first Norman dukes) was an account of how, with God's help, a divinely-chosen people, initially pagan and then Christian, had secured their kingdom. It was structured around four lives, in effect two paired *vitae*: Hasting (a tyrannical, pagan ruler who failed to establish a permanent settlement) and Rollo (a convert who succeeded); William Longsword (whose sanctity was such that he was, in fact, too peaceable, too merciful, and was thus martyred before he could establish either order within Normandy or autonomy from the French) and Richard I (whose violence and justice succeeded where William's peace and mercy had failed, who completed the process of Christianisation, and who united Normandy and gave it effective independence from French kings). Dudo wrote his history in the 990s, as someone who was closely connected to the court of Richard I's heir, duke Richard II, and his immediate political agenda is clear – he presents the association between Normans and French as voluntary rather than subservient, stresses the independence of Normandy from royal control, emphasises Christianisation as part of a divine mandate, and underlines the unity, loyalty and peace of all Normans as the product of effective ducal governance. As a series of deliberative *exempla*, the resonance of such judgments would have served the duke of Normandy very well.[537]

---

[536] L. Shopkow, *History and Community: Norman Historical Writing in the Eleventh and Twelfth Centuries* (Washington, DC, 1987); E. Albu, *The Normans in Their Histories: Propaganda, Myth and Subversion* (Woodbridge, 2001).

[537] Dudo of St Quentin, *History of the Normans*, trans. E. Christiansen (Woodbridge, 1998); cf. E. Searle, 'Fact and Pattern in Heroic History – Dudo of Saint-Quentin', *Viator*, 15 (1984), pp. 119–37; E. Albu, 'Dudo of Saint-Quentin – The Heroic Past Imagined', *Haskins Society Journal*, 6 (1994), pp. 111–18; Albu,

The historiography which resulted from the Norman conquest of England followed a similar path. Much of this (predominantly monastic) writing has been read either as some sort of psychological compensation for a world which had been lost, with pockets of Anglo-Saxon monks preserving a threatened and vanishing culture, or as a strategic means of holding on to rights and privileges which had hitherto existed in custom rather than in writing.[538] Just as, if not more, important, however, was the political context in which it was being written, as part of a larger and more complex social process in which both an identity and a legitimacy were being constructed for a new 'Anglo-Norman' ruling elite. Henry of Huntingdon, for example, declares that his goal is to narrate the *gesta* of the kingdom of the English and the origin of his *gens*; he therefore explicitly ties his work to that of Bede (from whom he takes his title and much of his material), but also to Gildas's *Ruin of Britain*. Like Gildas (and indeed like Orosius, Gregory of Tours, Bede and Thietmar of Merseburg), Henry saw the lessons of God as *plagae* – they represented His discipline and chastisement of a sinful people.[539] The organising theme of Henry's *History of the English* is accordingly that of five successive invasions of England which are considered as *plagae* inflicted by God on a faithless *gens*. The Normans, as a result, are the fifth and last in a long line of scourges, beginning with the Romans, the Picts and Scots, then the Angles and Saxons, and the Danes. To Henry's mind, however, there was nothing permanent in this most recent series of events and his history could therefore be just as scathing about the vices of the Normans – as far as he was concerned, the fate of the English was a warning from history which continued to be pertinent. God could punish the Normans too.[540]

Henry of Huntingdon's equivocal attitude to the recent history of the 'English' people indicates the complexity of the process by which 'Norman', 'Anglo-Norman' and, ultimately, 'Angevin' rule

---

The Normans in their Histories, ch. 1; Shopkow, *History and Community*, pp. 68–79, 146–53, 174–8, 181–8.
538 See pages 226–7.
539 Henry of Huntingdon, *Historia Anglorum*, I.4, p. 15, I.47, p. 75, II.35, p. 123, IV.25, p. 255, IV.30, p. 265, V.prol., pp. 273–5, V.27, p. 325, VI.1, p. 339; Gildas, *De Excidio Britanniae*, XLVII–XLIX, p. 43, LV–LVII, p. 47; see also pages 67, 81; cf. Psalm 78.
540 Henry of Huntingdon, *Historia Anglorum*, VII.1, p. 413.

could be grafted onto an emerging political reality in order to create a new political identity.[541] Henry himself was well aware of the significance of what he was doing, not least when drawing attention to the pointed absence of such historiography on the part of the British. 'The knowledge of past events has further virtues', Henry writes, 'especially in that it distinguishes rational creatures from brutes, for brutes, whether men or beasts, do not know, nor indeed do they wish to know about their origins, their race and the events and deeds in their native land'.[542] Henry is actively invoking Sallust here, but he is also engaged in word-play and at the expense of the British, the descendants of Brutus who are themselves therefore 'brutes' (*bruti*).[543] It was probably no accident, therefore, that very soon after Henry of Huntingdon had written these words, Geoffrey of Monmouth claimed to have discovered precisely what Henry had said did not exist, setting it down in his own *History of the Kings of Britain* and giving it all the formal characteristics of historiography – genealogies, chronology, deeds of individual rulers and descriptions of battles.[544] Indeed, in many respects, Geoffrey's 'history' put the seal on a complex process of cultural and historiographical accommodation and appropriation which, in the 1140s, also witnessed the composition of Gaimar's *Estoire des Engleis* (a verse history of 'the English' but written in Old French and for an Anglo-Norman

---

541 J. Gillingham, 'The Beginnings of English Imperialism', *Journal of Historical Sociology*, 5 (1992), pp. 392–409); reprinted in J. Gillingham, *The English in the Twelfth Century: Imperialism, National Identity and Political Values* (Woodbridge, 2000), pp. 3–18.
542 Henry of Huntingdon, *Historia Anglorum*, prol., p. 5; cf. Sallust, *Catiline*, I, p. 3 (see page 42).
543 *Historia Anglorum*, I.9, p. 27.
544 Geoffrey of Monmouth, *Historia Regum Britanniae*, ed. M.D. Reeve, trans. N. Wright, *The History of the Kings of Britain* (Woodbridge, 2007); cf. C.N.L. Brooke, 'Geoffrey of Monmouth as Historian', C.N.L. Brooke, D.E. Luscombe, G.H. Martin and D. Owen (eds), *Church and Government in the Middle Ages* (Cambridge, 1976), pp. 77–91; N. Wright, 'Geoffrey of Monmouth and Gildas', *Arthurian Literature*, 2 (1982), pp. 1–40; J. Gillingham, 'The Context and Purposes of Geoffrey of Monmouth's *History of the Kings of Britain*', *Anglo-Norman Studies*, 13 (1990), pp. 99–118; reprinted in J. Gillingham, *The English in the Twelfth Century*, pp. 19–39; V.I.J. Flint, 'The *Historia Regum Britanniae* of Geoffrey of Monmouth – Parody and Its Purpose. A Suggestion', *Speculum*, 54 (1979), pp. 447–68.

audience),[545] soon followed in the 1150s and 1160s by Old French versions of Geoffrey's own work on 'the British' by Wace (in verse) and by Benoît de Sainte-Maure.[546]

Even from a brief outline of demonstrative, judicial and deliberative rhetoric, it is clear that the principles which underpinned each category were, in many cases, very similar. Whilst it may be convenient to separate rhetoric into these three forms, therefore, there is still a considerable amount of common ground, most notably in a concern with moral character and the narrative of deeds and, more importantly, in the close connection which was understood to exist between them, that is, as a combination of *ethologia* with *narratio rei gestae*. Cicero, Quintilian and the author of the *Rhetorica ad Herennium* all make this observation. Deliberative rhetoric and judicial rhetoric both involve the praise or castigation of individuals, and the narrative of their deeds follows similar principles in each case.[547] Both deliberative rhetoric and judicial rhetoric, moreover, are concerned with evaluating an action (*quale sit*) in terms of whether it is morally worthy or advantageous.[548] In this respect, they share the same criteria as demonstrative rhetoric. Indeed, as such, all three types of rhetoric can concern themselves with what is morally worthy, what is advantageous and what is just.[549] Where differences are acknowledged, they are sometimes simply a matter of emphasis. Deliberative rhetoric, for example, should, in Quintilian's view, be plain and serious and it ought to be ornamented more by its reflections (*sententiae*) than

---

545 Geffrei Gaimar, *Estoire des Engleis*, ed. and trans. I. Short, *History of the English* (Oxford, 2009).
546 Wace, *Roman de Brut*, ed. and trans. J. Weiss, *Wace's Roman de Brut, A History of the British* (2nd edn, Exeter, 2002); cf. Wace, *Roman de Rou*, trans. G.S. Burgess (Woodbridge, 2004); M. Bennett, 'Poetry as History? The *Roman de Rou* of Wace as a Source for the Norman Conquest', *Anglo-Norman Studies*, 5 (1992), pp. 21–39, and, more generally, D.B. Tyson, 'Patronage of French Vernacular History Writers in the Twelfth and Thirteenth Centuries', *Romania*, 100 (1979), pp. 180–222. For the English adaptation of Wace, see Layamon, *Brut*, trans. R. Allen (London, 1992).
547 *Rhetorica ad Herennium*, III.4.7, p. 169, III.8.15, pp. 183–5.
548 See pages 180–1, 230–7.
549 Quintilian, *Institutio Oratoria*, III.4.14–16, pp. 395–7.

by its words.[550] Quintilian allows more 'colour' in demonstrative rhetoric than in either deliberative or judicial rhetoric because he regards demonstrative rhetoric to be geared solely to the pleasure and entertainment of an audience – its proper function lies in display (*ostentatio*), that is, in giving amplification and ornamentation to its subject-matter.[551] Appeals to the emotions, meanwhile, were considered to be particularly necessary in deliberative rhetoric. Otherwise, most rhetorical precepts are, as Cicero had argued, common to speeches both of praise and of persuasion.[552]

An examination of what classical manuals had to say about the three types of rhetoric – demonstrative, judicial or forensic and deliberative, each with distinctive goals and principles but also with a large amount of common ground between them – suggests at least some of the ways in which an education in classical rhetoric presupposed certain ways of speaking and writing about deeds done in the past and, as a result, could profoundly affect the writing of history in the Middle Ages. The result was a historiography which is morally, judicially and politically engaged. In its most basic form, this influence entailed the use of epideictic or demonstrative rhetoric – speaking or writing to praise or blame individuals, as a means of preserving their memory for posterity but also as a means of putting forward *exempla* of virtue and vice to be imitated or avoided by one's audience. Rather more complex was forensic or judicial rhetoric – speaking or writing in order to defend or accuse individuals on a charge of having done something in the past, narrating their deeds as a means of restoring or castigating their reputation (*fama*), and using the testimony of human witnesses and documentation in order to do so. Third, and last, there was deliberative rhetoric – speaking or writing for or against a particular course of political action, appealing to precedents in the past as a means of establishing the relationship between *honestum* and *utile*, between what is morally worthy and what is advantageous in the present and in the future. Individuals could therefore be praised and blamed for commemoration by posterity

---

550 Quintilian, *Institutio Oratoria*, III.8.65, p. 511, quoting Cicero, *Partitiones Oratoriae*, trans. H. Rackham (Loeb, 1942), XXVII.97, p. 383.
551 *Institutio Oratoria*, III.7.1–6, pp. 465–7, VIII.3.11–14, pp. 217–19, XI.1.48, p. 183; cf. page 172.
552 Cicero, *De Oratore*, II.81.333, p. 451.

but also so that they could be imitated or avoided by one's audience; individuals could be accused or defended by relating the quality of their character to the nature of their deeds; specific courses of political action could be put forward by citing precedents in the past; groups and communities could be legitimated, even constructed, by narratives of their ancestors and origins. When viewed from the perspective of classical rhetoric, in short, the range of historical writing which constitutes medieval 'historiography' reveals some very complex and sophisticated texts. The more problematic and contentious their subject-matter, the more subtle their message and, as a result, the more closely they need to be read.

⚜ 3 ⚜

INVENTION AND NARRATIVE

The categorisation of classical rhetoric into its demonstrative, judicial and deliberative forms reveals significant differences in emphasis, but also significant similarities in approach, in the way in which the relationship between an individual's character (*mores*) and deeds (*res gestae*) could, and should, be described by a speaker or writer. The principles which these three categories of rhetoric shared as common ground, however, exerted an impact on medieval historiography that went well beyond engineering the specific didactic, legal or political goals of particular works of history. This influence can be gauged by means of the two standard schemes according to which the contents and the form of all three types of rhetorical speech or text were traditionally classified. In the first instance, the contents of a speech or text were divided according to five aspects through which the presentation of its subject-matter should normally be considered: *inventio* (the discovery and construction of true or verisimilar arguments, that is, arguments which would make what is being said or written convincing or probable); *dispositio* (the arrangement of these arguments into an order); *elocutio* (the choice of language and vocabulary appropriate to these arguments); *memoria* (the memorisation of the actual speech or text); and *pronuntiatio* (the delivery or performance of the speech or text). In the second instance, the formal structure of a speech or text which was constructed on the basis of these five aspects of presentation was conventionally divided into six parts: introduction (*exordium*); narrative (*narratio*); division (*divisio* or *partitio*); proof (*confirmatio*); refutation (*confutatio* or *refutatio*); and conclusion (*conclusio* or *peroratio*). Within these two classificatory schemes, the methodological principles which informed a classical rhetorical analysis of, respectively, *inventio* and *narratio* came to have a central bearing on the medieval understanding of argumentation and narrative and, as such, on the concept and practice of writing history in the Middle Ages.

Invention

According to Cicero and the *Rhetorica ad Herennium*, the discovery or 'invention' of arguments is the most important of the five aspects of rhetoric because, in every type of case, it is the most influential. It was also regarded as the most difficult.[1] This was the subject which accordingly occupied the five central books (III–VII) of Quintilian's *Institutio Oratoria*; it was also the subject of, not one, but two works by Cicero – the first of these was entitled *De Inventione*, whilst the second was called *Topica*, after the Greek term for the place (*topos*) or location (in Latin, *locus*) from which an argument is drawn.[2] Cicero's *Topica* was, in turn, the subject of an influential commentary by Boethius and the basis for a work of Boethius' own, *De Topicis Differentiis*.[3] Since book IV of *De Topicis Differentiis* provided a summary analysis of the rhetorical topics contained in *De Inventione*, Boethius' account was often copied separately alongside both *De Inventione* and the *Rhetorica ad Herennium* and it effectively became the standard teaching text for the subject in the Middle Ages.[4] Given that rhetorical invention was defined by Cicero as the discovery of true or plausible arguments in order to make a case convincing or probable,[5] an understanding of *inventio* depends,

---

1 Cicero, *De Inventione*, trans. H.M. Hubbell (Loeb, 1949), I.7.9, p. 21; *Rhetorica ad Herennium*, trans. H. Caplan (Loeb, 1954), II.1.1, p. 59, III.8.15, p. 185.
2 Cicero, *Topica*, trans. H.M. Hubbell (Loeb, 1949); cf. ed. and trans. T. Reinhardt, *Cicero's Topica* (Oxford, 2006).
3 Boethius, *In Ciceronis Topica*, trans. E. Stump (Ithaca, 1988); Boethius, *De Topicis Differentiis*, trans. E. Stump (Ithaca, 1978); cf. N.J. Green-Pedersen, *The Tradition of the Topics in the Middle Ages: The Commentaries on Aristotle's and Boethius' Topics* (Munich, 1984).
4 J.J. Murphy, *Medieval Eloquence: Studies in the Theory and Practice of Medieval Rhetoric* (Berkeley, 1978), ch. 4.
5 Cicero, *De Inventione*, I.7.9, p. 19; *Rhetorica ad Herennium*, I.2.3, p. 7; cf. Martianus Capella, *The Marriage of Philology and Mercury*, trans. W.H. Stahl, R. Johnson and E.L. Burge (New York, 1977), V, p. 162: 'the prudent and searching

first and foremost, on an understanding of the precise nature of its connection with argumentation (*argumentatio*).[6] As a result, any discussion of invention has to start, first, with what qualifies something to be categorised under the heading of an 'argument' and, second, with the principles which govern the deployment of that *argumentum*. 'Invention', in other words, centres on an analysis of what makes particular arguments suitable or appropriate (*aptum*) for a particular case, and on how these arguments should then be ordered relative to one another in the arrangement or *dispositio* of the speech or text which that case produces.

An argument is defined by Cicero as a principle or reason which establishes faith (*fides*) in something that is otherwise in doubt; it is therefore a means of providing credence or believability.[7] An argument cannot produce belief in something which is in doubt, however, unless it is expressed in speech and unless it is arranged within an interweaving (*contextio*) of propositions that signify whether something is true or false. It is this expression and arrangement of arguments by means of interwoven propositions which is termed *argumentatio*.[8] Rhetorical argumentation consists of five elements (proposition, reason, confirmation of the reason, development or ornamentation and a summing-up),[9] whilst judgment of its validity is the role of dialectic. The arguments themselves can be drawn from a number of different sources, from a number of different 'topics', that is, from different places (*topoi*) or locations (*loci*). Cicero accordingly devotes much of his effort in the *Topica* to going through a long list of these 'foundations' or 'sources' for arguments (*sedes argumenti*)[10] and, in the process, two basic distinctions emerge: on the one hand, between

---

collection of issues and arguments' (*quaestionum argumentorumque sagax investigatrixque comprehensio*).

6 *De Inventione*, I.30.50, p. 91.

7 Cicero, *Topica*, I.8, p. 387; Boethius, *In Ciceronis Topica*, I, p. 29; Boethius, *De Topicis Differentiis*, I, pp. 30, 39, III, p. 63; Martianus Capella, *Marriage of Philology and Mercury*, V, p. 183; cf. Conrad of Hirsau, *Dialogue on the Authors*, trans. A.J. Minnis and A.B. Scott, in A.J. Minnis and A.B. Scott (eds), *Medieval Literary Theory and Criticism c.1100–c.1375* (Oxford, 1988), p. 44. See also page 338, note 297.

8 Boethius, *In Ciceronis Topica*, I, p. 35; cf. Boethius, *De Topicis Differentiis*, I, p. 30.

9 *Rhetorica ad Herennium*, II.18.28, p. 107.

10 Cf. Boethius, *De Topicis Differentiis*, II, p. 46, III, p. 63.

'topics' and 'common topics' (or 'commonplaces', *loci communes*) and, on the other, between intrinsic and extrinsic arguments.

According to Cicero, the distinction between a topic and a common topic or 'commonplace' is best understood as a distinction between a particular argument which is specific to one subject, act or event, and a generic argument which is applicable to many subjects, acts or events. Topics and common topics, particular arguments and generic arguments, are subject to the same precepts but they differ in the way in which they are handled. Topics or arguments are thus treated with greater restraint, plainness and precision; their goal is simply to ensure that a particular argument will appear to be true. Common topics or commonplaces, on the other hand, are treated with greater seriousness and more ornamentation, with both the language and the sense operating at a higher level; their goal is also for the argument to appear to be true but, in addition, it is to make that argument more all-embracing in its scope, to give it what was termed 'fullness' or *amplitudo*. In this sense, whether a subject is open to doubt or whether it is something certain, the goal towards which 'commonplaces' are directed is defined as amplification (*amplificatio*).[11] As a result, common topics or common arguments can be invested with all those ornaments of style which make something attractive as well as serious and weighty. This is the first point that needs to be underlined – not all arguments receive the same rhetorical treatment: a generic or typical argument involves greater scope for elaboration than one which is specific or unique to a particular case.

The second basic distinction, between arguments which are intrinsic to a case and arguments which are extrinsic, constitutes the core of judicial testimony and, as such, was the subject of a lengthy and, at times, complex analysis. Intrinsic arguments concern three basic questions: did something happen (*an sit*), what was it that happened (*quid sit*), and what was the nature of what happened (*quale sit*, that is, was it good or bad, morally worthy or morally reprehensible, advantageous or disadvantageous)? Each of these fundamental questions presupposes a particular approach to determining where, when, why and how something might have happened and the language with which it should therefore be

---

11 Cicero, *De Inventione*, II.16.51, p. 213, II.22.68, p. 233.

defined and evaluated.[12] Although all three questions are required in judicial rhetoric, one or more of them, according to Quintilian, is also asked of everything which is handled by demonstrative and deliberative rhetoric too.[13] Cicero's *Topica* accordingly gives a long list of possible sources for these intrinsic arguments: they can be drawn, for example, from the etymological definition of the word by which a particular subject or event is denoted;[14] from the genus or species to which the subject belongs; from what makes it similar and/or different; from the adjuncts or circumstances which are in some way connected with it (that is, from what preceded it and from what followed it – in other words, from its causes and effects); and, finally, from a comparison with other things which are of greater, lesser or equal importance.[15] Establishing what it was that happened (*quid sit*) may therefore turn on the precise definition of words, but such definitions can be established either by examining the etymology of a particular word or through comparing the subject or event with something similar. This similarity can be gathered from several things - in which case it constitutes an inductive argument (*inductio*) - or simply from one thing which is likened to something else as its equal (*collatio*).[16]

Viewed from the perspective of the writing of history, the importance of the rhetorical guidelines for discovering intrinsic arguments lay, in the first instance, in the clarity with which they defined the role of individual *exempla* in providing a comparative or inductive approach to a narrative of events. According to Cicero, comparison with something similar can be figurative, that is, it can proceed through the use of metaphor (*per translationem verbi ex similitudine*), or it can involve the recollection of similar examples (*commemoratio exemplorum*). The latter will involve the citation of deeds done in the past, namely the commemoration of historical events, but it can also include examples which are made

---

12 See pages 179–80.
13 Quintilian, *Institutio Oratoria*, trans. H.E. Butler (Loeb, 1920–22), III.6.81, p. 451; see also pages 262–3.
14 For the biblical exegetical tradition, see Eusebius (translated and revised by Jerome), *Onomasticon*, ed. and trans. R.S. Notley and Z. Safrai (Leiden, 2005).
15 Cicero, *Topica*, II.8–III.11, pp. 387–91; cf. Quintilian, *Institutio Oratoria*, V.10.54–94, pp. 229–53.
16 *Topica*, IV.26, p. 399, VII.32, p. 405, X.41–45, pp. 413–15; cf. Boethius, *In Ciceronis Topica*, IV, pp. 114–16 (see also page 384, note 122).

up (*ficta exempla*). Indeed, according to Cicero, it is permissible in this context for orators, philosophers and (to a lesser extent) lawyers to make mute objects speak, to raise the dead to life, to relate something which could not possibly happen and many other 'surprising things' (*mirabilia*), all for the sake of strengthening or weakening a particular proposition.[17] According to Quintilian, it is the act of comparison, as much as definition, which lies at the heart of rhetorical argumentation because of the particular operation of analogy. The demonstrative role of analogy, he explains, lies in the way in which something that is subject to doubt can be referred, or compared, to something similar about which there is no question – it provides proof of what is not certain by means of what is.[18] Induction, meanwhile, is a form of argumentation, according to Boethius, by means of which an argument progresses from particular to universal propositions; although it does not possess the same degree of certainty as a syllogism, and may sometimes lack truth, it is generally the most credible or probable kind of argument. The *exemplum*, finally, is simply an incomplete form of induction, the distinction being that an example produces a conclusion from no more than one, singular item or event.[19]

In the second instance, rhetorical principles of argumentation provided medieval authors with a clear set of guidelines for approaching the question of causation. According to Cicero, an intrinsic argument which is drawn from adjuncts or circumstances takes the form of inquiring into what happened before an event, what happened at the same time, and what happened afterwards.[20] This type of argumentation involves a discussion both of efficient causes and of what they have brought about or effected. This is the sort of exposition, Quintilian explains, which is deployed most frequently by historians when they analyse the

---

17 *Topica*, IV.26, p. 399, VII.32, p. 405, X.41–5, pp. 413–15.
18 Quintilian, *Institutio Oratoria*, I.6.4, p. 113.
19 Boethius, *De Topicis Differentiis*, II, pp. 43–6. For the origins of these definitions, see Aristotle, *Topica* trans. W.A. Pickard-Cambridge (Princeton 1984), I.12 105a13–19, p. 175; *Prior Analytics*, trans. A.J. Jenkinson (Princeton 1984), II.23–4 68b15–29, 68b38–69a19, pp. 109–10; *Posterior Analytics*, trans. J. Barnes (Princeton 1984), I.1 71a5–11, p. 114, I.18 81a38–b9, p. 132.
20 Cicero, *Topica*, XI.50–XII–51, p. 419 (see page 269, note 15).

origins of war, sedition or pestilence.[21] For Cicero, the rhetorical categorisation of causation necessarily influenced the classification of effects, because things that happen are either voluntary or involuntary – either they are done deliberately (throwing a weapon) or unintentionally, that is, through necessity or fortune (hitting someone with this weapon when there was neither a desire nor an intention to strike them). Knowledge of causes will therefore produce a knowledge of results, and vice versa – just as the cause shows what has been effected, so the effect will demonstrate the nature of the cause. This principle extends to results in the future – a subject, Cicero observes, on which orators and poets have much to say.[22] Whilst the discussion of efficient causes covers those causes which necessarily produce particular effects through their own force, it also extends to those which cannot in themselves produce an effect but without which this effect cannot be produced – in other words, causes such as place, time, material and means. Cicero points out that these secondary causes – things which assist an effect, but which do not necessarily produce that effect – are what the Stoics call 'fate' (*fatum*). Some of these causes produce their effect without assistance from elsewhere, that is, without the desire or will or opinion of any individual human being; others proceed from desire, will, disposition, nature, artifice or accident. Some causes are clear, some lie hidden: those which are clear are those which pertain to human desire and judgment; those which are hidden are those which are subject to what is called 'fortune'. For Cicero, this final term merely serves as shorthand for unknown causes: 'since nothing happens without a cause, fortune is simply what is effected by an obscure and hidden cause' (*cum enim nihil sine causa fiat, hoc ipsum est fortuna qui eventus obscura causa et latenter efficitur*).[23]

---

21 Quintilian, *Institutio Oratoria*, IV.2.2, p. 51.
22 Cicero, *Topica*, XIV.58–XVIII.67, pp. 425–33; cf. Boethius, *In Ciceronis Topica*, V, pp. 154–9.
23 *Topica*, XV.58–XVII.63, pp. 425–31; cf. Valerius Maximus, *Facta et Dicta Memorabilia*, trans. D.R. Shackleton Bailey (Loeb, 2000), I.7, p. 95, where fate is treated simply as a synonym for necessity; cf. Bernardus Silvestris, *Commentary on the First Six Books of Virgil's Aeneid*, trans. E.G. Schreiber and T.E. Maresca (Lincoln, 1979), VI, p. 43 ('fate is the temporal outcome of things foreseen.... Therefore "to ask the fates" is to inquire philosophically about the origins of generation,

When Boethius came to comment on Cicero's discussion of intrinsic arguments about causation, he brought to his analysis of efficient causes a well-defined vocabulary which he had developed in the course of distinguishing between the terms 'fortune', 'chance', 'providence' and 'fate'. The exactness which he sought to give this terminology, and the wider debate on which he drew in order to do so, were to have a profound impact on subsequent readers of his work and, as a result, on how the intrinsic argumentation of cause and effect was understood. Like Augustine, Boethius was responding to the extensive discussion of a divine ordering of the world which had been produced by Stoic and Neoplatonic writers. In the Stoic tradition, reflected in part by Cicero's *Topica*, an underlying cosmic order meant that humans should respond to the apparent vagaries of this world by adapting themselves to whatever external circumstances they were presented with – on this reckoning, the concept of 'fortune' was equivalent to those events which the order of the universe made necessary. Viewed from this perspective, in fact, there was, strictly speaking, no such thing as 'good' or 'bad' fortune, since prosperity and adversity each presented dangers of their own to the virtuous individual; what mattered was how the individual chose to accommodate their rational and emotional responses to these necessary changes in the material world. Fortune was thus not, in itself, an agent, even though it could be presented loosely and figuratively as a fickle and slippery goddess – such personification simply served as shorthand for when the efficient causes of a particular event or set of events were unclear or unknown. This was the definition recorded by Cicero and discussed at length by Boethius – fortune is what is effected by obscure and hidden causes.[24]

---

alteration and corruption in things'), VI, p. 81 ('*fata*: temporal events'), VI, p. 90, VI, p. 95, VI, p. 98.
24 See page 271. Cf. Augustine, *Retractationes*, trans. M.I. Bogan, *Retractions* (Washington, DC, 1968), I.1.2, pp. 6–7: 'I regret that ... I mentioned fortune so often, although I did not intend that any goddess be understood by this term, but a fortuitous outcome of events in good and evil circumstances, either in our bodies or extraneous to them. It is from this that we have those words which no religious scruple forbids us to use – perchance [*forte*], possibly [*forsan*], peradventure [*forsitan*], perhaps [*fortasse*], fortuitously [*fortuito*] – but all of these should be applied to divine providence. Furthermore, at the time I was not silent on this point for I said [*Contra Academicos*, trans. P. King (Indianapolis, 1995),

When Boethius came to discuss Cicero's use of the word 'fate', he glossed this term as 'a certain intricate interweaving and chain-like connection of antecedent causes and consequent events'.[25] Like Cicero, however, Boethius was concerned to retain a notion of the freedom of the human will against any idea of the necessity of *all* events, and he did so by distinguishing between different types of antecedent cause. When he came to Cicero's classification of the term 'fortune', therefore, as a word which should be used to denote causes that are hidden and as an index of epistemological ignorance, he thought it incomplete and put forward, in its place, an alternative formulation of his own, this time based on Aristotle. By substituting this much fuller definition, according to which 'fortune' describes the unintended consequences of other causes, Boethius brought it together with the definition of 'chance' (*casus*). For Boethius, both 'fortune' and 'chance' are terms which denote the unintended consequence of some other cause: 'we locate chance and events occasioned by fortune among those things which, although they occur fairly rarely, nonetheless do happen, but by accident, within the group of things that occur for the sake of something else.... Although fortune often undertakes its acts among things that are willed and directed to some end, nevertheless what pertains to fortune supervenes externally and does not come from the end that the mind in advance had constructed for itself'.[26] As the unintended consequence of a particular action, or as the result of a conjunction of separate

---

I.1.1, pp. 1–2] "and indeed perhaps what is commonly referred to as fortune is governed by a certain hidden order and in events we do not term anything chance unless its reason and cause are unknown".'

25 Boethius, *In Ciceronis Topica*, V, p. 155; cf. Plato, *Timaeus*, trans. R. Waterfield (Oxford, 2008), 41d–43e, pp. 31–3; Cicero, *De Fato*, trans. H. Rackham (Loeb, 1942); Seneca, *De Providentia*, trans. J.W. Basore (Loeb, 1928); and, more generally, M.L. Colish, *The Stoic Tradition from Antiquity to the Early Middle Ages* (2nd edn, Leiden, 1990), vol. I, pp. 109–26, vol. II, pp. 286–9.

26 Boethius, *In Ciceronis Topica*, V, pp. 161–3. For the distinction between *fortuna* and *casus*, see Calcidius, *Commentary on Plato's Timaeus*, ed. J.H. Waszink, *Plato Latinus* (Leiden, 1972), CLIX, vol. IV, p. 193: 'fortune can be correctly defined as follows: it is the simultaneous concurrence of two causes ... from which something unexpected and surprising results...; chance is a simultaneous concurrence of accidents that do not possess the principle of causality' (*quare sic etiam fortuna recte definiri potest: fortuna est concursus simul cadentium causarum duarum..., ex quo concursu provenit aliquid praeter spem cum admiratione...; casus [est] concursus simul atque una accidentium sine ratione causarum*). Cf. K.M. Fredborg, 'Abelard on Rhetoric', in

causes whose combined consequences may have been unforeseen by the individuals who performed the original actions, 'chance' was therefore defined in terms of a recognisable chain of causes, not as a purely random force. Boethius reiterates the point in his *Consolation of Philosophy*, citing two possible interpretations of the term *casus*. 'If someone were to define chance as an event produced by random motion', he writes, 'and not by any chain of causes, then I assert that chance is nothing at all, and I judge that, apart from signifying the subject-event it refers to, it is a sound entirely empty of meaning'.[27] Instead, Boethius repeats the definition he had found in book II of Aristotle's *Physics*: 'whenever something is done for the sake of some given end, and another thing occurs, for some reason or other, different from what was intended, it is called chance.... Now this is indeed believed to have happened by chance but it does not come from nothing; for it has its proper causes, and their unforeseen and unexpected coming together appears to have produced a chance event'.[28]

Belief in an underlying principle of cosmic rationality and order placed Boethius' definitions of fate, fortune and chance within a much broader understanding of the overarching operation of divine providence. In this respect, too, the influence of his discussion on the subsequent analysis of causation in rhetorical argumentation was profound. According to Boethius, 'we may ... define chance as the unexpected event of concurring causes among things done for some purpose; now causes are made to concur and flow together by that order which, proceeding with inevitable connection and coming down from its source in providence [*providentia*], disposes all things in their proper places and times'.[29] In Neoplatonic writings, the ideas of such cosmic order had been refined through the numerological and geometrical harmonies of Plato's *Timaeus* but also through the distinction which was drawn, on this basis, between 'providence' and 'fate'. Providence, in this account, was a term which applied to God and

---

C.J. Mews, C.J. Nederman and R.M. Thomson (eds), *Rhetoric and Renewal in the Latin West 1100–1540* (Turnhout, 2003), p. 65.
27 Boethius, *Consolation of Philosophy*, trans. S.J. Tester (Loeb, 1973), V.1, p. 387.
28 *Consolation of Philosophy*, V.1, pp. 387–9; cf. Aristotle, *Physics*, trans. R. Waterfield (Oxford, 1996), II.4–6, 195b31–198a13, pp. 42–8.
29 *Consolation of Philosophy*, V.1, p. 389.

to the governance and motion of the higher spheres, whereas fate was a term which applied to the sublunary sphere and the governance of the world. Whilst Augustine had explicitly distanced his own account of providence from such a division, and from the implications of such two-tier terminology,[30] Boethius retained and justified its use. According to his *Consolation of Philosophy*, the processes of generation, movement and change which characterise the world may seem random, confused and disordered, but they are all features which are caused and ordered by God. The multiple manner in which they take place is called 'providence' when it is located in the divine mind, but 'fate' when it is related to what is actually being moved and ordered. Providence, on this reckoning, should be understood as 'the divine reason itself ... which disposes all things which exist', whereas fate is 'the disposition inherent in movable things through which providence binds all things together, each in its own proper ordering'. Providence is thus all-inclusive and united in the simplicity of the divine mind, whereas fate is distributed across individuals, space and time. God orders and arranges events in a single and unchanging way, whereas fate effects them in their multiple ways across space and time. Fate is thus 'the movable interweaving and temporal ordering [*mobilis nexus atque ordo temporalis*] of those things which the simplicity of divine providence disposes to be done', binding the acts and fortunes of humans in 'an indissoluble chain of causes' (*indissolubilis causarum connexio*).[31] For Boethius, therefore, 'God disposes all things towards the good through the course of the necessity of fate' (*per fatalis seriem necessitatem*).[32] This is how the world is governed – not by chance events (*a fortuitis casibus*), but by divine reason.[33]

As a central part of the process of discovering intrinsic arguments, Boethius' explanatory lexicon for identifying and understanding

---

30 Augustine, *De Civitate Dei*, trans. H. Bettenson (2nd edn, Harmondsworth, 1984), V.1, pp. 179–80, V.8–11, pp. 188–96.
31 Boethius, *Consolation of Philosophy*, IV.6, pp. 359–63; cf. Calcidius, *Commentary on Plato's Timaeus*, CXLXI, p. 184: 'the order of God is ... reason, in my opinion, containing a perpetual ordinance which is called fate, and that has its origin in providence' (*iussum dei ... ratio est, opinor, continens ordinationem perpetuam quae fatum vocatur, idque trahit originem ex providentia*).
32 *Consolation of Philosophy*, IV.6, p. 371.
33 *Consolation of Philosophy*, I.6, p. 171, III.12, p. 299, IV.5, pp. 353–5.

the causes of events had far-reaching consequences for the writing of history. It was not just the responsibility of philosophy, after all, to 'unfurl the causes of hidden things and to unfold explanations veiled in mist'.[34] This task applied to rhetoric and to historiography as well. In reconciling divine foreknowledge with human free will, for example, Boethius, like Augustine, appealed to the idea that God is beyond time (that is, to the principle that God is outside of the temporal sequence of past, present and future) in order to explain how God's knowledge of what would happen (from a human perspective) 'in the future' did not necessarily serve to cause these events and thereby constrain the ability of human beings to will them and to act freely in time.[35] At a more practical level, this account of the relationship between providence and time set up an important theoretical connection between the conceptualisation of prudence and prophecy. According to Cicero, prudence was defined as a virtue which covered the past, the present and the future through its constituent elements of memory, understanding and foresight: '*memoria* is the faculty through which the mind recalls what has happened, *intelligentia* is the faculty through which it ascertains what is, *providentia* is the faculty through which something that will occur is seen before it has been done'.[36] Macrobius appealed to the same conjunction in order to explain the two faces of Janus ('a reference, no doubt, to the foresight and shrewdness of the king as one who knew not only the past but could also foresee the future') and the three-headed creature of Sarapis ('the lion's head is a symbol of time present, which, midway between the past and the future, has the strength and ardour of immediate action; time past is represented by the head of the wolf, because the memory of things that are over and done is swiftly borne away; so too the likeness of a fawning dog indicates the issue of time to come, the object of our hopes which are uncertain

---

34 *Consolation of Philosophy*, IV.6, p. 357. For the definition of Nature as a 'sequence of causes' (*causarum series natura vocatur*), see John of Salisbury, *Entheticus de Dogmate Philosophorum*, ed. and trans. J. van Laarhoven (Leiden, 1987), line 607, p. 144. Cf. Plato, *Timaeus*, 28a5 p.16.
35 *Consolation of Philosophy*, V.2–6, pp. 391–435; cf. Augustine, *De Civitate Dei*, V.9–11, pp. 190–6.
36 Cicero, *De Inventione*, II.53.160, p. 327; cf. Vincent of Beauvais, *Speculum Historiale* (Douai, 1624; reprinted Graz, 1964–65), VI.21, p. 181. For Augustine's discussion, see page 377.

but flatter us').[37] Human 'providence' was thus a combination of prudential memory and foresight, which could provide the basis for deliberative counsel and at least a degree of security against mutability and misfortune.[38] According to Macrobius, however, this combination culminated, not so much in the counsellor, as in the prophet (*vates*), since it was the role of prophets to use their prudence to explain the meaning of events in the future but also in the present and in the past – what will happen, but also what is happening and what has already been done. On this reckoning, an individual's understanding of the meaning of past and present events remained just as important a 'prophetic' function as any revelation of the future. Macrobius cited Vergil and Homer to demonstrate that the role of the prophet was, in fact, analogous to that of the doctor: 'to have knowledge of all things that are, or that have been, or that thereafter at their coming shall follow'; 'the things that are, and shall be, and that have been beforehand'.[39]

By treating memory and 'foresight' (*providentia*) as temporal aspects of prudence, Cicero and Macrobius opened the way for medieval authors to draw a close connection between the operation of prophecy amongst humans and their understanding of the 'providence' of God. According to the sixth-century writer Junilius Africanus, prophecy is the act of making hidden things clear through divine inspiration, but again this covered the past and present as well as the future.[40] This was a fairly typical definition, which was then glossed and refined throughout the Middle Ages: prophecy is 'the divine breath which proclaims with unshakeable truth the outcome of events through the deeds or words

---

37 Macrobius, *Saturnalia*, trans. P.V. Davies (New York, 1969), I.7.20, p. 58, I.9.4, p. 66, I.13.3, p. 91, I.20.13–15, p. 139. For Macrobius in the Middle Ages, see L.D. Reynolds (ed.), *Texts and Transmission: A Survey of the Latin Classics* (Oxford, 1983), pp. 223–35; D. Kelly, *The Conspiracy of Allusion: Disruption, Rewriting and Authorship from Macrobius to Medieval Romance* (Leiden, 1999), pp. 13–35.
38 For example, *Moralium Dogma Philosophorum*, ed. J. Holmberg, *Das Moralium Dogma Philosophorum des Guillaume de Conches, lateinisch, altfranzösisch und mittelniederfränkisch* (Uppsala, 1929), p. 9.
39 Macrobius, *Saturnalia*, I.20.5, p. 138, quoting Vergil, *Georgics*, trans. H.R. Fairclough, rev. G.P. Goold (Loeb, 2000), IV.392–3, p. 223, and Homer, *Iliad*, trans. M. Hammond (Harmondsworth, 1987), I.70, p. 5.
40 Junilius Africanus, *De Partibus Divinae Legis* (*PL* 68, cols 15–42), I.4, col. 17.

of certain persons'; it 'says or performs something concerning past, present or future times'; and it serves the threefold purpose of 'edification, exhortation and consolation' (cf. 1 Corinthians 14:3).[41] Defined in these terms, the role of the prophet became, not unnaturally, a prominent feature of saints' lives – this is the tradition which is reflected, for example, by Paschasius Radbertus when he applied it directly to the prudence and foresight of Adalard: 'he discerned at one and the same time things past, present and future, so that of each one he foresaw what should be done or followed by God's counsel'.[42] However, given that the definition of prophecy comprised, not only the visions, deeds and sayings of certain inspired individuals, but also what actually happened (*eventus rerum*), it was an equally natural step to extend the application of this term to the interpretation of the past which was put forward in the writing of history. If prophecy was defined, not just as explanation of the present and prediction of the future, but also as clarification of the significance of what had happened in the past, then the task of the historian, in explaining what had happened in the past and why, assumed considerable importance. If the apostle Paul had written of events in the Old Testament that 'these things happened as a sign [*in figura*] ... and were written down to warn us' (1 Corinthians 10:11), and Augustine had argued that events in the past intimate things that will happen in the future,[43] then it was only consistent to extend the same sort of language to the prophetic interpretation of history

---

41 Cassiodorus, *Explanation of the Psalms*, trans. P.G. Walsh (New York, 1990–91), pref.1, pp. 27–8; Haimo of Auxerre, *Explanatio in Psalmos* (*PL* 116, cols 193–696), I, col. 195; Peter Lombard, *Commentarium in Psalmos* (*PL* 191, cols 55–1296), pref., cols. 58–9; cf. Gregory the Great, *Homiliae in Hiezechihelem Prophetam*, ed. M. Adriaen (*CCSL* 142, Turnhout, 1971), I.1, p. 5; Aquinas, *Summa Theologiae*, ed. and trans. T. Gilby, *et al.* (Blackfriars edn, London, 1964–80), IIaIIae 171.1, pp. 5–9, 171.3, pp. 13–17.
42 Paschasius Radbertus, *Vita Adalhardi*, trans. A. Cabaniss, *Charlemagne's Cousins: Contemporary Lives of Adalard and Wala* (Syracuse, 1967), XVI, p. 36; cf. Eadmer, *Life of Anselm*, ed. and trans. R.W. Southern (Oxford, 1972), I.7, p. 12; Eadmer, *Historia Novorum in Anglia*, trans. G. Bosanquet (London, 1964), I.5, p. 5.
43 Augustine, *Enarrationes in Psalmos*, trans. M. Boulding (New York, 2000–04), CXIII, pp. 304–11; cf. Hilary of Poitiers, *Tractatus super Psalmos*, ed. J. Doignon (*CCSL* 61, Turnhout, 1997), LXII.4, p. 207: 'prophetic knowledge is the remembrance of what was done for the sake of what should be done' (*prophetiae scientia est pro gerendis gesta memorare*); Suger, *De Rebus in Sua Administratione Gestis* [*De Administratione*], ed. and trans. E. Panofsky (2nd edn, Princeton, 1979), XXIX,

outside of Scripture too. Richard of Devizes, for example, opens his *Chronicle* by explicitly juxtaposing 'prophecy' with made-up fable (*prophetare potius ... quam fabulari*),[44] whilst Gerald of Wales goes so far as to describe his account of the conquest of Ireland as a 'prophetic history' (*vaticinalis historia*). Gerald chose his adjective carefully. Of the series of prophetic utterances by 'Merlin' which he cites in this work, only one actually anticipates events in the future. The remainder serve as part of a much broader didactic message which Gerald was explicitly taking from the Bible. His own historiographical judgment was thus an extension of an admonitory lesson enshrined in Scripture: 'if you look through the entire Old Testament and [then] consider the history of more recent times, and particularly the *exempla* in that part of the world, you will always find that victory has been won, not by superior numbers of men or military resources, but by superiority in virtue and by grace of God rather than human might'.[45]

The difficulty of drawing too close a connection between rhetorical argumentation, historical causation, prophecy and providence (both human and divine) was, of course, the inscrutability of divine judgment to sinful human understanding. This fundamental reservation would always impose substantial restrictions on what medieval authors thought that the writing of history may, or may not, be able to reveal. Augustine had been careful to draw the line, after all, between *historia* and *haruspices* – history narrates

---

p. 53: 'the record of things past is a demonstration of things to come' (*praeteritorum enim recordatio futurorum est exhibitio*).
44 Richard of Devizes, *Chronicle*, ed. and trans. J.T. Appleby (London, 1963), p. 2.
45 Gerald of Wales, *Expugnatio Hibernica*, ed. and trans. A.B. Scott and F.X. Martin (Dublin, 1978), II.29, p. 211, II.39, p. 255; cf. Gerald of Wales, *Itinerarium Cambriae*, I.11, p. 145, and his *Descriptio Cambriae*, I.16, p. 250, both trans. L.Thorpe (Harmondsworth, 1978); R. Bartlett, 'Political Prophecy in Gerald of Wales', in M. Aurell (ed.), *Culture Politique des Plantagenêt (1154–1224)* (Poitiers, 2003), pp. 303–11. For the chronology of Gerald's works, see R. Bartlett, *Gerald of Wales, 1146–1223* (Oxford, 1982), pp. 213–21. For interest in the 'prophecies' of Merlin, as popularised by Geoffrey of Monmouth, *Historia Regum Britanniae*, ed. M.D. Reeve, trans. N. Wright (Woodbridge, 2007), VII, pp. 143–59, see, for example, Suger, *Gesta Hludowici*, trans. R.C. Cusimano and J. Moorhead (Washington, DC, 1992), XVI, p. 69; Orderic Vitalis, *Historia Ecclesiastica*, ed. and trans. M. Chibnall (Oxford, 1980), XII.47, pp. 381–9; Ralph de Diceto, *Imagines Historiarum*, ed. W. Stubbs (London, 1876), vol. I p. 384, vol. II pp. 64, 67; Roger of Howden, *Chronica*, ed. W. Stubbs (London, 1868–71), s.a 1173, vol. II, p. 47.

what has been done (*facta narrare*) in a faithful and useful way (*fideliter atque utiliter*), whereas books of soothsaying and the like set out to teach things that must be done (*facienda docere*) with the audacity of a counsellor and not the trustworthiness of a witness (*monitoris audacia non indicis fide*).[46] Medieval historians, including Gerald of Wales, therefore freely and repeatedly acknowledge the secrecy and subtlety of God's judgment ('it is never unjust but it is sometimes difficult to understand').[47] However, they also combine such admissions with instances where the cause and effect of divine judgment could, in their opinion, be clearly identified, thereby distinguishing between the hidden and the manifest judgments of God.[48] Such a prophetic and providential interpretation of historical events may, of course, itself require time in order to become clear. Orderic Vitalis, for one, points out that he saw his task to be one of recording events whose significance might become apparent only later on, or to those people who were blessed with greater discernment than his own.[49] For those historians who believed that the principle of number lay at the heart of the Neoplatonic order of the universe, an annalistic sequencing of events left open the same possibility, that is, when the entire course of world events was considered as an integral whole.[50] In both cases, the historian's responsibility in identifying divine causality in the events of the past, and in particular the action of God's active rather than permissive providence, was not to be taken lightly.

---

46 Augustine, *De Doctrina Christiana*, ed. and trans. R.P.H. Green (Oxford, 1995), II.28.109, p. 107; see also page 94.
47 Gerald of Wales, *Itinerarium Cambriae*, I.1, p. 74, II.13, pp. 204–5, II.14, p. 207; Gerald of Wales, *De Eruditione Principum*, trans. J. Stevenson (London, 1858; reprinted Felinfach, 1991), III.3 pp. 58–9; Gerald of Wales, *Expugnatio Hibernica*, II.28, p. 207; cf. Paschasius Radbertus, *Vita Adalhardi*, XXXV, p. 48; Liutprand of Cremona, *Antapodosis*, trans. F.A. Wright (London, 1930), I.36, p. 56, II.73, p. 104, IV.25–26, p. 161; Thietmar of Merseburg, *Chronicon*, trans. D.A. Warner (Manchester, 2001), I.8 p. 73, III.14, p. 139; Guibert of Nogent, *Monodiae*, trans. J.F. Benton (Toronto, 1984), I.24, p. 111; Guibert of Nogent, *Gesta Dei per Francos*, trans. R. Levine (Woodbridge, 1997), VI, p. 113.
48 For example, Henry of Huntingdon, *Historia Anglorum*, ed. and trans. D. Greenway (Oxford, 1996), III.39, p. 195, IV.20, pp. 245–7, IV.25, p. 255; cf. *Life of the Emperor Henry IV*, trans. T.E. Mommsen and K.F. Morrison (New York, 1962; rev. edn, 2000), V, p. 113, XI, p. 128.
49 Orderic Vitalis, *Historia Ecclesiastica*, prol., pp. 131–3.
50 See pages 53–4.

At the most basic level, Boethius' account of the relationship between providence, fate and fortune meant that historiographical contemplation of the fluctuations of this world could always serve the immediate purpose of providing consolation from the travails of the present.[51] As an application of rhetorical argumentation, however, as intrinsic arguments which could be discovered and deployed by an orator, Boethius' account of how providence (or fate) and fortune (or chance) served complementary functions within an overarching framework of causation also provided historians with a set of explanatory terms for narrating the course of events. According to *De Topicis Differentiis*, the issue of whether human beings are ruled by providence is thus a typical example of a commonplace argument 'from the whole'.[52] Divine providence comprehended all things and, as such, there was an underlying rationality to events – sometimes this order was open to human perception, at other times it was not, but even in the most adverse or inexplicable of circumstances the operation of 'fortune' and 'chance' represented the action of cause and effect and, as such, served a purpose, even if it was hard for humans to fathom and even if it was therefore simply in order to teach individuals to concentrate on true goodness, both in this world and in the next.

Read in conjunction with his commentary on Cicero's *Topica*, Boethius' *Consolation of Philosophy* raised fundamental questions about the relationship between human agency, temporal happiness and God's governance of events – of what happened to human beings and why.[53] Changeable fortune and the mutability of the things of this world were, for Boethius, perfectly compatible with a notion of divine providence – this much was also clear from Augustine and Orosius.[54] 'Fate' and 'chance', Boethius argued, needed to be understood in the same light. This was not necessarily an exclusively Christian insight. Macrobius, for example, contrasted Homer's attribution of the guidance of the universe to destiny (*decretum*) with Vergil's ascription of omnipotence to fortune (*fortuna*) in order to comment that philosophers maintain

---

51 See pages 77–8, 111.
52 Boethius, *De Topicis Differentiis*, II, p. 51.
53 Boethius, *Consolation of Philosophy*, V.2–6, pp. 391–435 (see also pages 79–80); cf. J. Marenbon, *Boethius* (Oxford, 2003), chs 6–9.
54 See pages 64–5, 97.

that fortune has, in fact, no power of its own but is the servant of destiny or providence (*decreti sive providentiae ministra*).[55] As a result, medieval historians were able to use Boethius' discussion of providence to draw on a repertoire of classical argument and argumentation which, they could claim, was entirely consistent with patristic exegesis. Thietmar of Merseburg, for example, comments on 'the fickleness by which the unstable course of this whole world is always impelled towards the depths', but he also juxtaposes such mutability with divine providence on the grounds that 'Scripture forbids us from believing that anything occurs through fate or accident'.[56] William of Malmesbury appeals to the same combination. In his view, such a capacity for revolution (*volubilitas*) meant that human affairs were the 'plaything' (*ludibrium*) of both fortune and providence. As far as William was concerned, this observation made, in itself, a valuable historiographical point, courtesy of Augustine's distinction between active and permissive providence: 'it is worthwhile to know the mutability of fortune and the changeability of the human lot, whether God permits it or commands it'.[57] Otto of Freising makes a very similar claim.[58]

Boethius' *De Topicis Differentiis* and *Consolation of Philosophy* provided medieval authors with a much wider theological and philosophical field in which to place the language of causality

---

55 Macrobius, *Saturnalia*, V.16.8, p. 356; cf. John of Salisbury, *Policraticus*, trans. J.B. Pike, *The Frivolities of Courtiers and the Footprints of Philosophers* (Minneapolis, 1938), III.8, p. 174. For Vergil, see *Aeneid* (trans. H.R. Fairclough, rev. G.P. Goold (Loeb, 2000), V.604, p. 487, XI.426–7, p. 267.
56 Thietmar, *Chronicon*, VI.7, p. 241; cf. *Gesta Stephani*, ed. and trans. K.R. Potter, rev. R.H.C. Davis (Oxford, 1976), II.91, p. 177, II.114, p. 221, II.116, p. 225.
57 William of Malmesbury, *Historia Novella*, ed. and trans. K.R. Potter (London, 1955), III.prol., p. 46; cf. I.457, p. 12, III.500, p. 61; see also William of Malmesbury, *Gesta Regum Anglorum*, ed. and trans. R.A.B. Mynors, R.M. Thomson and M. Winterbottom, *The History of the English Kings* (Oxford, 1999), I.2, p. 19, I.8, p. 27, I.17, p. 41, I.79, p. 115, II.107, p. 155, II.228, p. 417, III.251, p. 467, III.270, p. 499; Valerius Maximus, *Facta et Dicta Memorabilia*, VI.9, p. 99, VII.1, p. 103.
58 See page 111; cf. E. Mégier, '*Fortuna* als Kategorie der Geschichtsdeutung im 12. Jahrhundert am Beispiel Ordericus' Vitalis und Ottos von Freising', *Mittellateinisches Jahrbuch*, 32 (1997), pp. 49–70; T.M.S. Lehtonen, 'History, Tragedy and Fortune in Twelfth-Century Historiography with special reference to Otto of Freising's *Chronica*', in T.M.S. Lehtonen and P. Mehtonen (eds), *Historia: The Concept and Genres in the Middle Ages* (Helsinki, 2000), pp. 29–49.

than did Cicero's original analysis of intrinsic arguments in the *Topica*. At one level, reference to the 'fluctuations' of fortune and chance might reflect no more than an author's comparison of the world to the unpredictable character of the sea.[59] According to *De Inventione*, after all, a lament over the comprehensive power of fortune and the corresponding weakness of human beings is simply a commonplace argument which is designed primarily to elicit pity from an audience.[60] However, use of the terms 'fortune' and 'chance' could also indicate an author's recognition that unexpected events can arise from the conjunction of several different causes. Viewed from the perspective of rhetorical invention, these were categories of argument which could play a precise explanatory role in the course of uncovering antecedent, secondary and efficient causes. Boethius' commentary on Cicero's *Topica* certainly presupposed a clear sense of where the terminology of fortune and chance fitted into a series of different types of cause, intended or unintended, known or unknown.[61] This concern with aetiology was a central feature of rhetorical argumentation and, as such, it accommodated, rather than rejected, the epistemological uncertainty which might otherwise be acknowledged to characterise a particular course of events. An appeal to the terms providence and fortune, in other words, did not mark an admission of historiographical defeat; instead, it was based on two elements of a coherent scheme which was formulated to identify,

---

59 Cf. Boethius, *Consolation of Philosophy*, I.3, p. 43, I.5, p. 161, II.1, p. 179 (see also page 111); Calcidius, *Commentary on Plato's Timaeus*, CLIX, p. 193 (see also page 273). For the wave-wandering wheels of the world, see Paschasius Radbertus, *Vita Adalhardi*, XLIII, p. 52, and Paschasius Radbertus, *Epitaphium Arsenii*, trans. A. Cabaniss, *Charlemagne's Cousins: Contemporary Lives of Adalard and Wala* (Syracuse, 1967), II.12, p. 176; cf. Bernardus Silvestris, *Commentary on the First Six Books of Virgil's Aeneid*, VI, p. 50.
60 Cicero, *De Inventione*, I.55.106, p. 157, II.33.102, p. 269; cf. Geoffrey of Vinsauf, *Poetria Nova*, ed. and trans. E. Gallo, *The Poetria Nova and Its Sources in Early Rhetorical Doctrine* (The Hague, 1971), 181–4, p. 23. For the mutability of fortune (*volubilitas fortunae*), see Cicero, *De Divinatione*, trans. W.A. Falconer (Loeb, 1923), II.6.15, p. 387, quoted, for example, by William of Newburgh, *The History of English Affairs*, trans. P.G. Walsh and M.J. Kennedy (Warminster, 1988), I.10, p. 65; cf. Boethius, *Consolation of Philosophy*, II.1, p. 177, II.4, p. 197; Henry of Huntingdon, *Historia Anglorum*, X.11, p. 723; Gerald of Wales, *Expugnatio Hibernica*, I.1, p. 27, I.5, p. 39, I.23, p. 81, I.25, p. 85, II.31, p. 225.
61 Boethius, *In Ciceronis Topica*, V, pp. 161–3.

not deny, the interweaving of causes and the temporal ordering of what happens in a world that is ultimately governed by God.

If intrinsic arguments are drawn from sources which derive directly from the subject-matter of the case itself, the discovery of extrinsic arguments depends primarily on authority. This type of argumentation, Cicero states, is not an art or discipline (and is therefore not, in this strict sense, 'artificial'), but depends, instead, on testimony, where *testimonium* is defined as everything external which can be introduced into a case in order to create belief or credence (*fides*).[62] According to Boethius, this sort of argument is concerned with opinion and general report (that is, what people were actually saying).[63] Such testimony can take the form of divine testimony, be it through a specific divine utterance or action, through heavenly portents (including comets) or through divinely-inspired dreams.[64] Otherwise, as was the case in judicial rhetoric, this testimony is generally either material (that is, written documentation, often wills) or human.[65] According to Cicero, human witnesses should be given the greatest weight when they are eyewitnesses, or at least when the report of such eyewitnesses is relayed truthfully by truth-tellers (*veredici*). Not everyone has the weight to be a witness, since credence or belief depends on that person's authority. This authority depends, in turn, upon that person's nature (that is, primarily upon their virtue), upon circumstances (that is, upon their intelligence, wealth, age, fortune, knowledge and experience), upon necessity, or sometimes upon a concurrence of fortuitous events. In the case of virtue, however, Cicero makes a point of stating that it is the opinion of virtue which is more important than virtue itself, since opinion regards as virtuous not only those people who really are virtuous but also those who seem to be. It is thus 'popular opinion' or the opinion of the masses (*opinio vulgi*) that people who are intelligent, wealthy and who have lived a long and honourable life are people who are worthy of trust or belief. It may not, in fact, be correct that those who excel in these areas will also excel in virtue but, Cicero

---

62 Cicero, *Topica*, XIX.73, p. 439; cf. Boethius, *De Topicis Differentiis*, II, p. 61, III, p. 70.
63 Boethius, *De Topicis Differentiis*, II, p. 61.
64 Cicero, *Topica*, XX.77, p. 443.
65 Quintilian, *Institutio Oratoria*, V.7.1, p. 169; see pages 182–9.

remarks, popular opinion can hardly be changed. It is therefore this view which will guide those who are actually judging what is being said or written and, by extension, those who are doing the speaking or the writing.[66]

The extrinsic testimony provided by human witnesses extends to people who are no longer alive. It covers persons of intelligence, industry and learning whose conduct was consistent and proven, whether they held public office or whether they were orators, philosophers, poets or historians, whose sayings and writings are often sought for the authority to create belief or credence (*fides*).[67] This means that the sayings and deeds of the ancients, including works of history, can be used as material witnesses in support of a particular case.[68] It becomes clear from Cicero's *Topica*, however, that this type of extrinsic testimony also extends to reputation (*fama*) or rumour (*rumor*). Cicero concedes that popular repute (*fama vulgi*) sometimes cannot be refuted even by truth itself but is, in itself, a kind of public testimony (*quoddam multitudinis testimonium*).[69] Things that are readily believable depend on the judgment of the multitude because they represent those things that seem true to everyone, or to most people, or to the most famous or distinguished people, or to the experts in any particular art or science.[70] Orators do not themselves produce this opinion but they take the common talk which already exists, which has arisen spontaneously, and they use it to support their case. Such extrinsic authority, Boethius explains, comes either from nature or from the times. It derives either from things which are excellent and great and best by nature or from those things which hold an inferior place and have credibility, not because of the quality of their nature, but because of the beliefs held by common people.[71]

In extending the extrinsic legal testimony of human witnesses to include the evidence provided by rumour, Cicero's *Topica* reinforced an argument put forward by the *Rhetorica ad Herennium*.

---

66 Cicero, *Topica*, XIX.73–XX.78, pp. 439–43.
67 *Topica*, XX.78, p. 443.
68 See page 183.
69 *Topica*, XX.76, p. 441 (see pages 338–9); cf. Geoffrey of Vinsauf, *Poetria Nova*, 1700–03, p. 105; Guibert of Nogent, *Monodiae*, I.10, p. 57.
70 Cf. Boethius, *De Topicis Differentiis*, III, p. 70.
71 Boethius, *In Ciceronis Topica*, II, pp. 72–3, VI, p. 181.

This is certainly testimony which can, if necessary, be dismissed by a speaker or writer – if an individual's defence is hindered by their bad reputation (*fama*), for example, then these rumours can be dismissed as false opinion (*falsa opinio*) by means of the standard argument that rumours ought not to be believed because they are fables made up by one's enemies (*ficta fabula, conficta fabula*). Even if a rumour seems strongly probable, belief in it (*fides famae*) can be dismantled by argument.[72] By the same token, however, rumour can also be supported by a speaker or writer on the grounds that reputation (*fama*) always has some foundation, that there was no reason for anyone to make it up (*confingere*) in the first place, and that, even if other rumours are usually false, this particular one is true.[73] Quintilian makes the same point. Popular belief (*fama*), he writes, can be paired with rumours (*rumores*) in that both can certainly be dismissed as the false and deceptive product of malignity and credulity but both can also represent the common opinion of the community (*consensus civitatis*) and, as such, should be allowed to stand as public testimony (*publicum testimonium*).[74]

Extrinsic arguments from authority, according to Quintilian, can be derived from the views of nations, peoples, wise men, distinguished citizens and illustrious poets, but they also extend to popular sayings and beliefs because these, too, are a sort of testimony (*testimonia sunt ... quodammodo*). Indeed, in Quintilian's view, this type of testimony is all the more effective for the reason that, by its very nature, it has not been tailored to particular cases but represents words and deeds which are free from both hatred and favour (*gratia*, that is, remembering and returning services, respect

---

72 *Rhetorica ad Herennium*, II.3.5, p. 67; Cicero, *De Inventione*, II.11.37, p. 199; cf. *De Inventione*, II.16.50, p. 211; Boethius, *Consolation of Philosophy*, II.7, p. 221; Alan of Lille, *Anticlaudianus*, trans. J.J. Sheridan, *Anticlaudianus or the Good and Perfect Man* (Toronto, 1973), VIII.305, p. 200: 'rumour marries falsehood to truth'.
73 *Rhetorica ad Herennium*, II.8.12, p. 79. For the range of meanings which the term *fama* could have (public opinion, rumour, reputation, fame), including its role in law, see T. Fenster and D.L. Smail (eds), *Fama: The Politics of Talk and Reputation in Medieval Europe* (London, 2003), parts 1, 2.
74 Quintilian, *Institutio Oratoria*, V.1.2, p. 157, V.3.1, p. 163. Gerald of Wales defends his reliance on *fama* for parts of his *Topography of Ireland* on the grounds that Augustine had maintained that *fama* was neither to be completely accepted nor completely rejected: Gerald of Wales, *Retractationes*, ed. J.S. Brewer (London, 1861), vol. I, p. 425–6; cf. Augustine, *De Civitate Dei*, XXI.7, pp. 978–9.

and acts of friendship)[75] and which have been accepted because they appear to be the most morally worthy or the most true. This goes for the opinions of poets; it also applies to generally-received popular sayings which have lasted for such a long time precisely because they have seemed true to everyone.[76] The brief interjection of this sort of reflection (*sensus*) is therefore a technique which, according to Quintilian, is frequently used by orators and historians. These reflections (*sententiae*) are introduced in small clauses and, as such, they correspond in form to their oldest type, namely the aphorism or maxim. Because they are self-subsistent and isolated, such sayings should certainly be used sparingly, but they should not be avoided altogether. They are useful because they strike the mind, often with a single blow; they stick there because of their brevity and are persuasive through the pleasure they give.[77] The *Rhetorica ad Herennium* makes the same point. Reflections or *sententiae* are statements drawn from life which set out concisely either what happens or what ought to happen; they should be deployed sparingly so that orators will appear to be acting out their subject-matter (*actores rei*), not teaching the rules of life, but otherwise such expressions can produce considerable pleasure and ornamentation.[78]

The truth-content of the different types of rhetorical argument which can be discovered and cited in support of a particular case was clearly open to a very wide degree of variation. Like the dialectician, the orator can, of course, use the logic of a syllogism in order to prove a point, that is, by arguing from truth to truth. However, it was considered much more characteristic for the orator to resort to the enthymeme (*commentum* or *commentatio* in Latin) and the epicheireme – in other words, to weaker forms of syllogism which draw a conclusion from opposed propositions but which omit some part of the reasoning and are based

---

75 For this definition of favour (*gratia*), see Cicero, *De Inventione*, II.22.66, p. 231 (see also page 183).
76 Quintilian, *Institutio Oratoria*, V.11.36–41, pp. 293–5.
77 *Institutio Oratoria*, VIII.2.15, p. 205, VIII.5.1–34, pp. 281–301, XII.10.48, p. 477; cf. Macrobius, *Saturnalia*, V.16.6, p. 355; Priscian, *Praeexercitamina*, trans. J.M. Miller, in J.M. Miller, M.H. Prosser and T.W. Benson (eds), *Readings in Medieval Rhetoric* (Bloomington, 1973), III, p. 56; Geoffrey of Vinsauf, *Poetria Nova*, 142–5, p. 21.
78 *Rhetorica ad Herennium*, IV.17.24–5, pp. 289–91.

simply on what is credible rather than on what is necessarily true (Quintilian's example is 'virtue is a good in itself which no one can put to a bad use').[79] Cicero recognised that, in this respect, eloquence still requires a speaker or writer to possess a knowledge of dialectic. Even though rhetoric is broader and more expansive than disputation, it still presupposes familiarity with different categories and modes of words so that the speaker or writer can distinguish between truth and falsehood and is able to explain ambiguity. Take the second of the three judicial questions – what something is (*quid sit*) or what it is that has happened – and the way in which it is resolved by means of definition, that is, by demonstrating as briefly as possible what exactly it is that is being discussed. Analysed in these terms, according to Cicero, the definition produced by the rhetorician should possess a brevity and precision appropriate to dialectic, but it should also have a greater richness and be better adapted to common judgment and popular understanding (*commune iudicium, popularis intelligentia*).[80] Argumentation can, as a result, either demonstrate what is necessarily true (*necessaria demonstrare*) or set out what is probable (*probabilia ostendere*).[81] At one end of this sliding scale is the boundary which separates rhetoric from dialectic, that is, the use of probable argument as opposed to the citation of demonstrative proof; at the other end is common opinion, reputation, rumour, *sententiae* and the opinion of the masses.

The rhetorical discovery of arguments, in short, is a process of reasoning which provides proof, creating belief (*fides*) in something which is a matter of doubt on the basis of something which is not in doubt, namely from what is, or seems to be, true. It can be produced by logical argumentation, by a process of ratiocination, but it can also be provided by what is perceived through the senses (that is, via signs which are seen or heard), by the common agreement of public opinion (*communis opinio*),

---

79 Cicero, *Topica*, XIII.55, p. 423; Quintilian, *Institutio Oratoria*, V.10.1–8, pp. 203–7, V.14.1–2, p. 349, V.14.14, p. 357, V.14.24–5, p. 363; Boethius, *De Topicis Differentiis*, II, p. 45; cf. John of Salisbury, *Metalogicon*, trans. D.D. McGarry (Berkeley, 1955), III.10, p. 192.
80 Cicero, *Orator*, trans. H.M. Hubbell (Loeb, 1962), XXXIII.113–17, pp. 389–93.
81 Cicero, *De Inventione*, I.29.44, p. 83, I.42.79, p. 125.

and by what has been established in law and custom (*mos*).[82] Proof consists of signs or arguments or *exempla*.[83] Some signs are irrefutable. Others are not necessarily conclusive but, even though they may not be sufficient to remove doubt on their own, they can still carry considerable weight when taken in conjunction with other signs.[84] In producing *fides*, therefore, the 'proof' provided by rhetorical argumentation comes with varying degrees of certainty: it can be necessary, it can be credible, or it can simply be 'not inconsistent'.[85] Credibility has three gradations of its own: the first, and the strongest, is what usually occurs within the common understanding of everyone; second, there is what has a greater propensity to occur; third, and last, is what is not inconsistent, that is, when there is nothing to prevent it from being true. It is with credibility, Quintilian concludes, rather than with certainty, that the vast majority of arguments are concerned.[86]

In searching for arguments to give credibility to their narrative, medieval historians were well aware of the sensitivity which was required towards the reliability of the extrinsic testimony that was available to them. Bede provides one of the earliest, and most influential, statements of this principle when he runs through the range of material on which his *Ecclesiastical History* had drawn: eyewitnesses, the second-hand accounts of trustworthy authorities, documentary testimony and, last but not least, opinion – what people believed to have happened (*fama vulgans*). Bede acknowledged that when Stephen got Jacob's burial place wrong in Acts 7:16, he was tailoring his speech to the beliefs of his audience; likewise, when Luke spoke of Joseph as if he were the natural father of Jesus (Luke 2:33–4), Bede echoed Jerome's view that the apostle was accommodating his language to the *opinio vulgi* and in accordance with the 'true law of history' (*vera lex historiae*).[87] When Bede uses this last phrase (once more taken from Jerome)[88]

---

82 Quintilian, *Institutio Oratoria*, V.10.8–13, pp. 207–9.
83 *Institutio Oratoria*, V.9.1, p. 195.
84 *Institutio Oratoria*, V.9.8, p. 199.
85 *Institutio Oratoria*, V.8.6, p. 195; cf. Boethius, *In Ciceronis Topica*, I, pp. 25–6.
86 *Institutio Oratoria*, V.10.16–19, pp. 209–13.
87 Bede, *Commentary on the Acts of the Apostles*, trans. L.T. Martin (Kalamazoo, 1989), pp. 71–2; Bede, *In Lucae Evangelium Expositio*, ed. D. Hurst (*CCSL* 120, Turnhout, 1960). See also page 410.
88 Jerome, *Contra Helvidium*, trans. J.N. Hritzu (Washington, DC, 1965), p. 16.

in the prologue to his *Ecclesiastical History*, he is making a similar point. By including material which he had collected, not from eyewitness testimony, but from common report (*fama vulgans*), that is, from the oral traditions which had been handed down to the individuals and communities that he subsequently specifies as sources for his history, Bede is insisting that this is a legitimate approach, even if it might make his narrative unwittingly repeat any errors these sources may contain. Bede was not claiming that he would be altering his account in order to suit the opinion of his audience, but he was acknowledging that his narrative would include material whose truthfulness he could not guarantee.[89] Such an approach was entirely in accordance with the principles of rhetorical argumentation.

William of Malmesbury, who explicitly set his own historiography in a direct line of succession from Bede's work, illustrates the methodological sensitivity which an awareness of extrinsic argumentation could produce. 'Truthful eyewitnesses' provided, as ever, the best guarantee of accuracy,[90] although the truth of their account would also depend on the credibility of the individual witnesses concerned. 'This story', he writes, 'does not come from scattered references in untrustworthy writers but from eyewitnesses of mature years and the greatest reliability and learning'.[91] In doing so, William is self-consciously following

---

89 R. Ray, 'Bede's *Vera Lex Historiae*', *Speculum*, 55 (1980), pp. 1–21; cf. W. Goffart, 'Bede's *Vera Lex Historiae* Explained', *Anglo-Saxon England*, 34 (2005), pp. 111–16.
90 For example, William of Malmesbury, *Gesta Pontificum Anglorum*, ed. and trans. M. Winterbottom and R.M. Thomson, *The History of the English Bishops* (Oxford, 2007), IV.144, p. 435; William of Jumièges, *Gesta Normannorum Ducum* ed. and trans. E.M.C. van Houts (Oxford, 1992), Ep.ded., p. 7. Gerald of Wales, *Expugnatio Hibernica*, prol., states (p. 3) 'how much more trustworthy will be my account of those events which I have seen happen, the greater part of which I have actually witnessed, and which have happened too recently to admit of any doubt as to their really having happened' (*quanto magis ea quae vidimus quorumque maiori ex parte testes sumus et quorum de fide memoria tam recens hesitare non permittit*), and that he will report (p. 21) 'deeds which I have myself seen with my eyes or learned of from reliable witnesses' (*gesta quae vel certis ab indicibus audivi vel oculis ipse conspexi*). See also Joinville, *The Life of Saint Louis*, trans. M. Shaw, *Joinville and Villehardouin: Chronicles of the Crusades* (Harmondsworth, 1963), pp. 352–3.
91 William of Malmesbury, *Gesta Pontificum Anglorum*, V.263, p. 629 (see also page 187); cf. William of Malmesbury, *Gesta Regum Anglorum*, IV.372, p. 655. See also Gerald of Wales, *Gemma Ecclesiastica*, trans. J.J. Hagen, *The Jewel of the Church* (Leiden, 1979), pref., who states (pp. 1–2): 'eyewitness faith is usually stronger

Bede: 'there will be many, perhaps, in diverse parts of England, ready to say that they have heard or read about some things a different account from that which I have given. But if they judge aright, they will not therefore, with critical pen, dismiss me as worthless, for I have followed the true law of history [*vera lex historiae*] and have set down nothing but what I have learned from trustworthy reports or written sources'.[92] Henry of Huntingdon makes a point of appealing to the same principle and the same authority: for events up to his own lifetime (after which he relied on eyewitnesses and the testimony of others) he has diligently studied the collected writings of the past and thereby what is generally believed, 'for, as the learned Bede attests in his prologue to the *Ecclesiastical History*, the true law of history is essentially to make known to posterity in writing what is to be collected from common report [*fama vulgans*]'.[93]

A similar concern underpins William of Malmesbury's observations on the testimony furnished by written documentation – without the credence (*fides*) provided by the latter, William observes that reverence for an individual's holy reputation will remain simply opinion (*opinio*).[94] William also points out, for example, that Eadmer included the text of Anselm's letters in his book so that no one could criticise him for lying and so that the strength of his words should be considered unimpugnable.[95] His own inclusion of documentation for the primatial dispute between Canterbury and York is prefaced with the observation that this practice is not an attempt to steal someone else's *fama* but is, in fact, a necessary task of the historian; indeed, studious readers should be grateful for finding gathered in his history all the facts that it would be laborious to examine in their many documents, even supposing

---

and more trustworthy ... that which is present and visible to the eyes is assuredly observed and understood more certainly and exactly than something which is absent and unknown – this is the opinion of the poet'.
92 William of Malmesbury, *Gesta Regum Anglorum*, V.445, p. 797.
93 Henry of Huntingdon, *Historia Anglorum*, IV.14, p. 235; cf.VII.1, p. 413.
94 William of Malmesbury, *Gesta Pontificum Anglorum*, II.95, p. 317.
95 *Gesta Pontificum Anglorum*, I.59, p. 183. Compare Eadmer, *Life of Anselm*, II.71, pp. 147–9, and contrast *Life of Anselm*, II.46, pp. 123–5 ('considering the speaker's eminent sanctity and the respect due to him, we were obliged to have faith [*fides*] in what he said and for that reason we were content to trust his words alone and omitted to ask how he knew this').

they could ever happen to find them, which is doubtful.[96] This does not mean, of course, that such documentation was, in itself, unproblematic. Indeed, William explicitly acknowledges that his sources can themselves lie.[97] In describing the distant past, for example, he is happy to vouch for the truth of his sequence of years, but the credence of the remainder is left, as Sallust had put it, resting with the sources themselves.[98] When he discusses King Athelstan, for example, William registers the moment when his account moves from 'trustworthy books which have been written for the instruction of posterity' to the poetry of old songs (*cantilenae*) which have been eroded by the passage of time – he has included such material, he states, not to defend its truthfulness, but so as not to diminish the knowledge (*scientia*) of his readers.[99] William accordingly points out what he does *not* know, when he does not himself trust his sources because they are difficult or ambiguous,[100] however plausible (*veri similia*) they might seem,[101] and when he is therefore content to echo Sallust (and Bede) by stressing the limitations to the truth which he has been able to acquire,[102] or simply by putting his contradictory sources side by side.[103]

When William of Malmesbury discusses material for which he is reliant on reputation or report (*fama*) and opinion (*opinio*),

---

96   *Gesta Pontificum Anglorum*, I.28, p. 59; cf. William of Malmesbury, *Gesta Regum Anglorum*, III.294–303, pp. 529–39. Orderic Vitalis, *Historia Ecclesiastica*, I.22, states (p. 150): 'Whilst I have sometimes clung avidly to the same words which I saw in the original texts, generally I have changed the words for the sake of brevity, but have always made a supreme effort always to pursue the irrefutable truth [*invicta veritas*], and have never intentionally departed from the original meaning [*autentica sententia*]'. From the same source see also IV, pp. 287–93, V.5, pp. 27–35, IX.2, pp. 11–15, IX.3, pp. 21–3, XII.21, pp. 275–7, XII.48, p. 389.
97   William of Malmesbury, *Gesta Regum Anglorum*, III.248, p. 463.
98   *Gesta Regum Anglorum*, I.prol., p. 17; cf. Sallust, *Jugurthine War*, trans. J.C. Rolfe (Loeb, 1931), XVII.7, p. 171 (see also page 47).
99   *Gesta Regum Anglorum*, II.138, p. 225.
100 *Gesta Regum Anglorum*, V.prol., p. 709.
101 *Gesta Regum Anglorum*, II.140, p. 229.
102 *Gesta Regum Anglorum*, II.197–8, pp. 355–7, II.228, p. 417, III.238, pp. 445–7; cf. Widukind: 'It is beyond us to explain the cause of this defection and to reveal royal mysteries; our objective is to satisfy the truth of history [*verum historiae*] and, if we have sinned at all in this regard, may it be pardonable': *Res Gestae Saxonicae*, ed. and trans. E. Rotter and B. Schneidmüller (rev edn, Stuttgart, 1992), II.25, p. 138.
103 For example, *Gesta Regum Anglorum*, I.9, p. 29, I.44, p. 61.

his approach is therefore carefully calibrated. Knowledge and truth are, by definition, conceptually distinct from opinion.[104] Opinion is, by definition, 'uncertain'.[105] Reputation and *fama* can indeed be dismissed as trifles (*nugae*); so too can stories of King Arthur, which are also labelled old wives' tales (*antiquitas neniarum*) or deceitful fables (*fallaces fabulae*).[106] The uncertainty of *fama* can accordingly be juxtaposed with the credence of sight (*fides oculorum*),[107] or with what can be firmly asserted (*pro solido*).[108] Like Vergil, William could reinforce report or rumour with something of greater certainty or credibility (*fides*).[109] When he comes to the First Crusade, William thinks it advisable to point out that he is putting forward only what he has discovered in writing, because 'to believe everything from indulgent *fama* and to deceive the readiness [*facilitas*] of one's audience ought not to be the task of the truthful historian'.[110] Not believing everything he reads is, however, clearly not the same as excluding *fama* altogether. William is careful to acknowledge when his narrative does depend on *fama vulgans*,[111] or, where the truth remains in doubt because *fama* has produced two alternative accounts.[112] Indeed, he states that it is also as a 'truthful historian' that he will put down in writing 'the opinion of people in this part of

---

104 Cf. Macrobius, *Commentary on the Dream of Scipio*, trans. W.H. Stahl (New York, 1952), I.10, p. 127, I.12, p. 135; see also pages 417–19.
105 William of Malmesbury, *Gesta Regum Anglorum*, II.178, p. 309.
106 *Gesta Regum Anglorum*, I.8, p. 27, III.287, p. 521, IV.333, p. 575; cf. Thietmar, *Chronicon*, II.41, p. 122, VI.37, p. 263, VI.99, p. 303, VII.48, p. 341.
107 *Gesta Regum Anglorum*, II.213, p. 397; cf. Vergil, *Aeneid*, IV.287, p. 415; Einhard, *Vita Karoli*, trans. P.E. Dutton (Ontario, 1998), praef., p. 15 (see also page 158); Gervase of Tilbury, *Otia Imperialia*, ed. and trans. S.E. Banks and J.W. Binns, *Recreation for an Emperor* (Oxford, 2002), II.7, p. 249.
108 *Gesta Regum Anglorum*, II.188, p. 337; cf. Sidonius Apollinaris, *Letters*, trans. W.B. Anderson (Loeb, 1965), Ep.III.7.4 5, p. 31.
109 Vergil, *Aeneid*, X.510, p. 209, XI.511, p. 271.
110 William of Malmesbury, *Gesta Regum Anglorum*, IV.382, p. 681.
111 For example, *Gesta Regum Anglorum*, II.162, p. 267. For tales of Gerbert of Aurillac, see *Gesta Regum Anglorum*, II.167, p. 279, II.168, p. 283, II.169, p. 287, II.172, p. 293.
112 *Gesta Regum Anglorum*, I.8, p. 27, III.287, p. 521. cf. William of Malmesbury, *Historia Novella*, III.487, p. 47; Liutprand, *Antapodosis*, I.42, p. 59, III.47, pp. 135–6; Thietmar, *Chronicon*, V.32, pp. 226–7.

the country'.[113] In citing the different 'opinions' of the English and the Normans over the guilt of earl Waltheof, for example, William simply expresses the hope that *fama* and truth are not in conflict.[114] 'Solid truth' (*solida veritas*)[115] and something which is the subject of affirmation (*affirmatio*) or trust (*fides*) are conceptually distinct from something which is the subject of repute (*fama*) or opinion (*opinio*).[116] This applies to his sources but it also applies to William himself – something can be more probable in his own opinion (*magis opinor*); what he believes to be the case can be distinguished from what he affirms to be true.[117] When William is his own eyewitness, he can certainly vouch for 'complete truth' (*integra veritas*) in his account.[118] Otherwise, like Bede, the *vera lex historiae* comprises a wide spectrum of certainty and if, as in the case of some miracles, his narrative has to include what he has heard rather than seen, then not only are those events vouchsafed by the fact that what is being recorded has been universally believed from one generation to the next, but also, he points out, there is a precedent for such an approach in no less a work than the Gospel of Luke and Gregory the Great's *Dialogues*.[119] Gerald of Wales makes the same point about the marvellous and the miraculous by quoting Augustine: 'neither do I want everything which I have stated to be believed uncritically. For I myself do not believe in them as if I had no mental reservations regarding them, except in the case of those phenomena which I have myself experienced or which it is easy for anyone to experience. I believe in all other such only to the extent of judging that their existence is neither to be completely denied nor stoutly maintained'.[120]

---

113 William of Malmesbury, *Historia Novella*, I.452, p. 5.
114 *Gesta Pontificum Anglorum*, IV.182, p. 487; cf. *Historia Novella*, II.470, p. 28.
115 *Historia Novella*, III.514, p. 70.
116 *Gesta Regum Anglorum*, I.49, p. 75, II.126, p. 199; cf. Widukind, *Res Gestae Saxonicae*, III.15, p. 174, III.74, pp. 230–2.
117 *Historia Novella*, II, p. 26; *Gesta Regum Anglorum*, II.169, p. 289; cf. Thietmar, *Chronicon*, VII.71, p. 357.
118 *Historia Novella*, III.492, p. 52, III.501, p. 62.
119 *Gesta Pontificum Anglorum*, V.212, pp. 537–9. For Henry of Huntingdon's criteria for assessing the validity of miracle stories, see his *Historia Anglorum*, IX.1, p. 623.
120 Gerald of Wales, *Expugnatio Hibernica*, prol., p. 7, quoting Augustine, *De Civitate Dei*, XXI.7, pp. 978–9 (see pages 112–13, 411). For an emphasis on the significance of history, not as facts and events, but as collectively held opinion or

If 'invention', the discovery of arguments, was the most important of the five aspects of rhetoric, then the nature of these arguments was clearly understood to cover the entire range of what can produce faith in something that is in doubt. Credibility, rather than certainty, was the intended result. What are the criteria, then, which should guide the identification and selection of particular arguments for a particular case? Why choose some arguments rather than others? For classical manuals of rhetoric there was a simple, one-word answer. The choice of arguments will be made according to 'what is appropriate' (*aptum*). This is the fundamental principle which guides the process of rhetorical invention and is, in turn, governed by two considerations – the nature of the case and the nature of the audience.

The suitability of an argument for a particular case is established, in the first instance, by applying the technique of imitation (*imitatio*). It is a basic principle of training in rhetoric to study and imitate a model and to do so in such a way that the good qualities of the model are reproduced rather than its faults. Nor should this undertaking be confined to one single model – different qualities should be drawn from different authors in order to suit what is appropriate in different places. Such an approach is thus, strictly speaking, more than just imitation because otherwise no progress or growth would be possible. According to Quintilian, even those who do not seek the greatest heights of achievement should still contend with their models rather than simply be content to follow them. Instead of being copied slavishly, therefore, the model should be adapted in a spirit of creative rivalry (*aemulatio*).[121] This principle of imitation operates, first, at the level of style and of language (*elocutio*), in that different styles of speaking are appropriate for different purposes. Thus the three functions of rhetoric – to teach, to move and to give pleasure – have styles appropriate to each: the plain style (*subtilis*) is best for instruction and hence for narrative and for proof; the grand style (*grande*) is best for moving the emotions; whilst the intermediate

---

tradition, see S. Fleischman, 'On the Representation of History and Fiction in the Middle Ages', *History and Theory*, 22 (1983), p. 305; cf. Eadmer, *Historia Novorum in Anglia*, II.99, III.125–6, p. 131.
121 Quintilian, *Institutio Oratoria*, X.2.4–10, 26, pp. 77–9, 89; Cicero, *De Oratore*, II.22.90–96, pp. 265–71; Cicero, *De Inventione*, II.2.4–5, pp. 169–71.

style (*medium*) is best for pleasing and conciliating. All three styles will be used in the course of a given speech or text as the circumstances demand, from the introduction or *exordium* right through to the conclusion or *peroratio*. The circumstances of each case will inevitably vary – in some instances it will be necessary to instruct, in others to move, and different methods will be necessary for each – but the golden rule is that the words which are deployed will be clear, ornate and made suitable or appropriate to the effect which the speaker or writer is wishing to produce.[122]

Imitation extends to cover the exact choice of vocabulary. In the case of drawing an argument from antiquity, for example, the act of imitating a past orator, poet or historian will give dignity to words and will make a speech or text more distinguished (*sanctior*) and impressive. Only the best of such authors should be read, so that it is not just words which are imitated but those words which are the most suitable (*aptissima*). An individual's imitation of such authors should also, once again, not be confined to a single model; instead, different qualities from different authors should be combined. This principle is underlined in practice by the particular importance given to writing as a form of rhetorical exercise, especially when translating from one language into another or when turning verse into prose. Quintilian accordingly quotes Cicero's opinion that writing is the best way to learn how to speak, in order to support his own view that orators should write as much and as carefully as possible, frequently revising what they have written. It is in writing, he argues, that eloquence has its roots and its foundations. That said, both Quintilian and Cicero thought that, in imitating ancient authors, the language of the past should be used with care, in order to avoid the error of anachronism – the rhetorician should not employ those words, for example, which are no longer in current or customary use, except on the odd occasion and for the sake of ornamentation. The language of the past should be used sparingly and should not be preferred to that of the present day, least of all at the expense of clarity. However, with that proviso, it remains the case that the writer who has diligently read the writings of the past will be able to deploy the most appropriate words from amongst

---

122 *Institutio Oratoria*, VIII.1.1, p. 195.

them. In principle, the authority of antiquity (*auctoritas antiquitatis, auctoritas vetustatis*) will then give their style a certain majesty and produce no little pleasure.[123]

These principles of stylistic imitation and variation were, of course, not unique to medieval historiography, but their impact was still fundamental on the approach that was taken by writers of history. The plain style was best suited to instruction and hence for narrative and for proof. In Bede's view, it was in the nature of history to narrate words and deeds in plain language (*plano sermone*) and he accordingly describes his own prose life of Cuthbert as straightforward in style (*sermo simplex*).[124] Henry of Huntingdon subsequently incorporated great swathes of Bede's *Ecclesiastical History* within his own work but, in imitating this model, he also abbreviates and adapts the original, changing tenses and cases, for instance, and carefully updating the vocabulary.[125] William of Malmesbury, meanwhile, echoed Bede's original ideal. Simplicity of language, he states, is free from subterfuge (*tergiversatio*) and contrived splendour,[126] and he has therefore himself chosen a familiar style, as opposed to one which is overblown (*sufflata*).[127] Geoffrey of Monmouth justifies his own 'rustic' style on the grounds that, had he used the high-flown diction mentioned in Horace's *Ars Poetica*, not only would he have made his work tedious but his audience would also have spent more time expounding the words than in understanding the history.[128] In his *Deeds of Frederick Barbarossa*, by contrast, Otto of Freising explicitly draws attention to the fact that he will be using two

---

123 *Institutio Oratoria*, I.6.39–43, pp. 131–3, VIII.3.24–5, p. 225, X.1.8, p. 7, X.3.1–8, pp. 91–5 (quoting *De Oratore*), XII.10.58–60, pp. 483–5, XII.10.69–71, pp. 489–91; Cicero, *De Oratore*, II.23.96, p. 269, III.10.37–9, pp. 31–3.
124 Bede, *De Tabernaculo*, trans. A.G. Holder (Liverpool, 1994), I, p. 25; Bede, *Prose Life of Cuthbert*, ed. and trans. B. Colgrave (Cambridge, 1940), prol., p. 145; cf. William of Malmesbury, *Gesta Pontificum Anglorum*, III.126, p. 407; C. Cubitt, 'Memory and Narrative in the Cult of Early Anglo-Saxon Saints', in Y. Hen and M. Innes (eds), *The Uses of the Past in the Early Middle Ages* (Cambridge, 2000), pp. 39–50.
125 D. Greenway, 'Henry of Huntingdon and Bede', in J.-P. Genet (ed.), *L'Historiographie Médiévale en Europe* (Paris, 1991), pp. 43–50.
126 William of Malmesbury, *Gesta Regum Anglorum*, III.303, p. 539.
127 *Gesta Regum Anglorum*, II.132, p. 211.
128 Geoffrey of Monmouth, *Historia Regum Britanniae*, prol., p. 5. For rusticity of style, see page 28.

styles rather than one – the plain diction which is appropriate to historical narrative but also speech which is adapted to loftier philosophical heights.[129]

Imitation of authoritative models was regarded as stylistic, as a matter of language and vocabulary, but it could equally well be substantive, namely when it concerned the subject-matter of what was being treated. This is why Einhard's 'life' of Charlemagne reflects such a formal debt to Suetonius – in order to write about an emperor, Einhard went to the most appropriate model he could find in the library at Fulda, namely the *Lives of the Caesars*. Likewise, William of Poitiers made the subject of his *Deeds* of William of Normandy fit the pattern set by a previous conqueror of Britain, Julius Caesar;[130] so too William of Malmesbury who, in his *Deeds of the English Kings*, used the patterns established by both Suetonius and Einhard for his account of the rule of William Rufus and Henry I.[131] Rahewin, Otto of Freising's continuator, produces a much more straightforward narrative for his completion of the *Deeds of Frederick*, but he, too, applies the principles of imitation in describing the details of Frederick's campaigns in northern Italy by means of a deft interweaving of passages from Josephus' account of battles and sieges from the *Jewish War* with sections and phrases from Sallust's account of the *Jugurthine War* and *Catiline*.[132] Such stylistic and substantive imitation could also be deployed to make a political point. This was particularly true of those medieval historians who deliberately evoked Sallust and Lucan, that is, the classical writers who charted, respectively, the corruption of the Roman *res publica* and the baleful consequences of the *rabies* of civil strife. It was no accident, for example, that it was Lucan who provided such an influential model for many

---

129 Otto of Freising, *The Deeds of Frederick Barbarossa*, trans. C.C. Mierow (New York, 1953), prol., p. 28 (see also page 119).
130 William of Poitiers, *Gesta Guillelmi*, ed. and trans. R.H.C. Davis and M. Chibnall (Oxford, 1998), II.39–40, pp. 169–75; cf. *The Carmen de Hastingae Proelio of Guy Bishop of Amiens*, ed. and trans. F. Barlow (Oxford 1999), line 32, p. 5, lines 351–4, p. 23.
131 J.G. Haahr, 'William of Malmesbury's Roman Models: Suetonius and Lucan', in A.S. Bernardo and S. Levin (eds), *The Classics in the Middle Ages* (New York, 1990), pp. 166–70.
132 Rahewin, *The Deeds of Frederick Barbarossa*, trans. C.C. Mierow (New York, 1953), III–IV, pp. 170–334.

of the more resonant phrases and passages in accounts of the internecine strife which afflicted eleventh-century Germany (in Thietmar's *Chronicon* and the anonymous *Life of the Emperor Henry IV*) and twelfth-century England (in Henry of Huntingdon and the anonymous *Gesta Stephani*).[133] Likewise, Richard of Devizes invoked Statius' *Thebaid* in order to point up the comparison between the conduct of Henry II's sons and 'the confused house of Oedipus'.[134]

If the nature of the subject-matter should guide speakers or writers towards the model which it is 'appropriate' for them to imitate, then it also guides the selection and arrangement (*dispositio*) of the arguments which are actually put forward. Such order (*ordo*) is defined as the correct placement of things, so that one thing follows from another and their arrangement (*dispositio*) will be advantageous (*utilis*) to the case being made.[135] Such arrangement must therefore be, by definition, flexible and adaptable. The precepts which are established for each part of rhetoric are not immutable; most rules can be changed in order to suit the nature of the case, the time, the occasion and, as ever, in accordance with necessity. It is thus a distinguishing quality of rhetoricians to possess the strategy (*consilium*) which is required in order to make the changes that are demanded by the varying circumstances they encounter (*momenta rerum*). An introduction, for example, can be either necessary or superfluous. A narrative can be brief or extended, continuous or divided; it can follow the order of events as they actually occurred or it can shuffle that order about. Emotions can either be restricted to the conclusion (*peroratio*) or they can be distributed throughout the text. In each

---

133 Henry of Huntingdon, *Historia Anglorum*, X.1, p. 701, X.4, p. 707, X.7, p. 713, X.17, p. 737, X.33, p. 761; *Gesta Stephani*, I.27, p. 57, II.70, p. 141; Thietmar, *Chronicon*, II.32, p. 116, V.23, p. 221, V.41, p. 232, VI.59, p. 278, VIII.7, p. 366; *Life of the Emperor Henry IV*, I, p. 104, II, p. 105, 107, IV, p. 109–12, V, p. 112, VI, p. 115, VIII, p. 121, X, p. 127, XI, p. 128, XII, p. 132. For William of Malmesbury, see Haahr, 'William of Malmesbury's Roman Models', pp. 170–2; R.M. Thomson, *William of Malmesbury* (Woodbridge, 1987), p. 49; N. Wright, 'William of Malmesbury and Latin Poetry – Further Evidence for a Benedictine's Reading', *Revue Bénédictine*, 101 (1991), pp. 136–9; N. Wright, '*Industriae Testimonium* – William of Malmesbury and Latin Poetry Revisited', *Revue Bénédictine*, 103 (1993), pp. 492–6.
134 Richard of Devizes, *Chronicle*, pp. 3, 31.
135 Quintilian, *Institutio Oratoria*, VII.praef.1, pp. 5–7.

case, the orator has to decide what particular order to adopt, which particular testimonies and documents to include, and when to include them. The choice of any one of these alternatives will always be determined by the circumstances, by what is fitting or advantageous to the case being made. This is the golden rule for arrangement or disposition in the *Rhetorica ad Herennium* – departure from the normal order can always be justified when it is accommodated to the particular circumstances in which the speech or text is being delivered. It may be better, for example, to omit the *exordium* and to begin, instead, with the narrative, or with some very strong argument or with the recital of some text, particularly if the audience is already tired or if it is incapable of hearing an introduction with equanimity.[136]

Viewed from the perspective of the writing of history, adaptability in arrangement becomes a particularly significant principle when considering the order which an author chooses to give to the narrative of the events they are describing. Generally speaking, a narrative should follow the chronological sequence of what happened, the 'natural' order of events. According to Macrobius, this rule of historical writing is one which Homer had deliberately eschewed when he followed the technique of poetry and began his own narrative in the middle.[137] A much more important principle for Quintilian, however, is that a narrative should follow whatever order is most expedient or advantageous.[138] This becomes particularly evident when he considers the principles which should govern a narrative when the facts run contrary to a case that is otherwise just. In these circumstances, according to Quintilian, the best strategy for a speaker or writer is to deny some things, add some others, change some things, and pass over others in silence, admitting the truth in some places but putting forward different motives or intentions than the ones which have been alleged.[139] Where to begin a narrative, where to end it and the order in which the events are related are therefore all deliberate

---

136 *Rhetorica ad Herennium*, III.10.17, p. 187; cf. pages 170–1.
137 Macrobius, *Saturnalia*, V.2.9, p. 288; cf. V.14.11, p. 346.
138 Quintilian, *Institutio Oratoria*, II.13.1–8, pp. 289–93, IV.2.83–4, pp. 95–7, VII.10.11–13, p. 169.
139 Quintilian, *Institutio Oratoria*, IV.2.67–80, pp. 85–95, VII.4.3–15, pp. 107–13 (see also pages 181–2).

and self-conscious choices on the part of an author. The resulting changes to a 'natural' order can all be justified, Quintilian states, by a speaker or writer using certain figures of speech – the act of displacing a fact to where it is more useful to a case, for instance, can be legitimised by pretending that the event had previously escaped the author's notice, or by claiming to keep to the natural sequence in order to make things clear but then stopping to discuss the causes which preceded the event that is being expounded. There is no single prescriptive law; instead, the speaker must consider what benefits the nature and circumstances of their case.[140]

The practical consequences of such principles could be quite marked. The order of a narrative of events could, in the words of Conrad of Hirsau, be either natural or artificial;[141] it could be simple or complex.[142] William of Malmesbury, for example, insists that his *Gesta Regum* will include only what is necessary and, as a consequence, states that he has abbreviated much of the material from which he is quoting; the prologue to his *Gesta Pontificum* accordingly identifies truth, but additionally brevity, as its aim.[143] William is also explicit on the subject of how he is combining the thematic order of what he is narrating with the chronological sequence of events. He points out, for instance, that it is not his intention to pick out individually the 'inextricable labyrinths' of King Alfred's labours, since to relate them year by year might cause some confusion to his readers.[144] Likewise, when he inserts the text of some letters which had been exchanged between the king of Mercia and the pope, he acknowledges that he will be interrupting the chronological order of events but argues that this

---

140 *Institutio Oratoria*, IV.2.83–4, pp. 95–7.
141 Conrad of Hirsau, *Dialogue on the Authors*, p. 45; cf. Hugh of St Victor, *Didascalicon*, trans. J. Taylor (New York, 1961), III.8, pp. 91–2; Bernardus Silvestris, *Commentary on the First Six Books of Virgil's Aeneid*, pref., pp. 3–4 (Lucan follows the natural order, Vergil the artificial); Geoffrey of Vinsauf, *Poetria Nova*, II.87–100, p. 19; Geoffrey of Vinsauf, *Documentum de Modo et Arte Dictandi et Versificandi*, trans. R. Parr, *Instruction in the Method and Art of Speaking and Versifying* (Milwaukee, 1968), pp. 39–40.
142 *Rationes Dictandi*, trans. J.J. Murphy, *The Principles of Letter Writing*, in J.J. Murphy, *Three Medieval Rhetorical Arts* (Berkeley, 1971), VII p. 18.
143 William of Malmesbury, *Gesta Regum Anglorum*, I.5, p. 23, I.82, p. 119; William of Malmesbury, *Gesta Pontificum Anglorum*, I.prol., p. 5.
144 *Gesta Regum Anglorum*, II.121, p. 181.

is still preferable to the alternative: 'I therefore think it right to append part of the king's letter and part of the pope's, although I may seem to be taking things out of their chronological order; I will do it, however, for this reason, that it is more difficult to weave together [*contexo*] a story once interrupted than to finish what one has begun'.[145] Such chronological selectivity can also be used to make a particular political point. Suger's *Deeds of Louis*, whilst ostensibly covering the entirety of the king's reign until his death in 1145, in fact stops its narrative short, in *c*.1130, at precisely the point at which Louis VI's *gesta* became, like those of his father Philip I, much less worthy of imitation.[146]

For speakers or writers to observe the fundamental rhetorical principle of suitability (*quid deceat*) in their texts means consistently saying or writing what is appropriate to the subject-matter they are discussing and to the people whose actions they are describing. However, this rule also governs what is suitable or fitting for the character both of the speaker or writer themselves and of the audience to whom the text or speech is delivered. Orators, according to Cicero, need to display enough wisdom to moderate what they are saying so that it is suitable (*aptum*) for time, place and person – this goes for what they are describing but it also applies to the audience to whom they are delivering their speech or text.[147] Quintilian makes the same point. As far as he is concerned, there are two guiding principles in rhetoric – what is fitting and what is advantageous (*quid deceat et quid expediat*) – and it is their combination (and on those very rare occasions when they conflict, what is fitting always outweighs what is expedient) which produces what is appropriate (*aptum*). Different circumstances require different responses and the sheer variety of possibilities that result effectively precludes the imposition of hard-and-fast

---

145 *Gesta Regum Anglorum*, I.87, p. 125; cf. Widukind, *Res Gestae Saxonicae*, II.28, p. 142: 'since causes are conjoined with causes, and events with events, in such a way that they would not be sufficiently discernible from their ordered expression, no one will blame me for changing round their chronology if I put later deeds before earlier ones'. See also Gerald of Wales, *Expugnatio Hibernica*, II.27, p. 205: 'if, for the sake of greater clarity [*evidentia*], I may here briefly anticipate some events which in terms of chronological order happened later...'.
146 Suger, *Gesta Hludowici*, XIII, p. 61 (see also page 167).
147 Cicero, *Orator*, XXI.71, 74, pp. 359–61.

rules.[148] For Cicero, therefore, speaking and writing 'appropriately' (*apte*) becomes an all-important principle to master, where what governs whether or not something is suitable is defined by the views to which the speaker or writer wishes to guide the audience and the circumstances in which they are doing so. As a result, rhetorical ornamentation is governed, not only by its objective and by *what* is being said, but also by *where* it is being said. Different styles are appropriate for different people and occasions, and the wisdom and eloquence of the rhetorician lie, accordingly, in accommodating each part of what they are saying to what is fitting, to what is appropriate, both for the case and for the occasion.[149] Ornaments of speech are thus many and varied but they will be of no benefit unless they are in harmony with either the circumstances in which an individual is speaking or the views towards which the speaker wants to guide a judge. This is the substance of Quintilian's appeal to circumstance (*affectio*),[150] and he quotes Cicero's *De Oratore* and *Orator* to this effect. One single type of speaking does not suit every case or audience or person or time: first and foremost, it is necessary for the orator to understand that all rhetorical ornament is based, not on its own condition, but on the condition of the thing to which it is applied; *where* something is said is just as important as *what* is being said.[151]

The consequences of such adaptation to circumstance for both the spoken and the written word are numerous. According to Quintilian, it is a fault to say something which runs counter to the will of a judge or of one's audience and, as a result, words should always be made appropriate to people's opinions and *mores*. Different forms and manners of speaking will therefore be required when speaking before different types of people – before the learned as opposed to the unlearned, for example, before rulers and judges rather than the populace. Both the time and the place of an address demand attention, be it in public or in private – each requires its own form and style of rhetoric.[152] It is for this

---

148 Quintilian, *Institutio Oratoria*, XI.1.8–10, p. 159.
149 Cicero, *Orator*, XXXV.123–5, pp. 397–9.
150 See page 233.
151 Quintilian, *Institutio Oratoria*, XI.1.1–7, 43–7, pp. 155–9, 179–81.
152 *Institutio Oratoria*, VIII.3.43, p. 235; *Rhetorica ad Herennium*, II.27.43, p. 135; cf. Macrobius, *Saturnalia*, VII.1.15–25, pp. 443–5.

reason that Quintilian reports Cicero's judgment that the worst stylistic fault is to speak in a way that runs counter to popular ways of speaking and the usage of common understanding (*communis sensus*).[153] Syllogisms, enthymemes and epicheiremes are fine, therefore, if a speaker or writer is conducting a minute and scrupulous inquiry into the truth amongst the learned (*docti*). The rhetorician, however, is, by definition, frequently speaking or writing for an audience of people who are not learned (*imperiti*) and who are certainly ignorant of subjects such as dialectic. As a result, unless rhetoricians attract the audience through pleasure, stir them by emotion, or compel them by force, they will simply be unable to uphold what is nonetheless just and true.[154] A knowledge of dialectic and logic may be essential for the orator to be able to define the properties of words, clarify ambiguities, discern perplexities and judge what is false, but not to the same degree of detail, concision and subtlety as would be appropriate in a disputation proper. The goal of the orator is to move and to delight, not just to instruct.[155]

Adherence to this principle of suitability means, in short, that the identity and character of the audience will condition what is said and, just as importantly, what is not said. Sensitivity to this particular 'context' is used to justify a wide range of changes in otherwise 'normal' rules of speaking and writing. This is clear, for example, in the case of prologues which are written for a hostile audience, where an *insinuatio* will be used rather than a *proemium*.[156] However, it is just as important in every other part of a speech or text, including the content of the arguments which are 'invented' or discovered. At the most basic level, the principle of suitability means that certain expectations on the part of the audience must be met, not least that of entertainment or pleasure. This demand is what accounts for the inclusion of the set-piece depictions of battles, which are such a feature, for example, of Rahewin's continuation of the *Deeds of Frederick Barbarossa*, as well

---

153 *Institutio Oratoria*, VIII.praef.25, p. 191, quoting Cicero, *De Oratore*, I.3.12, p. 11; cf. *De Oratore*, I.12.54, p. 41 (*hominum sensibus ac mentibus accommodata*), I.23.108, p. 77 (*ad vulgarem popularemque sensum accommodata*).
154 *Institutio Oratoria*, V.14.27–32, pp. 365–7.
155 *Institutio Oratoria*, XII.2.10–14, pp. 387–9.
156 See pages 170–1, 191–3.

as the set-piece speeches with which they are often preceded. More significantly, perhaps, such considerations also account for the inclusion of digressions. Thietmar of Merseburg frequently apologises for disturbing the order of events and justifies himself on the grounds, not only of utility,[157] but also relief: 'I cannot place in its correct order everything that ought to be treated within the context of this book; in what follows, therefore, I will not be embarrassed to add a few recollections. Indeed, I will rejoice in the change of pace much as the traveller who, because of its difficulty or perhaps from ignorance, leaves the course of the more direct road and sets out on some winding secondary path'.[158]

The digression or *excursus* was defined in rhetoric as an incidental narrative which is inserted into a speech or text in order to achieve any one of a number of objectives: to secure credence or credibility (*fides*); to attack an adversary; to draw a comparison; to effect a transition from one subject to another; to entertain or give pleasure to an audience in a way which is germane to the subject under discussion; or in order to amplify a subject (*amplificare, amplitudo*), that is, to deepen its effect by giving it greater weight and dignity and thereby enhance the principal subject under discussion. This particular type of narrative (*egressus, egressio*) can accordingly take the form of the praise of individuals or of places, the description of regions, or the exposition of deeds (*res gestae*) or fabled events (*res fabulosae*).[159] The most familiar forms of such digression, at least in works of medieval history, were the geographical description and ethnographic survey, for which there were both classical and late-antique precedents. Three of the most influential were Sallust's description of Africa within his *Jugurthine War*, Caesar's description of Gaul in his *Gallic*

---

157 Thietmar, *Chronicon*, II.23, p. 108.
158 *Chronicon*, IV.55, p. 191. For the comparable image of a river filling up a valley, flowing in whatever direction the contours take it, see Gregory the Great, *Moralia in Job*, trans. J. Bliss (Oxford, 1843–50), Ep.miss.II, pp. 6–7, quoted, for example, in the fourteenth century, by Robert of Basevorn, *Forma Praedicandi*, trans. L. Kruhl, *The Form of Preaching*, in J.J. Murphy (ed.), *Three Medieval Rhetorical Arts* (Berkeley, 1971), prol. p. 116, XLI, p. 186.
159 Cicero, *De Inventione*, I.19.27, p. 55; *Rhetorica ad Herennium*, I.8.12, p. 23; Quintilian, *Institutio Oratoria*, IV.3.12, p. 127; cf. Martianus Capella, *Marriage of Philology and Mercury*, V, pp. 207–8; Isidore of Seville, *Etymologiae*, ed. and trans. P.K. Marshall (Paris, 1983), II.21.36, p. 92.

War and Orosius' description of the world at the beginning of his *Seven Books of History Against the Pagans*;[160] the basic template for combining topography, ethnography and marvels, meanwhile, was Pliny the Elder's *Natural History*.[161] Medieval writers were quick to follow suit. Paul the Deacon, who had read Pliny,[162] punctuates what he calls 'the order of narrative'[163] with a series of digressions, not least when he explains the etymology of 'the Lombards' themselves (why the long beard?).[164] Bede's opening description of Britain in his *Ecclesiastical History* owes much to the beginning he found in Orosius.[165] Henry of Huntingdon, meanwhile, includes digressions on the four great roads of Britain and on the river Ouse, culminating (unsurprisingly) in a description of Huntingdon. He also produces an incidental narrative on the Fens and its churches, as well as a graphic description of Stonehenge, one of the four great marvels of Britain (the other three being the Peak District, Cheddar Gorge and the rain).[166] William FitzStephen opens his *Life* of Thomas Becket with a

---

160 Sallust, *Jugurthine War*, XVII–XIX, pp. 169–77; Caesar, *Gallic War*, trans. H.J. Edwards (Loeb, 1917), I.1–2, pp. 3–5, IV.1–2, pp. 181–3, VI.11–28, pp. 333–55; Orosius, *Seven Books of History Against the Pagans*, trans. R.J. Deferrari (Washington, DC, 1964), I.2–3, pp. 7–21.
161 Pliny the Elder, *Natural History*, trans. H. Rackham, W.H.S. Jones and D.E. Eichholz (Loeb, 1938–63), VI.20–VII.2, pp. 377–527; cf. Solinus, *Collectanea Rerum Memorabilium*, ed. T.E. Mommsen (Berlin, 1895); Martianus Capella, *Marriage of Philology and Mercury*, VI, pp. 231–62. For Pliny the Younger's views on the writing of history, see Pliny the Younger, *Letters*, trans. W. Melmoth, rev. W.M.L. Hutchinson (Loeb, 1915), Ep.V.8, pp. 399–405 (see page 501), VII.33, pp. 85–9.
162 Paul the Deacon, *History of the Lombards*, trans. W.D. Foulke, rev. E. Peters (Philadelphia, 2003), I.2, p. 3, II.14–24, pp. 71–9.
163 *History of the Lombards*, I.6, p. 11, I.26, p. 49, II.24, p. 79, IV.37, p. 187.
164 *History of the Lombards*, I.8, p. 16.
165 Bede, *Historia Ecclesiastica Gentis Anglorum*, trans. B. Colgrave, rev. J. McClure and R. Collins (Oxford, 1994), I.1, pp. 9–12; cf. Gildas, *De Excidio Britanniae*, trans. M. Winterbottom, *The Ruin of Britain* (Chichester, 1978), III, pp. 16–17; Nennius, *Historia Brittonum*, ed. and trans. J. Morris (London, 1980), p. 18; Richer, *Historiae*, ed. and trans. R. Latouche (Paris, 1930–37), I.1–2, pp. 6–8; William of Jumièges, *Gesta Normannorum Ducum*, I.2, pp. 11–13, quoting Dudo of St Quentin, *History of the Normans*, trans. E. Christiansen (Woodbridge, 1998), I.1–2, pp. 15–16; Geoffrey of Monmouth, *Historia Regum Britanniae*, p. 6; Ralph de Diceto, *Abbreviationes Chronicorum*, ed. W. Stubbs (London, 1876), p. 3.
166 Henry of Huntingdon, *Historia Anglorum*, I.7, pp. 23–5, VI.6, p. 349. Ralph de Diceto omits the rain but extends Henry's list of *mirabilia* to a total of thirty-five in his *Abbreviationes Chronicorum*, pp. 11–15; cf. Nennius, *Historia Brittonum*, p. 40.

description of the *res publica* of London, for which he invokes both Plato and Sallust as his justification.[167] Thietmar of Merseburg describes the Liutizi and the Poles;[168] Adam of Bremen describes the lands and peoples of the North;[169] Ralph de Diceto includes detailed descriptions of Angers and Aquitaine,[170] Joinville of the Mongols and the river Nile.[171] For Ranulf Higden, descriptions of place (*descriptiones locorum*) formed, accordingly, the very first item on his list of eight components for the understanding of history.[172]

If digressions could be introduced, in Henry of Huntingdon's words, for the sake of pleasure and relief (*causa recreandi*),[173]

---

167 William FitzStephen, *Vita Sancti Thomae*, trans. H.E. Butler, *Description of London*, in F.M. Stenton, *Norman London: An Essay* (London, 1934), prol. pp. 25–35.
168 Thietmar, *Chronicon*, VI.23–25, pp. 252–4, VIII.2–3, pp. 361–3.
169 Adam of Bremen, *History of the Archbishops of Hamburg–Bremen*, trans. F.J. Tschan, rev. T. Reuter (New York, 2002), I.47, pp. 8–11, IV, pp. 186–223.
170 Ralph de Diceto, *Imagines Historiarum*, pp. 291–4; cf. A. Gransden, 'Realistic Observation in Twelfth-Century England', *Speculum*, 47 (1972), pp. 29–51; reprinted in A. Gransden, *Legends, Traditions and History in Medieval England* (London, 1992), pp. 191–4; P. Zanna, '*Descriptiones Urbium* and Elegy in Latin and Vernaculars in the Early Middle Ages', *Studi Medievali*, 32 (1991), pp. 523–96.
171 Joinville, *Life of Saint Louis*, pp. 211–13, 283–8.
172 Ranulf Higden, *Polychronicon*, ed. C. Babington and J.R. Lumby (London, 1865), I.prol.4, pp. 30–40. The other seven were: *status rerum* (the world before Christ and after Christ); *distinctiones temporum* (the times before the written law, under the written law, and under grace); *successiones regiminum* (the four world empires – Assyria, Persia, Macedonia and Rome); *variationes rituum* (five types of ritual observance, of which the fourth was Christianity, the fifth Islam); *decursiones aetatum* (Augustine's six ages); *qualitates actionum* (seven types of people whose actions are more often commemorated in histories – rulers, soldiers, judges, bishops, political officials, heads of household, and monks – together with their corresponding actions – construction of towns, defeat of enemies, establishment of laws, correction of criminals, organisation of public matters, arrangement of households, acquisition of merited salvation, and reward of the good and punishment of the wicked); *varias ... supputationes annorum* (eight ways in which years can be calculated, of which the eighth is the Christian *anno domini*).
173 Henry of Huntingdon, *Historia Anglorum*, V.19, p. 315; cf. Macrobius, *Saturnalia*, V.16.1, p. 354: 'a recital of facts and names is heavy-going and so, after such recitals, both Homer and Vergil introduce into their catalogues a story told in more pleasing verse in order to revive the spirits of the reader'. See also Widukind, *Res Gestae Saxonicae*, pref., p. 16 'in order that by reading this you might entertain your spirit, relieve your cares and spend your leisure well' (*ut in ea legendo animum oblectes, curas releves, pulchro otio vaces*); Liutprand, *Antapodosis*, I.1, pp. 31–2; Eadmer, *Historia Novorum in Anglia*, II.110, p. 114; John of Salisbury, *Policraticus*, trans. Pike, prol., p. 7; cf. Walter Map, *De Nugis Curialium*, ed. and trans. M.L.R. James, rev. C.N.L. Brooke and R.A.B. Mynors (Oxford, 1983), III.

then they could also be used to make a serious philosophical, moral or political point. Otto of Freising includes digressions on the nature of God, on Hungary (Pannonia) and on the Second Crusade, as well as on Gilbert of Poitiers and Abelard.[174] William of Malmesbury's digression on the First Crusade, a narrative which occupies more than half of book IV of his *Gesta Regum*, was introduced both for the sake of pleasure and to serve as a stimulus to virtue.[175] Suger's *Deeds of Louis* includes a digression on the dispute between the pope and the emperor Henry V over the issue of investiture.[176] The more significant the subject-matter, it was argued, the more amplification (*amplificatio*) is required; the more important the issue, the greater the need for ornamentation.[177] In these circumstances, digression was much more than 'just' a literary effect – it became a technique or strategy which was designed to secure approval and support from one's audience. In such situations, digressions were understood as one further example of a type of argument which could give credence to something that was in doubt. Once more, however, the determining factor was provided by the nature and character of the audience. Quintilian makes the point, for example, that it is a very easy task to persuade a group of virtuous people (*honesti*) to pursue a course of action that is morally worthy (*honestum*). It is a much more difficult goal to persuade an audience made up of people who are morally reprehensible. In trying to maintain such people on the correct path, a speaker must be wary of seeming to condemn their existing course of life, since they will remain unmoved by a simple discourse on virtue. For this sort of audience, therefore, a speaker should resort to the use of praise, to appeals to popular opinion

---

prol., p. 211; Gervase of Tilbury, *Otia Imperialia*, pref. pp. 13–15, I.1, p. 19, I.20 p.109, III.pref., pp. 559, 563, III.42, p. 641, III.81, p. 709, III.84, p. 717. For the utility of *recreatio*, see G. Olson, *Literature as Recreation in the Later Middle Ages* (Ithaca, 1982).

174 Otto of Freising, *Deeds of Frederick*, I.32, pp. 65–7, II.12–14, pp. 125–9; cf. J.O. Ward, 'Some Principles of Rhetorical Historiography in the Twelfth Century', in E. Breisach (ed.), *Classical Rhetoric and Medieval Historiography* (Kalamazoo, 1985), pp. 111–18.

175 William of Malmesbury, *Gesta Regum Anglorum*, IV.prol., p. 543; cf.II.173, p. 295; Henry of Huntingdon, *Historia Anglorum*, VII.5, p. 423.

176 Suger, *Gesta Hludowici*, X, pp. 46–54.

177 Quintilian, *Institutio Oratoria*, V.14.34, p. 369; cf. Cicero, *Orator*, XXIX.102, p. 381.

(*vulgi opinio*) and, failing that, to a demonstration that it will be to the audience's advantage to follow a recommended course of action, or rather to a demonstration of the disasters which will result from their non-compliance. Not only are fickle minds moved more by terror, Quintilian observes, but it remains a moot point whether most people are not, in fact, influenced more by fear of evil things than by hope for the good, in that they find it easier to understand wickedness than what is morally good. Fear, indeed, may prove the only means of constraining those people who cannot be led to better things by means of reason. This is why a knowledge of evil is necessary – in order for a speaker to be in a better position to defend what is right.[178]

Digressions are particularly important in view of the fact that, whereas dialectic might be fine for people of learning, it is necessary to deploy pleasure, compulsion and emotion in order to move an audience of the less learned. This is a consideration which justifies, for example, the inclusion of poetic fables (*poetici fabulae*) – although they will have less force as proof, such made-up fables (*fictae fabulae*) can be particularly useful if a speaker wants to guide the minds of the unlearned. If an audience is composed of the unlearned or ignorant (*rustici, imperiti*), therefore, a speaker will find it useful to include material such as the fables (*fabellae*) of Aesop or Hesiod, since an unlearned audience will listen with greater readiness to what is made up (*ficta*) and, captured by its pleasing nature, will then readily give their agreement to those things by which they are pleased. An unlearned audience, in short, will need to be both moved and led in ways that an audience of the wise will not. The wise simply need the subject-matter to be set out with proofs; the populace, on the other hand, will require every method which is capable of producing credence or belief, since the minds of the unlearned (*imperiti*) need to be moved and led. As a result, since judges – because they are either the people themselves or drawn from the people – are often uneducated (*indocti*) and sometimes *rustici*, Quintilian concludes that it is necessary for a speaker or writer to draw on every technique which will secure the intended goal of credibility.[179]

---

178 *Institutio Oratoria*, III.8.38–43, pp. 499–501, XII.7.2, p. 421; cf. Cicero, *De Oratore*, I.58.247, p. 181.
179 *Institutio Oratoria*, V.11.17–21, pp. 281–3, XII.10.52–3, pp. 479–81.

Given that the rhetorician's discovery of suitable arguments is determined by the nature of their audience as much as by the nature of their subject-matter, the identification of that audience naturally becomes a critical factor in understanding how, and why, a particular speech or text was composed in the way in which it was. Medieval historiography is, by extension, no exception. For many, perhaps most, works of medieval history, such a task remains a speculative venture, particularly for those texts which appear to have changed their audience in the course of composition – part of the difficulty with Suger's *Deeds of Louis VI*, for example, stems from the fact that it may have originated as *gesta* composed for a court audience and was only later combined with commemorative liturgical material following Louis VI's death and as a defence of the king's actions addressed to the bishop of Soissons.[180] Sometimes, however, an author makes the identity of their audience quite clear. Henry of Huntingdon, for instance, may have been writing in Latin but he states explicitly that he is writing for *minus docti*, that is, for the less well-educated, and, as a result, will use simple language rather than engage in debate by means of rhetoric or handle his subject-matter as if it were philosophy.[181] So too does William of Malmesbury: 'I will use daily and light language so that no one is caused by the obscurity of words to be rejected from knowing things'.[182] On other occasions, the indications are more oblique. Bede, for example, was thoroughly familiar with the notion that a narrative might have to reflect popular custom (*mos vulgi*) and the opinions of his audience.[183] A similar sensitivity lies behind the apparent contrast between Bede's *Ecclesiastical History* and his *Letter to Egbert*, the former a work of public edification written for, or at least dedicated to, the king of Northumbria, the latter a castigation of abuses within the Church which was addressed to the archbishop of York. It has always been an attractive means of bringing these two texts

---

180 L. Grant, *Abbot Suger of St-Denis: Church and State in Early Twelfth-Century France* (Harlow, 1998), pp. 38–42; see also Cusimano and Moorhead's introduction to their translation of Suger's *Gesta Hludowici*, pp. 5–8.
181 Henry of Huntingdon, *Historia Anglorum*, VIII (*De Contemptu Mundi*), p. 585.
182 William of Malmesbury, *Gesta Regum Anglorum*, IV.352, p. 615; cf. Widukind, *Res Gestae Saxonicae*, I.praef., p. 15; Eadmer, *Life of Anselm*, pref., p. 1.
183 See pages 289–90.

together to read the positive presentation of Aidan and Cuthbert in the *Ecclesiastical History* as a 'foil' to the negative depiction of abuses listed in the *Letter to Egbert*. Like Gregory of Tours, who declined to record a particular individual's evil deeds because he did not wish to appear as a detractor of his fellow churchman,[184] Bede wrote that it was wrong publicly to criticise even an evil priest.[185] Aidan and Cuthbert therefore do precisely what the contemporary priesthood stood accused of not doing – they embark on preaching tours and reject gift-giving and hospitality.[186] It is the nature of Bede's audience, in other words, which conditions the way in which he chooses to write his letter and his history.

One of the more striking attempts to shape historical material to suit the demands of different styles and audiences was provided by Gerald of Wales' descriptions of Wales and Ireland. Gerald studied in the schools of Paris for twelve years in the 1160s and 1170s, and his learning is not to be underestimated. Nor is his professed goal of making what he was writing embody Horace's combination of pleasure and utility,[187] and for an audience which could appreciate a text full of tropes and figures of speech but also one which enjoyed 'sarcasm, libel, word-play, allusions, ambiguity and equivocal statements'.[188] In placing history and poetry side by side, Gerald compares himself to a painter with his colours – successor to the Zeuxis described in *De Inventione* and adorning his subject with the 'flowers' of rhetoric.[189] Not that this translated into a completely free licence – in giving a mixed physical description of Henry II, for example, Gerald points out that, whilst he 'cannot allow such a splendid figure ... to pass from men's recollections in transitory fashion', he must also be permitted to set out the

---

184 Gregory of Tours, *Histories*, trans. L. Thorpe, *The History of the Franks* (Harmondsworth, 1974), V.5, p. 262.
185 Cf. Thietmar, *Chronicon*, VI.41, p. 266.
186 A. Thacker, 'Bede's Ideal of Reform', in P. Wormald, D. Bullough and R. Collins (eds), *Ideal and Reality in Frankish and Anglo-Saxon Society* (Oxford, 1983), pp. 130–53.
187 Gerald of Wales, *Topographia Hibernica*, trans. J.J. O'Meara, *The History and Topography of Ireland* (Harmondsworth, 1982), III.122, p. 125; cf. Gerald of Wales, *Descriptio Cambriae*, pref., p. 213, I.12, p. 241; Gerald of Wales, *Expugnatio Hibernica*, III.prol., p. 255.
188 *Descriptio Cambriae*, I.12, p. 242.
189 *Descriptio Cambriae*, pref., p. 212; cf. II.pref., p. 255; see also Gerald of Wales, *De Eruditione Principum*, II.29, p. 48.

truth, 'for, if it goes beyond the truth, all history not only loses its authority but also ceases to deserve the name history'. 'The painter who sets out to imitate nature by his art', Gerald explains, 'loses his reputation as a painter if he coyly passes over the less becoming features of his subject whilst carefully dwelling on those that suit his purpose'.[190] At the same time, however, Gerald also readily acknowledges that he still has to attract the attention of his audience and to hold it.[191] As was the case in his *Topography of Ireland*, a particular combination of prophecy, novelty and marvels would be carefully adapted to the expectations of his audience: 'human nature is such that only what is unusual and infrequent excites wonder or is regarded of value'.[192]

Gerald prefaces his *Description of Wales* with a definition of history which is ascribed to Seneca but clearly derived from Cicero's *De Oratore*: 'the recording of past events, the testimony of the ages, the light of truth, a living memory, a guide for conduct, and a reminder of what happened long ago'.[193] In identifying his work as history, Gerald also spells out the successive stages by which he had 'rescued from oblivion some of the remarkable events of our own times'.[194] The process he describes is shot through with an understanding of rhetoric. 'The work that is necessary', he writes, 'if one is to find out what really happened is not at all easy. Even when one has discovered the truth in all its detail, there still remains the task of ordering one's facts and this is difficult too. To maintain a correct balance from beginning to end and, indeed, throughout the whole course of one's narrative, and to exclude all irrelevant material, is not easy. Then there is the problem of the choice of words and expressions, and of how to perfect one's style if one wants to write well; it is one thing to set out the course of events in proper sequence but you still have the difficult problem of deciding what words to use and how best

---

190 *Expugnatio Hibernica*, I.46, p. 125.
191 *Itinerarium Cambriae*, pref., p. 66.
192 *Topographia Hibernica*, I.11, p. 42; cf. pages 192–3.
193 *Descriptio Cambriae*, pref., p. 217; cf. Gerald of Wales, Letter 3, to William de Montibus, Chancellor of Lincoln, ed. R.B.C. Huygens, trans. B. Dawson, in Y. Lefèvre and R.B.C. Huygens (eds), *Speculum Duorum or a Mirror of Two Men* (Cardiff, 1974), pp. 170–1; Gerald of Wales, *Expugnatio Hibernica*, prol., p. 11; Cicero, *De Oratore*, II.9.35–6, pp. 223–5 (see page 242).
194 *Descriptio Cambriae*, pref., p. 216.

to express what you want to say'. Writing, Gerald concludes, 'is a demanding task: first you decide what to leave out, and then you have to polish what you put in'.[195]

What follows in the *Description of Wales* is, at first sight, an extended digression modelled on Pliny the Elder's *Natural History*. Like the 'marvels of the West' contained in the *Topography of Ireland*, this is a history of the position and features of the land, its living creatures and the nature and customs of its peoples.[196] At the beginning of the *Description*, however, Gerald also invokes the model of Caesar's *Gallic War* – like Gaul, Wales is divided into three parts.[197] Like Caesar, in fact, Gerald has more than just topography and ethnography in mind. As the three concluding chapters make clear, his agenda is also explicitly political – how Wales can best be conquered and then governed.[198] The work of history with which Gerald explicitly aligns his own *Description* is accordingly Gildas' *On the Ruin of Britain* – this is the appropriate model he has imitated. 'For the subject I am now treating', Gerald writes, 'I have often had to consult Gildas. Of all the British writers, he seems to me to be the only one worth imitating'. The reason for Gerald's preference is spelled out. Gildas put in writing the things which he himself saw and knew but, instead of merely describing the ruin of his people, he deplored it and wrote a true, rather than ornate, history.[199] According to Gerald's account, Gildas, who revered the truth as every historian must, was not prepared to gloss over the weakness of his own people.[200] This did not mean that Gerald would go about the same task in exactly the same way: 'I only wish I could emulate his life and ways, but at least I can imitate what he tried to do, with more wisdom than eloquence, more in my soul than by my pen, more in my zeal than by my style, more in my life than by my words'.[201]

---

195 *Descriptio Cambriae*, pref., p. 216; cf.I.12, p. 242; *Expugnatio Hibernica*, prol., pp. 9–11.
196 *Topographia Hibernica*, pref., p. 31, I.27–II.33, pp. 54–7. For Manuel Comnenus, see Gerald of Wales, *Descriptio Cambriae*, I.8, p. 234.
197 *Descriptio Cambriae*, I.2, p. 221; cf. Ralph de Diceto, *Abbreviationes Chronicorum*, p. 24.
198 Cf. *Expugnatio Hibernica*, II.38–39, pp. 245–53.
199 *Descriptio Cambriae*, pref., p. 214.
200 *Descriptio Cambriae*, II.2, p. 257.
201 *Descriptio Cambriae*, pref., p. 214.

Gerald's ecclesiastical agenda, however, retains its underlying icy clarity. As in his *Itinerarium Cambriae*, Gerald will describe the failed leadership of a Church that has been corrupted by wealth and is under pressure from all sides. The result is a condemnation, both of temporal rule and of monastic observance, which not only echoes the failure of political and ecclesiastical leadership described by Gildas but also invites the same divine chastisement from the Angles. It was the same punishment that had recently been visited upon the Irish: 'read the book of Kings, read the prophets, go through the entire Old Testament, consider the familiar examples from our own times and our own country. You will never find that any race has ever been conquered except when their sins demanded this as a punishment'.[202]

Classical manuals of rhetoric provided medieval writers with a wide range of criteria through which to discover or 'invent' the arguments that they would need to deploy in the composition of their works. In assembling intrinsic arguments, writers of history found a language of causation (antecedent, secondary and efficient causes, intended and unintended causes, known and unknown causes, the conjunction of causes, fortune, chance, fate and providence), whilst, for their extrinsic argumentation, they found a range of different types of testimony and of varying degrees of reliability (eyewitnesses, legal records, public opinion, rumour and maxims). In classifying the different places or 'topics' where these arguments could be found, especially generic arguments or 'commonplaces', the single most important criterion by which a writer should judge which arguments should be selected and arranged was what was suitable or appropriate (*aptum*), both for a particular subject and for a particular audience. The discovery or invention of arguments accordingly encompassed the entire spectrum of material – from logical ratiocination through to histories, poetic fable, common opinion and rumour – depending on what was judged to be 'appropriate', both to the subject-matter of the case and to the audience before whom it was being presented. What is said or written must always be accommodated to the opinions and *mores* of people, especially if the audience is less learned – in the case of the latter, in fact, it may prove particularly

---

202 *Expugnatio Hibernica*, II.34, p. 233; cf.I.18, pp. 69–71.

helpful to cite what is fabulous or made up (*ficta*). The ultimate goal of such adaptation is that the arguments put forward should produce belief or credence (*fides*). Indeed, if it is the combination of *argumentum* and *aptum* which enables speakers or writers to construct what is probable or convincing (*probabilis*) in their work as a whole, then it is this last idea – of credibility, plausibility or verisimilitude – which provides the key to understanding that particular part of a text or speech which was the most germane to the writing of history, namely the narrative or *narratio*.

Narrative

Narrative is defined by both Cicero and the *Rhetorica ad Herennium* as 'the exposition of things which have been done or as if they have been done' (*narratio est rerum gestarum aut ut gestarum expositio*).[203] It comes in three forms. First, there is a narrative of the issue under discussion, that is, the exposition of the subject of controversy and of all the reasons why such differing views might exist. According to the *Rhetorica ad Herennium*, this type of narrative takes the form of expounding what has been done so that everything is turned to the advantage (*utilitas*) of the speaker or writer. Second, there is an incidental narrative, which takes the form of a digression or *excursus*. Third, there is a narrative which is not connected to any particular legal or political case but which is being written or delivered for the sake of entertainment and which is also considered to provide useful training in the principles of rhetoric, in that it enables individuals to engage in the first two types of narrative more effectively.[204]

Narrative may come in three forms but each of them, in turn, falls into two general types, namely narrative which is primarily concerned with individual people and narrative which is concerned with events.[205] There are also narratives of place, time and causation, but these can all be subsumed within this basic division

---

203 Cicero, *De Inventione*, I.19.27, p. 55, as cited, for example, by Vincent of Beauvais, *Speculum Historiale*, VI.21, p. 181; cf. *Rhetorica ad Herennium*, I.3.4, p. 9: *narratio est rerum gestarum aut proinde ut gestarum expositio*.
204 *De Inventione*, I.19.27, p. 55; *Rhetorica ad Herennium*, I.8.12, p. 23; cf. Quintilian, *Institutio Oratoria*, IV.3.12, p. 127.
205 *De Inventione*, I.19.27, p. 55; *Rhetorica ad Herennium*, I.8.13, p. 23.

between *narratio in personis* and *narratio in negotiis*. 'Narrative of persons' comprises the deeds of individuals but also their words and the motivation provided by their character. It should exhibit liveliness of style, it should include people with contrasting types of character and it should record the diversity of events which is produced by changeability of fortune, unexpected disaster, sudden joy and pleasing outcomes.[206] 'Narrative of events', meanwhile, is divided into three basic categories of material – history, argument and fable.[207] The term 'history' (*historia*) is given, in this particular context, to a narrative of things which have been done in the past but at some remove from the remembrance of the present age. This type of narrative, the exposition of what has been done (*expositio rei gestae*), should be the starting-point for rhetoricians, according to Quintilian, because the truer something is, the stronger (more forceful) it will be. The term 'argument' (*argumentum*), meanwhile, denotes a narrative of events which have been shaped or 'made up' (*ficta res*) but which nevertheless could have happened. This type of material is characteristic of the narrative which is found in comedies, in the sense that what is made up (*fingere*) is false (*falsa*) but similar to the truth (*vero simile*). Lastly, there is what is termed 'fable' (*fabula*), that is, a narrative of events which neither happened nor could have happened. This type of material is characteristic of the narrative which occurs in tragedies and in verse (*carmina*), in the sense that it is removed, not only from truth, but also from the form of the truth. This last category of narrative is accordingly what Quintilian calls 'poetic' (*poetica*) and is primarily the responsibility of the grammarian.[208]

---

206   *Rhetorica ad Herennium*, I.8.13, p. 25.
207   Cicero, *De Inventione*, I.19.27, pp. 55–7; *Rhetorica ad Herennium*, I.8.13, pp. 23–5; Quintilian, *Institutio Oratoria*, II.4.2, p. 225; cf. Isidore of Seville, *Etymologiae*, trans. S.A. Barney, W.J. Lewis, J.A. Beach and O. Berghof (Cambridge, 2006), I.44.5, p. 67 (see page 123); John of Salisbury, *Metalogicon*, I.24, p. 66; John of Garland, *Parisiana Poetria*, ed. and trans. T. Lawler (New Haven, 1974), V.315–32, p. 101; Vincent of Beauvais, *Speculum Doctrinale*, III.109, col. 287, III.127, col. 297.
208   Quintilian, *Institutio Oratoria*, II.4.2, p. 225. For fable, see Marie de France, *Fables*, ed. and trans. H. Spiegel (Toronto, 1994); Odo of Cheriton, *Fables*, trans. J.C. Jacobs (New York, 1985). Cf. Isidore, *Etymologiae*, trans. S.A. Barney, *et al.*, I.40.1–7, pp. 60–7; Priscian, *Praeexercitamina*, I, pp. 52–3; Conrad of Hirsau, *Dialogue on the Authors*, pp. 44, 47; Huguccio of Pisa, *Derivationes*, ed. E. Cecchini, *et al.* (Florence, 2004), p. 449.

This broad classificatory scheme is found across the board in classical manuals of rhetoric – in Cicero, in Quintilian and in the *Rhetorica ad Herennium* – and it came to underpin most medieval analyses of the nature of narrative.[209] Its influence on the way in which history was written (and, by extension, on the way in which it was taught, read and understood) was similarly far-reaching. In whatever form or type a narrative appears, whether it is expository, digressive or composed for the sake of training and entertainment, whether it concerns people or events, and whether it is historical, argumentative or poetic, this narrative will always need to possess three fundamental qualities. These are what Quintilian called the three 'virtues' of narrative, namely that it should be brief (*brevis*), open (*aperta, dilucida, lucida, perspicua*) and probable, credible or verisimilar (*probabilis, credibilis, verisimilis*). These three qualities are also important in other parts of the speech or text (in the sense that everything should always be said moderately, clearly and credibly) but, in the eyes of both Cicero and Quintilian, these virtues are particularly important in the narrative.[210]

Brevity is a means of making an audience remember a narrative of events and, as such, is closely tied to the nature of memory. A narrative will be brief if it begins and ends where it is necessary to begin and end, as opposed to being taken back to events in the remotest past or taken forward beyond what is necessary, or indeed allowed to stray sideways into other events. A narrative will also be brief if each thing is said once rather than repeatedly, beginning again each time it has been stopped. It will be brief, moreover, if it states the essence of what happened (*summa, summatim*) without stating all the details of how it happened,

---

209 For the importance of this tripartite division, and for the flexibility and permeability of its three categories, see P. Mehtonen, *Old Concepts and New Poetics: Historia, Argumentum and Fabula in the Twelfth- and Thirteenth-Century Latin Poetics of Fiction* (Helsinki, 1996). For the range and complexity of the genres which narrative could comprise, see T. Davenport, *Medieval Narrative: An Introduction* (Oxford, 2004). Cf. D. Kelly, 'Theory of Composition in Medieval Narrative Poetry and Geoffrey of Vinsauf's *Poetria Nova*', *Mediaeval Studies*, 31 (1969), pp. 117–48.
210 Quintilian, *Institutio Oratoria*, IV.2.31-5, 61, pp. 67–9, 83; Cicero, *De Inventione*, I.20.28, p. 57; *De Oratore*, II.80.326-9, pp. 445-7; *Topica*, XXVI.97, pp. 457–9. Cf. Paschasius Radbertus, *Vita Adalhardi*, LXIII, p. 63 (see page 197); Ralph de Diceto, *Abbreviationes Chronicorum*, p. 19; Vincent of Beauvais, *Speculum Historiale*, VI.21, p. 181.

if what is *not* said can nonetheless be understood from what *is* said, and if what hinders (or simply does not help) the truth is omitted. Indeed, according to Quintilian, everything should be omitted which does not contribute either to the understanding (*cognitio*) or to the advantage (*utilitas*) of the case.[211] This pairing of comprehension with advantage is important. Saying a multitude of things with brevity amounts to being prolix if many of those things are themselves simply unnecessary details; conversely, obscurity can result from excessive abridgement. It is therefore better, on balance, to say a little more than what is necessary than a little less, because it is dangerous to omit what is necessary and only tiresome to include what is superfluous. However attractive the brevity of a narrative such as Sallust's, in other words, a learned reader at leisure represents a different audience than an unlearned judge brought in from the country.[212]

A similar list of specifications governs the second virtue of narrative, namely openness. Lucidity or perspicacity is, first and foremost, a means of making an audience understand what is being said. A narrative will be 'open' or clear if the deeds in

---

211 Cf. Vergil, *Aeneid*, I.341–2, p. 265: 'long would be the tale of injury, long its winding course, but I will follow the main points of what happened' (*longa est iniuria, longae ambages; sed summa sequar fastigia rerum*). Compare William of Malmesbury, *Gesta Regum Anglorum*, III.prol., p. 425; cf. Otto of Freising, *Chronicle*, trans. C.C. Mierow, *The Two Cities: A Chronicle of Universal History* (New York, 1928; reprinted 2000), Ep.ded., p. 90.

212 Cicero, *De Inventione*, I.20.28, pp. 57–9; *Rhetorica ad Herennium*, I.9.14, pp. 25–7; Quintilian, *Institutio Oratoria*, IV.2.40–45, pp. 73–5. Cf. E.R. Curtius, *European Literature and the Latin Middle Ages* (London, 1953), pp. 487–94; G. Simon, 'Untersuchungen zur Topik der Widmungsbriefe mittelalterlicher Geschichtsschreiber bis zum Ende des 12. Jahrhunderts', *Archiv für Diplomatik*, 5–6 (1959–60), pp. 82–7. For obscure brevity, see, for example, Ralph de Diceto, *Abbreviationes Chronicorum*, p. 34; Petrarch, *De Viris Illustribus*, ed. and trans. B.G. Kohl, 'Petrarch's Prefaces to *De Viris Illustribus*', *History and Theory*, 13 (1974), pref., p. 143. For Sallustian brevity distinguished from Ciceronian abundance, see Macrobius, *Saturnalia*, V.1.7, p. 283. Cf. Wipo, *Deeds of Conrad* trans. T.E. Mommsen and K.F. Morrison (New York, 1962; rev. edn 2000), XXXIX, p. 98: 'We have written briefly.... If we have passed over anything and left it entirely untouched, let it be believed that we had not heard of it. If, however, something has been said in a more condensed fashion than the greatness of the matters would warrant, we will aver truthfully that this has been done for the convenience [*commoditas*] of the reader'; Eadmer, *Life of Anselm*, I.35, p. 62; Suger, *Gesta Hludowici*, XXX, p. 138: 'a brief narrative will show what he did but not how he did it' (*brevi narratione memorare non quomodo sed quid fecerit significantes proposuimus*).

question are set out one after another in their chronological order, that is, if the narrative observes the actual or probable sequence so that the events are narrated in the way in which they were done or could have been done. Otherwise, the precepts for openness follow those for brevity. A narrative should not be jumbled up, contorted or novel; it should not go too far backwards nor too far forwards; it should not switch to another subject; it should not omit anything pertinent but should set out facts, persons, time, place and cause; it should use a style and a language which are not rarefied or unusual but appropriate and meaningful; and it should be delivered in a way which facilitates comprehension (that is, by the speaker staying still, lightly moving the right hand, and expressing the emotion appropriate to each subject).[213]

A narrative, finally, will be plausible or probable if it follows the guidelines which establish belief or credence (*fides*). Credibility is produced by a number of factors: when the narrative contains things which usually appear to be true and which are in accordance with Nature; when actions and words are described which are appropriate to the standing and character of the individuals who perform and deliver them; when the causes and reasons for their actions are set out; when ability, motive and opportunity are established for the individuals concerned; and when the time and place are appropriate for the events which are being narrated.[214] A close connection is made here between the virtue of credibility and the nature of *argumentum*.[215] As Boethius puts it, 'an argument is believable or probable if it seems true to everyone or to most people or to the wise (and, of the wise, either to all of them or to most of them or to those most famous and distinguished) or to an expert in a particular field or, finally, if it seems true to one's audience or judge'.[216] And yet, as Boethius concludes, 'in this, the truth or falsity of the argument makes no difference if only it has the appearance of truth'.[217] Sometimes a narrative will

---

213 Cicero, *De Inventione*, I.20.29, pp. 59–61; *Rhetorica ad Herennium*, I.9.15, p. 27; Quintilian, *Institutio Oratoria*, IV.2.36–9, pp. 69–71 (see also pages 22–3).
214 Cicero, *De Inventione*, I.21.29, p. 61; *Rhetorica ad Herennium*, I.9.16, p. 29; Quintilian, *Institutio Oratoria*, IV.2.52–60, pp. 79–83.
215 See page 267.
216 See page 285.
217 Boethius, *De Topicis Differentiis*, I, p. 39; cf. Aristotle, *Topica*, I.1.100b21–3, p. 167.

need to be strengthened by briefly including arguments which will be developed at greater length in the proof itself (that is, in the *confirmatio* or *probatio*, the fourth part of a speech or text),[218] and which are drawn from a consideration of person, cause, place, time, instrument and opportunity. This proof contains all the topics or arguments through whose persuasiveness a case is given credibility, authority and a firm basis.[219] No other part of a speech or text follows on as closely from its predecessor as does the proof from the narrative. Defined in these terms, whereas proof is confirmation congruent with what has been narrated, the narrative is 'proof put forward in continuous form' (*narratio est probationis continua propositio*).[220] An audience can be made to believe a narrative of events, in other words, if seeds of the proof are scattered throughout the narrative and people are led to expect what follows next. An audience's belief in the narrative will also be secured through the presentation of what is circumstantially probable. This does not mean the necessary proofs of dialectic. Far from it. According to Cicero, it can be argued that the entire activity of the orator concerns opinions (*opiniones*) rather than knowledge (*scientia*).[221] Rhetoric has to be accommodated to the ears of the multitude in order to charm people's minds, in order to urge them to do something, or in order to prove things by weighing them (to use Cicero's own image), not in the scales of a goldsmith, but according to common scales (*non artificis statera sed populari quadam trutina*).[222] What this means in practice is that, once again, the speaker is able to deploy a wide range of arguments, extending all the way from enthymemes to fables.[223]

In order to provide a narrative with the requisite quality of probability or credibility, a speaker or writer needs to appeal to three basic categories – the natural (*natura*), the usual (*mos*) and the anticipated (*opinio*). Plausibility will result, in other words, if the subject of the narrative conforms to nature (that is, if it is in accordance with the nature of the people who did the deeds and

---

218 See page 265.
219 Cicero, *De Inventione*, I.24.34, p. 69; Cicero, *Topica*, XXVI.98, p. 459.
220 Quintilian, *Institutio Oratoria*, IV.2.55, p. 81, IV.2.79, p. 93, IV.3.5, p. 125.
221 Cicero, *De Oratore*, II.7.30, p. 219.
222 *De Oratore*, II.38.159, p. 313.
223 See page 309.

the place where they did them), to popular custom (*mos vulgi*) and to the expectation or opinion of the audience (*opinio eorum qui audient*). The combined effect of ensuring that a narrative follows these three principles will be to give it the appearance, or similitude, of truth (*verisimilitudo*).[224] It is in order to fulfil all three of these categories, therefore, that the speaker or writer will need to be familiar with the huge range of knowledge that rhetoric demands – varieties of human nature, types of conduct or behaviour (*mores*), principles by which humans are aroused or assuaged, history (*historia*), antiquity (*antiquitas*), the governance of the *res publica* and civil law.[225]

The three fundamental virtues of narrative – brevity, openness and plausibility – are not mutually exclusive. Quintilian, for example, insists that brevity should be understood in relative terms, to mean the inclusion of as much material as the task requires and as much as is sufficient. It should not be understood to mean only as much as is strictly necessary, since brevity must be accompanied by rhetorical ornamentation. In Quintilian's view, the pleasure which is derived from the latter has the capacity to deceive us (*fallere*) by making a narrative *seem* shorter, just as a pleasant and enjoyable short journey is less tiring than a hard and arid longer one.[226] Brevity should not be so dominant a concern, moreover, that it precludes the use of those figures of speech (or indeed of any other rhetorical element) which make an exposition of events credible. Quintilian summarises the argument from

---

224 Cicero, *De Inventione*, I.21.29, p. 61; *Rhetorica ad Herennium*, I.9.16, p. 29. Cf. Alcuin, *Disputatio de Rhetorica et de Virtutibus*, ed. and trans. W.S. Howell, *The Rhetoric of Alcuin and Charlemagne* (Princeton, 1941), lines 538–62, pp. 100–2: 'narrative is the exposition of what was done or could have been done, and it ought to possess three qualities, namely it should be brief, open and probable.... Narrative will be probable [*probabilis*] if those things which are usually apparent in true occurrences [*in veritate*] are seen to be present in the narrative too, if people's standings [*dignitates personarum*] are maintained, if the causes of events [*causae factorum*] are made plain, if the ability to act [*facultates faciundi*] is seen to be present, if the time [*tempus*] is suitable, if there is enough space [*spatium*], if the place [*locus*] in which the narrative occurs is shown to be opportune for the event described, and if the subject is accommodated to the nature of those who act it out and to common repute and to the opinions of those who listen to it [*si res et ad eorum qui agent naturam et ad vulgi rumorem et ad eorum qui audient opinionem accommodabitur*]'; see also pages 178–9.
225 Cicero, *De Oratore*, I.36.165, p. 113 (see page 243).
226 Quintilian, *Institutio Oratoria*, IV.2.46–7, p. 75.

Cicero's *Partitiones Oratoriae* – narrative should possess charm, surprise, anticipation, unexpected results, speeches and appeals to all the emotions; it might not take the form of argumentation, even though it will sometimes include arguments; the purpose of the narrative, after all, is not just to instruct a judge or an audience but to move them as well.[227]

Once again, it is the criterion of what is suitable or appropriate (*aptum*), both to the case and to the audience, which governs the way in which a narrative should be constructed and which will make that narrative believable or plausible. A narrative should not be included, therefore, if it is of no benefit, it should not be put in the wrong place, and it should have no form other than the one which the particular case demands. This might mean omitting a narrative altogether if the events are already familiar to the audience. A narrative will be counter-productive, moreover, if an exposition of the events will cause considerable offence to an audience. In the face of such hostility, its impact can still be softened if the narrative is distributed bit by bit throughout a speech or text and if, at each point, a mitigating explanation is offered for each event.[228] Where a long narrative is necessary, it can be shortened by postponing some of the facts until later, having first mentioned what it is that is being deferred. Alternatively, weariness can be averted by revealing the sections into which the narrative is divided (*partitio*) or by using interjections ('you have heard what happened before, now learn what followed').[229] Or, if it is still a long narrative even after all these remedies have been applied, then it is advantageous to add a brief summary (*commonitio*) at the very end.[230]

Likewise, the order of events can be changed in order to suit the nature and circumstances of the case. Everything in the narrative, in short, should be turned (*torquere*) to one's advantage

---

227 *Institutio Oratoria*, IV.2.46, 107–15, pp. 75, 109–13; cf. Cicero, *Partitiones Oratoriae*, trans. H. Rackham (Loeb, 1942), IX.31–2, pp. 335–7. For the act of composition as a journey, see, for example, William of Malmesbury, *Gesta Pontificum Anglorum*, III.110, p. 373, IV.prol., p. 421, V.prol., p. 499.
228 Cicero, *De Inventione*, I.21.30, pp. 61–3.
229 Quintilian, *Institutio Oratoria*, IV.2.48–51, pp. 77–9.
230 For example, William of Malmesbury, *Gesta Regum Anglorum*, I.105, p. 149; Henry of Huntingdon, *Historia Anglorum*, IV.31, p. 265, VI.42, p. 411 ('for the sake of order and clarity'); cf. Thietmar, *Chronicon*, V.2, p. 207.

(*commodum*) such that, when the speaker or writer is able to do so, they will pass over those facts that run counter to their position, touch on them lightly when they have no option but to mention them, and otherwise narrate what is helpful to their case carefully and smoothly.[231] When the facts are against the speaker, then they should deny some things, add others, change some things and pass over others in silence.[232] The act itself can be admitted in some circumstances but different motives can be adduced for doing it, or it can be described with different terminology – by using the word 'liberality', for example, instead of 'luxury', or 'simplicity' instead of 'negligence'.[233]

It is in order to underline the overriding importance of this principle of utility or advantage that Quintilian was prompted to adapt and extend Cicero's original definition of narrative. Narrative, Quintilian states, is 'the exposition of something which has been done, or as if it has been done, in a way which is advantageous to the goal of persuasion' (*narratio est rei factae aut ut factae utilis ad persuadendum expositio*).[234] This principle of narrative utility extends to 'forming', 'shaping' and 'making things up' (*fingere*). 'Going beyond the truth' is thus the definition given by Quintilian to 'hyperbole', the figure of speech which should be deployed when the subject that is being spoken about itself exceeds a natural measure. When it is simply not possible to say how great something is, he explains, it is permissible to amplify what is being said and it is certainly better if, rather than falling short, the language goes further than what is true.[235] More generally, if narratives have the function of countering an alternative construction of events and confirming the speaker's own account

---

231 Cicero, *De Inventione*, I.21.30, p. 63. See also page 318.
232 See page 300.
233 Quintilian, *Institutio Oratoria*, IV.2.66–77, pp. 85–93; see also page 180. Read in this context, for example, *simplicitas* is an interesting term to be applied to Edward the Confessor by both Henry of Huntingdon (*Historia Anglorum*, VI.20, p. 373) and William of Malmesbury (*Gesta Regum Anglorum*, II.196, p. 349, III.259, p. 479, III.300, p. 535; *Gesta Pontificum Anglorum*, I.23, p. 47, III.115, pp. 381–3), particularly when William describes Edgar the Ætheling's conduct as *ignavia*, only to point out that *simplicitas* would be a more gentle term to describe the same characteristic (*Gesta Regum Anglorum*, III.251, p. 467).
234 Quintilian, *Institutio Oratoria*, IV.2.31, p. 67.
235 *Institutio Oratoria*, VIII.6.76, p. 345.

in its stead, then this can be done by making use, not just of what has been recorded in annals (*monumenta annalium*), but also of what has been handed down in *fabula* or poetry.[236] First and foremost, the rhetorician certainly needs to be able to draw on a wealth of *exempla*, in the past and in the present, from a knowledge of what has been written in histories and what happens in daily life. However, the speaker should not neglect those *exempla* which have been made up (*ficta*) by the more distinguished of the poets. Historical and quotidian *exempla*, Quintilian explains, may have attained the status of testimony, or even legal judgment, but poetic *exempla* carry weight because either they have been preserved by the belief of antiquity or they are credited with having been made up by great personages in order to serve the function of precepts.[237] The more true something is, the stronger it is, but it is still permissible to introduce into the construction of a plausible argument something which has been formed, shaped or made up (*fingere, ficta*). Sometimes a made-up narrative (*ficta narratio*) is introduced in order to stir up the judges or to assuage them with some urbanity – when the audience already knows what was done, the purpose of the narrative becomes, not to instruct, but to move.[238] If the event being described did actually happen as the narrative describes it, then the guidelines for making something verisimilar should be observed all the same, because it is often the case that, without their assistance, the truth itself is not able to produce belief (*fides*). If the event being described is made up (*ficta*), however, then these stipulations need to be followed all the more closely. According to Quintilian, there are many things which are true but scarcely credible, just as there are false things which are frequently plausible; it therefore requires just as much labour to make a judge or an audience believe a narrative when what is being said is true as when it is made up (*fingere*).[239] Or, as

---

236 *Institutio Oratoria*, II.4.18, p. 233.
237 *Institutio Oratoria*, XII.4.1–2, pp. 407–9 (see pages 285–7).
238 *Institutio Oratoria*, IV.2.19–21, pp. 59–61.
239 *Institutio Oratoria*, IV.2.34, p. 69; cf. *Rhetorica ad Herennium*, I.9.16, p. 29. Compare Jerome, *Letters*, ed. and trans. J. Labourt (Paris, 1949–63), Ep.LXXII.2, p. 15: 'there are many other things said in Scripture which seem incredible but which are nevertheless true' (*multa et alia dicuntur in scripturis quae videntur incredibilia et tamen vera sunt*). This observation was then quoted and expanded, for example, by Gerald of Wales (*Itinerarium Cambriae*, I.8, p. 136; *Expugnatio*

Cicero puts it more pithily in *De Oratore*, were truth sufficient to be effective on its own, there would be no need for art.[240]

So where do the rhetorical principles of narrative leave the writing of history as a narrative of events (*narratio in negotiis*)? In the first instance, they produce a clear and carefully-argued justification for introducing a mixture of truth and verisimilitude, of understanding and advantage, such that deeds are described as they happened (*gestae*) but also as they might have happened (*ut gestae*), using historical *exempla* but also poetic *fabulae*. This combination of qualities is analysed at some length in *De Inventione*. What is probable, Cicero states, needs to be distinguished from what is necessary and it is defined by three criteria. First, there is the measure provided by what generally tends to happen, that is, by what is in accordance with Nature (Cicero's example here is 'if she is his mother, then she loves him'). This criterion of probability is revealed by answering the three judicial questions: did it happen, what was it that happened, and what was the quality of what happened? Second, there is the probability which is measured by what is established in common opinion – it is actually a fault to say something which runs counter to the will of a judge or an audience (Cicero's example here is 'punishment awaits the wicked'). Third, and last, is the probability which is produced by what possesses some similitude to the subject under discussion, in the sense of being its opposite, or of being on a par with it, or of sharing the same defining principle (*ratio*) and thus having an analogical identity with the object to which it is being compared. This last criterion of probability is applicable irrespective of whether the object of comparison is true ('if there is a scar, there must have been a wound'), plausible ('if he has dust on his feet, he must have been on a journey') or false. The probability which is deployed in argumentation, in short, derives from a number of sources: from a sign (that is, from something perceived by one of the senses); from something credible (that is, from something which is confirmed by the opinion of the audience without any other testimony being required); from a previous judgment (that is, from what has been

---

Hibernica, prol., p. 7, II.23, p. 195) and Ranulf Higden (*Polychronicon*, I.prol.1, p. 16): 'you will find many things incredible and lacking verisimilitude which are nevertheless true'. Likewise, Otto of Freising, *Chronicle*, II.25, p. 152.
240 Cicero, *De Oratore*, III.56.214, p. 171.

judged by some person, or some persons, and sanctioned by religion, by common human observance or by a specific decision); or from something comparable (that is, from something which contains some principle of similarity between different things).[241]

Of Cicero's three basic criteria for establishing something as probable, consistency with Nature and consistency with the opinion of one's audience are both governed by straightforward guidelines of what is *aptum*.[242] It is his third criterion – similitude – which requires a rather more careful exposition. Plausibility through similitude or comparison takes three forms: likeness (*imago*), which demonstrates similarity in form or nature; parallel (*collatio*), which juxtaposes one thing with something else on the basis of their similarity; and example (*exemplum*), which strengthens or weakens something on the basis of either authority or experience and which involves either an individual or an event.[243] When viewed from the perspective of the writing of history, there are two particular aspects of Cicero's discussion of similitude which invite further comment: the combination of likeness and parallel, on the one hand, with *exemplum* on the other; and the concession that *similitudo* through similarity or comparison can constitute similitude with something which is either true, plausible or false.

According to Boethius' commentary on Cicero's *Topica*, arguments from similarity are particularly suitable for persuasion and are therefore useful to orators and philosophers, because a judge or audience can readily believe that what generally occurs in other cases is also appropriate to the case in question.[244] Comparison with something gives credibility to an argument by the appeal to similarity (*similitudo*). This can take the form of an image (*imago*), a juxtaposition or parallel (*collatio*) and an example (*exemplum*), and all three are listed accordingly as related figures of speech, namely

---

241 Cicero, *De Inventione*, I.29.46–30.49, pp. 85–91.
242 See pages 320–1.
243 Cicero, *De Inventione*, I.30.49, pp. 89–91; see page 245; cf. Macrobius, *Saturnalia*, IV.5.1–12, pp. 271–4 (where parallel comparison or *parabole* is described as better suited to poetry) and, more generally, N. Palmer, 'Exempla', in F.A.C. Mantello and A.G. Rigg (eds), *Medieval Latin: An Introduction and Bibliographical Guide* (Washington, DC, 1996), pp. 582–8.
244 Boethius, *In Ciceronis Topica*, IV, p. 114.

as simile, metaphor and example.[245] According to the *Rhetorica ad Herennium*, comparison (*similitudo*) is a form of speech which transfers something similar (*simile*) from one thing to another. This similarity need not extend to the entirety of each thing but it must apply to the particular point which is being compared. Such *similitudo* is deployed for one of four purposes: ornamentation, proof, clarification or vividness.[246] Likeness or image, meanwhile, is defined as the juxtaposition (*collatio*) of one form with another on the basis of a certain similarity.[247] In every such juxtaposition or parallel (in Greek, *parabole*), the comparison either precedes or follows the subject to which it is similar; alternatively, it can be free and detached. Best of all, however, at least according to Quintilian, is when this likeness (*imago*) is connected to its subject, with the juxtaposition responding in both directions. This is achieved by what he calls reciprocal opposition or, in its Greek form, 'antapodosis'. Such reciprocity sets out the things which are being compared side by side, placing them, as it were, before one's eyes.[248]

Metaphor (*translatio*) is defined as the process by which a word that applies to one thing is 'transferred' to something else because of some similarity between them; it is a shorter or abbreviated form of comparison since, rather than being compared to the thing which a speaker or writer wants to describe, the metaphor is used instead. Bold metaphors should be introduced by the phrase 'if I may put it thus' (*ut ita dicam, si licet dicere*) in order to prevent them from seeming like an error of judgment. Otherwise they are included for the sake of brevity or ornamentation (Quintilian calls metaphor the most common, but also the greatest and most beautiful, ornament of speech) but primarily for vividness – once again, in order to put something 'before one's eyes' (*ante oculos*).[249]

Example (*exemplum*), finally, is defined as putting forward something said or done in the past together with the precise name of its author. The *Rhetorica ad Herennium* lists comparison

---

245 Cf. Macrobius, *Saturnalia*, IV.5.1, p. 271.
246 *Rhetorica ad Herennium*, IV.45.59, p. 377, IV.48.61, p. 383; cf. Quintilian, *Institutio Oratoria*, VIII.3.72, p. 251.
247 *Rhetorica ad Herennium*, IV.49.62, p. 385; Quintilian, *Institutio Oratoria*, V.11.24, p. 285.
248 Quintilian, *Institutio Oratoria*, VIII.3.77–9, p. 255.
249 *Rhetorica ad Herennium*, IV.34.45, p. 343; Quintilian, *Institutio Oratoria*, VIII.2.6, p. 199, VIII.3.37, p. 231, VIII.3.81, p. 257, VIII.6.4–9, 19, pp. 303–5, 311.

and *exemplum* side by side on the basis that these two figures of speech share the same four goals: they can serve as a means of embellishing and ornamenting a narrative, giving it greater weight or dignity; or they can serve as a means of clarification, making something less obscure; or they can serve as a means of making it more plausible, by giving it greater likeness to the truth; or they can serve as a means of putting something before the eyes of the judge or audience in such a way that the subject can, as it were, be touched by the hand.[250]

Plausibility through likeness is a form of argumentation which was intrinsic to the 'exemplary' nature of historiography. Such a comparative methodology, however, was clearly understood to operate in different ways and, as a result, could serve a number of different purposes. At the most straightforward level, citation of an *exemplum* from the past provided as a vivid and weighty illustration of an otherwise abstract moral precept – its immediacy and authority would move an audience to action in a way in which reasoning on its own would not.[251] However, Orosius explicitly used historical comparison as a measure of both definition (the nature of political power and of empire) and degree (calamity and suffering) in order to prove the arguments which he was putting forward for the providential significance of Rome and for consolation from present woes.[252] More complex still was Liutprand of Cremona, who used antapodosis both as a rhetorical strategy and as the actual title for his work. For Liutprand, this approach (he translates antapodosis into Latin as *retributio* or 'repayment') involves, first and foremost, setting out the just rewards and punishments which fall to good and bad rulers.[253] This is primarily as a means of convincing bishop Reccemund, the dedicatee of the work, of the dangers presented by Christian accommodation with Saracens in the Iberian peninsula.[254] However, the force of

---

250 *Rhetorica ad Herennium*, IV.49.62, pp. 383–5.
251 See pages 153–4.
252 See pages 76–8.
253 Liutprand, *Antapodosis*, III.1, pp. 109–10.
254 K. Leyser, 'Ends and Means in Liudprand of Cremona', in K. Leyser, *Communications and Power in Medieval Europe: The Carolingian and Ottonian Centuries* (London, 1994), pp. 125–42; K. Leyser, 'Liudprand of Cremona – Preacher and Homilist', in D. Wood and K. Walsh (eds), *The Bible in the Medieval World* (Oxford, 1985), pp. 43–60; reprinted in Leyser, *Communications and Power*, pp. 111–24.

his argument depends upon a comparative history of east Francia and the Italian peninsula which juxtaposes the lessons to be learned from dealing with, on the one hand, Magyars and, on the other, the Saracens of Fraxinetum – in other words, a reciprocal comparison which applies in more than one direction.[255]

If comparison through likeness served as a form of proof, much of its impact was held to depend upon its success in attaining vividness. According to Cicero, one of the qualities which makes narrative such a difficult technique is that it has to describe and present before one's eyes (*ante oculos*) things that possess the similitude of truth (*verisimilia*). This is its particular function and its chief challenge.[256] The immediacy of such a description – placing an event before one's eyes – is thus a primary goal of the orator. Take, for example, deliberative rhetoric and its defining activity of analysing whether an action is morally worthy (*honestum*) or advantageous (*utile*).[257] In the first instance, according to Cicero, the persuasiveness of such a discussion will involve the speaker setting out with what intention, at what time and for what purpose a particular action was done. In the second instance, the speaker will demonstrate, and expand upon, the greatness of this action by referring to its advantageousness, moral worth and necessity. These first two topics are, perhaps, to be expected. The prominence of a third 'commonplace' is therefore all the more striking. In the third instance, according to Cicero, the event or action under discussion will be brought before the eyes of the audience through the words of the speaker so that the audience will judge that they would have done the same thing themselves were they to have been faced by the same event, the same cause for action and at the same time.[258] A similar principle also governs judicial rhetoric, in particular where the process of accusation and defence involves controversy over a disputed will. In such cases, the time, the place, the circumstances and the defendant's deliberation will all be set before the eyes (*ante oculos*) of the accusers and judges in order that

---

255 For example, Liutprand, *Antapodosis*, IV.15, p. 153, V.12, p. 184; cf. Liutprand, *Relatio de Legatione Constantinopolitana*, trans. F.A. Wright, in *The Works of Liutprand of Cremona* (London, 1930), IX, p. 240, XL, p. 259.
256 Cicero, *De Oratore*, II.66.264, p. 397.
257 See pages 230–7.
258 Cicero, *De Inventione*, II.26.77–8, p. 243.

the orator can ask *them* what *they* would have done if faced with a similar situation.[259] Likewise, in upholding the will and intentions of the deceased, orators will do nothing less than use their rhetoric to raise that individual from the dead and set that person before the eyes (*ante oculos*) of the judge or audience.[260]

Quintilian quotes from *De Oratore* to demonstrate the great effect on the emotions which is produced by explaining things in such a way that it is as if they were being done practically before one's gaze.[261] As with the actual delivery of a narrative, the point of varying the voice is that it will give the impression that everything is being narrated just as it was done.[262] The particular figure of speech which denotes this critical technique of narrative is *enargeia* – literally the quality of being bright, distinct, visible – and it refers to the means by which something is described with such words that the subject or event under discussion seems to exist or to be being done before one's eyes. This is achieved, according to the *Rhetorica ad Herennium*, by describing what has preceded, followed and accompanied the event itself, or simply by keeping to its circumstances and consequences. As a technique of ornamentation, *enargeia* is useful because it serves both to amplify a subject and to secure an emotion, such as pity, through setting out the whole event practically before one's eyes.[263] The *Rhetorica ad Herennium* translates *enargeia*, the transliterated Greek term for this trope, with the Latin term 'demonstration' (*demonstratio*), that is, the quality of being shown or pointed out.[264] Cicero uses the

---

259 *Rhetorica ad Herennium*, II.14.22, pp. 97–9.
260 Cicero, *De Oratore*, I.57.245, p. 179; Quintilian, *Institutio Oratoria*, XII.10.61, p. 485.
261 Quintilian, *Institutio Oratoria*, IX.1.26–7, p. 363, quoting Cicero, *De Oratore*, III.53.202, p. 161.
262 *Rhetorica ad Herennium*, III.14.24, pp. 199–201 (see page 22).
263 *Rhetorica ad Herennium*, IV.55.68–9, pp. 405–9; Quintilian, *Institutio Oratoria*, IX.1.45, p. 373, quoting Cicero, *Orator*, XL.139, p. 413; cf. Macrobius, *Saturnalia*, IV.6.13–14, p. 278 (*adtestatio*).
264 Cf. Geoffrey of Vinsauf, *Poetria Nova*, 1277–80, p. 83. For *demonstratio* as distinct from *descriptio*, see *Rhetorica ad Herennium*, IV.55.68–9, pp. 405–9, IV.39.51, pp. 357–9; Isidore, *Etymologiae*, ed. and trans. Marshall, II.20.4, p. 72, II.21.33, p. 90. Cf. Martianus Capella, *Marriage of Philology and Mercury*, V, p. 197: 'diatyposis is description [*descriptio*] ... in which we express the very look and appearance of the people or things under discussion, as Cicero does in *Pro Milone* [trans. N.H. Watts (Loeb, 1931), XX.54 p. 65], "if you were not listening to his deeds, but seeing them depicted...".'

word 'illustration' (*illustratio*).²⁶⁵ Quintilian, meanwhile, reports that other people call it 're-presentation' (*repraesentatio*), in the sense that it makes something present for a second time. Both Cicero and Quintilian, however, also deploy another term, and one which is much more revealing – *enargeia* can also be translated, and more literally, as *evidentia*, the quality of being seen. According to Quintilian, such 'evidence' contributes to the narrative quality of lucidity and is a great virtue when something true needs, not just to be stated (*dicere*), but also, in some sense, to be shown (*ostendere*).²⁶⁶ Thus *enargeia* or *evidentia* seems, not so much to 'state' something, as to 'show' it.²⁶⁷ In so doing, 'evidence' contributes to the plausibility of what is being narrated. Much will be added to the truth of what has happened, he concludes, if a credible likeness (*imago*) of what occurred is introduced and which seems to bring the audience to the deed as if it were physically present.²⁶⁸

For Cicero and Quintilian, *enargeia* or *evidentia* was clearly an important means of moving one's audience. The primary utility of all figures of speech lies in the way in which they make what is being said credible (*credibilia*), because they work their way into a judge's mind undetected and because there is no more powerful method of guiding the emotions.²⁶⁹ This is particularly true of vividness, however, and it is therefore particularly appropriate to deploy it in that part of the speech or text – the conclusion or *peroratio* – in which the emotions play a key persuasive role. According to the *Rhetorica ad Herennium*, such a concluding summary can be deployed at no fewer than four points – in the introduction, after the narrative, after the strongest argumentation and in the conclusion proper. Its purpose is to enumerate all the points which have been made in order to aid the memory of the audience, in order to amplify what has been said so that the audience is stimulated by having the event described as if it was happening before their eyes, and in order to move the audience to pity by recounting the variability and changeability of fortune,

---

265 Cf. John of Salisbury, *Metalogicon*, I.24, p. 66 (*illustratio/picturatio*).
266 Quintilian, *Institutio Oratoria*, IV.2.63–5, p. 85.
267 *Institutio Oratoria*, VI.2.32, p. 435.
268 *Institutio Oratoria*, IV.2.123, p. 117. Compare Valerius Maximus, *Facta et Dicta Memorabilia*, I.7, p. 99, where *evidentia* is applied to the graphic nature of a dream.
269 *Institutio Oratoria*, IX.1.19–21, p. 359.

comparing former prosperity with present adversity.[270] Words should be used which bring the events in question before the eyes of the judge or audience so that their reaction will be the same as if they had been present and seen it for themselves. Misfortunes can be placed, one by one, before an audience's eyes so that the person who hears the words seems to see them and is moved to pity, not by the words alone, but by the event itself 'as if they were present'. Such appeals to the emotions are particularly necessary when there are no other means of attaining what is true, just and of general benefit.[271]

In order to create emotions such as anger, hatred, fear, jealousy or pity, the orator needs to describe things which are seen (*visiones*), namely images (*imagines*) of absent things which are re-presented and represented to the audience's mind in such a way that the audience will seem to be seeing those things with their own eyes and actually to have them 'present' before them. How is this achieved? By shaping or making things up (*fingere*) – be they events, voices or actions – to the best effect but also according to what is true. The result is that an audience will have before its eyes what can be believed to have happened, what is credible. By deploying this technique of *enargeia* or *evidentia*, an audience's emotions will become no different from those it would have experienced had it actually been present at the events. Quintilian reports that he was himself frequently so moved by speaking in this way that he had not only been seized with tears but had also turned pale and shown verisimilar grief (*veri similis dolor*).[272] For Quintilian, this strategy is clearly more than simply a matter of securing lucidity for a narrative. It is the difference between making something clear (*patere*) and actually showing it to be the case (*ostendere*). It is certainly a great virtue to speak or write clearly, he states, but it is also a great virtue to do this as if the things being described are actually seen, so that judges will believe that facts or events are not just being heard by them as a narrative but actually being

---

270 *Rhetorica ad Herennium*, II.30.47–31.50, pp. 145–53.
271 Quintilian, *Institutio Oratoria*, VI.1.7, p. 387, VI.2.1–5, pp. 417–19; Cicero, *De Inventione*, I.54.104–55.107, pp. 157–9; Cicero, *Topica*, XXVI.98–9, p. 459.
272 Quintilian, *Institutio Oratoria*, VI.2.29–32, pp. 433–7, VI.2.36, p. 439; cf. Augustine, *Confessions*, trans. H. Chadwick (Oxford, 1991), III.2–4, pp. 35–7.

shown to the eyes of their mind (*oculi mentis*).²⁷³ Placing an event before one's eyes (*sub oculos subiectio*) accordingly lies at the heart of Quintilian's understanding of what he, at least, understands by the term 'evidence'. This particular figure of speech does not just indicate something which has been done (*res gesta*), but shows how it might have been done (*ut res gesta*), and not just in general terms but in full detail. The entire likeness (*imago*) of the things described is, in this sense, 'painted' with words; it is expressed in such a way that its form is seen, rather than heard. Such 'evidence' can also be used to create an image of what might happen, or what might have happened, in the future. It can also be applied to topography, to the clear description of places as well as events. In each case, the goal is to represent the event to the eyes of the mind (*oculi mentis*).²⁷⁴

Narrative of events (*narratio in negotiis*) comprises a wide range of different types of argument, each one of which must be expounded briefly, lucidly and plausibly. It is this final quality of plausibility or verisimilitude which provides the key to making a narrative of events convincing. One way to secure credibility for one's account can be to use logical argumentation or it can be to make sure that what is being described is in accordance with Nature and congruent with the common opinion of one's audience. Above all, credibility is secured by deploying 'evidence', but this is evidence of a very specific sort – what can be shown, represented, to the audience before their very own eyes, as if they had been physically present at the events being described. This is therefore the first point which needs to be made concerning the nature of historical narrative. Quintilian concedes that there are times when a picture can even reach the deepest emotions and in a way that seems superior to the power of speaking itself.²⁷⁵ He was not alone in this assessment. Valerius Maximus, for example, reports how 'men's eyes are riveted in amazement when they see the painting [of a distinguished act] and renew the features of

---

273 Quintilian, *Institutio Oratoria*, VIII.3.61–2, p. 245; cf. Gregory the Great, *Regula Pastoralis*, trans. H. Davis, *Pastoral Care* (Washington, DC, 1950), I.11, pp. 40–2, III.35, p. 222, IV.1, p. 237.
274 *Institutio Oratoria*, IX.2.40–4, pp. 397–9; cf. Priscian, *Praeexercitamina*, X, pp. 65–6.
275 *Institutio Oratoria*, XI.3.67, p. 281.

the long by-gone incident in astonishment at the spectacle now before them, believing that in those silent outlines of limbs they see living and breathing bodies'. 'This must needs happen to the mind also', he continues, 'admonished to remember things long past as though they were recent by painting which is considerably more effective than literary memorials'.[276] Valerius' own *exempla* are accordingly described as 'likenesses' (*imagines*).[277] Vergil similarly describes how Aeneas grieved at the events of the Trojan wars which were depicted (*pictura*) in such graphic detail in the temple to Juno at Carthage; how Dido had the brave deeds of her ancestors engraved in gold on silver plate, 'a very long series of events traced through many men from the ancient origin of her people'; and how Vulcan fashioned a shield for Aeneas which vividly depicted the sequence (*in ordine*) of Roman wars and triumphs that would culminate in the battle of Actium, as an image (*imago*) of the fame and fates of his descendants.[278] Josephus, meanwhile, in relation to the triumph of Titus, describes a number of painted tableaux which showed the successive stages of the war in Palestine – the art and marvellous craftsmanship of these constructions, he comments, now revealed the incidents to those who had not seen them happen 'as clearly as if they had been there'.[279]

Medieval historians made similar observations and drew similar conclusions. Thus, Gregory of Tours describes histories painted on walls; Paul the Deacon describes Theudelinda having the deeds of the Lombards painted in her palace; Ermoldus Nigellus how Louis the Pious had the *maxima gesta virum* from Orosius painted on the walls of his hall at Ingelheim, joining the acts of caesars to the great deeds of the Franks.[280] Liutprand records the vividness of a triumph in battle which had been painted 'so that you can see it, not as it might have happened, but as it actually

---

276 Valerius Maximus, *Facta et Dicta Memorabilia*, V.4, pp. 501–3.
277 *Facta et Dicta Memorabilia*, IX.11, p. 359.
278 Vergil, *Aeneid*, I.455–93, pp. 273–5, I.640–2, p. 285, VIII.626–731, pp. 105–13; cf. Walter of Châtillon, *Alexandreis*, trans. D. Townsend (Philadelphia, 1996), II.575–630, pp. 68–9, IV.222–342, pp. 94–9.
279 Josephus, *De Bello Iudaico*, trans. G.A. Williamson, *The Jewish War* (Harmondsworth, 1970), VII.5, p. 372.
280 Gregory of Tours, *Histories*, II.17, pp. 131–2; Paul the Deacon, *History of the Lombards*, IV.22, p. 166; Ermoldus Nigellus, *In Honorem Hludowici Pii*, ed. and trans. E. Faral, *Poème sur Louis le Pieux* (Paris, 1964), lines 2126–63, pp. 163–5.

occurred'.[281] Suger points out how painting an event provided a means of keeping a memory fresh.[282] Otto of Freising describes a painting of a battle in Merseburg, Rahewin a picture recording the notorious 'good deed' (*beneficium*) at Besançon.[283] The impact on their own works of history was direct. It was not just poetry which could serve as 'painting that speaks',[284] but also the narrative of events itself.[285] William of Malmesbury, for example, credits Eadmer with writing 'such a lucid account of all the events that they seem, as it were, to have been placed before our

---

281 Liutprand, *Antapodosis*, II.31, p. 86.
282 Suger, *Gesta Hludowici*, XXVII, p. 121.
283 Otto of Freising, *Chronicle*, VI.18, p. 379; Rahewin, *Deeds of Frederick*, III.10, p. 184, III.17, p. 193. For public paintings of historical, political and judicial events, see, for example, H. Wieruszowski, 'Art and the Commune in the Time of Dante', *Speculum*, 19 (1944), pp. 21–2; for living tableaux, see Froissart, *Chroniques*, trans. G. Brereton (Harmondsworth, 1968), IV, pp. 355–8; F. Avril, *Manuscript Painting at the Court of France: The Fourteenth Century (1310–1380)* (London, 1978), pp. 106–7; A.D. Hedeman, 'Restructuring the Narrative – The Function of Ceremonial in Charles V's *Grandes Chroniques de France*', in H.L. Kessler and M.S. Simpson (eds), *Pictorial Narrative in Antiquity and the Middle Ages* (Hanover, 1985), pp. 177–9; B. Guenée, *Histoire et Culture Historique dans l'Occident Medieval* (Paris, 1980), p. 327; L.H. Loomis, 'Secular Dramatics in the Royal Palace, Paris, 1378, 1389 and Chaucer's "Tregetoures"', *Speculum*, 33 (1958), pp. 242–55; D.A. Bullough, 'Games People Played – Drama and Ritual as Propaganda in Medieval Europe', *Transactions of the Royal Historical Society*, 24 (1974), pp. 97–122.
284 *Rhetorica ad Herennium*, IV.28.39, p. 327. For painting as 'silent poetry', see Horace, *Ars Poetica*, trans. H.R. Fairclough (Loeb, 1929), line 361, p. 481: *ut pictura poesis* (see page 359); cf. M. Carruthers, *The Book of Memory: A Study of Memory in Medieval Culture* (Cambridge, 1990), p. 230. For painting as living writing or living narrative, see Bede, *De Templo*, trans. S. Connolly, *On the Temple* (Liverpool, 1995), II, p. 91. According to Gregory the Great, pictures were placed in churches so that those who could not read might at least read by seeing on the walls what they were unable to read in books: Gregory the Great, *Letters*, trans. J.R.C. Martyn (Toronto, 2004), Ep.XI.10. pp. 745–6, cf. Ep.IX.209, p. 674. See also C.M. Chazelle, 'Pictures, Books and the Illiterate – Pope Gregory I's Letters to Serenus of Marseilles', *Word and Image*, 6 (1990), pp. 138–53. For the literal comparison of the act of writing history with the act of painting, see, for example, William of Tyre, *A History of Deeds Done Beyond the Sea*, trans. E.A. Babcock and A.C. Krey (New York, 1941), prol., p. 55; Gerald of Wales, *Expugnatio Hibernica*, I.46, p. 125 (see page 312). For the painter as a witness (*testis*), providing testimony of the truth of what they depict, see Gervase of Tilbury, *Otia Imperialia*, II.25, p. 527.
285 K.F. Morrison, *History as a Visual Art in the Twelfth-Century Renaissance* (Princeton, 1990); Gransden, 'Realistic Observation in Twelfth-Century England'; cf. E. Auerbach, 'Figura', in E. Auerbach, *Scenes from the Drama of European Literature* (New York, 1959), pp. 11–76.

eyes'.[286] That this was more than just an aesthetic claim is made clear by the terminology which William uses in his own *Gesta Regum* when he describes a miracle on the First Crusade – the fact that only four Christian soldiers were killed, he writes, will make his audience feel it almost as something visible (*visibile*), rather than doubt it as an opinion (*opinabile*).[287] Sallust had made it a feature of his narrative of events to introduce a particularly vivid description with an apostrophe to the reader or audience, exclaiming 'you would have seen...' (*cerneres*).[288] Paul the Deacon, Suger, Guibert of Nogent, Galbert of Bruges, William of Malmesbury and Otto of Freising all use the same technique.[289] So too does Henry of Huntingdon, when he describes the battle of Beorhford in 752. 'You would have seen [*videres*]', he writes, 'the battle-lines that were heaving with breastplates, pointed with swords, bristling with lances, coloured with banners, glittering with gold, in a short time become moistened with blood, destitute of lances, broken up by disaster, bespattered with brains, frightful to behold...'.[290]

The second point which is raised by the rhetorical principles that governed the narration of events concerns the relationship between the terms *fingere* and *ficta*, that is, between the act of 'shaping' or 'forming' or 'making up' and the product that results. This particular means of creating verisimilitude was explicitly envisaged to encompass both true and false constructions of events which happened, or may have happened, in the past. Belief or credence (*fides*) in a narrative derives from the authority

---

286 William of Malmesbury, *Gesta Pontificum Anglorum*, I.45, p. 109.
287 William of Malmesbury, *Gesta Regum Anglorum*, IV.376, p. 669.
288 For example, Sallust, *Catiline*, trans. J.C. Rolfe (Loeb, 1931), LXI, p. 127.
289 Paul the Deacon, *History of the Lombards*, II.4, p. 57; Paschasius Radbertus, *Vita Adalhardi*, XXVII, p. 42; *Encomium Emmae Reginae*, ed. and trans. A. Campbell (Cambridge, 1949), II.6, p. 23; Eadmer, *Life of Anselm*, I.10, p. 17, II.9, p. 72, II.25, p. 101; Suger, *Gesta Hludowici*, XIX, pp. 87, 91, XXI, p. 102, XXIV, p. 107; Guibert of Nogent, *Gesta Dei per Francos*, III, p. 65, VII, pp. 139, 158, 161, 163; Galbert of Bruges, *The Murder of Charles the Good*, trans. J.B. Ross (New York, 1959), XXII, p. 139, XLVI, p. 186; William of Malmesbury, *Gesta Regum Anglorum*, II.197, p. 353; *Gesta Stephani*, I.66, p. 135, II.78, p. 153; Otto of Freising, *Chronicle*, II.49, p. 214, IV.3, p. 279, VI.9, p. 370, VII.9, p. 413; Otto of Freising, *Deeds of Frederick*, I.47, p. 81, I.57, p. 95, II.26, p. 142, II.32, p. 150, II.33, p. 151.
290 Henry of Huntingdon, *Historia Anglorum*, IV.19, p. 243; cf. V.2, p. 277, V.12, p. 297, VI.7, p. 351, X.18, p. 737.

of its narrator, first and foremost because of the narrator's life but also because of their style of speech, since the more serious and distinguished it is, the more weight it will add to what is being affirmed. This means that it is particularly important in the narrative to avoid any suspicion of guile (*calliditas*). Nothing in what an orator says must *seem* to be shaped or made up (*fictum*), nothing should *seem* to be the product of care and concern (*sollicitus*); instead, everything should be believed to derive from the case itself rather than from the speaker.[291] Self-questioning (*dubitatio*), for example, can therefore produce a belief that what is being said is true (*aliqua fides veritatis*), that is, when speakers pretend to ask themselves where they should begin, where they should end, and what should be said, or not even said at all.[292] Nonetheless, in re-presenting the images of absent things, Quintilian still suggests that it can be appropriate to shape or make things up (*fingere*), be they events, voices or actions, according to what is true. Such things will be manifest, they will seem to be present before an audience's eyes, if they possess the similitude of truth, if they are verisimilar. To this end, Quintilian argues that it is also permissible to make up (*adfingere*) something false when it is of the kind that usually occurs. Such clarity of re-presentation is, in his judgment, the greatest virtue and can be readily attained if a speaker or writer simply looks at, and follows, Nature.[293]

Viewed in this light, it is very revealing what Quintilian does when he takes up Cicero's classification of the three forms of narrative as history, argument and fable.[294] Quintilian states that, whilst historical narrative is the starting-point for the rhetorician and poetic narrative the preserve of the grammarian, he will discuss what he thinks are the best principles of narrative when he comes to discuss the subject of *judicial* rhetoric.[295] Martianus Capella picks up the implication; so too does Priscian. Either there is a fourth category of narrative that is being indicated here or it is specifically judicial narrative which corresponds to *argumentum*, to a narrative which expounds things which were done or which

---

291 Quintilian, *Institutio Oratoria*, IV.2.125, pp. 117–19.
292 *Institutio Oratoria*, IX.2.19, p. 385.
293 *Institutio Oratoria*, VIII.3.70–1, pp. 249–51.
294 See pages 316–17.
295 *Institutio Oratoria*, II.4.3, p. 225.

can be believed to have been done.[296] In doing so, however, both Martianus Capella and Priscian make a revealing move – they change the term *argumentum* to *fictio*. 'Fiction', as well as 'argument', is thus a term which can be used, in their eyes at least, to describe the narration of what *could* have been done rather than what was actually done. In the twelfth century, when Thierry of Chartres commented on *De Inventione*, he underlined the point still further, defining *argumentum* as 'the narrative of something made-up and verisimilar' (*narratio rei fictae et verisimilis*).[297] When John of Garland then came to offer his own version of Cicero's definition, he made the connection explicit: 'narrative is an exposition of events which have taken place or seem to have taken place; I say "seem to have taken place" in order to allow for fabulous narratives' (*narratio est rerum gestarum vel sicut gestarum expositio. sicut gestarum dicitur propter fabulosas narrationes*).[298]

For *fictio* to be classified as a narrative form which is technically distinct from *fabula* means that, strictly speaking, argument or rhetorical 'fiction' should always be distinguished from fable or poetic 'fiction'. Fables were understood as a sort of public testimony, as a particularly useful authority to which a speaker or writer could appeal in order to persuade a less educated audience – *fabula* is material which has been made up (*ficta*) by poets, but it

---

296 Martianus Capella, *Marriage of Philology and Mercury*, V, p. 207; Priscian, *Praeexercitamina*, II, pp. 53–4.
297 Thierry of Chartres, *Commentarius Super Libros De Inventione*, ed. K.M. Fredborg (Toronto, 1988), I.21.29, pp. 122–3. William of Conches, in his commentary on Macrobius, considers *argumentum* to have two meanings: reasoning which proves something which is in doubt; and something made up which could not have happened. See P. Dronke, *Fabula: Explorations into the Uses of Myth in Medieval Platonism* (Leiden, 1974), p. 69; Mehtonen *Old Concepts and New Poetics*, p. 152). According to Huguccio, *Derivationes*, pp. 78–9, *argumentum* can be understood in three senses: as proof of something which is in doubt; as a distillation of the subject of a particular work; and as something which is made up but which could have happened.
298 John of Garland, *Parisiana Poetria*, IV.197–8, p. 67. Compare, too, the classification put forward by Servius, *In Vergilii Carmina Commentarii*, ed. G. Thilo and H. Hagen (Leipzig, 1881–1902), I.235 p. 89, where *fabula* is defined as something said to occur against nature, whether or not it actually happened, and *historia* is defined as something said to occur in accordance with nature, whether or not it actually happened. History, on this reckoning, specifically includes verisimilar *argumentum* within its scope.

could never actually have happened.[299] Fiction, however, in the strictest sense of the term, could also be understood as verisimilar argument which is put forward in order to reconstruct the sequence and significance of events in the past – *fictio* describes what can be plausibly or credibly made up, what might actually have happened. Quintilian is certainly wary of the potential abuse of *fabulae* which are included in the teaching of grammar. Unscrupulous teachers, he suggests, exploit their licence to make things up (*licentia fingendi*) in such a way that they can get away with lying about entire books and authors.[300] Indeed, on this basis, it is a permissible line of defence for a speaker or writer to attack any ancient *exemplum* which has been put forward by their opponents as 'fabulous'.[301] In its strictest sense, however, a definition of rhetorical *fictio* is one which Quintilian is quite happy to sanction in order to explain the Greek term 'hypothesis', that is, a type of argument or proposition which is made up (*fingere, ficta*) and which, if true, would solve a problem or contribute to its solution.[302] More broadly, this definition also covers what Quintilian terms 'false exposition' (*falsa expositio*), that is, a narrative which is made up (*fingere*), which the speaker knows is not true, but which they have taken care to ensure is still capable of happening and conforms with what might be expected to have been true.[303]

The most straightforward, and perhaps most familiar, example of the application of rhetorical *fictio*, in both its strictest and its broadest sense, is the invented speech – *sermocinatio* was the term given to the trope of putting language into the mouths of people which is appropriate to their standing and character.[304] This can involve making up (*fingere*), not just the words, but even the

---

299 See page 309.
300 Quintilian, *Institutio Oratoria*, I.8.21, pp. 155–7.
301 *Institutio Oratoria*, V.13.24, p. 325; cf. Otto of Freising, *Deeds of Frederick*, I.29, p. 63, dismissing the historical claims put forward by Arnold of Brescia.
302 *Institutio Oratoria*, V.10.95–6, pp. 253–5.
303 *Institutio Oratoria*, IV.2.88, p. 99; cf. Cicero, *Topica*, X.45, p. 139; Boethius, *In Ciceronis Topica*, IV, p. 116: 'and other instances of this sort are found amongst lawyers, although they are of most use for orators, among whom it is so acceptable to make things up [*in tantum fingere licet*] that often the dead are even roused from the underworld in their speeches'.
304 *Rhetorica ad Herennium*, IV.43.55, p. 367, IV.52.65, pp. 395, 399.

people expressing them. Made-up speeches (*fictae orationes*) and impersonation (*fictio personarum* or *prosopopoeia*) were thought to constitute very useful exercises, and not just for poets but historians too.[305] They were also regarded as essential training for orators – in judicial rhetoric, for example, when speeches are put into the mouths of clients, and in deliberative rhetoric, when a controversy involves historical figures as speakers or when historical or poetic subjects of debate (*contiones*) are set as an exercise.[306] This technique of *sermocinatio* was designed to add variety and excitement to a narrative but it always had to be made up credibly – words, style and *mores* all had to be made appropriate to the character and circumstances of the person to whom they were being attributed.[307] As a narrative strategy, *sermocinatio* is thus closely connected both to physical depiction (*effictio*), namely when words are used to express and construct (*effingere*) someone's bodily appearance with sufficient clarity that they can be recognised,[308] and to personification (*conformatio*), namely when an absent person is conjured up (*confingere*) as if they are actually present.[309]

As types of fictive narration, the rhetorical strategies of hypothesis, *falsa expositio* and *sermocinatio* could all take the form of shaping or making up, not just words, but writings (*scripta*) as well. This approach could also extend to making mute objects speak. Such a technique licensed speakers or writers to personify abstractions (Virgil's *fama* and *furor* were perhaps the most famous examples from the *Aeneid*)[310] in such a way that these were given both a form and a speech or action which would be appropriate to their character. This included making cities or countries 'speak'. Orosius provided one of the most influential historiographical models here with his graphic personification of an exhausted

---

305 For example, Geoffrey of Vinsauf, *Poetria Nova*, 461–531, pp. 39–43; cf. Priscian, *Praeexercitamina*, IX, pp. 64–5.
306 Quintilian, *Institutio Oratoria*, III.8.49–54, pp. 503–7, VI.1.25, p. 399.
307 *Institutio Oratoria*, IX.2.29–31, pp. 391–3, XI.1.39, p. 177.
308 *Rhetorica ad Herennium*, IV.49.63, p. 387.
309 *Rhetorica ad Herennium*, IV.53.66, p. 399; cf. Geoffrey of Vinsauf, *Poetria Nova*, 1265–74, p. 83.
310 Vergil, *Aeneid*, I.294–6, p. 261, IV.173–97, pp. 407–9, VI.274–81, p. 525; cf. VIII.31–67, pp. 63–5, IX.719, p. 165, XII.335–6, p. 325. See also, for example, Liutprand, *Antapodosis*, V.18, p. 188, V.27, p. 195; Gerald of Wales, *Expugnatio Hibernica*, I.25, p. 87.

Gaul, placing her before his reader's eyes (*ante oculos*) and giving her words of an emotive lament.[311] According to Quintilian, however, such a technique required considerable powers of eloquence because, by their very nature, false and unbelievable things will necessarily produce one of two effects: either they will move people all the more because they go beyond what is true, or they will be treated as vain things because they are not true.[312] Writers of history were keen to take up the challenge, particularly of *sermocinatio*. The anonymous *Life of the Emperor Henry IV*, for example, included set-piece speeches by its protagonists; Gerald of Wales' *Conquest of Ireland* contained paired speeches, for and against a particular course of action.[313] Henry of Huntingdon composed several speeches for leaders exhorting their followers to war – Julius Caesar, William the Conqueror before Hastings, and King Stephen (and his opponents) on the eve of the battle of Lincoln.[314] Suger's *Deeds of Louis* included a whole series of speeches alongside his vivid descriptions of places and battles.[315]

'False exposition' (*falsa expositio*) has an important place in judicial rhetoric and Quintilian gives rules for it, whether it is based on extrinsic witnesses or on the rhetorician's own abilities. He certainly thought that care should be taken in order to ensure that what is made up in this way is something that could have happened; otherwise it would simply be *fabula*. Dreams and superstitions, for example, he regarded as having lost their

---

311 Orosius, *Seven Books of History*, VI.12, pp. 255–6; cf. Thietmar, *Chronicon*, I.28, p. 88, V.prol., p. 205, V.17, pp. 216–17; Wipo, *Deeds of Conrad*, I, p. 58; William of Malmesbury, *Gesta Regum Anglorum*, II.207, p. 387, V.397, p. 721; Henry of Huntingdon, *Historia Anglorum*, X.33, pp. 761–3; Otto of Freising, *Deeds of Frederick*, II.25, p. 140.
312 Quintilian, *Institutio Oratoria*, IX.2.32–7, pp. 393–5.
313 *Life of the Emperor Henry*, XI, pp. 129–30, XIII, pp. 132–3; Gerald of Wales, *Expugnatio Hibernica*, I.7, p. 43, I.8, p. 45, I.14, p. 59.
314 J. Bliese, 'Rhetoric and Morale – A Study of Battle Orations from the Central Middle Ages', *Journal of Medieval History*, 15 (1989), pp. 201–26; J. Bliese, 'The Battle Rhetoric of Aelred of Rievaulx', *Haskins Society Journal*, 1 (1989), pp. 99–107. Cf. William of Poitiers, *Gesta Guillelmi*, II.15, p. 125: 'we do not doubt that the exhortation ... was outstanding, even though it has not been transmitted to us in all its distinction'.
315 Suger, *Gesta Hludowici*, X, pp. 49–50, XVI, pp. 72–4, XVII, pp. 77–8, XIX, p. 85, XXIV, pp. 107–8, XXVIII, pp. 129–30, XXIX, pp. 136–7, XXXI, p. 143, XXXIII, pp. 152, 155. Cf. Orderic Vitalis, *Historia Ecclesiastica*, IV, pp. 313–15, VII.7, pp. 33–9, VII.15, pp. 81–95, VIII.2, pp. 121–5, VIII.26, pp. 313–21.

authority because of the ease with which they can be made up. In Quintilian's view, 'false exposition' must therefore be made congruent with person, place and time. It should have a credible line of reasoning and a credible order or arrangement. If possible, it should also be made consistent with something which *is* true or which can be confirmed by an argument that is already in the case. Above all, there should be no internal self-contradiction, something, Quintilian observes, which often happens to those who make things up (*fingentes*). There should certainly be no contradiction with those things which have already been established as true or with what can be proven otherwise by material and human testimony. In putting forward *falsa expositio*, therefore, the speakers or writers need to remember what they have made up, since people tend to forget things that are false. Quintilian quotes the popular saying that 'a liar [*mendax*] ought to have a memory'. The term *mendax* is not a slip of his pen. He uses it twice. What is made up in this way, he states, should not be sought entirely from outside the matter under discussion because, if that happens, the speaker will be betraying what Quintilian calls 'the licence to lie' (*licentia mentiendi*).[316]

The terminology here is very interesting: *argumentum*, or rhetorical *fictio*, can be distinguished from *fabula*, or poetic *fictio*; the act of making something up (*fingere*) can comprise something which is false (*falsa*) and a lie (*mendacium*). Analysed in the context of deliberative rhetoric, dissimulation and lying were already classified as one of several strategies to secure what is advantageous (*utile*).[317] Quintilian repeats the connection with military matters when he points out that a commander (*imperator*) – his example is Hannibal – often has to make use of what is false (*falsa*).[318] He also draws a parallel between the way in which commanders divide their forces in order to cover all the different arenas of war and the way in which orators arrange the different parts of a speech.[319] Quintilian, in fact, has rather a lot to say about a category of lying

---

316 Quintilian, *Institutio Oratoria*, IV.2.88–94, pp. 99–101.
317 See page 231.
318 *Institutio Oratoria*, II.17.19, pp. 333–5. For the original connection see page 231.
319 *Institutio Oratoria*, VII.10.13, pp. 169–71; cf. XII.9.2, p. 437.

which is 'useful'. He is certainly prepared to accept that there are some people who think that rhetoric has been used to undermine the position of political communities, and even to overthrow them, by making falsehood prevail against truth.[320] He himself confesses that rhetoric does indeed, on occasion, put forward false things (*falsa*) rather than true. When orators substitute falsehood for truth, however, Quintilian points out that they *know* that it is a falsehood and that it is being used instead of the truth. These orators do not themselves possess that false opinion and therefore do not deceive themselves, even though they deceive others. Nonetheless, for Quintilian, in this case at least, the end justifies the means. He draws the comparison with painting, pointing out that artists project three dimensions even though, in truth, they work on a two-dimensional plane. Given the metaphors which were used to describe the visual nature of *enargeia* or *evidentia*,[321] this was a significant parallel to invoke. It is not morally reprehensible (*turpe*), he concludes, to make use of vices in order to secure a good end; it is not a vice (*vitium*) to say something false in order to move the emotions, *provided* the principle for doing so is good. Even a wise man, Quintilian suggests, is at times permitted to tell a lie. The orator may be obliged to arouse the passions if this is the only way to lead a judge or an audience to justice and, if that judge or audience is lacking in wisdom (*imperitus*), then they will often *have* to be deceived in this way if their judgment is not to err. If every judge and every audience were wise, of course, if every court and political assembly were made up of wise people, then this would not be necessary, since there would be no enmity, no partiality, no preconceived opinions and no false witnesses. In such an eventuality, the scope of eloquence would effectively be limited to serving as a source of pleasure. However, this is clearly not the case. Not only is truth assailed by a large number of evils but also human minds are changeable.[322] As a result, although Quintilian suggests that the orator will be much more frequently called upon to defend the truth, he accepts that this does not always happen. There *are* times when the advantage of everyone

---

320 *Institutio Oratoria*, II.16.2, p. 319; cf. page 366.
321 See pages 330–3.
322 *Institutio Oratoria*, II.17.19–29, pp. 333–7.

(*communis utilitas*) will actually *require* that a speaker should defend what is false.[323] There is a fine line separating the virtues from the vices but orators will redescribe rashness, for example, as bravery, or classify prodigality as generosity, only when they are drawn to do so by considering what is to the common advantage.[324] Rhetoric, in short, may not always have as its aim telling the truth but it does always aim at describing things which have verisimilitude, which possess the similitude of truth. Orators will always know themselves when what they are saying is verisimilar.[325]

Quintilian goes to some considerable lengths to control the practical application of his 'licence to lie'. That art can be used to deceive an audience if 'advantage' (*utilitas*) demands it, for example, is a principle which he reports Aristotle classifying under judicial rhetoric. Deliberative rhetoric, by contrast, giving counsel or advice in a political assembly, always requires good faith (*fides*) and prudence alone.[326] Above all, Quintilian insists on the fact that individuals engaged in such a deception should themselves be morally virtuous. The aim of the orator, he states, is always to convince the judge or audience that what is being proposed seems both true and morally worthy. The morally worthy individual will generally speak or write what is true and *honestum* more frequently than a wicked individual. As a result, even if it sometimes happens that orators are led by duty (*officium*) to make use of things which are false in order to confirm what is true and morally worthy, these individuals will still necessarily be listened to with greater credence because they are themselves morally worthy people. The orator is skilled in rhetoric but he is, first and foremost, a virtuous individual, 'a good man skilled in speaking' (*vir bonus dicendi peritus*), and, of the two halves of this definition, the more important is that he should be a *vir bonus* – he will never be an orator unless he is. *This* is the prerequisite which

---

323 *Institutio Oratoria*, II.17.36, p. 341.
324 *Institutio Oratoria*, III.7.25, p. 477. For the redescription of rashness as bravery, and prodigality as generosity, see, for example, William of Malmesbury, *Gesta Regum Anglorum*, IV.374, p. 663, V.418, p. 757; cf. page 180. See also Isidore, *Etymologiae*, ed. and trans. Marshall, II.21.9, p. 80.
325 *Institutio Oratoria*, II.17.39, p. 343.
326 *Institutio Oratoria*, III.8.63, p. 511; cf. Aristotle, *On Rhetoric*, trans. G.A. Kennedy (Oxford, 1991), III.12, p. 256. See also page 464.

will prevent rhetoric from becoming an enemy to the truth and a danger to the community.[327]

The moral probity of the speaker or writer is thus, for Quintilian, the all-important safeguard on granting rhetoric a licence to lie. This is why he maintains that orators will primarily concern themselves with the cultivation of their own *mores* and with mastering the entirety of moral virtue and justice. Without this, an orator can neither be a 'good man' nor 'skilled in speaking'.[328] Nonetheless, and despite the additional argument that it is useful to know about falsehood and injustice in order to be able to detect and defeat them with greater ease, Quintilian clearly recognises that he is on dodgy ground. Quintilian, like Cicero, knew and accepted the arguments contained in Plato's *Gorgias* and *Phaedrus* that rhetoric could be, and was being, used for evil purposes, that it led people to side with falsehood against the truth, when it was separated from justice and preference was shown to verisimilitude over truth.[329] At first sight, Quintilian concedes, it does indeed seem hard to accept that

---

327 *Institutio Oratoria*, XII.1.1–3, pp. 355–7, XII.1.11–12, pp. 361–3, XII.1.27–32, pp. 371–3; cf. Cicero, *De Inventione*, I.1.1, pp. 3–5. For the subsequent transmission of the phrase 'a good man skilled in speaking', see, for example, Cassiodorus, *Institutiones*, trans. J.W. Halporn, *Institutions of Divine and Secular Learning* (Liverpool, 2004), II.2.1, p. 178; Isidore, *Etymologiae*, ed. and trans. Marshall, II.3.1, p. 24; Alcuin, *Disputatio de Rhetorica et de Virtutibus*, lines 33–51, p. 68; Hrabanus Maurus, *De Clericorum Institutione*, ed. D. Zimpel (Frankfurt, 1996), III.27, pp. 488–9; Dominicus Gundissalinus, *De Divisione Philosophiae*, ed. A. Fidora and D. Werner, *Über die Einteilung der Philosophie* (Freiburg, 2007), p. 146; Vincent of Beauvais, *Speculum Historiale*, I.55, p. 22. Originally taken from Seneca the Elder, *Controversiae*, ed. and trans. M. Winterbottom and W.C. Wright, *Declamationes* (Loeb, 1974), I.praef.9, pp. 9–11, it was applied, for example, to Bede by William of Malmesbury (*Gesta Regum Anglorum*, I.59, p. 91) and to Bernard of Clairvaux by Wibald of Stavelot, abbot of Corvey, in *Letters*, trans. G. Ellspermann, in J.M. Miller, M.H. Prosser and T.W. Benson (eds), *Readings in Medieval Rhetoric* (Bloomington, 1973), Ep.147, p. 213. For the close connection between rhetoric and the life of virtue in the eleventh and twelfth centuries, see C.S. Jaeger, 'Humanism and Ethics at the School of St. Victor in the Early Twelfth Century', *Mediaeval Studies*, 55 (1993), pp. 51–79; reprinted in C.S. Jaeger, *Scholars and Courtiers: Intellectuals and Society in the Medieval West* (Aldershot, 2002); C.S. Jaeger, *The Envy of Angels: Cathedral Schools and Social Ideals in Medieval Europe 950–1200* (Philadelphia, 1994). For Petrarch, see pages 480–1. Cf. Robert of Basevorn, *Forma Praedicandi*, I, p. 120.
328 Quintilian, *Institutio Oratoria*, XII.2.1–4, p. 383; Cicero, *De Oratore*, III.14.55, p. 45.
329 *Institutio Oratoria*, II.15.24–32, pp. 311–15; cf. Cicero, *De Inventione*, I.1.1, pp. 3–5, I.2.3–4.5, pp. 9–13; Plato, *Gorgias*, trans. R. Waterfield (Oxford, 1994); *Phaedrus*, trans. R. Waterfield (Oxford, 2002), 257c–279c, pp. 43–75.

there can be *any* reason why a morally virtuous individual should wish, on occasion, to conceal the truth from a judge and to speak in defence of falsehood or even injustice. Quintilian immediately counters this objection, however, by asking whether this should really be a source of surprise, given that there are many things which can become either morally worthy or morally reprehensible, not because of the acts themselves, but because of their causes, the reasons for which they are done. If it can sometimes be virtuous to kill another human being, or even one's own children (for which the classical *exemplum* was Brutus),[330] then it has to be conceded that still more unspeakable deeds might be justified when the general advantage (*communis utilitas*) demands it, as soon as one examines, not the act itself, but the reason why a morally good individual should have done such a deed.[331] Everyone, even the strictest of Stoics, has to concede that the virtuous individual will, on occasion, tell a lie (*mendacium*), sometimes for the most superficial of reasons – making things up (*fingere*) for the benefit of sick children, for example, promising them many things that the individual will not, in fact, do – let alone when the reason is to prevent someone being killed or when deception is practised on an enemy in order to preserve the fatherland (*patria*). Quintilian extends this list of extenuating circumstances. Certain acts, he argues, which are just by nature can nonetheless become disadvantageous to the political community depending on the circumstances of the times (*condicio temporum*). By the same token, it can become justifiable to use things that are false (*falsa*) in order to defend someone who has, for example, acted against a tyrant, when that person would otherwise be condemned. In the same way, it is justifiable to defend the guilty if their acquittal will result in the reformation of their character, or to acquit a guilty person when he is a good military leader and is therefore someone whom the orator is required to defend out of consideration for the general advantage (*communis utilitas*). However rarely such situations may arise, Quintilian

---

330 Vergil, *Aeneid*, VI.820–3, p. 565; Livy, *Ab Urbe Condita*, trans. B. O. Foster, *et al.* (Loeb, 1919–59), II.5, pp. 233–5.
331 For Machiavelli's development of this argument, see his *Discourses on Livy*, trans. J.C. Bondanella and P. Bondanella (Oxford, 1997), I.16, p. 63 (see also pages 507–8).

concludes, it is reasoning of this kind which compels the orator to act in this way. Such considerations are not inconsistent with a definition of the rhetorician as a morally worthy individual, as the *vir bonus dicendi peritus*. If orators defend what is false, then their actions will remain *honestum* provided they have acted with this good intention.[332]

This is therefore the third and final point which needs to be made with regard to narrative and its relationship to the writing of history in the Middle Ages. Something which is 'made up' (*fingere, ficta*) is, in rhetorical terms, a very elastic category indeed – hardly surprisingly, perhaps, given that, as Gregory the Great pointed out when discussing Christ's actions on the road to Emmaus, the verb *fingere* could also serve as a synonym for 'compose' (*componere*).[333] The term *fictio* could thus traverse the whole sweep of argumentation – from hypothesis, through plausible or credible reconstruction, false exposition, all the way to the poetic, the fabulous and the mendacious. According to Dominicus Gundissalinus, the subject-matter of poetry consisted either of what had been done (*res gesta*, for which Vergil is his prime example) or what had been made up (*res ficta*). Events in this second category (*res ficta*) were then subject to a further distinction between things which could have occurred (in which case they were to be classified as 'argument', like the parables in the Gospels) and things which could not (in which case they were 'fable'). This last category, *fabula*, was subdivided, in turn, according to the purpose for which it was composed – pleasure (such as Terence) or moral edification (such as Horace) and, if it was the latter, then it could be defined as 'fictive in principle but true in meaning' (*ficta quadam ratione sed veraci significatione*).[334] Where exactly the boundary lies between these different types of *fictio* (and the absence of this term as a

---

332 Quintilian, *Institutio Oratoria*, XII.1.34–44, pp. 375–81, XII.7.7, p. 423; cf. Cicero, *De Oratore*, III.29.113, p. 91.
333 Gregory the Great, *XL Homiliae in Evangelia*, trans. D. Hurst, *Forty Gospel Homilies* (Kalamazoo, 1990), II.23.1, p. 177. See also page 384.
334 Dominicus Gundissalinus, *De Divisione Philosophiae*, p. 126; cf. Macrobius, *Commentary on the Dream of Scipio*, I.2, pp. 84–5 (see page 383); Augustine, *Contra Mendacium*, trans. H. Browne, *To Consentius: Against Lying* (in Augustine, *Seventeen Short Treatises*, Oxford, 1847), XXVIII, pp. 454–6 (and see page 385); Mehtonen, *Old Concepts and New Poetics*, p. 43.

noun from the writings of both Cicero and Quintilian is, in itself, striking) will depend on the particular circumstances in which it is being deployed. Once again, the exact form which will be given to such an account will be governed by what is suitable or appropriate (*aptum*), both for the subject-matter and, above all, for the audience to whom it is directed.

Each one of the three types of rhetoric – demonstrative, judicial and deliberative – involves the discovery or 'invention' of arguments, that is, the inclusion of material which will make the narrative of deeds done in the past more plausible or convincing. The key criterion that governs which one of a whole range of possible arguments – particular or generic, 'topics' or commonplaces – should be selected and included is appropriateness or suitability (*aptum*), that is, what is required by the nature of the subject-matter but also, just as importantly, by the nature of the audience which is being addressed. The result is a vast array of techniques and strategies which are designed to make a narrative plausible, to give persons and deeds the quality of verisimilitude, the 'likeness' of truth. This involves accommodating a narrative account to Nature, to what generally happens, but also to what is in accordance with the beliefs or opinions of the audience. This also involves making it pleasurable and entertaining. Above all, however, it means making a narrative account realistic, using *enargeia* or *evidentia* to give the impression that an audience or judge is witnessing, with their very own eyes, the people and the events being narrated. The range of rhetorical strategies which is contained in this single term 'verisimilitude', together with the appeal to belief or credence (*fides*) in what is being narrated, combine to form the methodological basis on which history could be written in the Middle Ages.

Given the prominence of eyewitness testimony to Isidore's original definition of the truth of historiography, as well as of the accepted etymology of the Greek verb 'historein', the visual quality of evidence or *enargeia*, of presenting something before the eyes of an audience or reader, became all-important common ground between rhetoric and the writing of history. According to Conrad of Hirsau, for example, the term 'writer of history' (*historiographus*) should be understood as a writer of something seen (*rei visae scriptor*).[335] The resulting verisimilitude necessarily raised all sorts of difficult questions about the truth-content of a historical narrative. The very last thing which classical manuals of rhetoric suggest, however, is that the nature of such narrative presented a neat polarity of true and false, of 'history' and 'fiction'.[336] Between these categories there was an all-important middle ground – between historical truth and impossible fable there was plausible argument. It was this tripartite classification, therefore – history, argument and fable – which governed a medieval understanding of narrative, both of persons and of deeds, and, as a result, extended to the understanding, reading and writing of history.[337] Gerald of Wales suggested that his readers should not be too quick to take offence or level accusations if his material appeared to turn from history to fables (*ab historia tamquam ad fabulas*), on the grounds that not everything which presents the image of falseness (*imago falsitatis*) is fabulous and not everything which is verisimilar (*verisimilia*) should immediately be accepted as true (*pro veris*).[338] How exactly the boundary between these three qualities was to be negotiated was clearly no less complex a question for medieval historians than it is now, since within the context of historiography, if not elsewhere, this middle category of verisimilitude invited the simple question 'what is truth?' (John 18:38).

---

335 Conrad of Hirsau, *Dialogue on the Authors*, p. 43; cf. Aulus Gellius, *Noctes Atticae*, trans. J.C. Rolfe, *Attic Nights* (Loeb, 1927), V.18, pp. 433–7; Servius, *In Vergilii Carmina Commentarii*, I.373, pp. 125–6.
336 Cf. Walter Map, *De Nugis Curialium*, I.31, p. 129: 'history, which is founded on truth, and fable, which weaves together what is made up' (*historia qua veritate nititur et fabula que ficta contexit*). For Walter's views on the moral–didactic purpose of his own collection of *exempla*, both historical and fabulous, see *De Nugis Curialium*, I.12, p. 37 and, more generally, M. Otter, *Inventiones: Fiction and Referentiality in Twelfth-Century English Historical Writing* (Chapel Hill, 1996), pp. 111–28; B. Weiler, 'Royal Virtue and Royal Justice in Walter Map's *De Nugis Curialium* and William of Malmesbury's *Historia Novella*', in I. Bejczy and R. Newhauser (eds), *Virtue and Ethics in the Twelfth Century* (Leiden, 2005), pp. 317–39; R. Levine, 'How to Read Walter Map', *Mittellateinisches Jahrbuch*, 23 (1988), pp. 91–105.
337 Cf. R. Morse, *Truth and Convention in the Middle Ages: Rhetoric, Representation and Reality* (Cambridge, 1991); J. Beer, *Narrative Conventions of Truth in the Middle Ages* (Geneva, 1981); Fleischman, 'On the Representation of History and Fiction in the Middle Ages'; M. Otter, 'Functions of Fiction in Historical Writing', in N. Partner (ed.), *Writing Medieval History* (London, 2005), pp. 109–30.
338 Gerald of Wales, *Expugnatio Hibernica*, III.prol., p. 255.

4

VERISIMILITUDE AND TRUTH

In setting out the principles by which arguments could be found in order to construct a narrative of people and of events, classical manuals of rhetoric gave central importance to the criterion of verisimilitude. Quintilian may have disagreed with those who thought that the *sole* concern of the orator was verisimilitude,[1] but otherwise medieval authors were presented with a very clear agenda: truth requires the art of rhetoric in order to make it plausible or convincing, in order to give it the appearance or similitude of truth. This may involve composing or making things up (*fingere*) and the resulting *ficta* can cover a very wide range of possibilities indeed. These start with the strictest sense in which such 'fiction' (*fictio*) can be understood, namely as hypothesis (that is, the plausible reconstruction of events which, if true, would explain a matter that is otherwise subject to doubt), but they extend all the way to an account which is knowingly false (*falsa expositio*) and a lie which is intended to deceive (*mendacium*). Where exactly a particular argument and, by extension, a particular narrative should be placed along this 'sliding scale'[2] is determined or conditioned by one of three factors: by the nature of the subject-matter under discussion; by what generally happens according to nature; and by what is in accordance with the opinions or beliefs of the audience or judge to whom the narrative is being addressed. It is on the basis of the third factor that a writer may have to move

---

[1] Quintilian, *Institutio Oratoria*, trans. H.E. Butler (Loeb, 1920–22), II.15.32, p. 315; cf. page 345.
[2] M. Otter, *Inventiones: Fiction and Referentiality in Twelfth-Century English Historical Writing* (Chapel Hill, 1996), pp. 12, 60, 160.

away from rhetorical *fictio* or verisimilitude, from making things up that could have happened, to making things up that could never have happened, namely poetic *fictio* or *fabula*. This final type of 'fiction' is particularly suitable when an audience or judge is ignorant, or less well-educated, a situation in which it becomes not only appropriate but advantageous to make the truth of a narrative more plausible, more credible, by exploiting a 'licence to lie' and drawing on the authority of fable.

Given the proximity of the relationship between rhetoric and the writing of history in the Middle Ages, the consequences of such a comprehensive principle of verisimilitude for the nature of the 'truth' which that historiography was held to contain were naturally far-reaching. Indeed, in many respects, they went to the heart of what *historia* was considered to be, especially when it was precisely this sort of strategic ornamentation which was being identified as the main criterion that differentiated the writing of history from the writing of annals or chronicles.[3] These consequences – and the debate they triggered – are best approached by examining the respective relationships between truth and utility, truth and opinion, truth and 'fiction' and, finally, between truth and lies.

Rhetoric itself possesses utility or advantage in that, according to Quintilian, it was essential both to the origins of human association in political communities (when founders of cities used learned speech in order to bring wandering multitudes together and unite them into peoples) and to the subsequent task of legislation (when the highest powers of oratory were used to make people bind themselves to serve the law). The precepts by which life is led may have an intrinsic moral worth of their own, Quintilian observes, but they are better able to inform human minds when they are illuminated by the splendour of rhetoric.[4] This account of the usefulness of rhetoric to human 'civilisation' took its cue from the opening to *De Inventione*. In Cicero's view, human beings originally wandered in the fields like wild animals, administering their lives, not from reason, but mostly from physical strength; they possessed no religion, no sense of

---

3 See pages 88–91.
4 Quintilian, *Institutio Oratoria*, II.16.9–10, pp. 321–3.

duty to other humans, no legitimate marriage and no sense of the benefits of justice or equity; instead, they lived in ignorance and error and were ruled by cupidity. It was only when reason was combined with eloquence, Cicero argued, that a wise individual could bring such feral humans together in one place and induce into these brutes everything that is morally worthy and advantageous, thereby transforming them from the savage state of wild beasts. Only persuasive eloquence, in other words, could produce justice and good faith (*fides*); only rhetoric could make humans see the reason in obeying others voluntarily, in working, and even in sacrificing their lives, for the common benefit.[5]

Whilst rhetoric was seen to serve the utility of the human community as a whole, its advantages could also be directed towards more specific ends and, in this respect, the principle of verisimilitude was also capable of being deployed in the service of particular truths. The use of plausible or verisimilar arguments was thus acknowledged to produce, not just understanding (*cognitio*), but also utility or advantage (*utilitas*).[6] Verisimilitude was therefore deployed to secure what was advantageous to a particular case, as a means of narrating what would persuade an audience to believe the truth of what was being said. Analysis of the precise nature of the 'useful' arguments which could be discovered in the course of 'invention' indicated that the boundary between the utility of rhetoric and the truth of dialectic could be pretty flexible – *argumentum* could start with the enthymeme, with the looser form of syllogism, but it also covered a long list of

---

5 Cicero, *De Inventione*, trans. H.M. Hubbell (Loeb, 1949), I.2–3, pp. 5–7; cf. Cicero, *De Oratore*, trans. E. Sutton and H. Rackham (Loeb, 1948), I.8.32–3, p. 25; Alcuin, *Disputatio de Rhetorica et de Virtutibus*, ed. and trans. W.S. Howell, *The Rhetoric of Alcuin and Charlemagne* (Princeton, 1941), lines 33–51, p. 68; Rufinus [of Bologna], *Summa Decretorum*, in R. Somerville and B.C. Brasington, *Prefaces to Canon Law Books in Latin Christianity: Selected Translations 500–1245* (New Haven, 1998), pref., pp. 191–2; John of Salisbury, *Metalogicon*, trans. D.D. McGarry (Berkeley, 1955), I.1, p. 11; Gerald of Wales, *Topographia Hibernica*, trans. J.J. O'Meara, *The History and Topography of Ireland* (Harmondsworth, 1982), III.93, pp. 101–2. Otto of Freising combined this account from *De Inventione* with a Christian version (Christ is the *vir magnus et sapiens*), which he took from Eusebius: Otto of Freising, *Chronicle*, trans. C.C. Mierow, *The Two Cities: A Chronicle of Universal History* (New York, 1928); reprinted 2000), I.6, p. 130, III.prol., pp. 217, 220; cf. Eusebius, *Ecclesiastical History*, trans. G.A. Williamson (Harmondsworth, 1965), I.2.19, pp. 38–9.
6 See pages 315, 318, 344.

other proofs, which comprised arguments of successively smaller degrees of demonstrative certainty down to, and including, common report and reputation (*rumor, fama*). In part, this range of possibilities was created by the intellectual capacity of different types of audience. According to Cicero, the defining principle of oratory was concerned, in some measure, with common practice, with the custom and speech of humankind. As a result, whereas, in all other disciplines, a superior rank was given to whatever was furthest removed from the understanding and sense of the untrained (*imperiti*), in rhetoric the greatest sin was to depart from the popular manner of speaking and the usage of common sense (*communis sensus*).[7] In Cicero's view, the eloquence of orators had accordingly always been controlled by the prudence of their audience, in the sense that speakers who wanted to secure assent would always examine the will (*voluntas*) of those who were listening to them, making things up (*fingere*) and accommodating themselves entirely to what would secure their audience's approval (*nutum*) and judgment.[8]

Truth, for Cicero, is part of the law of nature. He defines it as the means by which things that exist in the past, present and future are stated unchanged (*immutata*); it provides the means by which a speaker ensures that there is no difference between what happened, is happening or will happen and what that speaker is affirming to be the case.[9] The truth, however, is not, in itself, enough; it has to be made convincing, and this will necessarily mean being accommodated to the opinion of an audience. If this audience is a group of like-minded intellectuals, such accommodation need go no further than deploying the rules of logic and dialectic; in all other cases, however, it will extend to using the techniques and strategies of rhetoric, not least as a means of providing pleasure. This is, after all, simply an expression of one of the fundamental goals of rhetoric. Instruction on its own is not enough. In order that people will be inspired to *act* upon what they are being taught, it is also necessary to move an

---

[7] Cicero, *De Oratore*, I.3.12, p. 11 (see also page 304).
[8] Cicero, *Orator*, trans. H.M. Hubbell (Loeb, 1962), VIII.24, p. 323, cited by Quintilian, *Institutio Oratoria*, XII.2.23, p. 395.
[9] Cicero, *De Inventione*, II.53.161, p. 329; II.22.66, p. 231; cf. Huguccio of Pisa, *Derivationes*, ed. E. Cecchini, *et al.* (Florence, 2004), p. 1263.

audience's emotions, and one of the best ways of achieving this is to make a series of precepts attractive, to win that audience's goodwill by making what is being said a source of pleasure. In the case of narrative, this pleasure-principle means providing invented speeches and set-piece battle scenes, as well as deploying the *excursus*, or digression.[10] The harsher a subject is in terms of its nature, in fact, the more it will have to be seasoned (*condire*) with things that give pleasure.[11] Indeed, according to Quintilian, whilst argumentation is made less suspect to an audience by the employment of such dissimulation, pleasure is of great assistance in creating belief or credence (*fides*).[12]

If an ability to draw on the full range of argumentation, from enthymeme to rumour, is demanded by the nature of a rhetorician's audience, it is also, in part, a question of the subject-matter, in the sense that, by its very nature, rhetoric deals with things which are the subject of controversy, which are subject to differing views precisely because they are open to doubt. Verisimilitude is thus more than just a technique of vivid and realistic description and of strategic accommodation to the beliefs and expectations of one's audience; it also marks a recognition of the limited degree of epistemological certainty which might be attainable for a given event or phenomenon. As Quintilian observes, it often happens that there is a question over the time or the place at which something is said to have been done (*gesta res*) and sometimes over the person who did it. He chooses the example of historiography to make the point: Livy is very frequently in doubt, he states, and some historians have a different opinion from others.[13] This explicit acknowledgment therefore provides a second strand to the significance of plausibility or verisimilitude (*verisimilitudo*) for the writing of history – its own epistemological status, as opinion (*opinio*) rather than as knowledge (*scientia*), and, as a result, its close connection to the philosophical scepticism of the Academy.

---

10 See pages 305, 315.
11 For William of Malmesbury's use of this metaphor, see his *Gesta Regum Anglorum*, ed. and trans. R.A.B. Mynors, R.M. Thomson and M. Winterbottom, *The History of the English Kings* (Oxford, 1998–9), I.prol., p. 15.
12 Quintilian, *Institutio Oratoria*, V.14.35, p. 369.
13 *Institutio Oratoria*, II.4.19, p. 235; cf. John of Salisbury, *Policraticus*, trans. J.B. Pike, *The Frivolities of Courtiers and the Footprints of Philosophers* (Minneapolis, 1938), VII.prol., p. 215 (see also page 424).

Direct familiarity with epistemological scepticism was made possible in the Middle Ages primarily through the arguments outlined in Cicero's *Academica*, a work which claimed that the wise man assents to nothing because the truth cannot be known, that the sublunary world contains only the appearance of truth, and that it would not be wise to assent to something which is erroneous or false.[14] Cicero himself drew a close connection between such a philosophy and the nature of rhetoric when he acknowledged that whatever rhetorical ability he himself possessed came, not from any specific training in the 'workshops' of orators, but from the various fields of philosophical debate in the Academy.[15] This affiliation also forms the substance of his closing remarks to the *Orator* – he is not, he states, asserting that the views on rhetoric which he has just expounded are more true than those of his reader; what he is claiming as the basis for his judgment is the fact that they seemed to be most *like* the truth (*simillimum veri*). This is a principle, he concludes, which, in fact, applies to all the most important subjects and not just to a subject, such as eloquence, which is concerned with securing popular assent (*assensus vulgi*) and pleasure.[16] According to Cicero's *De Oratore*, it can also be argued that rhetoric, on this basis, is not actually an art because, whereas an art is concerned with things that are known, the activity of orators is concerned with opinions (*opiniones*), rather than with knowledge (*scientia*), and is exercised about things of which speakers or writers are themselves not certain and in front of people who lack knowledge of them. Strictly speaking, therefore, rhetoric is, as Aristotle had argued, a faculty, not an art, or, if it is to be called an art, then this is only in a loose or approximate

---

14 Cicero, *Academica*, trans. H. Rackham (Loeb, 1967); cf. Cicero, *De Oratore*, III.36.145, p. 115; Cicero, *Tusculan Disputations*, trans. J.E. King (Loeb, 1945), II.2.4, p. 151, quoted, for example, by John of Salisbury, *Metalogicon*, II.14, p. 106; cf. L.D. Reynolds(ed.), *Texts and Transmission: A Survey of the Latin Classics* (Oxford, 1983) and, more generally, P. MacKendrick, *The Philosophical Books of Cicero* (London, 1989), pp. 149–68. Compare Paschasius Radbertus, *Epitaphium Arsenii*, trans. A. Cabaniss, *Charlemagne's Cousins: Contemporary Lives of Adalard and Wala* (Syracuse, 1967), I.8, p. 104: 'perhaps, like certain philosophers, we hold all things doubtful and we philosophise that nothing can be held certain'.
15 Cicero, *Orator*, III.12, p. 313.
16 *Orator*, LXXI.237, p. 509.

sense (*quasi ars quaedam*).[17] Quintilian disagreed (rhetoric is an art, he states, and Aristotle's *On Rhetoric* proves it),[18] but not before he summarised and repeated the objections from *De Oratore* – rhetoric cannot be an art because orators are concerned entirely with *opinio*, not with *scientia*, and because orators sometimes relate things of which they have no knowledge in front of people who have no knowledge of them; rhetoric therefore does not always have as its aim things that are true, even though it does always aim at saying things that are *verisimilia*.[19]

The rhetorical 'fiction' which is produced by implementing the principles of verisimilitude in the course of finding arguments that are appropriate to a particular case and a particular audience is, strictly speaking, distinct from the practice of 'making up' material which could simply never have happened. The degree to which such a distinction between *verisimilitudo* and *fabula* was acknowledged and maintained, however, could vary. In the *Topica*, for example, Cicero runs both concepts of *fictio* together in the course of describing the use of *ficta exempla similitudinis*. It is permissible, he states, for orators and philosophers to make mute things speak, to raise the dead, or to relate something which simply could not have happened, and many other amazing things (*mirabilia*), all in order to strengthen a case.[20] This licence is particularly important in the case of *enargeia* or 'evidence', the visual quality of narrative which moves the emotions precisely because it makes its contents so vivid.[21] It is on this basis that a combination of rhetorical fiction and poetic fiction was permitted to those

---

17 Cicero, *De Oratore*, II.7.30–8.33, pp. 219–21; cf. Aristotle, *On Rhetoric*, trans. G.A. Kennedy (Oxford, 1991), I.2, pp. 36–7.
18 See pages 460–1.
19 Quintilian, *Institutio Oratoria*, II.17.14, pp. 331–3, II.17.36–9, pp. 341–3. For the distinction between an art (*ars*) and a discipline (*disciplina*), see Isidore of Seville, *Etymologiae*, trans. S.A. Barney, W.J. Lewis, J.A. Beach and O. Berghof (Cambridge, 2006), I.1.1–3, p. 39: 'an art consists of matters that can turn out in different ways, whilst a discipline is concerned with things that have only one possible outcome. Thus, when something is expounded with true arguments, it will be a discipline; when something merely resembling the truth and based on opinion is treated [*veris disputationibus ... disseritur verisimile atque opinabile*], it will have the name of an art'.
20 Cicero, *Topica*, trans. H. M. Hubbell (Loeb, 1949), X.45, p. 415 (see also page 270); cf. Boethius, *In Ciceronis Topica*, trans. E. Stump (Ithaca, 1988), IV, p. 116.
21 See pages 331–2.

who were writing history in accordance with the principles of rhetoric – different subjects, different parts of the text and different audiences could each require the adoption of a distinct approach. Naturally, there were different rules to be observed in poetry from those that applied to history – according to Cicero, it would be wrong, for example, to look for the truth of a witness from a poet.[22] Whereas 'everything' (*omnia*) in history aims at the truth, he points out, 'almost everything' (*pleraque*) in poetry aims at pleasure. However, Cicero also recognises that this had not prevented Herodotus, the father of history, from including countless fables in his writing.[23] Lucan, likewise, explicitly criticises anyone who demands true things from the poet but who also refuses to allow legend (*fama*) in the long-distant past.[24]

Given the fact that acknowledgment of a theoretical distinction between verisimilitude and fable did not prevent these two categories from being combined in practice, it is, in itself, revealing that the fluidity of the boundary between rhetoric and poetry was a subject on which classical manuals of rhetoric had quite a lot to say. Poetic *exempla* carry weight because they have either been preserved by the belief of antiquity or are credited with having been made up by great personages in order to take the place of precepts.[25] The poet 'borders' (*finitimus*) on the orator, both stylistically and linguistically. Poets may have stricter rules of metre and greater freedom of vocabulary but otherwise they are almost on a par with orators in their shared use of many types of ornamentation and figures of speech. The poet can thus be described as a companion (*socius*), even next of kin (*proxima cognatio*), to the orator.[26] Poets are explicitly conceded greater licence to say

---

22 Cicero, *De Legibus*, trans. J.E.G. Zetzel, *On the Commonwealth* (Cambridge, 1999), I.4–5, p. 106.
23 *De Legibus*, I.4–5, p. 106.
24 Lucan, *Pharsalia*, trans. J.D. Duff, *The Civil War* (Loeb, 1928), IX.359–60, p. 531; cf. Vergil, *Aeneid*, trans. H.R. Fairclough, rev. G.P. Goold (Loeb, 2000), IX.79, p. 119: 'belief in the deed is ancient, but its reputation is everlasting' (*prisca fides facto, sed fama perennis*).
25 See page 324.
26 Cicero, *De Oratore*, I.16.70, pp. 51–3, III.7.27, p. 23; cf. Rufinus of Antioch, *On Word Arrangement and Metres in Oratory*, trans. I. Thomson, in J.M. Miller, M.H. Prosser and T.W. Benson (eds), *Readings in Medieval Rhetoric* (Bloomington, 1973), p. 38.

more than is strictly sufficient,[27] or to say what is demanded by the metre,[28] and therefore orators should not follow poets in the freedom with which they use vocabulary and figures of speech. Besides, in seeking to secure its single goal of pleasure, poetry makes up things that are not only false (*falsa*) but also beyond belief (*incredibilia*).[29] Nonetheless, although poets may have greater freedom in creating and arranging words, the principles which govern the judgment and choice of those words are the same.[30] This is why Quintilian thought that the study of the poets (*lectio poetarum*) would confer many benefits on the orator.[31] Of the epic poets, for example, he suggests that Homer provided a model and a starting-point for all the parts of rhetoric, be it demonstrative or deliberative, and whether it concerned the introduction, the narrative, the proof, or the task of moving the emotions. Of the comic poets, meanwhile, Menander provided the best example of how to castigate vice. Indeed, Quintilian proceeds to run through a long list of both Greek and Roman poets, evaluating each one of them for their specifically rhetorical qualities.[32] Orators can draw upon poetry in this way both to give trustworthiness or credibility (*fides*) to their case and to provide ornamentation for their eloquence. Quintilian points out that Cicero himself included quotations from Ennius, Terence and other poets; these excerpts are inserted, he remarks, not just for the sake of instruction and learning, but also to please his audience, since the charms of poetry provide a pleasant relief from the severity of his forensic eloquence. There is no little advantage in making such additions, Quintilian comments, since the reflections (*sententiae*) of poets serve as a sort of testimony in strengthening what is being put forward.[33] This close relationship extends to the specifics of training and educating an orator – translation or *conversio*, and especially the paraphrase of verse into prose, is a valuable exercise, according to Quintilian, because the sublime spirit of poetry can

---

27 *Rhetorica ad Herennium*, trans. H. Caplan (Loeb), II.22.34, pp. 119–21; Cicero, *Orator*, LX.202, p. 477.
28 Quintilian, *Institutio Oratoria*, I.6.2, p. 113.
29 *Institutio Oratoria*, X.1.28, p. 19.
30 Cicero, *Orator*, XX.68, p. 355.
31 Quintilian, *Institutio Oratoria*, X.1.27, pp. 17–19.
32 *Institutio Oratoria*, X.1.46–72, 85–100, pp. 29–43, 49–59.
33 *Institutio Oratoria*, I.8.11–12, p. 151 (and see pages 286–7, 309, 324).

elevate a work of rhetoric. Rhetoric has its strength enhanced by adding the reflections of poetry, once it has restricted the greater effusiveness and licence of poetic vocabulary, and supplies what poetry lacks.[34]

The proximity of the relationship between rhetoric and poetry was pointed up by classical manuals of poetry too. Horace's *Ars Poetica*, for example, makes claims for the nature and purpose of poetry, each one of which stood in parallel to those that Cicero had made for rhetoric. According to Horace, poetry is founded on a combination of pleasure, utility and instruction;[35] its source and guiding principle are provided by wisdom; and it uses appropriate styles for different subjects (including a Homeric style – that is, epic hexameter – when describing the deeds of kings). Poetry is a mixture of true things with false, the one proviso being that there should be internal consistency between them (*sibi convenientia*); material which is 'made up' (*ficta*) for the sake of pleasure may certainly be described by the term *fabula*, but its contents should at least approximate to the truth (*proxima veris*). Poetry should be characterised by the qualities of simplicity, clarity, order and brevity; it prefers action to narrative, characterisation to abstraction, because an audience is moved more sharply by seeing action with their own eyes than by simply hearing a narrative.[36] It is this visual quality which makes poetry comparable to painting and sculpture (*ut pictura poesis*). The social and political utility of poetry should therefore not be underestimated. According to Horace, in fact, it tames wild men, inscribes laws, instils virtue and sets out the path of life (*via vitae*).[37] The impact of such claims

---

34 *Institutio Oratoria*, X.5.4, p. 115.
35 Horace, *Ars Poetica*, trans. H.R. Fairclough (Loeb, 1929), line 333, p. 479. For the popularity of this particular pairing of utility and pleasure, see, for example, Walter Map, *De Nugis Curialium*, ed. and trans. M.L.R. James, rev. C.N.L. Brooke and R.A.B. Mynors (Oxford, 1983), III.prol., p. 211; John of Salisbury, *Metalogicon*, II.8, p. 92 (where it is combined with the *Rhetorica ad Herennium*); Gerald of Wales, *Topographia Hibernica*, III.122, p. 125.
36 Cf. Guibert of Nogent, *Gesta Dei per Francos*, trans. R. Levine, *The Deeds of God Through the Franks* (Woodbridge, 1997), IV, p. 73; Gerald of Wales, *Descriptio Cambriae*, trans. L. Thorpe, *The Journey Through Wales and the Description of Wales* (Harmondsworth, 1978), I.17, p. 252.
37 For medieval commentary, see S. Reynolds, *Medieval Reading: Grammar, Rhetoric and the Classical Text* (Cambridge, 1996), pp. 12–15; K. Friis-Jensen, 'The *Ars Poetica* in Twelfth-Century France – the Horace of Matthew of Vendôme,

on medieval writers was considerable. For example, Richer says that Gerbert of Aurillac regarded the study of poetry (by which he meant Vergil, Statius, Terence, Juvenal, Persius, Horace and 'the historian Lucan') to be preparatory to the study of rhetoric,[38] whilst Geoffrey of Vinsauf composed the *Poetria Nova* as part of his attempt to combine the precepts of Horace with those of Cicero.[39] Poetry and rhetoric, in short, were essentially regarded as verse and prose forms of the same principles of writing.[40]

In view of the relationship which existed (or was thought to exist) between poetry and rhetoric, it is perhaps not surprising that, over and above their proximity in the actual teaching of grammar, a comparable affinity was thought to exist between the writing of poetry and the writing of history. The *Rhetorica ad Herennium*, for instance, in a lengthy excursus on the stylistic examples which can be used to illustrate the ornaments of rhetoric, consistently places orators and poets side by side as sources for such *exempla*,[41] but it also pairs poets with writers of history (*scriptores historiarum*).[42] This is the context in which Quintilian made his famous observation that history 'is very close to poetry and is even, in a sense, a prose song' (*est enim proxima poetis et quodam modo carmen solutum*).[43] He points out that Greek histories, in particular, often display a freedom or

---

Geoffrey of Vinsauf, and John of Garland', *Cahiers de l'Institut du Moyen Âge Grec et Latin*, 60 (1990), pp. 319-88; K. Friis-Jensen, 'Horatius Liricus et Ethicus – Two Twelfth-Century School Texts on Horace's Poems', *Cahiers de l'Institut du Moyen Âge Grec et Latin*, 57 (1988), pp. 81-147; cf. Bernardus Silvestris, *Commentary on the First Six Books of Virgil's Aeneid*, trans. E.G. Schreiber and T.E. Maresca (Lincoln, 1979), VI, pp. 54-5.
38 Richer, *Historiae*, ed. and trans. R. Latouche (Paris, 1930-37), III.47-8, p. 56.
39 Geoffrey of Vinsauf, *Poetria Nova*, ed. and trans. E. Gallo, *The Poetria Nova and its Sources in Early Rhetorical Doctrine* (The Hague, 1971).
40 C.S. Baldwin, *Medieval Rhetoric and Poetic* (New York, 1928), ch. 3; E.R. Curtius, *European Literature and the Latin Middle Ages* (London, 1953), pp. 145-66; P. Zumthor, *Essai de Poétique Médiévale* (Paris, 1972), trans. P. Bennett, *Toward a Medieval Poetics* (Minneapolis, 1992), pp. 24-35; cf. ed. A. Michel, *Rhétorique et Poétique au Moyen Âge* (Turnhout, 2002); Bernardus Silvestris, *Commentary on the First Six Books of Virgil's Aeneid*, VI, p. 35 ('poetics is the knowledge of poets and has two parts – verse and prose'), VI, p. 36 ('eloquence is brighter than poetics; philosophy is the brightest').
41 *Rhetorica ad Herennium*, IV.1.1, p. 229, IV.1.2, p. 231, IV.1.3, p. 233, IV.1.5, p. 237, IV.5.7, p. 243.
42 *Rhetorica ad Herennium*, IV.5.7, p. 245.
43 Quintilian, *Institutio Oratoria*, X.1.31, p. 21 (see also page 126).

licence which is similar to that of poetry.[44] Horace's combination of utility with pleasure was therefore one which medieval writers could say applied both to Vergil and to the writing of history.[45] It is thus history, rather than poetry, which was termed the *via vitae* by, for example, Gerald of Wales.[46] Although Horace (and, through him, Isidore) maintained that the epic hexameter of heroic verse was the form best suited to describing the acts and deeds (*res gestae*) of great men and kings,[47] verse historical narrative was far from being limited to this one type of poetry. It could also cover tragedy, satire, invective, elegy, epitaph, bucolic and georgic. Conrad of Hirsau, for example, distinguished between tragic verse (*carmen tragicum*), which was used to describe public events and wicked deeds of the powerful, and chronicling verse (*cronicum carmen*), which was used to describe historical events or periods (*tempora*).[48]

Whilst poets, historians and orators, in short, each have their own guidelines and their own principles of what is fitting, Quintilian concludes that *all* eloquence has something in common and it is this commonality which should be sought in education.[49]

---

44 *Institutio Oratoria*, II.4.19, p. 233.
45 Bernardus Silvestris, *Commentary on the First Six Books of Virgil's Aeneid*, p. 4: 'Some poets, such as the satirists, write for instruction; some, such as the comic playwrights, write for delight; and some, such as the historians, write for both. Horace speaks about this: "poets aim either to benefit or to amuse or to utter words at once both pleasing and helpful to life" [*Ars Poetica*, lines 333–4, p. 479]. The *Aeneid* gives pleasure ... and also ... the greatest examples of, and inspiration for, pursuing virtue and avoiding vice'.
46 Gerald of Wales, Letter 3, to William de Montibus, Chancellor of Lincoln, ed. R.B.C. Huygens, trans. B. Dawson, in Y. Lefèvre and R.B.C. Huygens (eds), *Speculum Duorum or a Mirror of Two Men* (Cardiff, 1974), p. 171 (cf. page 359).
47 Horace, *Ars Poetica*, lines 73–4, p. 457; Isidore, *Etymologiae*, I.39.9, p. 65; cf. *Accessus ad Auctores*, trans. A.J. Minnis and A.B. Scott, 'Introductions to the Authors', in A.J. Minnis and A.B. Scott (eds), *Medieval Literary Theory and Criticism c.1100–c.1375* (Oxford, 1988), p. 28: 'tragedy is the goddess of poetry about the deeds of nobles and kings'. See also William of Malmesbury, *Gesta Pontificum Anglorum*, ed. and trans. M. Winterbottom and R.M. Thomson, *The History of the English Bishops* (Oxford, 2007), V.214, p. 541, quoting Aldhelm, *Letters*, ed. R. Ehwald (Hanover, 1919), Ep.3, p. 479.
48 Conrad of Hirsau, *Dialogue on the Authors*, trans. A.J. Minnis and A.B. Scott, in A.J. Minnis and A.B. Scott (eds), *Medieval Literary Theory and Criticism c.1100–c.1375* (Oxford, 1988), p. 44. For John of Garland's definition of the different types of historical poetry, see his *Parisiana Poetria*, ed. and trans. T. Lawler (New Haven, 1974), V.333–72, pp. 101–3.
49 Quintilian, *Institutio Oratoria*, X.2.21–2, p. 87.

The effect of such an argument on both the theory of medieval poetry and the practice of medieval historiography was marked. Gregory of Tours, for example, explicitly envisages history being written in either prose or verse and, perhaps as a compliment to Venantius Fortunatus (who had produced a verse rendition of Sulpicius Severus' *Life of Martin*), conceded that his own *Histories* could be rewritten accordingly, provided its substance was kept intact.[50] Paul the Deacon incorporated verse within his *History of the Lombards*, including his own epitaph on Venantius Fortunatus.[51] Liutprand of Cremona included fourteen verse compositions of his own and in a variety of different metres. The interweaving of poetry into prose historiography was an even more prominent feature in Dudo of St Quentin's *History of the Normans*, where four books of prose narrative are interspersed with no fewer than eighty-nine passages of verse.[52] Writing history as a mixture of prose and verse (the so-called prosimetric genre) may, of course, simply have been the result of a particular author taking Martianus Capella or Boethius as their model – both *The Marriage of Philology and Mercury* and the *Consolation of Philosophy*, after all, alternated passages of prose with passages of verse; so, too, as Bede pointed out, did the book of Job.[53] Bede and, following him, Henry of Huntingdon, both justified the inclusion of their own verse within their historiography on the grounds that it was the custom of Scripture to intersperse poetry (*carmina*) with history proper.[54] However (in addition to the scriptural model),

---

50 Gregory of Tours, *Histories*, trans. L. Thorpe, *The History of the Franks* (Harmondsworth, 1974), pref., p. 63, X.31, p. 603. Lampert of Hersfeld concludes his *Annals*, ed. O. Holder-Egger (Hanover, 1894), pp. 303–4, by echoing Sulpicius Severus' comparison of his historiographical activity to that of the poet who is wearied by the scale of his undertaking; cf. Sulpicius Severus, *Life of Martin of Tours*, trans. C. White (Harmondsworth, 1998), XXVI.1, p. 158.
51 Paul the Deacon, *History of the Lombards*, trans. W.D. Foulke, rev. E. Peters (Philadelphia, 2003), I.26, p. 48, II.13, p. 70.
52 Dudo of St Quentin, *History of the Normans*, trans. E. Christiansen (Woodbridge, 1998); cf. *The Life of King Edward Who Rests at Westminster*, ed. and trans. F. Barlow (2nd edn, Oxford, 1992).
53 P. Dronke, *Verse with Prose from Petronius to Dante: The Art and Scope of the Mixed Form* (London, 1994); Bede, *De Arte Metrica*, ed. C.B. Kendall (*CCSL* 123A, Turnhout, 1975), I.25, pp. 139–41 (see page 57).
54 Bede, *Historia Ecclesiastica Gentis Anglorum*, trans. B. Colgrave, rev. J. McClure and R. Collins, *The Ecclesiastical History of the English People* (Oxford, 1994), IV.20,

its inclusion could also be a quite deliberate argumentative strategy. In his prologue, Henry of Huntingdon explicitly calls Homer a historian and claims that poetry and historiography not only share the same didactic goal of the reformation of moral conduct (*puritas morum*) but actually secure it with greater clarity and greater pleasure than philosophy. He then concludes with a verse recapitulation of the themes he has just outlined in prose.[55] Henry considered poetry to provide a cure for both sloth and vice, rather than simply an exercise for children, and he cites the Psalms and the prophets as examples to prove the point.[56] Henry proceeds in the main body of his *History of the English* to incorporate no fewer than twenty-four poems of his own, as well as to translate significant portions of Old English verse into Latin prose. This is much more than a literary exercise – Henry is using his poems, much as he uses the technique of digression, in order to highlight events of significance within his narrative. The battle of Brémule, for example, the sinking of the White Ship, the deaths of distinguished individuals, the marriage of Henry I, and the accession of the bishop of Lincoln, are all elevated, 'amplified', with passages of verse.[57]

The proximity of poetry to historiography, however, clearly made some writers of history nervous. A poet was, by definition, someone who composed or shaped verse (*fictor vel formator*) and a poem was thus the product of such formation (*fictio*). Whilst poetry could cover things which had actually happened (*res gesta*), it also extended to material which was presented as true even if it did not exist, and had not existed, in reality (*res ficta*). This equivocation was fundamental to its definition. According to Conrad of Hirsau,

---

p. 205; Henry of Huntingdon, *Historia Anglorum*, ed. and trans. D. Greenway, *History of the English* (Oxford, 1996), IX.34, p. 665.

55 Henry of Huntingdon, *Historia Anglorum*, prol., pp. 3–9; cf. Horace, *Epistles*, trans. H.R. Fairclough (Loeb, 1929), Ep.I.2 lines 3–4, p. 263 (see page 241), also quoted by John of Salisbury, *Metalogicon*, I.22, p. 63. For Henry's verse treatise on figures of speech, tropes and versification, see D. Greenway, 'Authority, Convention and Observation in Henry of Huntingdon's *Historia Anglorum*', *Anglo-Norman Studies*, 18 (1996), p. 106.

56 *Historia Anglorum*, XI.1, p. 781.

57 See D. Greenway's introduction to her translation of Henry of Huntingdon, *Historia Anglorum*, pp. cvii–cxii; cf. A.G. Rigg, 'Henry of Huntingdon's Metrical Experiments', *Journal of Medieval Latin*, 1 (1991), pp. 60–72. For amplification, see pages 268, 308.

for example, poets say what is false rather than what is true *or* they sometimes mix truth with falsehood (*vel pro veris falsa dicat vel falsis interdum vera commisceat*).[58] In defining the range of different types of poetic fable which result, Conrad accordingly distinguishes between fables of the sort written by Aesop (that is, those moral and pleasurable tales which could never have happened) and the fictions composed by comic poets such as Terence and Plautus (that is, those things which did not happen but which nevertheless correspond to the truth 'in a certain sense', *aliquo modo*). This last category, however, Conrad calls 'lying fabrications' (*commentis mendacibus*).[59] For some historians, the risks which were posed by having this sort of language associated with their texts were too serious to be ignored. William of Poitiers, for example, provides an account of the *Deeds* of William the Conqueror which, he claimed, however difficult some of those *res gestae* may be for posterity to believe, will teach future ages good actions to be imitated and less good actions to be avoided.[60] In doing so, however, William of Poitiers goes out of his way to distance his own composition from the writing of poetry. It is permissible for poets, he notes, to write down wars which are produced from their imagination and to amplify (*amplificare*) whatever is known by wandering through the fields of what is made up (*figmenta*).[61] William himself, by contrast, will simply praise the duke and king, never taking a single step beyond the bounds of truth (*a veritatis limite*). When he comes to the battle of Hastings, therefore, he makes a point of differentiating himself from the likes of Statius and Vergil. The writers of the *Thebaid* or the *Aeneid*, he states, 'who in their books sing of great events and make them greater according to the law of poetry [*poetica lex*], could compose a more worthy work by singing what is true about the equally great actions of this man'.[62] William,

---

58 Conrad of Hirsau, *Dialogue on the Authors*, p. 43; cf. Isidore, *Etymologiae*, VIII.7.1–10, pp. 180–1.
59 *Dialogue on the Authors*, p. 47; cf. page 383.
60 William of Poitiers, *Gesta Guillelmi*, ed. and trans. R.H.C. Davis and M. Chibnall (Oxford, 1998), I.4, p. 7, I.25, p. 39.
61 *Gesta Guillelmi*, I.20, p. 29; cf. Isidore, *Etymologiae*, VIII.7.10, p. 181.
62 *Gesta Guillelmi*, II.22, p. 137; cf. J. Beer, *Narrative Conventions of Truth in the Middle Ages* (Geneva, 1981), ch. 1. Orderic Vitalis points out that William of Poitiers wrote his history in order to secure royal favour, but he otherwise praises the *Gesta Guillelmi* for its polish, profundity and subtle imitation of Sallust; Guy of

however, will content himself with using his feeble prose in order to bring a brief and truthful end to his account of the battle. In part, William of Poitiers' attempts at demarcation are prompted by considerations of audience and genre. William the Conqueror 'will live ... in our pages', he states, 'which we are happy to write in a simple style of speech [*tenui orationis figura*] so that many people will easily understand such shining deeds, particularly since you will find that the greatest orators who have a great capacity for writing in a weighty style [*graviter*] use a plain style when they are writing history'.[63] In part, however, William's concerns are also prompted by considerations of truthfulness. As Reginald of Canterbury freely admitted when writing his verse epic on the life of Malchus, his poetic account added and made up (*confingere*) much that was not present in the prose historical account which had originally been written by Jerome.[64]

Similar concerns over the boundaries between truthful history and poetic *fabula* are expressed by Richard of Devizes, in the twelfth century, when he prefaces his *Chronicle* with the opposition of fables to prophecy (that is, to divine and therefore truthful knowledge of what is done in the world).[65] William of Newburgh was more vociferous still. An Augustinian canon writing in *c.*1196–98, William devoted much of the prologue to his *History of English Affairs* to a sustained attack on Geoffrey of Monmouth's *History of the Kings of Britain*, dismissing it as a series of ridiculous fabrications (*ridicula figmenta*).[66] His particular

---

Amiens' poetic praise of the king, meanwhile, he saw as an imitation of Vergil and Statius; Dudo of St Quentin, on the other hand, is explicitly categorised as panegyric: Orderic Vitalis, *Historia Ecclesiastica*, ed. and trans. M. Chibnall (Oxford, 1980), III.prol., p. 3, III, p. 79, pp. 185–7, IV, pp. 259–61. William of Jumièges states that, in his own abbreviation of Dudo's work, he has excised some material on the grounds that it is mere flattery (*adulatoria*) and does not offer a model of what is either *honestum* or *utile*: William of Jumièges, *Gesta Normannorum Ducum*, ed. and trans. E.M.C. van Houts (Oxford, 1992–95), Ep.ded., p. 7.
63 *Gesta Guillelmi*, II.32, p. 159. For history in the plain style, see pages 295, 297–8.
64 A.G. Rigg, *A History of Anglo-Latin Literature 1066–1422* (Cambridge, 1992), pp. 25–6.
65 Richard of Devizes, *Chronicle*, ed. and trans. J.T. Appleby (London, 1963), p. 2 (see page 279); cf. N. Partner, *Serious Entertainments: The Writing of History in Twelfth-Century England* (Chicago, 1977), pp. 143–79.
66 William of Newburgh, *History of English Affairs*, trans. P.G. Walsh and M.J. Kennedy (Warminster, 1988), I.prol. p. 29; cf. Partner, *Serious Entertainments*, pp. 51–140.

charge is that Geoffrey augmented fables drawn from what the British had made up with the colour (*color*) of the Latin language and, in doing so, had cloaked them with the morally worthy name of history. Worse still, rather than observe the *fides* of historical truth, Geoffrey had produced, not just fabrications, but also lies. William can only guess at his motives for doing so – either this was in order to give pleasure to the British or it was simply out of his own unrestrained 'lust for lying' (*libido mentiendi*).[67] Geoffrey of Monmouth's 'history', in short, was the product of what William terms a 'licence to lie' (*licentia mentiendi*); it is the work of a fabulist (*fabulator*) and a shameless liar.[68]

In acknowledging the complexity of the relationship between truth, verisimilitude and fable, and the consequent fluidity of the boundary between history, argument and poetry, classical manuals all recognised the potential of rhetoric to do damage. Eloquence without wisdom is mere cunning (*calliditas*); it is sophistry and trickery – this is what produces harm, by causing lying to be placed above the truth.[69] Medieval writers were well aware of this critique, which had originally been put forward in Plato's *Gorgias* and then summarised by, amongst others, Quintilian.[70] Yet, according to Quintilian, provided it is a virtuous individual who is doing it, the act of lying is permissible if it serves the truth, secures a higher good, or produces what is generally advantageous. Cicero drew an explicit connection with history in his *Brutus*: 'it is permissible for orator to lie in their historical accounts

---

67 *History of English Affairs*, I.prol., p. 33.
68 *History of English Affairs*, I.prol., pp. 35, 37; cf. Henry of Huntingdon, *Historia Anglorum*, VIII, p. 559; Ailred of Rievaulx, *The Mirror of Charity*, trans. E. Connor (Kalamazoo, 1990), II.51, p. 199; Gerald of Wales, *Itinerarium Cambriae*, trans. L. Thorpe, *The Journey Through Wales and the Description of Wales* (Harmondsworth, 1978), I.5, p. 117; Gerald of Wales, *Descriptio Cambriae*, I.7, p. 232. For Geoffrey of Monmouth's own acknowledgment that, according to Gildas, the British indulged in the sin which overthrows the very essence of all virtue, namely hatred of truth and of those who maintain the truth, together with the love of lying and those who fabricate lies, see his *Historia Regum Britanniae*, ed. M.D. Reeve, trans. N. Wright, *The History of the Kings of Britain* (Woodbridge, 2007), XI.195, p. 268.
69 Cicero, *De Inventione*, I.3.4, p. 9; cf. Cicero, *De Oratore*, II.7.30, p. 219; Boethius, *In Ciceronis Topica*, I, pp. 25–6; *Moralium Dogma Philosophorum*, ed. J. Holmberg, *Das Moralium Dogma Philosophorum des Guillaume de Conches, lateinisch, altfranzösisch und mittelniederfränkisch* (Uppsala, 1929), p. 21, quoting Cicero, *De Officiis*, trans. M.T. Griffin and E.M. Atkins, *On Duties* (Cambridge, 1991), II.14.51, p. 82.
70 Quintilian, *Institutio Oratoria*, II.15.18, 24–32, pp. 309–15 (see page 345).

in order to be able to say something with greater sharpness'.[71] Seneca was even more forthright. In his opinion, some historians ensured commendation by relating incredible events, exciting their audience with some wonder (*miraculum*) on the grounds that their readers would do something else if they were simply taken through humdrum, quotidian matters. Some historians are therefore credulous, others are negligent; some do not avoid the lying which creeps up on them, others actively seek it out – either way, Seneca's distrust is profound. This, he concludes, is what the whole tribe (*natio*) of historians has in common: they do not think that their work can be approved and become popular unless it is sprinkled with lies.[72]

The concept of rhetorical verisimilitude clearly raised a series of fundamental questions about the relationship between truth, on the one hand, and utility, opinion, fable, poetry and lies, on the other. Take, for example, Alan of Lille's *Anticlaudianus*, a work which, as its title indicated, recast the content of Martianus Capella's *Marriage of Philology and Mercury* as a response to Seneca's *Claudian*. Alan of Lille's summary of the art of rhetoric runs through all of its central features: the distinction between moral worth and utility; its division into five parts; the importance of making an audience teachable, benevolent and attentive; the different types of case which can be argued according to the letter or the spirit of the text; the attributes of persons and of events.[73] When Alan comes to narrative, however, he defines it as 'a brief exposition either of the truth or of falsehood which lurks beneath the image of truth' (*sub brevibus verbis narratio verum explicat aut latitans veri sub imagine falsum*).[74] Likewise, in drawing a parallel between the 'colours' of rhetoric and the art of painting, Alan defines the fictive nature of the latter as making the false and non-existent appear true, thereby changing individual lies

---

71 Cicero, *Brutus*, trans. G.L. Hendrickson (Loeb, 1962), X.42, p. 47.
72 Seneca, *Quaestiones Naturales*, trans. T.H. Corcoran (Loeb, 1972), VII.16, p. 261; cf. *Suasoriae*, ed. and trans. M. Winterbottom and W.C. Wright (Loeb, 1974), VI.16, 21–2, pp. 577–9, 585 (see page 15); Seneca, *Letters*, trans. R.M. Gummere (Loeb, 1920), Ep.88, p. 351 (see page 124).
73 Alan of Lille, *Anticlaudianus*, trans. J.J. Sheridan, *Anticlaudianus or the Good and Perfect Man* (Toronto, 1973), III.166–224, pp. 98–101.
74 *Anticlaudianus*, III.188–9, p. 99.

to truth.[75] Poetry posed this question of lying in its most acute form. This is why Alan regarded the poetry of Vergil to have been made up of lies, weaving a cloak for falsehood from the appearance of truth.[76] For all of Alan of Lille's positive appreciation of the refinements of rhetoric – the ornaments of style by means of which words shine like stars, discourse clothes itself in beauty and conclusions shine forth in a flood of light[77] – he could also inveigh against the lies, trickery, deceit, fraud and hypocrisy of sophistry.[78] There was always a flip-side. For all William of Malmesbury's familiarity with the rhetorical precepts of Cicero and Quintilian, he, too, recognised the cunning of contemporary Romans who 'resort to orators' ploys [*versutiae*] and use empty ambiguities in order to keep their meaning in suspense'.[79] 'Commonplaces', he observes, 'can be directed towards either side of an argument according to the linguistic ability of the orator'.[80]

The challenge of rhetoric for medieval writers of history was clear. The problems presented by poetry and fable were indicative of a much wider debate about the nature and purpose of verisimilitude. Truth, the narration of 'what actually happened' (*narratio rei gestae*), was clearly understood to form the basis of the writing of history, but it was also acknowledged to be only the beginning of a complex and sophisticated process. This was encapsulated by the nature and purpose of also narrating what *might* have happened (*narratio ut rei gestae*), by the task of constructing or 'making up' a 'fictive' and plausible account of events.[81] In

---

75 *Anticlaudianus*, I.122–30, p. 49, II.200–4, p. 74, III.149–50, 168–9, pp. 97–8. For 'painting' with the colours or tropes of rhetoric, see, for example, Geoffrey of Vinsauf, *Poetria Nova*, IV.877, p. 61.
76 *Anticlaudianus*, I.142–3, p. 50; Alan of Lille, *De Planctu Naturae*, trans. J.J. Sheridan, *Plaint of Nature* (Toronto, 1980), VIII.124–42 pp. 139–40; cf. W. Wetherbee, 'The Function of Poetry in the *De Planctu Naturae* of Alain de Lille', *Traditio*, 25 (1969), pp. 87–125. For 'Vergilian lies', see Alcuin, *Letters*, ed. E. Dümmler (Berlin 1895), Ep.309.15, p. 475; Conrad of Hirsau, *Dialogue on the Authors*, p. 63 (cf. page 435). The prime example of preferring such fictions to the truth was, according to Macrobius, Vergil's account of Dido: Macrobius, *Saturnalia*, trans. P.V. Davies (New York, 1969), V.17, p. 359.
77 *Anticlaudianus*, VII.270–5, p. 181.
78 *Anticlaudianus*, III.38–41, p. 92.
79 William of Malmesbury, *Gesta Pontificum Anglorum*, I.70, p. 209.
80 William of Malmesbury, *Gesta Regum Anglorum*, V.406, p. 735.
81 See pages 245, 315, 323.

part, the outcome depended on whether a writer of history saw themselves as a judge (*iudex*), whose goal was always, as Cicero argued, the truth, or as an advocate (*patronus*), who sometimes defended what was plausible (*veri simile*), even if it might be less true.[82] Otherwise, in order to understand what medieval writers of history did with the problems posed by verisimilar argumentation – by utility, opinion, 'fiction' and lies – it is necessary to recognise that they were not the first people to try to make sense of the 'truth' of history, or to integrate the views of classical rhetoricians with the principles set down by Christian authorities, either in Scripture itself or in the models of historiography that were subsequently engendered by the biblical narrative. Direct engagement with the classical pagan past did not start in the eighth or ninth century; it originated in the fourth and fifth. Just as Charlemagne or Frederick II understood the Roman Empire by going back, not just to Augustus, but to Constantine and Justinian, that is, to previous *Christian* Roman emperors, so medieval historians understood the relationship between rhetoric and historiography by going back, not just to classical writers, to Sallust and Josephus, but to late-antique *Christian* Roman writers, that is, to Eusebius, Orosius and, above all, to Augustine.

When Augustine is presented in his traditional 'historiographical' guise, as the author of the *City of God*, he provides perhaps the single most important influence on a conception of universal history and its division into the six (ultimately seven) ages of man.[83] What makes Augustine all the more interesting, however, is that he was a trained rhetorician, teaching in Milan until his conversion in 386. As a Christian writer who was steeped in classical rhetoric, including the works of Cicero and Quintilian and the *Rhetorica ad Herennium*, Augustine had rather a lot to say on each of the issues – utility, opinion, 'fiction' and lies – which had a direct bearing on the truth-content of a verisimilar narrative of events. In this regard, Augustine's views on the writing of history are often best approached by means of texts *other* than the *City of God*. His discussion of the relationship between truth and utility, for example, an analysis on which, in many respects, his primary

---

82 Cicero, *De Officiis*, II.14.51, p. 82, quoted, for example, in the *Moralium Dogma Philosophorum*, p. 21.
83 See page 102.

understanding of historiography depended, is contained in his treatise *On Christian Teaching* (*De Doctrina Christiana*). Written as a short reflection on the relationship between words and things and, as a result, on how the relationship between language and reality is dependent upon a proper understanding of signs, *De Doctrina Christiana* set out to demonstrate how a basic knowledge of grammar, dialectic and rhetoric could, and should, be used to explain the meaning of the Bible. In expounding the utility of these branches of pagan learning (according to his famous image, the 'gold' and 'clothing' of the Egyptians which the chosen people took with them to the Promised Land [Exodus 3:22, 12:35–6]), Augustine is certainly careful to point out their limitations. Some humanly-instituted knowledge is self-indulgent and, as such, should simply be avoided by his Christian audience. Nonetheless, as a means of understanding the divine truths which are contained in the Old and New Testaments and, equally importantly, as a means of communicating these truths to others, the disciplines of grammar, dialectic and rhetoric remain, in Augustine's view, fundamental to Christian teaching.[84]

De Doctrina Christiana itself did not attempt to provide this sort of introduction. Indeed, Augustine issued explicit disclaimers on this score. 'This is not the proper place', he writes, 'to present [figures of speech] to people not familiar with them; I do not wish to look as if I am giving a course on grammar'.[85] 'At the outset', he continues, 'I must curb the expectations of any readers who think that I am going to present the rhetorical rules which I learned and taught in pagan schools, and warn them ... not to expect that sort of thing from me. This is not because the rules have no

---

84 See K. Pollmann and M. Vessey (eds), *Augustine and the Disciplines: From Cassiciacum to Confessions* (Oxford, 2005), and, more generally, D.W.H. Arnold and P. Bright (eds), *De Doctrina Christiana: A Classic of Western Culture* (Notre Dame, 1995); E.D. English (ed.), *Reading and Wisdom: The De Doctrina Christiana of Augustine in the Middle Ages* (Notre Dame, 1995); cf. M.M. Gorman, 'The Diffusion of the Manuscripts of Saint Augustine's *De Doctrina Christiana* in the Early Middle Ages', *Revue Bénédictine*, 95 (1985), pp. 11–24; reprinted in M.M. Gorman, *The Manuscript Traditions of the Works of St Augustine* (Florence, 2001), pp. 265–78; cf. Cassiodorus, *Explanation of the Psalms*, trans. P.G. Walsh (New York, 1990–91), pref.1.15, pp. 38–9, citing Augustine, *De Doctrina Christiana*, ed. and trans. R.P.H. Green (Oxford, 1995), III.87, p. 171.
85 Augustine, *De Doctrina Christiana*, III.87, p. 171.

practical use but because such practical uses as they do have must be learned separately ... and not sought from me either in this or any other work'.[86] Even with these caveats, however, Augustine's recommendation is clear: 'as for the relevant observations and rules which, together with a skilful manner of speaking that uses an abundance of words and verbal ornament, constitute what we mean by eloquence, these should be learned independently of this work by those who can do so quickly, by setting aside an appropriate period of time at a suitable and convenient stage of their lives'.[87] The remainder of *De Doctrina Christiana* is devoted, accordingly, to a demonstration of how the interpreter and teacher of divine Scripture can use different types of style (*elocutio*) to defend the Christian faith and defeat error, to communicate what is good and to eradicate what is bad.[88]

Augustine registers profound concerns over the potential abuse of eloquence when it has no goal other than pleasure and when it is placed in the service of falsehood rather than truth. In this respect, the stipulations contained in *De Doctrina Christiana* on the essential connection between eloquence (*eloquentia*) and wisdom (*sapientia*) provide a Christian reprise of the opening to Cicero's *De Inventione* and the conclusion to Quintilian. As such, they were to prove hugely influential throughout the Middle Ages.[89] Delight in words, for Augustine, should only ever constitute a means to further the primary goals of persuasion, namely instruction in truth and inspiration to good action. It is strictly within these terms of reference, he insists, that rhetoric serves a useful purpose (*utilis*).[90] Just because the rules of eloquence can be used to

---

86 *De Doctrina Christiana*, IV.3, p. 196; cf. Augustine, *Letters*, trans. R. Teske (New York, 2001–05), Ep.118, pp. 103–24. Both Alcuin and Hrabanus Maurus took the hint and accordingly followed their own digests of *De Doctrina Christiana* with summaries of the arts of grammar, dialectic and rhetoric.
87 *De Doctrina Christiana*, IV.6, p. 198. Compare the very similar remarks of Quintilian, *Institutio Oratoria*, VIII.praef.1, p. 177.
88 *De Doctrina Christiana*, IV.14, p. 200.
89 See pages 229, 344–5, 352; cf. Isidore of Seville, *Differentiae* ed. M.A. Andrés Sanz (*CCSL* 111A, Turnhout, 2006), XXXVII, pp. 95–6, and, more generally, C. Nederman, 'The Union of Wisdom and Eloquence Before the Renaissance – The Ciceronian Orator in Medieval Thought', *Journal of Medieval History*, 18 (1992), pp. 75–95.
90 Augustine, *De Doctrina Christiana*, IV.143–4, 149–50, pp. 272, 274–6; cf. Boethius, *Consolation of Philosophy*, trans. S.J. Tester (Loeb, 1973), II.1, p. 177.

commend falsehood does not make them invalid. 'Since they can also be used to commend the truth', Augustine states, 'it is not the subject itself that is reprehensible but the perversity of those who abuse it'.[91] Truth should not stand unarmed in its fight against falsehood; rhetoric should not be left to those who serve iniquity and error. Rhetorical ability, he concludes, needs to be acquired by good and zealous Christians in order to fight for the truth.[92]

Augustine's concentration on scriptural exegesis and on the dangers of sophistry should not be allowed to obscure his conviction of just how useful a knowledge of rhetoric could be. This is a point which deserves greater emphasis than it is sometimes given. It is underscored by the range of *non*-scriptural contexts in which Augustine clearly considered familiarity with classical rhetoric could, and would, be 'useful'. In providing a list of the purposes for which rhetoric proves valuable, Augustine envisages a much wider scope than the exposition of scriptural texts in sermons and homilies – it also comprises entreaties (*obsecrationes*), rebukes (*increpationes*), rousing speeches (*concitationes*) and solemn admonitions (*coercitationes*).[93] Rhetoric is required, he concludes, whenever an individual wishes to give instruction on, and to advocate, something which is to be acted upon.[94] It can be deployed in public or in private, with one person or with several, with friends and opponents, in continuous speech and debate, in treatises and books, in letters of great length or extreme brevity; in other words, wherever, and in whatever form, instruction in Christian truths and exhortation to a Christian way of life are demanded.[95]

When it comes to the questions raised by rhetoric concerning the relationship between truth and opinion, Augustine's central arguments are contained in his *Contra Academicos* (*Against*

---

91 *De Doctrina Christiana*, II.132, p. 118, a passage cited, for example, by Coluccio Salutati, *Letters*, ed. F. Novati, *Coluccio Salutati Epistolario* (Rome, 1891–1911), Ep.XIV.23, p. 204.
92 *De Doctrina Christiana*, IV.4–5, pp. 196–8.
93 *De Doctrina Christiana*, IV.15, p. 202; cf. Cicero, *De Oratore*, III.30.118, pp. 306–7; 1 Timothy 2:1. Hrabanus Maurus quotes Augustine's list in his own teaching manual for the clergy, much of which is drawn from *De Doctrina Christiana*: Hrabanus Maurus, *De Clericorum Institutione*, ed. D. Zimpel (Frankfurt, 1996), III.28, pp. 489–90).
94 *De Doctrina Christiana*, IV.79, pp. 230–2.
95 *De Doctrina Christiana*, IV.102, p. 242.

the Academics) and *De Magistro* (*On the Teacher*).[96] The former is a dialogue devoted to refuting the central claim of Cicero's *Academica* that the wise man assents to nothing because the truth cannot be known.[97] Central to Augustine's critique are two terms (in this instance treated as synonyms), namely *verisimilitudo* and *probabile* – what has the likeness of truth and what is plausible or probable. Augustine's main contention is that the truth is *not*, in fact, unknowable by human beings. Indeed, he ends up concluding that the Academics were not sceptics after all, but closet Platonists – they knew the truth all along but chose to keep it hidden. In the course of putting forward his critique of Academic scepticism, however, Augustine also tackles some important issues for the relationship between rhetoric and historiography. In the first instance, he uses the distinction between knowledge and opinion as a means of stressing the untrustworthy and unreliable nature of sense experience. Significantly (at least from the perspective of the methodological analogy which was most frequently invoked by writers of history themselves), the illustration that Augustine uses, and discusses, is the sense of sight. In the case of the oar of a boat, he argues, what is actually seen with the eyes when the oar is underwater is a distorted image; even though we know with our intellect that the oar is straight, it actually appears to the senses to be bent.[98] Truth, Augustine concludes, is therefore, strictly speaking, the preserve of the mind, of the intellect, and not of the senses. In the second instance, Augustine, like Cicero, draws a clear connection between the teachings of the Academics and his own career as a professional rhetorician, by commenting that it was his knowledge and practice of rhetoric which attracted him to the scepticism of the Academy in the first place. It is this intellectual affinity between epistemological scepticism and the

---

96 Augustine, *Contra Academicos* and *De Magistro*, trans. P. King, *Against the Academicians and The Teacher* (Indianapolis, 1995). More generally, see C. Atherton, *Stoics on Ambiguity* (Cambridge, 1993).
97 See page 355; cf. MacKendrick, *The Philosophical Books of Cicero*, pp. 114–30; M.A. Rouse and R.H. Rouse, 'The Medieval Circulation of Cicero's "Posterior Academics" and the *De Finibus Bonorum et Malorum*', in M.A. Rouse and R.H. Rouse, *Authentic Witnesses: Approaches to Medieval Texts and Manuscripts* (Notre Dame, 1991), pp. 61–98.
98 Cf. Macrobius, *Saturnalia*, VII.14.20, p. 505; Walter Map, *De Nugis Curialium*, I.22, p. 69.

study of rhetoric which Augustine, like Cicero, sees embodied in the single term 'verisimilitude', the likeness of truth.

Augustine's distinction between the knowledge which is denoted by intellectual truth and the opinion which is derived from sense experience also underpins the argument he puts forward in his treatise *On the Teacher*. *De Magistro* is primarily concerned with the role of words in teaching and, as in the *Contra Academicos*, Augustine again adopts (and adapts) a Platonist argument, in this case, the position that words act as signs of things which we already know – they are triggers which prompt us to remember, in the sense of 'unforget' (*anamnesis*).[99] Towards the end of the treatise, however, Augustine shows a particular interest in so-called 'past sensibles', that is, in the question of how, in the present, we talk about what we have experienced, in the past, through the senses. The term which Augustine uses to describe these past sensibles is *falsa* – they are 'false' in the technical sense that what we are referring to when we talk about these experiences is not, in fact, the things themselves but the mental images of the things being remembered. Whilst we may not be 'lying' about the nature of these images, we may still be in error about what they represent; unlike so-called intelligibles (which are not open to the vagaries of sense experience and which are therefore true), these sensibles (*sensibilia*) are, as in the case of the bent oar, deceptive by their very nature.[100]

The consequences of Augustine's views on language and on epistemology have been extensively discussed in terms of the fundamental questions they raise about how human beings come to know things and then communicate that knowledge to one another.[101] It is the consequences of Augustine's account of human knowledge *of the past* which repay rather closer attention when they are read in terms of their particular implications for the writing of history. If it can be argued, for example, that the

---

99   Cf. Plato, *Phaedo*, trans. D. Gallop (Oxford, 1993), 72e–76e, pp. 21–7; Plato, *Meno*, trans. R. Waterfield (Oxford, 2005), 80d–86c, pp. 113–24; Plato, *Phaedrus*, trans. R. Waterfield (Oxford, 2002), 249c, p. 32; Cicero, *Tusculan Disputations*, I.24.57–8, pp. 67–9; Boethius, *Consolation of Philosophy*, III.2, p. 235, III.11, p. 297.
100 Augustine, *De Magistro*, XII.39, p. 140.
101 For what follows, see R.A. Markus, *Signs and Meanings: World and Text in Ancient Christianity* (Liverpool, 1996).

Confessions tell us as much about Augustine's view of historiography as the *City of God*,[102] then the degree of certain knowledge (*scientia*) which the former contains is recognised by Augustine himself to be far from absolute. As is the case in *Contra Academicos* and *De Magistro*, Augustine was acutely aware of the distinction between knowledge and opinion. Indeed, it is because he is so sensitive to the capacity of sense experience to mislead and deceive that he takes great care to incorporate into the *Confessions* an extended reflection on the problematic nature of memory, on the difficulties which 'knowledge' of past *sensibilia* can present. Having opened book X by speculating why other people might benefit from the confession of his own past sins, Augustine describes the 'vast storehouse' of memory in which innumerable things exist but where the ease of their retrieval will vary – some things are hidden and disordered, whilst others come unbidden and arranged. Memory stores the images of objects perceived by the senses but it also stores images of what it has heard from other people. Augustine's primary concern at this point is to analyse how knowledge of self is related to knowledge of God but, in book XI, he returns to the nature of memory in the context of a more general analysis of time.

Augustine's difficulties with the nature of time stem, in part, from the fact that the human experience of time is a consequence of sin – in contrast to God's absolute simplicity and unity (where simultaneity and eternity coexist, where past, present and future are as one), humans experience time as a stretching-out, a 'distension'. Human salvation, in this regard, will accordingly be characterised by, among other things, freedom from the variation and change of the world which time represents. However, Augustine's difficulties with time are also definitional, in the sense that, strictly speaking, neither the past nor the present nor the future 'exists' – the past no longer has existence, the future has yet to come into existence, whilst the present is merely a fleeting instant tending from, and to, non-existence. If past, present and future can be said to 'exist', then it is only as a present experience of the mind – the past is present in the memory, the future is present in expectation, and the present is present as immediate

---

102 See page 98.

awareness. The past 'exists' only in the memory, therefore, and, as such, what is narrated about the past is made up, once again, of the images of what happened in the past, rather than the past itself. However, if the past exists only in the memory, then, as Augustine has already demonstrated in book X, the memory itself is very difficult to fathom.[103] The consequences for human understanding of events in time and, by extension, for the recording of those events as 'history', are clear. Belief, rather than certainty, is what characterises an individual's knowledge even of their own past life. Certainty is the preserve of God; so too is knowledge of the totality of human existence in time (*totum saeculum filiorum hominum*).[104]

Augustine stages his most extensive discussion of the relationship between knowledge and memory in *De Trinitate*, a work which was, by definition, devoted to understanding the triune nature of God but which, because humankind is created in the image or likeness of God, also turns into a treatise on the philosophy of mind. In books X and XI, Augustine accordingly develops, and extends, several of the observations which he had made in *De Magistro* and the *Confessions*. On the 'false' nature of past sensibles, for example, Augustine reiterates his position that the form of an object which is perceived by the human mind as it exists in reality is different from the form which is impressed upon the senses and thereafter retained in the memory – what is remembered is a 'fiction' or 'likeness' (*figmentum, effigies*) of the object, rather than the object itself. In setting up this model for how, and what, humans know about the sensible world, Augustine's principal interest is, again, knowledge of self and knowledge of God, but Augustine also acknowledges the self-generative capacity of this mental process. A memory of an image can be created, not just by an individual's own sense perception, but also by hearing *other* people narrate what *they* have seen. This fictive likeness (*figmentum*) can also be turned into something false (*falsa*) simply by the

---

103 Augustine, *Confessions*, trans. H. Chadwick (Oxford, 1991), X–XI, pp. 179–245. Walter Map opens *De Nugis Curialium* (I.1, p. 3) by echoing Augustine's perplexity: 'In time I exist, and of time I speak ... [but] what time is, I do not know'.
104 *Confessions*, XI.28.38, p. 243; cf. Augustine, *De Catechizandis Rudibus*, trans. C.L. Cornish, *Of the Catechizing of the Unlearned* (in Augustine, *Seventeen Short Treatises*, Oxford 1847), III.5, p. 191, where Augustine refers to the complete narrative (*narratio plena*) of the Christian religion, from the act of Creation to the present, which is then summarised and expounded selectively in the course of instruction.

action of that individual's will. The gaze of cognition, Augustine explains, can construct images of things in the mind which do not, in reality, exist (a green sun, for example, a square sun or, Augustine supposed, a black swan), but these images can be made so vivid, in dreams or in a frenzy, that the human body will react as if they did exist. Most important of all, however, at least in terms of its consequences for the writing of history, was the way in which Augustine then developed his reflections from books X and XI of the *Confessions* into a trinitarian model for the human mind. According to *De Trinitate*, memory, understanding and will are three interdependent faculties within each human being – the unity which binds them together is such that each one is contained in, and by, the others. Memory, in other words, is impossible without both understanding and will – in order to be understood, what is perceived and remembered has first of all to be related to what is already known; this process of comprehension, however, is not enjoyed as an end in itself (otherwise it would be curiosity rather than learning), but is put to good use by the action of the will.[105]

With the conjunction of memory, awareness and anticipation, and with the interdependence of memory, understanding and will, Augustine's *Confessions* and *De Trinitate* set up a hugely influential epistemological paradigm for the manner, degree and purpose of human knowledge about the past. Coupled with the tripartite definition of prudence (memory, understanding and foresight) which was already familiar from Cicero's *De Inventione* and which was propagated by Macrobius' *Saturnalia*,[106] Augustine's analysis provided medieval writers with a comprehensive intellectual framework for explaining both the way in which the remembrance of the past operated and the functions which it could then serve.

What, then, were Augustine's views on the challenges posed by verisimilitude and, in particular, on the relationship between fiction and lies? Augustine approached this issue, first and foremost, from the perspective of Scripture and, as such, created a quite distinctive and, again, influential set of difficulties of his own. When applied to the study of the Bible, Augustine's

---

105 Augustine, *De Trinitate*, trans. E. Hill, *The Trinity* (New York, 1991).
106 See pages 276–7.

sensitivity to the limitations of linguistic and epistemological understanding crystallised into a distinction between the literal truth of a particular event and its spiritual or allegorical meaning. From his training in classical rhetoric, Augustine was thoroughly familiar with the definition of allegory or *permutatio* as language which demonstrates one thing with the words themselves but something else in the meaning that lies behind them (*sententia*).[107] He was also familiar with the principle that, as a figure of speech, allegory possessed no fewer than three aspects: comparison (in the form of metaphor), argument (when likeness is drawn from a person, place or object in order to magnify or minimise something) and contrast (by referring to the opposite of what is being described).[108] From his exposure to the teaching of Ambrose, moreover, and above all from the latter's exegesis of the Bible, Augustine also knew that the use of allegory in Scripture had been explicitly sanctioned by the apostle Paul in his letter to the Galatians (4:21–31).[109] It was the potential consequences of this last connection, between rhetorical and scriptural allegory, which served as the occasion for Augustine's investigation into the nature and function of verisimilitude.

The distinction between the letter and the spirit of the Bible (the epistle to the Hebrews; 2 Corinthians 3:6) was discussed extensively by both Augustine and Ambrose, in part as a response to Origen, but it was subsequently given its clearest definition by Gregory the Great, when he classified the four senses in which Scripture could be interpreted. First, there was the literal or historical sense, that is, what actually happened, what was actually done (*gesta*); second, there was the moral or tropological sense, that is, the significance of what was being described for the way in which an individual should conduct their life on this earth; third, there was the anagogical sense, that is, the indication which something gave of higher, heavenly things in the life to come and

---

107 For example, *De Trinitate*, XV.3.15, pp. 406–7; *De Diversis Quaestionibus LXXXIII*, trans. B. Ramsey, *Miscellany of Eighty-Three Questions* (in Augustine, *Responses to Miscellaneous Questions*, New York, 2008), 65, p. 101.
108 *Rhetorica ad Herennium*, IV.34.46, p. 345.
109 See, more generally, P. Rollinson, *Classical Theories of Allegory and Christian Culture* (Pittsburgh, 1981); J. Whitman, *Allegory: The Dynamics of an Ancient and Medieval Technique* (Oxford, 1987).

therefore the way in which it 'led' humans to them; fourth, and last, was the allegorical sense, that is, where the event described stood for something else, where the word indicated one thing but signified something different.[110] To ask what is the 'truth' of a scriptural text, in other words, depended, first of all, on which particular truth was being sought. There were different types of truth, different levels of exegesis on which a narrative could operate, amongst which the 'historical' was one of four. In establishing the principles by which the 'truths' of the Bible could be unveiled, the approach that was set out by Augustine raised several fundamental questions. Do all these levels of truth have to be present at one and the same time in a scriptural text? Does the presence of allegory in Scripture extend to verisimilitude and, if so, to making up plausible material and even lies? The answers to these questions had repercussions, not only for the truth-content of the biblical narrative of events, but, by extension, for the truth-content of non-biblical history as well.

In *De Doctrina Christiana*, at least, the term 'verisimilitude' is striking for its absence. However, the one occasion on which it does occur, in book IV, is revealing for the immediate context in which

---

110 G.W.H. Lampe (ed.), *The Cambridge History of the Bible. Vol. II: The West from the Fathers to the Reformation* (Cambridge, 1969), pp. 155–219; H. de Lubac, *Medieval Exegesis: The Four Senses of Scripture*, trans. M. Sebanc (Edinburgh, 1998); cf. Augustine, *De Genesi ad Litteram Libri Duodecim*, trans. J.H. Taylor, *The Literal Meaning of Genesis* (New York, 1982), I.1.1, p. 19; Augustine, *De Utilitate Credendi*, trans. R. Kearney, *The Advantage of Believing* (in Augustine, *On Christian Belief*, New York, 2005), III.5, pp. 119–20; Gregory the Great, *Moralia in Job*, trans. J. Bliss (Oxford, 1843), Ep.ded., pp. 4–5, 7; Bede, *De Tabernaculo*, trans. A.G. Holder, *On the Tabernacle* (Liverpool, 1994), I, pp. 25–6; Bede, *De Schematibus et Tropis*, trans. G.H. Tannenhaus, *Concerning Figures and Tropes*, in J.M. Miller, M.H. Prosser and T.W. Benson (eds), *Readings in Medieval Rhetoric* (Bloomington, 1973), p. 119; John Cassian, *Collationes*, trans. E.C.S. Gibson (Michigan, 1964), XIV.8, pp. 437–8; Hrabanus Maurus, *Expositio in Epistolam ad Galatas* (*PL* 112, cols 245–382), IV, cols 330–1; Hrabanus Maurus, *Commentaria in Exodum* (*PL* 108, cols 9–246), III.11, cols 147–8; Conrad of Hirsau, *Dialogue on the Authors*, pp. 45–6; *Glossa Ordinaria*, ed. A. Rusch (Strassburg, 1480–81; reprinted Turnhout, 1992), prol., p. 6; Alexander of Hales, *Summa Theologica. Tractatus Introductorius*, trans. A.J. Minnis and A.B. Scott, in A.J. Minnis and A.B. Scott (eds), *Medieval Literary Theory and Criticism c.1100–c.1375* (Oxford, 1988), I.4.3–4, pp. 217–21; Bonaventure, *Breviloquium*, trans. E.E. Nemmers (London, 1946), prol.4.1, pp. 12–14; Aquinas, *Summa Theologiae*, ed. and trans. T. Gilby, *et al.* (Blackfriars edn, London, 1964–80), Ia.1.10, pp. 37–40; Aquinas, *Quaestiones de Quolibet* (Leonine edn, Rome, 1996), VII.6.15, pp. 29–32.

it is used. Those who try to make falsehood persuasive, Augustine writes, produce a narrative which is brief, clear and plausible (*verisimiliter*).[111] The reason why Augustine seems to have wanted to associate verisimilitude at this point *only* with what is false is indicated by his earlier analysis of how the relationship between words and things will depend upon a proper understanding of signs and signification. In the course of this discussion, in book II, Augustine had discussed signs which are of purely human institution. There are, he writes, thousands of made-up fables (*fictae fabulae*) and falsehoods (*falsitates*) which are human creations – these are lies (*mendacia*) which serve to give humans pleasure; they are specific to human beings and should be thought of as false and mendacious (*falsa atque mendacia*).[112] Augustine then proceeds to make clear what exactly falsehood might constitute in this context. We call something 'false', he argues, when the signification of something is not what is signified, and it comes in two forms – those things which cannot exist and those things which do not exist even though it is possible that they could.[113] In other words, these two types of falsehood are, respectively, *fabula* and verisimilitude.

Augustine's sensitivity to the dangers associated with poetic *fabula* and rhetorical *fictio* is a consistent feature of his thinking and produced one of its most influential expressions in the hostility to acting and to the theatre which is recorded in the *Confessions*.[114] It is Augustine's suspicion of verisimilitude, however, of false things which do not exist but might, which is the striking feature of this part of his argument in *De Doctrina Christiana*. Its immediate roots lie in the series of letters which Augustine exchanged with Jerome on the meaning of Paul's letter to the Galatians, the original context in which allegory had been given explicit biblical sanction (Galatians 4:21–31). In this instance, however, the source of Augustine's concern, and the subject of his disagreement with Jerome, lay in the precise significance of Paul's correction of Peter

---

111 Augustine, *De Doctrina Christiana*, IV.4, p. 197.
112 *De Doctrina Christiana*, II.25, p. 103. For Augustine's theory of signs, see J.M. Rist, *Augustine: Ancient Thought Baptized* (Cambridge, 1994), pp. 23–40, and, more generally, Markus, *Signs and Meanings*, pp. 1–43.
113 *De Doctrina Christiana*, II.130, p. 117.
114 Augustine, *Confessions*, III.1.1–2.4, pp. 35–7.

and Barnabas for their judaising customs in Galatians 2:11–21.[115] In essence, Jerome had argued that either Peter was simulating his accommodation of Jewish customs or Paul was making up the episode in order to make an instructive point to his audience – in other words, that the event itself had not actually happened as it was described in Scripture but either Peter or Paul pretended it had in order to illustrate a moral or spiritual truth. This might seem a very specific point of exegesis but it is one which Augustine clearly believed went to the heart of how a Christian should use the tools of classical rhetoric in order to interpret the Bible. So much so, in fact, that not only was Galatians the one book of the Bible for which Augustine provided a complete, formal commentary,[116] but he also subsequently generalised the points which he made in his correspondence with Jerome into, first, one treatise on lying, *De Mendacio*, and then a second, *Contra Mendacium*.[117]

What worried Augustine about Jerome's position was the possibility that it could allow a justification of lying in Scripture, either in the conduct of Peter and Paul themselves or in the way in which the text of Scripture was subsequently written down. Augustine proceeds to identify eight types of lie, classifying them in decreasing order of gravity. It is the ones which come towards the end of this list which are the most revealing, in that they are lies which do not harm another person; indeed, they may even be designed to benefit them, by providing some sort of utility or advantage.[118] The language Augustine uses here and in *De Doctrina Christiana* – securing utility as well as providing pleasure – strongly suggests that he has, not just Galatians, but rhetorical verisimilitude firmly in mind. Augustine ends up taking his stand on two fundamental principles. The first is a distinction between the Old Testament and the New Testament, according to which the deeds narrated in the former should be approached

---

115 For the dispute, see J.N.D. Kelly, *Jerome: His Life, Writings and Controversies* (London, 1975), pp. 217–18, 263–72.
116 E. Plumer (ed.), *Augustine's Commentary on Galatians* (Oxford, 2006); cf. S.A. Cooper, *Marius Victorinus' Commentary on Galatians* (Oxford, 2005).
117 Augustine, *De Mendacio*, trans. H. Browne, *On Lying* (in Augustine, *Seventeen Short Treatises*, Oxford, 1847); Augustine, *Contra Mendacium*, trans. H. Browne, *To Consentius: Against Lying* (in Augustine, *Seventeen Short Treatises*, Oxford, 1847).
118 Cf. Gratian, *Decretum*, ed. E. Friedberg, *Corpus Iuris Canonici* (Leipzig, 1879–81), II.22.2.4–20, cols 867–75.

with a greater degree of leeway than those in the latter. Some instances of conduct and action which are described in the Old Testament may, in themselves, be wicked, but this does not mean that they are being put forward for imitation. It is this principle, Augustine argues, which should be applied to those instances of lying which are described in Scripture. To draw this conclusion, however, is not the same as maintaining that such actions, being primarily of figurative significance, might therefore not have actually happened. Even if their true signification resides in their figurative, rather than their literal, meaning, these were events and actions which historically did still take place. Or, as Gregory the Great was subsequently to put it, David's action in sending Uriah to his death may signify the triumph of the Church over the Devil, but Uriah's death was still an evil deed which actually occurred.[119] Having drawn this conclusion for the Old Testament, Augustine proceeds to point out that the need for such figurative signification in the prophetic books of Scripture had then been superseded in the New Testament by the narrative of the Gospels. Indeed, by the time the 'sacred history' of the book of Acts was written, and certainly by the time Paul was writing his epistles, the deeds being narrated were being proffered as a literal and exemplary form of life to be imitated by all Christians. This is what made Jerome's intimation of the presence of verisimilitude in the letter to the Galatians so dangerous – if Paul is allowed to have lied on one occasion, either by describing something which did not in fact actually happen or by dissimulating in his own or Peter's actions, then the result would be to undermine both the truth of the entire New Testament narrative and the truth which should characterise the life of every individual Christian.[120]

Is it the case, then, that *everything* which is made up, not just poetic *fabula* but also rhetorical *fictio*, is technically a lie? This question, Augustine knew, had a long pedigree in the Neoplatonic

---

119 Cf. Augustine, *Contra Faustum*, trans. R. Teske, *Answer to Faustus, a Manichean* (New York, 2007), XXII.87, pp. 364–5; Gregory the Great, *Moralia in Job*, XXXIII.12.23, pp. 578–9; and, more generally, de Lubac, *Medieval Exegesis*, vol. II, pp. 65–7.
120 Cf. Augustine, *De Civitate Dei*, trans. H. Bettenson (2nd edn, Harmondsworth, 1984), XV.27, pp. 645, 648: 'no one should think that ... these things did not happen at all but are mere figures of speech' (*non tamen quisquam putare debet ... haec omnino gesta non esse sed solas esse verborum figuras*).

principle that some truths could be communicated under a fictive veil (*involucrum*) or covering (*integumentum*), a tradition which was summarised by Macrobius in his *Commentary on the Dream of Scipio* when discussing the role of made-up material in philosophy. According to Macrobius, fables come in two forms – those which serve no other function than that of pleasure (and which should therefore be restricted to young children) and those which inspire their audience to perform virtuous deeds. Within the second category, there is a further distinction between fables (such as Aesop's) which are entirely made up, and which therefore have no place in philosophy, and those which have a foundation of truth and which present morally-worthy subject-matter beneath a covering of allegory. It is this second category of fabulous narrative, Macrobius concludes, which can, in fact, be deployed by the philosopher.[121] Augustine was clearly troubled by this issue, and by his own handling of it in *De Mendacio*, and, as a result, he tackles it head on when he returns to the subject of lying in *Contra Mendacium*.

Lying, Augustine states, of whatever sort (although he repeats his concession that some forms are worse than others), is wrong. There is no justification for it. That said, there are two qualifications which need to be made. First of all, concealing the truth (*occultare veritatem*) is not the same as lying and, second, there is an important distinction to be drawn between apparent examples of lying in the Old Testament and those which have been adduced in the book of Acts and the epistles of Paul. Augustine gives a reprise of his earlier argument from *De Mendacio*. Some lies recorded in Scripture are the acts of wicked people and, although they may not be explicitly condemned as such in the text, they are not to be imitated by Christians. Other lies which have been recorded are the acts of weak and ignorant people – these acts are forgiven by God precisely because they were committed by Egyptians or

---

121 Macrobius, *Commentary on the Dream of Scipio*, trans. W.H. Stahl (New York, 1952), I.2, pp. 84–5 (see page 347); cf. Vergil, *Aeneid*, VI.100, p. 513, where the Sibyl is described as 'wrapping up truth in obscurity' (*obscuris vera involvens*). See also A.J. Minnis and A.B. Scott (eds), *Medieval Literary Theory and Criticism c.1100–c.1375* (Oxford, 1988), pp. 113–19; Bernardus Silvestris, *Commentary on the First Six Books of Virgil's Aeneid*, pref., p. 5 (see page 212, note 355), VI, p. 51; John of Garland, *Parisiana Poetria*, V.394, p. 104.

Israelites who had not yet reached spiritual and moral illumination. A third category of lies recorded in Scripture is represented by the episode in which Jacob pretended to be Esau (Genesis 27:1–40) – this is an act which has a true, figurative signification. On a literal level (and, once again, Augustine never denies that these events actually happened), such acts may seem to be lies but, because of their figurative truth, they become something else. Strictly speaking, Augustine states, an act such as Jacob's is not a lie but a mystery (*non est mendacium sed mysterium*). Then comes the crunch. If actions such as Jacob's dissimulation were, indeed, to be counted as lies (*mendacia*), then so too should all parables;[122] the same would be true of all figures of speech, all literary tropes, and especially the use of metaphor, whose proper signification lies beyond the literal meaning of its words. All these modes of speaking, Augustine suggests, will have to be thought of as lies once figurative speech or action is described as mendacious. This is not the case, however, and this is not what he wants to argue.[123]

It is from this perspective that Augustine proceeds to interpret the action on the road to Emmaus, when Christ 'made as if' (*finxit*) to go further (Luke 24:28).[124] Not everything which is made up, Augustine now states, is a lie. Many things are made up truthfully so that one thing can be signified by another; this covers those things which are narrated as if they actually happened when, in fact, they did not, in order to signify something else (*quasi mendacium sit omne quod fingitur cum veraciter aliud ex alio significandi causa tam multa fingantur*). This is the type of 'fictive composition' (*genus fingendi*) which covers the parable of the prodigal son in the New Testament (Luke 15:11–31), for example, or the fable of the trees attempting to institute kingship in the Old Testament (Judges 9:7–15). These are made-up narratives which nonetheless

---

122 For the translation of the Greek term 'parabole' by *collatio*, see Quintilian, *Institutio Oratoria*, V.11.23, p. 285 (see page 327).
123 Augustine, *Contra Mendacium*, XXIII–IV, pp. 447–50; cf. Augustine, *De Civitate Dei*, XVI.37, pp. 700–1.
124 For the broader significance of this particular biblical passage, see F.C. Gardiner, *The Pilgrimage of Desire: A Study of Theme and Genre in Medieval Literature* (Leiden, 1971), pp. 1–52; cf. Wisdom 1:5: 'the holy spirit of discipline will flee from deceit' (*sanctus spiritus disciplinae effugiet fictum*), quoted, for example, by William of Malmesbury, *Gesta Regum Anglorum*, I.59, p. 91.

have a true signification (*fictae narrationes sed veraci significationes*). Augustine draws an explicit connection with Horace's *Ars Poetica*, and throws in the fables of Aesop for good measure. There is no one, he writes, who is so lacking in learning that they would call this sort of writing 'lies', since a lie is a false signification which has been introduced in order to deceive. A parable is a made-up narrative (*ficta narratio*), not a lying narrative (*mendax narratio*), because its signification is true (*quod totum utique fingitur ut ad rem quae intenditur ficta quidem narratione non mendaci tamen sed veraci significatione veniatur*).[125]

There is a lot that can be teased out of Augustine's reflections on the nature of lying.[126] In his *Soliloquies*, for example, Augustine defined falsehood as that which makes itself out to be what it is not, but he then immediately draws a distinction between falsehood which is intended to deceive (*fallax, fallere*) and falsehood which is simply a lie (*mendacium, mentire*). Not everyone who lies, he points out, wishes to deceive, 'for mimes and comedies and many poems are full of lies with the intent to give pleasure rather than to deceive, and almost all those who jest utter a lie'. Those people who do not aim to deceive but nevertheless make something up (*aliquid fingunt*) are simply mendacious (*mendaces*,

---

125 Augustine, *Contra Mendacium*, XXVIII, pp. 454–6; cf. Augustine, *Quaestiones Evangeliorum*, ed. A. Mutzenbecher (*CCSL* 44, Turnhout, 1980), II.51.1, pp. 116–17.
126 For more extensive discussion of Augustine's views on rhetoric and lying, see J.J. Murphy, 'Saint Augustine and the Debate about a Christian Rhetoric', *Quarterly Journal of Speech*, 46 (1960), pp. 400–10; J.J. Murphy, *Rhetoric in the Middle Ages: A History of Rhetorical Theory from St Augustine to the Renaissance* (Berkeley, 1974), pp. 46–64; E. Fortin, 'Augustine and the Problem of Christian Rhetoric', *Augustinian Studies*, 5 (1974), pp. 85–100; R. Ray, 'Christian Conscience and Pagan Rhetoric – Augustine's Treatises on Lying', *Studia Patristica*, 22 (1989), pp. 321–5; C.J. Swearingen, *Rhetoric and Irony: Western Literacy and Western Lies* (New York, 1991), pp. 175–214; M.L. Colish, 'The Stoic Theory of Verbal Signification and the Problem of Lies and False Statement from Antiquity to St. Anselm', in L. Brind'Amour and E. Vance (eds), *Archéologie du Signe* (Toronto, 1983), pp. 17–43; M.L. Colish, *The Stoic Tradition from Antiquity to the Early Middle Ages* (Leiden, 1990), vol. II, pp. 190–8; M.L. Colish, 'Rethinking Lying in the Twelfth Century', in I. Bejczy and R. Newhauser (eds), *Virtue and Ethics in the Twelfth Century* (Leiden, 2005), pp. 155–73; T. Feehan, 'Augustine on Lying and Deception', *Augustinian Studies*, 19 (1988), pp. 131–9; T. Feehan, 'Augustine's Moral Evaluation of Lying', *Augustinian Studies*, 21 (1990), pp. 67–81); T. Feehan, 'Augustine's Own Examples of Lying', *Augustinian Studies*, 22 (1991), pp. 165–90.

mentientes).[127] Augustine remains adamant that plausible or verisimilar narrative should not be introduced into a reading of the New Testament, either in the book of Acts or in Paul's letter to the Galatians – this is literal and historical narrative, not prophetic or figurative language, and, as such, the events described *both* have a true signification *and* actually happened. However, whereas in *De Doctrina Christiana* fables (*fabulae*) are clearly described as both false and mendacious, in *Contra Mendacium* both fable (*fabula*) and made-up narrative (*ficta narratio*) are explicitly defended from the charge of lying provided that they carry a true signification. This apparent inconsistency is resolved by the fact that the 'fables' which Augustine dismisses in *De Doctrina Christiana* are explicitly defined as *fabulae* which have been created for pleasure, and pleasure alone; there is no mention of the utility or truth that Augustine is so careful to introduce as his proviso in *Contra Mendacium*. Nonetheless, the line between falsehood (*falsa*), made-up narrative (*ficta narratio*), fable (*fabula*) and lies (*mendacia*) was clearly a fine one for Augustine to tread. The complexity and subtlety of his treatment of all four categories reveal the problems which he himself encountered in thrashing out some sort of resolution. Indeed, Augustine himself acknowledges in his *Retractationes* that much of what he has written in *De Mendacio* was hard to understand and, whilst it remained a useful work, such obscurity and difficulty had made him prefer the *Contra Mendacium* instead.[128]

Set alongside the account of epistemological verisimilitude outlined in *Contra Academicos*, Augustine's attitude to the status of non-scriptural narrative reveals a particularly nuanced position – objects of the intellect (intelligibles, *intelligibilia*) represent what can be truly known, whereas objects of sense perception (sensibles, *sensibilia*) are simply the subject of opinion; past sensibles, meanwhile, that is *sensibilia* which are remembered, are mediated by mental images which are, by definition, false (*falsa*) and which

---

127 Augustine, *Soliloquies*, trans. C.C. Starbuck (New York, 1888), II.16, p. 552; cf. Richard of Devizes, *Chronicle*, p. 46: 'he reported what he saw as the truth ... he did not lie, for he thought that what he said was true'; Walter Map, *De Nugis Curialium*, I.25, p. 113: 'I confess myself an inept and silly poet, yet not a writer of falsehood [*falsigraphus*]; for he does not lie who recites a tale, but he who makes it up [*non enim mentitur qui recitat sed qui fingit*]'.
128 Augustine, *Retractationes*, trans. M.I. Bogan, *Retractions* (Washington, DC, 1968), I.26, p. 117; cf. II.86, pp. 244–55.

can also generate erroneous images of their own. At the very least, Augustine's observations suggest that he considered the 'truth' of the past to be very problematic for any individual human being both to establish and to describe. From his training in rhetoric, Augustine knew that truth, in itself, is not enough, that it needs to be made persuasive if it is to be of any use, to be advantageous, if it is to move an audience both to conviction and to action. He also knew, however, that knowledge of truth was different from probable opinion. Following the scepticism of the Academy, therefore, or at least a recognition that the evidence of sense experience (and, above all, the memory of sense experience) can be intrinsically misleading, it may well be that the most which can ever be attained in this world is a likeness of truth, not the truth as such. According to the principles of rhetoric, such verisimilitude could involve shaping or making things up (*fingere, fictio, ficta, figmentum*) but there was a difference here between making things up that could have happened and making things up that could not. Poetic *fabula* could still carry authority, it could still play an important role, particularly when the audience was less educated, but the plausible reconstruction of the past, making something up as hypothesis, was different from making something up when the speaker knew it to be false, when it was intended to deceive, when it was a lie (*mendacium*).

Augustine's examination of these issues – the need for truth to be made plausible, the distinction between truth and probability, the permeable boundary between fiction and deceit – was, in the first instance, a function of his exploration of the truth of the Bible, or, rather, of the truths (plural) of 'sacred history' (*sacra historia*). Throughout his analysis, Augustine is concerned to distinguish between figurative and allegorical interpretation so that he could retain the literal truth of the historical events described in Scripture. The historical event, Augustine maintained, represented the literal truth, and it could also signify an additional, figurative truth, but both these truths were contained in the event itself (*res*), rather than in the words with which they were described (*verba*); this is what made them different from the allegorical truth, which is signified by something that is made up, that has no real existence other than in the words with which it is communicated. In allegory, as an extended metaphor or parable, the events described need not actually have happened.

Figuratively, by contrast, events in Genesis or in Galatians did actually happen and, as such, their meaning is contained in the things themselves, not in the words with which they are narrated.

First and foremost, *De Doctrina Christiana* is concerned with understanding the words and meaning of Scripture and the historical events which it narrates (*divina eloquentia*). However, Augustine's argument also extends beyond the Judaeo-Christian past and to the human experience of Creation as a whole, that is, to the eloquence of things (*eloquentia rerum*). Historical events are themselves an expression of divine eloquence, in the sense that the deeds of God in Creation are one of the means by which He communicates with human beings: 'the order of the ages is like a very beautiful poem', its beauty comprising 'the eloquence, not of words, but of things' (*non verborum sed rerum eloquentia*).[129] In narrating the order of events in time (*ordo temporum*), therefore, historians do not themselves compose that sequence but are narrating a divinely instituted pattern.[130] This last step is the crucial one as far as historiography is concerned, since it raises the question of how a model of scriptural interpretation can be applied to the signification of non-scriptural events. It is the consequences of this agenda for the writing of history *outside* of Scripture, therefore, which, in many respects, provide the key to understanding the nature of medieval historiography; what happened, in other words, when Augustine was mixed with Cicero and shaken, rather than stirred. In the hands of a less careful reader (or a more selective one), the notions Augustine discussed, and the conceptual terminology in which he discussed them, created all sorts of possibilities, and indeed difficulties, particularly if the difference between a truth and a lie was to be located in its signification rather than in whether it actually happened. For subsequent writers, for people who had read enough Cicero and Quintilian to want to join Augustine in putting the scriptural and classical traditions together, Augustine's analysis of classical rhetoric was one of the major reasons why the narration of past events remained so complex a subject in the Middle Ages.

---

129 Augustine, *De Civitate Dei*, XI.18, p. 449.
130 Augustine, *De Doctrina Christiana*, II.121, p. 113.

This complexity is illustrated best (and perhaps most appropriately) by example rather than by precept. One of the earliest, and most influential, demonstrations of the range of methodological issues which underpinned the truth-content of historiography is provided by Bede. The approach which informs Bede's *Ecclesiastical History*, it has been argued, is best understood as a combination of two strands in his thinking. On the one hand, there are the principles of sacred history which Bede adopted in the course of his exegesis of individual books of the Bible – on 1-2 Samuel and 1- 2 Kings, for example, or on the book of Ezra.[131] On the other hand, there are the principles of rhetoric which Bede derived (either at first- or at second-hand) from his familiarity with Cicero, Marius Victorinus and other classical authors.[132] This combination of biblical and rhetorical methodology had as its foundation the validation of using eloquence in the service of wisdom and truth which Bede found set out in Augustine's *De Doctrina Christiana*. As a result, in order to understand why Bede wrote history in the way in which he did, it is necessary to look, not so much to Eusebius, Orosius and Gildas (important though these authors were to Bede),[133] as to the knowledge of classical grammar and rhetoric which is revealed by his own work on figures of speech and tropes, *De Schematibus et Tropis*,[134] and

---

131 R. Ray, 'Bede, the Exegete, as Historian', ed. G. Bonner (ed.), *Famulus Christi: Essays in Commemoration of the Thirteenth Centenary of the Birth of the Venerable Bede* (London, 1976), pp. 125–40; A. Thacker, *Bede and Augustine of Hippo: History and Figure in Sacred Text*, Jarrow Lecture (Jarrow, 2005); J. McClure, 'Bede's Old Testament Kings', in P. Wormald, D. Bullough and R. Collins (eds), *Ideal and Reality in Frankish and Anglo-Saxon Society* (Oxford, 1983), pp. 76–98.

132 R. Ray, 'Bede and Cicero', *Anglo Saxon England*, 16 (1987), pp. 1–15; R. Ray, *Bede, Rhetoric and the Creation of Christian Latin Culture*, Jarrow Lecture (Jarrow, 1997); R. Ray, 'The Triumph of Greco-Roman Rhetorical Assumptions in Pre-Carolingian Historiography', in C. Holdsworth and T.P. Wiseman (eds), *The Inheritance of Historiography 350–900* (Exeter, 1986), pp. 75–81.

133 For Bede's imitation, and adaptation, of Eusebius, see R.A. Markus, *Bede and the Tradition of Ecclesiastical Historiography*, Jarrow Lecture (Jarrow, 1975); reprinted in R.A. Markus, *From Augustine to Gregory the Great: History and Christianity in Late Antiquity* (London, 1983); R.A. Markus, 'Church History and the Early Church Historians', in D. Baker (ed.), *The Materials, Sources and Methods of Ecclesiastical History* (Oxford, 1975), pp. 1–17.

134 Cf. R. Ray, 'Bede, the Exegete, as Historian', pp. 130–2. See also J. Davidse, 'On Bede as Christian Historian', in L.A.J.R. Houwen and A.A. MacDonald (eds), *Beda Venerabilis: Historian, Monk and Northumbrian* (Groningen, 1996), pp. 1–15;

to his reading of Augustine's *De Consensu Evangelistarum* (*On the Harmony of the Four Gospels*), a work in which Augustine defended the trustworthiness of the truth of the Gospel narratives on the grounds that any apparent factual differences between them simply reflected their different purposes and their different permutations of eyewitness and second-hand sources.[135]

Like Augustine, Bede left his own biblical commentary open to the possibility that there was more than one authoritative interpretation, and for the same reason – the truths it contains will grow and multiply and thus, whilst some truths would always remain veiled secrets, the course of exegesis will otherwise produce a progressively fuller understanding.[136] Central to this approach to the narrative of Scripture was the sanction provided by the apostle Paul: 'these things happened as a sign [*in figura*] for us' (1 Corinthians 10:11).[137] What was distinctive about Bede's approach, however, was his emphasis on the significance, not just of words and deeds, but also of what he terms the 'circumstances' in which things were said and done, that is, the details of time, place and person – all of these, Bede argues, could function as what he terms the allegory of fact (*allegoria facti*).[138] Bede's conception of the truth of a narrative of events outside of Scripture, in his own historical writing, accordingly operates on more than one level. Much of the form of the *Ecclesiastical History*, for example, is dependent upon a figurative understanding of the Old Testament – like Gildas, Bede saw the history of Britain

---

J. Davidse, 'The Sense of History in the Works of the Venerable Bede', *Studi Medievali*, 23 (1982), pp. 647–95.

135 Augustine, *De Consensu Evangelistarum*, trans. S.D.F. Salmond, *The Harmony of the Gospels* (New York, 1888); cf. R. Ray, 'Augustine's *De Consensu Evangelistarum* and the Historical Education of the Venerable Bede', *Studia Patristica*, 16 (1985), pp. 557–63. For the methodological influence of this text on, for example, Orderic Vitalis, see M. Chibnall's general introduction to Orderic Vitalis, *Historia Ecclesiastica*, I, pp. 49–51.

136 For example, Bede, *De Tabernaculo*, I, p. 18; cf. page 96.

137 Bede, *De Tabernaculo*, I prol., p. 1; Bede, *Homilies on the Gospels*, trans. L.T. Martin and D. Hurst (Kalamazoo, 1991), II.24, p. 249; Bede, *De Templo*, trans. S. Connolly (Liverpool, 1995), I.2, p. 7.

138 Bede, *De Tabernaculo*, I prol., p. 1; Bede, *De Schematibus et Tropis*, pp. 116–21; cf. Ray, 'Bede, the Exegete, as Historian', pp. 128–9. For the created world as a book written by God, see, for example, Alexander Neckham, *De Naturis Rerum*, ed. T. Wright (London, 1863), II.prol., p. 125; cf. Gregory the Great, *Moralia in Job*, XXVI.17–18, pp. 144–5.

fulfilling both the historical and the moral sense of Scripture.[139] A structure of five books was therefore consciously modelled on the Pentateuch, in the sense that it was designed to provide an account of how a chosen people with particular tribal and familial structures adopted the covenant of God's laws and how the observance of this covenant then brought that people to the threshold of the Promised Land.[140] Still more precisely, Bede's historical account of how the Church was built up amongst the people of the English was designed to provide a literal narrative to be read alongside his separate treatment of the figurative interpretation of the Temple in Jerusalem.[141] Just prior to composing the *Ecclesiastical History* in 731, Bede had been examining the significance of both Tabernacle and Temple in the light of Gregory the Great's interpretation of Ezekiel's vision, that is, of a restored Jerusalem as a prefigurement of a restored and reformed Christian Church. In *De Tabernaculo* (721–25), *De Templo* (729–31) and in his commentary on Ezra and Nehemiah (725–31), Bede accordingly presented the Tabernacle as a prefiguration of the Church being carried through the wilderness to the Promised Land and the successive Temples in Jerusalem as prefigurements of the Church Triumphant and the Heavenly City.[142]

For all Bede's dependence on a scriptural and exegetical approach to the writing of history, many of the principles which inform the narrative in the *Ecclesiastical History* also depend on a clear familiarity with principles of classical rhetoric. The preface to the *Ecclesiastical History* contains his famous and influential

---

139 Cf. Gildas, *De Excidio Britanniae*, ed. and trans. M. Winterbottom, *The Ruin of Britain* (Chichester, 1978), XXIV, p. 27, LXIX–LXX, p. 55, LXXXIII, p. 64, XCIII–XCIV, p. 70 (see pages 162–3).
140 N. Brooks, *Bede and the English*, Jarrow Lecture (Jarrow, 1999), p. 2; H.E.J. Cowdrey, 'Bede and the "English People"', *Journal of Religious Studies*, 11 (1981), pp. 501–23; reprinted in H.E.J. Cowdrey, *Popes, Monks and Crusaders* (London, 1984).
141 P. Meyvaert, *Bede and Gregory the Great*, Jarrow Lecture (Jarrow, 1964); H. Mayr-Harting, *The Venerable Bede, the Rule of St. Benedict, and Social Class*, Jarrow Lecture (Jarrow, 1976), pp. 12–13, 19–22; cf. Gregory of Tours, *Histories*, I.15, p. 79.
142 Bede, *De Tabernaculo*, II.1, pp. 45–6; Bede, *De Templo*, I, p. 6; cf. Augustine, *Enarrationes in Psalmos*, trans. M. Boulding, *Expositions of the Psalms* (New York, New York, 2000–04), LXXXVI, pp. 246–56; Augustine, *De Civitate Dei*, XVII.3, pp. 713–15; Bede, *On Ezra and Nehemiah*, trans. S. DeGregorio (Liverpool, 2006). See also Paschasius Radbertus, *Epitaphium Arsenii*, I.15, p. 122, I.18, p. 127, I.20, p. 129.

statement of the moral–didactic value of writing history, of the importance of eyewitness testimony and of the citation of written documentation, but also a striking acknowledgment of the importance of *communis opinio*, that is, of the beliefs or opinion of the audience for whom he was writing.[143] Likewise, in the main body of the narrative, Bede's account of the pivotal synod of Whitby provides a prime example of biblical and rhetorical principles acting in tandem. On the one hand, Bede's narrative is modelled on the report of the council held at Jerusalem in Acts 15 – it is deliberately constructed, in other words, as a description of the moment at which a newly-established Church puts aside mixed customs in favour of a universal religious observance.[144] On the other hand, Bede's account of the events at Whitby also reflects the principles of deliberative rhetoric – the issue with which the synod is concerned, the dating of Easter, is explicitly termed a *quaestio, controversia* and *contio* and, as such, is resolved by a carefully staged set of paired speeches, one for and one against, the proposed course of action.[145]

Writing some five hundred years later, Guibert of Nogent provides a useful point of comparison to Bede in terms of the methodological range which could be displayed across a combination of historical and exegetical works. Although Guibert may have been less technically accomplished than Bede as a commentator on the Bible, both his narrative of the First Crusade (which Guibert entitled *The Deeds of God Through the Franks*) and his 'memoirs' of his own life (which Guibert entitles *Monodiae*) are, in and of themselves, revealing works of 'historiography', the first a rewriting of earlier accounts of the expedition of 1095–99, the second an account of Guibert's own spiritual life and of the social, political and ecclesiastical fabric of north-eastern France in the early years of the twelfth century.[146] What is particularly interesting about this historiography, indeed, is the methodological connection which

---

143 See pages 289–90.
144 Ray, 'Bede and Cicero', p. 9; R. Ray, 'What Do We Know About Bede's Commentaries?', *Recherches de Théologie Ancienne et Médiévale*, 49 (1982), pp. 5–20.
145 Bede, *Historia Ecclesiastica*, III.25, pp. 153–9; Ray, 'The Triumph of Greco-Roman Assumptions', pp. 79–81.
146 Guibert of Nogent, *Gesta Dei per Francos*; Guibert of Nogent, *Monodiae*, trans. J.F. Benton (Toronto, 1984); cf. J. Chaurand, 'La Conception de l'Histoire de Guibert de Nogent (1053–1124)', *Cahiers de Civilisation Médiévale*, 8 (1965),

exists *between* these texts, a connection which Guibert himself makes explicit through his role as an exegete and as a homilist, that is, as an interpreter of Scripture who was charged with the pastoral care and instruction both of the clergy in his monastery and of the laity. These connections are encapsulated in the work with which Guibert chose to preface his commentary on the book of Genesis and which describes, quite simply, 'how a sermon ought to be given' (*Liber quo ordine sermo fieri debeat*).[147]

At the heart of Guibert's approach to preaching was the, by now conventional, exegetical distinction between the different senses of Scripture. 'There are four ways of interpreting Scripture', he writes, 'and on them, as though on so many scrolls, each sacred page is rolled. The first is history, which speaks of actual events as they occurred; the second is allegory, in which one thing stands for something else; the third is tropology, or moral instruction, which treats of the ordering and arranging of one's life; and the last is ascetics, or spiritual enlightenment, through which we who are about to treat of lofty and heavenly topics are led to a higher way of life'.[148] As an illustration (predictably, perhaps, but nonetheless revealingly for the author of an account of the First Crusade), Guibert chooses the city of Jerusalem: 'historically, it represents a specific city; in allegory it represents the holy Church; tropologically, or morally, it is the soul of every faithful human who longs for the vision of eternal peace; and anagogically it refers to the life of the heavenly citizens who already see the God of Gods revealed in all His glory in Sion'.[149] The point which

---

pp. 381–95; and, more generally, J. Rubinstein, *Guibert of Nogent: Portrait of a Medieval Mind* (London, 2002).
147 Guibert of Nogent, *Liber Quo Ordine Sermo Fieri Debeat*, trans. J.M. Miller, *A Book About the Way in Which a Sermon Ought To Be Given*, in J.M. Miller, M.H. Prosser and T.W. Benson (eds), *Readings in Medieval Rhetoric* (Bloomington, 1973), pp. 162–81. For Guibert's scriptural commentaries, see B. Smalley, 'William of Middleton and Guibert de Nogent', *Recherches de Théologie Ancienne et Médiévale*, 16 (1949), pp. 281–91; Rubinstein, *Guibert of Nogent*, pp. 26–60, 182–99.
148 Guibert of Nogent, *Liber Quo Ordine*, pp. 170–1; cf. H. Caplan, 'The Four Senses of Scriptural Teaching and the Medieval Theory of Preaching', *Speculum*, 4 (1929), pp. 282–90.
149 *Liber Quo Ordine*, p. 171; cf. Cassian, *Collationes*, XIV.8, pp. 437–8; Bede, *In Cantica Canticorum Allegorica Expositio* (PL 91, cols 1065–236), IV, col. 1142; Hrabanus Maurus, *Expositio in Epistolam ad Galatas*, IV, cols 331–2; Sedulius Scottus, *Collectanea in Epistolam ad Galatas* (PL 103, cols 181–94), IV, col. 191;

Guibert himself takes pains to emphasise, however, is that not all of these levels of truth will always be appropriate for a preacher to expound.

It had long been a fundamental principle of pastoral care that different audiences needed to be taught in different ways, according to particular considerations of time, condition and capacity. Gregory the Great had devoted much of book III of the *Regula Pastoralis*, his treatise on the subject, to going through an analysis of these different audiences one by one.[150] Gregory of Tours had likewise drawn attention to the care which had been taken by the apostle Paul to speak in accordance with the intellectual level of the person whom he was addressing (1 Corinthians 3:2; 1 Corinthians 14:9; Hebrews 5:12),[151] and Gregory had, as a result, used the preface and conclusion to his own *Histories* to stress that he had written in a humble, rustic and straightforward style. 'Few people', Gregory points out, 'can understand a rhetorical speechifier, whereas many can follow a blunt speaker'.[152] Guibert of Nogent follows suit. As a general rule, he states, given the nature and circumstances of a preacher's typical audience, it is the moral or tropological sense which should be privileged in a sermon. 'Granted', he writes, 'that all four of these methods of interpretation are valid and can be used, either together or singly, yet the most appropriate and prudent for use in matters referring to the lives of men seems to be the moral approach'.[153] Guibert's reasoning is that 'among the less intelligent, error can result from preaching which is too esoteric; but in moral instruction, we can

---

Honorius of Autun, *De Animae Exsilio et Patria* (*PL* 172, cols 1241–6), XII, col. 1245; *Glossa Ordinaria*, prol., p. 6; Robert of Basevorn, *Forma Praedicandi*, trans. L. Kruhl, *The Form of Preaching*, in J.J. Murphy (ed.), *Three Medieval Rhetorical Arts* (Berkeley, 1971), XXXIX, p. 183.
150   Gregory the Great, *Regula Pastoralis*, trans. H. Davis (Washington, DC, 1950), III.prol., pp. 89–90, quoted, for example, by Bede, *De Tabernaculo*, I, p. 27; cf. *De Tabernaculo*, II, p. 90, citing 1 Peter 2:2 and Hebrews 5:14.
151   Gregory of Tours, *Histories*, VI.40, p. 373; cf. Otto of Freising, *Chronicle*, VIII.33, p. 508: 'milk for the simple so that they can be led from the visible to the invisible'; Hugh of St Victor, *Didascalicon*, trans. J. Taylor (New York, 1961), VI.4, p. 139.
152   Gregory of Tours, *Histories*, pref., p. 63, I.prol., p. 67, V.6, p. 263, X.31, p. 603; cf. Gregory of Tours, *Glory of the Confessors*, trans. R. van Dam (Liverpool, 1988), pref., pp. 16–17.
153   Guibert of Nogent, *Liber Quo Ordine*, p. 171.

especially learn the utility of discretion'.[154] 'When the secrets of the Scriptures are interpreted for the unlettered and uneducated', he explains, 'they quickly forget'. The unlettered and uneducated, he continues, 'are accustomed to dealing with physical objects, so it is of no great wonder that they do not possess the same power of understanding the spiritual, which they cannot see, as they possess for the material substances, which they can see and touch. Some of them are almost animals and scarcely comprehend anything, unless it is material and evident even to beasts; they are completely ignorant of the vices of their bodies and souls, unless someone explains this to them'.[155] What clearly interests Guibert here is the practical reality that the preacher's audience will be mixed, in the sense that it will tend to comprise both the educated and the less educated, the intelligent and (in Sallust's sense) the bestial.[156] This means that the preacher's own rhetoric will have to operate at more than one level of truth at once:

> although he preaches simple and uncomplicated matter to the unlettered, at the same time he should try to reach a higher plane with the educated; let him offer to them what they are capable of understanding. When he expounds such things by explaining them in detail, he will make clear and lucid for the peasants and common people ideas which at first seem difficult and confusing even to the very learned.... So also the preacher who offers simple doctrine to the people and at the same time adds something more substantial on which the more educated can exercise their intellects – by so doing, he is able both to feed with his words the dull and sluggish of mind and also to inject weightier ideas by adding something more solid to the milk, thus delighting the educated audience as well.[157]

Gerald of Wales was to make a very similar point to Guibert's when he defended the utility of his writings on Ireland. In the case of the *Expugnatio Hibernica*, Gerald argued, he had deliberately

---

154 *Liber Quo Ordine*, p. 171.
155 *Liber Quo Ordine*, p. 172.
156 *Liber Quo Ordine*, pp. 172, 178; Guibert of Nogent, *Monodiae*, I.2, p. 40; cf. page 42. For John of Salisbury, what distinguished human understanding from the mental images experienced by animals was the ability to analyse the reasons and causes of those images (*Metalogicon*, IV.16, p. 227); cf. Robert of Basevorn, *Forma Praedicandi*, XLIX, p. 205.
157 *Liber Quo Ordine*, p. 170; cf. 1 Corinthians 3:2; Eadmer, *Life of Anselm*, ed. and trans. R.W. Southern (Oxford, 1972), I.22, pp. 38–9, I.31, pp. 55–6.

produced something 'clear, straightforward and easily understood by all', because he was adapting his language to make it suitable for lay people and rulers who were little educated in letters. 'It is therefore written in a plain and easy style', he explains, 'and needs to be made simple, with the sole purpose of being understood. For it will always be permissible to use popular words when the deeds of the people, and of the leaders among the people, are being set down in writing'.[158] In the case of the *Topographia Hibernica*, on the other hand, he encouraged the diligent reader to find both moral and allegorical meanings in this otherwise apparently 'juvenile' historical work.[159] Like the Book of Kells, he observes, 'delight is open only to those with a fine perception and careful scrutiny, as opposed to those who look without seeing and hear without being able to understand what appears to them to be confused and disordered noise'. As far as his own work is concerned, therefore, like the study of birds, 'the careful observing mind will clearly grasp the differences which exist between similar things and the similarities between different things'.[160] Whether the three different groups of people to whom Gerald claims he recited the *Topographia* actually existed in reality,[161] or whether, like John of Garland's, these were theoretical audiences, each with a different level of understanding,[162] the idea of including more than one level of interpretation within a single text was not restricted to Scripture.

The notion that a narrative could operate at two levels simultaneously, a historical sense which would use examples to nourish those who were slower in understanding and an allegorical sense which would feed the intellectually refined, was a long-established principle in scriptural exegesis: 'the historical sense should nourish

---

[158] Gerald of Wales, *Expugnatio Hibernica*, ed. and trans. A.B. Scott and F.X. Martin, *The Conquest of Ireland* (Dublin, 1978), prol., pp. 3–4.
[159] Gerald of Wales, Letter 3, to William de Montibus, p. 171 (see page 2); cf. Gerald of Wales, *Topographia Hibernica*, I.9–10, p. 40, III.106, p. 114.
[160] Gerald of Wales, *Topographia Hibernica*, III.94, p. 104, I.13, p. 43.
[161] Gerald of Wales, *De Rebus a Se Gestis*, trans. H.E. Butler, *The Autobiography of Giraldus Cambrensis* (London, 1937; reprinted Woodbridge, 2005), XVI, p. 97 (see pages 24–5). He names his three groups as 'the poor, the doctors of the faculties, and then other scholars, knights and a number of the citizens'.
[162] John of Garland, *Parisiana Poetria*, II.93–5, p. 37.

young minds, the mystical sense those of adults'.[163] As John Cassian put it, the simple and pure narrative of historical reading is like 'grass for cattle' (*faenum iumentis*) (Psalm 103 [104]:14), that is, it is food for those with simpler minds, who are less capable of perfect and sound understanding, and who will thereby be strengthened for the task and labour of living according to their position and the measure of their understanding.[164] Likewise, Hrabanus Maurus thought that, whereas an allegorical reading is for the quick (*velociores*), history is for the slow (*tardiores*), for the mass of the people (*turba populi*) whose minds are set on the things of this world (*mentes carnalium*).[165] The consequences of this distinction for the writing of history outside of scriptural exegesis were clear. Wipo, for example, selects one specific deed of Conrad II and explicitly gives it what he terms a mystical significance – in this case the emperor's encounter with a poor farmer, an orphan and a widow, which signifies the true justice of Christian rule in accordance with the injunctions of Deuteronomy. 'Certain things must be told', he writes, 'which [Conrad] did on the very day of his consecration. For although they may seem small, nonetheless they are eminently significant in a mystical way [*mysterio quodam*]. But since this is written as public history [*historia publica*] which makes the spirit of the reader more attentive to the new turns of events than to the figurative meaning of words, it seems more fitting simply to follow this affair through in its entirety instead of mixing in some comment with mystical reasonings [*mysticis rationibus*]'.[166] History, in other words, makes a moral or spiritual point better when this point is being made to a specifically public audience.

The ultimate goal of concentrating on the moral or tropological sense is, by definition, a knowledge of virtue and vice. As Hugh of St Victor explained, echoing Gregory the Great's gerundive, 'tropology is when, in that action which we hear was done, we

---

163 For example, Abelard, *Hymni Nocturni* (*PL* 178, cols 1775–80), II, col. 1776; cf. Murphy, *Rhetoric in the Middle Ages*, p. 313.
164 Cassian, *Collationes*, VIII.3, p. 376.
165 Hrabanus Maurus, *Commentaria in Exodum*, II.15, col. 106.
166 Wipo, *Deeds of Conrad*, trans. T.E. Mommsen and K.F. Morrison, in *Imperial Lives and Letters of the Eleventh Century* (New York, 1962; rev. edn 2000), V, p. 70; cf. Deuteronomy 14:29, 24:19–21, 26:12–13; Psalm 146:9. For Suger's emphasis on the same theme, see page 26.

recognise what we should be doing. It is rightly called tropology, that is, speech that has changed direction ... or folded back upon itself, because without a doubt we turn the word of history about other people to our own instruction when, having read of the deeds of others, we conform our life to their example'.[167] Guibert of Nogent, for one, understood this principle to be applicable in a very direct way, as the practical application of that knowledge to one's *own* life. The purpose of focusing on the moral sense is therefore, for him, not just as an effective means of preaching, but also for a knowledge of oneself. 'It seems to me', Guibert writes, 'that no preaching is more efficacious than that which would help man to know himself, that which brings out into the open all that is deep within him, in his innermost heart, that which will shame him, finally, by forcing him to stand clearly revealed before his own gaze'.[168] This applies to the audience but also to the preacher: 'through these points, and others of like nature, anyone having the office of teacher can, if he wishes, be prepared in every detail, first by knowing himself and, second, through the lessons his experience of interior struggles has taught him; this training will be far richer than anything I could express. In this way, the events of his life, both good and bad, are indelibly imprinted on his memory; because of them he is able to act wisely for his own salvation and that of others'.[169] Armed with these twin methodological principles – different levels of truth for different or mixed audiences, together with the moral priority of self-knowledge – it thereby becomes possible to read

---

167 Hugh of St Victor, *De Tribus Maximis Circumstantiis Gestorum*, trans. M. Carruthers, in M. Carruthers and J.M. Ziolkowski (eds), *The Medieval Craft of Memory* (Philadelphia, 2002), p. 265; cf. page 249.
168 Guibert of Nogent, *Liber Quo Ordine*, p. 173; cf. Thietmar of Merseburg, *Chronicon*, trans. D.A. Warner (Manchester, 2001), where the author twice quotes the proverb 'know thyself' (taking it from Macrobius, *Saturnalia*, I.6.6, p. 50) and interweaves an explicitly confessional element throughout his text (*Chronicon*, I.20, p. 82, V.1, p. 206, VI.42–3, p. 267, VI.45, p. 269, VII.14, p. 317, VII.33–4, pp. 330–1, VIII.24, p. 377), over and above more straightforwardly familial and 'autobiographical' material; cf. Boethius, *Consolation of Philosophy*, II.5, p. 205; John of Salisbury, *Metalogicon*, IV.40, p. 270, quoting Cicero, *De Finibus*, trans. H. Rackham, *On Ends* (2nd edn, Loeb, 1931), V.16.44, p. 443.
169 *Liber Quo Ordine*, p. 175.

the 'history' of both the *Monodiae* and *The Deeds of God Through the Franks* in a more complex, and revealing, fashion than the contents of each of these narratives might, at first sight, suggest.

At the most straightforward level, Guibert's *Monodiae* amount to an act of penance – they are given this title, after all, because they represent a penitential psalm sung by the author on his own.[170] Self-knowledge is the first step in confession (the opening word of the entire text is *confiteor* – 'I confess') and 'know thyself' is a maxim quoted in the very first chapter.[171] Whilst Guibert's work is thus clearly modelled on Augustine's *Confessions* (as Guibert himself notes, confession of past sins is the beginning of good deeds),[172] Guibert, like Augustine, is putting forward a history of his own life not only as an act of personal confession but also as an account which will be useful to others, even as a moral–didactic *exemplum*. 'I do not utter destructive and hateful words with pleasure...,' he writes, 'and I have undertaken to tell the tale of my fortunes and misfortunes for what help it may be to others'.[173] These were memoirs, therefore, with an explicitly homiletic purpose, namely to provide examples which would be useful in sermons.[174] However, if it was a moral interpretation of events which Guibert thought would be more useful in the present age,[175] such utility also had a more specific target in mind. In recounting his own, rather belated, conversion to the study of Scripture, Guibert records the assiduousness with he had read the works of Gregory the Great and thereby learned 'according to the rules of ancient writers, to treat the words of the prophets and the Gospels in their allegorical, their moral, and finally their anagogical meaning'.[176] This invocation of Gregory's exegetical

---

170 Guibert of Nogent, *Monodiae*, I.14, p. 76; cf. Isidore, *Etymologiae*, VI.19.6, p. 147.
171 *Monodiae*, I.1, p. 37; cf. Juvenal, *Satires*, trans. S.M. Braund (Loeb, 2004), XI.27, p. 403; Hugh of St Victor, *Didascalicon*, I.1, p. 46; Bernardus Silvestris, *Commentary on the First Six Books of Virgil's Aeneid*, pref., p. 5; and, more generally, P. Courcelle, 'Nosce Teipsum du Bas-Empire au Haut Moyen-Âge', *Settimane di Studio*, 9 (1962), pp. 265–95.
172 *Monodiae*, I.14, p. 75, I.23, p. 110, II.3, p. 129.
173 *Monodiae*, II.3, p. 130.
174 *Monodiae*, II.3, p. 130, III.13, p. 195; cf. I.8, p. 53, I.10, p. 58.
175 *Monodiae*, I.17, pp. 90–2.
176 *Monodiae*, I.17, p. 92; cf. G.R. Evans, 'Guibert of Nogent and Gregory the Great on Preaching and Exegesis', *The Thomist*, 49 (1985), pp. 534–50;

method sets up one further reason for Guibert remembering the history of his past life – so that the act of remembrance can provide a means of avoiding pride, the besetting sin of all those who, like Guibert himself, were charged with the ministry of pastoral care and who exercised authority over other Christians. The memory of virtue and, more importantly, the memory of weakness and vice, served as a corrective to assuming one's own moral superiority over those people who had been placed in one's care. Guibert, again like Augustine, acknowledges that he continued to be assailed by the temptation to sin, as Paul's letter to the Romans (7:7–25) had suggested he would be: 'although I am forever sinning, compelled by my weakness and not through the wilfulness of pride, yet I in no way lose the hope of amendment'.[177] Guibert's primary source of inspiration here, however, remained Gregory the Great, and for one important reason.

Throughout his *Pastoral Care*, Gregory the Great had emphasised that individuals who exercise authority over others should first exercise authority over themselves, so that their lives can provide an exemplary demonstration of the content of their teaching. This is a necessary precaution against pride that is achieved, first and foremost, by looking at oneself.[178] In the first instance, such introspection will involve individuals calling to mind their past actions, remembering what they have done in obedience to others, in order to assess their suitability to assume a position of authority.[179] Thereafter, it becomes a matter of committed self-examination (*studium suae inquisitionis*), such that individuals in authority will never be ignorant of their own selves but will always be brought back to a memory of who, and what, they are (*memoria sui*). In reproving the infirmity of others, therefore, individuals in authority must never be forgetful of their

---

R. Wasselynck, 'Les *Moralia in Job* dans les Ouvrages de Morale du Haut Moyen Âge Latin', *Recherches de Théologie Ancienne et Médiévale*, 31 (1964), pp. 6–11; R. Wasselynck, 'L'Influence de l'Exégèse de Saint Grégoire le Grand Sur les Commentaires Bibliques Médiévaux (VIIe–XIIe Siècles)', *Recherches de Théologie Ancienne et Médiévale*, 32 (1965), pp. 157–204.

177 *Monodiae*, I.16, p. 86.
178 Gregory the Great, *Regula Pastoralis*, I.2, pp. 23–5, I.4, pp. 27–9; cf. Gregory the Great, *Moralia in Job* XXV.7.12–18, pp. 101–8; Paschasius Radbertus, *Epitaphium Arsenii*, I.9, p. 108.
179 *Regula Pastoralis*, I.9, pp. 36–7.

own (*oblitus sui*).[180] According to Gregory, the act of remembering one's virtues is thus a vital component of exercising office, for the sake of self-knowledge, and not just for the edification of others. Crucially, however, Gregory was quick to recognise that such recollection could also become a pitfall of the soul, in the sense that this sort of *memoria virtutis* can readily serve as a temptation to pride.[181] Gregory of Tours went back to Proverbs 26:27 in order to make the same point – recording a good deed can promote vainglory as you can 'fall into a pit of your own making'.[182] John of Salerno records the same anxiety in Odo of Cluny – his life may have served as 'the example of all virtues' and his conduct may have instructed others 'as if from an open book', but Odo himself was extremely reluctant to have his own deeds narrated unless they were attributed to some anonymous third person.[183] With the performance of any good action, there is a balance to be struck between keeping that action secret in order to preserve one's own humility and making it public so that it can serve as an example to others.[184]

Presented with the pitfalls of personal remembrance, the solution, for Gregory the Great, was to accompany the recollection of one's own virtue with the recollection of one's own infirmity (*memoria infirmitatis*). The memory of the physical weakness to which an individual has been subject in the past is thus the means by which the human mind is brought to a knowledge of itself in the present *without* succumbing to the sin of pride.[185] This is the point, therefore, with which Gregory chooses to open and close the entire argument of his treatise on pastoral care. For some

---

180 *Regula Pastoralis*, I.3, p. 26, I.4, pp. 26–7, II.6, p. 61, II.10, p. 82; cf. Guibert of Nogent, *Monodiae*, I.23, p. 108: 'when we had forgotten these things and had become sluggish and careless'.
181 *Regula Pastoralis*, IV.1, pp. 234–5.
182 Gregory of Tours, *Histories*, IV.34, p. 228, IX.9, p. 491.
183 John of Salerno, *Life of Odo of Cluny*, trans. G. Sitwell (London, 1958), I.14, p. 16, I.17, p. 19, II.2, p. 42, II.16, p. 60; cf. Odo of Cluny, *Life of Gerald of Aurillac*, trans. G. Sitwell (London, 1958), II.33 p. 159; Eadmer, *Life of Anselm*, I.32, p. 58, II.41, p. 119, II.72, p. 150.
184 Gregory the Great, *Regula Pastoralis*, III.35, pp. 222–6; cf. Gregory the Great, *Dialogues*, trans. O.J. Zimmerman (Washington, DC, 1959), I.9, pp. 35–6.
185 *Regula Pastoralis*, III.12, pp. 123–5; cf. Bede, *De Tabernaculo*, II, p. 59; Henry of Huntingdon, *Historia Anglorum*, III.8, p. 153 (quoting Bede citing Gregory the Great); 2 Corinthians 12:9.

people, he argues, the greatness of their virtue has become the occasion of their fall once the Devil has listed all the things which that individual has done well (*omne quod bene gessit*). Such individuals fall prey to pride as soon as their souls start to seek their own praise, rather than that of God, attributing to themselves the good which they have received from God and disseminating the glory of their own reputation through their lust for praise. In this situation, whenever individuals are endangered by the abundance of their own virtues, they need to recall, not the things which they have done, but the things which they have left undone. This is why, Gregory suggests, God often leaves some imperfection in people who exercise authority – so that when they shine in outstanding virtues they may also be repelled by their own weakness. Their struggle against the lowest and the least of difficulties will thus keep them humble even amidst the greatest of their achievements. It is the remembrance of their weakness, *memoria infirmitatis*, which prevents them from otherwise taking pride in the virtues which they have received from God.[186]

Guibert of Nogent's emphasis on introspective remembrance as a precondition for exercising office opens the strong possibility that the original motivation behind the composition of his *Monodiae* was closely tied to the period of Guibert's 'retirement' from Nogent in 1107–08.[187] The two examples he gives of his own sermons or homilies within the text, after all, are both concerned with his own unsuitability for office (Isaiah 3:6–8).[188] However, this work was also designed to be more generally applicable, at least through its division into three books dealing, respectively, with self, household (or monastery) and the political community.[189]

---

[186] *Regula Pastoralis*, praef., pp. 20–1, IV.1, pp. 234–7; cf. Gregory the Great, *Dialogues*, III.14, pp. 134–5. For the application of this principle to the life of a temporal ruler, see M.S. Kempshall, 'No Bishop, No King – The Ministerial Ideology of Kingship and Asser's *Res Gestae Aelfredi*', in R. Gameson and H. Leyser (eds), *Belief and Culture in the Middle Ages* (Oxford, 2001), pp. 106–27. As Guibert points out, however, such remembrance has to be handled with great care, since picturing a past sin in the memory can also cause individuals to relapse into slavery to such sculpted idols; see Rubinstein, *Guibert of Nogent*, p. 179.

[187] Guibert of Nogent, *Monodiae*, II.4, p. 133; cf. Rubinstein, *Guibert of Nogent*, pp. 87–95, 101–6.

[188] *Monodiae*, II.3, pp. 131–2, III.6, pp. 161–2.

[189] For a similar tripartite division, see Giles of Rome, *De Regimine Principum* (Venice, 1502) (see page 465).

Guibert's own moral and spiritual decline is therefore set up as a mirror to that of his age, not least in its inclusion of cautionary tales of exemplary monastic wrongdoing (*terribile exemplum*).[190] If Augustine had taught Guibert the close connection between memory, knowledge of self and knowledge of God, and if Gregory the Great had taught him the utility both of a fourfold exegesis of Scripture and of remembrance as a corrective to pride, then it is Anselm of Bec who is credited by Guibert with teaching him how 'to divide the mind in a threefold or fourfold way, to treat the operations of the interior mystery under the headings of appetite, will, reason and intellect'.[191] Augustine's *De Trinitate* had exercised considerable influence on Anselm, not least in Anselm's *Monologion*, and it is this teaching on the composition of the soul which sets up one final level of interpretation for Guibert's *Monodiae*. Guibert's early life is presented as a complicated tripartite relationship between himself, his mother and his tutor and, read in the light of the explicit citation of Anselm's psychology, it appears that Guibert was recasting the history of his own life in order to make a moral and anagogical point about a three-way struggle between affection, will and reason, which ultimately produces a fourth goal – intellectual understanding.[192]

The Deeds of God Through the Franks is ostensibly a much more conventional work of historiography than the *Monodiae*, but its connections to Guibert's works of scriptural exegesis are no less clear. Indeed, there is a revealing point of comparison here with Guibert's contemporary, Orderic Vitalis. In recounting the last days of William the Conqueror, Orderic explains that his narrative has amounted to a careful investigation and a truthful description of what God's disposition of events has revealed. Orderic has composed, he states, 'neither a fictitious tragedy nor a wordy comedy but simply a true record of the diversity of events for studious readers' (*non fictilem tragediam ..., non loquaci comedia ..., sed studiosis lectoribus varios eventus veraciter intimo*). This disclaimer,

---

190 Guibert of Nogent, *Monodiae*, II.6, p. 141; cf. III.11, pp. 188–9.
191 *Monodiae*, I.17, p. 89.
192 Rubinstein, *Guibert of Nogent*, chs 2–3. For the further application of this theme to Guibert of Nogent's *Deeds of God Through the Franks* (where success is made dependent on the affection of goodwill and where Jerusalem is interpreted as the intellect at peace), see Rubinstein, *Guibert of Nogent*, pp. 98–100.

however, does not preclude a moral lesson being drawn from what he was describing. In the particular case of King William, Orderic makes it explicit – do not put your trust in false princes (quoting Psalm 145 [146]:3 though with Orderic adding 'false'), but meditate on the books of the Old and New Testaments and from them compile *exempla* to teach you what to shun (robbery and oppression) and what to pursue (true riches rather than the transitoriness of worldly power).[193] Nonetheless, Orderic would clearly prefer his 'studious readers' to make such moral–didactic connections for themselves. 'I find many things in the pages of Scripture', he writes, 'which, when they are carefully interpreted, seem to be similar to the events of our own time'. However, he continues, 'I leave the allegorical readings and interpretations appropriate to human conduct to be expounded by the studious, setting myself the task of now relating a little further the straightforward history [*simplex historia*] of Norman affairs'.[194] Guibert of Nogent's *Deeds of God* are not so restrained.

In his dedicatory letter, Guibert sets out exactly why he has written this work and, in the first instance, draws attention to the fact that he will be using a more elaborate style than the one he had employed in his biblical commentary. Not only will it be more self-consciously rhetorical but it may even include poetic diction. 'No one should be surprised', he writes, 'that I make use of a style very much different from that of the commentaries on Genesis, or the other little treatises; for it is proper and permissible to ornament a history with the crafted elegance of words; however, the mysteries of sacred eloquence should be treated, not with poetic loquacity, but with ecclesiastical plainness'.[195]

---

193 Orderic Vitalis, *Historia Ecclesiastica*, VII.16, pp. 107–9; cf. page 194.
194 *Historia Ecclesiastica*, VIII.16, p. 229; cf. I.prol., p. 133: 'I strive ... to explain truthfully and straightforwardly the things which I have seen in our own times, or know to have occurred in nearby provinces. I firmly believe, following the conjectures of earlier writers, that in time someone will come with greater understanding than myself, and greater capacity for interpreting the various events taking place on earth, who will perhaps derive something from my writings and those of others like me, and will graciously insert this in their chronography or narrative [*chronographiae narrationique*] for the information of future generations'. For Orderic's audience, see R. Ray, 'Orderic Vitalis and His Readers', *Studia Monastica*, 14 (1972), pp. 16–33.
195 Guibert of Nogent, *Gesta Dei per Francos*, Ep.ded., p. 23.

Guibert explains his desire to find linguistic ornamentation that is fitting for the truth of what happened – what is appropriate, in this instance, means that the style should be varied in order to match the events being described, using harsh words for martial deeds and more temperate words for divine matters. Guibert accordingly promises to use both modes of writing.[196] Indeed, such is the glorious nature of the events he will be describing that, in his opinion, they deserve to be narrated with greater dignity than Josephus managed or the book of Maccabees. These are, in short, exceptional events and, in providing them with a frame of reference from the ancient past (the siege of Troy, Alexander the Great's expedition to the East, Caesar's Gallic wars and Titus' sack of Jerusalem),[197] Guibert is also at pains to point out that they are still unprecedented, in terms of both their glory and their suffering: 'no example can be adduced from the past'.[198]

As becomes clear in the main body of the narrative, such rhetorical ornamentation is made necessary, in part, by the inadequacy, even crudeness, of the account of the First Crusade which had been given by Fulcher of Chartres and which Guibert was choosing to rewrite in a style much more appropriate to the nature of its subject-matter.[199] Guibert accordingly intersperses his narrative with passages of verse, sometimes of his own composition.[200] In part, however, such strategies are also conditioned by the identity of his intended audience. In alerting his readers to the change of style from his scriptural commentaries, Guibert anticipates a hostile reaction, but it is one for which he has a ready response – he is writing for the benefit of more than just simple minds. 'Furthermore', he states, 'if anyone accuses me of writing obscurely, let him fear inflicting on himself the stigma of weak intellect, since I know for certain that no one trained in letters

---

196 *Gesta Dei per Francos*, pref., p. 24; cf. VII, p. 155.
197 *Gesta Dei per Francos*, I, p. 27, II, p. 54, III, p. 64, V, p. 103, VII, pp. 129, 131; cf. William of Malmesbury, *Gesta Regum Anglorum*, IV.372, p. 655.
198 *Gesta Dei per Francos*, I, p. 28, V, p. 104, VII, pp. 128, 135, 143, 145, 147.
199 Cf. William of Malmesbury, *Gesta Regum Anglorum*, IV.374, p. 661; J.O. Ward, 'Some Principles of Rhetorical Historiography in the Twelfth Century', in E. Breisach (ed.), *Classical Rhetoric and Medieval Historiography* (Kalamazoo, 1985), pp. 122–48.
200 For example, Guibert of Nogent, *Gesta Dei per Francos*, II, pp. 47, 50, III, pp. 59, 63, IV, pp. 78, 83; cf. pages 362–3.

can raise a question about whatever I may have said in the following book'.[201] As was the case in his instructions on giving a sermon, Guibert's remarks indicate that he recognised that he, too, needed to write at more than one level, for more than one audience at the same time. In *The Deeds of God*, he states explicitly that it is his desire to produce something which, like Scripture, will exercise the mind through its difficulties and complexities.[202] Once again, Guibert was given his cue by Gregory the Great: 'if the spirit of the reader seeks to know something moral or something historical [in Scripture], this moral sense of history follows; if it seeks something typical, the figurative language is soon understood; and if it seeks something contemplative, ... the heavenly sense of the words of the sacred text is revealed'.[203] The practical consequences for Guibert's own historical writing can be seen towards the end of *The Deeds of God*, where, having provided an allegorical interpretation of the sufferings of hunger and thirst,[204] Guibert first of all invokes Judges 6–8 as a prefigurement of the events he is describing and then, having described the capture of Jerusalem, makes his entire narrative culminate in a figural interpretation of Zechariah 12:2–10.[205]

If the first point which Guibert wishes to make about *The Deeds of God* concerns the style in which it was written, the second concerns its historical contents. Guibert accordingly devotes the rest of his prologue to elaborating the authoritative basis for his narration of the causes, as well as the course, of events – the extrinsic testimony for what happened but also the intrinsic testimony for why and how. He writes:

> In setting out to correct, or perhaps corrupt, the model [*exemplar*] for this history I have first attempted to consider the causes [*causae*]

---

201 *Gesta Dei per Francos*, praef., p. 25.
202 *Gesta Dei per Francos*, V.praef., p. 90.
203 Gregory the Great, *Homiliae in Hiezechihelem Prophetam*, ed. M. Adriaen (*CCSL* 142, Turnhout, 1971), VII.9, p. 246.
204 Guibert of Nogent, *Gesta Dei per Francos*, VII, p. 131.
205 *Gesta Dei per Francos*, VII, pp. 141–4; cf. Alan of Lille, *Anticlaudianus*, prol., pp. 40–1: 'the sweetness of the literal sense will soothe the ears of boys, the moral instruction will inspire the mind on the path to perfection, the sharper subtlety of the allegory will whet the advanced intellect'; Richard FitzNigel, *Dialogus de Scaccario*, ed. and trans. E. Amt (Oxford, 2007), I.5, p. 39: 'for it is a worthy thing to seek flowers of mystic meaning among the thistles of worldly matters'.

and necessities [*necessitates*] that brought about this expedition, as I have heard them, and then, having set out the circumstances [*occasiones*], to relate the deeds [*res gestae*] themselves. I learned the story, related with great veracity, from the previous author whom I follow [Fulcher of Chartres] and from those who were present on the expedition. I have often compared the book's version of events with what was said by those who saw what happened with their own eyes and, beyond a doubt, I have seen that neither testimony was discordant with the other. Whatever I have added, I have learned from eyewitnesses, or have found out for myself.[206]

Despite not himself being an eyewitness, Guibert defends the accuracy and trustworthiness of the testimony on which his own narrative is founded, including where it is based on the opinion of others:

If anyone objects that I did not see, he cannot object on the grounds that I did not hear, because I believe that, in a way, hearing is almost as good as seeing. For although 'what has been thrust into the ears stirs the mind more slowly than those things which have appeared before reliable eyes' [Horace, *Ars Poetica*, 180–1], nevertheless, who doubts those historians who wrote the lives of the saints, who wrote down not only what they saw with their own eyes but what they drank from what others have understood and told them? For if the narrator is reliable and, as one reads, 'testifies to what he saw and heard' [John 3:32], then stories told by those who speak the truth about events no one has seen are clearly acceptable as true.[207]

Guibert concludes his prologue by anticipating one final objection which might be raised regarding the accuracy of his historical narrative, caused, on this occasion, not by any hostility to the use of rhetorical ornamentation, but by sensitivity to the boundary with what is made up, false and deceitful. Significantly, Guibert does so on the Augustinian basis that sense-memory is fallible even when it concerns one's own actions and motives. He states:

If anything is described as false, no clever critic may rightly accuse me of lying, I say, since he cannot argue, as God is my witness, that I have spoken out of a desire to deceive. How can it be surprising if we make errors, when we are describing things done in a foreign land, when we are clearly unable, not only to express in words our

---

206 Guibert of Nogent, *Gesta Dei per Francos*, praef., p. 25.
207 *Gesta Dei per Francos*, IV.praef., p. 73; cf. I, p. 32, VII, pp. 133, 166.

own thoughts and actions, but even to collect them in the silence of our own minds? What can I say, then, about intentions, which are so hidden most of the time that they can scarcely be discerned by the acuity of the inner man? Therefore we should not be severely attacked if we stumble unknowingly in our words; but relentless blame should be brought to bear when falsity is wilfully woven into the text, in an attempt to deceive or out of a desire to disguise something.[208]

Guibert had a clear sense of the distinction between the seriousness of true history and the triviality of vulgar fables,[209] and in basing his narrative on the reports made by others his approach was methodologically defensible. 'If', he concludes, 'following the opinions of other men, we have said anything false, we have not done so with the intention of deceiving anyone'.[210] Verisimilitude, *fama* and *falsa* are one thing, intentional lies quite another.

A third, and final, illustration of the complexity with which the writing of history could be both understood and practised is provided by John of Salisbury. Educated at the schools in Paris in the 1130s and 1140s, John was thoroughly versed in the principles of classical rhetoric, largely as a result of having been taught by Thierry of Chartres and Petrus Helias, both of whom had commented on the *Rhetorica ad Herennium* and Cicero's *De Inventione*, but also through his own direct acquaintance with *De Oratore*, Marius Victorinus and Quintilian.[211] Indeed, John's 'Defence of Logic' or *Metalogicon* was written as an eloquent demonstration of the need to integrate rhetoric, alongside grammar and dialectic, within an all-inclusive discipline of language, where 'logic' is defined (after Boethius), in its broadest sense, as the science of verbal expression and reasoning, which includes all instruction

---

208 *Gesta Dei per Francos*, praef., pp. 25–6.
209 *Gesta Dei per Francos*, VII, p. 156.
210 *Gesta Dei per Francos*, VII, p. 165.
211 R. Ray, 'Rhetorical Scepticism and Verisimilar Narrative in John of Salisbury's *Historia Pontificalis*', in E. Breisach (ed.), *Classical Rhetoric and Medieval Historiography* (Kalamazoo, 1985), p. 95. For John of Salisbury's knowledge and use of Cicero and Quintilian, see B. Munk Olsen, 'L'Humanisme de Jean de Salisbury, un Cicéronien au 12e Siècle', in M. Gandillac and E. Jeauneau (eds), *Entretiens sur la Renaissance du 12e Siècle* (Paris, 1968), pp. 53–69; H. Liebeschutz, *Medieval Humanism in the Life and Writings of John of Salisbury* (London, 1950).

concerning words.[212] Faced with those who would restrict a definition of logic exclusively to the rules of dialectic, John produced his own version of the Ciceronian and Augustinian argument that wisdom and truth needed to be communicated through eloquence and rhetoric.[213] The *Metalogicon* opens, accordingly, with a vigorous defence of the mutual dependence of eloquence and wisdom, together with a reminder that it was this union which provided the premise for the poetic fiction of Martianus Capella's 'marriage' of Mercury (eloquence) to Philology (reasoned knowledge). [214] If philosophy required rhetoric, then, by the same token, eloquence which existed without wisdom was futile.[215] The second half of the *Metalogicon* is then devoted to providing a summary of the 'logical' contents of Aristotle's *Topics*, *Analytics* and *De Sophisticis Elenchis* (all three of which had already been translated by Boethius but which had also all been given new Latin versions in the 1120s) in order to prove just how important they are to an overarching science of words (*ratio dicendi*). Familiarity with *De Sophisticis Elenchis*, John argued, was useful, for example, in understanding the nature of 'equivocation', that is, how different contexts could affect the meaning of the same word. However, of Aristotle's three treatises, it is the *Topics* in particular which, in John of Salisbury's view, is most necessary for his readers to know, 'because all the principles and examples set out in this work can usefully be applied to all branches of learning'.[216] Indeed, John points out that both Cicero and Quintilian had acknowledged that Aristotle's *Topics* had not merely been helpful to practising rhetoricians but had served as a crucial starting-point for the systematic study of their subject.[217]

It is from this polemical context that John of Salisbury emerges as a prime example of a writer who actively engaged with, and

---

212 John of Salisbury, *Metalogicon*, I.10, p. 32, I.13, p. 37, II.prol., p. 73; cf. Hugh of St Victor, *Didascalicon*, I.11, pp. 57–9.
213 Cf. M. Bride, 'John of Salisbury's Theory of Rhetoric', *Studies in Medieval Culture*, 2 (1966), pp. 56–62; Ray, 'Rhetorical Scepticism and Verisimilar Narrative', pp. 63–5.
214 John of Salisbury, *Metalogicon*, I.1, pp. 10–11, II.3, p. 79, II.9, p. 94; cf. Bernardus Silvestris, *Commentary on the First Six Books of Virgil's Aeneid*, VI, p. 83.
215 *Metalogicon*, II.9, p. 93; cf. Cicero, *Orator*, IV.14, p. 315.
216 *Metalogicon*, III.5, pp. 171–2.
217 *Metalogicon*, III.10, p. 190.

applied, the issues which had been raised by Augustine concerning the relationship between truth, utility, opinion, 'fiction' and lies. In doing so, John took his lead from Abelard and, in particular, from the latter's distillation of *De Doctrina Christiana*, *De Mendacio*, *Contra Mendacium* and Augustine's original disagreement with Jerome over the letter to the Galatians which had been epitomised in the prologue to Abelard's *Sic et Non*.[218] Faced with the difficulty of understanding and reconciling problematic passages from the Bible and from the Church Fathers (the *Sic et Non* was itself a collection of 158 obscure and apparently discordant excerpts), Abelard used the prologue to his work in order to establish some basic ground rules for the interpretation of texts. He echoes cautionary remarks from both Augustine and Jerome, for example, concerning the possibility that any text can become corrupted through scribal error. Citing Augustine's own *Retractions*, he also points out that patristic authors sometimes pose provisional questions, rather than definitive solutions, and report the opinions of other people, rather than their own. Even in Scripture, Abelard observes, some things appear to have been set down (like Bede, he cites the example of Joseph being called the 'father' of Christ) which agree with people's opinions rather than with the true state of affairs. This principle, in fact, provides Abelard with his essential starting-point, namely that language will vary according to the nature of the audience for which it is intended. If the purpose of a particular text is teaching or instruction, for example, then clarity of understanding will always be its primary goal. Abelard quotes Cicero on the need to recognise what level of truth will be appropriate in different circumstances: 'one degree of precision is required when the truth itself is being debated and refined, but another when discourse is being adapted to common opinion'.[219] The key distinction here, he points out, is between opinion and truth and, in order to assess which of the two is applicable in a particular text, it will be necessary to examine the intention of the author. Error and ignorance, Abelard comments, are not the same as deliberate deceit and, in this regard, no statement which is prompted

---

218 Abelard, *Sic et Non*, trans. A.J. Minnis and A.B. Scott, in A.J. Minnis and A.B. Scott (eds), *Medieval Literary Theory and Criticism c.1100–c.1375* (Oxford, 1988), prol., pp. 87–100.
219 Cicero, *De Officiis*, II.9.35, p. 76.

by love and which has the goal of edification can be classified as sinful. For the latter, Abelard quotes Augustine's definition from *Contra Mendacium* (lying occurs when a false meaning is given to a word with the intention to deceive), together with Augustine's case-study of Jacob. According to Augustine's *Enchiridion*, in fact, 'no one is to be considered a liar who says something which is false, but which he believes to be true, because, as far as he himself is concerned, he does not deceive but is the victim of deception. So the person who, without exercising sufficient caution, trusts false statements and regards them as true, should not be accused of lying but sometimes of rashness'.[220] These are therefore the lessons which Abelard draws from Augustine's exchange with Jerome over Paul's letter to the Galatians. A clear distinction should, in any case, always be drawn between the canonical books of the Bible and all other writings. As far as the latter are concerned, Augustine's *Retractions* provide the model for all open-ended inquiry into the truth – individual authors accept that what they write may well require emending and correcting by subsequent readers.[221]

Abelard may not have written the work on rhetoric which some of his remarks seem to promise or, if he did do so, it has not survived. However, the fact that he was writing a commentary on Boethius' *De Topicis Differentiis* in 1120–22, at the same time as he was starting the first version of the *Sic et Non* (c.1121–26), suggests that there was a close correlation between the two.[222] What particularly interests Abelard about the subject-matter of the *Topics* (both in Cicero's text and in Boethius' commentary) is the notion that an argument, strictly speaking, is concerned, not with truth, but with opinion and probability, that is, with what possesses the similitude of truth according the perception or understanding

---

220 Abelard, *Sic et Non*, prol., p. 95, quoting Augustine, *Enchiridion de Fide et Spe et Caritate*, trans. B. Harbert, in Augustine, *On Christian Belief* (New York, 2005), XVIII, pp. 283–4.
221 Cf. Otto of Freising, *Chronicle*, VIII.34, p. 511, VIII.35, p. 513, quoting Augustine, *De Civitate Dei*, XXI.7, p. 978; cf. Augustine, *Letters*, Ep.148, p. 358; Augustine, *Retractationes*, prol., pp. 3–5. For active encouragement to read Augustine's *Retractions*, see Cassiodorus, *Institutiones*, trans. J.W. Halporn, *Institutions of Divine and Secular Learning* (Liverpool, 2004), I.16, pp. 148–9.
222 K.M. Fredborg, 'Abelard on Rhetoric', in C.J. Mews, C.J. Nederman and R.M. Thomson (eds), *Rhetoric and Renewal in the Latin West 1100–1540* (Turnhout, 2003), pp. 55–80.

of an audience.[223] An argument is therefore, in Abelard's view, a process of reasoning which creates faith (*fides*) in something that is otherwise in doubt, but, in doing so, such argumentation is concerned more with the capabilities of individual human beings than with the actual truth of the matter itself.[224] In the case of the Bible, this principle led Abelard to observe, at the beginning of his commentary on Romans, that all Scripture is intended to teach or to warn (through either persuasion or dissuasion) 'in the manner of rhetorical language' (*more orationis rhetoricae*). As such, it is always critical in the interpretation of a scriptural text to recover its author's original intention – in this case, that of the apostle Paul, who was writing this epistle as an instrument of admonition specifically for the circumstances presented by the church at Rome – in order to understand what was appropriate both to the subject-matter and to the audience of that particular text.[225] This principle also meant that Abelard could endorse the position outlined by Macrobius and argue that to cover or conceal the truth in fable (*fabulosa involucra*) was an activity distinct from creating poetic 'fictions' (*figmenta*), in that the former served the useful purpose of inspiring and attracting the reader or audience

---

223 For the distinction between truth and verisimilitude, see Abelard, *Theologia*, ed. E.M. Buytaert and C.J. Mews (*CCCM* 13, Turnhout, 1987), II.prol.26–7, p. 123: 'we do not promise to teach the truth, which neither we nor any mortal can know, but at least we may put forward something verisimilar and close to human reason which is not contrary to sacred Scripture.... What the truth is, God will know; what I am about to say is, I consider, what is verisimilar and in particular congruent with the philosophical reasoning which we are looking for'; cf. Seneca, *Letters*, Ep.118.8, p. 365: 'That which is true [*verum*] differs from that which looks like the truth [*veri simile*]; hence the good is connected with the true, for it is not good unless it is also true. But that which attracts and allures is only like the truth – it steals your attention, demands your interest and draws you to itself'. See also Seneca, *De Beneficiis*, trans. J.W. Basore (Loeb, 1935), IV.33.2, p. 273: 'our answer to this will be that we never wait for absolute certainty, since the discovery of truth [*verum*] is difficult, but follow the path that the similitude of truth [*veri similitudo*] shows. All the business of life proceeds in this way'.
224 C. Mews, 'Peter Abelard on Dialectic, Rhetoric and the Principles of Argument', in C.J. Mews, C.J. Nederman and R.M. Thomson (eds), *Rhetoric and Renewal in the Latin West 1100–1540* (Turnhout, 2003), pp. 37–53.
225 P. von Moos, 'Literary Aesthetics in the Latin Middle Ages – The Rhetorical Theology of Peter Abelard', in C.J. Mews, C.J. Nederman and R.M. Thomson (eds), *Rhetoric and Renewal in the Latin West 1100–1540* (Turnhout, 2003), pp. 81–97; cf. W.S. Campbell, P.S. Hawkins and B. Schildgen, *Medieval Readings of Romans* (London, 2007).

to seek the truth.[226] The golden rule here, as far as Abelard was concerned, was provided by 1 Thessalonians 5:21: 'test everything and keep what is good'.[227]

It is in the context of the tradition reflected in Abelard's teaching that the implications of John of Salisbury's engagement with the issues raised by Augustine and his approach to language, truth and logic become fully apparent. John of Salisbury had learned enough from the approach to written texts which had been embodied in the *Accessus ad Auctores*, then championed by Abelard,[228] to know that what is said or written should always be interpreted in the light of *why* it is being said or written.[229] Indeed, according to John, in order to understand the rationale behind anything said or written by someone, it is necessary to assess the occasion, the sort of person, the nature of the audience, the place, the time and various other pertinent circumstances that must be taken into account by anyone who seriously seeks the truth.[230] The two works by which John himself is best known, namely the *Policraticus* (a moral–didactic treatise which was written over a period of time before 1159 and which was designed to instruct both political and ecclesiastical courtiers on the principles of virtue and vice in the temporal sphere) and the *Historia*

---

226 von Moos, 'Literary Aesthetics in the Latin Middle Ages', p. 91; cf. Macrobius, *Commentary on the Dream of Scipio*, I.2, pp. 84–5 (see page 383); A.J. Minnis, *Medieval Theory of Authorship: Scholastic Literary Attitudes in the Later Middle Ages* (2nd edn, Aldershot, 1988), pp. 9–72, especially pp. 58–63.
227 von Moos, 'Literary Aesthetics in the Latin Middle Ages', p. 94.
228 See pages 126–7.
229 John of Salisbury, *Metalogicon*, prol., pp. 6–7; III.2, p. 152, quoting Hilary of Poitiers, *De Trinitate*, trans. S. McKenna (New York, 1954), IV.14, p. 103: 'we shall not attempt to deceive or mislead our unlearned listeners by merely citing some quotations from the texts without explaining all the attendant circumstances. The understanding of the words is to be deduced from the reasons why they were spoken, because the words are subordinated to the event, not the event to the words. But we shall examine everything while at the same time we shall explain the reasons why they were said and the meaning of the words'; cf. John of Salisbury, *Historia Pontificalis*, ed. and trans. M. Chibnall (London, 1956), XIV, pp. 39, 41
230 *Metalogicon*, I.19, p. 58; cf.III.3, p. 157, where twelve questions (whether something is, what it is, of what kind, how great, what relation, where, when, place, condition, what it does, what it undergoes, and why) are presented as 'comprising all knowledge'; cf. Aristotle, *Categories*, trans. J.L. Ackrill (Princeton, 1984), 1b25–2a4, p. 4 (see also page 127).

Pontificalis (completed in 1164 as a narrative of events at the papal curia between 1148 and 1152),[231] are no exceptions to this rule. However, as was the case with Guibert of Nogent, the best way to approach these two texts is, not to view them in isolation, but to see how they fit together, as well as in the light of the linguistic philosophy which was outlined in the *Metalogicon*.

There is certainly no better example than the *Policraticus* of an application of Cicero's contention that the art of rhetoric formed part and parcel of political knowledge (*civilis scientia*).[232] Or, as John of Salisbury put it in the *Metalogicon*, whereas dialectic is concerned with what is true or seems to be true, *civilis scientia* is necessary in order to estimate justice, utility and goodness.[233] Indeed, the encyclopaedic range of subjects which the *Policraticus* covers, and which has traditionally made it so hard to categorise, stems precisely from the encyclopaedic range of subjects on which Cicero and Quintilian thought that the trained rhetorician should be equipped to speak.[234] There is also no better illustration than the *Policraticus* of the way in which moral conduct was thought to be taught more effectively in the form of examples rather than precepts, through entertainment rather than with systematic logic.[235] *Policraticus* is designed, not just to instruct and to teach,[236] but also to move and to give pleasure; it is intended to be enjoyable, even funny, but this pleasure serves a serious didactic purpose. Humour, as John was well aware, had a strategic goal as a means of persuasion.[237] The truths which John wished to

---

231 Ray, 'Rhetorical Scepticism and Verisimilar Narrative'; Ward, 'Some Principles of Rhetorical Historiography', pp. 107–11; J. Coleman, *Ancient and Medieval Memories: Studies in the Reconstruction of the Past* (Cambridge, 1992), pp. 305–16.
232 See page 229.
233 John of Salisbury, *Metalogicon*, I.15, p. 46.
234 See pages 243, 321.
235 See pages 152–6.
236 For example, John of Salisbury, *Policraticus*, trans. J. Dickinson, *The Statesman's Book of John of Salisbury* (New York, 1927), VI prol., pp. 171–2.
237 Quintilian, *Institutio Oratoria*, VI.3.22–35, pp. 449–57; Cicero, *De Oratore*, II.54.216–71.290. William of Malmesbury praised archbishop Lanfranc for the way in which he successfully combined humorous with serious language in order to guide William the Conqueror when straightforward reproof would have had no effect. William of Malmesbury, *Gesta Pontificum Anglorum*, I.42.6, p. 91; cf. R.M. Thomson, 'Satire, Irony and Humour in William of Malmesbury', in C.J. Mews, C.J. Nederman and R.M. Thomson (eds), *Rhetoric and Renewal in the Latin West 1100–1540* (Turnhout, 2003), p. 120; and, more generally, R.M. Thomson, 'The

communicate therefore had to be made both convincing and appealing in order for his work to be useful or advantageous to the audience of ecclesiastical and lay courtiers towards whom it was primarily directed. John says as much as in his prologue. 'If anything here departs extensively from true faithfulness [*fides vera*]', he writes, 'I am confident that I ought to be forgiven, since I promise that not all the things which have been written down here are true, but that, whether they are false or true, they will serve the reader as useful'.[238]

The *Historia Pontificalis* was likewise written by John of Salisbury with a particular didactic agenda in mind. The striking feature of this work, however, is that, in the prologue, this agenda is kept largely hidden. John states that his work will provide supplementary and explanatory historical material which has been omitted from other accounts (namely a clarification of the decrees issued at the Council of Rheims, an analysis of what had gone wrong on the Second Crusade, a correction of the misunderstandings surrounding the trial of Gilbert of Poitiers, a narrative of what had happened to Arnold of Brescia, a discussion of the disputes over royal rights in the English and Sicilian churches, and a specification of what had actually been granted as privileges to various sees by popes Innocent II and Eugenius III). Indeed, in this sense, the prologue to the *Historia Pontificalis* provides a good example of an *insinuatio* rather than a *proemium*, of disguising what the speaker or writer is about to say, or introducing it

---

Origins of Latin Satire in Twelfth-Century Europe', *Mittellateinisches Jahrbuch*, 13 (1978), pp. 73–83.

[238] John of Salisbury, *Policraticus*, trans. Pike, prol., p. 9; cf.I.8, pp. 38–9: 'the wise man's mind detects what is beneficial or fitting in particular cases as they occur; nor does he shun fables [*apologi*], stories [*narrationes*] or spectacles in general, provided that they possess the requirements of virtue and honourable utility [*honesta utilitas*]'. For Gerald of Wales' recognition of the particular demands of the courtly audience for whom he was writing, see *Itinerarium Cambriae*, p. 67; cf. Walter Map, *De Nugis Curialium*, I.12, pp. 35–7; and, more generally, P. Dronke, 'Peter of Blois and Poetry at the Court of Henry II', *Medieval Studies*, 28 (1976), pp. 185–235; K. Bate, 'La Littérature Latine d'Imagination à la Cour d'Henri II d'Angleterre', *Cahiers de Civilisation Médiévale Xe–XIIe Siècles*, 34 (1991), pp. 3–26; J. Gillingham, 'The Cultivation of History, Legend, and Courtesy at the Court of Henry II', in R. Kennedy and S. Meecham-Jones (eds), *Writers of the Reign of Henry II: Twelve Essays* (New York, 2006), pp. 25–52 .

only indirectly.[239] It becomes clear from the main body of this work, for example, that John of Salisbury was writing his history as deliberative rhetoric, as a contribution to a particular political and ecclesiastical debate in the early 1160s.[240] In describing the pope's role within the Christian community, John was presenting the pope as judge and administrator, as reformer, as leader of the Crusade, as defender of orthodoxy and as regulator of temporal rulers. As such, the *Historia Pontificalis* needs to be read alongside more prescriptive works by his contemporaries – Bernard of Clairvaux's *De Consideratione*, for example, or even Gratian's *Decretum* – as an exemplary illustration of how a good pope should act, how he should embody the principles of the reformed papacy of the 1130s.[241] What John actually says in his prologue to the *Historia*, however, is altogether more limited. What he explicitly states is that he will simply be providing a continuation of the universal chronicle of Sigebert of Gembloux, from the point at which it had left off, and thereby give a general demonstration of both the workings of providence and moral–didactic *exempla*, as well as a judicial instrument for the defence of rights and privileges. He writes:

> My aim, like that of other chroniclers before me, shall be to profit my contemporaries and future generations. For all these chroniclers have had a single purpose – to relate noteworthy matters, so that the invisible things of God may be clearly seen by the things that are done [Romans 1:20] and so that people may, by examples of reward or punishment, be made more zealous in the fear of God and the pursuit of justice.... For, as the pagan says, 'the lives of others are our teachers' [*Disticha Catonis*] and whoever knows nothing of the past hastens blindly into the future. Besides, the records of the chronicles are valuable for establishing or abolishing customs, for strengthening or destroying privileges; and nothing, after knowledge of the

---

239 See pages 170–1, 191–3.
240 For the political and ecclesiastical context of the work, see I.S. Robinson, *The Papacy 1073–1198* (Cambridge, 1990); C. Morris, *The Papal Monarchy: The Western Church from 1050 to 1250* (Oxford, 1989), pp. 177–236, 404–9.
241 John of Salisbury, *Policraticus*, trans. Dickinson, VI.24, pp. 252–7; Ray, 'Rhetorical Scepticism and Verisimilar Narrative'; Ward, 'Some Principles of Rhetorical Historiography in the Twelfth Century', pp. 107–11; cf. Bernard of Clairvaux, *De Consideratione ad Eugenium Papam*, trans. J.D. Anderson and E.T. Kennan, *Five Books on Consideration: Advice to a Pope* (Kalamazoo, 1976).

grace and law of God, teaches the living more surely and soundly than knowledge of the deeds of the departed.[242]

John of Salisbury accordingly ends his prologue to the *Historia* with a conventional statement of the sort familiar from Guibert of Nogent. 'In what I am going to relate', he concludes, 'I shall, by the help of God, write nothing but what I myself have seen and heard and know to be true, or have on good authority from the testimony or writings of reliable men'.[243]

Underpinning both the *Policraticus* and the *Historia Pontificalis* is the same concern with variability in the truth-content of human knowledge which runs right through the *Metalogicon*. If knowledge of the truth is the greatest good in human life, then John of Salisbury is keen to stress that this also involves 'careful investigation into the nature of all things, so as to determine which should be avoided as evil, discounted as useless, sought after as good, or preferred as better, and finally which are called good or bad according to circumstances'.[244] This investigation, in turn, involves a threefold division of the linguistic tools which are required for it – demonstrative logic, probable logic and sophistry – that John takes directly from Boethius' *De Topicis Differentiis*.[245] Demonstrative logic is concerned with necessity, namely with that which cannot be otherwise, a truth which is determined irrespective of what any particular audience might think or assent to.[246] Probable logic is concerned with propositions which seem to be true, either to everyone or to many people or to the wise; such 'opinion' is the field of both dialectic and rhetoric. Sophistry, finally, is concerned merely with the appearance of probability and not at all with the truth; it involves disguise, delusion and the appearance of wisdom – although it may, on occasion, use true and probable arguments, it is a shrewd deceiver, sweeping an audience along from the evident and the true to the doubtful and the false.[247] Although John concedes that sophistry has its pedagogic place in the schoolroom, it is otherwise, in his view, an

---

242 John of Salisbury, *Historia Pontificalis*, prol., p. 3 (see also page 155).
243 *Historia Pontificalis*, prol., p. 4.
244 John of Salisbury, *Metalogicon*, II.2, p. 76.
245 *Metalogicon*, II.3, p. 79; cf. Hugh of St Victor, *Didascalicon*, III.1, p. 83.
246 *Metalogicon*, II.3, p. 79, II.6, p. 86, II.13, p. 104.
247 *Metalogicon*, II.5, p. 83.

adulteress, betraying her blinded lover by exposing him to errors and leading him to the precipice with her deceit – 'one who speaks sophistically [*sophistice*] is hateful' (Ecclesiasticus [Sirach] 37:20).[248]

Of Boethius' three categories of linguistic tool, John of Salisbury is interested, first and foremost, in the probable opinion which underpins the study of both dialectic and rhetoric. John justifies this concentration on the basis of Aristotle's *Posterior Analytics* – the degree of epistemological certainty in any area will be conditioned by the changeable nature of its subject-matter and, as a result, whereas demonstrative logic will be applicable to mathematics, probable logic is better suited to the corporeal and therefore changeable substance of Nature.[249] For his definition of 'probable opinion', however, John of Salisbury turned from Boethius (and Aristotle) back to Cicero's *Topica*: 'probable opinion is that which always, or usually, happens or is thought to be true by many, or at least by persons of good judgment'.[250] 'A proposition is probable', John explains, 'if it seems obvious to a person of judgment, and if it occurs thus in all instances and at all times, or is otherwise only in exceptional cases and on rare occasions. Something that is always, or usually, so either is, or seems, probable, even though it could possibly be otherwise. And its probability is increased in proportion as it is more easily and surely known by one who has judgment.... A wide knowledge of probabilities prepares expeditious access to all things'.[251] The difference here between judgment (*sententia*) and opinion (*opinio*) is that, whereas judgment is always on the side of the truth, opinion frequently errs.[252] However, this does not mean that opinion cannot turn into belief (*fides*), or even approach certitude. Even though opinion is, by definition, less than knowledge, it becomes its equivalent as far as the certainty of human judgment is concerned, given the dependence of the latter on what is perceived through the senses.[253] For this last observation (and its illustration – that it is 'known' that the sun

---

248 *Metalogicon*, IV.22, p. 237.
249 *Metalogicon*, II.13, p. 105.
250 Cicero, *Topica*, XIX.73–4, p. 439; Boethius, *De Topicis Differentiis*, trans. E. Stump (Ithaca, 1978), III, p. 70 (see page 285); cf. John of Salisbury, *Metalogicon*, II.3, pp. 78–9, II.12–15, pp. 101–9, IV.11–13, pp. 220–3.
251 *Metalogicon*, II.14, pp. 106–7; cf. III.9, p. 188, IV.5, p. 210.
252 *Metalogicon*, II.5, p. 83.
253 *Metalogicon*, II.14, pp. 106–7.

will always rise tomorrow), John is indebted to Aristotle's *Topics*, a work, he observes, which serves as the source of investigation into the *probabilia* which comprise most of human knowledge.[254]

Since the category of probable opinion covers the disciplines of both dialectic and rhetoric, John spends some time clarifying the distinction between the two subjects, on this occasion by summarising the discussion contained in book IV of Boethius' *De Topicis Differentiis*. Dialectic, he points out, is concerned with the abstract and general, rhetoric with the particular circumstances (who, what, where, by what means, why, how and when); dialectic expresses itself succinctly and by means of deductive reasoning, whereas rhetoric uses extended speech and inductive reasoning because it is usually addressed to a larger number of people and seeks the assent of the crowd.[255] This last observation proves to be of particular interest. Since it is a necessary part of prudence for a speaker or writer to assess the nature of their audience, John concludes that the learned and the unlearned must be treated in different ways. This means that a speaker or writer will use syllogisms for the former and inductive examples for the latter.[256] Induction, therefore, is defined in one of two ways – either an argument which proceeds from several individual instances to a universal proposition or an argument which proceeds by inference, from one thing to another, by means of a single example. In both cases, John concludes, inductive argumentation is more suited to rhetoric than it is to dialectic because it persuades rather than convinces.[257]

John of Salisbury, like Augustine, reveals himself to be acutely sensitive to the limitations of human knowledge. There are, in his view, many impediments to human understanding. First and foremost, there are the consequences of sin, but there is also the brevity of human life, neglect of what is useful, conflict of probable opinions and the sheer multitude of subjects to be investigated.[258] To grasp the truth 'as it is actually is' is a task

---

254 *Metalogicon*, III.5, pp. 171–2, III.9, p. 187, III.10, p. 201.
255 *Metalogicon*, II.12, p. 102; cf. Boethius, *De Topicis Differentiis*, IV, pp. 79–80 (see page 463).
256 *Metalogicon*, III.10, p. 200.
257 *Metalogicon*, III.10, p. 192; cf. page 270.
258 *Metalogicon*, IV.40, p. 269.

that pertains only to divine and angelic perfection. Certitude or true reason is therefore possessed only by God and by those to whom He grants the privilege of genuine certainty and divine judgment.[259] Like Augustine, John of Salisbury also points out the capacity of human 'imagination' to generate 'images' for itself (fashioned from the storehouse of memory in such a way that they 'conform' to those images which it has actually recorded from experience), as well as the deceptive nature of the senses, exemplified by the oar which is distorted in water.[260] The solution to such confusion, as far as John of Salisbury is concerned, lies in the exercise of prudence, a virtue which he defines (following Cicero) as the investigation, perception and skilful utilisation of the truth.[261] Even with prudence, however, the changeable and transitory nature of human affairs will still present difficulties, since, although opinion on these subjects can be reliable, it is only rarely the case that individuals can be certain that their opinion is correct. What John is left with, therefore, is what he terms faith or belief (*fides*), a category which is defined (again with reference to Aristotle's *Topics*) as 'exceedingly strong opinion' (*vehemens opinio*).[262] Such *fides* is, of course, necessary in religion (John quotes Hebrews 11:1), but it is also most necessary in human affairs, because 'belief' is an intermediate stage between 'opinion' and 'knowledge'. For this last definition John is dependent on Hugh of St Victor: faith is a voluntary certitude concerning something which is not present, a certitude which is greater than opinion but which falls short of knowledge.[263] Knowledge, after all, on Boethius' account, must necessarily be free from any falsehood (*mendacium*), because it represents intellectual apprehension of something which cannot be otherwise than as it is known.[264] Human prudence, John concludes, will therefore always be hindered by the errors which are produced by sense perceptions

---

259 *Metalogicon*, III.10, p. 201, IV.30, p. 249.
260 *Metalogicon*, IV.9, p. 217.
261 Cf. Cicero, *De Officiis*, I.5.15, p. 7.
262 *Metalogicon*, IV.13, p. 223, quoting Aristotle, *Topica*, trans. W.A. Pickard-Cambridge (Princeton 1984), IV.5 126b18, p. 212.
263 *Metalogicon*, IV.13, p. 223, quoting Hugh of St Victor, *De Sacramentis Christianae Fidei*, trans. R.J. Deferrari, *On the Sacraments of the Christian Faith* (Cambridge, MA, 1951), I.10.2, p. 168; cf. John of Salisbury, *Historia Pontificalis*, XIII, p. 32.
264 Boethius, *Consolation of Philosophy*, V.3, p. 399.

and opinions and, as a result, it can hardly proceed with confidence in its investigation of the truth. This does not mean, however, that reason cannot be engaged in a constant effort to overcome these limitations – the very defining activity of reason, after all, is to judge principles (*rationes*) whose essence is *different* from the nature of sensible and particular things. Nonetheless, human beings generally operate in what John of Salisbury terms 'the slipperiness of uncertainty' (*incertitudinis lubricum*) – at times their opinions are true and accurate representations of reality, but at other times they are deceptive and illusory.[265]

For all the professed alignment of the *Historia Pontificalis* with the annalistic tradition of the chroniclers, John of Salisbury was clearly writing his narrative from the perspective of a more complex understanding of what the nature of such historiography might involve. If 'making clear the invisible things of God' was John's professed 'single purpose', for example, then it is certainly a striking feature of what follows that there is only one episode in his whole narrative where a particular act – the spilling of a consecrated chalice – is given a figural or prophetic interpretation.[266] Augustine had been very wary about detecting God's active providence at work in the course of historical events outside of what had been narrated in the Bible; he had also expressed his scepticism over the epistemological uncertainty of past sensibles.[267] What makes the *Historia Pontificalis* more than 'just' a chronicle is the way in which it reflects very similar concerns. 'Since human affairs are transitory', John remarks in the *Metalogicon*, 'our opinion about them will lack certainty of judgment, except on rare occasions'.[268] The routine of certain natural occurrences, the rising and setting of the sun, produces belief (*fides*), not certainty, that the same phenomenon will always happen again. This is why John uses the notions of 'fortune' and 'chance' as shorthand terms which would be familiar to his audience but which also represented the intrinsic argumentation of causality – in order to reflect the inability of the human mind to measure the constant

---

265 John of Salisbury, *Metalogicon*, IV.33, p. 254.
266 John of Salisbury, *Historia Pontificalis*, V, p. 11; Ray, 'Rhetorical Scepticism and Verisimilar Narrative', p. 72.
267 See pages 97, 374–6.
268 John of Salisbury, *Metalogicon*, IV.13, p. 223.

fluctuations of life and the hidden nature of causes.[269] Such mutability covers one's own motives and intentions, let alone those of other people, let alone the events themselves. This is why John uses the term *opinio* to describe the interpretation of the spilled chalice as an event which did, indeed, bode ill for the Church, as the failure of the Second Crusade revealed.[270]

Similar epistemological concerns emerge from the *Policraticus*, where John of Salisbury remains nervous about any human claim to be able to identify the overt workings of divine providence. Only God knows how freedom of the will fits in with predestination, he argues, and this is particularly true for the events of post-biblical history, where God 'paints periods of time with the movement and variation of events as if with different colours'.[271] God makes His own actions look as if they are the acts of human beings, yet all that humankind itself can see is the outward appearance. Beyond Scripture, in other words, God's will is inscrutable. In the *Metalogicon*, John had accordingly already aligned himself with a moderate form of Academic scepticism: 'those of us who do not precipitate an opinion concerning questions which are doubtful to a wise man'.[272] This affiliation is echoed in the *Policraticus*: 'in statements made from time to time with regard to providence, fate, freedom of the will and the like, I am to be regarded as a disciple of the Academy, rather than as a rash exponent of those things which are still a matter of doubt'.[273] Indeed, such scepticism is given an extended discussion by John in the prologue to book VII. 'Certain things', he writes, 'which I have not found in the books of the authorities, however, I have excerpted from daily usage and the experience of things, as though from a sort of

---

269 John of Salisbury, *Policraticus*, trans. Pike, III.8, pp. 173–5; cf. pages 271–2.
270 John of Salisbury, *Historia Pontificalis*, V, p. 11; cf. VII, p. 14 (*nescio*), VIII, p. 16 (*incertum habeo*; *varia opinio est*), XI, p. 25 ('no human judgment is competent to decide this'), XXI, p. 51 (*nescio*; *arbitror*), XXIII, p. 53 (*incertum est*), XXV, p. 57 (*alii … alii*), XXXV, p. 70 (*incertum est*), XXXVII, p. 73 (*quod magis creditur*), XXXIX, p. 77 (*ut credebatur a plurimis*); Ray, 'Rhetorical Scepticism and Verisimilar Narrative', p. 72.
271 John of Salisbury, *Policraticus*, trans. Pike, II.24, p. 119. For the universe itself as *eloquentia rerum*, see Alexander Neckham, *De Naturis Rerum*, II.prol., p. 125 (see page 388).
272 John of Salisbury, *Metalogicon*, prol., p. 6, II.20, pp. 128–9, III.prol., p. 145, IV.7, p. 213.
273 John of Salisbury, *Policraticus*, trans. Pike, prol., p. 10.

history of conduct [*quadam morum historia*]. It will be understood that such questions as appear to belong to the field of weightier philosophy have been put forward in the spirit of the Academics, rather than in that of a stubborn partisan, so that each person is to retain their freedom of judgment in the examination of truth, and an authority is to be discounted as useless where a more powerful argument contradicts it'.[274]

The consequences of such intellectual affiliation for the actual argument of the *Policraticus* are manifold. Viewed as moral and political counsel, for example, as a work of deliberative rhetoric, such scepticism provides one very good reason why it is not only impossible but misguided to extract a systematic theory of, say, tyrannicide – the sheer range of situations in which tyranny can be exercised, a range which extends all the way from the political to the ecclesiastical, the domestic and the private, yields too varied a set of circumstances to submit to a single prescriptive 'theory'.[275] Viewed from the perspective of historiography, meanwhile, what is so striking is the range of the subjects on which John of Salisbury thought that such scepticism should be brought to bear. 'Those things are doubtful for the man of wisdom,' he writes, 'which are supported by the authority of neither faith, sense nor manifest reason and for which there are arguments on both sides of the question. Such are questions which are asked about providence, about the substance, quantity, power, efficacy and origin of the soul; about fate and the inclination of nature; chance and free will; the material, movement and elements of bodies...; about time and place; about number and speech ... and about the use, end and beginning of virtues and vices ... likewise about the cause of things and their attraction and repulsion...'.[276] 'And so', he concludes, 'I readily believe that the Academics express doubt with a restraint proportionate to the pains I find they have taken to avoid the pitfall of rashness. So true is this,

---

274 *Policraticus*, trans. Pike, VII.prol., p. 216.
275 Ray, 'Rhetorical Scepticism and Verisimilar Narrative', pp. 75–6; cf. R.H. Rouse and M.A. Rouse, 'John of Salisbury and the Doctrine of Tyrannicide', *Speculum*, 42 (1967), pp. 693–709; C.J. Nederman, 'A Duty to Kill – John of Salisbury's Theory of Tyrannicide', *Review of Politics*, 50 (1988), pp. 365–89.
276 John of Salisbury, *Policraticus*, trans. Pike, VII.2, pp. 221–2; cf. Ray, 'Rhetorical Scepticism and Verisimilar Narrative', p. 76.

indeed, that when writers in passages not ordinarily subject to doubt use words of a certain ambiguity, such as "maybe" [*forte*], "probably" [*fortasse*] and "perhaps" [*forsitan*],[277] they are said to have used them with "Academic" moderation. The reason for this is that the Academics were more restrained than others, for they shunned both the stigma of rash definition and the pitfall of falseness'.[278] The consequences for John of Salisbury's view of historiography are clear – in the diversity of individual events, histories report mutually contradictory things.[279] This is also what informs his own approach to the *Historia Pontificalis* – probable opinion about human affairs; what is likely, or at least thought, to have taken place; in short, verisimilitude.

It is from this perspective, finally, that John of Salisbury tackles the question of the relation of verisimilitude to fictive narrative and to lies, an issue exemplified in the *Policraticus* by his decision to 'make up' the *Institutes of Trajan* as an authoritative source for his argument.[280] John is quite explicit on the subject in his preface, where, for his justification, he appeals to a particular category of deceit. 'I confess', he writes, 'that I have had recourse to lies when they have been required [*officiosa mendacia*]'.[281] In the *Metalogicon*, John had given a very broad, ultimately Macrobian, definition to the role played by what is composed or 'made up' in several different branches of learning. In the study of logic, for example, John writes that the categories of genus and species 'are, as it were, fictions' (*quasi quaedam sunt figmenta*), which are employed by reason as it investigates and teaches things with greater subtlety. Reason does so in good faith (*fideliter*), however, because it always produces an actual example whenever there is a need to substantiate it. The study of civil law, likewise, has its own

---

277 Cf. page 272, note 24.
278 John of Salisbury, *Policraticus*, trans. Pike, VII.2, p. 222. For the terms used in his *Historia Pontificalis*, see Ward, 'Some Principles of Rhetorical Historiography', p. 107; Ray, 'Rhetorical Scepticism and Verisimilar Narrative', p. 78.
279 *Policraticus*, trans. Pike, VII.prol., p. 215; cf. Augustine, *De Civitate Dei*, XXI.6, p. 974.
280 H. Liebeschutz, 'John of Salisbury and Pseudo-Plutarch', *Journal of the Warburg and Courtauld Institutes*, 6 (1943), pp. 33–9; J. Martin, 'John of Salisbury as Classical Scholar', in M. Wilks (ed.), *The World of John of Salisbury* (Oxford, 1984), pp. 179–201.
281 John of Salisbury, *Policraticus*, trans. Pike, prol., p. 9; cf. page 344.

'fictions' (*figmenta*). So too, in fact, do all branches of learning, which, John states, 'unhesitatingly devise them in order to further their investigations, each of them, in a way, priding itself on its own special *figmenta*'.[282] In the *Policraticus*, John stages a reprise of his position, on this occasion in the form of a direct address or apostrophe to his audience. He writes:

> The simplicity of my style shall be worthy of your approval and you, as a faithful reader [*fidelis lector*], will not note the superficial sense that the words first signify, but the source of their sense and the sense to which they are directed. The serious is mingled with the trivial, the false with the true [*falsa veris*], in such a way that all may logically contribute to the attainment of supreme truth [*summa veritas*]. Let it cause no disquiet if any of those things which are written here are found stated differently elsewhere, since even histories, in the diversity of events, are found to be mutually contradictory; yet they are serviceable for the single fruit of utility and moral worth [*utilitas et honestas*]. I do not care to run the risk of formulating truth [*verum*]; my intention is merely to share ungrudgingly for the utility of my readers [*utilitas legentium*] what I have read in different writers. For even the Apostle does not say 'whatever is written is true' [*quaecumque scripta sunt vera sunt*] but 'whatever is written is written for our instruction' [*quaecumque scripta sunt ad nostram doctrinam scripta sunt*] [Romans 15:4].[283]

'Utility', 'opinion', 'verisimilitude' and 'lies' are all terms which John of Salisbury deliberately deploys in the course of acknowledging the complexities that are involved in writing about the past – narrating what has happened, or may have happened, in order to communicate a moral, intellectual or doctrinal truth. At the heart of John's approach was a concept of *fides* – belief or trustworthiness – which comprised both an epistemological claim for the validity of historical understanding (it marked the highest degree of certainty that human knowledge could attain about

---

282 John of Salisbury, *Metalogicon*, II.20, p. 135; cf. Aristotle, *Categories*, V.3b20, p. 6; Colish, 'Rethinking Lying in the Twelfth Century', pp. 171–3.
283 *Policraticus*, trans. Pike, VII.prol., p. 215; cf. III.8, p. 175. For this use of Romans 15:4, see also Gervase of Canterbury, *Chronica*, ed. W. Stubbs, in *Opera Historica* (London, 1879), prol. p. 86; Gervase of Tilbury, *Otia Imperialia*, ed. and trans. S.E. Banks and J.W. Binns, *Recreation for an Emperor* (Oxford, 2002), III.101, p. 757; Ranulf Higden, *Polychronicon*, ed. C. Babington and J.R. Lumby (London 1865), I.prol.1, p. 18.

Nature) and a linguistic strategy of rhetorical argumentation (the plausibility or verisimilitude that could be given to the narrative of what may have or had actually happened). For John, what is true and what is 'made up' were not necessarily mutually exclusive categories, especially when the audience was less learned or courtly. Unlike some of his contemporaries, he did not simply polarise veracity with lies, the truth of what had been done with the fictions of fable. Instead, he carefully negotiated the middle ground of argument – what was needed in order to make the truth both believable and convincing.

In appealing to 'belief' in the writing of history, John of Salisbury reflected a longstanding tradition of biblical exegesis which originated in the patristic acknowledgment that there were two basis components to the historical sense of Scripture – the truth of what happened (*veritas factorum*) and the fidelity of the account in which it was relayed (*fides relationis, fides dictorum*).[284] As a result, it had become a staple approach – in Augustine, for example, but also in Jerome, Isidore, Bede, Hrabanus Maurus and Alcuin – to insist upon the 'believability' or 'trustworthiness' of history (*fides historiae, fides historica, fides gestorum, fides rerum gestarum, historica fides rerum gestarum*).[285] However, John of Salisbury was also reflecting a similarly longstanding classical approach – in Valerius Maximus, for example, and in Boethius – when he recognised that, whilst truthfulness may itself inculcate belief, it may also have to be strengthened and reinforced by intrinsic and extrinsic arguments, by argumentation and testimony.[286] This was the significance, and contribution, of John's education in the principles of classical rhetoric, in the writings of Cicero, Quintilian and Boethius. In the twelfth century, a commitment to belief in, and not just the truth of, 'history' was accordingly a marked, and requisite, feature of historical writing – Hugh of St Victor referred to the credibility of deeds done (*fides rerum gestarum*), Rahewin to the 'demanded' or 'measured' trustworthiness of history (*exacta*

---

284 de Lubac, *Medieval Exegesis*, vol. I, pp. 98, 138, 141.
285 de Lubac, *Medieval Exegesis*, vol. II, pp. 117, 338–41; *Glossa Ordinaria*, prol., pp. 6–8.
286 Valerius Maximus, *Facta et Dicta Memorabilia*, trans. D.R. Shackleton Bailey, *Memorable Doings and Sayings* (Loeb, 2000), III.2, p. 261; Boethius, *Consolation of Philosophy*, IV.2, p. 319.

fides historiae).[287] These were not naïve or transparent appeals. Finding the appropriate argument which would make a narrative plausible and convincing presupposed a commitment to the truth of what was being narrated, but also an awareness of the limitations on the certainty of its attainment and its verisimilar expression. The concerns which had been expressed, on both counts, by Augustine were no less valid and applicable in 1200 than they had been in 400. So too was the self-conscious historiographical sophistication of the response.

---

287 Hugh of St Victor, *De Sacramentis Christianae Fidei*, I.prol.3, p. 4; Rahewin, *Deeds of Frederick Barbarossa*, trans. C.C. Mierow (New York, 1953), III.prol., p. 171.

5

HISTORIOGRAPHY AND HISTORY

The influence of classical rhetoric on the writing of history in the Middle Ages centred on the relationship between the depiction of character (attributes of person) and the description of deeds (attributes of events), on the invention of arguments (causation, testimony and proof), and on the construction of a brief, lucid and, above all, verisimilar narrative. This does not mean, of course, that all the principles involved in each one of these areas were applied either simultaneously or consistently across the broad range of writings which the single term *historia* could comprise and across the conventional periodisation of a thousand years of 'The Middle Ages'. The transmission and interpretation of classical rhetoric had a history of their own between $c.400$ and $c.1500$. The knowledge and application of Cicero, Quintilian and the *Rhetorica ad Herennium* accordingly took various forms as their ideas – singly, collectively or in particular combinations – were distilled, adapted and taught in order to make them practicable for changing circumstances and appropriate for different audiences. The study and utility of history naturally followed suit.

Like any other discipline, the writing of history reflected broader changes and developments in the intellectual, literary, social and political culture of the time. The convenient homogeneity of the phrase 'medieval historiography' must therefore, at some point, recognise and accommodate this potential for diversification and refinement. One candidate for such a shift has traditionally been sought in the period between $c.1050$ and $c.1200$ – years which are often given the convenient, if problematic, modern appellation 'the twelfth-century renaissance' – since the 'long' century denoted by this characterisation witnessed a significant clarification of the conceptual categories within which the writing of history came to be discussed. The same may also be said, however, of the thirteenth, fourteenth and fifteenth centuries, as similarly far-reaching claims have been made, with each of them, for the distinctiveness of certain developments in the conceptualisation and practice of historiography (a sharper differentiation between genres of 'historical' writing, the reception of Aristotle, and the emergence of a 'Renaissance' sense of the past), all of which are alleged to have culminated in the supersession of 'the medieval' by, as ever, 'the modern'.

The twelfth century

In the course of the twelfth century, both the meaning and the importance of the study of history were influenced by the emergence of an approach to biblical exegesis which placed renewed emphasis on the literal sense of Scripture, as a truth to be uncovered in its own right, rather than as a superficial level to be skipped over in order to reach the treasures of a tropological, anagogical or allegorical interpretation of events.[1] Whilst the novelty of such an approach should not be exaggerated (Augustine had already stressed the importance of the literal sense in biblical exegesis as the 'foundation' on which the entire structure of spiritual signification rested; so too had Bede, who, for all his debt to Gregory the Great's allegorical and moral interpretation, had also insisted that the historical sense was just as important as a figurative reading and who had explicitly criticised allegory which went beyond the *fides historiae*),[2] the twelfth century did

---

1 M.-D. Chenu, 'Theology and the New Awareness of History', in M.-D. Chenu, *Nature, Man and Society in the Twelfth Century: Essays on New Theological Perspectives in the Latin West* (Chicago, 1968), pp. 162–201; cf. B. Smalley, *The Study of the Bible in the Middle Ages* (2nd edn, Oxford, 1952); G.R. Evans, *The Language and Logic of the Bible: The Earlier Middle Ages* (Cambridge, 1984).
2 For example, Augustine, *Sermons*, trans. E. Hill (New York, 1990–95), II.7, pp. 179–80, VIII.1–2, pp. 240–1; Augustine, *Letters*, trans. R. Teske (New York, 2001–05), Ep.93.8.24, p. 392; Bede, *De Tabernaculo*, trans. A.G. Holder (Liverpool, 1994), II, p. 47; and, more generally, A. Thacker, *Bede and Augustine of Hippo: History and Figure in Sacred Text*, Jarrow Lecture (Jarrow, 2005). For Gregory the Great's own note of caution against spiritual interpretation at the expense of the literal and historical, see, for example, *Moralia in Job*, trans. J. Bliss (Oxford,

see a number of influential works putting considerable emphasis on this point and a number of influential theologians developing the linguistic and philological skills which were necessary to support it. Hugh of St Victor's *Didascalicon*, for example, a treatise of the 1130s which was intended to summarise the purpose and content of Christian learning and which was therefore strongly influenced by Augustine's *De Doctrina Christiana*, explicitly sought to restrain those scholars who viewed the four senses of Scripture as an interpretative *carte blanche*. All things in the divine utterance, Hugh argued, must not be wrenched in order to provide an interpretation in which every word is held to contain history, allegory and tropology all at once.[3] The literal, historical sense of Scripture was not simply a peg on which to hang a spiritual treatise, a transparent medium through which a deeper signification was readily accessible; the Bible was, in itself, much more difficult and problematic, a text whose language concealed as much as it revealed and which was, as Augustine had put it, both many-layered and complex (*multiplex et multimoda*).[4]

If the twelfth century was characterised by a reinvigoration of the importance of the historical sense of Scripture, what Gregory the Great had called the bare and unadorned sense, the exterior 'plane' or 'surface' (*superficies*),[5] then it is certainly tempting to tie such a development to a corresponding reassertion of the value of historiography outside of Scripture too. Writing at some

---

1843–50), Ep.miss.IV, p. 9, I.37, p. 66, XX.41.79, p. 512; cf. *Glossa Ordinaria*, ed. A. Rusch (Strassburg, 1480–81; reprinted Turnhout, 1992), prol., p. 8.
3 Patristic theologians alternated between four and three senses of Scripture, sometimes eliding the anagonical with the allegorical (see chapter 4).
4 Hugh of St Victor, *Didascalicon*, trans. J. Taylor (New York, 1961), V.2–3, pp. 120–2, VI.3, pp. 135–9, VI.11, pp. 149–50; Augustine, *De Trinitate*, trans. E. Hill (New York, 1991), II.prol., p. 97; cf. Hugh of St Victor, *De Archa Noe*, in *Selected Spiritual Writings* (New York, 1962), IV.9, pp. 147–52; Hugh of St Victor, *De Vanitate Mundi* (*PL* 176, cols 703–40), IV, cols 730–40); G.R. Evans, 'Hugh of St Victor on History and the Meaning of Things', *Studia Monastica*, 25 (1983), pp. 223–34. For Hugh's influence on Petrus Comestor, see Smalley, *Study of the Bible*, pp. 178–9; cf. S.R. Daly, 'Peter Comestor – Master of Histories', *Speculum*, 32 (1957), pp. 62–73; D.E. Luscombe, 'Peter Comestor', in K. Walsh and D. Wood (eds), *The Bible in the Medieval World* (Oxford, 1985), pp. 109–29.
5 Gregory the Great, *Moralia in Job*, IV.pref., pp. 177–8, XVI.19.24, p. 239, XVIII.39.60, pp. 360–1, XX.3.8, p. 450, XX.9.20, pp. 463–4, XXXV.14.24, p. 677; Gregory the Great, *In Librum Primum Regum Expositio*, ed. and trans. A. de Vogüé (Paris, 1989), praef.7.4, p. 158.

point in the decade before 1135, for example (that is, at more or less the same time as Hugh of St Victor), Peter the Venerable expressed both sadness and anger at 'the torpor of a great number of men who, though distinguished for their knowledge of learning and eloquence are yet so lazy that they do not hand down in writing for remembrance by posterity the marvellous works of Almighty God which repeatedly occur in different parts of the world for the instruction of the Church'. Unlike the first fathers of the Church, and indeed unlike the pagans of antiquity, Peter's contemporaries were ignoring both the commemorative and the utilitarian function of recording the results of active and permissive providence; instead, they 'nonchalantly allow to die out the memory of everything that is happening in their times and which could be so useful to those who will come after them.... How are they able to remain in the memory of receding and succeeding times if they are not written down? All the good or bad things that occur in the world by the will or the permission of God ought to serve for His glorification or the edification of the Church'. The contrast drawn by Peter the Venerable with the patristic, late-antique and classical approach to the past was stark: 'the barren idleness [*infructuosa segnities*] of this silence has borne such fruit that everything which has happened for four or almost five hundred years, whether in the Church of God or in Christian kingdoms, is practically unknown to us and to everyone else. In fact, our times are so distant from former times that, whilst we are very well informed about everything that was done [*gesta*] five hundred or a thousand years ago, we know nothing about later events, or even what has taken place during our own day. Thus we have a great number of ancient histories, ecclesiastical deeds, and multiple books of patristic doctrine containing precepts and examples [*instructiones et exempla*]; but as for the events which have occurred in periods close to our own, I am not at all certain that we possess even one'.[6] A generation later, Peter the Venerable would not have been in such despair.

---

6 Peter the Venerable, *De Miraculis Libri Duo*, ed. D. Bouthillier (*CCCM* 83, Turnhout, 1988), II.prol., p. 93; cf. I.prol., p. 3; J. Leclercq, *The Love of Learning and the Desire for God: A Study of Monastic Culture* (3rd edn, New York, 1982), pp. 156–7; Walter Map, *De Nugis Curialium*, ed. and trans. M.L.R. James, rev. C.N.L. Brooke and R.A.B. Mynors (Oxford, 1983), V.prol., pp. 405–7.

The proliferation of historical writing in the twelfth century may, of course, be a reflection of no more specific a phenomenon than the expansion of literacy and growth in the authority of *all* forms of the written word. The increase in the quantity of historiography may, in turn, be enough to explain why twelfth-century authors then felt the need to clarify the different forms in which the past was now being written down – reconceptualisation would seem, after all, a natural response to the stimulus provided by the sheer range of material which was now being presented as 'history'. Some of this new writing about the past, however, clearly had a conceptual and methodological impact all of its own. Biblical exegesis (and, by extension, the grammatical and historical tools of the *accessus ad auctores* which were developed to service it) may have been the primary cause of a more refined sense of the importance, and difficulty, of understanding 'what actually happened', but the writing of history was also responding to the challenges presented by the emergence of vernacular romance and, with it, a hitherto unknown category of 'literary fiction'. In practical terms, this came about as a consequence of histories being written, not just in prose and in Latin, but in verse and in the vernacular. In theoretical terms, it was accompanied by a renewed concentration on defining the exact nature of the relationship between historiography, rhetoric and poetry. Discussion of this relationship came to focus on the nature and function of the concept of verisimilitude and, in particular, on its clear suggestion that this particular aspect of narrative constituted a form of writing which could comprise material that had been made up (*ficta*). As a consequence, the nature of what was actually denoted by the terms *fingere* and *fictio* became subject to increasingly precise and extensive discussion.[7]

---

7 For what follows, see P. Nykrog, 'The Rise of Literary Fiction', in R.L. Benson and G. Constable (eds), *Renaissance and Renewal in the Twelfth Century* (Oxford, 1982), pp. 593–612; W. Haug, *Vernacular Literary Theory in the Middle Ages: The German Tradition 800–1300 in Its European Context* (Cambridge, 1997), pp. 91–106; D.H. Green, *The Beginnings of Medieval Romance: Fact and Fiction 1150–1220* (Cambridge, 2002). For an examination of self-conscious concepts of fictionality in Latin historiography, see M. Otter, *Inventiones: Fiction and Referentiality in Twelfth-Century English Historical Writing* (Chapel Hill, 1996); M. Otter, 'Functions of Fiction in Historical Writing', in N. Partner (ed.), *Writing Medieval History* (London, 2005), pp. 109–30; for the shifting relationship between history and 'fiction' when

The issues raised by verisimilitude, like those presented by a renewed emphasis on the literal sense of Scripture, were not necessarily a new challenge for writers of history in the twelfth century. They had originally been formulated, once again, by Augustine, in this instance as part of his controversy with Jerome over Paul's letter to the Galatians. Faced with the concerns aired by Augustine and the distinctions drawn by Macrobius,[8] writers of extra-scriptural history in the twelfth century were accordingly presented with a clear conceptual challenge. The close relationship with rhetoric which had characterised historiography since late antiquity rested, in large part, on the ontological claims that could be made for verisimilitude, both as an epistemological category and as a strategic argument – that is, both as something plausible which could have happened (and which was therefore the subject of opinion) and as something made up which would give credibility to a matter that was otherwise in doubt (and which would therefore itself create opinion). The plausible reconstruction of what might have happened (*narratio ut rei gestae*) was just as important as what actually did (*narratio rei gestae*). According to handbooks of rhetoric, this combination was epitomised in the classical distinction between three types of narrative, namely history (*historia*), argument (*argumentum*) and fable (*fabula*). On the basis of this categorisation, *historia* should, in theory, be defined strictly as a narrative of what actually happened; *argumentum* as a narrative of events which have been shaped or made up but which nevertheless could have happened (in Thierry of Chartres' formulation, it is termed 'hypothesis', the narrative of something made up and plausible, *narratio rei fictae et verisimilis*); and *fabula*, finally, as a narrative of events which neither happened nor could have happened.[9] Establishing the connection between history and verisimilar argument was therefore a critical task for anyone who wanted to narrate what happened, or may have happened,

---

viewed from the perspective of epic and romance, see S. Fleischman, 'On the Representation of History and Fiction in the Middle Ages', *History and Theory*, 22 (1983), pp. 278–310. More generally, see J. Beer, *Narrative Conventions of Truth in the Middle Ages* (Geneva, 1981) and, especially, P. Mehtonen, *Old Concepts and New Poetics: Historia, Argumentum and Fabula in the Twelfth- and Thirteenth-Century Latin Poetics of Fiction* (Helsinki, 1996).
8 See pages 380–5.
9 See pages 337–8.

in the past, but so too was distinguishing it from fable, from what did not happen or could never have happened in reality. Familiarity with Augustine may, on its own, have been sufficient to convince twelfth-century writers of the delicacy and importance of acknowledging these boundaries. What this threefold classification of rhetorical narrative precipitated in the course of the twelfth century, however, was a turf-war between the two forms of writing which were otherwise busily laying claim to either end of this measure, namely historiography and poetry.

Conflict between historiography and poetry over the middle ground of verisimilitude was difficult to avoid once the teaching of rhetoric had been subsumed within the teaching of grammar in the course of the early Middle Ages. Given that grammar was taught via both the *enarratio historiarum* and the *enarratio poetarum*, the lines of demarcation between the two forms of exposition inevitably became blurred. As the twin components of learning how to write correctly and to write well, historical and poetic narrative came to be regarded as prose and verse applications of the same rhetorical principles. Plotted onto the tripartite categorisation of *historia, argumentum* and *fabula*, therefore, the writing of history and poetry could not, in practice, keep discretely to their respective ends of the spectrum, and verisimilar argument was where they naturally overlapped. Take, for instance, the three elements which governed what would make a narrative 'appropriate' (*aptum*):[10] the subject-matter of what was being narrated could be shared by both history and poetry (particularly the epic poetry used for the deeds of kings); so too could conformity with what generally happens in the circumstances being described; as for conformity with the expectations, opinion and ability of one's audience, both history and poetry were understood to provide material for use primarily with *imperiti*, with a less well-educated group. In terms of their truth value, moreover, historical reality and poetic fable were not necessarily the polar opposites which the scheme *historia–argumentum–fabula* suggested. It had, of course, long been commonplace to refer to poetry in terms of its 'Vergilian lies' (*virgiliaca mendacia*). According to Conrad of Hirsau, for example, whilst there had never been an author greater than Vergil in

---

10 See pages 320–1.

terms of style and metre, there was also no one, when forced to give way to truth, who lied in a more polished and civil fashion.[11] By the same token, there was also a tradition of reading Vergil's historical narrative in the allegorical sense suggested by Servius and Macrobius and, above all, in accordance with the allegorical interpretations of Aeneas' journeys put forward, in the early sixth century, by Fulgentius.[12] For some writers, truth and fable were, on this basis, *not* necessarily incompatible. Set against a backdrop of a longstanding historiographical tradition of prosimetric composition, therefore, of combining prose and verse within the same work of history, there was every reason why, in the course of the twelfth century, the relationship between 'historical' and 'poetic' narratives of the past should have come under close scrutiny.

The twelfth century has traditionally been viewed as the moment at which poetry began to be treated with a greater degree of autonomy than its subservience to the teaching of grammar and rhetoric had hitherto permitted.[13] What this process can sometimes obscure is the consequences it had for its erstwhile twin and, indeed, the extent to which an equivalent process of self-determination also came to be applied, through imitation or by default, to the writing of history. As far as verse narrative was concerned, combining the principles of composition drawn from *De Inventione* and the *Rhetorica ad Herennium* with the theoretical summary outlined in Horace's *Ars Poetica* (and, to a lesser extent, in Ovid) certainly had some very important consequences for the language of 'forming', 'shaping' or 'making up'. The terms

---

11 See page 368; Alcuin, *Letters*, ed. E. Dümmler (Berlin 1895), Ep.309, p. 475; Conrad of Hirsau, *Dialogue on the Authors*, trans. A.J. Minnis and A.B. Scott, in A.J. Minnis and A.B. Scott (eds), *Medieval Literary Theory and Criticism c.1100–c.1375* (Oxford, 1988), p. 63; cf. Alan of Lille, *Anticlaudianus*, trans. J.J. Sheridan (Toronto, 1973), I.142, p. 50; Richard of Devizes, *Chronicle*, ed. and trans. J.T. Appleby (London, 1963), p. 66: 'they lie like Vergil'.
12 A.J. Minnis and A.B. Scott (eds), *Medieval Literary Theory and Criticism c.1100–c.1375* (Oxford, 1988), pp. 120, 150, 153; cf. J.W. Jones, 'Allegorical Interpretation in Servius', *Classical Journal*, 56 (1961), pp. 218–22; Macrobius, *Commentary on the Dream of Scipio*, trans. W.H. Stahl (New York, 1952), I.9.8, p. 126; Fulgentius, *The Exposition of the Content of Vergil According to Moral Philosophy*, trans. L.G. Whitbread (Colombus, 1971), pp. 119–35.
13 For example, C.S. Baldwin, *Medieval Rhetoric and Poetic* (New York, 1928); P. Zumthor, *Essai de Poétique Médiévale* (Paris, 1972), trans. P. Bennett, *Toward a Medieval Poetics* (Minneapolis, 1992).

fingere and *fictio* were categories which, for Thierry of Chartres at least, were clearly commensurable with constructing a plausible and convincing historical narrative of events, but they could also be correlated, in other contexts, with falsehood (*falsa*) and lies (*mendacia*). For those twelfth-century authors who now wanted to make a case for poetic truth *without* exposing themselves to Augustine's accusations of falsehood, the fusion of Cicero with Horace required a shift in the concept of verisimilitude from being an ontological to an aesthetic category of narrative. Under their influence, a narrative of events which did not happen, nor could ever have happened, accordingly began to appropriate the language of plausibility which had hitherto been reserved for verisimilar argument, for a narrative of events which was defined by the fact that those events could actually have happened in reality. The 'historical' romances of Chrétien de Troyes are often held, in this regard, to mark the point in the late twelfth century at which 'fiction' about the past began to be written without necessarily being equated with the language of lies.[14] Writing at the very beginning of the thirteenth century, Geoffrey of Vinsauf and John of Garland epitomised the theoretical transformation that had been taking place. According to the formulation put forward by Geoffrey, fabulous narrative (*fabula*) should be defined as lying with probability: 'if the narrative is fable, then we ought to lie with probability, that is, in order that false things should be narrated as if they were true' (*si contingent narrationem esse fabulosam, debemus probabiliter mentiri, ut scilicet narratio falsa narretur ut esset vera*).[15] Such narrative, however, in Geoffrey's eyes, remained different from deceit (*mendacium*). Or, as John of Garland put it, 'avoiding vice in fabulous narratives means lying with probability; as it says in the *Ars Poetica* [119], either follow tradition [*fama*] or make up a consistent story [*sibi convenientia*]'.[16]

---

14 Chrétien de Troyes, *Arthurian Romances* [Erec et Enide, Cligés, Yvain, Lancelot], trans. W.W. Comfort (London, 1914); cf. N.J. Lacy and J.T. Grimbart (eds), *A Companion to Chrétien de Troyes* (Cambridge, 2005).
15 T. Lawler, 'The Two Versions of Geoffrey of Vinsauf's *Documentum*', in T. Lawler, *The Parisiana Poetria of John of Garland* (New Haven, 1974), pp. 331–2; cf. E. Faral (ed.), *Les Arts Poétiques du XIIe et du XIIIe Siècles: Recherches et Documents sur la Technique Littéraire du Moyen Age* (Paris, 1924), pp. 265–320.
16 John of Garland, *Parisiana Poetria*, ed. and trans. T. Lawler (New Haven, 1974), V.318–20, pp. 101–2; Mehtonen, *Old Concepts and New Poetics*, pp. 124, 130–4, 155.

Viewed from a historiographical perspective, the theoretical challenge presented by this new, poetic understanding of verisimilitude was clear. Once a concept of verisimilitude could be separated from any necessary relation to reality, and thereby from any claim to mimetic realism (that is, to what actually happened, to what might have actually happened, or to what generally tends to happen), and once it became, instead, simply a matter of correspondence to literary convention, an issue of purely internal consistency with agreed aesthetic criteria of representation (such that even the fantastic – a centaur, say – could be said to be described with verisimilitude), then it became a much more problematic strategy for writers of otherwise 'truthful' history to deploy.[17] For writers of prose historical narrative, in other words, this sort of language created a real difficulty for their 'plausible' reconstruction of events. Poetic verisimilitude involved a form of representation which could be termed a likeness (*similitudo*), but not in the sense of an image (*imago*), since an image, by definition, had to possess some sort of ontological or existential connection with what it was representing.[18] The emergence of vernacular romance as a practical, and popular, means of narrating 'events' from the past presented this generic challenge in concrete and written form.[19] Once verisimilitude could be construed as a purely aesthetic category, rather than a claim about reality, some writers

---

17 Cf. E. Auerbach, *Mimesis: The Representation of Reality in Western Literature* (Princeton, 1953).
18 For this distinction, see Augustine, *De Diversis Quaestionibus LXXXIII*, trans. B. Ramsey, *Miscellany of Eighty-Three Questions* (in Augustine, *Responses to Miscellaneous Questions*, New York, 2008), 74, p. 137: 'image and equality and likeness must be differentiated because where there is an image [*imago*] there is necessarily a likeness [*similitudo*] but not necessarily equality; where there is equality there is necessarily a likeness but not necessarily an image; where there is a likeness there is not necessarily an image and not necessarily equality'; cf. Gilbert Crispin, *Disputatio Iudei et Christiani*, ed. A.S. Abulafia and G.R. Evans, *The Works of Gilbert Crispin* (Oxford, 1986), p. 52: *sicut enim littere quodam modo fiunt verborum figure et note, ita et picture scriptarum rerum existunt similitudines et note*; M. Carruthers, *The Book of Memory: A Study of Memory in Medieval Culture* (Cambridge, 1990), pp. 23–4.
19 G.M. Spiegel, *Romancing the Past: The Rise of Vernacular Prose Historiography in Thirteenth-Century France* (Berkeley, 1993); E.B. Vitz, *Orality and Performance in Early French Romance* (Woodbridge, 1999); S. Gaunt, 'Romance and Other Genres', in R.L. Krueger (ed.), *The Cambridge Companion to Medieval Romance* (Cambridge, 2000), pp. 45–59; K. Busby, 'Narrative Genres', in S. Gaunt and S. Kay (eds), *The Cambridge Companion to Medieval French Literature* (Cambridge, 2008), pp. 139–52.

of history became nervous of using this rhetorical strategy, for fear of being branded, not only fabulous, as writers of fable, but also as liars. It was not just a case of William of Newburgh, in other words, being alarmed by the 'lies' of Geoffrey of Monmouth;[20] his reaction was indicative of much more systemic concern over the literary re-presentation of historical truth in narrative.

The historiographical response to poetic verisimilitude took various forms. Some writers felt obliged to issue disclaimers that their verse historical narratives did not contain lies.[21] Others simply abandoned verse altogether. One long-term consequence was that prose began to assume a more definitive status as the form of writing best suited to communicating the historical truth.[22] This certainly seems to be the attitude some two centuries later, when Froissart opened his *Chronicles* by observing that he could be scrupulous in his historical record only once he had abandoned his earlier commemoration of deeds of war in verse.[23] It is thus the same concern which may have precipitated the retreat that is sometimes identified as a feature of twelfth-century historical writing, away from the sort of ambitiously literary narratives which characterised the first half of the century to the more limited chronicling of the second. On this account, a rigorous analytical interest in the writing of history which was characteristic of the first half of the twelfth century gradually petered out, especially once Peter Comestor's *Scholastic History* appeared to provide theologians with all that they needed for the

---

20 See pages 365–6.
21 For example, Jordan Fantosme, *Chronicle*, ed. and trans. R.C. Johnston (Oxford, 1981), line 667, p. 51; *Histoire de Guillaume le Maréchal*, ed. A.J. Holden, trans. S. Gregory (London, 2004), lines 16401–12, p. 323; Herald of John Chandos, *Life of the Black Prince*, ed. and trans. M.K. Pope and E.C. Lodge (Oxford, 1910), line 1602, p. 48. Compare Marie de France, *Lais*, trans. E. Mason, *Medieval Lays and Legends of Marie de France* (London, 1911; reprinted New York, 2003), p. 90 (Bisclaveret), pp. 102, 104 (Chevrefoil), p. 31 (Eliduc); and, for the equivalence of fable and lies, Marie de France, *Fables*, ed. and trans. H. Spiegel (Toronto, 1994), p. 125 ('The Lion and the Peasant'); cf. Fleischmann, 'On the Representation of History and Fiction', pp. 296, 302; Beer, *Narrative Conventions of Truth*, ch. 5.
22 Cf. Zumthor, *Toward a Medieval Poetics*, pp. 69, 302; D. Hay, *Annalists and Historians: Western Historiography from the VIIIth to the XVIIIth Century* (London, 1977), p. 62; R. Ainsworth, 'Legendary History – *Historia* and *Fabula*', in D.M. Deliyannis (ed.), *Historiography in the Middle Ages* (Leiden, 2003), pp. 411–15.
23 Froissart, *Chroniques*, trans. G. Brereton (Harmondsworth, 1968), prol., p. 38.

literal exegesis of Scripture, and once the initiative was seized by courtiers composing history in both prose and verse, as a form of entertainment as well as instruction, for royal, episcopal and aristocratic households. Only when historiography became the primary vehicle for political advice and education in the thirteenth and fourteenth centuries did it regain its earlier intellectual and scholarly integrity.[24]

Not all writers of history, however, responded to the intrusion of poetic lies with a complete abandonment of verisimilitude. Many authors continued to champion the ontological claims which underpinned the rhetorical tradition drawn from Cicero and Quintilian, namely that the composition of a historical narrative depended on both truthful and verisimilar argument, on a combination of what actually happened with what might reasonably and plausibly be believed to have happened. They did so on the understanding that the narrative of history-writing could be separated from the fabulous narrative of poetry without being separated from the application of rhetoric itself. This tradition is best illustrated by John of Salisbury and his classification of three approaches to knowledge of the truth. Demonstrative logic, he argued, is concerned with necessity, namely with that which cannot be otherwise, a truth which is determined irrespective of what any particular audience might think or assent to. Probable logic, meanwhile, is concerned with propositions which seem to be true either to everyone or to many people or to the wise; such opinion is the field of both dialectic and rhetoric. Sophistry, finally, is concerned merely with the appearance of probability and not at all with the truth; although it may, on occasion, use true and probable arguments, it otherwise deals in deceit and falsehood (*fallacia, insidiae, dubia, falsa, mendacia*). Of the three categories, John of Salisbury is interested, first and foremost, in the probable opinion that underpins both dialectic and rhetoric. The degree of epistemological certainty in any area will be conditioned by whether or not the subject-matter is changeable and, as a result, whereas demonstrative logic will be applicable to mathematics,

---

24 B. Guenée, 'Y a-t-il une Historiographie Médiévale?', *Revue Historique*, 258 (1977), pp. 261–75; reprinted in B. Guenée, *Politique et Histoire au Moyen Age: Recueil d'Articles sur l'Histoire Politique et l'Historiographie Médiévale 1956–1981* (Paris, 1981), pp. 205–19.

probable logic is better suited to the corporeal, and therefore changeable, substance of Nature – in other words, to the substance of historical narrative. This does not mean, he states, that opinion cannot be turned into belief (*fides*), or even approach certitude (at least as far as human judgment is concerned), but, in theory, probability and verisimilitude are the closest humans will ever get to knowledge of Nature and, by extension, to history.[25]

The debate over poetic and rhetorical verisimilitude may not have been resolved in the twelfth century but it did serve to crystallise and clarify the terms in which different narratives of past events would need to be discussed. Indeed, once the *fabula* of poetry became associated with a purely aesthetic definition of verisimilitude ('lying with probability'), Augustine's original concerns over the potential consequences of this rhetorical category for the historical truth of Scripture assumed an even sharper edge. Jacob's 'lie' (Genesis 27:24) and the kingship of trees (Judges 9:7–15) accordingly remained test-cases for the possible presence of falsehood and the fabulous in Scripture well into the thirteenth and fourteenth centuries.[26] In 1277, for example, the commission set up by the bishop of Paris to investigate the teaching of erroneous doctrines within the faculty of arts included two propositions which indicated that the Neoplatonic tradition expressed by Macrobius – that truth could be communicated under the covering of *fabulosa narratio* – was continuing to find its adherents as a tool of biblical exegesis.[27] Extra-scriptural narrative followed suit. Histories of past events remained susceptible to accusations of falsehood and lies once they moved beyond what had actually happened to 'hypothesise' or 're-present' what could have happened. If, in response, the lines of demarcation between history and fiction could be construed differently by different individuals, then the conceptual challenge remained much the same as it had been for Augustine. In this regard, historical writing in the period *after c.*1200 suggests that the twelfth century was a moment

---

25 See pages 417–19.
26 Minnis and Scott (eds), *Medieval Literary Theory*, pp. 209–11.
27 *Condemnation of 219 Propositions*, trans. E.L. Fortin and P.D. O'Neill, in R. Lerner and M. Mahdi (eds), *Medieval Political Philosophy: A Sourcebook* (Toronto, 1963), p. 352; cf. R. Hissette, *Enquête sur les 219 Articles Condamnés à Paris le 7 Mars 1277* (Louvain, 1977), pp. 274–5.

which accentuated, rather than transformed, a number of existing methodological issues that then continued to prove central to how the nature of historiography was understood. Indeed, once the relationship between rhetoric and the writing of history is regarded from the perspective of these fundamental continuities, including continuities in debate and difference of opinion, some of the more conventional, if not entrenched, lines of 'progress' which are usually identified in traditional histories of 'medieval historiography' lay themselves open to substantive reconsideration. The writing of history in the twelfth century did highlight a number of issues – of theory and practice, of epistemology and genre – but these were methodological issues which had been central to the conceptualisation and understanding of historical narrative since late antiquity. The writing of history between c.1200 and c.1500 bore the imprint of the sharper focus that those twelfth-century debates had introduced, and subsequent works of historiography reflected the impact, sometimes positively and sometimes negatively, of these reconfigured terms of engagement. Nonetheless, viewed, in particular, from the perspective of the disciplinary and methodological differentiation between history, rhetoric and poetry, the questions raised by twelfth-century historiography invite a reassessment of three traditional characterisations of the 'innovations' of the period which followed: a developing understanding of the relationship, and distinction, between annals, chronicle and history; the particularising impact of Aristotle's inductive empiricism; and the distinctiveness of a specifically 'Renaissance' or 'humanist' historiography.

Annals, chronicles and history

Modern commentators have long looked for consistency of classification and distinction in the various ways in which medieval authors categorised their different types of historical writing. There is, in consequence, tangible frustration at the apparent permeability of the three most pervasive terms – annals, chronicles and history.[28] In theory, after all, it should have been so much

---

28 B. Lacroix *L'Historien au Moyen Âge* (Montreal, 1971), pp. 33–40; B. Guenée, 'Histoires, Annales, Chroniques. Essai sur les Genres Historiques au Moyen Âge', *Annales*, 28 (1973), pp. 997–1016; reprinted in B. Guenée, *Politique et Histoire*

more straightforward, either following the example provided by Eusebius (and Bede), who first compiled a chronicle and then wrote a separate history, or courtesy of the distinction set down by Aulus Gellius – annals are a brief record of the names, facts and events in the chronological sequence in which they occurred, whereas history keeps broadly to the same *series temporum* but also reconstructs the causes and motives (*causae et consilia*) which made those events happen in the way in which they did.[29] In practice, however, it is clear that the relationship between the recording of annals and the writing of history was constantly shifting, in both conceptual and practical terms.

In his *Derivationes*, a hugely influential book of etymologies composed in the second half of the twelfth century, Huguccio of Pisa provided separate entries for 'annals' (*annales*), 'chronicles' (*cronica*), 'chronography' (*cronographia*), 'history' (*hystoria*) and 'historiography' (*hystoriographia*). Annals denoted a book in which the deeds done in a particular year were written down; chronicles and chronography were defined by their brief description of the times, or of deeds done in various times, which followed a chronological sequence or order (*temporum series vel ordo*); whilst history and historiography were defined by their root verb 'to see' or 'to know' and comprised a description or depiction (*describere vel depingere*) of deeds done (*res gesta*). In antiquity, Huguccio points out, no one wrote 'history' who had not lived through, or seen in person, the events they were describing, but the term could also apply to deeds long past, which were therefore remote from people's memories but which had now come to their knowledge. Current usage, however, restricted the term to what had been done recently or only a short time ago.[30]

---

au Moyen Age (Paris, 1981), pp. 279–98; cf. M. McCormick, *Les Annales du Haut Moyen Âge* (Typologie des Sources 14, Turnhout, 1975); B. Roest, 'Medieval Historiography – About Generic Constraints and Scholarly Constructions', in B. Roest and H. Vanstiphout (eds), *Aspects of Genre and Type in Pre-Modern Literary Cultures* (Groningen, 1999), pp. 47–61.
29 See pages 82–9.
30 Huguccio of Pisa, *Derivationes*, ed. E. Cecchini, *et al.* (Florence, 2004), pp. 55, 295, 575. The word 'paralipomenon' is defined separately (p. 902) as a book of days or of the things which have been left over or missed out and then briefly summarised (see page 55); cf. Osbern of Gloucester, *Derivationes*, ed. F. Bertini, *et al.* (Spoleto, 1996), p. 175.

Writing in London in 1188–90, Ralph de Diceto explicitly envisaged his own practical contribution to 'chronography' and 'historiography' comprising both causes and events (*tam causis quam casibus*), and he prefaced his work with definitions from Hugh of Fleury (deeds which are committed to writing without the certainty of a king-list or other chronology must be classed as old-wives' tales), Aulus Gellius (history differs from annals because, although each of them constitutes a narrative of deeds, history concerns itself strictly with those deeds which were done in the lifetime of the narrator, whereas annals are so called when the deeds of several years are then set down whilst observing the sequence of each year) and Cassiodorus (chronicles are sketches of history or very brief summaries of the past).[31] Although Ralph goes on to highlight the five central issues from the reign of Henry II which he was particularly concerned to elucidate (the right to consecrate and crown the English king, the privileges granted to Canterbury by the papacy, the expansion of Anjou, the issues that arose between kingdom and priesthood under Anselm and Becket, and the settlement of the long dispute between king Henry and his sons),[32] it is these theoretical definitions which determine the form that his chronicles (*chronica*) ultimately take – the first part a 'digest' of other chronicles (*Abbreviatio Chronicorum*) dealing with the history of the world up to 1147, the second part 'sketches' of history (*Imagines Historiarum*) covering events after 1149 which occurred during his lifetime and of which he had first-hand experience.

Ralph de Diceto's exact contemporary, Gervase of Canterbury, chose to open his own *Chronica* (covering events from 1100 to 1188) by eliding the terms 'annals' and 'chronicles' and then distinguishing them both from the writing of history on the basis that history made much greater use of the techniques of rhetoric. He concluded his remarks, however, by observing that, in

---

31 Ralph de Diceto, *Abbrevationes Chronicorum*, ed. W. Stubbs (London, 1876), pp. 3, 15, 34; cf. pages 87–8.
32 *Abbrevationes Chronicorum*, p. 34; cf. Smalley, *Historians in the Middle Ages*, pp. 114–19; C. Duggan and A. Duggan, 'Ralph de Diceto, Henry II and Becket', in B. Tierney and P. Linehan (eds), *Authority and Power* (Cambridge, 1980), pp. 59–81.

practice, such a clear distinction was hard to sustain given that the results were so frequently a mixture of the two.[33] In and of itself, Gervase's concession might not be so surprising if even the most straightforwardly paratactic sequences of annals are read within the broader intellectual framework for which they were intended, that is, less as simple annotations of computus or Easter tables or commemorative necrologies, and more as deliberate evocations of the exterior decay of Augustine's sixth age,[34] or as conscious statements of the providential vagaries of Boethius' understanding of fortune,[35] or simply, with Orderic Vitalis, as preparatory material compiled with a disclaimer of the expertise (or presumption) best left to others, in this case to exegetes and to prophets.[36] Bonaventure, for one, considered chronological completeness to be a prerequisite for the meaning of human history: 'one can view, following the sequence of time, the variety, multiplicity and symmetry, order, rectitude and beauty of the many judgments proceeding from the wisdom of God governing the world'. This was the model provided by Scripture, after all, where 'the whole world is described in a most orderly sequence ... as proceeding from beginning to end, in accordance with the peculiar beauty of its well-designed song'.[37] There could clearly be sophisticated reasons for organising a record of events in an otherwise apparently 'simple' chronological order.[38] However, it might also not be surprising to find flexibility over where exactly to draw the line between annals, chronicles and history when medieval authors were so clearly in disagreement over how far history should incorporate plausible argumentation, or whether such verisimilitude was appropriate only to the fables, or lies, of the poets.

---

33 See pages 89–91.
34 See page 102.
35 See pages 272–5.
36 Orderic Vitalis, *Historia Ecclesiastica*, ed. and trans. M. Chibnall, *The Ecclesiastical History of Orderic Vitalis* (Oxford, 1980), VIII.16, p. 229 (see also page 404).
37 Bonaventure, *Breviloquium*, trans. E.E. Nemmers (London, 1946), prol.2.4, p. 10.
38 According to Auerbach, *Mimesis*, pp. 70–6, the paratactic arrangement of events expresses a preference for moral or allegorical interpretation over causality or aetiology; cf. H. White, 'The Value of Narrativity in the Representation of Reality', *Critical Inquiry*, 7 (1980), pp. 5–27; reprinted in H. White, *The Content of the Form: Narrative Discourse and Historical Representation* (Baltimore, 1987), pp. 1–25.

The hierarchy which was so trenchantly expressed by Aulus Gellius proved to be an enduring and influential means of discrimination – annals constituted a form of writing which set down the substance of events within a fixed chronological framework but made no attempt to establish any thematic or causal connection between them; they were thus merely stories for children; history, on the other hand, narrated what happened, but also how and why.[39] This classification was not the only alternative on offer, however. Indeed, Augustine's distinction between 'history', on the one hand, and causality or 'aetiology', on the other, suggested that 'history' could, in fact, denote precisely what Aulus Gellius had called 'annals'.[40] The distinction of annals from history could also be presented in terms of authorial involvement (as Aulus Gellius observed, annals were, according to Cicero, a record of events which the author had not personally witnessed, whereas history was a matter of contemporary testimony) or linguistic style (in rewriting Flodoard in the tenth century, for example, Richer acknowledged the debt of his own histories to the latter's annals but also stressed their departure in terms of vocabulary and presentation).[41] Moreover, even if the deeper significance of a distinction between these two types of historical writing remained rooted in the difference in approach between noting down deeds and explaining the *causes* of those deeds, the superiority of such causal history over paratactic annals did not go uncontested. The centrality of computus and the championing of a universal chronography meant that an equally strong ecclesiastical tradition continued to claim superiority for compilations of annals over the fabrication of 'old-wives' tales' (*aniles fabulae*). This did not necessarily exclude causality. In quoting Hugh of Fleury, Ralph de Diceto makes it clear that his own chronography will be dealing with causes (*causae*) and not just events (*casus*).[42] In his *Chronicle*

---

39 See pages 82–3.
40 See page 95.
41 Richer, *Historiae*, ed. and trans. R. Latouche (Paris, 1930–37), prol., p. 4; Flodoard of Reims, *Annals (919–966)*, trans. S. Fanning and B.S. Bachrach (Ontario, 2004); cf. J. Glenn, *Politics and History in the Tenth Century: The Work and World of Richer of Reims* (Cambridge, 2004); M. Sot, *Un Historien et Son Église au Xe Siècle: Flodoard de Reims* (Paris, 1993).
42 Ralph de Diceto, *Abbreviationes Chronicorum*, p. 3: 'the condition of chronography is always infinitely open-ended and, with new causes as much as new

of c.908, Regino of Prüm devotes his first book to an annalistic account of what was done, when and where, between the year of Christ's birth and the year 741. In his second book, however, which deals with the deeds of the Frankish kings between 741 and 906, when Regino comes to the events leading up to his own expulsion from Prüm in 899, he points out that it would be absurd were he to pass over in silence a matter which concerned him directly when otherwise he had been explaining the actions of others and the *causes* of their deeds (*aliorum actiones et rerum gestarum causas*). Nonetheless, Regino continues, he is still inclined to maintain his silence for fear of giving offence to people who are still alive or of incurring the charge of flattery and lying. As a result, he states that he will leave it to posterity to provide a fuller explanation and restrict his own account simply to a summary of what actually happened (*res tantum gestas ex parte summatim adnotare*).[43]

It did not require twelfth-century concerns over poetic licence, moreover, to make the use of rhetoric inherently suspicious as a defining characteristic of specifically 'historical' writing about the past. The disclaimers which were issued, on these grounds, by the likes of Gervase of Canterbury tapped into a countervailing Christian tradition to the one sanctioned by Augustine's *De Doctrina Christiana*, a longstanding hostility to rhetoric which went back to 1 Corinthians 2:4–5 and 2 Corinthians 11:6 and which was expressed most famously, perhaps, by Jerome ('you are a Ciceronian, not a Christian').[44] A Platonic tension between

---

events arising, it is usual to note down new entries' (*chronographiae conditio semper in infinitum decurrat et novis emergentibus tam causis quam casibus novae fieri soleant annotationes*); cf. Herbert of Bosham, *Vita Sancti Thomae*, ed. J. C. Robertson, in J. C. Robertson and J. B. Sheppard (eds), *Materials for the History of Thomas Becket* (London, 1875–85), III.18, vol. III, p. 248: '*non solum ... opera sed et causas operum explicare: quasi non solum facta sed et animum facientis*'.

43 Regino of Prüm, *Chronicon*, trans. S. MacLean, *History and Politics in Late Carolingian and Ottonian Europe: The Chronicle of Regino of Prüm and Adalbert of Magdeburg* (Manchester, 2009), I.pref., pp. 61–2; II (s.a 892), pp. 213–14; cf. II (s.a 899), p. 224: 'we have decided to record the deeds done ... and not to explain their causes with specific testimony of the reasons for them' (*res enim gestas ... notare statuimus, non rerum gestarum causas certis rationum indiciis enucleare*).

44 Jerome, *Letters*, trans. W.H. Fremantle, G. Lewis and W.G. Martley (Oxford, 1893), Ep.XXII, pp. 22–41. For Jerome's defence of his own use of pagan authors, citing, *inter alia*, Hilary of Poitiers' mastery of Quintilian, see Jerome, *Letters*, ed. and trans. J. Labourt (Paris, 1949–63), Ep.LXX, pp. 209–15 (quoting Deuteronomy 21:10–13).

the knowledge being communicated and its rhetorical presentation had also been a theme of non-Christian prefaces, to Solinus' *Collectanea*, for example, and Macrobius' *Saturnalia*.[45] Thus, whilst there was certainly a distinctively Christian content to any contrast between the rude simplicity of truth and the cultivation of colourful eloquence (a comparison made by ascetic writers such as Cyprian, Sulpicius Severus and John Cassian), it is the classical disclaimer which Cassiodorus chose to echo when he suggested that his own *Institutions* represented an account of what was necessary rather than any affected eloquence (*non affectata eloquentia sed relatio necessaria*).[46]

Given that it was a recommended feature of rhetorical ornamentation to keep linguistic strategies hidden and at least to claim the virtues of spontaneity and plain-speaking,[47] expressions of artlessness by medieval historians should not necessarily always be read at face value. Nonetheless, when they are read in the context of Augustine's Platonic concerns over the boundary between verisimilitude and deceit, a more general suspicion towards the 'cosmetic' colouring of rhetoric could clearly serve, in some quarters, as a significant restraint on its application to the writing of history. Salvian had made this point in the 440s, and with characteristic moderation, in his *On the Governance of God*. In a dedicatory letter, Salvian attacked writers of both prose and verse who concentrated all their efforts and attention on the splendour of the words with which they embellished the chain of events (*series rerum*). Rather than focus on the utility of their

---

45 Solinus, *Collectanea Rerum Memorabilium*, ed. T. Mommsen (Berlin, 1895), praef. pp. 1–2; Macrobius, *Saturnalia*, trans. P.V. Davies (New York, 1969), I.pref., pp. 26–8.
46 Cassiodorus, *Institutiones*, trans. J.W. Halporn, *Institutions of Divine and Secular Learning* (Liverpool, 2004), I.pref., p. 105; cf. Athanasius, *Life of Antony*, trans. C. White (Harmondsworth, 1998), LXXX, p. 58, quoting 1 Corinthians 2:4–5; Sulpicius Severus, *Life of St Martin*, trans. C. White (Harmondsworth, 1998), Ep.ded., p. 134; Cassian, *Institutes*, trans. E.C.S. Gibson (Michigan, 1964), pref., pp. 199–200. More generally, see H. Hagendahl, *Latin Fathers and the Classics: A Study on the Apologists, Jerome and Other Christian Writers* (Gothenburg, 1958), II, pp. 309–28; G.L. Ellspermann, *The Attitude of the Early Christian Latin Writers Toward Pagan Literature and Learning* (Washington, DC, 1949); T. Janson, *Latin Prose Prefaces: Studies in Literary Conventions* (Stockholm, 1964), pp. 133–41.
47 See page 190.

subject-matter or on its moral worth, he complained, their goal was to be praised for the elegance of their poetry or for the glittering language of their narrative; rather than be considered wholesome or beneficial, they wanted to be thought of as erudite and distinguished. As a result, their writing was swollen with pride, notorious for falsehood, sordid in expression and sinful in its material. Salvian, by contrast, stated that, in his own narrative of events, he would eschew the vanity of worldly embellishments and the idleness of meretricious ornaments (*lenocinia*) in favour of healthy rewards and profitable remedies. For his own part, he was devoted more to the things themselves than to the words in which they were expressed, to the pursuit of utility rather than plaudits from others (*nos autem qui rerum magis quam verborum amatores, utilia potius quam plausibilia sectamur*).[48]

It was the same polarisation of words and things which continued to leave writers of a similarly ascetic stamp profoundly suspicious of allowing any place within the monastic life either for the study of grammar and rhetoric in general or for the cultivation of history-writing in particular. In the 1060s, for example, Peter Damian vociferously criticised those monks who were forsaking their spiritual studies for 'the absurdities of Donatus' and compared their desire for the worldly art of grammar to the act of abandoning 'the chaste spouse in the marriage-bed of faith' for prostitution with 'painted harlots'. Dismissing any claim that the liberal arts might enable monks to profit more fully from their devotional and theological studies, he castigated these 'superficial' and 'theatrical' disciplines as 'vain' and 'superfluous teaching'.[49] A case in point, he argued, was the taste being exhibited by some monks, particularly those who had taken their vows late in life, for histories and 'the poisonous banquets of fables'. Tongues which have been dedicated to God, he complained, were being taken up instead, not with salvific prayer, but with 'the ridiculous recitation of vain and superstitious annals' (*ridiculose vani ac supersitiosi recitentur annales*). These were people, he suggested, who were

---

48 Salvian, *De Gubernatione Dei*, trans. J.F. O'Sullivan, *The Governance of God* (Washington, DC, 1947), Ep.ded., p. 25; cf. D. Lambert, 'The Uses of Decay – History in Salvian's *De Gubernatione Dei*', *Augustinian Studies*, 30 (1999), pp. 115–30.
49 Peter Damian, *Letters*, trans. O.J. Blum and I.M. Resnick (Washington, DC, 1989–2005), Ep.153 (*De Perfectione Monachorum*), vol. VII, pp. 37–9.

so preoccupied with fabulous tales (*fabulosae neniae*) that they were both harmful to themselves and seemed deranged to their listeners: 'sometimes they weave fancy pleats of deeds done [*rerum gestarum lacinia*], sometimes they relate the sayings or victories of kings from the past [*regum antiquorum edicta vel victoriae*], and in this way they consume the entire day in the inappropriate recitation of old-wives' tales [*nugae aniles*]'.[50]

One practical effect of the expression of such anxiety towards the admixture of rhetoric and historiography was for the chronicle to emerge as some sort of a compromise position, occupying the middle ground in the polarisation between 'truthful' annals and 'false' romance which might otherwise result from twelfth-century disagreement over the relationship between *historia*, *argumentum* and *fabula*.[51] As a consequence, and despite Gervase of Canterbury's explicit elision of chronicles with annals,[52] a distinction between three types of writing, rather than two, began to open up in the course of the thirteenth and fourteenth centuries, in more reflective 'chronicles' by Roger of Wendover, Matthew Paris and Thomas Walsingham,[53] for example, or by Ranulf Higden and Adam Usk.[54] To that extent, an ascetic suspicion of rhetoric served to reinforce the concerns created by an aesthetic conception of verisimilitude. The result, not surprisingly, was a lack of

---

50   Peter Damian, *Letters*, Ep.153, p. 66.
51   Ainsworth, 'Legendary History – *Historia* and *Fabula*', p. 389: 'most historians in the Middle Ages seem only to have retained the first- and last-mentioned of these categories'; cf. Smalley, *Historians in the Middle Ages*, p. 180; B. Guenée, *Histoire et Culture Historique Dans l'Occident Medieval* (Paris, 1980), pp. 204–7; B. Guenée, 'Histoire et Chronique. Nouvelles Réflexions sur les Genres Historiques au Moyen Age', in D. Poirion (ed.), *La Chronique et l'Histoire au Moyen Age* (Paris, 1984), pp. 3–12; J. Blacker, *The Faces of Time: Portrayal of the Past in Old French and Latin Historical Narrative of the Anglo-Norman Regnum* (Austin, 1994), pp. xi, 201.
52   See page 90.
53   V.H. Galbraith, *Roger of Wendover and Matthew Paris* (Glasgow, 1944); Matthew Paris, *Chronica Maiora*, trans. J.A. Giles (London, 1853); Thomas Walsingham, *Chronica Maiora*, ed. and trans. J. Taylor, W.R. Childs and L. Watkiss (Oxford, 2003–10); cf. R. Vaughan, *Chronicles of Matthew Paris: Monastic Life in the Thirteenth Century* (Gloucester, 1984); R. Vaughan, *The Illustrated Chronicles of Matthew Paris* (Stroud, 1993); J.G. Clark, *A Monastic Renaissance at St Albans: Thomas Walsingham and His Circle c.1350–1440* (Oxford, 2004).
54   C. Given-Wilson, *Chronicles: The Writing of History in Medieval England* (London, 2004); cf. Adam Usk, *Chronicle*, ed. and trans. C. Given-Wilson (Oxford, 1997); J. Taylor, *The Universal Chronicle of Ranulf Higden* (Oxford, 1966).

clarity over where a specific 'genre' of history-writing actually lay. Self-conscious disagreement, however, should not be mistaken for intellectual sloppiness or conceptual confusion. For some writers, the identification of causes and the deployment of rhetoric were precisely what distinguished, and elevated, the writing of history from the mere noting and compilation of events; for others, aetiology and cosmetics suggested levels of, respectively, discernment and deceit which were best left to others – to theologians and to poets, rather than to historians.

If the shifting nature of the boundary between annals, chronicles and history from the twelfth to the fourteenth centuries reflected a theoretical debate over the relationship between truth, verisimilitude and fable, then this flexibility also reflected the practical consequences of the changing social and political contexts for which different types of historical narrative were being written. 'Chronicles' were no exception. In fourteenth-century northern Europe, for example, Froissart's four books of *Chroniques* represented a chivalric form of the chronicle, a vernacular genre which, like its verse predecessors amongst the sagas and *chansons de geste* of the twelfth century, was devoted to preserving the *fama* of outstanding *gesta*, glorious deeds which had been done by named individuals – in Froissart's case, between 1307 and 1400 and primarily in the course of the Hundred Years War, or in the case of Chandos Herald, a verse life of the Black Prince.[55] South of the Alps, meanwhile, the same period witnessed the emergence of the civic or communal chronicle, a type of historical record which, in the case of a city such as Genoa, could also date back, continuously or intermittently, to the twelfth century and, in this case, to the annalistic compilation of a chronological sequence of events. In the case of Florence, this tradition rested on a series of late thirteenth-century chronicles and culminated in the fourteenth-century *Chronicle* of Giovanni Villani.[56] Sometimes these civic chronicles were in Latin, but they

---

55 J.J.N. Palmer (ed.), *Froissart: Historian* (Woodbridge, 1981); P. Ainsworth, *Jean Froissart and the Fabric of History: Truth, Myth and Fiction in the Chroniques* (Oxford, 1990); P. Ainsworth, 'Contemporary and "Eyewitness" History', in D.M. Deliyannis (ed.), *Historiography in the Middle Ages* (Leiden, 2003), pp. 264–75.

56 Giovanni Villani, *Chronicle*, trans. R.E. Selfe and P.H. Wicksteed, *Villani's Chronicle: Selections from the First Nine Books of the Croniche Fiorentine of Giovanni*

were mostly in the vernacular; generally they were official, but sometimes they mixed the communal with the personal and the familial. All of them, however, tended to take the form of annals, that is, year-by-year accounts of significant events within the city.[57]

There was, therefore, no clear or consistent line of demarcation between rhetorical 'histories' and chronographic 'annals', and any middle ground claimed by 'chronicles', be they monastic, chivalric or civic, could expand or contract according to the particular tradition with which individual authors were choosing to align themselves.[58] In theory, at least, what distinguished the writing of history from the compilation of annals was the investigation of the causes of events (*rationes* or *causae*) and the deliberations (*consilia*) which motivated an individual to perform one action rather than another. 'Happy is the man who has been able to understand the causes of things' (*felix qui potuit rerum cognoscere causas*) was the Vergilian line quoted by both Otto of Freising and Gerald of Wales.[59] In the thirteenth and fourteenth centuries, this distinction could be as clearly maintained as it had been by Eusebius or Bede. Matteo Palmieri, for example, composed a chronicle of Florentine affairs for the years 1432–74 which simply described what had been done and how, but then moved on to write a history of the conquest of Pisa by Florence which put in all the reasons why (*rationes, consilia*).[60] In practice, however, a universally strict differentiation in genre was much harder to police. To say that medieval writers of 'history' were aware of this

---

Villani (London, 1906); cf. L. Green, *Chronicle into History: An Essay on the Interpretation of History in Florentine Fourteenth-Century Chronicles* (Cambridge, 1972); S. Dale, A.W. Lewin and D.J. Osheim (eds), *Chronicling History: Chroniclers and Historians in Medieval and Renaissance Italy* (University Park, 2007).
57 E. Cochrane, *Historians and Historiography in the Italian Renaissance* (Chicago, 1981).
58 Cf. A. Gransden, 'The Chronicles of Medieval England and Scotland', *Journal of Medieval History*, 16 (1990), pp. 129–50; 17 (1991), pp. 217–43; reprinted in A. Gransden, *Legends, Traditions and History in Medieval England* (London, 1992).
59 Vergil, *Georgics*, trans. H.R. Fairclough, rev. G.P. Goold (Loeb, 2000), II.490, p. 150; Otto of Freising, *The Deeds of Frederick Barbarossa*, trans. C.C. Mierow (New York, 1953), I.4, p. 31; Gerald of Wales, *Topographia Hibernica*, trans. J.J. O'Meara, *The History and Topography of Ireland* (Harmondsworth, 1982), II.41, p. 63, where it is paired with Vergil, *Eclogues*, trans. H.R. Fairclough, rev. G.P. Goold (Loeb, 2000), VIII.63, p. 60: 'not all of us know everything' (*non omnia possumus omnes*).
60 Cochrane, *Historians and Historiography*, pp. 25–6.

frontier, however, and recognised the need to situate their works somewhere within this permeable zone of contact, is *not* the same as saying that the period 1200–1500 was characterised by a move from simplicity to complexity, by a linear development *away* from the 'medieval' chronicle and *towards* 'Renaissance' history, as if the only types of historiographical causality known before 1300 had been the capitalised abstractions of active Providence and mutable Fortune.[61]

The work of Philippe de Commynes serves, in this respect, to illustrate the difficulties of drawing too hard or fast a set of distinctions between 'chronicle' and 'history', between vernacular and Latin, or indeed any arbitrary line of 'progress' from paratactic annals to history 'proper'. Commynes was a layman writing in the vernacular in the 1490s, and his account of the reigns of Louis XI of France and Charles the Bold of Burgundy (and subsequently of his own embassies in northern Italy) certainly lacks the self-conscious classicism of his contemporary Thomas Basin, bishop of Lisieux and author of a Latin history of the deeds of Charles VII and Louis XI which drew on Sallust, Suetonius and Caesar.[62] Nevertheless, for all the self-deprecatory remarks about his limited learning, Commynes' communication with his classically educated contemporaries, together with his familiarity with at least some classical texts (his library included French translations of a digest of Sallust, Livy and other ancient historians, as well as of Valerius Maximus' *Facta et Dicta Memorabilia*, the latter providing him with inspiration for the title of his very own *Mémoires*), left him conversant enough with some of the central methodological

---

61 See M.M. Phillips, 'Representation and Argument in Florentine Historiography', *Storia della storiografia*, 10 (1986), pp. 48–63; cf. S. Bagge, *Kings, Politics and the Right Order of the World in German Historiography c.950–1150* (Leiden, 2002), pp. 7–8, 412.
62 Thomas Basin, *Historiae*, ed. and trans. C. Samaran, *Histoire de Charles VII* (Paris, 1933–44), *Histoire de Louis XI* (Paris, 1963–72), prol., pp. 2–4; cf. P. Archambault, 'Sallust in France – Thomas Basin's Idea of History and of the Human Condition', *Papers on Language and Literature*, 4 (1968), pp. 227–57; P. Archambault, 'Thomas Basin – History *Cum Ira et Studio*', in P. Archambault, *Seven French Chroniclers: Witnesses to History* (New York, 1974), pp. 87–99; B. Guenée, *Between Church and State: The Lives of Four French Prelates in the Late Middle Ages* (Chicago, 1991), ch. 4, especially pp. 260–8; M. Spencer, *Thomas Basin: The History of Charles VII and Louis XI* (Nieuwkoop, 1997).

assumptions of classical and medieval historiography.[63] Commynes was adamant, for example, in emphasising the truth-value of eye-witness testimony rather than hearsay or rumour, and it was on these grounds that he took care to point out what he did not, and could not, know for certain.[64] His work was also peppered with a series of proverbial *sententiae*.[65] As an explanatory framework of causation, moreover, Commynes was particularly drawn to the Sallustian and Orosian idea that peace and prosperity posed their own grave dangers, both for communities and for individuals. Whilst he was well aware, therefore, that what he called the *fiction poétique* of fortune could substitute for the mystery of a divine judgment which was at times inscrutable, there were other occasions on which he read an explicit didactic lesson straight out of the pages of the Old Testament.[66] For those in his audience who thought that God no longer intervened directly in the world in the manner described in the Bible, and that prophets were no longer on hand to speak with His voice ('I believe indeed that He does not speak directly to men as He used to, for He has left enough examples in the world to be believed'), Commynes' understanding of history in practice, and of the corresponding vocation of historians, suggested otherwise.[67]

Ostensibly written simply in order to comply with a request to furnish raw material for the archbishop of Vienne to incorporate

---

63 Cf. R.H. Lucas, 'Medieval French Translations of the Latin Classics to 1500', *Speculum*, 45 (1970), pp. 225–53. For the teaching of rhetoric in Paris in the 1460s, see G.A. Kennedy, 'The *Rhetorica* of Guillaume Fichet', *Rhetorica*, 5 (1987), pp. 411–18; and, more generally, F. Simone, *The French Renaissance: Medieval Tradition and Italian Influence in Shaping the Renaissance in France* (London, 1969). For the distinction between things which are memorable (*memorabilia*) and things which should be remembered (*memoranda*), see Gervase of Canterbury, *Chronica*, ed. W. Stubbs, *Opera Historica* (London, 1879), prol., p. 89 (see page 89).
64 Philippe de Commynes, *Mémoires*, ed. S. Kinser, trans. I. Cazeaux, *The Memoirs of Philippe de Commynes* (Columbia, 1969–73), I.4, p. 110, I.4, p. 111, I.6, p. 120, I.8, p. 125, I.16, p. 143, II.6, p. 169, III.8, pp. 226, 228, V.8, p. 324, VI.5, p. 395; cf. P. Archambault, 'Commynes – History as Lost Innocence', in P. Archambault, *Seven French Chroniclers: Witnesses to History* (New York, 1974), pp. 101–15); J. Blanchard, *Philippe de Commynes* (Paris, 2006).
65 For example, Commynes, *Mémoires*, I.3, p. 108, II.6, p. 168 ('war between two great princes is easy to start but difficult to stop'), III.3, p. 205, III.11, p. 240.
66 *Mémoires*, I.2, p. 100, I.3, p. 108, I.7, p. 123, IV.12, pp. 291–2, IV.13, pp. 294–5, V.9, p. 325.
67 *Mémoires*, III.4, p. 211; cf. V.18, pp. 356–7.

into his own Latin history, it therefore becomes rapidly apparent that Commynes' 'memoirs' were designed to serve a didactic purpose all of their own. Commynes is certainly careful to distinguish his own narrative both from the chronographic compilation of annals and from the unalloyed praise which he found characteristic of some chroniclers (Commynes probably had Froissart in mind). 'I am not observing the order of writing used in histories', he states, 'and I am not mentioning the years or the exact times during which these events took place, nor do I draw examples from history for you know them well enough'; 'chroniclers commonly write only things which reflect credit on those whose actions they record, and they omit many things, or they do not know about them sometimes as they truly happened. But I have decided not to speak of anything which is not true and which I have not seen or heard from such great people that they are worthy of being believed, and without having any regard to praises'.[68] Instead, Commynes furnishes his own account of events with two overarching goals.

In the first instance, Commynes repeatedly expresses a commitment to the principle that history is a useful storehouse of *exempla* from which his audience – rulers and princes in particular – can and should be instructed: 'it is ... to their advantage if [princes] have studied history in their youth.... One of the surest means to make a man wise is to have him read ancient history and learn how to conduct and to guard himself and how to manage his affairs wisely according to the histories and examples of our ancestors'.[69] Indeed, as the distillation of human experience, historical *exempla* constituted a concentration of profitable knowledge which it would otherwise be impossible for individuals to acquire on their own: 'all the books that have been written would be useless if they did not serve to bring to mind past events. And one man can learn more in three months' time from reading a book than twenty men living successively could observe and understand from experience'.[70] The lack of such education is, in Commynes' view, one major reason why so many people in positions of power ultimately come to grief. The other is the quality of the political

---

68 *Mémoires*, III.4, p. 210, V.13, p. 335.
69 *Mémoires*, II.6, p. 169; cf.III.9, p. 232, IV.9, p. 279, VI.1, p. 378.
70 *Mémoires*, II.6, p. 170.

advice, and advisers, to which they choose to listen. In the second instance, therefore, Commynes designs his historical narrative, his *'bons advertissemens'*,[71] as an extended commentary on the nature of good and bad political counsel, on the need for good advice rather than flattery, and, as such, on the importance of understanding utility and practicability in a world characterised by dissimulation, stratagem, cunning and deceit. 'It is necessary', he writes, 'to be informed of the deceit and the wickedness of this world as well as the goodness, not in order to make use of them, but to protect ourselves against them'.[72] Commynes' exemplary historiography is, in this regard, itself an exercise in deliberative rhetoric. Such an approach to the lessons of the past may, of course, prove an ultimately thankless task and, as an *apologia* for his own career advising both Charles the Bold and Louis XI, Commynes is quick to point out that truthful but unwelcome counsel will often end in failure and the withdrawal of princely favour.[73] Nevertheless, as an instruction manual for the education of rulers, the *Mémoires* also constituted his own testament to the need for historiography to teach a pragmatic realism in a world in which even the best individuals were flawed and where the historical disjunction between the appearance and the reality of causation and human motivation ('great princes, or at least the wise ones, always look for a good pretence and one which is not too obvious') meant that both counsellors and historians should always act with the most prudent circumspection.[74]

In terms of 'genre', the picture presented by historiography between 1200 and 1500 is very fluid. It is not clear that there was any consensus on its definition, any convergence in a 'horizon of expectations',[75] still less a neat and simple demarcation between the recording of events or deeds, on the one hand, and their narration, on the other. When Guarino da Verona invoked the distinction between 'history' and 'annals' in the 1440s, therefore, it is perhaps not surprising that, as a humanist scholar, he should have cited Cicero's observation that history is a description of

---

71 *Mémoires*, III.8, p. 228.
72 *Mémoires*, III.4, p. 213, III.5, p. 214; cf.III.9, p. 233.
73 *Mémoires*, III.12, p. 245.
74 *Mémoires*, III.1, p. 199; cf.IV.6, p. 265.
75 H.R. Jauss, *Toward an Aesthetic of Reception* (Brighton, 1982), p. 88.

the times and the events which the author saw, or could have seen, for himself, whereas annals are an exposition of those years which are remote from the author's own age. What is rather more revealing is the rider which Guarino goes on to add, in a clear echo of Servius' commentary on the *Aeneid*. Other people, he points out, have thought and argued otherwise and the usage of such a distinction has become confused.[76] Sensitivity, and indeed anxiety, over the issues raised by the boundary, and the relationship, between words and things, between narrative and events, between verisimilitude and reality, between ornamentation and truth, was no less acute in the fifteenth century than it had been in the twelfth. The terms of the debate may have become clearer and, as the example of Commynes suggests, more widely disseminated, but, as far as the methodology of writing about past events was concerned, the fundamental issue continued to pivot on the relationship between *historia*, *argumentum* and *fabula*, between history, rhetoric and poetry. In theoretical terms, the one novel element that could now be added to this twelfth-century equation was the authority provided by Aristotle.

The reception of Aristotle

The translation of Aristotle's works of natural philosophy into Latin in the course of the twelfth and thirteenth centuries is traditionally seen as having had a decisive impact on both the form and the content of the teaching of the liberal arts in late medieval schools and universities. It might seem only reasonable, therefore, to expect this intellectual development to have exerted a comparable influence on the way in which the writing of history was both conceived and practised in the period 1200–1500. If the operation of memory was largely a technical issue in classical manuals of rhetoric, for example, then this certainly changed under the combined impact of the translations of Aristotle's *De Anima* and *De Memoria et Reminiscentia*.[77] The ties between the

---

76 Guarino da Verona, *Letters*, Ep.796, trans. I. Thomson, 'Guarino's Views on History and Historiography', *Explorations in Renaissance Culture*, 3 (1976), p. 59; cf. Servius, *In Vergilii Carmina Commentarii*, ed. G. Thilo and H. Hagen (Leipzig, 1878), I.373, pp. 125–6.
77 Carruthers, *The Book of Memory*.

processes of remembrance and the recording of the past had, in practice, always been close. Once writing came to be viewed as an aid to memory, historiography could be expected to have developed some of the formal qualities which were understood to characterise the latter: the ordered arrangement of material in a vast 'treasury', or storehouse, that would make the processes of both selection and retrieval much easier; the epistemological status of what was remembered as a representation, or image, of what was experienced, rather than the experience itself; the importance of retaining *res* rather than precise *verba*; the significance of registering the specifics of circumstance, of time, place and person, not necessarily as a claim to accuracy of reporting, but as a means of making something memorable; and, above all, the vividness of the mental image with which it was retained, even when that image had been created artificially or when it was generated by what had been heard from someone else rather than seen with one's own eyes. With the translation of *De Anima* and *De Memoria et Reminiscentia*, such connections between the act of memorisation and the writing of history were established on a much more analytical basis than they had been in rhetorical handbooks.[78] Memory was not a passive receptacle, a reiterative store of experience, but an active process of investigation and understanding. Recollection was therefore understood to be an ethical activity, a cognitive act of intellection and, as such, the basis of the virtue of prudence. The formal recording of what happened – the writing of history – followed suit and, as a result, Aristotle's works on memory came to form part of an on-going critical dialogue with Augustine's understanding of the means by which the past only 'exists' in the present.[79] Memory on its own was a simple record of events (annals, chronicles); reminiscence (history) was the application to those events of understanding and of will.

Just as, if not more, significant than Aristotle's account of memory and epistemology, however, was what he had to say about the truth-content of the historical *exemplum*. Classical manuals of rhetoric had included several theoretical reflections on the nature and role of the paradigmatic 'example'. Cicero set out

---

[78] J. Coleman, *Ancient and Medieval Memories: Studies in the Reconstruction of the Past* (Cambridge, 1992).
[79] See pages 375–6.

the alternatives in the clearest fashion. In defining something by comparing it to something similar, he argued, this similarity or similitude is either gathered from several things (in which case it is an inductive argument or *inductio*) or it is a simple comparison between one thing and another (in which case it is a parallel or *collatio*). Similitude takes three forms: image (*imago*), which demonstrates similarity in form or nature; parallel (*collatio*), which juxtaposes one thing with something else on the basis of their similarity; and example (*exemplum*), which is drawn either from authority or from experience and involves either an individual or an event. All three forms of similitude are accordingly listed as figures of speech – as simile, metaphor and example, respectively – and, in each case, the comparison can be with something which is true, plausible or false.[80] The *Rhetorica ad Herennium* hesitated to equate the citation of examples with the force of proof or testimony – *exempla* demonstrate the nature of what is being said, whereas testimony proves that what is being said is actually the case. Quintilian had fewer qualms – experience, in his view, served as the testimony of reason; an appeal to similar things in the past is a comparative argument and amounts to proof from similarity.[81]

Aristotle's most significant statement on the exemplary nature of events in the past and, as a consequence, on the status of history-writing occurred in the course of a contrast he drew with the nature of poetry in book IX of his *Poetics*. He wrote:

> The poet's function is to say, not what did happen [*gesta*], but the sort of thing that would happen, that is, what can happen in a strictly probable or necessary sequence [*qualia utique fierent et possibilia secundum verisimile aut necessarium*]. The difference between the historian and the poet is not merely that one writes verse and the other prose – one could turn Herodotus' work into verse and it would be just as much history as before. The essential difference is that the one

---

80 See pages 269, 326–7. For four types of argumentation (syllogism, induction, enthymeme, example), see Peter of Spain, *Tractatus (Summulae Logicales)*, trans. N. Kretzmann and E. Stump, *The Cambridge Translations of Medieval Philosophical Texts. Vol. I: Logic and the Philosophy of Language* (Cambridge, 1988), V.3, pp. 227–8: induction proceeds from particulars to a universal (*inductio est progressus particularibus ad universale*); example is when one particular is proved by means of another because of something similar found in them (*exemplum est quando per unum particulare probatur aliud particulare propter simile repertum in ipsis*).
81 See pages 244–5.

tells us what happened (*gesta*) and the other the sorts of thing that would happen (*qualia utique fierent*). This is why poetry is more like philosophy and more worthwhile than history, since poetry tends to make general statements, whereas those of history are particular. A general statement is one that tells us what sort of person would, in all probability or necessity [*secundum verisimile aut necessarium*], say or do what sort of thing, and this is what poetry aims at, although it attaches proper names. A particular statement, on the other hand, simply tells us what Alcibiades did, for instance, or what happened to him.[82]

There were at least two elements in this passage, when viewed from the perspective of the issues which had already been raised by twelfth-century discussions of the relationship between history, rhetoric and poetry, that struck a particular chord with a thirteenth-century readership. The first was the clear association of poetry with the narrative of what could happen or what would have happened – in other words, not with fabulous or fantastic narrative, but with the plausible reconstruction of events covered by rhetorical verisimilitude. The second was the corresponding limitation of history, not just to a narrative of who did what and what actually happened, but to the uniqueness of the particular series of events or actions that it recorded.

Despite its translation into Latin in 1278, the subsequent influence of Aristotle's *Poetics* in the later Middle Ages was, in itself, rather muted. Quite why that should have been the case is, in the history of literary criticism, open to speculation.[83] Viewed from the perspective of historiography, however, the significance

---

82 Aristotle, *Poetics*, trans. M.E. Hubbard, in *Classical Literary Criticism* (rev. edn, Oxford, 1989), IX 1451a38–b7, p. 62; Aristotle, *Poetics*, ed. L. Minio-Paluello, *De Arte Poetica, cum Averrois Expositione* (*Aristoteles Latinus* 33, Brussels, 1968), pp. 12–13.
83 Minnis and Scott (eds), *Medieval Literary Theory*, p. 277. More influential than the *Poetics* themselves, for example, was Averroes' commentary on the work, translated into Latin in 1256, which argued that the value of poetry lay in its capacity to move the emotions of an audience for whom logical reasoning would not be as effective, but also that, as a part of logic, it did *not* have the licence to create false fictions or fables because what it represents has to be possible and verisimilar in order to be persuasive. Averroes also made *enargeia* definitively a quality of poetic, rather than historical, narrative – when things occur as if before one's eyes, they almost have the credibility which derives from being seen. See Averroes, *Middle Commentary on Aristotle's Poetics*, trans. O.B. Hardison, in A. Preminger, O.B. Hardison and K. Kerrane (eds), *Classical and Medieval Literary Criticism: Translations and Interpretations* (New York, 1974), pp. 358–60, 362–3, 369–70; Averroes,

of this text lay in the reinforcement it gave to a much broader 'Aristotelian' view of the inherent particularism of a strictly 'historical' narrative. Aristotle's attention to the epistemological status of empirical sense data was clearly a concern which ran through many of his other works – this was, after all, the technical meaning of the term *historia* in the Latinised title of Aristotle's *History of Animals* (and, for that matter, of Pliny the Elder's Latin *Natural History*). According to Aristotle, however, individual facts are, by themselves, incapable of providing formal or demonstrative proof and, as a result, a collection of *exempla* on their own – in a narrative, say – will never produce certainty and understanding. The consequences of this approach for the position of history-writing were encapsulated by what Aristotle had to say about the *exemplum*, not in his treatise on *Poetics*, but in his own work *On Rhetoric*, a treatise which was translated into Latin at some point in the 1260s.[84] Its impact is best tracked through the influential interpretation, and application, which it received from its first scholastic commentator, Giles of Rome.

Giles of Rome produced his analysis of Aristotle's *Rhetoric* as one of a series of commentaries on Aristotle in the period before 1277 but, in this case, he chose to make a particularly close exposition of the original.[85] Nowhere is this more apparent than in Aristotle's very first sentence, an opening which encapsulated much of what had been distinctive about his own approach to the subject: 'rhetoric is the counterpart of dialectic'.[86] Aristotle himself had defended this claim on the grounds that both rhetoric and dialectic are disciplines which are concerned with things that lie within the comprehension of all people and which use logical reasoning in order to produce probable conclusions. For rhetoric,

---

Middle Commentary on Aristotle's Poetics, trans. C.E. Butterworth (Princeton, 1986), pp. 83–6, 93–4, 108–10; Mehtonen, *Old Concepts and New Poetics*, p. 71.
84 Aristotle, *On Rhetoric*, trans. G.A. Kennedy (Oxford, 1991); Aristotle, *Rhetorica, Translatio Anonyma sive Vetus et Guillelmi de Moerbeka*, ed. B. Schneider (Leiden, 1978).
85 Giles of Rome, *Super Libros Rhetoricorum* (Venice, 1542); cf. J.R. O'Donnell, 'The Commentary of Giles of Rome on the *Rhetoric* of Aristotle', in T.A. Sandquist and M. Powicke (eds), *Essays in Medieval History presented to Bertie Wilkinson* (Toronto, 1969), pp. 139–56.
86 Aristotle, *Rhetoric*, I.1.1 1354a1, p. 159; Giles of Rome, *Super Libros Rhetoricorum*, f.1r.

this means using enthymemes (a less formal type of deductive syllogism) and paradigms or *exempla* (a looser form of inductive reasoning), and it means taking as its starting-point what is contingent, doubtful or debatable. The result is that rhetoric is based on 'endoxa' (that is, on commonly-held opinions), rather than on tightly-reasoned arguments deduced from definite premises and *a priori* truths. The difference between a paradigm and an enthymeme, meanwhile, was clarified with a reference to Aristotle's own *Topics*: 'to show on the basis of many similar instances that something is so is induction in dialectic, paradigm in rhetoric; to show that if some premises are true, something else beyond them results from these, because they are true either universally or for the most part, is called syllogism in dialectic and enthymeme in rhetoric'.[87] Both rhetoric and dialectic, moreover, are methods or disciplines which do not possess any subject-matter which is specific to themselves. Rhetoric, in this respect, since it is a practical discipline which is usually applied to human conduct, adopts as its subject-matter the propositions described by ethics and politics. Indeed, in Aristotle's view, rhetoric thereby clothes itself (*induit*) in the form (*figura*) of political science.[88]

In his commentary on the *Rhetoric*, Giles of Rome used the opening statement of Aristotle to examine, and in some detail, the various ways in which rhetoric could be related to the method of dialectic and to the subject-matter of politics and ethics. In reinforcing Aristotle's account of what rhetoric has in common with these three disciplines, however, Giles went much further than Aristotle in setting out exactly where they differed. Rhetoric, he argued, is concerned with arousing the emotions as a means of persuading the will; dialectic is concerned exclusively with reason and with the intellect. Rhetoric seeks to secure belief (*fides*) or credibility (*credulitas*) through persuasion; dialectic to secure opinion (*opinio*) through probable reasoning (*rationes probabiles*). Rhetoric persuades by means of enthymemes and *exempla*; dialectic proceeds by means of syllogisms and induction. Rhetoric

---

[87] *Rhetoric*, I.1.1–14 1354a1–1355b23, pp. 159–63; I.2.9 1356b11–18, p. 165; cf. Aristotle, *Topica*, trans. W.A. Pickard-Cambridge (Princeton, 1984), I.1, pp. 167–8, I.12, pp. 174–5; Aristotle, *Topica*, ed. L. Minio-Paluello (*Aristoteles Latinus* V.1–3, Brussels, 1969), pp. 5–7, 18–19.
[88] *Rhetoric*, I.2.7 1356a25–28, p. 164.

has an audience which is simple and rough (*simplex et grossus*); dialectic has an audience which is intelligent and refined (*ingeniosus et subtilis*).[89] Likewise, in accepting Aristotle's view that rhetoric is the part of dialectic which is applicable to human behaviour in the political community and that it is therefore subordinate to the architectonic discipline of politics, Giles also established in what respects it should be regarded as different. Rhetoric is not a part of politics, he states, because rhetoric discusses particular political propositions in so far as they can be reduced to common principles (*principia communia*), whereas politics discusses them in so far as they are particular issues of debate applicable only to particular circumstances.[90]

Giles of Rome's discussion of the relationship between rhetoric, dialectic and politics has attracted considerable attention from modern scholars, both for what is said in the commentary on the *Rhetoric* itself and for a rather brusque letter with which it was followed up, when Giles reiterated his position (and in even more unequivocal terms) to Oliverius, a Dominican *lector* from Angers. Although rhetoric shares common ground with both dialectic and politics, Giles wrote, it still has a greater affinity to dialectic, as Aristotle had argued, than it does to politics, as Cicero had suggested,[91] because rhetoric conveys knowledge only of general principles applied to human behaviour and, as such, deals only indirectly with particular moral actions.[92] In tackling the exact relationship between rhetoric, politics and dialectic, Giles was contributing to a debate which stretched back to the twelfth century, and to writers such as John of Salisbury, and which was to continue well into the fourteenth and fifteenth centuries.

---

89 Giles of Rome, *Super Libros Rhetoricorum*, f.1r–7r; cf. S. Robert, 'Rhetoric and Dialectic According to the First Latin Commentary on the *Rhetoric* of Aristotle', *New Scholasticism*, 31 (1957), pp. 484–98; J.J. Murphy, 'The Scholastic Condemnation of Rhetoric in the Commentary of Giles of Rome on the *Rhetoric* of Aristotle', in *Arts Libéraux et Philosophie au Moyen Age* (Montreal, 1969), pp. 833–41; P. von Moos, 'Rhetorik, Dialektik und *Civilis Scientia* in Hochmittelalter', in J. Fried (ed.), *Dialektik und Rhetorik im früheren und hohen Mittelalter: Rezeption, Überlieferung und gesellschaftliche Wirkung antiker Gelehrsamkeit vornehmlich im 9. und 12. Jahrhundert* (Munich, 1997), pp. 133–55.
90 *Super Libros Rhetoricorum*, f.17r.
91 See pages 229, 414.
92 G. Bruni, 'The *De Differentia Rhetoricae, Ethicae et Politicae* of Aegidius Romanus', *New Scholasticism*, 6 (1932), pp. 5–12.

To this extent, Giles was effectively using the newly translated text of Aristotle's *Rhetoric* to comment on a discussion of disciplinary boundaries which had been precipitated, and sustained, from early in the Middle Ages by familiarity with Cicero's *Topics*, Boethius' commentary on Cicero's *Topics* and, above all, Boethius' own *De Topicis Differentiis* (whose fourth book had opened with an analysis of the similarities, differences and relationship between the subjects of rhetoric and dialectic).[93] The subsequent transmission and circulation of Aristotle's *Rhetoric*, however (the Latin text was frequently bound up in the same manuscript as the *Ethics* and the *Politics*; a new Latin translation was subsequently printed in 1477), together with Giles of Rome's commentary (there are some twenty-six extant manuscripts, one of which was owned by Coluccio Salutati; it was printed twice in the fifteenth century, as indeed was Giles' letter to Oliverius),[94] proceeded to give an extra edge to what soon became a critical issue of demarcation between 'humanism' and 'scholasticism'.[95]

Viewed from the particular perspective of historiography, Giles of Rome's reading of Aristotle's *Rhetoric* is also significant for what it reveals about the methodology of history-writing as a sub-section of rhetoric which deals with ethical and political subject-matter. Perhaps the most striking illustration of its consequences is provided by the effects which Giles' detailed knowledge of Aristotle had on the work which he promptly went on to compose (and for which he was subsequently, courtesy of its wide circulation in both Latin and in a large number of vernacular translations, best

---

93 Cicero, *Topica*, trans. H.M. Hubbell (Loeb, 1949); Boethius, *In Ciceronis Topica*, trans. E. Stump (Ithaca, 1988); Boethius, *De Topicis Differentiis*, trans. E. Stump (Ithaca, 1978), IV, pp. 79–80; cf. page 419.
94 C.H. Lohr, 'Medieval Latin Aristotle Commentaries', *Traditio*, 23–30 (1967–74), pp. 334–5; Bruni, 'The *De Differentia Rhetoricae, Ethicae et Politicae*', pp. 1–2; P.D. Brandes, *A History of Aristotle's Rhetoric with a Bibliography of Early Printings* (Metuchen, 1989). More generally, see J.J. Murphy and M. Davies, 'Rhetorical Incunabula – A Short-Title Catalogue of Texts Printed to the Year 1500', *Rhetorica*, 15 (1997), pp. 355–470; J.J. Murphy, 'Rhetoric in the Fifteenth Century – From Manuscript to Print', in C.J. Mews, C.J. Nederman and R.M. Thomson (eds), *Rhetoric and Renewal in the Latin West 1100–1540* (Turnhout, 2003), pp. 227–41.
95 For example, E. Rummel, *The Humanist–Scholastic Debate in the Renaissance and Reformation* (Harvard, 1995); W.A. Rebhorn, *Renaissance Debates on Rhetoric* (Ithaca, 2000).

known for the next two hundred years), *De Regimine Principum* (*On the Governance of Rulers*).[96] Traditionally, the significance of the discipline of rhetoric for the 'mirror-for-princes' genre and, by extension, for the writing of history lay in the guidelines it provided for describing *exempla* of good and bad conduct. Both demonstrative rhetoric (the language used to praise or castigate an individual) and judicial rhetoric (the strategies deployed to accuse or defend an individual) necessarily involve establishing a set of virtues and vices, narrating good and bad deeds, which are to be imitated or avoided by one's audience. This was the moral–didactic tradition which was inherited from the *Rhetorica ad Herennium* and Cicero's *De Inventione* and which accounts for the prominence, within the mirror-for-princes genre, of *encomia* and the writing of history.[97] Indeed, it had become axiomatic for some writers who used this method of approach to claim that an *exemplum virtutis* was, in fact, a better means of instruction than a precept or a prohibition.[98] Giles of Rome certainly does not deny the value of also reading Aristotle's *Rhetoric* in this way – the great utility of this treatise, he writes, is that it provides a knowledge of how to praise people or to castigate them.[99] From the outset of his commentary, moreover, Giles reveals that he also wants to take what Aristotle had said about the value of deploying this knowledge of virtue in the depiction of character and apply it to the speaker or writer themselves, not just to the individual who is being described, because people tend to put their faith in those who are morally virtuous. Making oneself credible to an audience as a means of making one's argument credible was, again, a well-established principle in Ciceronian rhetoric.[100] Giles uses Aristotle to make the same point: knowledge of the virtues enables a speaker or writer to make both themselves and any other person whom they are describing worthy of trust, or credence, in regard to virtue.[101] This self-reflexive justification firmly connects

---

96 Giles of Rome, *De Regimine Principum* (Venice, 1502).
97 See pages 166–8.
98 See pages 152–6.
99 Giles of Rome, *Super Libros Rhetoricorum*, f.31r.
100 See pages 140, 190–1, 227, 246.
101 Aristotle, *Rhetoric*, I.9.1 1366a24–28, p. 189, II.1.2–7 1377b21–1378a20, pp. 220–1; cf.I.2.4 1356a5–14, pp. 163–4.

Giles' views on rhetoric to a line of argument which went back to Augustine's *De Doctrina Christiana* and Gregory the Great's *Regula Pastoralis*. Rhetoric needs to be connected with virtue because eloquence needs to be united with wisdom; the individual who is skilled in speaking also needs to be a morally good person.[102] This is, in the first instance, in order to prevent the abuse of rhetoric. However, it is also to ensure that the individual who is in authority over others will teach by example as well as by word and, in order to do that, such an individual will need to be virtuous themselves in order that they can teach others. As is made clear by book I of *De Regimine Principum*, it is the presence of these virtues in oneself which is both a prerequisite and a means for instilling these virtues in others.[103]

A second point which emerges from Giles' reading of Aristotle's *Rhetoric* had a still more significant bearing on the writing of *De Regimine Principum* but, in this instance, it derived from a feature of Aristotle's text which, when viewed from a Ciceronian perspective, appears both novel and distinctive. This is Aristotle's concentration, not on demonstrative or on judicial rhetoric, but on deliberative rhetoric, that is, on the language which is used in the governance of the political community in order to offer counsel (*consilium*) or to engage in debate (*contio*).[104] It had been a major goal of Aristotle's own analysis of rhetoric to wrest it away from the sophistry of the law courts; this is why he had been so keen to provide it with the logical rigour which would derive from the direct connection with dialectic with which his treatise had so emphatically opened. This is also why Aristotle had devoted so much of his treatise to deliberative rhetoric in particular. Not only is it a finer subject than judicial rhetoric, he explains, but it is also more central to the political community.[105] Aristotle's *Rhetoric* accordingly prompted Giles of Rome to consider the best

---

102 See pages 10, 116, 229, 246, 344–5, 352, 371, 409.
103 See pages 400–1; cf. Gerald of Wales, *Expugnatio Hibernica*, ed. and trans. A.B. Scott and F.X. Martin, *The Conquest of Ireland* (Dublin, 1978), I.45, p. 123: 'a ruler will derive no renown from a triumph over his enemies until he conquers himself'.
104 Aristotle, *Rhetoric*, I.5–6 1360b3–1363b4, pp. 174–82. Compare, for example, the relatively small amount of space devoted to deliberative rhetoric by Cicero in *De Inventione*, trans. H.M. Hubbell (Loeb, 1949), II.51.155–58.176, pp. 323–43.
105 *Rhetoric*, I.1.10 1354b23–25, p. 161.

way in which rhetoric could be used to inculcate virtue in one's audience. The subject-matter of ethics and politics may provide the propositions which serve as the basis for its inductive and deductive arguments, but it is rhetoric itself which provides the understanding of the emotions that will enable those arguments to be adapted to the particular character of an audience and thereby, for example, made appropriate to people who may be young, in their prime, or old.[106] Aristotle had acknowledged that, even if an individual were to possess the most exact knowledge, it would not be easy to use that knowledge in order to teach or to persuade some types of audience, most notably the mass of the people.[107] It was this last point which Giles chose to pick up on in the introduction to his own *De Regimine Principum*.[108]

In writing a work which communicates knowledge of the art of governance, Giles states that his mode of procedure will be 'outline and rough' (*figuralis et grossus*). Why is it necessary to move across such matters in a general and outline fashion (*typo et figuraliter*)? Because, he writes, moral deeds in their entirety (*gesta moralia completae*) do not fall within the scope of narrative (*narratio*). Giles justifies such an approach on three grounds, each of which was drawn from the medieval *accessus ad auctores*: the nature of the subject-matter, the nature of its goal, and the nature of the audience to which it is directed.[109] First of all, therefore, Giles explains that moral conduct is, by definition, material which is indeterminate; the subject-matter of ethical and political analysis is simply not susceptible to the sort of certitude and detailed examination (*perscrutatio subtilis*) which is appropriate, say, in mathematics or in geometry. Giles' cross-reference here is to book I of Aristotle's *Ethics* ('it will be satisfactory if we can demonstrate the truth roughly and in outline; since we argue from, and about, what is true for the most part, it will be satisfactory if we

---

106 *Rhetoric*, II.12–14 1388b31–1390b14, pp. 246–50.
107 *Rhetoric*, I.1.12 1355a24–29, p. 162. Aristotle makes the cross-reference to his own *Topics*, I.1, p. 167.
108 Giles of Rome, *De Regimine Principum*, I.i.1–3. There are translations of the *proemium* in Minnis and Scott (eds), *Medieval Literary Theory*, pp. 248–50, and in A.S. McGrade, J. Kilcullen and M.S. Kempshall (eds), *The Cambridge Translations of Medieval Philosophical Texts. Vol. II: Ethics and Political Philosophy* (Cambridge, 2001), pp. 203–12.
109 Minnis and Scott (eds), *Medieval Literary Theory*, pp. 201–2; see pages 126–7.

can draw conclusions of the same sort'),[110] following the interpretation of the phrase *grosse et figuraliter* which had been set out by Albertus Magnus in his own commentary on this text some twenty years earlier. According to Albertus, a 'rough' demonstration entails using *exempla* which appeal to the emotions, as well as popular proverbs (*proverbia vulgaria*); a 'sketched' or 'outline' demonstration involves incomplete or imperfect argumentation (that is, the use of enthymemes rather than syllogisms).[111]

Giles' second justification for adopting a rough or outline approach is that ethical and political knowledge is designed to be put into practice. Its goal is therefore not just to know what virtue is, but actually to lead a virtuous life. Ethical and political analysis must move human wills to the good rather than just convince human intellects of the truth, and it must therefore appeal to the emotions, not just to reason. Again, Giles' cross-reference is to the *Ethics*: 'the end aimed at in political science is, not knowledge, but action'.[112] Giles' third, and final, justification for his approach to the art of governance is that any discussion of ethical and political material must be made appropriate to its intended audience. In the first instance, this means appropriate to the king, and to a young king at that, but, in writing *De Regimine Principum*, Giles also makes it clear that his goal is to inculcate the principles of a life of virtue into the king's subjects as well, that is, into the whole populace (*totus populus*). This is why he envisages a vernacular version of his treatise;[113] this is also why his approach will be, not detailed, but in outline. His is a simple and rough audience (*simplex et grossus*), Giles explains, which cannot understand refined argumentation (*subtilia*); instead, it needs to be instructed by arguments that are sketched and which appeal to the emotions (*rationes superficiales et sensibiles*). These are not pejorative terms. Giles goes out of his way to say so. Because people generally hate a discussion that goes into great detail, he writes, most audiences

---

110 Aristotle, *Ethica Nicomachea*, ed. R.A. Gauthier (Brussels, 1972–73), I.3 1094b11–14, 19–22, 25–27, p. 376; trans. R. Crisp (Cambridge, 2000), pp. 4–5.
111 Albertus Magnus, *Super Ethica Commentum et Quaestiones*, ed. W. Kübel (Münster, 1968), I.2, p. 12.
112 Aristotle, *Ethica Nicomachea*, II.2 1103b27–29, trans. Crisp, p. 24, ed. Gauthier, p. 397.
113 Giles of Rome, *De Regimine Principum*, II.iii.20.

are favourably disposed towards one which is easy and sketched (*facilis et superficialis*). This may be a corruption of the appetite in other branches of knowledge but, in moral matters, where the nature of the subject requires treatment which is *figuralis et grossus*, it is the correct arrangement. Giles proceeds to argue that the laity, and especially the young, are simply not able to cope with detailed analysis (*subtilis perscrutatio*) and, as a result, the instruction which they receive from their ecclesiastical teachers should always be general (*grossus*).[114] A chain of syllogistic reasoning is not necessarily an easy argument to follow and yet the audience for rhetoric is generally assumed to be 'simple' (*simplex*).[115] Giles accordingly echoes the definition of rhetoric which, he states, Aristotle originally suggested in the *Rhetoric*: it is, as it were, a 'rough' form of dialectic. Whereas subtle reasoning (*subtiles rationes*) characterises natural philosophy and other speculative branches of knowledge, rough reasoning (*grossae rationes*) characterises the moral sciences, which deal with actions. Rhetoric teaches a mode of argumentation which is rough and in outline and it is therefore particularly important for rulers to learn this discipline because of their position in communicating with, and exercising authority over, the populace – that is, through their contact with people who can understand only such an outline form of reasoning.[116]

If Aristotle's *Rhetoric* provided Giles of Rome with the general means by which virtue could, and should, be inculcated in his own audience, then its account of deliberative rhetoric provided him with guidelines for the actual content of the principles which would thereby be instilled. The study of ethics established happiness – activity in accordance with perfect or complete virtue – as the ultimate goal of humankind. According to Aristotle, however, since human beings deliberate over the means to an end, rather than over the end itself, the goal of deliberative rhetoric is to secure what contributes to this happiness, namely what it is advantageous (*conferens*) to do in order to attain the good which

---

114 *De Regimine Principum*, II.ii.5; cf. John of Salisbury, *Policraticus*, trans. J. Dickinson, *The Statesman's Book of John of Salisbury* (New York, 1927), IV.6, pp. 28–9.
115 Aristotle, *Rhetoric*, I.2.13 1357a12, p. 166.
116 Giles of Rome, *De Regimine Principum*, II.ii.8.

is otherwise chosen as an end in itself. As such, the deliberative rhetoric of political counsel is concerned with the constituent elements of happiness – with nobility of birth, a multitude of good friends, wealth, a good wife and children, a good old age, physical health and vigour, glory, honour and good fortune, as well as with the exercise of the cardinal virtues.[117] It is also particularly important for deliberative rhetoric to understand how to compare different actions as more or less advantageous, as greater or lesser goods.[118] Having defined happiness as the ultimate goal, Aristotle identified five topics as essential to deliberative rhetoric: material resources; war and peace; the import and export of goods; the security of the community; and, finally, the framing of laws as the means by which virtue can be instilled in the political community.[119] It is in the course of mastering these subjects, Aristotle also pointed out, that the utility of historiography becomes apparent: it is necessary to make use of the history of one's own political community, as well as the histories of others, because similar results follow naturally from similar causes. Written histories, Aristotle concluded, are therefore particularly useful to political counsel (*sunt utiles ... ad civilia autem consilia historiae scribentium gesta*).[120]

Aristotle's discussion of deliberative rhetoric presented Giles with a clear agenda for any work of political counsel – presuppose that the life of virtue is the goal of the political community, list the constituent elements of this happiness, discuss peace and security as its material preconditions, and then analyse legislation as the means by which it can be effected. These are the most important subjects, Aristotle suggested, on which someone who is going to

---

117 Aristotle, *Rhetoric*, I.5.1–4 1360b3–30, pp. 174–5. For the close relationship between deliberation (*consilia*) and praise (*laus*), see I.9.35–6 1367b36–1368a3, p. 193: 'praise and deliberation are part of a common species in that what might be proposed in counsel becomes commendation when the form of expression is changed. When, therefore, we know what should be done and what sort of person someone should be, the form of expression should be changed and what is said converted into propositions'; cf. page 249.
118 *Rhetoric*, I.6–7 1362a17–1365b20, pp. 179–88.
119 *Rhetoric*, I.4.7 1359b19–22, p. 172; cf. Giles of Rome, *De Regimine Principum*, III.ii.19.
120 *Rhetoric*, I.4.8–13 1359b22–1360b1, pp. 172–4; cf.I.8.1–3 1365b23–31, p. 188.

proffer political counsel ought to have propositions.[121] Aristotle's advice is accordingly taken to heart in *De Regimine Principum*, where Giles establishes *consilium* on the same five subjects as a vital means of averting the disintegration of a kingdom. Offering advice, he states, not on the goal of virtue and happiness, but on the means towards that end, is intended to be persuasive, to produce credibility (*credulitas*) and belief (*fides*). It is the counsel of good and wise men which will provide a safeguard against kingship turning into tyranny.[122] In his commentary on the *Rhetoric*, Giles kept closely to these five categories of political counsel (*consiliabilia*). Deliberation on legislation, he argues, requires knowledge of other types of political community and therefore of forms of government and laws different to one's own, up to and including those microcosmic communities represented by the household and the individual. It is thus comparison with other constitutions and laws, as well as with the deeds of one's predecessors, the deeds of those who have written histories, or the deeds which have been written down as histories (*gesta eorum qui praecesserunt; gesta scribentium historias sive gesta scripta historialiter*), which will reveal what is advantageous to one's own political community.[123]

Aristotle's prescriptions on deliberative rhetoric were not limited to the contents of political counsel. Book III of the *Rhetoric* argued that it is especially important for the style of deliberative rhetoric to avoid becoming excessively detailed. Unlike the exactness used in the law courts, deliberative rhetoric should proceed, once again, in outline, like a sketch in painting (*protracture umbre*). The reason? Because – and this is the argument to which Giles appeals directly in his introduction to *De Regimine Principum* – the bigger the audience is for political counsel, the further it is from understanding.[124] As Giles explains in his commentary on the *Rhetoric*, the 'sketched' nature of deliberative rhetoric derives from the fact that it is sufficient for this type of language to have some appearance in outline but not to concern itself with any

---

121 *Rhetoric*, I.4.13 1360b1, p. 174.
122 Giles of Rome, *De Regimine Principum*, III.ii.15–19.
123 Giles of Rome, *Super Libros Rhetoricorum*, f.17r–18v; cf. Giles of Rome, *De Regimine Principum*, II.i.4.
124 Aristotle, *Rhetoric*, III.12.5 1414a8–10, p. 306; cf. Giles of Rome, *De Regimine Principum*, I.i.1.

depth because it is addressed to the populace and to the multitude. For such an audience, excessive detail and subtlety would be redundant. Political deliberation, therefore, like rhetoric in general, is by definition 'rough' (*grossus*).[125] Aristotle had pointed out how difficult it is for the educated (*eruditi*) to persuade masses of people (*turbae*), because educated people reason on the basis of axioms and universals, whereas the uneducated do so on the basis of the particulars which they know and of instances drawn from their own experience. The solution, in Aristotle's view, was to recommend that arguments should be based on well-respected authorities, that the truth of what is said should be clear to all or to most people, and that conclusions should be drawn not only from what is necessarily valid but also from what is true for the most part.[126] This extends to the use of maxims (*sententiae*) as a type of enthymeme, once again because of the uncultivated minds of the audience (*ruditas auditorum*), because people are pleased if someone in a general observation hits upon opinions which they themselves hold about a particular instance.[127]

Aristotle's concern to exclude excessive depth and detail from deliberative rhetoric was echoed and reinforced by Giles of Rome's commentary on the *Rhetoric*. Its consequences can be traced throughout *De Regimine Principum*, from the moment Giles declares that his approach will be *grossus et figuraliter*. What remains intriguing about his use of this particular phrase, however, is the way in which Giles of Rome appears to have understood the second of the two terms. It is certainly tempting to interpret this pairing as Giles' shorthand for the twin elements with which Aristotle had defined the approach that should be adopted by rhetoric in general – the use of enthymemes and of paradigmatic *exempla*. This is, after all, how Albertus Magnus had glossed the phrase from the *Ethics* which Giles quotes in his introduction.[128] However, this does not appear to be how Giles himself wanted the second term to be understood and certainly not how he proceeds to incorporate *exempla* of his own into the main body of his argument. In his own *speculum principis*, Giles refrains

---

125 Giles of Rome, *Super Libros Rhetoricorum*, f.108r.
126 *Rhetoric*, II.22.1–3 1395b20–1396a2, p. 262.
127 *Rhetoric*, II.21.15 1395b1–11, p. 261; cf. page 287.
128 See page 467.

from appealing to a mass of illustrative *exempla* drawn from the past, either in the form of written history or as individual cases. He does not appeal to examples drawn from the Old and New Testaments and from the histories of non-Christian kings (David, Solomon, Trajan and Charlemagne, as paradigms of good rulers or, as paradigms of the wicked, Alexander the Great and Julius Caesar).[129] Giles certainly does not deny the didactic value of such an approach. On the contrary, he explicitly endorses reading the praiseworthy deeds of kings (*laudabilia gesta*) as a useful alternative to the instructive principles which are contained in his own *De Regimine Principum*. The king, he argues, ought frequently to contemplate the history of his kingdom and to remember what happened to his predecessors in order to learn how he ought to rule and what he ought to avoid as injurious to his governance – if the king is ignorant of such matters, he will be unable to govern his kingdom correctly.[130] Nonetheless, such *exempla* are notable for their absence from *De Regimine Principum* itself. Indeed, this is one of the qualities that made his treatise so distinctive. Giles chose neither to praise particular individuals of outstanding virtue as subjects for imitation nor to castigate their wicked counterparts as paradigms to be avoided. As a result, *De Regimine Principum* remains a logical and systematic sequence of arguments, a patient, even painstaking, demonstration of the principles which underpin the good governance of kings and kingdoms.

By adopting such a rigorous method of approach, by keeping to an abstract level of dispassionate, generally-applicable observation, rather than by narrating particular illustrative *exempla* drawn

---

129 For this contrasting approach, see, for example, the works by Giles of Rome's immediate predecessors: Vincent of Beauvais, *De Morali Principis Institutione*, ed. R.J. Schneider (*CCCM* 137, Turnhout, 1995); Guibert of Tournai, *Eruditio Regum et Principum*, ed. A. de Poorter (Louvain, 1914); and Guillelmus Peraldus, *De Eruditione Principum*, in R. Busa (ed.), *Thomae Aquinatis Opera Omnia* (Stuttgart-Bad Canstatt, 1980), vol. VII, pp. 89–121. Compare Joinville, *Life of Saint Louis*, trans. M.Shaw, *Joinville and Villehardouin: Chronicles of the Crusades* (Harmondsworth, 1963), p. 336: 'before he went to bed, the king used to send for his children and tell them of the deeds of good kings and emperors, at the same time pointing out that they should take such men as an example. He would also tell them of the deeds of wicked princes who, by their dissolute lives, their rapacity and their avarice had brought ruin on their kingdoms. "I'm drawing your attention to such things", he would say, "so that you may avoid them, and not make God angry with you".'
130 Giles of Rome, *De Regimine Principum*, II.iii.20, III.ii.15.

from history, still less by writing a history of his own, Giles set out to privilege a systematic exposition of the logical principles which underpin good governance. The reason he chose to do so lies, once again, in the closeness with which he had read Aristotle's account of deliberative rhetoric. Aristotle had raised the issue of the relative weight which might be given to *exempla*, as opposed to enthymemes, at various stages in his argument in the *Rhetoric* but especially when deliberative rhetoric was being discussed in comparison to judicial rhetoric. According to Aristotle, within the three types of rhetoric, narrative is least common in deliberative rhetoric, because no one narrates future events; if narrative does appear, then it is a narrative of events in the past, so that, by being reminded of these things, an audience will take better counsel over what is to come, either by criticising or by praising what has happened (at which point, however, Aristotle concedes that the rhetoric involved is no longer functioning as counsel).[131] Aristotle certainly maintains that fables (*fabulae*) can be used in deliberative rhetoric, since they can be easier to find than actual events (*negotia*) which are similar to the situation under discussion. However, whilst *exempla* which are put forward through fables may be easier to find, those which are drawn from actual events are more useful, since, in general, future events will be similar to those that have happened in the past. Whilst particular *exempla* can provide support for the argument of enthymemes, therefore, Aristotle concludes that they should be used sparingly. In the absence of a supply of enthymemes, then paradigmatic *exempla* should be used as a means of demonstration but, if there are enthymemes, then paradigms should be used simply as testimony (*testimonia*), as a supplement to the enthymemes. Arguing by means of paradigmatic *exempla* is no less persuasive a use of rhetoric, but enthymemes will generally produce a more rousing response from an audience (*magis turbantur*).[132]

At no point, either in his commentary on Aristotle's *Rhetoric* or in his own *De Regimine Principum*, does Giles of Rome deny the value of an exemplary didactic method. Nonetheless, as far as his own work is concerned, it is the enthymematic, quasi-syllogistic

---

131 Aristotle, *Rhetoric*, III.16.11 1417b11–15, p. 316.
132 *Rhetoric*, I.2.10 1356b22–24, p. 165, II.20.8–9 1394a2–15, p. 258. However, see also I.9.40 1368a30–33, pp. 194–5, III.17.5 1418a1–5, p. 316.

form of reasoning to which he wishes to give priority. This is why he eschews historiography himself. According to Giles, deliberative rhetoric, unlike judicial rhetoric, is concerned with general principles rather than with particulars. Deliberative rhetoric deals with particular propositions only in so far as specific details can be reduced to common principles; compared to the person actually involved in political activity, the approach should be general and sketched.[133] In fact, Giles has some harsh words to say about the value of narrating particulars on their own. He did not think that historical *exempla* could ever provide a sufficiently rigorous means of analysing political subjects. This can be seen from his letter to Oliverius, where narrative *exempla* takes the form, not of historiography, but of law. The science of politics, Giles argues, may consist of instituting and maintaining laws but it considers legislation in so far as it is a subordinate part of moral philosophy. The study of law, by contrast, is conducted, not in a 'scientific' fashion, but as a narrative (*per modum narrativum*). In their use of moral philosophy, in fact, students of law are to students of politics what the masses and the laity (*vulgares et laici*) are to dialecticians trained in logic. Indeed, Giles issues a warning against descending from general principles to particular eventualities – to do so is to practise exactly the sort of unreflective political expertise which characterises sophistry.[134] Giles' use of this final term ties his retort, in turn, to the passage in book X of the *Ethics* in which Aristotle had bluntly dismissed the claims of sophists to teach political science. This sort of rhetorician, Aristotle insisted, is completely ignorant of the knowledge which underpins the act of legislation; they assume that politics is the same as, or subordinate to, rhetoric and that legislation is therefore simply a matter of collecting examples of good laws. Instead, such rhetoricians should realise that both the acquisition of political knowledge and the capacity to discern which laws are good require systematic reflection on the underlying assumptions of politics.[135] To put it another way, if rhetoric is not to become sophistry, then it needs

---

133 Giles of Rome, *Super Libros Rhetoricorum*, f.17r.
134 Giles of Rome, *De Differentia Rhetoricae Ethicae et Politicae*, ed. G. Bruni, 'The *De Differentia Rhetoricae Ethicae et Politicae* of Aegidius Romanus', p. 8.
135 Aristotle, *Ethica Nicomachea*, X.14 1180b29–1181b12, trans. Crisp, p. 203, ed. Gauthier, pp. 586–7.

to be firmly connected to dialectic, rather than to historiography, to the narrative of particulars.

Giles of Rome's more general analysis of the relationship between rhetoric and politics provides significant insights into how he may have seen his own task in writing a work of counsel for a future king of France. The contents of *De Regimine Principum* certainly suggest that he took on board many of the central lessons of Aristotle's *Rhetoric*. Giles does not deny that rhetoric can, and should, be used to discuss the particulars of political action; what he does insist on is that they should be resolved into common principles. When Giles came to compose his own political treatise, therefore, this is precisely the form which he gives to the counsel which it puts forward. His was a work which would confine itself to the general and the typical in an attempt to persuade both ruler and populace of the benefits of leading a life of virtue. It is not a narrative collection of empirical moral *exempla*; it is not history. Nor is it a refined and subtle dialectical exposition of politics and ethics. It is, instead, a work of rhetoric, that is, the product of a broadly logical method which has been applied to the moral conduct of humans in order to persuade a wider audience of the general principles of the life of virtue. If Giles ended up writing a 'mirror-for-princes', therefore, a work which instructed kings and rulers on the principles of good governance, then this was a treatise which was produced in accordance with some very specific guidelines. Giles wanted to give his work much greater philosophical rigour than he thought could be provided by historiography, by the particulars of narrative *exempla*. By the same token, Giles also recognised that a purely dialectical demonstration of the material contained in Aristotle's *Ethics* and *Politics* would convince only the intellect, and a refined and highly-trained intellect at that. To learn easily (*facile*), Aristotle had informed him, is by nature pleasing to everyone[136] and, in order to be persuasive, Giles realised that his work would have to draw, not just on true or probable arguments, but also on moral character and on the emotions of his audience. In order to convince a wider audience, therefore, in order to move that audience to act, to persuade them to lead a life of virtue, he

---

136   Aristotle, *Rhetoric*, III.10.2 1410b10, p. 298.

needed to do something else. He found that approach, he found that something else, in Aristotle's *Rhetoric*. It was the combination of political analysis with deliberative rhetoric which gave *De Regimine Principum* its distinctive character and, by extension, reconfigured the fourteenth- and fifteenth-century genre of the *speculum principis* with a character all of its own.

Giles of Rome's commentary on Aristotle's *Rhetoric* reveals how much of this newly translated text served to reinforce precepts that were already familiar from Cicero, Quintilian and the *Rhetorica ad Herennium*. Certainly there were significant differences in emphasis – most notably, the explicit subordination of rhetoric to dialectic, the concentration on deliberative rhetoric, and the priority given to the emotions – but otherwise there was a considerable degree of common ground. Viewed from the perspective of the writing of history, Aristotle's *Rhetoric* served, in this regard, simply to strengthen the conviction of thirteenth- and fourteenth-century writers that nothing could be a better guide to political counsel and deliberation, in the present and for the future, than 'the remembrance of, and induction from, past deeds' (*memoria et inductio rerum gestarum*).[137] Engelbert of Admont, for example, writing at the end of the thirteenth century, defined history as the ordered narrative of what was done, just as it actually happened (*historia autem est rei gestae, prout gesta est, ordinate narratio*). It was particularly useful in the course of deliberation and offering advice, he continued, since past events gave certainty to conjecture about what would happen in the future as a consequence of a particular action being taken. In order to create credence (*fides*) in what is being proposed, Engelbert explains, histories of past events are brought forward (*inducuntur*) as testimony for people to believe and as *exempla* to be imitated – the difference between testimony and example lying in the fact that testimony confirms that something is as it is said to be, whereas an *exemplum* is used to declare what sort of action is being recommended.[138] At the same time, Engelbert is also careful to echo Aristotle's clarification of the distinction between historical *exempla* and *fabula* with

---

137 Engelbert of Admont, *Speculum Virtutum Moralium*, ed. B. Pez, in *Bibliotheca Ascetica Antiquo-Nova* (Regensburg, 1724), X.17, vol. III, pp. 343–4, cited by G.B. Fowler, *The Intellectual Interests of Engelbert of Admont* (New York, 1947), p. 150.
138 Cf. pages 244–5.

his concession that it is easier and more pleasurable to make up something similar to what is being advised than to cite an inductive factual example because nothing can be added or taken away from the truth of the historical fact.[139] A parable, meanwhile, is different again, in that it transfers an event or actions from definite to indefinite persons – whereas history is the narrative of a deed done by certain named individuals, a parable is something which could be done by any individual; as such, although a parable is not true in terms of the action it describes as having happened, it is true in terms of its signification, as a likeness of what is done or should be done.[140]

Giles of Rome and Engelbert of Admont demonstrate how, at one level, the writing of history retained its instrumental political value in the later Middle Ages and, as a result, how Aristotle's authority could be dovetailed neatly with an existing Ciceronian tradition. Historical *exempla* thus continued to be deployed, for example, in the deliberations of civic counsels in northern Italy,[141] in the arguments over conciliarism,[142] to justify and legitimise the respective claims of kings of England and France over the course of the Hundred Years War,[143] and to support Philip the Good's campaign to secure a royal title for the 'Lotharingian' dukedom of Burgundy from the emperor Frederick III in 1447–48.[144] At

---

[139] Engelbert of Admont, *Speculum Virtutum Moralium*, X.18, pp. 347–8.
[140] *Speculum Virtutum Moralium*, X.19, p. 348; cf. Augustine, *Contra Mendacium*, trans. H. Browne, *To Consentius: Against Lying* (in Augustine, *Seventeen Short Treatises*, Oxford, 1847), XXVIII, pp. 454–6 (see page 385).
[141] V. Cox, 'Ciceronian Rhetoric in Italy 1260–1350', *Rhetorica*, 17 (1999), pp. 239–88.
[142] B. Tierney, *Foundations of the Conciliar Theory: The Contribution of the Medieval Canonists from Gratian to the Great Schism* (Cambridge, 1955; rev. edn, Leiden, 1998); B. Tierney, '"Only the Truth Has Authority": The Problem of Reception in the Decretists and in Johannes de Turrecremata', in B. Tierney, *Church, Law and Constitutional Thought in the Middle Ages* (London, 1979); F. Oakley, *The Conciliarist Tradition: Constitutionalism in the Catholic Church 1300–1870* (Oxford, 2003), ch. 2.
[143] C.T. Allmand, *The Hundred Years War* (Cambridge, 1988), pp. 144–7.
[144] Guenée, *Histoire et Culture Historique*, p. 336. For Philip the Good's subsequent commissioning of Georges Chastelain, Jean Molinet and Olivier de La Marche as 'official' court historiographers, see G. Small, *George Chastelain and the Shaping of Valois Burgundy: Political and Historical Culture at Court in the Fifteenth Century* (London, 1997); C. Emerson, *Olivier de La Marche and the Rhetoric of Fifteenth-Century Historiography* (Woodbridge, 2004), ch. 3.

the same time, however, Giles of Rome also reveals that Aristotle's discussion of the relationship of rhetoric to dialectic had at least one other consequence which acted *against* the continuation of such a positive appreciation of the value of historiography – the downgrading of the narrative *exemplum* to what was unique and particular and, as such, to something which was not, by itself, susceptible to 'scientific' knowledge. Coupled with his trenchant remarks in the *Poetics*, in fact, this principle now made the authority of Aristotle available to those writers who wanted to *exclude* the plausible and the verisimilar from the recording of history. From the outset, this was clearly how some other thirteenth-century scholars understood Aristotle's position. Vincent of Beauvais, for example, saw fit to include Aristotle's reservations in his *Speculum Historiale*. The 'historical' part of this hugely influential encyclopaedia was a chronological account of *res gestae* from the beginning of the world to the present day, arranged according to their *series temporum*, but, Vincent states, this did not pertain directly to philosophy because it narrated only individual events (*singularia rerum gesta tantum enarrat*). Although the result would be the source of much wonder (*admiratio*), refreshment (*recreatio*) and benefit (*utilitas*), it remained the case that, according to Aristotle, an art does not result from particulars.[145] In Padua, in the early fourteenth century, Peter of Abano went one step further. 'History', he remarked, 'is merely a laborious and pointless piling up of examples'.[146]

Given the centrality of Aristotle's teaching to the late medieval university curriculum, and given the centrality of Giles of Rome's *De Regimine Principum* to the late medieval mirror-for-princes genre, the strictures issued against the narrative of particular historical *exempla* constituting the basis for any properly 'scientific' study formed a potent counterweight to any academic appreciation of the scholarly value of the subject. For all Aristotle's

---

145 Vincent of Beauvais, *Speculum Maius* (Douai, 1624; reprinted Graz, 1964–65), prol.XVI, col. 13; cf. III.109 (*Speculum Doctrinale*), col. 287. More generally, see J. Schneider, 'Recherches sur une Encyclopédie du XIIIe Siècle: Le *Speculum Maius* de Vincent de Beauvais', *Comptes Rendus de l'Académie des Inscriptions et Belles-Lettres* (1976), p. 180; T.R. Eckenrode, 'Vincent of Beauvais – A Study on the Construction of a Didactic View of History', *The Historian*, 46 (1984), pp. 339–60.
146 N.G. Siraisi, 'The *Expositio Problematum Aristotelis* of Peter of Abano', *Isis*, 61 (1970), pp. 321–39, cited by Smalley, *Historians in the Middle Ages*, p. 181.

concession that historical *exempla* could still play a useful role in political counsel, therefore, the result for historiography, in some quarters at least, was the beginning of what has been memorably termed 'the Aristotelian freeze'.[147]

The 'Renaissance'

A combination of aesthetic verisimilitude in the twelfth century and Aristotelian empiricism in the thirteenth might be thought sufficient, in and of themselves, to have broken the close relationship between rhetoric and the writing of history which had otherwise informed the theory and practice of historiography in the Middle Ages. Once poetry began to lay claim to the construction of plausible and fictive narrative, and once philosophy was considered to have a monopoly on propagating general or universal precepts, it might be expected that the nature and purpose of historiography would be limited simply to chronography and compilation. For those writers brought up on an ascetic suspicion of all rhetorical ornamentation, this was certainly grist to their mill and may indeed have contributed to the annalistic restraint which is evident in some later medieval chronicles. The difficulty with generalising, or even totalising, such a line of interpretation is, of course, the fact that one of the striking features of so much fourteenth-century historiography is its vigorous *re*statement of the twelfth-century connection between history and rhetoric, especially for the role of moral–didactic *exempla*. Even Aristotle, after all, had conceded an important role to historical material in the delivery of political counsel and, as Philippe de Commynes demonstrated, this particular combination continued to produce significant works of 'history' long after 1300 and well beyond an exclusively ecclesiastical and Latinate elite. The profound influence which classical rhetoric came to exercise on the understanding of historiography in the Renaissance may therefore be a well-established feature of many modern accounts of the emergence and development of a 'truly' historical discipline,

---

147 R.W. Southern, 'Aspects of the European Tradition of Historical Writing I – The Classical Tradition from Einhard to Geoffrey of Monmouth', *Transactions of the Royal Historical Society*, 20 (1970), p. 177.

but it remains questionable whether this connection had to wait until the fourteenth and fifteenth centuries in order to be rediscovered or whether, in fact, it represents the continuation of a well-established, and resilient, relationship which had already been in existence for much of the Middle Ages.[148]

Traditional accounts of Renaissance humanism and, as a result, of Renaissance humanist historiography tend to begin with the work of Petrarch, a writer whose reaction against the technical logic of fourteenth-century scholasticism prompted him to express a principle which came to dominate much of the learning and writing of his successors. Knowing the truth was not enough, he argued; it had to be put into practice. Knowledge must be translated into action; it should lead to a virtuous life. As far as Petrarch was concerned, true philosophy therefore involved a Ciceronian and Augustinian union of wisdom with eloquence, of *sapientia* with *eloquentia*; its goal was to teach, certainly, but it was also to move an audience to action and it could do so only by making what was being said attractive. Indeed, if it came down to a choice between knowledge and virtuous action, then, according to Petrarch, it would be better to will the good than to know the truth. This was the point at which Petrarch appealed to the study of rhetoric, since this was the discipline that enabled someone, not just to instruct an audience, in the sense of convincing their intellect, but also to persuade them, in the sense of moving them to action by means of appealing to their emotions as well. The function of rhetoric was to teach, to move and to provide pleasure (*docere, movere, delectare*)

---

148 For a sharp distinction *between* 'medieval' and 'Renaissance' approaches to the relationship between rhetoric and the writing of history, see N. Struever, *The Language of History in the Renaissance: Rhetoric and Historical Consciousness in Florentine Humanism* (Princeton, 1970), pp. 36–7, 81–3; cf. H. Gray, 'Renaissance Humanism – The Pursuit of Eloquence', *Journal of the History of Ideas*, 24 (1963), pp. 497–514; J.O. Ward, 'Classical Rhetoric and the Writing of History in Medieval and Renaissance Culture', in F. McGregor and N. Wright (eds), *European History and Its Historians* (Adelaide, 1977), pp. 1–10. For continuity in the rhetorical tradition, see P.O. Kristeller, 'Humanism and Scholasticism in the Italian Renaissance', in P.O. Kristeller, *Renaissance Thought and Its Sources* (New York, 1979), pp. 85–105; J. Monfasani, 'Humanism and Rhetoric', in A. Rabil (ed.), *Renaissance Humanism: Foundations, Forms and Legacy* (Philadelphia, 1988), vol. III, pp. 171–235; R. Black, 'Humanism', in C.T. Allmand (ed.), *The New Cambridge Medieval History* (Cambridge, 1998), vol. VII, pp. 243–77.

and its practice pertained to the morally good individual who was skilled in the art of language (*vir bonus dicendi peritus*).[149]

Petrarch's understanding of the centrality of rhetoric to the communication of knowledge carried significant consequences for the literary forms in which he himself chose to write between the 1330s and 1360s, all of which came to exert a tremendous influence on the subsequent development of 'Renaissance' humanism in Italy. Poetry, letters and historiography provided the all-important means by which the truths of moral philosophy could be translated into virtuous action, or at least more effectively than those essayed by scholastic philosophers in all their commentaries and treatises. Fundamental to Petrarch's approach to these three forms of writing was the principle of creative imitation which he had discovered in Seneca.[150] The results can be found in Petrarch's *Africa* (an epic narrative of the deeds of Scipio which was intended to emulate Vergil's *Aeneid*), several collections of *Letters* (after the models provided by Cicero's letters to Atticus and to Quintus, *Ad Familiares*) and two works of history, *De Viris Illustribus* and *De Gestis Caesaris* (following Plutarch, Jerome and Gennadius).[151] In doing so, Petrarch was, in part, responding to the discovery of 'new' classical texts – a twelfth-century manuscript of *Pro Archia* (Cicero's

---

149 Petrarch, *Invectiva Contra Medicum*, ed. and trans. D. Marsh, *Against a Physician*, in Petrarch, *Invectives* (Cambridge, MA, 2003), pp. 1–179; Petrarch, *De Sui Ipsius et Multorum Ignorantia*, ed. and trans. D. Marsh, *On His Own Ignorance and That of Many Others*, in Petrarch, *Invectives* (Cambridge, MA, 2003), pp. 222–363; cf. Petrarch, *Rerum Familiarum Libri*, trans. A.S. Bernardo, *Letters on Familiar Matters* (Albany, 1975), I.7, pp. 37–40; Hugh of St Victor, *Didascalicon*, V.6, pp. 127–8. More generally, see K. Foster, *Petrarch: Poet and Humanist* (Edinburgh, 1984); C.E. Quillen, *Re-Reading the Renaissance: Petrarch, Augustine and the Language of Humanism* (Ann Arbor, 1998); J. Seigel, *Rhetoric and Philosophy in Renaissance Humanism: The Union of Eloquence and Wisdom, Petrarch to Valla* (Princeton, 1968).
150 Petrarch, *Rerum Familiarum Libri*, XXIII.19, pp. 301–2; cf. Seneca, *Letters*, trans. R.M. Gummere (Loeb, 1920), Ep.84, pp. 277–85. For the subsequent significance of this passage, see E.H. Gombrich, 'The Style *all'Antica* – Imitation and Assimilation', in E.H. Gombrich, *Norm and Form: Studies in the Art of the Renaissance* (London, 1966), pp. 122–8.
151 Petrarch, *Africa*, ed. N. Festa (Florence, 1926); Petrarch, *Rerum Familiarum Libri*; Petrarch, *De Viris Illustribus*, ed. G. Martellotti (Florence, 1964); cf. A.S. Bernardo, 'The Selection of Letters in Petrarch's *Familiares*', *Speculum*, 35 (1960), pp. 280–8.

defence of the moral utility of poetry),[152] a collection of Cicero's own letters[153] and two manuscripts of Livy's history (which enabled Petrarch to construct the most complete version of Livy's *Ab Urbe Condita* to date).[154] Petrarch was also responding to the particular intellectual stimulus provided by the earlier Paduan humanism of Albertino Mussato and Lovato Lovati in the 1280s and 1290s, a milieu in which historiography and poetry had been regarded as literary and moral–didactic genres but also as instruments of political counsel and debate. Mussato had written a history of Henry VII of Luxembourg, for example, and had proffered Ezzelino da Romano as a cautionary historical *exemplum* of the clear and present danger embodied by Can Grande della Scala.[155] Viewed from the perspective of twelfth-century historiography, however, what is so striking about Petrarch's motivation in a work such as *De Viris Illustribus* is the conventional nature of so many of the principles which informed it. His written style may have been of a qualitatively different order to that of his predecessors, in other words, but the contents and inspiration of his historiography would not have been out of place two hundred years earlier.

In the preface to *De Viris Illustribus*, Petrarch spells out the goals for which it was written. Like Valerius Maximus, Petrarch states

---

152 Cicero, *Pro Archia*, trans. N.H. Watts (Loeb, 1923). For Petrarch's own defence of poetry against the charge of being useless and mendacious, see his *Invectiva Contra Medicum*; cf. Petrarch, *Rerum Familiarum Libri*, I.12, pp. 55–6.
153 Cicero, *Letters to Atticus*, ed. and trans. D.R. Shackleton Bailey (Loeb, 1999).
154 Livy, *Ab Urbe Condita*, trans. B.O. Foster, *et al.* (Loeb, 1919–59); cf. G. Billanovich, 'Petrarch and the Textual Tradition of Livy', *Journal of the Warburg and Courtauld Institutes*, 14 (1951), pp. 137–208; G. Billanovich, *La Tradizione del Testo di Livio e le Origini dell'Umanesimo: Tradizione e Fortuna di Livio tra Medioevo e Umanesimo* (Padua, 1981). For Nicholas Trevet's early fourteenth-century commentary on Livy (he also wrote commentaries on Boethius' *Consolation of Philosophy*, Augustine's *City of God*, Seneca's *Controversiae* and Seneca's *Tragedies*, as well as writing *Annals* of his own for the years 1135–1307 and a universal *Chronicle* from creation to the birth of Christ), see R.J. Dean, 'Nicholas Trevet, Historian', in J.J.G. Alexander and M.T. Gibson (eds), *Medieval Learning and Literature* (Oxford, 1976), pp. 328–52; R.J. Dean, 'The Earliest Known Commentary on Livy', *Medievalia et Humanistica*, 3 (1945), pp. 86–98; B. Smalley, *English Friars and Antiquity in the Early Fourteenth Century* (Oxford, 1960), pp. 58–65.
155 R.G. Witt, *'In the Footsteps of the Ancients': The Origins of Humanism from Lovato to Bruni* (Leiden, 2000), chs 3–4; cf. G. Billanovich, 'Il Petrarca e Gli Storici Latini', in *Tra Latino e Volgare. Per C. Dionisotti* (Padua, 1974), pp. 67–145.

that he had decided 'to collect, or rather almost to compress, the praise of the illustrious men who flourished with outstanding glory' but whose remembrance he had found spread far and wide in various volumes.[156] Like Livy's historical work, this assemblage of *exempla* was primarily intended to serve a moral–didactic purpose, because, 'through the remembrance of virtue, we censure vice'.[157] This, in Petrarch's opinion, was the profitable goal which defined the historian: 'to point up ... those things that are to be followed and those to be avoided, with plenty of distinguished examples provided on either side'. Petrarch's aim throughout, therefore, was to embody Cicero's prescription that history must be true, but also Horace's poetic combination of pleasure with utility. In both cases, however, the point was to avoid the mere accumulation of events in annals.[158] His own history would accordingly be characterised by brevity, clarity and order, rather than the sort of sterile diligence and curiosity which was produced when simply collecting everything in an exhaustive compilation.[159]

In one of his 'familiar' letters, Petrarch echoed similar goals, and a similar understanding of the relationship between rhetoric and the writing of history, when he set out to underline the authority of moral–didactic *exempla*, their particular combination of pleasure and utility, and the centrality of teaching, moving and pleasing to both demonstrative and deliberative rhetoric. Guidance taken from the illustrious examples of history, he argues, is the next best thing to being taught by the certainty of experience; it provides the pleasure gained from conversing with individuals in the past as if they were still alive; above all, it has the benefit of actually moving people to action. If, as Sallust observed, physical images possess the capacity to inspire the viewer to imitate the people whose material form they had represented before them,[160] then the example of their actual deeds will have a still greater effect, since such *exempla* provide, as it were, the images of their virtues.

---

156 Petrarch, *De Viris Illustribus*, preface, ed. B.G. Kohl, 'Petrarch's Prefaces to *De Viris Illustribus*', *History and Theory*, 13 (1974), p. 138; cf. pages 36–7.
157 *De Viris Illustribus*, pref., p. 138; cf. Livy, *Ab Urbe Condita*, I.pref., p. 7, VI.1, p. 195, XXI.1, p. 3, XXXI.1, pp. 3–5.
158 *De Viris Illustribus*, pref., p. 141.
159 *De Viris Illustribus*, pref., pp. 139–40, 143.
160 See pages 44–5.

Petrarch cites the case of Cicero emulating Demosthenes and Vergil following Homer, but he concludes his argument, revealingly, with the Augustine who 'burned to imitate', not just a saint, Antony of Egypt, but Marius Victorinus, the rhetorician (*Victorini rethoris ... exemplum*).[161]

Petrarch's interest in Livy contributed to a concerted effort in fourteenth-century Italy to recover and consolidate the history of Rome from the foundation of the city to the reign of Augustus. Petrarch's interest in Plutarch, meanwhile, helped prompt Coluccio Salutati and Leonardo Bruni to secure better and more complete Latin translations of the text of the *Lives* (a task which was finally realised in 1462) and thereby helped stimulate the vogue for individual 'biography' which became such a marked feature of fifteenth-century humanist historiography.[162] The intention which informed this approach to history, however, remained couched in traditional rhetorical terms. When the didactic values espoused by Petrarch were reiterated and reinforced by Salutati, for example, in a letter of the early 1390s, Salutati runs through the three branches of rhetoric – demonstrative, judicial and deliberative – showing how each of them revolves around a narrative of what has, or has not, been done. What is it, Salutati asks, that is brought forward for praise or blame except that which can be said to have been done with virtue or perpetrated with vice? What else is sought in judgment except the penalty or reward which is given deservedly for what has been done? What do we counsel through persuasion except what we think ought to happen, or not to happen, for private or public utility? Salutati may have gone on to lament the loss of those works of classical history which he knew only from the names provided by Aulus Gellius and the *Historia Augusta* (a loss he ascribes to either the neglect or the malevolence of an earlier age), but this was accompanied by a vigorous statement of the instruction, utility and pleasure which

---

161 Petrarch, *Rerum Familiarum Libri*, VI.4, pp. 314–17; cf. Augustine, *Confessions*, trans. H. Chadwick (Oxford, 1991), VIII.2.3–7.17, pp. 134–45; Otto of Freising, *Chronicle*, trans. C.C. Mierow (New York, 1928; reprinted 2000), IV.8, p. 287.
162 M. Pade, *The Reception of Plutarch's Lives in Fifteenth-Century Italy* (Copenhagen, 2007); R.G. Witt, 'Salutati and Petrarch', in S. Bertelli and G. Ramakus (eds), *Essays Presented to Myron P. Gilmore* (Florence, 1978), I, pp. 335–46.

are provided, in principle (and in a phrase deliberately chosen for its contradiction of Aristotle), by the *scientia rerum gestarum*.[163]

The remembrance of deeds, Salutati argues, is designed to ensure that exemplary virtues are imitated and thereby equalled or exceeded by posterity. Works of history form a branch of knowledge (*scientia*, once again, is the term which he uses) that advises rulers, teaches peoples and instructs individuals how to conduct themselves in public and in private; it tempers prosperity and consoles in adversity; it provides counsel; it shows the evil acts that should be shunned; and it provides the most reliable testimony of the good deeds that should be done. In fact, as a means of instruction in what is (or is not) morally virtuous and advantageous, histories are actually a better vehicle than the precepts of philosophy. Virtues and vices can be demonstrated with historical examples; so too can the fortunes of individuals and the rise and fall of kingdoms. There is no virtue or vice, indeed, no action, no warning, no ruse and no counsel which cannot be drawn from history and established with distinguished *exempla*. Salutati bases this argument, as indeed Henry of Huntingdon had done, on the authority of Cicero and Horace.[164] Knowledge drawn from history gives order to the present, he continues, but it also enables conjecture for the future. For this judgment, however, Salutati cites neither Cicero nor Horace, but Ecclesiastes 1:9–10: 'there is nothing new under the sun'. The goal of history, Salutati concludes, is not just an intellectual apprehension of what has happened in the past but the application and use of what has happened. This is the great benefit of narrating *exempla* – they will please people and move them to action, and in a way that subtlety, complexity and abstraction cannot. Scripture, Salutati points out, is no exception. Unlike other branches of knowledge,

---

163 Salutati, *Letters*, ed. F. Novati, *Coluccio Salutati Epistolario* (Rome, 1891–1911), Ep.VII.11, pp. 289–302; cf. Struever, *The Language of History in the Renaissance*, p. 98. More generally, see R.G. Witt, *Hercules at the Crossroads: The Life, Works and Thought of Coluccio Salutati* (Durham, 1983); R.G. Witt, 'In the Footsteps of the Ancients', ch. 7. In *c*.1402–03, Pier Paolo Vergerio issued a similar lament for the loss of Latin historical texts and a comparable plea for the utility of studying the subject: Pier Paolo Vergerio, *De Ingenuis Moribus et Liberalibus Adulescentiae Studiis Liber*, trans. C.W. Kallendorf, *The Character and Studies Befitting a Free-Born Youth*, in C.W. Kallendorf, *Humanist Educational Treatises* (Cambridge, MA, 2002), pp. 47–9.
164 Cf. page 241. Salutati also invokes Frontinus, *Strategemata* (see page 154, note 133).

in short, there is practically no intellect so obtuse or recalcitrant that it is incapable of understanding histories, that does not derive pleasure from the narration of such matters, and that cannot elicit from them either testimony of vices which should be avoided or examples of virtue to be imitated.[165]

Following in the footsteps of Petrarch and Salutati, it is the same moral–didactic tradition of historiography, finally, which informed the composition of Leonardo Bruni's official *History of the Florentine People*.[166] Completed in 1442 (and subsequently continued by Poggio Bracciolini before being translated into the vernacular in 1476), the classical models for this work were dominated, once again, by Livy's *Ab Urbe Condita*. Bruni's preface accordingly rehearses many of the familiar and conventional reasons why he should have embarked upon such a work. History is a source of great wisdom, he remarks, provided it is read correctly: 'for there the deeds and deliberations [*facta consiliaque*] of many ages may be scrutinised; from its pages we may learn with ease what behaviour we should imitate and avoid, while the glory won by great men, as therein recorded, inspires us to perform acts of virtue'.[167] Bruni proceeds to deploy the rhetorical techniques of arrangement (*dispositio*) and style (*elocutio*) in order to construct a history of the Florentine people in twelve books, six of which amounted to a rhetorical rewriting of the factual information contained in Giovanni and Matteo Villani's *Chronicle*.[168] What followed was a combination of admonition and castigation, a narrative of pivotal events in Florence (Giano della Bella's

---

165 Salutati, *Letters*, Ep.VII.11, pp. 289–302.
166 Leonardo Bruni, *History of the Florentine People*, ed. and trans. J. Hankins (Cambridge, MA, 2001–07); cf. B. Ullman, 'Leonardo Bruni and Humanistic Historiography', *Medievalia et Humanistica*, 4 (1946), pp. 45–61; reprinted in B. Ullman, *Studies in the Italian Renaissance* (2nd edn, Rome, 1955); D.J. Wilcox, *The Development of Florentine Humanist Historiography in the Fifteenth Century* (Cambridge, MA, 1969), pp. 1–128; Struever, *The Language of History in the Renaissance*; G. Ianziti, 'Leonardo Bruni – First Modern Historian?', *Parergon*, 14 (1997), pp. 85–99; G. Ianziti, 'Challenging Chronicles – Leonardo Bruni's History of the Florentine People', in S. Dale, A.W. Lewin and D.J. Osheim (eds), *Chronicling History: Chroniclers and Historians in Medieval and Renaissance Italy* (University Park, 2007), pp. 249–72.
167 Bruni, *History of the Florentine People*, pref., p. 3.
168 G. Ianziti, 'Bruni on Writing History', *Renaissance Quarterly*, 51 (1998), pp. 367–91.

Ordinances of Justice, Walter of Brienne, the Ciompi, the war with Lucca), with speeches arguing for and against the moral worth and practical advantage of particular courses of action.[169] Bruni's approach to the exemplary moral didacticism of the past clearly owed much to the historiographical tradition of demonstrative rhetoric which had been vigorously championed by both Petrarch and Salutati. It was the deliberative element in this approach, however, which gave his historiography its cutting edge and provided the immediate rationale for the composition of his *History*. In writing down the deeds of the Florentine people at home and abroad, in peace and at war, Bruni explicitly set up a parallel with the Roman people by comparing Florence's enemy, Sforza Milan, to 'another Carthage'.[170] Bruni's phraseology highlights the fact that his stylistic imitation of Livy was also designed to serve an immediate political purpose and, in particular, to acknowledge the force of the idea that the wars between Rome and Carthage had constituted a 'whetstone of virtue'.[171] Indeed, in this respect, Bruni's historiography was designed to contribute to a pressing diplomatic and military debate about the values of glory and territorial expansion.

Imitation of the models of historiography provided by Livy and Sallust presented fifteenth-century humanist historians with an agenda which was both literary and political. In the first instance, it meant that writers of history should concern themselves with a combination of domestic politics and foreign wars (*domus et militia*); it also meant couching their history within certain terms of interpretative analysis, the most prominent of which was the relationship between virtue and fortune, between what outstanding individuals could, and did, achieve, and what fortune or fate allowed them to do. Imitating *both* Livy *and* Sallust, however,

---

169 For example, Bruni, *History of the Florentine People*, I.32, p. 43, II.28–9, pp. 135–41, II.39, pp. 151–9, II.55, p. 163, II.69, pp. 177–81, II.88, pp. 199–205, XII.27–31, 33–7, pp. 279–91; cf. Bruni's 1405 preface to the Latin translation of Plutarch's life of Mark Antony, where he specifically rules out invention in the writing of history – see Wilcox, *The Development of Florentine Humanist Historiography*, p. 106; Ianziti, 'Bruni on Writing History', p. 374.
170 Bruni, *History of the Florentine People*, pref., p. 3.
171 Cf. pages 40, 68. For the influence of Sallust, see A. La Penna, 'Il Significato de Sallustio nella Storiografia e nel Pensiero Politico di Leonardo Bruni', in A. La Penna, *Sallustio e la 'Rivoluzione Romana'* (Milan, 1968), pp. 409–31.

affected more than just the form of historiography. Putting these two classical historians together also affected its contents, since pairing the substance of Livy and Sallust raised leading political questions. Both these authors had been historians of the Roman republic, after all, but they had produced strikingly different works. Livy's history was a monumental study of the origins of Rome, from the founding of the city (*ab urbe condita*), which charted the virtue and the love of liberty that had caused Rome's rise to greatness, then traced its preservation and transformation under the guiding hand of Fortune and, when republican institutions began to decline, through the virtues of the emperor Augustus (a point which was subsequently given even more explicit endorsement with the Latin translation of Appian's *Roman History* in the early 1450s).[172] Sallust's history, on the other hand, provided a much bleaker vision, a snap-shot of the Roman republic in decline, a political community whose original virtues had been corrupted by wealth and luxury and whose martial vigour had been sapped and softened by peace.[173] Livy's history of Rome was thus a celebration of liberty and virtue; Sallust's was a critique of a corrupt and factional republic on the brink (as it turned out) of being replaced by a principate. Put the two together and the result was a form of historiography which was concerned, not just with foreign wars and domestic politics, with virtue and fortune, but also with the nature of a republican government, with those qualities and institutions which made it flourish and with those qualities and institutions which would see it decline and decay. Put together in the immediate political context of the history of fifteenth-century Florence, in other words, the combination of Livy and Sallust embodied a historiographical analysis of acute contemporary relevance. The sharp polemical exchange between Poggio Bracciolini and Guarino da Verona on the relative merits of Scipio Africanus and Julius Caesar concentrated only on the most prominent of several possible examples. This was not so much a scholarly discussion of the relative virtues of republican

---

172 P.G. Walsh, *Livy: His Historical Aims and Methods* (Cambridge, 1961); T.A. Dorey (ed.), *Livy* (London, 1971); T.J. Luce, *Livy: The Composition of His History* (Princeton, 1977); C.S. Kraus and A.J. Woodman, *Latin Historians* (Oxford, 1997), pp. 51–81.
173 See pages 39–42.

and monarchical forms of governance as a political commentary on the politics of the northern Italian peninsula in the 1430s.[174] Bruni's *History of the Florentine People* was no exception and placed itself firmly within the same pragmatic terms of reference – this was historiography as a work of political counsel.

If a reason is being sought for why the impact on fourteenth- and fifteenth-century historiography of the empiricism of Aristotle's *Poetics*, and indeed of Aristotle's *Rhetoric*, was more muted than might have been expected, then the continuing vigour of the moral–didactic tradition of historiography provides one explanation. Any 'freeze' in the literary ambition, and academic status, of written histories seems therefore to have remained confined to certain scholastic quarters. Elsewhere, the writing of history, in theory and in practice, remained closely tied to the traditions of both demonstrative and deliberative rhetoric that continued to be championed by humanist writers, from Petrarch and Salutati through to Leonardo Bruni. All three of these writers were faithful to a medieval conception of historiography which had drawn on the same Latin tradition embodied in Cicero, Quintilian and the *Rhetorica ad Herennium*. Indeed, if the strength of this continuing relationship served as a powerful counterweight to Aristotelian particularism, then it also might explain the scholarly reaction to the rediscovery of another potentially critical Greek text, Lucian's essay on how to write history, when it, too, came into circulation, this time amongst humanist writers at the beginning of the fifteenth century.

It is, of course, always methodologically problematic to ask why certain texts, such as Aristotle's *Poetics*, do not get the reception which modern commentators might otherwise expect them to have had, but Lucian's summary of the methodology of history would seem to constitute a genuine case in point. Cicero, after all, had wondered out loud in *De Oratore* just why it was that no one had tried to assemble precepts of history-writing into a single set of rules and, *faute de mieux*, he had attempted to put one together,

---

174 J.W. Oppel, 'Peace *vs* Liberty in the Quattrocento: Poggio, Guarino and the Scipio–Caesar Controversy', *Journal of Medieval and Renaissance Studies*, 4 (1974), pp. 221–65. For the influence of Sallust on Poggio, see Wilcox, *The Development of Florentine Humanist Historiography*, pp. 130–69, and, for Poggio's deliberative rhetoric, pp. 167–9.

albeit very brief, himself.[175] As a self-contained work, composed in Greek in c.166 AD, Lucian's discussion would seem, *prima facie*, to fill precisely this historiographical gap, and at rather greater length. In the first half of the fifteenth century, a series of humanist scholars – Guarino da Verona, Poggio Bracciolini, Giovanni Aurispa (who brought the complete text of Lucian's works to Italy in 1423), Leon Battista Alberti and Lapo da Castiglionchio – all became very interested in Lucian and busily translated many of his works into Latin.[176] And yet, although Guarino da Verona and Lapo da Castiglionchio can be shown to have read Lucian's treatise on historiography, both scholars seemed content to leave it in Greek, excerpting its contents into letters of advice, rather than translating and transmitting it in its entirety. Why?

Lucian wrote his treatise in two parts. The first half is devoted to demonstrating what history is *not* and, for him, this meant explicitly distancing it, first, from demonstrative rhetoric (that is, from panegyric, where Lucian suggests that the sole priority is praise and pleasure, even to the extent of lying) and, secondly, from poetry (that is, from a form of writing whose rules extend as far as a licence to exaggerate and to invent fabulous and flattering material). To confuse history with poetry, he writes, is to make up a rugged athlete with the cosmetics of a courtesan. It is on this basis that Lucian maintains that those people who claim history should rest on a combination of pleasure and utility are, in fact, mistaken; it is utility alone which should guide the historian and this utility derives exclusively from truth. This is not to deny that pleasure may not be present in history at all. Lucian's point is that it should be an accidental by-product, not a primary goal. Elegance of style, he suggests, should therefore not be eschewed altogether, since all that would then be left is a flat, bare record of events, notes or commentaries of the sort that a soldier would record in a diary.[177] What really concerns Lucian is *excessive* praise, *completely* false and fabulous material, *exhaustive* descriptions of place, comprehensive and indiscriminate catalogues of *all* events,

---

175 See pages 136–7.
176 D. Marsh, *Lucian and the Latins: Humor and Humanism in the Early Renaissance* (Ann Arbor, 1998), ch. 1; cf. C. Robinson, *Lucian and His Influence in Europe* (London, 1979), pp. 81–95.
177 Cf. pages 63, 123.

trivial as well as important, vivid and self-indulgent depictions of what the author has never *actually* seen – it is thus as much a matter of degree as it is of substance but, with this qualification, the force of his opening critique is allowed to stand.

The second half of Lucian's work sets out the positive qualities required of the historian, most notably knowledge of political and military matters and, above all, independence of mind. Historians, he argues, should be free from both fear and expectation, such that their commitment to truth is placed above all other considerations, including those of self-interest, friendship, animosity and every personal and political affiliation. Such impartiality, Lucian writes, is exemplified by Thucydides, a historian who embodies the goal of writing a true account of what happened and for the benefit of posterity. A historian's style, Lucian continues, should be clear and measured and, in so far as it does become elevated or even poetic, will do so only in order to match the grandeur of its subject-matter. The mind of the historian, in short, should be like a mirror, in the sense that it should display what actually happened in the form that those events originally occurred, without any alteration and without any trace of distortion or cosmetics. With the exception of invented speeches, Lucian concludes, historians do not write on the same terms as orators; they are sculptors, not painters; what they have to say is in front of them and will be said because it has already happened; their task is simply to organise it and to shape it. Unlike orators, after all, historians do not have to seek the goodwill of their audience. All historians need to do is to make their readers teachable and attentive, and all they require to achieve that end is to concentrate on causality and to stress the utility and importance of what they are writing.[178]

Lapo da Castiglionchio began to read and translate various works of Lucian when he came to Florence as part of the papal curia in 1434. In 1437, however, in a letter to Flavio Biondo, he carefully adapts the content of Lucian's treatise, incorporating into his own guidance for the writing of history those elements

---

178 Lucian, *How to Write History*, trans. C.D.N. Costa, in *Selected Dialogues* (Oxford, 2005). For the earliest Latin translation, *Quomodo Historia Conscribenda Sit* (Bologna, 1507), see C. Ligota, 'Lucian on the Writing of History – Obsolescence Survived', in C. Ligota and L. Panizza (eds), *Lucian of Samosata Vivus et Redivivus* (London, 2007), p. 59.

which could be harmonised with the rhetorical tradition of historiography that could already be epitomised from Cicero's *De Oratore*. Like Lucian, Lapo stresses the utility of history and, like Petrarch and Salutati, he locates this benefit in the appeal of moral–didactic *exempla* to a wider group of people than would otherwise be able to comprehend, say, the self-referential subtleties of philosophy. In doing so, however, Lapo is also careful to pair such utility with pleasure, and in a way which strategically modifies Lucian's original – it is the combination which Lapo stresses, not the priority of one consideration over the other. History remains superior to poetry, and to painting, in that its moral–didactic *exempla* are true rather than made up, but otherwise Lapo appropriates for historiography the claims which had been made for the utility of poetry by Cicero's *Pro Archia*. Likewise, once again following Salutati, Lapo transfers to the writing of history many of the comprehensive claims for communicable knowledge which had been made for rhetoric by Cicero's *De Oratore* and Quintilian's *Institutio Oratoria* – the capacity of historiography to include material and approaches drawn from other disciplines is what makes it at once so distinctive and so useful in inspiring and guiding individuals towards a virtuous life. When Lapo comes to list the 'laws' which are incumbent upon writers of history, he therefore fuses the prescriptions of Lucian with those made by Cicero – an impartial commitment to the truth, but also an account of causes and motives, descriptions of place and speeches that will all make a historical narrative *probabilis*.[179]

Guarino da Verona was familiar with Lucian from an even earlier date than Lapo da Castiglionchio and had started translating a number of his works into Latin during a sojourn at

---

179 M. Regoliosi, '*Res Gestae Patriae e Res Gestae ex Universa Italia*: La Lettera di Lapo da Castiglionchio a Biondo Flavio', in C. Bastia and M. Bolognani (eds), *La Memoria e la Città: Scritture Storiche tra Medioevo ed Età Moderna* (Bologna, 1995), pp. 292–305; cf. M. Miglio, 'Una Lettera di Lapo da Castiglionchio', in M. Miglio (ed.), *Storiografia Pontificia del Quattrocento* (Bologna, 1975), pp. 33–59. For Lapo's life, see Vespasiano, *Memoirs*, trans. W. George and E. Waters, *Renaissance Princes, Popes and Prelates. The Vespasiano Memoirs: Lives of Illustrious Men of the XVth Century* (New York, 1963), pp. 424–5; C.S. Celenza, *Renaissance Humanism and the Papal Curia: Lapo da Castiglionchio the Younger's De Curiae Commodis* (Ann Arbor, 1999), ch.1. For Lapo's translations of Plutarch, see Pade, *The Reception of Plutarch's Lives*, pp. 269–306.

Constantinople between 1403 and 1408. It was only towards the end of his life, however, when teaching in Ferrara, that Guarino directly tackled Lucian's treatise on the writing of history. In a letter of 1446, to Tobias dal Borgo, his former pupil and recently-appointed historian to Sigismondo Malatesta at Rimini, Guarino picked up on many of the same themes which had been highlighted by Lapo and took as his starting-point the commemorative value of history that he found epitomised in Cicero's defence of poetry – according to *Pro Archia*, when Alexander the Great visited the tomb of Achilles, he commented on how fortunate the latter had been in finding Homer to proclaim his virtue.[180] In a clear echo of Lucian, Guarino then proceeded to distinguish the writing of history from both the exaggerated praise of individuals in panegyric and the falsehoods involved in poetry. For the truth of history, however, Guarino explicitly quotes, not Lucian, but Cicero. It is thus Cicero's commitment to the truth of history which he contrasts with the licence that Horace afforded both to poetry and to painting, a licence Guarino defines as excessive praise, invention of the fabulous, but also an approach which goes *beyond* what is plausible or verisimilar (*plusquam verisimilia*). Like Lucian, Guarino maintains that the first and only goal of history is its utility in making people both more knowledgeable and more disposed towards the life of virtue. However, whereas Lucian had invoked the analogy of a rugged athlete to point up the incongruity of cosmetics, Guarino chooses to accentuate Lucian's subsequent concession that exercise by athletes will often bring 'a pleasing colour' to their cheeks. Praise or blame are accordingly not prohibited in the writing of history; they should simply be introduced in moderation. Descriptions of place and circumstance should likewise not be self-indulgent, but extend only as far as is useful for the narrative of what was done – within

---

180 Cicero, *Pro Archia*, X.2.4, p. 33; Cicero, *Epistulae ad Familiares*, trans. D.R. Shackleton Bailey, *Letters to Friends* (Loeb, 2001), V.12, p. 165. The same episode was cited by Jerome, *Life of Hilarion*, trans. W.H. Fremantle, G. Lewis and W.G. Martley (Oxford, 1893), prol., p. 303 (see page 44, note 36); cf. Walter Map, *De Nugis Curialium*, V.prol., p. 405; Walter of Châtillon, *Alexandreis*, trans. D. Townsend (Philadelphia, 1996), I.549–78, p. 48; John of Salisbury, *Policraticus*, trans. J.B. Pike, *The Frivolities of Courtiers and the Footprints of Philosophers* (Minneapolis, 1938), prol., pp. 6–7: 'no one has ever gained permanent fame except as a result of what he has written or of what others have written of him'.

these limits, they make the narrative clearer and more certain. Guarino continues to echo those prescriptions of Lucian which dovetail with Cicero's *De Oratore*: history should be free from any partiality or enmity; it should be concerned with causes (*causae*), with the intentions which prompt actions (*consilia*) and with the results which follow from them (*eventus*). In contrast to Lucian, however, Guarino proceeds to demonstrate that historians do, in fact, share this commitment to causality with poets, and quotes both Vergil and Lucan to prove the point. Guarino completes his advice by aligning himself with Cicero's observation that it is not enough to say what was done, rather than how it was done, and, as a result, he concludes by invoking, not truth, but probability. It often happens, Guarino points out, that what should be commemorated is, in fact, incredible because it goes beyond what usually occurs or what is natural. In these cases, Guarino argues, the historian has to find a way of making those things probable (*probabile*), in this instance by using rhetoric and deploying the figure of speech known as prolepsis, or *praeoccupatio*, by means of which the doubts of the reader are explicitly acknowledged.[181]

The reaction of Lapo and Guarino to Lucian's critique of the relationship between rhetoric, poetry and the writing of history is very revealing. The way in which both these humanist scholars read his text indicates that they were concerned to elicit and to copy only as much as could be readily harmonised with the account of the nature and purpose of historiography with which they were

---

181 Guarino da Verona, *Letters*, ed. R. Sabbadini, *Guarino Veronese Epistolario* (Venice, 1915–19), Ep.796, pp. 58–63; cf. Ep.439, pp. 616–18; and, more generally, M. Regoliosi, 'Riflessioni Umanistiche sullo "Scrivere Storia"', *Rinascimento*, 31 (1991), pp. 8–16. For Guarino himself, see E. Garin, *Ritratti di Umanisti* (Florence, 1967), pp. 69–106; R. Schweyen, *Guarino Veronese* (Munich, 1973); however, see also A. Grafton and L. Jardine, 'Humanism and the School of Guarino – A Problem of Evaluation', *Past and Present*, 96 (1982), pp. 51–80. For the place of classical historians in Guarino's educational programme, see Battista Guarino, *De Ordine Docendi et Scribendi* (1459), ed. and trans. C.W. Kallendorf, *A Program of Teaching and Learning*, in C.W. Kallendorf, *Humanist Educational Treatises* (Cambridge, MA, 2002), pp. 269, 285–7. Taught alongside poetry and as part of grammar, students were to start with Valerius Maximus and Justin and 'then they should read the remaining historians in order, from whom they will excerpt the customs, manners and laws of various peoples, the various fortunes that befell individuals of genius and their vices and virtues. This practice is of great use in producing eloquence in daily speech and a reputation for prudence in a wide range of affairs'.

already familiar from Cicero. Set alongside the moral didacticism and political counsel which were so central to the composition of Bruni's historiography at more or less the same time (and, in Lapo's case, in the same place),[182] this would suggest that any Greek or Aristotelian 'derhetoricisation', or even 'depoeticisation', of the writing of history exercised a distinctly limited appeal. In the light of a taste for Plutarch's *Lives*, several of which (Theseus, Romulus, Solon, Publicola, Fabius Maximus, Aratus, Artaxerxes, Themistocles) Lapo himself had translated,[183] this was not an unnatural reaction. The excesses of panegyric and the licence of poetry certainly presented dangers which were well worth warning against but, just as it had done in the twelfth century, this did not necessarily require an abandonment of rhetoric altogether, rather than a recognition that historiography needed to negotiate and clarify its boundaries with care. Moving and pleasing did not have to exclude utility and truth; history did not have to restrict itself to annals; 'how' and 'why' remained just as important as 'what'; verisimilar argument was not necessarily the preserve of the fabulous and the false.

If the centrality of demonstrative and deliberative rhetoric to humanist historiography suggests the continuing strength of a medieval rhetorical tradition in the 'Renaissance' writing of history, or at least the recognition by some writers that history could not simply be separated (or be simply separated) from rhetoric and from poetry, a similar issue is raised by a second methodological feature which is often cited as a characteristic that is distinctive to fifteenth-century historiography. It is advertised, once again, in the preface to Leonardo Bruni's *History of the Florentine People*, where he points out that there are 'gaps and obscurities in our knowledge of certain times'.[184] Bruni states that he will make it his goal 'to relate what I think is the most correct tradition concerning the city's founding and its origins' and, as

---

182 For the relationship between Bruni, Alberti, Valla, Biondo and Lapo, see E.M. McCahill, 'Finding a Job as a Humanist – The Epistolary Collection of Lapo da Castiglionchio the Younger', *Renaissance Quarterly*, 57 (2004), pp. 1308–45.
183 C.S. Celenza, 'Parallel Lives – Plutarch's Lives, Lapo da Castiglionchio the Younger (1405–1438) and the Art of Italian Renaissance Translation', *Illinois Classical Studies*, 22 (1997), pp. 121–55.
184 Bruni, *History of the Florentine People*, pref., p. 3.

a result, warns that 'this will involve rejecting some popular and fabulous opinions' (*vulgaribus fabulosisque opinionibus*).[185] Although, as far as Bruni himself was concerned, his subsequent analysis of the various surviving sources for the foundation of Florence appears to have been a necessary conjectural excursus rather than the fundamental point of his narrative, it is this analytical aspect of his historiography which has sometimes been heralded as a departure from, or a transformation of, the critical method with which the writing of history was now being approached.

In purely formal terms, Bruni's interest in the origins of Florence clearly belonged to an existing, and longstanding, tradition of deliberative historiography that concerned itself with establishing the *origo gentis*.[186] Bruni's scholarly assessment of the historical evidence for these origins, however, took its cue, in part, from an awareness of the importance of the surviving material evidence from the classical past and of the means by which that evidence could now be understood and assessed. This material sensibility was exemplified, and extended, by Flavio Biondo, one of Bruni's students and the addressee of Lapo da Castiglionchio's letter. Biondo was not the first humanist to follow Petrarch's interest in the physical remains of classical Rome (Cyriac of Ancona had already started the trail), but his descriptions of what survived, principally in his *Roma Instaurata* (1443–46) and *Roma Triumphans* (1452–59), and the connection of this ancient past to contemporary history in his *Italia Illustrata* (1448–58), were to prove hugely influential. In the *Decades* (composed between 1439 and 1453), his history of the Roman Empire, Biondo also argued that the year 1410, the one-thousandth anniversary of the sack of Rome, marked a new period in the history of Italy which should be distinguished from the age 'in the middle' (*medium aevum*).[187] Leonardo Bruni's scholarly evaluation of the historical evidence owed less to Biondo, however, than to the development of techniques of philological criticism, which were epitomised in 1440 by Lorenzo Valla's demonstration that the

---

185 *History of the Florentine People*, pref., pp. 5–6.
186 See page 257.
187 D. Hay, 'Flavio Biondo and the Middle Ages', *Proceedings of the British Academy*, 45 (1960), pp. 97–128; reprinted in D. Hay, *Renaissance Essays* (London, 1988), pp. 35–63.

Donation of Constantine was a forgery.[188] This strand of textual scholarship and 'source criticism' was also applied by Valla to classical literature, in his *De Elegantiis Linguae Latinae* (1441), and to the Bible, in his *Collatio Novi Testamenti* (1442), but it was the specifically historiographical ramifications of his *Declamation on the Donation of Constantine* which makes Valla, even more so than Bruni, a test-case for what was, and was not, different or distinctive in the approach of Renaissance humanists to the act of writing history.[189]

Valla's analysis of the Donation of Constantine served a particular political purpose in 1440, in that it was designed to support Alfonso V, king of Naples, against pope Eugenius IV. First and foremost, however, it was a virtuoso exercise in judicial rhetoric. Proving the Donation to be a forgery required a demonstration of its philological inaccuracies and its terminological anachronisms, but the case also turned on an argument for the historical implausibility and rhetorical incongruity of such a testamentary deposition ever having been made on the part of both donor and beneficiary. Before Valla embarks upon his philological critique, he accordingly establishes the sort of person (*qualis*) who would have made, and received, such a donation, providing set-piece speeches for both the individuals concerned, emperor and pope, all as a means of establishing what would have been plausible (*verisimile*) in the historical circumstances of the fourth century. It was Valla's debt to the analytical approach of judicial rhetoric, therefore, just as much as his philological expertise, which made him acutely sensitive to the historical context within which the language and actions of the past had taken place.[190]

Valla's interest in the deliberative and judicial application of historiography did not stop at the Donation of Constantine. In 1445–46, he composed the deeds (*gesta*) of Alfonso's father, Ferdinand I, king of Aragon, and the prologue to this work

---

188 Lorenzo Valla, *Declamation on the Donation of Constantine*, trans. C.B. Coleman, *The Treatise of Lorenzo Valla on the Donation of Constantine* (Yale, 1922; reprinted Toronto, 1993); ed. and trans. G.W. Bowersock, *On the Donation of Constantine* (Cambridge, MA, 2007).
189 Cf. L.G. Janik, 'Lorenzo Valla – The Primacy of Rhetoric and the Demoralization of History', *History and Theory*, 12 (1973), pp. 389–404.
190 C. Ginzburg, *History, Rhetoric and Proof* (Hanover, 1999), ch. 2; cf. pages 187–9.

provided him with the opportunity to outline his own understanding of the relationship between history, rhetoric and poetry. Whilst it is unclear whether Valla had read Lucian, he had certainly read Aristotle's *Poetics* and *Rhetoric* and was, as a result, all too aware of the historiographical challenges presented by the philosopher's firmly empirical view of *exempla*. Valla used the prologue to his *Gesta Ferdinandi* to tackle Aristotle's charge of particularism from book IX of the *Poetics* head on.[191]

Valla's opening sentence emphasises not just the utility of history to the reader but also the difficulty involved in actually writing it. And yet, he writes, 'some philosophers, and not just any philosophers but the greatest and most ancient amongst them, have placed history beneath poetry on the grounds that poetry is closer to philosophy because it deals with what is general and sets down universal precepts on the basis of made-up *exempla*; Homer actually teaches people to become good and wise, whereas Thucydides merely narrates what Pericles did next'. Valla's response was to use his prologue to turn Aristotle's hierarchy of philosophy, poetry and history upside down, by comparing, first, poets to philosophers, then poets to historians and, finally, historians to philosophers. Like Salutati (and, indeed, like Henry of Huntingdon), Valla quotes Horace to the effect that poetry provides a greater incentive to virtue than any number of precepts put forward by philosophy – commanding others to do something, after all, reeks of arrogance and presumption, whereas people will readily submit to the same instruction through examples when they are struck by the desire to emulate the people they see depicted. Historians, however, not only have a claim to be chronologically prior to poets but, in addition to having the same goals of utility and pleasure, they also practise a discipline which is all the stronger for being more truthful. Aristotle was therefore simply wrong to claim that history does not deal with universal propositions, and Valla quotes Cicero to prove it: history has no other function than that it should instruct by means of *exempla*; it is witness to the ages, the light

---

191 Lorenzo Valla, *Gesta Ferdinandi Regis Aragonum*, ed. O. Besomi (Padua, 1973), proem., pp. 3–8; cf. C. Vasoli, 'Osservazioni sulle Teorie Umanistiche sulla Storiografia', *Nuova Rivista Storica*, 76 (1992), pp. 495–516; M. Regoliosi, 'Lorenzo Valla e la Concezione della Storia', in *La Storiografia Umanistica* (Messina, 1992), pp. 549–71.

of truth, the life of remembrance, the teacher of life, the herald of antiquity.[192] Speeches, testimony, praise, castigation and many other things, Valla continues, are all designed to teach universal precepts of wisdom. For Valla, therefore, the histories of Sallust and Livy contain more weight, more prudence and more political philosophy than the precepts of any philosopher; history, in fact, produces greater knowledge of the nature of things, of ethics and indeed of every branch of wisdom. Historians are thus superior to philosophers, both in principle and as authorities, a point which can be proven both from Scripture (Moses and the authors of the Gospels were all historians) and from Quintilian (the superiority of Romans to Greeks derived from the fact that they taught by example rather than by precept).[193]

Having demonstrated the moral and political utility of history, Valla then moves on to the second half of his opening statement – the difficulties involved in writing it. First of all, he argues, it requires care, insight and judgment to find out about something when it is the subject of so much disagreement; it is very rare for the same action or event to be narrated in the same way by several people, because different individuals have different reasons for demonstrating either ignorance or credulity; it is also hardly possible for one person to perceive with their five senses all the circumstances which surround a particular deed. A historian's investigation of the truth is, in this regard, an activity which, in epistemological terms, 'requires no less accuracy and wisdom than that which is shown by a judge or a doctor'.[194] The writing of history accordingly requires trustworthiness (*fides*) and application (*constantia*); it should be free from hope and fear, favour and envy. It is on this basis, Valla concludes, that historians should, in fact, be placed above both poets and philosophers in any hierarchy of the three disciplines. Valla's defence of historiography against Aristotle is resolute. In championing the forensic rigour and intellectual veracity which are required by historians, Valla could also not have been more explicit on the source of this

---

192 See page 242.
193 Cf. page 155.
194 Lorenzo Valla, *Gesta Ferdinandi*, proem., p. 7; cf. A. Momigliano, 'History Between Medicine and Rhetoric', in *Ottavo Contributo alla Storia degli Studi Classici e del Mondo Antico* (Rome, 1987), pp. 13–25.

integrity. The art of rhetoric, he states, is the mother of history (*mater historiae*), a filiation which is evident both from classical rhetoricians and from the books written by historians themselves.

Whilst the immediate impact of the *Gesta Ferdinandi* seems to have been itself geographically limited, the methodological principles which underpinned its composition were given a much wider airing by the characteristically intemperate humanist exchange that it precipitated with Bartolomeo Facio (a pupil of Guarino and a rival scholar at the Neapolitan court, whose surname Valla could not resist transliterating into Latin as *Fatuous*).[195] Facio complained that a historical narrative of events should be pure and minimally coloured and that any tropes and figures of speech should instead be reserved for that part of the text which deals with confirmation or refutation. It was his view, therefore, that Valla's *Gesta Ferdinandi* was a work, not of history, but of satire and tragedy. Valla's response was to accuse Facio of having read only the *Rhetorica ad Herennium* and Alan of Lille; had he also read *De Oratore*, *Orator* and the *Institutio Oratoria*, he might have realised that rhetorical ornamentation should be present *everywhere* in a historical narrative. Indeed, in the critique that follows, Valla effectively provides a running commentary on the precise relationship that should exist between rhetoric and historiography, in order to demonstrate why Facio had been so misguided with his criticism and especially with his repeated accusation that Valla's historical narrative had failed to display the key attributes of verisimilitude and brevity.

Valla vigorously defends the verisimilitude of his own historical narrative against the charge that the words, speeches and actions he had described were inappropriate to the people to whom they had been ascribed. Like Guarino and Lapo, Valla explicitly distinguishes writing *gesta* from composing a panegyric and he contrasts historical sincerity with the poetic licence of making things up. He also defends his judicious choice of witnesses (*testes*) on whose authority he had chosen to base part of his account. However, Valla also maintains that the use of digression is appropriate to history in the manner of poets (*more poetarum*); so too is

---

[195] Lorenzo Valla, *Antidotum in Facium*, ed. M. Regoliosi (Padua, 1981), especially book III, pp. 211–301; cf. Regoliosi, 'Riflessioni Umanistiche', pp. 16–27.

the deployment of *sententiae*, which had such a clear precedent in Sallust and Thucydides. His defence against the charge of prolixity is thus to produce extended quotations from both Cicero and Quintilian on the true nature of brevity – where no word is redundant but also where obscurity is avoided, where economy should not come at the expense of clarity or credibility, and where pleasure can make a long journey seem shorter.[196] Indeed, it is the issue of brevity, not verisimilitude, which prompts Valla to acknowledge the differences that *do* still exist between history and oratory, by quoting Quintilian and then Pliny on precisely this subject. According to the *Institutio Oratoria*, he states, history may drink from rhetoric like a smooth and pleasing juice, but it should also avoid some things which are considered virtues in oratory; history, in this respect, is closest to poetry and is like continuous verse; it is written to narrate, rather than to prove, and for the benefit of posterity, rather than the present day. Sallustian brevity and the milky fullness of Livy represent two stylistic extremes and, as such, both should both be avoided.[197] According to Pliny the Younger, meanwhile, history and oratory have many things in common, yet, in the midst of their apparent similarities, they also have several differences. Both are concerned with narrative but in different ways: oratory deals with the ordinary and the mean, history with the exceptional and the lofty; oratory is more often bones, muscles and nerves, whereas history is all flesh and display; oratory pleases most when it is forceful, sharp and immediate, history when it is shaped, mellifluous and even sweet; words, sound and periodisation are therefore different in each type of writing.[198]

Valla's sensitivity to the complexity of the relationship between rhetoric, poetry and the writing of history is intended to stand in stark contrast to the much more simplistic understanding which was demonstrated by Facio (and then exemplified in the latter's own *Deeds* of Alfonso V). This much might have been expected from a scholar who had started his public career by launching a

---

196 See page 321.
197 Quintilian, *Institutio Oratoria*, trans. H.E. Butler (Loeb, 1920–22), X.1.31–4, p. 21 (see pages 135–6).
198 Pliny the Younger, *Letters*, trans. W. Melmoth, rev. W.M.L. Hutchinson (Loeb, 1915), Ep. V.8, pp. 399–405.

comparison between Cicero and Quintilian and, as a consequence, a controversy with Poggio Bracciolini over his conclusions.[199] Viewed from a historiographical perspective, the combination of Valla's *Gesta Ferdinandi* and *Declamation on the Donation of Constantine* reveals an author who was highly attuned both to the demonstrative and the deliberative value of written history, but also to the judicial and forensic rigour with which it should always be pursued. At the same time, Valla's response to Facio's critique of his own venture into historiography also reveals an author who, whilst acknowledging the kinship of historiography to the compositional methods of both rhetoric and poetry, recognised that both rhetoric and poetry included narrative techniques that were, and should remain, distinct. In both instances, the depth and range of Valla's philological expertise and textual erudition marked a departure in terms of the quality of his historical writing but in neither case was the intention behind it revolutionary. In *c.*1450, history, rhetoric and poetry remained as closely intertwined and interrelated as they had done three hundred years earlier. Valla's treatise on the Donation of Constantine showed what could be done with a historical document by applying the forensic principles of judicial rhetoric. His *Gesta Ferdinandi* demonstrated the debt owed by historical narrative to the techniques of rhetorical verisimilitude. What is striking about his *Antidotum in Facium* is that it reflects an argument, not over whether to deploy rhetorical strategies in the course of writing history, but over how exactly this should be done. Valla is certainly prepared to acknowledge that rhetoric and the writing of history are not identical, but nor are they mutually exclusive, and they are certainly no more mutually exclusive than history and poetry, even though poetry had the licence to make things up. The similarity, and continuity, with the debates of the twelfth century is clear. The distinctions may have become more refined, the language of 'lies' and 'falsehood' may have been modified, but the categories within which the debate was conducted remained recognisably the same.

---

[199] J. Monfasani, 'Episodes of Anti-Quintilianism in the Italian Renaissance – Quarrels on the Orator as a *Vir Bonus* and Rhetoric as the *Scientia Bene Dicendi*', *Rhetorica*, 10 (1992), pp. 127–35; cf. J.O. Ward, 'Quintilian and the Rhetorical Revolution of the Middle Ages', *Rhetorica*, 13 (1995), pp. 245–7.

The final contention which is generally put forward to support the notion that there was some sort of paradigm-shift in the writing of history over the course of the fourteenth and fifteenth centuries is provided by the claim that Renaissance humanism developed a hitherto unprecedented sense of the past. From the moment Petrarch characterised the preceding age as one of 'darkness' or 'shadows' (*tenebrae*), it became possible, so it is argued, to view the historical past as a qualitatively different period, a time which should be differentiated from the present and, as such, in a manner that was quite distinct from a 'medieval' approach, which, it is alleged, simply moulded the past to fit its own standards and preoccupations.[200] A more modest, and perhaps more accurate, version of the same claim is that what changed was the way in which the past was represented.[201]

According to the principles of classical rhetoric, the moral-didactic value of writing about the past was held to depend upon using language appropriate to a particular audience in the present. In historiographical terms, this naturally meant avoiding anachronism and, as a result, translating ancient material into terms which would be comprehensible to the present.[202] As Macrobius put it, 'let us show in our lives the manners of the past, but speak in the language of our own day'.[203] With the development of the scholarly humanist philology exemplified by Valla (and after him Politian),[204] the language and grammar of ancient texts began to

---

200 P. Burke, *The Renaissance Sense of the Past* (London, 1969); cf. E. Garin, *Italian Humanism: Philosophy and the Civic Life in the Renaissance* (Oxford, 1965), pp. 7–9; E. Panofsky, *Renaissance and Renascences in Western Art* (Stockholm, 1960); T.E. Mommsen, 'Petrarch's Concept of the "Dark Ages"', *Speculum*, 17 (1942), pp. 226–42; R. Black, 'The New Laws of History', *Renaissance Studies*, 1 (1987), pp. 126–56.
201 Cf. G. Constable, 'Past and Present in the Eleventh and Twelfth Centuries – Perceptions of Time and Change', in *L'Europa dei Secoli XI e XII fra Novità e Tradizione: Sviluppi di una Cultura* (Milan, 1989), pp. 135–70; R. Vaughan, 'The Past in the Middle Ages', *Journal of Medieval History*, 12 (1986), pp. 1–14; D.R. Kelley, 'Clio and the Lawyers – Forms of Historical Consciousness in Medieval Jurisprudence', *Medievalia et Humanistica*, 5 (1974), pp. 25–49; reprinted in D.R. Kelley, *History, Law and the Human Sciences* (London, 1984); Carruthers, *The Book of Memory*, pp. 193–4; Coleman, *Ancient and Medieval Memories*, p. 455.
202 See page 296.
203 Macrobius, *Saturnalia*, I.5.1–3, p. 45; cf. Spiegel, *Romancing the Past*, pp. 101–6.
204 A. Grafton, 'On the Scholarship of Politian and Its Context', *Journal of the Warburg and Courtauld Institutes*, 40 (1977), pp. 150–88.

be historicised and contextualised and, as such, acknowledged to possess a temporal value of its own which could be separated from the use to which it was then put in order to support a moral or political goal. Within these terms of reference, in fact, a stylistic challenge was soon mounted against the slavish Atticism of those humanists who wanted to champion a fixed, prescriptive and ultimately ahistorical Latin.[205] One consequence of this heightened sensitivity to the evolution of language over time was that the historian's insistence on *enargeia*, on the priority of providing a vivid depiction of a past event for didactic purposes,[206] began to compete with other considerations, not least an appreciation of the importance of providing a temporal perspective on a particular historical text, respecting the time and the place in which an event originally occurred and the linguistic terms in which it was originally described. In one respect, this philological development was, once again, a matter of degree rather than substance – the *accessus ad auctores*, after all, had long ago insisted on the priority of such circumstantial contextualisation for the interpretation of classical and patristic texts; so too had the principles of judicial rhetoric for the evaluation of witnesses and wills.[207] Viewed from the perspective of fifteenth-century historiography, what was to prove crucial was the connection which could then be forged between this philological relativism and the appreciation of the particularism, rather than the generality, of the past. What *was* different, in other words, was the empirical view of *historia* which had been set out, not by Cicero, but by Aristotle.

Transformation of the way in which historical events came to be represented in writing in the course of the fifteenth century owed much to the way in which the centrality of *enargeia* to historiography also began to interact with the actual visual depiction of the past, in painting and (for Valla at least) in sculpture. Parallel developments in both historiography and art are perhaps only to be expected, given the way in which the composition and narrative content of a visual image had often served as a metaphor

---

205 Cf. Cicero, *Brutus*, trans. G.L. Hendrickson (Loeb, 1962), 82.284–84.291, pp. 247–55.
206 See pages 330–3.
207 See pages 126–8, 187–9.

for the writing of history.[208] It is certainly striking that, in both areas, attempts were made to develop a historical and a visual language which would reflect a sharpened philological recognition that events in the past had their own circumstantial context, their own form of expression. In both areas, however, it is equally striking that whether or not a contextualised or historicised form was replicated remained dependent on the purpose of the re-presentation of the events that was being made in a particular case.[209] A visual or literary depiction of the past, in other words, continued to be conditioned by the goal it was designed to serve, not by any innate temporal sensitivity on the part of the artist or writer who was producing it. As Valla's own historiographical output demonstrates, what remains so noteworthy is the length of time it took for historical relativism and particularism to influence the theory and practice of historiography as the *defining* characteristics of its truthfulness, rather than as qualities which could be accommodated within its existing classification as part and parcel of rhetoric. That development, when it did occur, was itself the result of a conjunction of a quite specific set of intellectual and historical circumstances.

Writing some fifty years after Lorenzo Valla, in the 1490s, Giovanni Pontano, humanist scholar and former chancellor at the court in Naples, could approach the writing of history within substantially similar terms of reference. He continued to echo Cicero's expression of surprise that the rules of history-writing had not been systematically arranged, and continued to produce commentary on the equivalence of poetry and historiography on the basis of Quintilian's classification of history as a prose song (*carmen solutum*).[210] By the 1490s, however, it is also clear that analysis of, and disagreement over, the exact nature of the

---

208 See pages 197, 200, 216, 311–12, 333–5, 367–8.
209 For history as a form of visual depiction, see, for example, A. Grafton, *Leon Battista Alberti: Master Builder of the Italian Renaissance* (London, 2001), ch. 4, and, for the relationship between rhetoric and painting, J.R. Spencer, 'Ut Rhetorica Pictura – A Study in Quattrocento Theory of Painting', *Journal of the Warburg and Courtauld Institutes*, 20 (1957), pp. 26–44; and, more generally, M. Baxandall, *Giotto and the Orators: Humanist Observers of Painting in Italy and the Discovery of Pictorial Composition, 1350–1450* (Oxford, 1971).
210 Giovanni Pontano, *Actius*, ed. C. Previtera, in *I Dialoghi* (Florence, 1943), pp. 192–239; cf. Paolo Cortesi, *De Hominibus Doctis*, cited by Wilcox, *The Development*

relationship between rhetoric, poetry and historiography was beginning to encounter a rather different approach. Pontano's dialogue on poetry and historiography was a largely conventional digest of principles that no longer reflected the way in which some people, at least, were now choosing to write their histories. This shift in practice, when it becomes fully apparent, is exemplified by the works of two authors who are otherwise often taken to mark the culmination of 'Renaissance' historiography – Machiavelli's *Florentine Histories* (written 1520–24) and Guicciardini's *History of Italy* (written 1537–40).[211]

Interpretation of the actual contents of Machiavelli's historiography has traditionally turned on the delicacy and ambivalence of his relationship to the Medici family. His *Florentine Histories* are no exception.[212] Indeed, they raise the question in its most acute form, given that this was a work which was actually commissioned by, and presented to, cardinal Giulio de' Medici. Methodologically at least, Machiavelli's preface to the *Florentine Histories* would seem to place his work firmly within a longstanding rhetorical tradition of moral–didactic historiography, of pleasure combined with utility in order to teach, move and entertain. 'If nothing else delights or instructs in history', he writes, 'it is that which is described in detail; if no other lesson is useful to the citizens who govern republics, it is that which shows the causes.... And if every example of a republic is moving, those which one reads concerning one's own are much more so and much more useful'.[213] What exactly the substance of those instructive and emotive *exempla* might be, however, is an altogether different matter and it is here

---

of *Florentine Humanist Historiography*, pp. 18–19. For the debate to which Pontano was contributing, see Black, 'The New Laws of History', pp. 130–42.

211 Machiavelli, *Florentine Histories*, trans. L.F. Banfield and H.C. Mansfield (Princeton, 1988); Guicciardini, *The History of Italy*, trans. S. Alexander (New York, 1969); cf. F. Gilbert, *Machiavelli and Guicciardini: Politics and History in Sixteenth-Century Florence* (Princeton, 1965), especially pp. 203–35; M. Phillips, 'Machiavelli, Guicciardini and the Tradition of Vernacular Historiography in Florence', *American Historical Review*, 84 (1979), pp. 86–105.

212 J.M. Najemy, 'Machiavelli and the Medici – The Lessons of Florentine History', *Renaissance Quarterly*, 35 (1982), pp. 551–76; cf. F. Gilbert, 'Machiavelli's *Istorie Fiorentine* – An Essay in Interpretation', in M.P. Gilmore (ed.), *Studies on Machiavelli* (Florence, 1972), pp. 73–99; reprinted in F. Gilbert, *History: Choice and Commitment* (Cambridge, MA, 1977).

213 Machiavelli, *Florentine Histories*, pref., p. 6.

that Machiavelli's text becomes at once more problematic and more revealing.

Machiavelli's first foray into history-writing had taken place a decade earlier than the *Florentine Histories* and in the particular form of a commentary on the first ten books of Livy's *Ab Urbe Condita*. In the preface to these *Discourses*, Machiavelli had already given a clear indication of where he stood with regard to the tradition of fifteenth-century humanist historiography. Considering how much honour is attributed to antiquity, Machiavelli writes, considering how much is revealed by ancient historians to have been achieved by virtuous individuals, by kings, generals, citizens and lawgivers, he professes himself as amazed as he is saddened by the fact that people's attitude to these examples was simply to admire rather than to imitate. 'The example of the ancients', he writes, 'will show you how to organise republics, maintain states, govern kingdoms, institute a citizen militia, and conduct a war', and yet the deliberative counsel provided by these classical examples was not being put into practice by his contemporaries. Why not? For Machiavelli, it is the result, quite simply, of a failure to possess 'a true understanding of those histories'.[214] It is not the historiographical principles which are at fault, in other words, but the failure to learn from, and indeed to be taught, the correct examples and, as a consequence, an inability to put those examples into practice. This, then, is the task on which Machiavelli is going to embark in the *Discourses* – he will establish a true understanding of those ancient histories. In the process, he will make use of the same material, the same historiographical conventions, as his humanist predecessors, but he will deploy them to real, practical effect.

Perhaps the most significant of Machiavelli's didactic lessons from the past was the relationship between a course of action which is morally worthy (*honestum*) and a course of action which is advantageous (*utile*), a relationship which, according to classical and medieval manuals on rhetoric, lay at the heart of deliberative counsel. Speaking for or against a course of action in a political assembly demanded an analysis of the extent to which a proposed action was morally worthy and the extent to which it

---

214 Machiavelli, *Discourses on Livy*, trans. J.C. Bondanella and P. Bondanella (Oxford, 1997), pref., pp. 15–16.

was advantageous; above all, however, it demanded consideration of which of these two criteria should be given the greater weight at a time, and in circumstances, which made such action both necessary and practicable.[215] When Machiavelli made these criteria central to his own studies in 'war and the governance of the *res publica*',[216] that is, in his works of political advice (the *Prince*) and historical commentary (the *Discourses*), he was therefore participating in a longstanding debate over the practical relationship between the terms *honestum* and *utile*. What Machiavelli did was, quite simply, to exploit the twin considerations of necessity and practicability in order to turn the argument of Cicero's *De Officiis* on its head. According to Machiavelli, what is morally virtuous can, in certain circumstances, be positively disadvantageous. In taking a political course of action, therefore, an individual should always be guided first by what is advantageous and by what is necessary; this comes before any consideration of what is morally worthy. As a result, Machiavelli makes a point of redefining what virtue is – in his view, what is advantageous is what is virtuous, and not, as Cicero had maintained, the other way around. What constitutes a virtuous or successful action is therefore conditioned, even determined, by the practical political circumstances in which it is performed.

Much has, of course, been written on the particular political and personal circumstances which prompted Machiavelli to put forward such a stark prescription for political success.[217] As a conceptual possibility, it had clearly always been present in deliberative rhetoric and, as a practical recommendation, it had at least one historical precedent, in Lucan's account of the advice

---

215 See pages 230–7. For deliberative rhetoric in the *Florentine Histories*, see B. Richardson, 'Notes on Machiavelli's Sources and His Treatment of the Rhetorical Tradition', *Italian Studies*, 26 (1971), pp. 36–48; for *The Prince*, see J.F. Tinkler, 'Praise and Advice – Rhetorical Approaches in More's *Utopia* and Machiavelli's *Prince*', *Sixteenth Century Journal*, 19 (1988), pp. 187–207; V. Cox, 'Machiavelli and the *Rhetorica ad Herennium* – Deliberative Rhetoric in *The Prince*', *Sixteenth Century Journal*, 28 (1997), pp. 1109–41; and, more generally, M. Viroli, *Machiavelli* (Oxford, 1998), pp. 75–113.
216 See page 469.
217 Q. Skinner, *Machiavelli* (Oxford, 1981); cf. A.H. Gilbert, *Machiavelli's Prince and its Forerunners:* The Prince *as a Typical Book De Regimine Principum* (2nd edn, New York, 1968).

given to Ptolemy of Egypt.[218] Viewed in specifically historiographical terms, however, the attention paid to the particular demands of utility and circumstance reflects a broadening of Machiavelli's classical perspective, away from the canonical examples of Livy and Sallust[219] and towards the alternative models which were now provided by the histories of Polybius and Tacitus.

Writing in the mid-second century BC, Polybius had set out to explain to his fellow Greeks 'by what means, and under what system of government, the Romans succeeded in less than fifty-three years [220–167 BC] in bringing under their rule almost the whole of the inhabited world, an achievement which is without parallel in human history'.[220] Thirty books followed on 'the formation and growth of the Roman Empire', subsequently extended by a further ten books in order to accommodate the years 167–146 BC (ostensibly as a means of analysing just how well Rome had proceeded to use that power and therefore whether it should be welcomed or rejected by his contemporaries, and indeed praised or condemned by succeeding generations).[221] Leonardo Bruni had used books I–II of Polybius in 1420 in order to supplement what had been lost from Livy in his own account of the First Punic War, but it was the Latin translation of the first five books which was made in the early 1450s (with a printed edition appearing in 1473) that gave Polybius' *Histories* a much wider audience still.[222] Indeed, of the series of translations of Greek historians which were commissioned in this decade by pope Nicholas V (Polybius from Niccolò Perotti, Thucydides and Herodotus from Lorenzo Valla, and Appian from Pier Candido

---

218 See pages 293–40. For an emphasis on the distinction between *tutum* and *laudabile*, rather than between *honestum* and *utile*, see Cox, 'Machiavelli and the *Rhetorica ad Herennium*'.
219 J.H. Whitfield, 'Machiavelli's Use of Livy', in T.A. Dorey (ed.), *Livy* (London, 1971), pp. 73–96; Q. Skinner, 'Machiavelli's Discorsi and the Pre-Humanist Origins of Republican Ideas', in G. Bock, Q. Skinner and M. Viroli (eds), *Machiavelli and Republicanism* (Cambridge, 1990), pp. 121–41.
220 Polybius, *Histories*, trans. I. Scott-Kilvert, *The Rise of the Roman Empire* (Harmondsworth, 1979), I.1, p. 41; cf. III.1, p. 178, VI.2, p. 302; and, more generally, F.W. Walbank, *Polybius* (Berkeley, 1972).
221 Polybius, *Histories*, II.2, p. 112, III.4, p. 181.
222 *Historiae Polybii Libri Quinque* (Rome, 1473). See B. Reynolds, 'Bruni and Perotti Present a Greek Historian', *Bibliothèque d'Humanisme et Renaissance*, 16 (1954), pp. 108–18.

Decembrio), it was the work of Polybius that appears to have registered the deepest methodological impact.[223]

As a vigorous restatement of Thucydides' insistence that politics and war should be the chief subject matter of history-writing, there was much in Polybius' approach which would already have been familiar to a fifteenth-century readership brought up on the *domus et militia* of Livy. The study of history was, in itself, a moral and political education, and the lessons of the past provided useful guidance and instruction for the conduct of both private and public affairs. As Polybius himself put it, right at the start of his work, 'there is no easier path to an education in life than a knowledge of deeds done in the past'.[224] 'The person who is willing to consider these things correctly', he states, 'will find many things which are most useful for the betterment of human life'. Given that there are clearly two ways in which people can reform themselves, either by learning from their own errors or by learning from those of others, it seemed preferable to Polybius for people to avoid the danger and pain of the former in favour of the safety of the latter: 'for this reason, when considered correctly, the best education for real life [*ad veram vitam*] would seem to consist of the experience we acquire from the remembrance of deeds done by others because it makes us the best judges of what is the truly good [*veri boni*] without causing us any harm'.[225] Such moral didacticism was, in part, a legacy of the classical commemoration of the deeds of one's ancestors, just as the virtues and achievements of the dead were recalled to an audience's mind in the ritual of a Roman funereal oration, 'brought before their eyes', as an incentive to

---

223   E.B. Fryde, 'Some Fifteenth-Century Translations of Ancient Greek Historians', in E.B. Fryde, *Humanism and Renaissance Historiography* (London, 1983), pp. 99–102; A. Momigliano, 'Polybius' Reappearance in Western Europe', in E.Gabba (ed.), *Polybe* (Geneva, 1974), pp. 345–72; reprinted in A. Momigliano, *Sesto Contributo alla Storia degli Studi Classici e del Mondo Antico* (Rome, 1980), vol. I, pp. 103–23, and A. Momigliano, *Essays in Ancient and Modern Historiography* (Oxford, 1977), pp. 79–98. For Thucydides, see P.O. Kristeller, F.E. Cranz, V. Brown, *et al.* (eds), *Catalogus Translationum et Commentariorum: Medieval and Renaissance Latin Translations and Commentaries* (Washington, DC, 1960–), vol. VIII, pp. 103–81. For the wider intellectual context, see J.F. D'Amico, *Renaissance Humanism in Papal Rome: Humanism and Churchmen on the Eve of the Reformation* (Baltimore, 1983); C. Stinger, *The Renaissance in Rome* (Bloomington, 1985).
224   Polybius, *Histories*, I.1, p. 41; cf. III.21, p. 199, III.31, p. 207.
225   *Histories*, I.35, pp. 79–80; cf. page 153.

perform similar actions of their own. 'By this constant renewal of the good report of brave men', Polybius comments, 'the fame of those who have performed any noble deed is made immortal'.[226] For Polybius, however, it also constituted an object-lesson in how to deal directly with both prosperity and adversity. This meant that his *Histories* would express the true test of virtue (that is, 'the capacity to bear with spirit and dignity the most complete transformations of fortune'),[227] but would also make them a trustworthy source of consolation ('the only effective method of being taught how to bear the vicissitudes of fortune with equanimity is to learn from the examples of disasters suffered by others').[228]

For the methodology which underpinned this moral and political instruction, Polybius appealed first and foremost to the principle of causality, the aetiology by which history could be distinguished from a mere narrative of events and through which people could learn what they should do in a given situation. 'The particular aspect of history which both attracts and benefits its readers', he argues, 'is the examination of causes, and the capacity (which is the reward of this study) to decide in each case the best policy to follow'.[229] To establish 'when' and 'by what means' something happened must, in his opinion, always be accompanied by the question 'why', because the latter provides the basis of any moral evaluation: 'our first judgment of good and evil is decided in every case, not by the actions themselves, but by the purpose and intention [*finis et intentio*] of those who perform them'.[230] For Polybius, this had the quite practical consequence of making it vitally important for his narrative to distinguish between a beginning [*principium*] and a cause [*causa*]: 'the word "beginning" I shall use to refer to people's initial actions in matters which have already been judged and deliberated upon; and the word "cause" to what precedes judgment and deliberation, that is, those factors which make us judge and deliberate in this manner, namely thought [*cogitationes*], counsel [*consilia*], reasoning [*ratiocinationes*],

---

226 *Histories*, VI.53, pp. 346–7.
227 *Histories*, VI.2, p. 302.
228 *Histories*, I.1, p. 41; cf. pages 77–80.
229 *Histories*, VI.2, p. 302.
230 *Histories*, II.56, p. 169.

and other things of this sort'.[231] As a result, in Polybius' view, 'by far the most important part of history lies in considering those things which preceded a series of events, those which followed them, and, above all, those which pertain to their causes'.[232]

Causation, however, was far from being a straightforward intellectual or historiographical exercise. Much of the methodological force of Polybius' *Histories* stemmed from an awareness of the epistemological difficulties which could be caused by the disjunction between appearance and reality. In distinguishing a cause from a beginning, for example, Polybius was keen to give equal weight to what he termed a 'pretext' or occasion (*occasio*), an explanatory category which, he pointed out, could be in defiance of the real reason why people did things.[233] He was also well aware of the demands of political expediency which might make the pretext more evident than the cause: 'kings do not look on anyone either as an enemy or a friend on account of their nature, but measure friendship or enmity in terms of the advantage [*commodum*] they bring'. As a result, it could prove necessary for someone 'not only to reveal his counsel to no one, but also to do and say many things which were at variance with his real opinion and so suggest the opposite of what he was striving towards'.[234] Such an acknowledgment also prompted a complex and, at times, ambivalent attitude to the role of fortune, an agency which Polybius sometimes credits with directing the affairs of this world as if it were the theatre or the games,[235] but which he could also use as shorthand for an unexpected or unpredictable turn of events.[236] Alternatively, it could simply be dismissed altogether: 'it would be very stupid to assert that this was done through fortune; we must rather seek the cause of such a thing since, without a cause, none of those things which occur through reason, or seem to be done beyond reason, can be completed'.[237] Causal argumentation thus remained key

---

231 *Histories*, III.6, p. 184.
232 *Histories*, III.32, p. 208.
233 *Histories*, III.7, p. 185; cf. III.15, p. 192.
234 *Histories*, II.47, p. 159.
235 *Histories*, I.4, p. 44, I.58, p. 103; cf. II.70, p. 176, III.118, p. 275.
236 *Histories*, II.4, p. 114, II.7, p. 117; cf. pages 271–4.
237 *Histories*, II.38, pp. 149–50.

to Polybius' understanding of what the writing of history should involve:

> I believe that those who write histories and those who are concerned with reading them ought to concentrate their attention, not so much on the deeds, as on what preceded them and what followed them. For if we remove from history the analysis of what, where, and for what purpose actions were done, and what was their result, what is left is a sort of competitive display, not a lesson [*veluti contentio quaedam non doctrina*], and this, although it may perhaps be a source of some pleasure in the present, is of no benefit to human life in the future.[238]

For all its emphasis on moral didacticism, counsel, consolation and causality, there were clearly aspects to Polybius' approach to the writing of history which would have struck a rather different note from the historiography with which earlier fifteenth-century historians had hitherto been familiar. In Polybius' eyes, much of what was cogent and distinctive about his own work was provided by its universal scope. He was therefore explicit in claiming to improve upon existing historical narratives by drawing together particular accounts which had been written of individual episodes in separate parts of the world – in Italy, Africa, Asia and Greece: 'while various historians have dealt separately with particular wars and the things done in each of them, nobody up to the present day has attempted, so far as I am aware, a universal and conjoined account of what was done, when it began, whence it originated, how it was done, and what was the result'.[239] By integrating such isolated histories into a systematic and organic whole, Polybius sought not only to relate these discrete histories to one another but also to compare them: 'it is only by combining things ... and noting their resemblances and differences, that we shall arrive at an awareness and knowledge of the whole'.[240] Indeed, this was one of the reasons why he suggested that, rather than tackle shorter narratives of individual episodes, a reader would actually find it easier to ready all forty books of his *Histories*: 'by comparing simultaneous events with one another, the truth

---

238 *Histories*, III.31, p. 207.
239 *Histories*, I.4, p. 44; cf. I.3, p. 43, II.37, p. 148.
240 *Histories*, I.4, p. 45; cf. I.13, p. 54.

can be discerned much more clearly'.[241] The originality of such comparative history may have resonated a little less forcefully with those amongst his fifteenth-century readers who had been brought up on the universalism of Orosius, but the substance of Polybius' second claim to distinction was a quite different matter, since the first five books of the *Histories* were also punctuated by repeated criticism of the distortions to which the discipline of history had been subjected through the application of literary, and specifically rhetorical, techniques.

Polybius did not think that reading history should be tedious or unenjoyable. Precisely the opposite. It is to a combination of pleasure and utility that he frequently appeals as its defining value.[242] However, this did not extend to the inclusion of material which Polybius believed to be more germane to tragedy and to fable. In the first instance, this criticism is applied to those writers who introduced graphic scenes into a narrative in order to arouse pity and enlist sympathy from their audience. One historian, Polybius points out, 'reproduces this kind of effect again and again in his history, striving on each occasion to recreate the horrors before our eyes [*ante oculos*]'.[243] Visualisation nonetheless clearly had a place in the narration of events: 'the battlefield proved truly terrible and marvellous, not only by sight to those who were actually present, but also by report to the others who heard about it afterwards'.[244] However, the extremes to which it had been taken by some writers was completely alien to what Polybius considered to be the nature and utility of historiography. Likewise with the use, and abuse, of topography. The physical description of place and circumstance played an important role in Polybius' narrative, but it was also one which he believed needed to be handled with some restraint in order to prevent a geographical excursus from becoming an ill-advised interruption and distraction. Indeed, he writes, 'those readers who insist on such topographical digressions at every point fail to understand that they are acting like the type of gourmand [*gulosus*] at a dinner who samples everything on the table at once and, as a result, is able to derive neither pleasure at

---

241 *Histories*, III.32, p. 208.
242 For example, *Histories*, I.4, p. 45, III.4, p. 181.
243 *Histories*, II.56, p. 168.
244 *Histories*, II.28, p. 139.

the time nor benefit in the future.... Those who treat history in this fashion likewise receive no true pleasure at the moment of reading, nor do they retain any benefit for the future'.[245] Such depictions could also provide yet another temptation to engage in competitive display. In Polybius' view, this had certainly proved to be the case with Hannibal's crossing of the Alps. 'Some of the writers who have reported this crossing', he suggests, 'through their desire to instil fear into the minds of their readers with descriptions of the scale of the achievement, have not noticed that they have fallen into the two vices which are most alien to the law of history, namely to write things that are false and things that are clearly self-contradictory'.[246] The same criticism also applied, finally, to the introduction of invented speeches, and in a manner which (as Niccolò Perotti pointed out in the *proemium* to his Latin translation) directly echoed the criticism originally voiced by Pompeius Trogus.[247] When news of Hannibal's capture of Saguntum arrived in Rome, for example, Polybius was drawn to observe that 'there was no debate in the senate on the question of whether or not to go to war, as some people have written, adding the reasons and causes which compelled people to adopt views on both sides'. 'What could be more inconsistent or incredible?', Polybius asks. 'All these things are neither true nor plausible [*neque vera sunt neque verisimilia*].... This would seem to be, not so much history, as old-wives' tales [*fabulae anicularum*], similar to what is generally recounted at the barber's [*in tonstrinis*]'.[248]

Polybius' views on the relationship between rhetoric and the writing of history were cut from the same cloth as those of Lucian but, in his case, they were supported by a demonstration of the form which such historiography should actually take in practice. 'It is not fitting', Polybius concludes, 'for historians [*scriptores rerum gestarum*] to move people's emotions, nor should they try to search out speeches which are suitable for the occasion [*oratio apta*], nor to rail at the calamities of mortal beings as writers of tragedies do'. Instead, the historian should 'recount truthfully the words and deeds of humans [*dicta factaque hominum vere*

---

245 *Histories*, III.57–8, pp. 229–30.
246 *Histories*, III.47, p. 220.
247 See page 87.
248 *Histories*, III.20, p. 197.

referre], however unremarkable they may be'.[249] The result, from Polybius' perspective, was a fundamental difference in purpose:

> the goal of tragedy is not the same as that of history but clearly the contrary. The tragic poet seeks to thrill and charm his audience for the moment by expressing through his characters the most plausible words possible, but the historian's task is to strive with all his powers to recount truly the words and deeds of people for committed readers.... For the former, it is all about presenting verisimilar things in order that the spectator may be more easily deceived, but for the latter it is all about presenting true things in that what is written is for the benefit of the reader.[250]

Polybius' opposition of probability to truth, of deception to utility, and his critique of the strategic use of *enargeia*, *descriptio loci* and *sermocinatio*, were all part and parcel of his demonstration of the trustworthiness (*fides*) of his own writings.[251] This went beyond the more conventional criticism of writers who had failed to report the truth as they should because of partisan zeal or favour: 'once a man takes up the task of writing history, he must moderate all considerations of this kind ... because, just as if a living creature is deprived of its eyes the remainder of its body is useless, so if history is deprived of the truth its entire narrative is useless'.[252] As with his criticism of untrustworthy witnesses to geographical truth, Polybius' goal was that 'we should not be obliged by lack of knowledge to listen in the manner of children [*more puerorum*], but that, being in possession of some elements of the truth, we may discern the truth or falsity of what is being narrated'.[253] Such concerns extended even to apparently authoritative historians, where Polybius exhorted his readers to concentrate, not so much on the author themselves, as upon the deeds narrated (*series rerum gestarum*): 'my opinion is that we should certainly have belief [*fides*] in an author on many matters

---

249 *Histories*, II.56, p. 168; cf. XII.25, p. 440.
250 *Histories*, II.56, p. 168; cf. III.48, p. 221.
251 *Histories*, III.33, p. 210.
252 *Histories*, I.14, p. 55; cf. XII.12, p. 432. The avoidance of partisan favour or enmity was the one methodological principle from Polybius which Leonardo Bruni explicitly echoed in the preface to his own account of the First Punic War, *De Primo Bello Punico* (Pairs, 1512), in 1420.
253 *Histories*, IV.42, p. 287.

but this does not mean that they should be believed in absolutely everything; consideration should be given instead to what agrees with the nature and quality of the facts themselves'.[254] For a fifteenth-century readership, an overarching concern with the moral and political didacticism of historiography may have prevented Polybius from completely endorsing Aristotle's emphasis on the particularism of history, but his sustained attack on 'tragic' historians took Lucian's methodological invective to a different level of scholarly endeavour. Reading Polybius carried a trenchant warning against the inappropriate use of rhetoric but also a powerful model of how this could be avoided in practice.

Although Tacitus, unlike Polybius, had been available from well before the beginning of the fifteenth century,[255] he seems to have exerted little influence on the conception and practice of historiography in the Middle Ages, at least when compared with Sallust and (especially from the fourteenth century) with Livy, authors who remained the dominant classical paradigms for the writing of prose history in this period.[256] Where Tacitus was read, there was certainly much in his approach which would have served as a reprise of themes that were already familiar from other sources. According to Tacitus, for example, the writing of history should be concerned with committing events to the remembrance of posterity and, as such, with securing the reputation of individuals: 'I consider a historian's foremost duty is to ensure that virtue is not silenced and to confront evil deeds and words with the fear of

---

254 *Histories*, III.9, pp. 186–7.
255 L.D. Reynolds (ed.), *Texts and Transmission: A Survey of the Latin Classics* (Oxford, 1983), pp. 406–11; Kristeller, *et al.* (eds), *Catalogus Translationum et Commentariorum*, vol. VI, pp. 87–174; cf. R. McKitterick, *History and Memory in the Carolingian World* (Cambridge, 2004), pp. 40–2; R. McKitterick, *Charlemagne* (Cambridge, 2008), pp. 17–20. For Tacitus in the fifteenth and, above all, in the sixteenth centuries, see P. Burke, 'Tacitism', in T.A. Dorey (ed.), *Tacitus* (London, 1969), pp. 149–71; K.C. Schellhase, *Tacitus in Renaissance Political Thought* (Chicago, 1976); D.R. Kelley, 'Tacitus Noster – The *Germania* in the Renaissance and Reformation', in T.J. Luce and A.J. Woodman (eds), *Tacitus and the Tacitean Tradition* (Princeton, 1993), pp. 152–7.
256 For Livy, see page 482, note 154; for Sallust, see Kristeller, *et al.* (eds), *Catalogus Translationum et Commentariorum*, vol. VIII, pp. 183–326; P.J. Osmond, 'Princeps Historiae Romanae – Sallust in Renaissance Political Thought', *Memoirs of the American Academy in Rome*, 40 (1995), pp. 101–43.

posterity's denunciation'.[257] Such commemoration, as illustrated by Tacitus' eponymous epideictic account of his father-in-law Agricola, could serve an exemplary moral–didactic purpose.[258] It could also fulfil the explicitly deliberative function of giving guidance on appropriate courses of political action: 'few people have the prudence to distinguish what is right [*honesta*] from what is wrong, what is expedient [*utilia*] from what is harmful; most people are taught by the experience of others'.[259] The surviving books of Tacitus' *Histories* and *Annals* accordingly interspersed a narrative of political and military activity with speeches, vivid descriptions and a series of pithy epigrammatic *sententiae*, whilst Tacitus' *Germania* provided a lesson in martial (and marital) virtue and a case-study in ethnography.[260] This was historiography which promised, once again, to be free from both commitment (*studium, amor*) and animosity (*odium*), and to be devoted to describing, not just what happened and its outcome (*casus eventusque rerum*), but the reasons and causes behind it (*ratio ... causaeque*).[261]

For all this ostensible familiarity, however, Tacitus proved a much more problematic and elusive historian when it came to the actual substance of what he was writing, namely a narrative of events in Rome under the successors of Augustus between 14 and 96 AD, when the causal relationship between liberty and virtue had been broken and a republican façade of senatorial governance served to conceal the reality of monarchical rule: 'savage edicts, repeated accusations, treacherous friendships, innocent people ruined, always for the same reasons – a path choked by monotony and satiety'.[262] Like Sallust, and like Livy, Tacitus was well aware of the corrupting effects of peace and wealth, particularly on a

---

257 Tacitus, *Annals*, trans. J. Jackson (Loeb, 1931–37), III.65, p. 625; cf. IV.38, p. 69: 'contempt for fame is contempt for virtue'.
258 Tacitus, *Agricola*, trans. M. Hutton, rev. R.M. Ogilvie (Loeb, 1970), XLVI, pp. 113–15.
259 Tacitus, *Annals*, IV.33, p. 57.
260 Tacitus, *Histories*, trans. C.H. Moore (Loeb, 1925–31); *Germania*, trans. M. Hutton, rev. E.H. Warmington (Loeb, 1970).
261 *Histories*, I.1, pp. 3–5, I.4, p. 9; *Annals*, I.1, pp. 243–5. For Tacitus' conception of history, see A.J. Woodman, *Rhetoric in Classical Historiography* (London, 1988), ch. 4; and, more generally, R.H. Martin, *Tacitus* (London, 1981); C.S. Kraus and A.J. Woodman, *Latin Historians* (Oxford, 1997), pp. 88–118.
262 *Annals*, IV.33, p. 59.

senatorial aristocracy upon whom the virtue and vitality of the Roman republic had hitherto depended.[263] Unlike Sallust, but like Livy, Tacitus was prepared to accept the proposition that rule by a single individual might provide a remedy for such decadence and therefore at least to countenance the argument that the institution of the principate could be regarded as the result of, if not the guiding hand of Fortune, then of political necessity rather than just bribery and indolence.[264] Unlike both Sallust and Livy, however, Tacitus' primary concern appears to have been to examine the relationship between the intrinsic worth of moral virtue and the utility of actually putting it into practice, and thereby to explore the disjunction between appearance and reality which could be expressed alike by individuals (the dissimulation of Tiberius), institutions (the vestigial 'authority' of the Roman senate) and, indeed, by the form of his own historical writing (a façade of republican annals which framed the [mis]deeds of individual emperors).[265]

Methodologically, Tacitus' sensitivity to political realities left his approach to causation as, if not more, problematic than it had been for Polybius. In Tacitus' case, it produced a narrative in which the cause of a given event could be left simply as one of a series of alternatives, or expressed from the relatively safe distance of indirect speech, insinuation and rumour. Substantively, this produced the sober counsel that, under a tyranny, when faced with the alternatives of servile obedience or rash contumacy, the virtuous individual (Agricola, or indeed Tacitus himself under Domitian) should seek out the path of cautious moderation.[266] Indeed, with the prosecution and death of Cremutius Cordus, Tacitus made a point of underlining just how dangerous for historians this sort of regime could be: 'you will find those who think that, because their own conduct is similar, the misdeeds of others are directed against themselves; even glory and virtue make enemies, by showing their opposites in too close a contrast'.[267] Other than a

---

263   Cf. *Agricola*, XI, p. 47, XV, p. 55, XXI, pp. 67; *Germania*, XLV, p. 209.
264   *Histories*, I.16, pp. 31–3; cf. *Annals*, I.1, p. 32.
265   *Annals*, I.81, p. 381, VI.51, p. 245.
266   *Histories*, I.1, p. 3–5; *Annals*, III.65, p. 625, IV.20, p. 39; *Agricola*, XLII, pp. 105–7.
267   *Annals*, IV.33, p. 59; cf. page 166.

politic reference to the freedom enjoyed under Trajan, therefore, Tacitus' *Histories*, and above all his *Annals*, read as a bleak vision of imperial power and of the moral and political degeneracy which had made such autocracy possible and, perhaps, even necessary. Or, as Guicciardini was to put it, 'Cornelius Tacitus explains very well how those living under a tyranny may live and conduct their affairs with prudence, just as he teaches tyrants the means by which they may found their tyrannies'.[268]

If Machiavelli proved, in practice, more sympathetic to Tacitus than to Polybius in his view of the role of rhetoric in the writing of history, he was fully in agreement with both writers over the political utility of studying the 'correct' examples from the past. In particular, Machiavelli was drawn to the fact that Polybius had identified the principal cause of the strength and success of Rome to be the way in which it had combined kingship, aristocracy and democracy in a mixed constitution (a combination which, unlike that of Sparta, was born of experience rather than reasoning and was suited to expansion rather than security).[269] Still more important for Machiavelli was the way in which Polybius had set this analysis within the context of what he termed a law of nature, whereby all political communities pass through a repeating cycle of growth, evolution, decay and subsequent regeneration. This was a point which seems to have fascinated Machiavelli and its imprint can be traced throughout his *Discourses on Livy*:

> this is the cycle through which all states that have governed themselves or that now govern themselves pass, but rarely do they return to the same forms of government because almost no republic can be so full of life that it may pass through these mutations many times and remain standing. But it may well happen that, in the course of its troubles, a republic ever lacking in counsel and strength becomes subject to a nearby state that is better organised; but if this were not

---

268 Guicciardini, *Ricordi*, trans. M. Grayson, in C. Grayson (ed.), *Francesco Guicciardini: Selected Writings* (London, 1965), 18, p. 9.
269 Polybius, *Histories*, VI.2–18, pp. 302–18, VI.43–57, pp. 338–50. Machiavelli's knowledge of Polybius was in all likelihood mediated through Bernardo Rucellai; cf. J.H. Hexter, 'Seyssel, Machiavelli and Polybius VI – The Mystery of the Missing Translation', *Studies in the Renaissance*, 3 (1956), pp. 75–96; J.M. Blythe, *Ideal Government and the Mixed Constitution in the Middle Ages* (Princeton, 1992), pp. 24–9, 265–9, 292–5, 298–300.

to occur, a republic would be apt to circle about endlessly through these types of government.[270]

This is therefore the historical framework within which Machiavelli's own analysis of events in the *Florentine Histories* is also set. It is described in the preface to book V, exactly the midpoint of Machiavelli's history.

> Usually, provinces go most of the time, in the changes they make, from order to disorder and then pass again from disorder to order, for worldly things are not allowed by nature to stand still. As soon as they reach their ultimate perfection, having no further to rise, they must descend; and similarly, once they have descended and through their disorders arrived at the ultimate depth, since they cannot descend further, of necessity they must rise. Thus they are always descending from good to bad and rising from bad to good. For virtue gives birth to quiet, quiet to leisure, leisure to disorder, disorder to ruin; and similarly from ruin, order is born; from order, virtue; and from virtue, glory and good fortune.... Thus provinces come by these means to ruin; when they have arrived there and men have become wise from their afflictions, they return, as was said, to order, unless they remain suffocated by an extraordinary force.[271]

This was the specific political context, therefore, into which Machiavelli wanted to insert the successful emergence of the Medici – these were the times and the circumstances, the point in the constitutional cycle, which made their actions both 'practicable' and 'necessary', and which meant that Cosimo and then Lorenzo de' Medici had prospered.

It is from this wider historiographical perspective that the preface to book I of the *Florentine Histories* begins to assume a rather different aspect. In his introductory remarks, Machiavelli invokes the work of Leonardo Bruni and Poggio Bracciolini as outstanding historians, but he also criticises them for what they have left out:

> My intent, when I at first decided to write down the things done at home and abroad by the Florentine people, was to begin my narration with the year of the Christian religion 1434, at which time the Medici family, through the merits of Cosimo and his father

---

270 Machiavelli, *Discourses*, I.2, p. 26.
271 Machiavelli, *Florentine Histories*, V.1, p. 185.

Giovanni, gained more authority than anyone else in Florence; for I thought that Messer Leonardo [Bruni] d'Arezzo and Messer Poggio [Bracciolini], two most excellent historians, had told everything in detail that had happened from that time backwards. But when I had read their writings diligently, so that by imitating them our history might be better approved by readers, I found that in the descriptions of the wars waged by the Florentines with foreign princes and peoples they had been very diligent, but as regards civil discords and internal enmities, and the effects arising from them, they were altogether silent about the one and so brief about the other as to be of no use to readers or pleasure to anyone. I believe they did this either because these actions seemed to them so feeble that they judged them unworthy of being committed to memory by the written word, or because they feared that they might offend the descendants of those they might have to slander in their narrations. These two causes ... appear to me altogether unworthy of great men, for if nothing else delights or instructs in history, it is that which is described in detail; if no other lesson is useful to the citizens who govern republics, it is that which shows the causes of the hatreds and divisions in the city so that when they have become wise through the dangers of others, they may be able to maintain themselves united. And if every example of a republic is moving, those which one reads concerning one's own are much more so and much more useful, and if in any other republic there were ever notable divisions, those of Florence are most notable.[272]

These apparent omissions or oversights were important to Machiavelli because he believed that it was precisely a knowledge of these civil discords and internal enmities which would be useful to his own audience. It would teach *them* how *they* could act effectively within a corrupt republic. This is accordingly what Machiavelli presents as Lorenzo de' Medici's defining achievement in book VIII of the *Florentine Histories* – to have survived conspiracies – and this is why he presents Lorenzo's defining virtue as the munificence and liberality which kept the Florentine people quiescent with peace, wealth and festivities.[273] It was the same sober lesson which Machiavelli also drew, in still more dramatic form, from the failure of the Pazzi conspiracy of 1478:

---

272   *Florentine Histories*, pref., p. 6.
273   *Florentine Histories*, VIII.36, p. 361. For 'bread and circuses', see Juvenal, *Satires*, trans. S.M. Braund (Loeb, 2004), X line 81, p. 373.

'Messer Jacopo ... mounted on a horse to make this last trial of their fortune ... and went to the piazza of the palace, calling to his aid the people and liberty. But because the former had been made deaf by the fortune and the liberality of the Medici and the latter was not known in Florence, he had no response from anyone'.[274]

All of this did not mean that Machiavelli was rejecting the humanist concern of Bruni and Poggio with the practical applicability of moral and political *exempla* which should instruct, but also move, one's audience. Far from it. However, it did mean that the substance of such writing should deal with the world as it is, not the world as it should be.[275] If Machiavelli's own history was to be useful, therefore, if his own deliberative rhetoric was to be convincing, it would have to reveal what course of action would be advantageous and necessary in a republic which had reached such depths of corruption in the constitutional cycle as Florence had in the late fifteenth and early sixteenth centuries. Either it would be reformed or it would stay where it was, 'suffocated by an extraordinary force'. It remains an open question just what or, more pertinently, who, Machiavelli considered that *'forza'* to be.

One of the characteristics which has traditionally made Guicciardini such a natural foil to Machiavelli is that he evidently shares a similar didactic pragmatism, a realism born of political experience, first as Florentine ambassador to Ferdinand II of Aragon and then as papal governor and counsellor to the Medici popes, Leo X and Clement VII.[276] Guicciardini contributed to the same public political debates over the governance of Florence in the 1520s;[277] he also commented directly on the lessons which Machiavelli had claimed could be drawn from the history of Rome in his own (unfinished) *Considerations on the Discourses of Machiavelli* in the 1530s.[278] Both authors shared a bitter frustration with the

---

274 *Florentine Histories*, VIII.8, p. 325.
275 Machiavelli, *The Prince*, trans. Q. Skinner and R. Price (Cambridge, 1988), XV, p. 54.
276 M. Phillips, *Francesco Guicciardini: The Historian's Craft* (Toronto, 1977).
277 Guicciardini, *Dialogue on the Government of Florence*, trans. A. Brown (Cambridge, 1994); cf. Machiavelli, *A Discourse on Remodelling the Government of Florence*, trans. A. Gilbert, in *Machiavelli: The Chief Works and Others* (Durham, 1958), vol. I, pp. 101-15.
278 Guicciardini, *Considerations on the Discourses of Machiavelli on the First Decade of T. Livy*, trans. M. Grayson, in C. Grayson (ed.), *Francesco Guicciardini: Selected Writings* (London, 1965), pp. 61-124.

pie-eyed idealism of rhetorical appeals to virtue and to moral worth. Guicciardini accordingly echoes Machiavelli's contrast between those people who wish to live ideally and those who wish to rule 'according to the common usage of the world, as they must'.[279] He also develops a series of comparable themes in his own *Ricordi* or *Maxims*, the observations and *sententiae* which he set down over the course of some twenty years between *c*.1510 and 1530. Guicciardini, like Machiavelli, comments on the influence of fortuitous events in human affairs; on the need for individuals to adapt their nature according to the conditions of the time; on the disjunction between theory and practice; on the advantages of practising dissimulation; on the fact that rulers act according to their nature and habit rather than their reason; and on how self-interest is generally stronger than reason in guiding people's actions.[280] These are also all recurrent themes in Guicciardini's *History of Italy*, the retrospective (and, in some respects, apologetic) narrative of events since 1494 which he composed in political retirement, and towards the end of his life, between 1537 and 1540. Viewed from the perspective of the tradition of fifteenth-century humanist historiography with which Guicciardini was familiar and to which, like Machiavelli, he was responding, there are two aspects to his approach which stand out.

The first distinctive quality to Guicciardini's historiography concerns the value of written history as a vehicle for moral–didactic *exempla*. Machiavelli may have thought that the political malaise of contemporary Italy was due to a failure to reach a true understanding of history, an inability to appreciate the real meaning of Roman historical examples and to imitate them, but Guicciardini went one step further. 'How mistaken are those who quote the Romans at every step', he exclaims, 'One would need to have a city with exactly the same conditions as theirs and then act according to their example. That model is as unsuitable for those lacking

---

279 Guicciardini, *Considerations on the Discourses*, I.1, p. 62; cf. I.10, p. 79: 'these ideas ... are more easily given form in books and in men's imaginations than carried into effect; rather, though private citizens have frequently discussed them, real examples are extremely rare'; Guicciardini, *Ricordi*, 179, p. 45: 'the world and its princes are not made as they should be, but as they are'.
280 *Ricordi*, 30, p. 13, 31, p. 13, 35, p. 14, 104, p. 28, 128, p. 34, 151, p. 39, 196, p. 49, 199, p. 50.

the right qualities as it would be useless to expect a donkey to run like a horse'.[281] Nor was such scepticism limited to Guicciardini's approach to the history of Rome. The basis for his objection lay in a profound sensitivity to the significance of historical circumstance. 'It is entirely fallacious to judge by examples', he comments, 'for, if they are not exactly alike in every detail, they are useless, since every slightest variation in the case may make a great difference in the result, and to distinguish these minute differences requires a keen and perspicacious eye'.[282] 'It is a great mistake', he suggests, 'to speak of the affairs of the world without distinction and absolutely and, as it were, by rule, since every case is different and exceptional because of the variety of circumstances which cannot be judged by the same measure. Such distinctions and exceptions are not written in books but must be revealed by discernment'.[283] Guicciardini directs the same critique towards Machiavelli himself in his commentary on the *Discourses*: 'one should not praise antiquity so far that one condemns all modern uses which were not current with the Romans, for experience has revealed many things not thought of by the ancients, and because, furthermore, their origins were different, certain things are needed by or suited to one country which were not to others'; 'thus one finds many examples on both sides, and each side has its good reasons.... These are decisions which cannot be taken by a firm rule, but conclusions must be drawn from the mood of the city, from the state of affairs which changes according to the state of the times, and other mutable circumstances'.[284] It is the same approach, finally, which Guicciardini chose to implement in his own *History of Italy* by including such density of circumstantial detail and by providing the cautionary example of Piero de' Medici: 'governing

---

281 *Ricordi*, 110, p. 30.
282 *Ricordi*, 117, p. 32.
283 *Ricordi*, 6, p. 7; cf. 69, p. 21, 76, p. 23: 'everything which was in the past and is now, will be in the future, but the names change, and the outward appearance of things, so that anyone who lacks perspicacity does not recognise them and cannot draw conclusions or form an opinion from what he observes'.
284 Guicciardini, *Considerations on the Discourses*, II.24, p. 117, I.40, p. 101; cf.II.12, p. 110: 'if in this Discourse one finds a number of examples on both sides, there are also many arguments which render it such a doubtful question that it is not easily resolved'. For the falsehood of counterfactual history, see *Ricordi*, 22, p. 11; and for the general impossibility of judging the future, 23, p. 11, 58, p. 19.

oneself by examples is undoubtedly very dangerous if similar circumstances do not correspond, not only in general but in all particulars, and if things are not managed with similar judgment, and if, aside from all other fundamentals, one does not have similar good fortune on one's side'.[285]

The second distinguishing feature of Guicciardini's historiography centres on his identification of those causes and deliberations (*causae et consilia*) which, according to Polybius, were the very essence of writing history and, according to Aulus Gellius, were precisely what distinguished history from annals, from setting down one damned thing after another. Guicciardini famously starts his *History of Italy* with a very clear statement of the cause of the present calamities – it was the greed and ambition of rulers within the Italian peninsula, in Venice, Florence, Milan, Naples and the papacy in Rome.[286] When he comes to the main body of his narrative, however, it becomes clear that, by charting the short-term and long-term effects of the French invasion of 1494, Guicciardini, like Polybius, was determined to draw attention to just how difficult a task it was to uncover what the real causes, the hidden causes, actually were. This is why, like Tacitus, he consistently gives more than one possible explanation of historical events. This produces a historiography where any particular occurrence is given several possible causes, an approach which one modern commentator has called 'corollary thrombosis'.[287] It also epitomises Guicciardini's reluctance to come to any instantaneous judgment: 'do not rush to criticise or commend according to the superficial aspect of things and what is immediately visible; you must see further into matters if you want your judgment to be true and well weighed'.[288] As in the works of Cicero and Boethius, unknown causes and conjunctions of events could certainly be denoted in Guicciardini's text by the single term 'fortune'; like Boethius, however, Guicciardini did not consider this incompatible either with the operation of divine providence or, like Augustine, with the observation that the justice of God's governance was

---

285 Guicciardini, *The History of Italy*, I, p. 57.
286 *History of Italy*, I, pp. 3–8; cf. *Ricordi*, 91, pp. 25–6.
287 Phillips, *Francesco Guicciardini*, p. 138; cf. *Ricordi*, 82, p. 24.
288 *Ricordi*, 215, p. 54.

inscrutable.[289] This is why Guicciardini dwells on the *un*intended consequences of individual actions, on events which have effects of their own, where the intended remedy ends up causing worse damage than the affliction it was originally designed to cure. The result is frustration, even despair, at the difficulties which are presented to any historian who has set themselves the task of unravelling the deliberations (*consilia*) which caused individuals to act in the way in which they did.

The process of deliberation, of political counsel, lies at the heart of Guicciardini's historiography and, like that of Commynes, is one of the defining characteristics of his historical narrative. This is why he spends so much time stage-managing debates, either by means of paired speeches, for and against a particular course of action, or through internal soliloquies which take place within a particular individual's own mind. Yet Guicciardini also explicitly acknowledges the difficulty of ever arriving at a true or complete explanation for actions or events when individuals are so adept at dissimulation, where there is such a disparity between words and deeds:

> Nothing certainly is more necessary in arduous deliberations and nothing, on the other hand, more dangerous than to ask advice. Nor is there any question that advice is less necessary to wise men than to unwise; and yet wise men derive much more benefit from taking counsel. For whose judgment is so perfect that he can always evaluate and know everything by himself and always be able to discern the better part of contradictory points of view? But how can he who is asking for counsel be certain that he will be counselled in good faith? For whoever gives advice, unless he is bound by close fidelity or ties of affection to the one seeking advice, not only is moved largely by self-interest but also by his own small advantages and by every slight satisfaction and often aims his counsel toward that end which turns more to his advantage or is more suitable for his purposes; and since these ends are usually unknown to the person seeking advice he is not aware, unless he is wise, of the faithlessness of the counsel.[290]

Guicciardini is therefore left to ruminate on his own reflection from the *Ricordi*:

---

289 See pages 97, 272–5; cf. *Ricordi*, 1, p. 4, 30, p. 13, 33, p. 14, 92, p. 26.
290 *History of Italy*, I, p. 63.

Do not be surprised that much is unknown about former ages or about what is happening in distant towns and provinces. For if you consider well, there is no accurate information to be had about present-day affairs or those done daily in the same city, and often between the palace and the public square there is such a dense fog or thick wall that, being impenetrable to the human eye, the people know as much of what those in power are doing and their reasons for it as of what is going on in India. Hence the world is easily filled with erroneous and vain opinions.[291]

For all his epistemological scepticism, Guicciardini, like Commynes, still thought that revealing the hypothetical content of deliberations or *consilia* could, in itself, prove an instructive and useful historiographical exercise. It is striking, for example, that Guicciardini points out how the Medici restoration of 1512 could, in fact, have been averted had the Florentines possessed a better understanding of the situation and the motives of their political opponents.[292] Like Machiavelli, Guicciardini did think that the course of Roman history provided important *exempla* from which contemporaries in Florence (and Venice) could learn valuable political lessons, even though he clearly wanted to temper some of the more extreme judgments to which Machiavelli had been drawn. A comparison between Machiavelli and Guicciardini suggests, indeed, that much of their historiography continued to be couched in conventional terms – the function of historical writing was to preserve deeds for the remembrance of posterity,[293] and its primary value was to serve as deliberative rhetoric, as a means of delivering political advice. At the same time, it is also a recurring theme of Guicciardini's commentary on Machiavelli's *Discourses* to stress the circumstantial context (political, cultural, geographical and temporal) that might end up qualifying the more general applicability with which a particular political principle or observation could be invested. It is this combination of the contingency of individual political events with the epistemological difficulties of uncovering the explicit and hidden causes of those events which also makes the course of Guicciardini's own historical narrative

---

291 *Ricordi*, 141, p. 37.
292 *History of Italy*, XI, pp. 266–7.
293 *Ricordi*, 143, p. 37.

particularly complex. What is so striking about Guicciardini, in other words, is his uncertainty and his particularism – in short, his acute sensitivity to the difficulties of ever discovering what actually happened and to the contingencies of time, place and circumstance which make generalisation and comparison of an *exemplum* so highly problematic. The former would not have been alien to Augustine or to John of Salisbury, but the latter, once again, strikes the distinctive note of Aristotelian empiricism.

No medievalist, however, partisan, is going to deny that something started to shift within historiography at the end of the fifteenth century and the beginning of the sixteenth. The critical point is to establish where, and why, such a conceptual transformation should have occurred and, most importantly, to distinguish any difference in kind from a difference in degree. Fourteenth- and fifteenth-century 'humanism' would seem to have possessed enough in common with its twelfth-century predecessor to rule out any sea-change in historiography resulting from a qualitatively different cognitive (as opposed to representational) approach to the deeds and events of the past. Fourteenth- and fifteenth-century historians remained committed to the same exemplary moral and political didacticism as their twelfth-century predecessors, a continuity in rhetorical tradition which extended to recognising the need to clarify the same permeable boundary between history and poetry and to express the same concerns over the ways in which verisimilitude should be allowed to supplement the truth. Writing at the very end of the fifteenth century, Pontano reveals just how resilient this conceptual framework for historiography could be. The explicitly forensic and diagnostic approach of Valla, meanwhile, demonstrated the potential of principles drawn from judicial rhetoric to provide the means by which events, deeds and particularly texts from the past could be evaluated and set out in the present. The rigour with which Valla set about his task certainly owed much to newly-developed instruments of philology but, in doing so, Valla's historiography was also party to a longstanding intellectual and instrumental association of history with judicial testimony which went back, in theory, to the rhetorical attributes of person and events and to the exegetical categories of the *accessus ad auctores* and, in practice, to the likes of Paschasius Radbertus, Galbert of Bruges and, more recently, to the processes of canonisation and inquisition.[294] It was the same longstanding forensic tradition which was soon to give rise to the historical and historiographical sensibilities of sixteenth-century jurists.[295]

Moral didacticism and judicial rhetoric, therefore, suggest that there were broad continuities in the way in which history was being written between 1200 and 1500. Demonstrative and deliberative rhetoric, on the other hand, offer a rather different picture. The writings of Machiavelli and Guicciardini suggest that late fifteenth- and early sixteenth-century historiography was beginning to express a much sharper disjunction between the values afforded to celebratory panegyric and to pragmatic political counsel. If the writing of history was now being located, by some writers at least, firmly within the sphere of deliberative rhetoric, rather than (and, in some cases, to the exclusion of) demonstrative rhetoric, then this would seem to mark a significant shift in emphasis from the twelfth, thirteenth and fourteenth centuries. Ideal and reality were being more explicitly disengaged and, as a result, both prescriptive exhortation and descriptive commemoration were becoming estranged from the business of basing political advice on an explanation of what actually happened and why. Given that the relationship between historiography and deliberative rhetoric had traditionally been so close, any changes in how their relationship was now viewed and, more precisely, handled become all the more revealing. Giles of Rome's approach to the mirror-for-princes genre is, in this respect, striking for what it does and, more importantly, does not acknowledge to be the value of narrative *exempla* drawn from the past.

The strength of the prevailing moral–didactic tradition, coupled with Aristotle's concession of the instrumental value of history to deliberative rhetoric, seems sufficient to have ensured that the charge of particularism expressed in the *Poetics* and the *Rhetoric* was fended off in the course of the fourteenth century, or at least effectively countered. It also meant that Lucian's invective against

---

294 For the latter, see M. Goodich, 'Biography 1000–1350', in D.M. Deliyannis (ed.), *Historiography in the Middle Ages* (Leiden, 2003), pp. 364–9; A.-M. Lamarrigue, *Bernard Gui (1261–1331): Un Historien et sa Méthode* (Paris, 2000).
295 For example, Jean Bodin, *Method for the Easy Comprehension of History*, trans. B. Reynolds (New York, 1945); cf. D.R. Kelley, *Foundations of Modern Historical Scholarship: Language, Law and History in the French Renaissance* (New York, 1970).

the use of rhetorical (and poetic) techniques, when it became known in the early fifteenth century, could be adapted, absorbed and ultimately left untranslated. This does not mean that there is no mileage left in pursuing Jacob Burckhardt's identification of a move away from rhetorical historiography in the course of the fifteenth century,[296] or a distinction between 'Latin' and 'Greek' traditions of writing history, but the terms of reference need to be significantly reconfigured. If there is a change in the fifteenth century, if there is a shift in understanding, then it seems to have been very gradual, the product of a particular conjunction of Aristotelian empiricism and philological expertise which took some considerable time to take effect.

What proved crucial for such a transformation to take place was, in the first instance, the critical mass of Greek histories in translation which began to filter through from around 1400, courtesy of an increased knowledge of both the Greek language and Greek manuscripts. This process had been initiated by the teaching of Manuel Chrysoloras in Florence between 1397 and 1400 and of George of Trebizond,[297] but it was given its decisive impetus in the 1450s by the translations made under the aegis of pope Nicholas V. One consequence was a clear encouragement to the cause of scholarly and disciplinary self-definition which ran counter to Aristotle's insistence that history, as the study of particulars, could, by definition, *never* be made the subject of an art, a systematic ordering of knowledge. A work such as Diodorus of Sicily's *Bibliotheca* or 'Library' of universal history, for example, when the first five books were translated into Latin by Poggio Bracciolini in 1449 (and then printed in 1472), put forward, in contrast to Aristotle, some very elevated claims for the utility of the subject. Historiography, Diodorus argued, covers every single aspect of human life and, as such, deserves to be called 'the metropolis of philosophy'. In fulfilling its primary didactic functions of commemorating the good, denouncing the wicked, inspiring people to virtue, instilling justice and providing a wealth of accumulated

---

296 J. Burckhardt, *The Civilization of the Renaissance in Italy*, trans. S.G.C. Middlemore (London, 1878; reprinted Harmondsworth, 1990), pp. 160–3.
297 I. Thomson, 'Manuel Chrysoloras and the Early Italian Renaissance', *Greek, Roman and Byzantine Studies*, 7 (1966), pp. 63–82; J. Monfasani, *George of Trebizond: A Biography and a Study of His Rhetoric and Logic* (Leiden, 1976).

experience to serve as guidance and advice for every possible circumstance, history is superior to all other forms of discourse, including poetry and law, both of which contain certain elements which detract from the utility and truth of what they are saying. Poetry is thus more pleasing than it is profitable, law punishes but does not instruct; only history succeeds in attaining a perfect harmony of word and fact and thereby embraces everything that is useful.[298] This sort of language dovetailed neatly with the claims which had already been articulated by Salutati (on the basis of Quintilian) and which received such a vigorous endorsement from Valla. Still more significant than such disciplinary ambition, however, was the methodological emphasis on political utility and truth which several of these newly-translated Greek works now embodied. This was the importance of the translations made of Thucydides (1452) and, above all, of Polybius (1452–54).[299]

Thucydides, the historian who was championed by name in Lucian's treatise, had been known to Leonardo Bruni but, when his work was translated into Latin by Lorenzo Valla, its immediate impact seems to have been substantially reduced (at least when compared with his subsequent popularity in the seventeenth century) for the simple reason that he had been writing about Athens, not Rome. The same reservation did not apply, however, to Polybius, a historian who had been writing in a self-consciously Thucydidean tradition but who, crucially, had been writing about the history of Rome and for a period which, as far as fifteenth-century humanists were concerned, was suffering from the gaps that had been left by an incomplete version of Livy. Polybius, moreover, even in the first five books that made it into Latin courtesy of Niccolò Perotti, had put forward, like Lucian, some trenchant observations on the theoretical relationship between history, rhetoric and poetry. In doing so, Polybius effectively applied pressure to what was already a sensitive area, courtesy of a longstanding ascetic and annalistic critique. What seems to have tipped the balance, and much more so than with Lucian,

---

298 Diodorus of Sicily, *Library of History*, trans. C.H. Oldfather (Loeb, 1933), I.1–5, pp. 5–23.
299 Cf. A. Momigliano, 'Polybius Between the English and the Turks', in A. Momigliano, *Sesto Contributo alla Storia degli Studi Classici e del Mondo Antico* (Rome, 1980), vol. I, p. 131.

was that, in Polybius, humanists now had an authoritative *model* for how history could, and should, be written without succumbing to the excesses of panegyric and poetry. It was a precedent which appears to have prompted them to read Tacitus' political realism in a new light. For those writers schooled in the principles of *imitatio* and *aemulatio*,[300] in other words, Polybius presented a qualitatively different proposition from Aristotle and Lucian – that is, from reading the precepts of a philosopher and the exclamations of a satirist, however much they may have been driving home the same point. It was the *exemplum* which made the difference.

This is the historiographical context within which Machiavelli and Guicciardini were reading, talking and writing at the turn of the fifteenth century. Both authors were firmly committed to the principle that history could furnish specific *exempla*, useful lessons which would provide their readers with instruction in the practical realities of politics. In and of itself, a pragmatic emphasis on the utility of historiography as deliberative rhetoric, as a vehicle for political counsel, was clearly not, in itself, either new or innovative – such a rationale would have been familiar three or four hundred years earlier. Nor did it necessarily require a reading of Thucydides or Polybius – Commynes, after all, demonstrated what could be achieved, within this pre-existing rhetorical tradition, from a combination of direct political experience with a reading of Valerius Maximus. Nonetheless, when Machiavelli and, above all, Guicciardini came to write continuous historical narratives of their own, alongside the *sententiae* which they supported with historical examples, what is so distinctive about the approach they chose to take was the way in which the didactic value of historiography was now accompanied by an acute sensitivity to, and explicit acknowledgment of, the particular conjunction of circumstances in which the events and deeds being described originally took place and which, by extension, would determine whether their repetition was *both* advisable *and* practicable. Likewise, whilst causation and intent (*causae et consilia*) remained the distinguishing features of their history-writing, as opposed to any 'simple' chronological record of events, it was now, as Valla had put it, the difficulty of the discipline as much

---

300 For *imitatio* and *aemulatio*, see page 295.

as its utility which needed to be stressed. It required discernment to identify the causes of events, and the reasons for human actions, through the fog of ignorance and dissimulation; it also required a detailed appreciation of the particular circumstances which were specific to the historical situation in which these deeds had been done, as this particularism might undermine their practical applicability as *exempla* in other contexts, be they in the present or in the future. If the historiography epitomised by Machiavelli and Guicciardini was characterised by a relativism and an empiricism which was born, in practice, of these authors' frustration with humanist idealism, then this approach had its roots, in theory, in a specifically fifteenth-century combination of philological contextualisation and Aristotelian particularism with the methodological prescriptions (and proscriptions) of Polybius.

By taking rhetoric seriously, as a discipline which is concerned with so much more than just style, which is all about the strategic use of language rather than mere trope-spotting, and by taking the writing of history back to its patristic roots, especially in Augustine, there are obvious dangers in allowing any, unquote, 'medieval' conceptualisation of the writing of history to flatten out both the twelfth and the fifteenth centuries as conventional period breaks. It is certainly striking, however, that modern commentators have tended to detect pretty similar features in both of these periods – for those schooled in post-Enlightenment paradigms, these are still centuries for which claims have been entered for a process of 'de-rhetoricisation'. This is a line, and a language, which needs considerable modification and refinement. Such a trend, if it exists in the twelfth century, is primarily a reaction to what poetry was doing to verisimilitude – *this* is what made historians rather more wary of this particular category of rhetorical presentation, not a desire to be free from rhetoric *per se*. Likewise, in the fifteenth century, it was the effect of philology on judicial rhetoric and of epistemology on deliberative rhetoric which reconfigured the relationship of historiography to the prescriptive idealism of demonstrative rhetoric – *this* is what concentrated historians' attention on circumstance, not a discovery of natural and human causation *per se*.

Viewed in this light, the similarities in the longstanding debate over the connections between history, rhetoric and poetry should become more striking, perhaps, than their differences. Twelfth- and fifteenth-century historians were responding to similar theoretical questions – where to draw a line of demarcation between historiography and poetry and, by extension, how much argument and verisimilitude to accommodate within a narrative whose truthfulness was always acknowledged to rest on credibility rather than certainty, on *fides* rather than *scientia*. A sharp polarisation of truth and fiction, the opposition of veracity to falsehood, fails to do justice to the complexity of both the medieval understanding and the medieval vocabulary for the problematic bit in the middle. What, in the end, seems to have forced the issue of genre for historiography, at least around 1500, is the cumulative pressure produced by linguistic relativism and epistemological empiricism – an Aristotelian 'freeze' and an early modern Ice Age perhaps, but a development whose origins are traceable to the thirteenth century, at least, and which took until the late fifteenth century to develop a truly critical momentum.

CONCLUSION

Medieval historiography was neither crude nor credulous nor conceptually unsophisticated. Such characterisations would be no more, and no less, applicable to the writing of history in the early modern and modern periods and, if only on this basis, medieval historians deserve better than to suffer the methodological condescension of posterity. The present study has been designed accordingly as an introduction to a set of interpretative criteria on which works of medieval historiography might be assessed, primarily through examining principles of classical rhetoric which would have been second-nature to writers who had been brought up, directly or indirectly, on the precepts of Cicero, Quintilian and the *Rhetorica ad Herennium*. In so doing, the aim of this digest, and this survey, has been to suggest just how complex the approach to the writing of history in the Middle Ages could be, primarily through its interweaving of these rhetorical principles with other historiographical traditions, drawn from ancient history, chronography and the Bible.

The writing of history in the Middle Ages was conditioned, in the first instance, by the three basic functions of rhetoric – to teach (*docere*), to move (*movere*) and to please (*delectare*) – each one of which, not least the pleasure principle, carried important consequences for the way in which a narrative of events could, and should, be constructed and presented. This meant that the writing of history was understood, in the second instance, to follow the division of rhetoric into its three basic categories – demonstrative, judicial and deliberative oratory. Demonstrative rhetoric concerned the praise and commemoration of distinguished individuals or the castigation and denunciation of the wicked; in both cases it was marked by an attention to reputation (*fama*) and to remembrance (*memoria posteritatis*). Holding up the deeds of individuals for praise in this way was intended to provide a model for imitation, on the grounds that an *exemplum* should be considered a better means of instruction than a precept, particularly for the less well-educated. One immediate historiographical consequence was the close relationship which thereby emerged between the writing of history and the 'mirror-for-princes' genre – deeds of predecessors were written down in order to be instructive, so that they would be imitated and emulated by sons and successors, sometimes with an explicit admonition that their intended audience should take care that the reflection actually matched. Judicial or forensic rhetoric, meanwhile, concentrated on setting out who, what, where, when, why, how, by what means and in what circumstances a particular action took place, all with a view to accusing or defending an individual charged with having done that particular deed. This extended to a consideration of the character of the individual, or individuals, performing the action under discussion and thus to an interest in combining a depiction of character with a narrative of what had been done. Describing what sort of person an individual was (*qualis est*), in other words, became central to establishing whether they would, or would not, have performed the deed in question. Again, the influence of this category of rhetoric on medieval historiography is marked, not least in the number of medieval 'lives' (*vitae*) or 'deeds' (*res gestae*) which were written as a defence of an individual against a certain set of accusations. However, judicial rhetoric also considered *everything* that was a subject of differing views, literally 'controversy' (*controversia*). It therefore extended to the interpretation of disputed documents, often the will of a dead person, but once again the approach was to use narrative in order to harmonise character with action and word: was this the sort of person (*qualis est*) who would have written such a text and what was the intention and meaning of their words? Judicial rhetoric accordingly also covered evaluation of the testimony of human witnesses, including the character of the speaker or writer themselves but also the evidence provided collectively by popular opinion (*fama*). Deliberative rhetoric, finally, comprised a speech or text which was written for, or against, a particular course of political action and, as such, underpinned a form of history-writing which was concerned, first and foremost, with delivering political counsel and advice. As with demonstrative rhetoric, narrating the deeds of the past could be deployed in the form of an appeal to precedent or to experience, not least as a means of judging what may happen in the future. What was specific to deliberative rhetoric were the criteria for evaluating whether or not a particular course of action should be taken: is it morally worthy (*honestum*), expedient or advantageous (*utile*) and is it necessary, practicable or even possible (*possibile*)?

One of the conceptual and disciplinary consequences of being credited with such a close association with the principles of rhetoric, and in each one of its three basic categories, was for the writing of history to be considered, in the main, as a secondary or auxiliary subject of learning. Definitions of *historia* in the Middle Ages therefore concentrated on its general qualities, as a narrative of something which had been done (*narratio rei gestae*), and, as such, 'history' was not (and perhaps could not be) regarded as an autonomous branch of knowledge. Considered in these terms, however, the writing of history was also understood to follow another tripartite distinction in rhetoric, this time between the three qualities by which *any* narrative could, and should, be defined – brevity, lucidity and what was termed plausibility or verisimilitude. Brevity and lucidity did what they said in the handbooks. Plausibility, however, was epistemologically and stylistically more complex. Verisimilitude was effected, first and foremost, through invention, that is, through finding the right argument for the point being made, be it specific to the case in question or one which was typical or commonplace to the sort of situation under discussion. What is appropriate for a narrative of events will thus be governed by three further considerations: the subject-matter of what is being narrated; what generally happens or conforms to Nature; and what corresponds to the opinion of one's audience. The goal of this probable argumentation is, not truth as such, but belief or credence (*fides*), a conviction that is derived both from the narrator of the deeds described (hence the credibility which needed to be established for the author in a prologue) and from the actual narrative of events which is then produced (hence the emphasis on causation and the testimony of witnesses and proof). Argument creates faith in something that is otherwise in doubt and, according to classical manuals of rhetoric, such plausibility and trustworthiness could be secured in a number of different ways. Prominent amongst these strategies was *enargeia*, that is, the vividness given to a narrative such that the events would seem to be happening before the audience's very eyes (*ante oculos*). This technique was also designed to move the audience – in the sense of appealing to their emotions rather than to their reason – but, as with Isidore's definition for the etymology of the word 'history' itself, it was primarily designed to make a narrative convincing as autopsy, as the product of eyewitness testimony. The term *enargeia* was translated into Latin as *evidentia*. Strictly speaking, then, this is what 'evidence' meant for medieval historiography and, as a result, definitions of 'history' as *narratio rei gestae* were qualified, and expanded, to read *narratio rei gestae aut ut rei gestae*, the narrative of what was done or might have been done.

If the plausible reconstruction of what might have happened was just as important as what actually did occur, then it could clearly include material which had been shaped or 'made up'. The rhetorical understanding of verisimilitude accordingly posed particular challenges both for the conceptualisation and for the practice of the writing of history, but these were challenges which were present from the outset. They had originally been aired by Augustine, for whom the status of verisimilitude, both as an epistemological category (how the reality of what has happened is understood) and as a rhetorical strategy (how that reality is then re-presented in writing), raised a series of fundamental questions. In *De Magistro*, for example, Augustine was interested in exploring the category of so-called 'past sensibles', and the fact that these *sensibilia* are, strictly speaking, 'false', because they are only the generated images of experience, not the experience itself. In *Contra Academicos*, he therefore discusses the epistemological status of these *sensibilia* as opinion rather than knowledge, *opinio* rather than *scientia*, whilst in *De Trinitate* and, most famously, in the *Confessions*, he set out to examine how this past experience is then stored, and understood, in the memory.

According to Augustine, although historical narrative recounts things which have been instituted by human beings, history itself should not be numbered among human constructions. Establishing the temporal order or sequence of events is therefore different from understanding their significance; a narrative of what has happened is conceptually distinct from explaining the causes of those events, the reason *why* a deed was done. Augustine was someone who knew all about the distinction between different types of 'historical' writing, between chronography, aetiology and narrative, but he was primarily concerned with acknowledging the inscrutability of divine providence, particularly when that providence was permissive, when it simply allowed things to happen, and particularly when it governed events in the sixth and final age of humankind, its old age (*senectus mundi*). In these circumstances, the act of writing history needed to steer well clear of presumption if it was to avoid assuming the mantle of prophecy – God's judgments are inscrutable and His ways are past searching out.

Verisimilitude is a term which is striking by its absence from *De Doctrina Christiana*, the text in which Augustine says most about the utility of classical rhetoric in the service of Christian truth. The one occasion on which it does occur is therefore all the more revealing. Those who try to make falsehoods persuasive, Augustine writes, produce a narrative which is brief, clear and plausible (*verisimiliter*). There are thousands of made-up fables and falsehoods, he observes; these are human creations, 'lies' which serve to give pleasure. Something is called false, he explains, when the signification of something is not what is signified, and it comes in two forms – those things which cannot exist as such (the fabulous) and those things which do not exist even though it is possible that they could (the verisimilar). Verisimilitude is clearly a category which Augustine found difficult and, in a specifically historiographical context, it assumed a central role in his disagreement with Jerome over the apostle Paul's account of his correction of Peter in the letter to the Galatians. According to Augustine, Jerome had argued that either Peter had been simulating his own actions or Paul was making up the episode in order to make an instructive point – in other words, that the event itself had not actually happened as it was narrated in Scripture but had been staged in order to illustrate a spiritual truth. As an exegetical principle, this was a point which Augustine clearly believed went to the heart of how Christians should, and should not, use classical rhetoric to elucidate the Bible – once rhetorical verisimilitude was allowed to explain Paul's actions on one occasion, the historical truth of the entire New Testament narrative would be called into question.

The need to clarify the boundary between verisimilitude, fable and falsehood prompted Augustine to write two treatises on the

❦ CONCLUSION ❦

nature of lying, *De Mendacio* and then *Contra Mendacium*. A made-up narrative (*ficta narratio*) which nonetheless has a true meaning or signification is not, he maintains, a lie, since a lie depends on the intention to deceive. Such a rhetorical strategy, however, should not be invoked as an explanation for the particular form given to the historical account of the apostles' actions in the New Testament – the events narrated there had a true signification *and* actually happened. For Augustine's immediate purposes, it remained vital to defend the literal, historical accuracy of Paul's account in Galatians. Whether the same constraints applied to extra-scriptural narrative, however, was left open to interpretation. Indeed, beyond the text of the New Testament, Augustine's discussion opened up a question which had a long pedigree in Neoplatonism and which was summarised by Macrobius when he analysed the role of similarly 'fictive' material in philosophy. According to Macrobius' *Saturnalia*, fables come in two forms: those which serve no other function than that of pleasure (this was the category of which Augustine was so dismissive in *De Doctrina Christiana*) and those which inspire their audience to perform virtuous deeds. Within this second, expressly didactic, category, Macrobius draws a further distinction between fables which are entirely made up (and which therefore have no place in philosophy) and those which have a foundation of truth and which present morally-worthy subject-matter beneath a 'covering' (*integumentum*), or veil, of allegory. It is this latter category of fabulous narrative, Macrobius concludes, which *can* be deployed by philosophers, which is *not* incompatible with truth.

Augustine himself acknowledges in his *Retractions* that, on the subject of lying, he did not explain himself as clearly as he might have done. From the perspective of medieval historiography, the important point to make is that, when it came to extra-scriptural events, Augustine's legacy ensured that the task of writing history necessarily involved taking a view on a set of terms in which it could, and should, be approached – truth, verisimilitude, fable, falsehood and lies. In the twelfth century, this debate came to centre on the distinction which was drawn in rhetorical manuals between three types of narrative – *historia*, *argumentum* and *fabula* – that is, between history, argument and fable. According to this distinction, *historia* should be defined as a narrative of what actually happened; *argumentum* as a narrative of events which have been shaped or made up but which nevertheless could have happened (in other words, hypothesis, the narrative of something made up and plausible, *narratio rei fictae et verisimilis*); *fabula*, finally, should be defined as a narrative of events which neither happened nor could have happened. What this threefold distinction prompts in the course of the twelfth century is, in many respects, a demarcation dispute between the two disciplines which otherwise laid claim to the narratives at either end of this scale, namely historiography and poetry. In part, this was unavoidable, given the way in which the teaching of rhetoric had been subsumed within the teaching of grammar, and as the dividing line between historiography and poetry accordingly became blurred. Given that grammar and rhetoric were taught via both the study of classical poets and the study of classical historians, the precise status of narrative verisimilitude was up for grabs between the two. It was also, in part, a reflection of the overlap between the two subjects in terms of the three factors which could determine verisimilitude: subject-matter could be shared by history and poetry, particularly in epic verse; so, too, was conformity with what usually happens, depending on the circumstances being described; conformity with the expectations and abilities of one's audience, meanwhile, would vary according to the exact identity of that audience, but history and poetic fable were both understood to provide material which was appropriate for use primarily with an ignorant, less well-educated or simply younger group of people.

Conflict over the rhetorical category of verisimilitude in the twelfth century was precipitated, therefore, by the rise of 'literary fiction' with which this period is often credited. The proximity of poetry to rhetoric meant that they were often regarded as verse and prose types of the same principles of writing. This had some very important consequences for the language of fiction – *fingere, ficta, figmenta* – terms which had hitherto been thought commensurable with constructing a plausible and convincing narrative of events, but which could also be correlated with falsehood (*falsa*) and lies (*mendacia*). Indeed, it had the quite practical result of making some authors attempt to shift the concept of verisimilitude from being an ontological to an aesthetic category of narrative. According to Geoffrey of Vinsauf's formulation, fabulous narrative should be defined as 'lying with probability' – poetic *fabula* presents a false narrative as if it were true. The significance of this move has been frequently highlighted by scholars of twelfth-century literature, but it also naturally posed a challenge to writers of history, for whom verisimilitude had hitherto played a central strategic role in the narrative plausibility of their accounts of events. This is the ontological claim best illustrated by John of Salisbury when he used Aristotle and Boethius to classify three types of approach to knowledge: demonstrative logic, probable logic and sophistry. Demonstrative logic is concerned with necessity, namely with that which cannot be otherwise, a truth which is determined irrespective of what any particular audience might think or assent to. Probable logic is concerned with propositions which seem to be true either to everyone or to many people or to the wise; such opinion is the field of both dialectic and rhetoric and, by extension, of history. Sophistry, finally, is concerned merely with the appearance of probability and not at all with the truth; although it may, on occasion, use true and probable arguments, it otherwise deals in deceit. Of these three categories, John of Salisbury is interested, first and foremost, in the second – in probable opinion on the grounds that the degree of epistemological certainty in dialectic and rhetoric will be conditioned by the changeable nature of their subject-matter. Thus, whereas demonstrative logic will be applicable to mathematics, and sophistry to poetics, probable logic is better suited to the corporeal and therefore changeable substance of Nature – in other words, to the substance of historical narrative. This does not mean, John states, that opinion cannot be turned into belief (*fides*), and even approach certitude, at least as far as human judgment is concerned, or, as Hugh of St Victor put it, 'a voluntary certitude concerning something which is not present, greater than opinion but falling short of knowledge'. Nonetheless, probability and verisimilitude are the closest humans are going to get to knowledge of Nature and, by extension, to knowledge of history.

What needs underlining here is the challenge which the shift in the poetic meaning of verisimilitude presented for the writing of history. Once it could be construed as a purely aesthetic category, as Geoffrey of Vinsauf suggested, rather than a claim about reality, as John of Salisbury maintained, verisimilitude made writers of history much more nervous of using this rhetorical strategy, for fear of being branded, not only as writers of fable, but also as liars. This is the charge which William of Newburgh levelled against the 'lies' of Geoffrey of Monmouth, but it also went much further. In the twelfth century, it was indicative of a more systemic concern over the literary 're-presentation' of historical truth in narrative. It is this concern which seems to have precipitated the historiographical retreat which has often been commented upon as a feature of twelfth-century writing, away from the sort of ambitiously literary historical narratives which characterised the first half of the century to the more limited chronicling of the second.

Historiographical verisimilitude is not a problem that was resolved in the twelfth or thirteenth centuries. If anything, the issue was made still more difficult by the recovery and circulation of Aristotle's contention that empirical narrative cannot, in any case, form the basis for any truly scientific discipline. This idea was already being applied to the study of law by Albertus Magnus in the 1250s, on the basis of the arguments he had found in the *Nicomachean Ethics*. In his own work on rhetoric, Aristotle had expressed a clear preference for the use of logical argumentation over historical *exempla* – whilst particular *exempla* can certainly provide support for an argument, they should be used sparingly, simply as supplementary testimony. Arguing inductively, by means of individual *exempla*, can still be persuasive, but enthymemes will generally produce a more rousing response from an audience. When Aristotle's *Ethics* was combined with his *Rhetoric*, the effects were striking, and they can be seen most clearly in Giles of Rome's *De Regimine Principum*, a hugely influential 'mirror-for-princes' which starts with an explicit statement that it will *not* proceed in a narrative manner. Giles wanted to give his work much greater analytical rigour than he thought could be provided by the writing of history, by the particulars of narrative *exempla*. This was a position which was reinforced still further by the circulation of Aristotle's *Poetics*, a text which compared history directly with poetry, and very much to the advantage of the latter: it is the function of the poet to say, not what did happen (*gesta*), but the sort of thing that would happen, that is, what can happen in a strictly probable or necessary sequence (*secundum verisimile aut necessarium*); as a result, only poetry can aspire to deal with universal propositions, whereas history deals simply with singulars.

In and of themselves, a combination of aesthetic verisimilitude and Aristotelian empiricism might be thought sufficient to have severed the relationship between rhetoric and the writing of history as soon as poetry started to lay claim to plausible narrative and universal precepts. The difficulty with this line of interpretation is the fact that one of the more striking features of fourteenth-century historiography was its vigorous restatement of the twelfth-century connection *between* history and rhetoric, especially for the role of moral–didactic *exempla*. This is what happens with Petrarch in the 1350s, when he stresses the value of *exempla* as inspirations to virtue, but also the combination of utility and pleasure which makes history such a superior vehicle for communicating the truths of moral philosophy to a wider audience. This is the line reiterated by Salutati in the 1390s, when he runs through the three branches of rhetoric – demonstrative, judicial and deliberative – showing how each of them revolves around a narrative of what has, or has not, been done. In the early fifteenth century, it is the same moral–didactic rhetorical tradition which is driving the demonstrative and deliberative historiography of Leonardo Bruni and which accounts for the subsequent popularity of the works of Sallust, Livy and Plutarch. It is an approach to the writing of history, however, which would not have been out of place three hundred years earlier.

If the vigour of the moral–didactic rhetorical tradition amongst humanist writers of history provides one explanation for the initially muted response to Aristotle's *Rhetoric* and *Poetics*, it also seems to account for the reaction, or non-reaction, to the introduction of another potentially momentous (and this time explicitly historiographical) Greek text, namely Lucian's essay on how to write history. When humanists read Lucian in the 1430s, they carefully adapted the content of his treatise, incorporating into their own guidance for the writing of history those elements which could be harmonised with the rhetorical tradition of historiography epitomised in Cicero's *De Oratore*. Much the same measured response is found in Lorenzo Valla. Valla may or may not have read Lucian, but he is too scrupulous a writer to pretend the challenge of Aristotelian empiricism did not exist, and too intelligent not to set out a response. Valla is, of course, best known in modern accounts of historiography for his virtuoso exercise in judicial rhetoric – proving the Donation of Constantine to be a forgery required a demonstration of its philological inaccuracies but also depended on an argument for the historical implausibility and rhetorical incongruity of such a testamentary deposition ever being made or received. Still more revealing for Valla's views on historiography, however, is his prologue to the deeds (*gesta*) of Ferdinand, king of Aragon and Sicily, where he tackles Aristotelian particularism head on. 'Some philosophers,' he writes, 'and not just any philosophers but the greatest and most ancient amongst them, have placed history beneath poetry on the grounds that poetry is closer to philosophy because it deals with what is general and sets down universal precepts on the basis of made-up *exempla*'. In response, Valla turns this judgment on its head. 'Speeches, testimony, praise, castigation and many other things', he writes, are all designed to teach universal precepts of wisdom. Indeed, for Valla, the histories of Sallust and Livy contain more political wisdom than the precepts of any philosopher. History, in fact, produces more knowledge than philosophy of the nature of things, of ethics and of every branch of wisdom.

Fifteenth-century humanist historiography, in short, reveals profound continuities with its twelfth-century predecessor, including the need to clarify the same permeable boundary between history and poetry and including the extent to which verisimilitude should be allowed to supplement the truth. If there is a change, if there is a shift, then it seems to have been much more gradual. What prompts it is an increasingly critical mass of Greek histories in translation which filtered through from around 1400 and above all from the 1450s. Aristotle's empirical particularism had been fended off, or at least effectively countered; Lucian's invective could be adapted and left untranslated; Thucydides' impact was softened by the fact that he was writing about Athens rather than Rome. The same could not be said, however, about Polybius, a historian who was not only writing about Rome but writing history which was needed in order to fill many of the gaps left by an incomplete text of Livy. Polybius, even in the first five books that made it into Latin in the 1450s, had some pretty trenchant things to say about the relationship between rhetoric and the writing of history. Whilst fully endorsing the view that history provided a moral and, above all, political education for real life (*vera vita*), and that it should combine such utility with pleasure, Polybius also insisted that historians should always stop short of deploying those rhetorical techniques which he associated exclusively with poetry, tragedy and fable. This list included moving and graphic visualisations *ante oculos*, descriptions of place, and the invention of appropriate speeches – in other words, all the techniques that historians used to adopt from their study of classical rhetoric in order to move and entertain their audience rather than just instruct them. The goal of poetry, Polybius explains, may be all about presenting verisimilitude, but this is in order that the audience will be more easily deceived. The goal of history, on the other hand, is all about presenting true things that will be of benefit to the reader. Arnoldo Momigliano suggested that the translations made from Greek into Latin in the 1450s caused a seismic shift in historiography. That view is worth repeating. What tipped the balance was that, with Polybius, and in conjunction with Thucydides, humanists now had authoritative *models* for how history should be written. For those schooled in rhetorical principles of *imitatio* and *aemulatio*, this presented an altogether different proposition, a qualitatively different challenge from Aristotle and Lucian, that is, from reading the precepts of a philosopher and the exclamations of a satirist, however much they may have been driving home the same point.

So where does all this leave the grand narrative for medieval and 'Renaissance' historiography? By taking rhetoric seriously as a discipline which is all about the strategic use of language, rather than just style, and by taking the writing of history back to its patristic roots, especially in Augustine, a distinctively 'medieval' conceptualisation of the writing of history would seem to soften both the twelfth and the fifteenth centuries as conventional period breaks. The similarities in their debates over the relationship between history, rhetoric and poetry certainly appear more striking than the differences, and a response to very similar theoretical questions – where to draw a line of demarcation between history and poetry and, by extension, how much argument and verisimilitude to accommodate within a narrative whose truthfulness was always acknowledged to rest on credibility rather than certainty, *fides* rather than *scientia*. Modern commentators have long looked for consistency of classification and distinction in the various ways in which medieval authors categorised their many and diverse types of historical writing, not least with the terminology of 'history', 'annals' and 'chronicles'. If these three genres were not as watertight as Aulus Gellius might have preferred, then, as even Gervase of Canterbury recognised, this was because causality and intention could not be written out of anything but the most paratactic of chronographic records. Rhetoric could be dismissed as cosmetics or it could be acknowledged as necessary argumentation. Either way, flexibility over where exactly to draw the line between history, annals and chronicles was hardly surprising when medieval authors were so clearly in disagreement over how far history should incorporate plausible argumentation, or whether such verisimilitude was appropriate only to the fables, or lies, of the poets. Flexibility of classification should not be confused with either ignorance or naïvety. At the very least, it should be recognised that the polarisation of truth and fiction, the opposition of veracity to falsehood, fails to do justice to the complexity of the medieval understanding of the problematic area between 'history' and 'lies', a language of *argumentum* and verisimilitude which it has taken until the last twenty or thirty years for modern historians to face up to once more.

The fact that there continues to be such slippage in modern English between the terms 'history' and 'historiography' remains a revealing facet of the methodology of this particular discipline of writing. The vitality of historiography within a western intellectual tradition stems, in part, from the longevity of the dialogue – and tension – between *res gestae* and *narratio*, between what actually happened and its verisimilar re-presentation in narrative. The debt to classical rhetoric that this reciprocity embodies is the fundamental point which this book has sought to address by surveying the conventions through which 'history' came to be written, from its inception in classical antiquity onwards. As a study of the relationship between historical content and literary form, however, this book might also end up providing a historical perspective on the resonance of this debt for more recent debates within modern historiography over the need (or otherwise) to acknowledge a connection between historical methodology and literary theory and, in particular, on the effects upon historiography of the modern 'linguistic turn' – effects which often run the risk of reinventing the textuality of history rather than discovering it for the first time.

As nineteenth- and twentieth-century positivist models for the writing of history came under pressure from Kuhnian paradigms and post-structuralist relativism, historians who wanted to challenge the certainties of historiography as a 'scientific' discipline frequently turned to philosophical analyses of the relationship between language and reality. Taking their cue, not this time from

Augustine, but from Saussure and Wittgenstein, these historians sought to apply a theoretical awareness of the complexity of the relationship between the occurrence (and experience) of events and the different ways in which they could be represented (and understood) by means of language.[1] The result was an increasingly self-conscious use of terms such as 'text' and 'discourse' and a flourishing, if controversial, literature on the connection between historiography and literary theory. What is often overlooked in such an account, however, is just how far back an appreciation and analysis of the specifically literary nature of the writing of history can, and should, be taken. In appealing to Hayden White's analysis of 'narratology', for example, or Hans Robert Jauss' formulation of 'reception theory', modern historians sometimes under-appreciate the acknowledged debt of both authors to the extensive discussion of the literary qualities of *narratio* and *aptum* which was second nature to medieval writers.[2] Likewise, in championing Paul Ricoeur's analysis of time and narrative, modern historians have tended to underplay the author's own debt to Augustine.[3]

---

[1] See, for example, J. Tully (ed.), *Meaning and Context: Quentin Skinner and His Critics* (Oxford, 1988); Q. Skinner, *Visions of Politics. Vol. I: Regarding Method* (Cambridge, 2002); G.M. Spiegel (ed.), *Practicing History: New Directions in Historical Writing After the Linguistic Turn* (London, 2005).
[2] H. White, *The Content of the Form: Narrative Discourse and Historical Representation* (Baltimore, 1987); H. White, 'Rhetoric and History', in H. White and F.E. Manuel, *Theories of History* (Los Angeles, 1978), pp. 7–25; H. White, 'The Fictions of Factual Representation', in A. Fletcher (ed.), *The Literature of Fact* (New York, 1976), reprinted in H. White, *Tropics of Discourse* (Baltimore, 1978), pp. 1–25; H. White, 'The Value of Narrativity in the Representation of Reality', *Critical Inquiry*, 7 (1980), pp. 5–27, reprinted in H. White, *The Content of the Form: Narrative Discourse and Historical Representation* (Baltimore, 1987), pp. 1–25; H.R. Jauss, 'Literary History as a Challenge to Literary Theory', *New Literary History* (1970), pp. 7–37, reprinted in H.R. Jauss, *Toward an Aesthetic of Reception* (Brighton, 1982), pp. 3–45. Cf. E.B. Vitz, *Medieval Narrative and Modern Narratology: Subjects and Objects of Desire* (New York, 1989); R.H. Canary and H. Kozicki (eds), *The Writing of History: Literary Form and Historical Understanding* (Madison, 1978); F.R. Ankersmit, 'Historiography and Postmodernism', *History and Theory*, 28 (1989), pp. 137–53; P. Zagorin, 'Historiography and Postmodernism: Reconsiderations', *History and Theory*, 29 (1990), pp. 263–74.
[3] P. Ricoeur, *Time and Narrative* [*Temps et Récit*] (Chicago, 1984–88), vol. I, pp. 5–30; P. Ricoeur, 'History and Rhetoric', in F. Bédarida (ed.), *The Social Responsibility of the Historian* (Providence, 1995), pp. 7–24; P. Ricoeur, 'L'Histoire comme Récit', in D. Tiffenau (ed.), *La Narrativité* (Paris, 1980), pp. 3–24. Cf. R. Kearney, 'Time, Evil and

A study of the relationship between classical rhetoric and the writing of history in the Middle Ages suggests that there has *always* been a critical dialogue between historiography and literary theory and that the influences on modern historiography of, respectively, positivism and post-modernism might usefully be viewed from this perspective. In each case, the substantial qualifications which need to be made for some of the more extreme claims on both sides – for scientific empiricism or for subjective textuality – deserve to be given a history of their own. Historiography has *never* been an autonomous discipline but, in the wake of recent methodological debates, it may prove salutary to be reminded of the central role of rhetoric in shaping how the writing of history has been understood, and practised, in the past. Historical method may now be regarded as inherently 'comparative',[4] but this, in turn, clearly presupposes a sophisticated lexicon for how such similitude should be understood. The distinct epistemological status of each of the three rhetorical categories – *exemplum*, parallel and image – itself invites comparison with modern claims for 'micro-history', as the inductive study either of unique particulars or of a generalisable, exemplary microcosm. The rhetorical concern with *imitatio* and *aemulatio* can likewise fruitfully be set alongside more modern concepts of 'langue' and intertextuality, of shared linguistic expectations and literary models to which individual authors then respond, and adapt. The status of *verisimilitudo* and *argumentum*, meanwhile, raises ever-present questions about the boundary between truth and plausibility and the relationship between epistemological incertitude and 'fictive' narrative. The rhetorical principle that any text is written to be appropriate and suitable (*aptum*), finally, resonates forcefully with contemporary concerns about both 'genre' and 'context' – that is, with the notion that words need to be located within a framework of particular intellectual expectations in order for their performative or illocutionary function to be established, where identifying a truly 'historical' meaning depends, first and foremost, on identifying the conceptual and literary conventions within which a text is

---

Narrative – Ricoeur on Augustine', in J.D. Caputo and M.J. Scanlon (eds), *Augustine and Post-Modernism: Confessions and Circumfession* (Bloomington 2005), pp. 144–58.

4 See, for example, C. Lorenz (ed.), 'Comparative History – Problems and Perspectives', *History and Theory*, 38 (1999), pp. 25–99.

working (or which it is subverting) and the nature and opinions of the audience for whom it is being written.

The key question in all these 'modern' debates remains exactly where to place historiography on a line which stretches from dialectic to rhetoric to scepticism to sophistry, from truth to plausibility to opinion to falsehood. It may have been phrased differently by Augustine, John of Salisbury, Giles of Rome, Lorenzo Valla and Guicciardini, but the underlying issue remains the same. History is not a Manichean discipline of truth and falsehood, of fact and 'fiction'. It is better understood, or at least more faithfully written, when it is viewed, not in terms of the bipolar categories of the nineteenth century, nor indeed of 2 Timothy 4:4 ('they have turned from truth to fables'),[5] but in terms of the tripartite categories of the twelfth and thirteenth centuries: history, verisimilitude and fable; memory, understanding and will; truth, belief and opinion. Accepting that historiography may, in consequence, owe no less (or possibly more) to the literary conventions of rhetoric than it does to the demonstrable 'scientific' proofs of dialectic, to enthymemes rather than to syllogisms, to paradigmatic *exempla* rather than to inductive propositions, does not mean, however, that it is necessary to succumb to the radical intellectual uncertainty of the Academy, still less to meretricious displays of sophistry. What prevents it from doing so is what patristic and medieval historians termed *fides historiae*. This is a lesson which some modern historians might still do well to listen to, if not, perhaps, to learn. In the sixth century, Junilius Africanus warned that history, defined as the narrative of past or present things, would appear quite plain and simple on the surface but would often be difficult to understand.[6] Five hundred years later, Thietmar of Merseburg agreed. 'We should not view ourselves as superior to our predecessors', he warned; 'we are not unequal because we are similarly deceived by the various faces of truth'.[7]

---

5 Odo of Cluny, *Life of Gerald of Aurillac*, trans. G. Sitwell (London, 1958), III.12, p. 171.
6 Junilius Africanus, *De Partibus Divinae Legis* (*PL* 68, cols 15–42), I.3, col. 17, I.6, col. 19.
7 Thietmar of Merseburg, *Chronicon*, trans. D.A. Warner, *Ottonian Germany* (Manchester 2001), VI.21, p. 251: *non videamur nostris antecessoribus meliores, quia pariter decepti in varia specie recti hiis sumus nimis inaequales.*

BIBLIOGRAPHY

Abbreviations

CCCM	*Corpus Christianorum, Continuatio Mediaevalis*
CCSL	*Corpus Christianorum, Series Latina*
CSEL	*Corpus Scriptorum Ecclesiasticorum Latinorum*
MGH	*Monumenta Germaniae Historica*
PL	*Patrologia Latina*, ed. J.P. Migne (217 vols, Paris, 1844–55).
Rolls Series	*Rerum Britannicarum Medii Aevi Scriptores*, or Chronicles and Memorials of Great Britain and Ireland During the Middle Ages, published by authority of Her Majesty's Treasury under the direction of the Master of the Rolls (99 vols, London, 1858–96).

Primary sources

Abelard, *Commentary on Paul's Letter to the Romans*, trans. A.J. Minnis and A.B. Scott, in A.J. Minnis and A.B. Scott (eds), *Medieval Literary Theory and Criticism c.1100–c.1375* (Oxford, 1988), pp. 100–5; ed. E.M. Buytaert, *Commentaria in Epistolam Pauli ad Romanos* (*CCCM* 11, Turnhout, 1969).

Abelard, *Ethics*, ed. and trans. D.E. Luscombe (Oxford Medieval Texts), Oxford, 1971).

Abelard, *Historia Calamitatum*, trans. B. Radice, *The Letters of Abelard and Heloise* (Penguin Classics, Harmondsworth, 1974), pp. 57–106; trans. J.T. Muckle, *The Story of Abelard's Adversities* (Toronto, 1964); ed. J. Monfrin (4th edn, Paris, 1978).

Abelard, *Hymni Nocturni* (*PL* 178, cols 1775–80).

Abelard, *Sic et Non*, prologue, trans. A.J. Minnis and A.B. Scott, in A.J. Minnis and A.B. Scott (eds), *Medieval Literary Theory and Criticism c.1100–c.1375* (Oxford, 1988), pp. 87–100; ed. B.B. Boyer and R. McKeon (Chicago, 1976).

Abelard, *Theologia*, ed. E.M. Buytaert and C.J. Mews (*CCCM* 13, Turnhout, 1987).

Accessus ad Auctores, trans. A.J. Minnis and A.B. Scott, 'Introductions to the Authors', in A.J. Minnis and A.B. Scott (eds), *Medieval Literary Theory and Criticism c.1100–c.1375* (Oxford, 1988), pp. 15–36; ed. R.B.C. Huygens (Leiden, 1970), pp. 19–54.

Adam of Bremen, *History of the Archbishops of Hamburg–Bremen*, trans. F.J. Tschan, rev. T. Reuter (New York, 2002); ed. B. Schmeidler (*MGH Scriptores Rerum Germanicarum*, Hanover, 1917).

BIBLIOGRAPHY

Adam Usk, *Chronicle*, ed. and trans. C. Given-Wilson, *The Chronicle of Adam Usk 1377–1421* (Oxford Medieval Texts, Oxford, 1997).
Adnotationes Super Lucanum, ed. J. Endt (Leipzig, 1909).
Aegidius Romanus – see Giles of Rome.
Agnellus of Ravenna, *The Book of Pontiffs of the Church of Ravenna*, trans. D.M. Deliyannis (Washington, DC, 2004); ed. D.M. Deliyannis (*CCCM* 199, Turnhout, 2006).
Ailred of Rievaulx, *The Mirror of Charity*, trans. E. Connor (Kalamazoo, 1990).
Alan of Lille, *Anticlaudianus*, trans. J.J. Sheridan, *Anticlaudianus or the Good and Perfect Man* (Toronto, 1973); ed. R. Bossuat (Paris, 1955).
Alan of Lille, *De Planctu Naturae*, trans. J.J. Sheridan, *Plaint of Nature* (Toronto, 1980); ed. N.M. Häring, in *Studi Medievali*, 19 (1978), pp. 806–79.
Alberic of Monte Cassino, *Flores Rhetorici*, trans. J.M. Miller, *Flowers of Rhetoric*, in J.M. Miller, M.H. Prosser and T.W. Benson (eds), *Readings in Medieval Rhetoric* (Bloomington, 1973), pp. 132–61; ed. D.M. Inguanez and H.M. Willard (Montecassino, 1938).
Albertus Magnus, *Super Ethica Commentum et Quaestiones*, ed. W. Kübel (*Opera Omnia*, ed. B. Geyer, *et al.*, Münster 1951–, vol. 14, 1–2).
Alcuin, *De Virtutibus et Vitiis* (*PL* 101, cols 613–38).
Alcuin, *Disputatio de Rhetorica et de Virtutibus*, ed. and trans. W.S. Howell, *The Rhetoric of Alcuin and Charlemagne* (Princeton, 1941), pp. 66–155.
Alcuin, *Letters*, ed. E. Dümmler (*MGH Epistolae* 4, Berlin, 1895).
Aldhelm, *Letters*, ed. R. Ehwald, in *Aldhelmi Opera* (*MGH Auctores Antiquissimi* 15, Hanover, 1919).
Alexander of Hales, *Summa Theologica* (4 vols, Quaracchi edn, Ad Claras Aquas, 1924–48); *Summa Theologica. Tractatus Introductorius*, trans. A.J. Minnis and A.B. Scott, , in A.J. Minnis and A.B. Scott (eds), *Medieval Literary Theory and Criticism c.1100–c.1375* (Oxford, 1988), pp. 217–21.
Alexander Neckham, *De Naturis Rerum*, ed. T. Wright (Rolls Series, London, 1863).
Alexander Neckham, *Sacerdos ad Altare Accessurus*, ed. C.H. Haskins, *Studies in the History of Medieval Science* (Cambridge, MA, 1927), pp. 372–6; ed. T. Hunt, *Teaching and Learning Latin in Thirteenth-Century England* (3 vols, Cambridge, 1991), vol. I, pp. 269–71.
Ambrose, *De Obitu Valentiniani Consolatio* (*PL* 16, cols 1357–84).
Ambrose, *Expositio Evangelii Secundum Lucan*, ed. C. Schenkl (*CSEL* 32, Vienna, 1902).
Aquinas, *Quaestiones de Quolibet* (Commissio Leonina, *Opera Omnia*, vol. XXV, Rome, 1996).
Aquinas, *Summa Theologiae*, ed. and trans. T. Gilby, *et al.* (Blackfriars edn, 61 vols, London, 1964–80).
Aristotle, *Categories*, trans. J.L. Ackrill, in J. Barnes (ed.), *The Complete Works of Aristotle: The Revised Oxford Translation* (2 vols, Princeton, 1984), vol. I, pp. 3–24; ed. L. Minio-Paluello, *Categoriae vel Praedicamenta* (*Aristoteles Latinus* I.1–5, Bruges, 1961).
Aristotle, *Nicomachean Ethics*, trans. R. Crisp (Cambridge, 2000); ed. R.-A. Gauthier, *Ethica Nicomachea* (*Aristoteles Latinus* XXVI.2–4, Brussels, 1972–73).
Aristotle, *On Rhetoric*, trans. G.A. Kennedy (Oxford, 1991); ed. B. Schneider, *Rhetorica, Translatio Anonyma sive Vetus et Guillelmi de Moerbeka* (*Aristoteles Latinus* XXXI.1–2, Leiden, 1978).
Aristotle, *Physics*, trans. R. Waterfield (Oxford, 1996).
Aristotle, *Poetics*, trans. M.E. Hubbard, in *Classical Literary Criticism* (rev. edn,

Oxford, 1989), pp. 51–90; ed. L. Minio-Paluello, *De Arte Poetica, Cum Averrois Expositione* (*Aristoteles Latinus* XXXIII, Brussels, 1968).
Aristotle, *Posterior Analytics*, trans. J. Barnes, in J. Barnes (ed.), *The Complete Works of Aristotle: The Revised Oxford Translation* (2 vols, Princeton, 1984), vol. I, pp. 114–66; ed. L. Minio-Paluello and B.G. Dod, *Analytica Posteriora* (*Aristoteles Latinus* IV.1–4, Bruges, 1968).
Aristotle, *Prior Analytics*, trans. J. Barnes, in J. Barnes (ed.), *The Complete Works of Aristotle: The Revised Oxford Translation* (2 vols, Princeton, 1984), vol. I, pp. 39–113; ed. L. Minio-Paluello, *Analytica Priora* (*Aristoteles Latinus* III.1–4, Bruges, 1962).
Aristotle, *Topica*, trans. W.A. Pickard-Cambridge, in J. Barnes (ed.), *The Complete Works of Aristotle: The Revised Oxford Translation* (2 vols, Princeton 1984), vol. I, pp. 167–277; ed. L. Minio-Paluello, *Topica* (*Aristoteles Latinus* V.1–3, Brussels, 1969).
Arnulf of Orleans, *Glosule Super Lucanum*, ed. B.M. Marti (Rome, 1958); trans. A.J. Minnis and A.B. Scott, in A.J. Minnis and A.B. Scott (eds), *Medieval Literary Theory and Criticism c.1100–c.1375* (Oxford, 1988), pp. 155–8.
Asser, *Res Gestae Ælfredi*, trans. S. Keynes and M. Lapidge, *Alfred the Great* (Penguin Classics, Harmondsworth, 1983), pp. 67–110; ed. W.H. Stevenson, rev. D. Whitelock, *Asser's Life of King Alfred* (Oxford, 1959).
Astronomer, *Life of Louis*, trans. A. Cabaniss, *Son of Charlemagne: A Contemporary Life of Louis the Pious* (Syracuse, 1961); ed. E. Tremp, *Vita Hludowici Imperatoris* (*MGH Scriptores Rerum Germanicarum* 64, Hanover, 1995).
Athanasius, *Life of Antony*, trans. C. White, in *Early Christian Lives* (Penguin Classics, Harmondsworth, 1998).
Augustine, *Confessions*, trans. H. Chadwick (Oxford, 1991); ed. J.J. O'Donnell (3 vols, Oxford, 1992).
Augustine, *Contra Academicos*, trans. P. King, *Against the Academicians and The Teacher* (Indianapolis, 1995); ed. W.M. Green (*CCSL* 29, Turnhout, 1970).
Augustine, *Contra Faustum*, trans. R. Teske, *Answer to Faustus, a Manichean* (New York, 2007); ed. J. Zycha (*CSEL* 25, Vienna, 1891).
Augustine, *Contra Mendacium*, trans. H. Browne, *To Consentius: Against Lying*, in Augustine, *Seventeen Short Treatises* (Library of the Fathers vol. 22, Oxford, 1847), pp. 426–69; ed. J. Zycha (*CSEL* 41, Vienna, 1900).
Augustine, *De Catechizandis Rudibus*, trans. C.L. Cornish, *Of the Catechizing of the Unlearned*, in Augustine, *Seventeen Short Treatises* (Library of the Fathers vol. 22, Oxford, 1847), pp. 187–242; ed. J. Bauer (*CCSL* 46, Turnhout 1969).
Augustine, *De Civitate Dei*, trans. H. Bettenson, *On the City of God Against the Pagans* (2nd edn, Penguin Classics, Harmondsworth, 1984); ed. B. Dombart and A. Kalb (*CCSL* 47–8, Turnhout, 1955).
Augustine, *De Consensu Evangelistarum*, trans. S.D.F. Salmond, *The Harmony of the Gospels* (Select Library of the Nicene and Post-Nicene Fathers vol. 6, New York, 1888, pp. 65–236); ed. F. Weihrich (*CSEL* 43, Vienna, 1904).
Augustine, *De Diversis Quaestionibus LXXXIII*, trans. B. Ramsey, *Miscellany of Eighty-Three Questions*, in Augustine, *Responses to Miscellaneous Questions* (New York, 2008), pp. 27–157; ed. A. Mutzenbecher (*CCSL* 44A, Turnhout, 1975).
Augustine, *De Diversis Quaestionibus ad Simplicianum*, trans. B. Ramsey, *Miscellany of Questions in Response to Simplician*, in Augustine, *Responses to Miscellaneous Questions* (New York, 2008), pp. 174–231; ed. A. Mutzenbecher (*CCSL* 44, Turnhout, 1970).
Augustine, *De Doctrina Christiana*, ed. and trans. R.P.H. Green, *On Christian Teaching* (Oxford, 1995).

Augustine, *De Genesi ad Litteram Libri Duodecim*, trans. J.H. Taylor, *The Literal Meaning of Genesis* (Ancient Christian Writers 41-2, New York, 1982); ed. J. Zycha (*CSEL* 28.1, Vienna, 1894).
Augustine, *De Genesi Contra Manicheos*, trans. R.J. Teske, *Two Books on Genesis Against the Manichees*, in Augustine, *On Genesis* (Fathers of the Church vol. 84, Washington, DC, 1991), pp. 45-141.
Augustine, *De Magistro*, trans. P. King, *Against the Academicians and The Teacher* (Indianapolis, 1995); ed. K.-D. Daur (*CCSL* 29, Turnhout, 1970).
Augustine, *De Mendacio*, trans. H. Browne, *On Lying*, in Augustine, *Seventeen Short Treatises* (Library of the Fathers vol. 22, Oxford, 1847), pp. 382-425; ed. J. Zycha (*CSEL* 41, Vienna, 1900).
Augustine, *De Ordine*, trans. R.P. Russell, in Augustine, *Divine Providence and the Problem of Evil* (Fathers of the Church vol. 5, New York, 1948), pp. 239-331; ed. W.M. Green (*CCSL* 29, Turnhout, 1970).
Augustine, *De Trinitate*, trans. E. Hill, *The Trinity* (New York, 1991); trans. S. McKenna, *On the Trinity: Books 8-15* (Cambridge, 2002); ed. W.J. Mountain (*CCSL* 50, Turnhout, 1968).
Augustine, *De Utilitate Credendi*, trans. R. Kearney, *The Advantage of Believing*, in Augustine, *On Christian Belief* (New York, 2005), pp. 116-48; ed. J. Zycha (*CSEL* 25, Vienna, 1891).
Augustine, *De Vera Religione*, trans. E. Hill, *True Religion*, in Augustine, *On Christian Belief* (New York, 2005), pp. 29-104; ed. K.-D. Daur (*CCSL* 32, Turnhout, 1962).
Augustine, *Enchiridion de Fide et Spe et Caritate*, trans. B. Harbert, in Augustine, *On Christian Belief* (New York, 2005), pp. 273-343; ed. E. Evans (*CCSL* 46, Turnhout, 1969).
Augustine, *Letters*, trans. R. Teske (4 vols, New York, 2001-05); ed. A. Goldbacher (*CSEL* 34-5, 44, 57, Vienna, 1895, 1904, 1923).
Augustine, *Enarrationes in Psalmos*, trans. M. Boulding, *Expositions of the Psalms* (6 vols, New York, 2000-04); ed. E. Dekkers and J. Fraipont (*CCSL* 38-40, Turnhout, 1956).
Augustine, *On the Literal Interpretation of Genesis: An Unfinished Book*, trans. R.J. Teske, in Augustine, *On Genesis* (Fathers of the Church vol. 84, Washington, DC, 1991), pp. 143-88; *De Genesi ad Literam Imperfectus Liber*, ed. J. Zycha (*CSEL* 28, Vienna, 1894).
Augustine, *Quaestiones Evangeliorum*, ed. A. Mutzenbecher (*CCSL* 44, Turnhout, 1980).
Augustine, *Retractationes*, trans. M.I. Bogan, *Retractions* (Fathers of the Church vol. 60, Washington, DC, 1968); ed. A. Mutzenbecher (*CCSL* 57, Turnhout, 1984).
Augustine, *Sermones*, trans. E. Hill, *Sermons* (10 vols, New York, 1990-95); *PL* 38-9.
Augustine, *Soliloquies*, trans. C.C. Starbuck (Select Library of the Nicene and Post-Nicene Fathers vol. 7, New York, 1888), pp. 537-60.
Aulus Gellius, *Noctes Atticae*, trans. J.C. Rolfe, *Attic Nights* (3 vols, Loeb Classical Library, Cambridge, MA, 1927).
Averroes, *Middle Commentary on Aristotle's Poetics*, trans. C.E. Butterworth (Princeton, 1986); trans. O.B. Hardison, in A. Preminger, O.B. Hardison and K. Kerrane (eds), *Classical and Medieval Literary Criticism: Translations and Interpretations* (New York, 1974), pp. 349-82.
Basin – see Thomas Basin.
Battista Guarino, *De Ordine Docendi et Scribendi*, ed. and trans. C.W. Kallendorf, *A Program of Teaching and Learning*, in C.W. Kallendorf, *Humanist Educational*

Treatises (Cambridge, MA, 2002), pp. 260–309; trans. W.H. Woodward, *Vittorino da Feltre and Other Humanist Educators* (Cambridge, 1905), pp. 161–78.
Bede, *Commentary on the Acts of the Apostles*, trans. L.T. Martin (Kalamazoo, 1989).
Bede, *De Arte Metrica*, trans. C.B. Kendall, *The Art of Poetry and Rhetoric* (Saarbrücken, 1991); ed. C.B. Kendall (*CCSL* 123A, Turnhout, 1975, pp. 81–141).
Bede, *De Schematibus et Tropis*, trans. G.H. Tannenhaus, *Concerning Figures and Tropes*, in J.M. Miller, M.H. Prosser and T.W. Benson (eds), *Readings in Medieval Rhetoric* (Bloomington, 1973), pp. 96–122; ed. C.B. Kendall (*CCSL* 123A, Turnhout, 1975, pp. 142–71).
Bede, *De Tabernaculo*, trans. A.G. Holder, *On the Tabernacle* (Liverpool, 1994); ed. D. Hurst (*CCSL* 119A, Turnhout, 1969).
Bede, *De Templo* trans. S. Connolly, *On the Temple* (Liverpool, 1995); ed. D. Hurst (*CCSL* 119A, Turnhout, 1969).
Bede, *De Temporibus*, ed. C.W. Jones (*CCSL* 123C, Turnhout, 1980, pp. 585–611).
Bede, *De Temporum Ratione*, trans. F. Wallis, *The Reckoning of Time* (Liverpool, 1999); ed. C.W. Jones (*CCSL* 123B, Turnhout, 1977).
Bede, *Historia Ecclesiastica Gentis Anglorum*, trans. B. Colgrave, rev. J. McClure and R. Collins, *The Ecclesiastical History of the English People* (Oxford, 1994); ed. B. Colgrave and R.A.B. Mynors (rev. edn, Oxford Medieval Texts, Oxford, 1991).
Bede, *Homilies on the Gospels*, trans. L.T. Martin and D. Hurst (2 vols, Kalamazoo, 1991).
Bede, *In Cantica Canticorum Allegorica Expositio* (*PL* 91, cols 1065–236).
Bede, *In Lucae Evangelium Expositio*, ed. D. Hurst (*CCSL* 120, Turnhout, 1960).
Bede, *On Ezra and Nehemiah*, trans. S. DeGregorio (Liverpool, 2006); ed. D. Hurst, *In Ezram et Neemiam* (*CCSL* 119A, Turnhout, 1969).
Bede, *Prose Life of Cuthbert*, ed. and trans. B. Colgrave, *Two Lives of Cuthbert* (Cambridge, 1940), pp. 141–307.
Bernard of Clairvaux, *De Consideratione ad Eugenium Papam*, trans. J.D. Anderson and E.T. Kennan, *Five Books on Consideration: Advice to a Pope* (Kalamazoo, 1976).
Bernardus Silvestris, *Commentary on the First Six Books of Virgil's Aeneid*, trans. E.G. Schreiber and T.E. Maresca (Lincoln, 1979); ed. J.W. Jones and E.F. Jones, *Commentum Super Sex Libros Eneidos Virgilii* (Lincoln, 1977).
Bodin, *Method for the Easy Comprehension of History*, trans. B. Reynolds (New York, 1945).
Boethius, *An Overview of the Structure of Rhetoric*, trans. J.M. Miller, in J.M. Miller, M.H. Prosser and T.W. Benson (eds), *Readings in Medieval Rhetoric* (Bloomington, 1973), pp. 70–6; *Speculatio de Cognatione Rhetoricae* (*PL* 64, cols 1218–25).
Boethius, *Consolation of Philosophy*, trans. S.J. Tester (Loeb Classical Library, Cambridge, MA, 1973); ed. L. Bieler (*CCSL* 94, Turnhout 1957).
Boethius, *De Topicis Differentiis*, trans. E. Stump (Ithaca, 1978); *PL* 64, cols 1173–222.
Boethius, *In Ciceronis Topica*, trans. E. Stump (Ithaca, 1988); *PL* 64, cols 1039–174.
Bonaventure, *Breviloquium*, trans. E.E. Nemmers (London, 1946); ed. Quaracchi, *Opera Theologica Selecta* (5 vols, Florence, 1934–64), vol. V, pp. 1–175.
Brunetto Latini, *Rettorica*, ed. F. Maggini (Florence, 1915).
Bruni – see Leonardo Bruni.
Bruno of Merseburg, *De Bello Saxonico*, ed. W. Wattenbach (*MGH Scriptores Rerum Germanicarum*, Hanover, 1880).
Byrhtferth of Ramsey, *Enchiridion*, ed. P.S. Baker and M. Lapidge (Early English Texts Society 15, Oxford, 1995).
Caesar, *Civil War*, trans. A.G. Peskett (Loeb Classical Library, Cambridge, MA, 1914).

Caesar, *Gallic War*, trans. H.J. Edwards (Loeb Classical Library, Cambridge, MA, 1917).
Calcidius, *Commentary on Plato's Timaeus*, ed. J.H. Waszink, *Plato Latinus* (Leiden, 1972), vol. IV, pp. 57–346.
Carmen de Hastingae Proelio of Guy Bishop of Amiens, ed. and trans. F. Barlow (Oxford Medieval Texts, Oxford 1999).
Cassian, *Collationes*, trans. E.C.S. Gibson (Select Library of the Nicene and Post-Nicene Fathers vol. 11, Michigan, 1964, pp. 291–545); ed. M. Petschenig, rev. G. Kreuz (*CSEL* 13, Vienna, 2004).
Cassian, *Institutes*, trans. E.C.S. Gibson (Select Library of the Nicene and Post-Nicene Fathers vol. 11, Michigan, 1964, pp. 199–290); ed. M. Petschenig, *De Institutis Coenobiorum* (*CSEL* 17, Vienna, 1888).
Cassiodorus, *Expositio Psalmorum*, trans. P.G. Walsh, *Explanation of the Psalms* (Fathers of the Church vols 51–3, New York, 1990–91); ed. M. Adriaen (*CCSL* 97–8, Turnhout, 1958).
Cassiodorus, *Institutiones*, trans. J.W. Halporn, intr. M. Vessey, *Institutions of Divine and Secular Learning and On the Soul* (Liverpool, 2004); ed. R.A.B. Mynors (Oxford, 1937).
Chandos Herald – see Herald of John Chandos.
Chrétien de Troyes, *Arthurian Romances*, trans. W.W. Comfort (London, 1914).
Cicero, *Academica*, trans. H. Rackham (Loeb Classical Library, Cambridge, MA, 1967, pp. 406–659).
Cicero, *Brutus*, trans. G.L. Hendrickson (Loeb Classical Library, Cambridge, MA, 1962, pp. 18–293).
Cicero, *De Amicitia*, trans. W.A. Falconer (Loeb Classical Library, Cambridge, MA, 1923, pp. 108–211).
Cicero, *De Divinatione*, trans. W.A. Falconer (Loeb Classical Library, Cambridge, MA, 1923, pp. 222–539).
Cicero, *De Fato*, trans. H. Rackham (Loeb Classical Library, Cambridge, MA, 1942, pp. 192–249).
Cicero, *De Finibus*, trans. H. Rackham, *On Ends* (2nd edn, Loeb Classical Library, Cambridge, MA, 1931).
Cicero, *De Inventione*, trans. H.M. Hubbell, *On Invention* (Loeb Classical Library, Cambridge, MA, 1949).
Cicero, *De Legibus*, trans. C.W. Keyes (Loeb Classical Library, Cambridge, MA, 1928, pp. 296–519); trans. J.E.G. Zetzel, *On the Commonwealth and On the Laws* (Cambridge, 1999).
Cicero, *De Natura Deorum*, trans. H. Rackham (Loeb Classical Library, Cambridge, MA, 1933, pp. 2–387).
Cicero, *De Officiis*, trans. M.T. Griffin and E.M. Atkins, *On Duties* (Cambridge, 1991); trans. W. Miller (Loeb Classical Library, Cambridge, MA, 1921); ed. M. Winterbottom (Oxford, 1994).
Cicero, *De Optimo Genere Oratorum*, trans. H.M. Hubbell (Loeb Classical Library, Cambridge, MA, 1949, pp. 354–73).
Cicero, *De Oratore*, trans. E. Sutton and H. Rackham (Loeb Classical Library, Cambridge, MA, 1948); ed. A.S. Wilkins, *Ciceronis De Oratore Liber I* (3rd edn, Oxford, 1895).
Cicero, *Epistulae ad Familiares*, trans. D.R. Shackleton Bailey, *Letters to Friends* (3 vols, Loeb Classical Library, Cambridge, MA, 2001).
Cicero, *Letters to Atticus*, trans. D.R. Shackleton Bailey (4 vols, Loeb Classical Library, Cambridge, MA, 1999).

Cicero, *Orator*, trans. H.M. Hubbell (Loeb Classical Library, Cambridge, MA, 1962, pp. 306–509).
Cicero, *Partitiones Oratoriae*, trans. H. Rackham (Loeb Classical Library, Cambridge, MA, 1942, pp. 310–421).
Cicero, *Pro Archia*, trans. N.H. Watts (Loeb Classical Library, Cambridge, MA, 1923, pp. 6–41).
Cicero, *Pro Milone*, trans. N.H. Watts (Loeb Classical Library, Cambridge, MA, 1931, pp. 6–123).
Cicero, *Pro Sestio*, trans. R. Gardner (Loeb Classical Library, Cambridge, MA, 1958, pp. 36–239).
Cicero, *Topica*, trans. H. M. Hubbell (Loeb Classical Library, Cambridge, MA, 1949, pp. 382–459); ed. and trans. T. Reinhardt, *Cicero's Topica* (Oxford, 2006).
Cicero, *Tusculan Disputations*, trans. J.E. King (Loeb Classical Library, Cambridge, MA, 1945).
Coluccio Salutati – see Salutati.
Commynes, *Mémoires*, ed. J. Calmette (3 vols, Paris, 1924–25); ed. S. Kinser, trans. I. Cazeaux, *The Memoirs of Philippe de Commynes* (2 vols, Columbia, 1969–73).
Condemnation of 219 Propositions, trans. E.L. Fortin and P.D. O'Neill, in R. Lerner and M. Mahdi (eds), *Medieval Political Philosophy: A Sourcebook* (Toronto, 1963), pp. 337–54.
Conrad of Hirsau, *Dialogue on the Authors*, trans. A.J. Minnis and A.B. Scott, in A.J. Minnis and A.B. Scott (eds), *Medieval Literary Theory and Criticism c. 1100–c.1375* (Oxford, 1988), pp. 39–64; ed. R.B.C. Huygens, *Dialogus Super Auctores* (Leiden, 1970), pp. 71–131.
Corpus Iuris Canonici, ed. E. Friedberg (2 vols, Leipzig, 1879–81).
Cosmas of Prague, *The Chronicle of the Czechs*, trans. L. Wolverton (Washington, DC, 2009); ed. B. Bretholz, *Cronica Boemorum* (*MGH Scriptores Rerum Germanicarum* 2, Berlin, 1923).
Dante, *Monarchia*, ed. and trans. P. Shaw (Cambridge, 1995).
Dares Phrygius, *De Excidio Troiae Historia*, trans. R.M. Frazer, *The Trojan War: The Chronicles of Dictys of Crete and Dares the Phrygian* (Bloomington, 1966); ed. F.O. Meister (Leipzig, 1873).
Decrees of the Fourth Lateran Council, ed. and trans. N.P. Tanner, *Decrees of the Ecumenical Councils* (2 vols, London, 1990), vol. I, pp. 230–71.
Dictys Cretensis, *Ephemeridos Belli Troiani Libri*, trans. R.M. Frazer, *The Trojan War: The Chronicles of Dictys of Crete and Dares the Phrygian* (Bloomington, 1966); ed. W. Eisenhut (Leipzig, 1973).
Diodorus of Sicily, *Library of History*, trans. C.H. Oldfather (12 vols, Loeb Classical Library, Cambridge, MA, 1933).
Disticha Catonis, ed. M. Boas, rev. H.J. Botschuyver (Amsterdam, 1952); trans. W.J. Chase, *The Distichs of Cato* (Madison, 1922).
Dominicus Gundissalinus, *De Divisione Philosophiae*, ed. L. Baur (Münster, 1903); ed. A. Fidora and D. Werner, *Über die Einteilung der Philosophie* (Freiburg, 2007).
Donatus, *Ars Maior*, ed. L. Holtz, *Donat et la Tradition de l'Enseignement Grammatical: Étude sur l'Ars Donati et sa Diffusion (IVe–IXe Siècle) et Edition Critique* (Paris, 1981), pp. 603–74.
Dudo of St Quentin, *History of the Normans*, trans. E. Christiansen (Woodbridge, 1998); ed. J. Lair, *De Moribus et Actis Primorum Normanniae Ducum* (Caen, 1865).
Eadmer, *Historia Novorum in Anglia*, trans. G. Bosanquet, *Eadmer's History of Recent Events in England* (London, 1964); ed. M. Rule (Rolls Series, London, 1884).

Eadmer, *Life of Anselm*, ed. and trans. R.W. Southern (Oxford Medieval Texts, Oxford, 1972).
Einhard, *Translatio et Miracula Marcellini et Petri*, trans. P.E. Dutton, *Charlemagne's Courtier: The Complete Einhard* (Ontario, 1998), pp. 69–130; ed. G. Waitz (*MGH Scriptores Rerum Germanicarum* 15, Hanover, 1888).
Einhard, *Vita Karoli Magni*, trans. P.E. Dutton, *Charlemagne's Courtier: The Complete Einhard* (Ontario, 1998), pp. 15–39; ed. L. Halphen (5th edn, Paris, 1981).
Encomium Emmae Reginae, ed. and trans. A. Campbell (Cambridge, 1949); rev. S. Keynes (Cambridge, 1998).
Engelbert of Admont, *De Ortu, Progressu et Fine Regnorum et Praecipue Regni Seu Imperii Romani*, trans. T. Izbicki and C. Nederman, *Three Tracts on Empire* (Bristol, 2000), pp. 37–93; ed. M. Goldast, *Politica Imperialia sive Discursus Politici* (Frankfurt, 1614), pp. 754–73.
Engelbert of Admont, *Speculum Virtutum Moralium*, ed. B. Pez, *Bibliotheca Ascetica Antiquo-Nova* (12 vols, Regensburg, 1723–40), vol. III, pp. 3–498.
Ennodius, *Vita Epiphani*, ed. W. Hartel (*CSEL* 6, Vienna, 1882, pp. 331–83).
Ermoldus Nigellus, *In Honorem Hludowici Pii*, ed. and trans. E. Faral, *Poème sur Louis le Pieux* (Paris, 1964).
Eusebius, *Chronicon*, ed. R. Helm, *Die Chronik des Hieronymus* (3rd edn, Berlin, 1984).
Eusebius, *Ecclesiastical History*, trans. G.A. Williamson (Penguin Classics, Harmondsworth, 1965).
Eusebius, *Laus Constantini*, trans. H.A. Drake, *In Praise of Constantine: A Historical Study and New Translation of Eusebius' Tricennial Orations* (University of California Publications Classical Studies 15, Berkeley, 1976), pp. 83–102.
Eusebius (with reworking by Jerome), *Onomasticon*, ed. and trans. R.S. Notley and Z. Safrai (Leiden, 2005)
Eutropius, *Breviarium ab Urbe Condita*, trans. H.W. Bird (Liverpool, 1993); ed. F. Ruehl (Leipzig, 1887).
Flodoard of Rheims, *Annals* (919–966), trans. S. Fanning and B.S. Bachrach (Ontario, 2004).
Florus, *Epitome of Roman History*, trans. E.S. Forster (Loeb Classical Library, Cambridge, MA, 1929).
Fortunatianus, *Ars Rhetorica*, trans. J.M. Miller, in J.M. Miller, M.H. Prosser and T.W. Benson (eds), *Readings in Medieval Rhetoric* (Bloomington, 1973), pp. 25–32; ed. K. Halm, *Rhetores Latini Minores* (Leipzig, 1863), pp. 81–134.
Freculf, *Historiae*, ed. M.I. Allen (*CCCM* 169A, Turnhout, 2002).
Froissart, *Chroniques*, trans. G. Brereton, *Chronicles* (Penguin Classics, Harmondsworth, 1968); ed. P.F. Ainsworth, G.T. Diller and A. Varvaro, *Chroniques* (2 vols, Paris, 2001–04).
Frontinus, *Strategemata*, trans. C.E. Bennett (Loeb Classical Library, Cambridge, MA, 1925).
Fulcher of Chartres, *Historia Hierosolymitana*, trans. F.R. Ryan, *A History of the Expedition to Jerusalem 1095–1127* (Knoxville, 1969); *Historia Hierosolymitana* book I, trans. M.E. McGinty, *Chronicle of the First Crusade* (Philadelphia, 1941).
Fulgentius, *The Exposition of the Content of Vergil According to Moral Philosophy*, trans. L.G. Whitbread, *Fulgentius the Mythographer* (Colombus, 1971), pp. 119–35; ed. A. Preminger, O.B. Hardison and K. Kerrane, *Classical and Medieval Literary Criticism: Translations and Interpretations* (New York, 1974), pp. 329–40.
Fulgentius, *Mythologies*, trans. L.G. Whitbread, *Fulgentius the Mythographer* (Colombus, 1971), pp. 39–99.

Gaimar, *Estoire des Engleis*, ed. and trans. I. Short, *History of the English* (Oxford, 2009).
Galbert of Bruges, *The Murder of Charles the Good*, trans. J.B. Ross (New York, 1959); ed. J. Rider, *De Multro Traditione et Occisione Gloriosi Karoli Comitis Flandriarum* (*CCCM* 131, Turnhout, 1994).
Geffrei Gaimar – see Gaimar.
Gennadius – see Jerome.
Geoffrey of Monmouth, *Historia Regum Britanniae*, ed. M.D. Reeve, trans. N. Wright, *The History of the Kings of Britain* (Woodbridge, 2007); trans. L. Thorpe (Penguin Classics, Harmondsworth, 1966).
Geoffrey of Vinsauf, *Documentum de Modo et Arte Dictandi et Versificandi*, trans. R. Parr, *Instruction in the Method and Art of Speaking and Versifying* (Milwaukee, 1968); ed. E. Faral, *Les Arts Poétiques du XIIe et du XIIIe Siècles: Recherches et Documents sur la Technique Littéraire du Moyen Age* (Paris, 1924), pp. 265–320.
Geoffrey of Vinsauf, *Poetria Nova*, ed. and trans. E. Gallo, *The Poetria Nova and Its Sources in Early Rhetorical Doctrine* (The Hague, 1971); trans. J.B. Kopp, *The New Poetics*, in J.J. Murphy (ed.), *Three Medieval Rhetorical Arts* (Berkeley, 1971), pp. 32–108; ed. E. Faral, *Les Arts Poétiques du XIIe et du XIIIe Siècles: Recherches et Documents sur la Technique Littéraire du Moyen Age* (Paris, 1924), pp. 197–262.
Gerald of Wales, *De Eruditione Principum*, trans. J. Stevenson (London, 1858; reprinted Felinfach, 1991); ed. J.S. Brewer, J.F. Dimock and G.F. Warner, *Giraldi Cambrensis Opera* (8 vols, Rolls Series, London, 1861–91), vol. VIII, pp. 3–329.
Gerald of Wales, *De Rebus a Se Gestis*, trans. H.E. Butler, *The Autobiography of Giraldus Cambrensis* (London, 1937; reprinted Woodbridge, 2005); ed. J.S. Brewer, J.F. Dimock and G.F. Warner, *Giraldi Cambrensis Opera* (8 vols, Rolls Series, London, 1861–91), vol. I, pp. 1–122.
Gerald of Wales, *Descriptio Cambriae*, trans. L. Thorpe, *The Journey Through Wales and the Description of Wales* (Penguin Classics, Harmondsworth, 1978), pp. 211–74; ed. J.S. Brewer, J.F. Dimock and G.F. Warner, *Giraldi Cambrensis Opera* (8 vols, Rolls Series, London, 1861–91), vol. VI, pp. 155–227.
Gerald of Wales, Letter 3, to William de Montibus, Chancellor of Lincoln, ed. R.B.C. Huygens, trans. B. Dawson, in Y. Lefèvre and R.B.C. Huygens (eds), *Speculum Duorum or a Mirror of Two Men* (Cardiff, 1974), pp. 168–75.
Gerald of Wales, *Expugnatio Hibernica*, ed. and trans. A.B. Scott and F.X. Martin, *The Conquest of Ireland* (Dublin, 1978).
Gerald of Wales, *Gemma Ecclesiastica*, trans. J.J. Hagen, *The Jewel of the Church* (Leiden, 1979).
Gerald of Wales, *Itinerarium Cambriae*, trans. L. Thorpe, *The Journey Through Wales and the Description of Wales* (Penguin Classics, Harmondsworth, 1978), pp. 63–209; ed. J.S. Brewer, J.F. Dimock and G.F. Warner, *Giraldi Cambrensis Opera* (8 vols, Rolls Series, London, 1861–91), vol. VI, pp. 3–152.
Gerald of Wales, *Retractationes*, ed. J.S. Brewer, J.F. Dimock and G.F. Warner, *Giraldi Cambrensis Opera* (8 vols, Rolls Series, London, 1861–91), vol. I, pp. 425–7.
Gerald of Wales, *Topographia Hibernica*, trans. J.J. O'Meara, *The History and Topography of Ireland* (Penguin Classics, Harmondsworth, 1982); ed. J.S. Brewer, J.F. Dimock and G.F. Warner, *Giraldi Cambrensis Opera* (8 vols, Rolls Series, London, 1861–91), vol. V, pp. 3–204.
Gervase of Canterbury, *Chronica*, ed. W. Stubbs, *Opera Historica* (2 vols, Rolls Series, London, 1879–80), vol. I, pp. 84–594.
Gervase of Canterbury, *Gesta Regum*, ed. W. Stubbs, *Opera Historica* (2 vols, Rolls Series, London, 1879–80), vol. II, pp. 3–106.

Gervase of Canterbury, *Mappa Mundi*, ed. W. Stubbs, *Opera Historica* (2 vols, Rolls Series, London, 1879–80), vol. II, pp. 414–49.
Gervase of Tilbury, *Otia Imperialia*, ed. and trans. S.E. Banks and J.W. Binns, *Recreation for an Emperor* (Oxford Medieval Texts, Oxford, 2002).
Gesta Francorum et Aliorum Hierosolimitanorum, ed. and trans. R. Hill (Oxford Medieval Texts, Oxford, 1962).
Gesta Romanorum, trans. C. Swann, rev. W. Hooper (London, 1906).
Gesta Stephani, ed. and trans. K.R. Potter, rev. R.H.C. Davis (Oxford Medieval Texts, Oxford, 1976).
Gilbert Crispin, *Disputatio Iudei et Christiani*, ed. A.S. Abulafia and G.R. Evans, *The Works of Gilbert Crispin* (Auctores Britannici Medii Aevi 8, Oxford, 1986), pp. 8–54.
Gilbert of Mons, *Chronicle of Hainaut*, trans. L. Napran (Woodbridge, 2005).
Gildas, *De Excidio Britanniae*, ed. and trans. M. Winterbottom, *The Ruin of Britain* (Chichester, 1978).
Giles of Rome, *De Differentia Rhetoricae Ethicae et Politicae*, ed. G. Bruni, 'The *De Differentia Rhetoricae Ethicae et Politicae* of Aegidius Romanus', *New Scholasticism*, 6 (1932), pp. 1–18.
Giles of Rome, *De Regimine Principum* (Venice, 1502); prologue, trans. M.S. Kempshall, in A.S. McGrade, J. Kilcullen and M.S. Kempshall (eds), *The Cambridge Translations of Medieval Philosophical Texts. Vol. II: Ethics and Political Philosophy* (Cambridge, 2001), pp. 203–12; trans. A.J. Minnis and A.B. Scott, *Medieval Literary Theory and Criticism 1100–1375* (Oxford, 1988), pp. 248–50.
Giles of Rome, *Super Libros Rhetoricorum* (Venice, 1542).
Giovanni Pontano – see Pontano.
Giovanni Villani, *Chronicle*, trans. R.E. Selfe and P.H. Wicksteed, *Villani's Chronicle: Selections from the First Nine Books of the Croniche Fiorentine of Giovanni Villani* (London, 1906).
[Glanvill], *Tractatus de Legibus et Consuetudinibus Regni Anglie Que Glanvilla Vocatur*, ed. and trans. G.D.G. Hall, *The Treatise on the Laws and Customs of England Commonly Called Glanvill* (London, 1965).
Glossa Ordinaria, ed. A. Rusch (Strassburg, 1480–81; reprinted Turnhout, 1992).
Gratian, *Decretum*, ed. E. Friedberg, *Corpus Iuris Canonici* (2 vols, Leipzig, 1879–81), vol. I.
Gregory the Great, *Dialogues*, trans. O.J. Zimmerman (Fathers of the Church vol. 49, Washington, DC, 1959); ed. A. de Vogüé (3 vols, Sources Chrétiennes 251, 260, 265, Paris, 1978–80).
Gregory the Great, *Homiliae in Hiezechihelem Prophetam*, ed. M. Adriaen, *Homilies on Ezekiel* (CCSL 142, Turnhout, 1971); ed. and trans. C. Morel (2 vols, Sources Chrétiennes 327, 360, Paris, 1986–90); trans. T. Gray, *The Homilies of Gregory the Great on the Book of the Prophet Ezekiel* (Etna, 1990).
Gregory the Great, *In Librum Primum Regum Expositio*, ed. and trans. A. de Vogüé (4 vols, Sources Chrétiennes 351, 391, 432, 449, Paris, 1989–2000).
Gregory the Great, *Letters*, trans. J.R.C. Martyn (3 vols, Toronto, 2004).
Gregory the Great, *Moralia in Job*, trans. J. Bliss, *Morals on the Book of Job* (Library of the Fathers vols 18, 21, 23, 31, Oxford, 1843–50); ed. M. Adriaen (CCSL 143, Turnhout, 1979–85).
Gregory the Great, *XL Homiliae in Evangelia*, trans. D. Hurst, *Forty Gospel Homilies* (Kalamazoo, 1990); ed. R. Etaix (CCSL 141, Turnhout, 1999).
Gregory the Great, *Regula Pastoralis*, trans. H. Davis, *Pastoral Care* (Ancient Christian Writers 11, Washington, DC, 1950); ed. F. Rommel (Sources Chrétiennes 381, 382, Paris, 1992).

Gregory of Tours, *Glory of the Confessors*, trans. R. van Dam (Liverpool, 1988).
Gregory of Tours, *Histories*, trans. L. Thorpe, *The History of the Franks* (Penguin Classics, Harmondsworth, 1974); ed. B. Krusch, W. Levison and W. Holtzmann, *Historiarum Libri Decem* (*MGH Scriptores Rerum Merovingarum*, 3 vols, Hanover, 1937–51).
Guarino da Verona, *Letters*, ed. R. Sabbadini, *Guarino Veronese Epistolario* (3 vols, Venice, 1915–19); trans. I. Thomson, 'Guarino's Views on History and Historiography', *Explorations in Renaissance Culture*, 3 (1976), pp. 49–69.
Guibert of Nogent, *Gesta Dei per Francos*, trans. R. Levine, *The Deeds of God Through the Franks* (Woodbridge, 1997); ed. R.B.C. Huygens (*CCCM* 127A, Turnhout, 1996).
Guibert of Nogent, *Liber Quo Ordine Sermo Fieri Debeat*, trans. J.M. Miller, *A Book About the Way in Which a Sermon Ought To Be Given*, in J.M. Miller, M.H. Prosser and T.W. Benson (eds), *Readings in Medieval Rhetoric* (Bloomington, 1973), pp. 162–81; ed. R.B.C. Huygens (*CCCM* 127, Turnhout, 1993).
Guibert of Nogent, *Monodiae*, trans. P. Archambault, *A Monk's Confession: The Memoirs of Guibert of Nogent* (Philadelphia, 1996); trans. J.F. Benton, *Self and Society in Medieval France* (Toronto, 1984); ed. and trans. E.R. Labande (Paris, 1981).
Guibert of Tournai, *Eruditio Regum et Principum*, ed. A. de Poorter (Louvain, 1914).
Guicciardini, *Considerations on the Discourses of Machiavelli on the First Decade of T. Livy*, trans. M. Grayson, in C. Grayson (ed.), *Francesco Guicciardini: Selected Writings* (London, 1965), pp. 61–124.
Guicciardini, *Dialogue on the Government of Florence*, trans. A. Brown (Cambridge, 1994).
Guicciardini, *The History of Italy*, trans. S. Alexander (New York, 1969).
Guicciardini, *Ricordi*, trans. M. Grayson, in C. Grayson (ed.), *Francesco Guicciardini: Selected Writings* (London, 1965), pp. 4–56; ed. R. Spongano (Florence, 1951).
Guillelmus Peraldus, *De Eruditione Principum*, in R. Busa (ed.), *Thomae Aquinatis Opera Omnia* (7 vols, Stuttgart, 1980), vol. VII, pp. 89–121.
Haimo of Auxerre, *Explanatio in Psalmos* (*PL* 116, cols 193–696).
Hegisippus, ed. V. Ussani, *Hegesippi Qui Dicitur Historiae Libri V* (*CSEL* 66, Vienna, 1932).
Henry of Andelys, *Psychomachia*, ed. and trans. L.J. Paetow, *Two Medieval Satires on the University of Paris: La Bataille des VII Ars of Henri d'Andeli and the Morale Scolarium of John of Garland* (Berkeley, 1914), pp. 37–60.
Henry of Huntingdon, *Historia Anglorum*, ed. and trans. D. Greenway, *History of the English* (Oxford Medieval Texts, Oxford, 1996).
Henry Knighton – see Knighton.
Herald of John Chandos, *Life of the Black Prince*, ed. and trans. M.K. Pope and E.C. Lodge (Oxford, 1910).
Herbert of Bosham, *Vita Sancti Thomae*, ed. J.C. Robertson, in J. C. Robertson and J. B. Sheppard (eds), *Materials for the History of Thomas Becket* (7 vols, Rolls Series, London, 1875–85), vol. III, pp. 155–534.
'Hibernicus Exul', *In Praise of Poetry*, ed. and trans. P. Godman, *Poetry of the Carolingian Renaissance* (London, 1985), pp. 174–9.
Higden, *Polychronicon*, ed. C. Babington and J.R. Lumby (9 vols, Rolls Series, London, 1865–86).
Hilary of Poitiers, *De Trinitate*, trans. S. McKenna (Fathers of the Church vol. 25, New York, 1954); ed. P.F. Smulders (*CCSL* 62, Turnhout, 1979–80).
Hilary of Poitiers, *Tractatus Super Psalmos*, ed. J. Doignon (*CCSL* 61, Turnhout, 1997).
Histoire de Guillaume le Maréchal, ed. A.J. Holden, trans. S. Gregory (London, 2004).

Historia Augusta, trans. D. Magie (3 vols, Loeb Classical Library, Cambridge, MA, 1924–32).
Homer, *Iliad*, trans. M. Hammond (Penguin Classics, Harmondsworth, 1987); *Ilias Latina*, ed. M. Scaffai (2nd edn, Bologna, 1997).
Honorius of Autun, *De Animae Exsilio et Patria* (*PL* 172, cols 1241–6).
Honorius of Autun, *De Decem Plagis Aegypti* (*PL* 172, cols 265–70).
Honorius of Autun, *Imago Mundi*, ed. V.I.J. Flint, 'Honorius Augustodunensis *Imago Mundi*', *Archives d'Histoire Doctrinale et Littéraire du Moyen Âge*, 49 (1983), pp. 7–153.
Horace, *Ars Poetica*, trans. H.R. Fairclough (Loeb Classical Library, Cambridge, MA, 1929), pp. 450–89.
Horace, *Epistles*, trans. H.R. Fairclough (Loeb Classical Library, Cambridge, MA, 1929).
Horace, *Epodes*, trans. N. Rudd (Loeb Classical Library, Cambridge, MA, 2004).
Horace, *Odes*, trans. N. Rudd (Loeb Classical Library, Cambridge, MA, 2004).
Horace, *Satires*, trans. H.R. Fairclough (Loeb Classical Library, Cambridge, MA, 1929).
Hrabanus Maurus, *Commentaria in Exodum* (*PL* 108, cols 9–246).
Hrabanus Maurus, *De Clericorum Institutione*, ed. D. Zimpel (Frankfurt, 1996).
Hrabanus Maurus, *Expositio in Epistolam ad Galatas* (*PL* 112, cols 245–382).
Hugh of Fleury, *Historia Ecclesiastica* (*PL* 163, cols 821–54).
Hugh of St Victor, *De Archa Noe*, in *Selected Spiritual Writings* (New York, 1962), pp. 45–153; ed. P. Sicard (*CCCM* 176, Turnhout, 2001).
Hugh of St Victor, *De Sacramentis Christianae Fidei*, trans. R.J. Deferrari, *On the Sacraments of the Christian Faith (De Sacramentis)* (Cambridge, MA, 1951).
Hugh of St Victor, *De Scripturis et Scriptoribus Sacris* (*PL* 175, cols 9–28).
Hugh of St Victor, *De Tribus Maximis Circumstantiis Gestorum*, ed. W.M. Green, 'De Tribus Maximis Circumstantiis Gestorum', *Speculum*, 18 (1943), pp. 484–93 (at pp. 488–92); ed. G. Waitz, *Archiv der Gesellschaft für ältere Deutsche Geschichtskunde*, 11 (1858), pp. 307–8; trans. M. Carruthers, in M. Carruthers and J.M. Ziolkowski (eds), *The Medieval Craft of Memory* (Philadelphia, 2002), pp. 33–40.
Hugh of St Victor, *De Vanitate Mundi* (*PL* 176, cols 703–40).
Hugh of St Victor, *Didascalicon*, trans. J. Taylor, *The Didascalicon of Hugh of St Victor: A Medieval Guide to the Arts* (New York, 1961); ed. C.H. Buttimer (Freiburg, 1997).
Hugo Falcandus, *Historia*, ed. and trans. G.A. Loud and T. Wiedemann, *The History of the Tyrants of Sicily by 'Hugo Falcandus' 1154–69* (Manchester, 1998).
Huguccio of Pisa, *Derivationes*, ed. E. Cecchini, *et al.* (2 vols, Florence, 2004).
Ilias Latina – see Homer.
Isidore of Seville, *Differentiae*, ed. M.A. Andrés Sanz (*CCSL* 111A, Turnhout, 2006).
Isidore of Seville, *Etymologiae*, trans. S.A. Barney, W.J. Lewis, J.A. Beach and O. Berghof, *The Etymologies of Isidore of Seville* (Cambridge, 2006); ed. and trans. P.K. Marshall, *Etymologies*, book II (Paris, 1983); *Etymologiarum Sive Originum Libri XX*, ed. W.M. Lindsay (Oxford, 1911).
Isidore of Seville, *Liber Numerorum* (*PL* 83, cols 179–200).
Isidore of Seville, *Sententiae*, ed. P. Cazier (*CCSL* 111, Turnhout, 1998).
Itinerarium Peregrinorum et Gesta Regis Ricardi, trans. H.J. Nicholson, *The Chronicle of the Third Crusade* (Aldershot, 1997); ed. W. Stubbs (Rolls Series, London, 1864).
Ivo of Chartres, prologue to the *Decretum* and *Panormia*, trans. B.C. Brasington, in R. Somerville and B.C. Brasington, *Prefaces to Canon Law Books in Latin Christianity: Selected Translations 500–1245* (New Haven, 1998), pp. 132–58.

Jacobus de Voragine, *The Golden Legend: Readings on the Saints*, trans. W.G. Ryan (2 vols, Princeton, 1993).
Jean Bodin – see Bodin.
Jerome, *Chronicon*, trans. M.D. Donalson (Lampeter, 1996).
Jerome, *Contra Helvidium*, trans. J.N. Hritzu, *On the Perpetual Virginity of the Blessed Mary Against Helvidius* (Fathers of the Church vol. 53, Washington, DC, 1965, pp. 11–43).
Jerome (with continuation by Gennadius), *De Viris Illustribus*, trans. T.P. Halton, *On Illustrious Men* (Fathers of the Church 100, Washington, DC, 1999); trans. E.C. Richardson, *Lives of Illustrious Men* (Select Library of the Nicene and Post-Nicene Fathers vol. 3, Oxford, 1892, pp. 359–84).
Jerome, *Letters*, trans W.H. Fremantle, G. Lewis and W.G. Martley (Select Library of the Nicene and Post-Nicene Fathers vol. 6, Oxford, 1893, pp. 1–295); trans. C.C. Mierow (Ancient Christian Writers vol. 33, Washington, DC, 1963); *Select Letters*, trans. F.A. Wright (Loeb Classical Library, Cambridge, MA, 1933); ed. and trans. J. Labourt (8 vols, Paris, 1949–63).
Jerome, *Life of Hilarion*, trans. W.H. Fremantle, G. Lewis and W.G. Martley (Select Library of the Nicene and Post-Nicene Fathers vol. 6, Oxford, 1893, pp. 303–15); trans. C. White, in *Early Christian Lives* (Penguin Classics, Harmondsworth, 1998), pp. 89–115; *PL* 23, cols 29–54.
Jerome, *Prologue to the Book of Job*, trans. W.H. Fremantle, G. Lewis and W.G. Martley (Select Library of the Nicene and Post-Nicene Fathers vol. 6, Oxford, 1893), pp. 491–2.
Jerome, *Prologue to the Books of Samuel and Kings*, trans. W.H. Fremantle (Select Library of the Nicene and Post-Nicene Fathers vol. 6, Oxford, 1893), pp. 489–90.
John of Biclaro, *Chronicle*, trans. K.B. Wolf, in *Conquerors and Chroniclers of Early Medieval Spain* (2nd edn, Liverpool, 1999), pp. 57–77; ed. C. Cardelle de Hartmann, *Chronicon* (*CCSL* 173A, Turnhout, 2001, pp. 57–83).
John of Garland, *Parisiana Poetria*, ed. and trans. T. Lawler, *The Parisiana Poetria of John of Garland* (New Haven, 1974).
John of Salerno, *Life of Odo of Cluny*, trans. G. Sitwell, in *St Odo of Cluny* (London, 1958).
John of Salisbury, *Entheticus de Dogmate Philosophorum*, ed. and trans. J. van Laarhoven, *Entheticus Maior and Minor* (3 vols, Leiden, 1987).
John of Salisbury, *Historia Pontificalis*, ed. and trans. M. Chibnall, *Memoirs of the Papal Court* (London, 1956).
John of Salisbury, *Metalogicon*, trans. D.D. McGarry, *The Metalogicon of John of Salisbury: A Twelfth-Century Defense of the Verbal and Logical Arts of the Trivium* (Berkeley, 1955); ed. J.B. Hall (*CCCM* 98, Turnhout, 1998).
John of Salisbury, *Policraticus*, trans. J.B. Pike, *The Frivolities of Courtiers and the Footprints of Philosophers* [books I, II, III, selections from VII and VIII] (Minneapolis, 1938); trans. J. Dickinson, *The Statesman's Book of John of Salisbury* [books IV, V, VI, selections from VII and VIII] (New York, 1927); ed. C.C.J. Webb (2 vols, Oxford, 1909).
Joinville, *The Life of Saint Louis*, trans. M. Shaw, in *Joinville and Villehardouin: Chronicles of the Crusades* (Harmondsworth, 1963), pp. 161–353; ed. and trans. J. Monfrin (Paris, 1995).
Jordan Fantosme, *Chronicle*, ed. and trans. R.C. Johnston (Oxford, 1981).
Joseph of Exeter, *De Bello Troiano*, trans. G. Roberts, *The Iliad of Dares Phrygius* (Cape Town, 1970); ed. and trans. A.K. Bate, *Trojan War* (Warminster, 1986); ed. L. Gompf (Leiden, 1970).

Josephus, *Antiquitates*, trans. W. Whiston, *The Works of Josephus* (Peabody, 1987), pp. 27–542; ed. F. Blatt, *The Latin Josephus*, vol. I [*Antiquitates* I–V] (Copenhagen, 1958); ed. G. Squarciafico (Venice, 1486).
Josephus, *De Bello Iudaico*, trans. G.A. Williamson, *The Jewish War* (Penguin Classics, Harmondsworth, 1970); ed. G. Squarciafico (Venice, 1486).
Julius Victor, *Ars Rhetorica*, ed. R. Giomini and M.S. Celentano (Leipzig, 1980).
Junilius Africanus, *De Partibus Divinae Legis* (*PL* 68, cols 15–42).
Justin, *Epitome of the Philippic History of Pompeius Trogus*, trans. J.C. Yardley (Atlanta, 1994); ed. O. Seel, *Epitoma Historiarum Philippicarum Pompeii Trogi* (Leipzig, 1972).
Justinian, *Codex*, ed. P. Krüger (Berlin, 1884).
Justinian, *Digest*, ed. T. Mommsen and P. Krüger, trans. A.Watson (4 vols, Philadelphia, 1985).
Justinian, *Institutes*, ed. P. Krueger, trans. P. Birks and G. McLeod (London, 1987); ed. and trans. J.A.C. Thomas (Amsterdam, 1975).
Juvenal, *Satires*, trans. S.M. Braund (Loeb Classical Library, Cambridge, MA, 2004).
Knighton, *Chronicon*, ed. J.R. Lumby (Rolls Series, London, 1889–95); ed. and trans. G.H. Martin, *Knighton's Chronicle 1337–1396* (Oxford Medieval Texts, Oxford, 1995).
Lambert of Ardres, *The History of the Counts of Guines and Lords of Ardres*, trans. L. Shopkow (Philadelphia, 2007).
Lampert of Hersfeld, *Annales*, ed. O. Holder-Egger (*MGH Scriptores Rerum Germanicarum*, Hanover, 1894).
Lapo da Castiglionchio, *Letter to Flavio Biondo*, ed. M. Regoliosi, 'Res gestae patriae e res gestae ex universa Italia – la lettera di Lapo da Castiglionchio a Biondo Flavio', in C. Bastia and M. Bolognani (eds), *La Memoria e la Città: Scritture Storiche tra Medioevo ed Età Moderna* (Bologna, 1995), pp. 273–305 (at pp. 292–305).
Layamon, *Brut*, trans. R. Allen (London, 1992).
[Leonardo Bruni], *Polybii Historici De Primo Bello Punico Leonardo Aretino Interprete Libri Tres* (Paris, 1512).
Leonardo Bruni, *History of the Florentine People*, ed. and trans. J. Hankins (3 vols, Cambridge, MA, 2001–07).
Li Fet des Romains, ed. L.-F. Flutre and K. Sneyders de Vogel (Paris, 1938).
Liber Eliensis, trans. J. Fairweather (Woodbridge, 2005); ed. E.O. Blake (Camden Society, Third Series, vol. 92, London, 1962).
Liber Pontificalis, trans. R. Davis, *The Book of Pontiffs* (2nd edn, Liverpool, 2000); *The Lives of the Eighth-Century Popes*, trans. R. Davis (Liverpool, 1992); *The Lives of the Ninth-Century Popes (Liber Pontificalis)*, trans. R. Davis (Liverpool, 1995); ed. L. Duchesne (2 vols, Paris, 1886–92).
Life of Gregory the Great, ed. and trans. B. Colgrave, *The Earliest Life of Gregory the Great* (Kansas, 1968).
Life of the Emperor Henry IV, trans. T.E. Mommsen and K.F. Morrison, in *Imperial Lives and Letters of the Eleventh Century* (New York, 1962; rev. edn, 2000), pp. 101–37; ed. W. Wattenbach and W. Eberhard (*MGH Scriptores Rerum Germanicarum*, Hanover, 1899).
Life of King Edward Who Rests at Westminster, ed. and trans. F. Barlow (2nd edn, Oxford Medieval Texts, Oxford, 1992).
Liutprand of Cremona, *Antapodosis*, trans. F.A. Wright, *The Works of Liutprand of Cremona* (London, 1930), pp. 25–212; trans. P. Squatriti, *The Complete Works of Liudprand of Cremona* (Washington, DC, 2007), pp. 41–202; ed. P. Chiesa (*CCCM* 156, Turnhout, 1998).

Liutprand of Cremona, *Gesta Ottonis*, trans. F.A. Wright, in *The Works of Liutprand of Cremona* (London, 1930), pp. 215–32; trans. P. Squatriti, in *The Complete Works of Liudprand of Cremona* (Washington, DC, 2007), pp. 219–37; ed. P. Chiesa (*CCCM* 156, Turnhout, 1998).

Liutprand of Cremona, *Relatio de Legatione Constantinopolitana*, trans. F.A. Wright, in *The Works of Liutprand of Cremona* (London, 1930), pp. 235–77; trans. P. Squatriti, *The Complete Works of Liudprand of Cremona* (Washington, DC, 2007), pp. 238–82; ed. and trans. B. Scott (Bristol, 1993); ed. P. Chiesa (*CCCM* 156, Turnhout, 1998).

Livy, *Ab Urbe Condita*, trans. B.O. Foster, *et al.* (14 vols, Loeb Classical Library, Cambridge, MA, 1919–59).

Lorenzo Valla, *Antidotum in Facium*, ed. M. Regoliosi, *Laurentii Valle Antidotum in Facium* (Padua, 1981).

Lorenzo Valla, *Declamation on the Donation of Constantine*, trans. C.B. Coleman, *The Treatise of Lorenzo Valla on the Donation of Constantine* (Yale, 1922; reprinted Toronto, 1993); ed. and trans. G.W. Bowersock, *On the Donation of Constantine* (Cambridge, MA, 2007).

Lorenzo Valla, *Gesta Ferdinandi Regis Aragonum*, ed. O. Besomi, *Laurentii Valle Gesta Ferdinandi Regis Aragonum* (Padua, 1973).

Lucan, *Pharsalia*, trans. J.D. Duff, *The Civil War* (Loeb Classical Library, Cambridge, MA, 1928).

Lucian, *How to Write History*, trans. C.D.N. Costa, in *Selected Dialogues* (Oxford, 2005), pp. 181–202; *Quomodo Historia Conscribenda Sit* (Bologna, 1507).

Machiavelli, *A Discourse on Remodelling the Government of Florence*, trans. A. Gilbert, in *Machiavelli: The Chief Works and Others* (3 vols, Durham, 1958), vol. I, pp. 101–15.

Machiavelli, *Discourses on Livy*, trans. J.C. Bondanella and P. Bondanella (Oxford, 1997).

Machiavelli, *Florentine Histories*, trans. L.F. Banfield and H.C. Mansfield (Princeton, 1988).

Machiavelli, *The Prince*, trans. Q. Skinner and R. Price (Cambridge, 1988).

Macrobius, *Commentary on the Dream of Scipio*, trans. W.H. Stahl (New York, 1952); ed. J. Willis (Leipzig, 1970).

Macrobius, *Saturnalia*, trans. P.V. Davies (New York, 1969); ed. J. Willis (Leipzig, 1963).

Marie de France, *Fables*, ed. and trans. H. Spiegel (Toronto, 1994).

Marie de France, *Lais*, trans. E. Mason, *Medieval Lays and Legends of Marie de France* (London, 1911; reprinted New York, 2003).

Marius Victorinus, *Explanatio in Rhetoricam Ciceronis*, ed. K. Halm, in *Rhetores Latini Minores* (Leipzig, 1863), pp. 155–304.

Martial, *Epigrams*, trans. D.R. Shackleton Bailey (Loeb Classical Library, Cambridge, MA, 1993).

Martianus Capella, *The Marriage of Philology and Mercury*, trans. W.H. Stahl, R. Johnson and E.L. Burge, *Martianus Capella and the Seven Liberal Arts* (New York, 1977); ed. J. Willis (Leipzig, 1983).

Matthew Paris, *Chronica Maiora*, trans. J.A. Giles, *Matthew Paris's English History* (London, 1853); ed. and trans. R. Vaughan, *Chronicles of Matthew Paris: Monastic Life in the Thirteenth Century* (Gloucester, 1984); R. Vaughan, *The Illustrated Chronicles of Matthew Paris* (Stroud, 1993).

Matthew of Vendôme, *Ars Versificatoria*, trans. R. Parr (Milwaukee, 1981); ed. E. Faral, *Les Arts Poétiques du XIIe et du XIIIe Siècles: Recherches et Documents sur la Technique Littéraire du Moyen Age* (Paris, 1924), pp. 109–93.

Moralium Dogma Philosophorum, ed. J. Holmberg, *Das Moralium Dogma Philosophorum des Guillaume de Conches, lateinisch, altfranzösisch und mittelniederfränkisch* (Uppsala, 1929).
Nennius, *Historia Brittonum*, ed. and trans. J. Morris (London, 1980).
Odilo of Cluny, *Epitaph of Adelheid*, trans. S. Gilsdorf, in *Queenship and Sanctity: The Lives of Mathilda and the Epitaph of Adelheid* (Washington, DC, 2004), pp. 128–43.
Odo of Cheriton, *Fables*, trans. J.C. Jacobs, *The Fables of Odo of Cheriton* (New York, 1985).
Odo of Cluny, *Life of Gerald of Aurillac*, trans. G. Sitwell, in *St. Odo of Cluny* (London, 1958).
Odo of Deuil, *De Profectione Ludovici VII in Orientem*, ed. and trans. V. Berry (New York, 1948).
Orderic Vitalis, *Historia Ecclesiastica*, ed. and trans. M. Chibnall, *The Ecclesiastical History of Orderic Vitalis* (Oxford Medieval Texts, Oxford, 1980).
Orosius, *Seven Books of History Against the Pagans*, trans. R.J. Deferrari (Fathers of the Church vol. 50, Washington, DC, 1964); ed. C. Zangemeister, *Historiarum Adversum Paganos Libri Septem* (*CSEL* 5, Vienna, 1882); ed. J. Bateley, *The Old English Orosius* (Oxford, 1980).
Osbern of Gloucester, *Derivationes*, ed. F. Bertini, *et al.* (2 vols, Spoleto, 1996).
Otto of Freising, *Chronicle*, trans. C.C. Mierow, *The Two Cities: A Chronicle of Universal History* (New York, 1928; reprinted 2000); ed. A. Hofmeister, *Chronica sive Historia de Duabus Civitatibus* (*MGH Scriptores Rerum Germanicarum*, Hanover, 1912).
Otto of Freising (with continuation by Rahewin), *The Deeds of Frederick Barbarossa*, trans. C.C. Mierow (New York, 1953); ed. G. Waitz, *Gesta Friderici I Imperatoris* (*MGH Scriptores Rerum Germanicarum*, Hanover, 1884).
Ovid, *Heroides*, trans. G. Showerman (Loeb Classical Library, Cambridge, MA, 1914).
Paschasius Radbertus, *Epitaphium Arsenii*, trans. A. Cabaniss, in *Charlemagne's Cousins: Contemporary Lives of Adalard and Wala* (Syracuse, 1967), pp. 83–204; ed. E. Dümmler, *Radberts Epitaphium Arsenii* (Berlin, 1900).
Paschasius Radbertus, *Expositio in Matheo Libri XII*, ed. B. Paul (*CCCM* 56, 3 vols, Turnhout, 1984).
Paschasius Radbertus, *Vita Adalhardi*, trans. A. Cabaniss, in *Charlemagne's Cousins: Contemporary Lives of Adalard and Wala* (Syracuse, 1967), pp. 25–82; *PL* 120, cols 1507–56.
Paul the Deacon, *History of the Lombards*, trans. W.D. Foulke, rev. E. Peters (Philadelphia, 2003); ed. G. Waitz, *Historia Langobardorum* (*MGH Scriptores Rerum Langobardicarum et Italicarum*, Hanover, 1878).
Paul the Deacon, *Historia Romana*, ed. A. Crivelluci (Rome, 1914).
Peter of Blois, *Epistolae* (*PL* 207, cols 1–560).
Peter Damian, *Letters*, trans. O.J. Blum and I.M. Resnick (7 vols, Fathers of the Church – Medieval Continuation, Washington, DC, 1989–2005); ed. K. Reindel (*MGH Briefe*, 4 vols, Munich, 1983–93).
Peter Lombard, *Commentarium in Psalmos* (*PL* 191, cols 55–1296).
Peter of Spain, *Tractatus* (*Summulae Logicales*), trans. N. Kretzmann and E. Stump, *The Cambridge Translations of Medieval Philosophical Texts. Vol. I: Logic and the Philosophy of Language* (Cambridge, 1988), pp. 217–61; ed. L.M. de Rijk (Assen, 1972).
Peter the Venerable, *De Miraculis Libri Duo*, ed. D. Bouthillier (*CCCM* 83, Turnhout, 1988).

Petrarch, *Africa*, ed. N. Festa (Florence, 1926).
Petrarch, *De Sui Ipsius et Multorum Ignorantia*, ed. and trans. D. Marsh, *On His Own Ignorance and That of Many Others*, in Petrarch, *Invectives* (Cambridge, MA, 2003), pp. 222–363.
Petrarch, *De Viris Illustribus*, preface, ed. and trans. B.G. Kohl, 'Petrarch's Prefaces to *De Viris Illustribus*', *History and Theory*, 13 (1974), pp. 132–44; ed. G. Martelloti (Florence, 1964).
Petrarch, *Invectiva Contra Medicum*, ed. and trans. D. Marsh, *Against a Physician*, in Petrarch, *Invectives* (Cambridge, MA, 2003), pp. 2–179.
Petrarch, *Rerum Familiarum Libri*, trans. A.S. Bernardo, *Letters on Familiar Matters* (3 vols, Albany, 1975–85); ed. V. Rossi and U. Bosco, *Le Familiari* (4 vols, Florence, 1933–42).
Philippe de Commynes – see Commynes.
Pier Paolo Vergerio, *De Ingenuis Moribus et Liberalibus Adulescentiae Studiis Liber*, trans. C.W. Kallendorf, *The Character and Studies Befitting a Free-Born Youth*, in C.W. Kallendorf, *Humanist Educational Treatises* (Cambridge, MA, 2002), pp. 2–91.
Plato, *Gorgias*, trans. R. Waterfield (Oxford, 1994).
Plato, *Meno*, trans. R. Waterfield (Oxford, 2005).
Plato, *Phaedo*, trans. D. Gallop (Oxford, 1993).
Plato, *Phaedrus*, trans. R. Waterfield (Oxford, 2002).
Plato, *Timaeus*, trans. R. Waterfield (Oxford, 2008); ed. J.H. Wazink, *Plato Latinus* IV (2nd edn, London, 1975).
Pliny the Elder, *Natural History*, trans. H. Rackham, W.H.S. Jones and D.E. Eichholz (10 vols, Loeb Classical Library, Cambridge, MA, 1938–63).
Pliny the Younger, *Letters*, trans. W. Melmoth, rev. W.M.L. Hutchinson (2 vols, Loeb Classical Library, Cambridge, MA, 1915).
Polybius, *Histories*, trans. I. Scott-Kilvert, *The Rise of the Roman Empire* (Penguin Classics, Harmondsworth, 1979); *Historiae Polybii Libri Quinque* (Rome, 1473).
Pontano, *Actius*, ed. C. Previtera, in *I Dialoghi* (Florence, 1943), pp. 121–239.
Porphyry, *Introduction*, trans. J. Barnes (Oxford, 2003); ed. L. Minio-Paluello, *Porphyrii Isagoge Translatio Boethii* (*Aristoteles Latinus* I.6–7, Bruges, 1966).
Prefaces to Canon Law Books in Latin Christianity: Selected Translations 500–1245, trans. R. Somerville and B.C. Brasington (New Haven, 1998).
Priscian, *Praeexercitamina*, trans. J.M. Miller, in J.M. Miller, M.H. Prosser and T.W. Benson (eds), *Readings in Medieval Rhetoric* (Bloomington, 1973), pp. 52–68; ed. K. Halm, *Rhetores Latini Minores* (Leipzig, 1863), pp. 551–60.
Priscian, *Institutiones Grammaticarum*, ed. M. Hertz, in H. Keil (ed.), *Grammatici Latini* (7 vols, Leipzig, 1855–80), vols II, III.
Proverbia Sententiaeque Latinitatis Medii Aevi, ed. H. Walther (5 vols, Göttingen, 1963–67).
pseudo-Augustine, *De Rhetorica*, trans. J.M. Miller, *On Rhetoric*, in J.M. Miller, M.H. Prosser and T.W. Benson (eds), *Readings in Medieval Rhetoric* (Bloomington, 1973), pp. 7–24; ed. K. Halm, *Rhetores Latini Minores* (Leipzig, 1863), pp. 137–51.
Quintilian, *Institutio Oratoria*, trans. H.E. Butler (4 vols, Loeb Classical Library, Cambridge, MA, 1920–22); ed. M. Winterbottom, *Institutionis Oratoriae Libri Duodecim* (2 vols, Oxford, 1970).
Rahewin – see Otto of Freising.
Ralph de Diceto, *Abbreviationes Chronicorum*, ed. W. Stubbs, *The Historical Works of Master Ralph de Diceto, Dean of London* (2 vols, Rolls Series, London, 1876), vol. I, pp. 3–263.
Ralph de Diceto, *Imagines Historiarum*, ed. W. Stubbs, *The Historical Works of Master*

Ralph de Diceto, Dean of London (2 vols, Rolls Series, London, 1876), vol. I, pp. 291–440, vol. II, pp. 3–174.

Ranulf Higden – see Higden.

Rationes Dictandi, trans. J.J. Murphy, *The Principles of Letter Writing*, in J.J. Murphy, *Three Medieval Rhetorical Arts* (Berkeley, 1971), pp. 5–25.

Regino of Prüm, *Chronicon*, trans. S. MacLean, *History and Politics in Late Carolingian and Ottonian Europe: The Chronicle of Regino of Prüm and Adalbert of Magdeburg* (Manchester, 2009); ed. F. Kurze (*MGH Scriptores Rerum Germanicarum*, Hanover, 1890).

Rhetores Latini Minores, ed. K. Halm (Leipzig, 1863).

Rhetorica ad Herennium, trans. H. Caplan (Loeb Classical Library, Cambridge, MA, 1954).

Richard of Devizes, *Chronicle*, ed. and trans. J.T. Appleby (London, 1963).

Richard FitzNigel, *Dialogus de Scaccario*, ed. and trans. E. Amt (Oxford Medieval Texts, Oxford, 2007).

Richer, *Historiae*, ed. and trans. R. Latouche (2 vols, Paris, 1930–37); ed. H. Hoffmann (*MGH Scriptores* 38, Hanover, 2000).

Robert of Basevorn, *Forma Praedicandi*, trans. L. Kruhl, *The Form of Preaching*, in J.J. Murphy (ed.), *Three Medieval Rhetorical Arts* (Berkeley, 1971), pp. 114–215.

Robert the Monk, *Historia Ierosolimitana*, trans. C. Sweetenham, *History of the First Crusade* (Aldershot, 2005).

Roger of Howden, *Chronica*, ed. W. Stubbs (4 vols, Rolls Series, London, 1868–71).

Rufinus [of Antioch], *On Word Arrangement and Metres in Oratory*, trans. I. Thomson, in J.M. Miller, M.H. Prosser and T.W. Benson (eds), *Readings in Medieval Rhetoric* (Bloomington, 1973), pp. 37–51.

Rufinus [of Aquileia], *Die Kirchengeschichte mit der lateinischen Übersetzung und Fortsetzung des Rufinus von Aquileja*, ed. E. Schwartz and T. Mommsen (Leipzig, 1903; reprinted Berlin, 1999).

Rufinus [of Aquileia], 'Preface to Books X–XI of Eusebius' *Ecclesiastical History*', trans. W.H. Fremantle (Select Library of the Nicene and Post-Nicene Fathers, vol. 3, Oxford, 1892), p. 565.

Rufinus [of Aquileia], P.R. Amidon *The Church History of Rufinus of Aquileia: Books X and XI* (Oxford, 1997).

Rufinus [of Bologna], *Summa Decretorum*, trans. R. Somerville and B.C. Brasington, *Prefaces to Canon Law Books in Latin Christianity: Selected Translations 500–1245* (New Haven, 1998), preface, pp. 189–93.

Rupert of Deutz, *De Gloria et Honore Filii Hominis Super Mattheum*, ed. R. Haacke (*CCCM* 29, Turnhout, 1979).

Salimbene, *Chronicle*, trans. J.L. Baird, G. Baglivi and J.R. Kane (Binghamton, 1986).

Sallust, *Catiline*, trans. J.C. Rolfe (Loeb Classical Library, Cambridge, MA, 1931).

Sallust, *Jugurthine War*, trans. J.C. Rolfe (Loeb Classical Library, Cambridge, MA, 1931).

Salutati, *De Laboribus Herculis*, ed. B.L. Ullman (Zurich, 1951).

Salutati, *Letters*, ed. F. Novati, *Coluccio Salutati Epistolario* (4 vols, Rome, 1891–1911).

Salvian, *De Gubernatione Dei*, trans. J.F. O'Sullivan, *The Governance of God* (Fathers of the Church vol. 3, Washington, DC, 1947); ed. and trans. G. Lagarrigue (Sources Chrétiennes 220, Paris, 1975).

Saxo Grammaticus, *The History of the Danes, Books I–IX*, trans. P. Fisher, ed. H.E. Davidson (Woodbridge, 1979–80); ed. K. Friis-Jensen, *Gesta Danorum* (2 vols, Copenhagen, 2005).

Scholia in Lucani Bellum Civile, ed. H. Usener (Leipzig, 1869).
Sedulius, *Carmen Paschale*, trans. G. Sigerson, *The Easter Song* (Dublin, 1922); ed. J. Huemer (*CSEL* 10, Vienna, 1885).
Sedulius Scottus, *Collectanea in Epistolam ad Galatas* (*PL* 103, cols 181–94).
Seneca the Elder, *Declamationes [Controversiae* and *Suasoriae]*, ed. and trans. M. Winterbottom and W.C. Wright (2 vols, Loeb Classical Library, Cambridge, MA, 1974).
Seneca the Elder, *Suasoriae*, ed. and trans. M. Winterbottom and W.C. Wright, in *Declamationes* (2 vols, Loeb Classical Library, Cambridge, MA, 1974), vol. II, pp. 484–611.
Seneca, *De Beneficiis*, trans. J.W. Basore, *Moral Essays* (3 vols, Loeb Classical Library, Cambridge, MA, 1928–35), vol. III, pp. 2–525.
Seneca, *De Providentia*, trans. J.W. Basore, *Moral Essays* (3 vols, Loeb Classical Library, Cambridge, MA, 1928–35), vol. I, pp. 2–47.
Seneca, *Letters*, trans. R.M. Gummere (Loeb Classical Library, Cambridge, MA, 1920).
Seneca, *Ludus de Morte Claudii [Apocolocyntosis]*, ed. and trans. P.T. Eden (Cambridge, 1984).
Seneca, *On Consolation to Polybius*, trans. J.W. Basore, *Moral Essays* (3 vols, Loeb Classical Library, Cambridge, MA, 1928–35), vol. II, pp. 356–415.
Seneca, *Quaestiones Naturales*, trans. T.H. Corcoran (Loeb Classical Library, Cambridge, MA, 1972).
Servius, *In Vergilii Carmina Commentarii*, ed. G. Thilo and H. Hagen, *Commentary on Vergil's Aeneid* (3 vols, Leipzig, 1878–1902); *Servianorum in Virgilii Carmina Commentariorum* [books I–V] (Lancaster, 1946, 1965).
Sidonius Apollinaris, *Carmina*, trans. W.B. Anderson, *Poems and Letters* (2 vols, Loeb Classical Library, Cambridge, MA, 1936), vol. I, pp. 2–327.
Sidonius Apollinaris, *Letters*, trans. W.B. Anderson, *Poems and Letters* (2 vols, Loeb Classical Library, Cambridge, MA, 1965).
Sigebert of Gembloux, *Chronica* (*PL* 160, cols 57–240).
Sigebert of Gembloux, *Liber de Scriptoribus Ecclesiasticis* (*PL* 160, cols 547–88).
Snorri Sturluson, *Heimskringla*, trans. L.M. Hollander, *Heimskringla: History of the Kings of Norway* (Austin, 1964).
Solinus, *Collectanea Rerum Memorabilium*, ed. T.E. Mommsen (Berlin, 1895).
Song of Roland: The Oxford Text, trans. D.D.R. Owen (London, 1972).
Statius, *Achilleid*, trans. D.R. Shackleton Bailey (Loeb Classical Library, Cambridge, MA, 2003).
Statius, *Thebaid*, trans. D.R. Shackleton Bailey (Loeb Classical Library, Cambridge, MA, 2003).
Suger, *De Rebus in Sua Administratione Gestis [De Administratione]*, ed. and trans. E. Panofsky, *Abbot Suger on the Abbey Church of St.-Denis and Its Art Treasures* (2nd edn, Princeton, 1979), pp. 40–81.
Suger, *Libellus Alter de Consecratione Ecclesiae Sancti Dionysii [De Consecratione]*, ed. and trans. E. Panofsky, *Abbot Suger on the Abbey Church of St.-Denis and Its Art Treasures* (2nd edn, Princeton, 1979), pp. 82–121.
Suger, *Gesta Hludowici*, trans. R.C. Cusimano and J. Moorhead, *The Deeds of Louis the Fat* (Washington, DC, 1992); ed. H. Waquet, *Vie de Louis le Gros* (2nd edn, Paris, 1964).
Sulpicius Severus, *Dialogues*, trans. B.M. Peebles (Fathers of the Church vol. 7, New York, 1949, pp. 161–251); ed. and trans. J. Fontaine (Paris, 2006).
Sulpicius Severus, *Life of Martin of Tours*, trans. C. White, in *Early Christian Lives*

(Penguin Classics, Harmondsworth, 1998), pp. 134–59; trans. F.R. Hoare, in *The Western Fathers* (London, 1954), pp. 10–44; ed. and trans. J. Fontaine, *Sulpice Sévère, Vie de Saint Martin* (3 vols, Paris, 1967–69).
Tacitus, *Agricola*, trans. M. Hutton, rev. R.M. Ogilvie (Loeb Classical Library, Cambridge, MA, 1970).
Tacitus, *Annals*, trans. M. Grant (rev. edn, Penguin Classics, Harmondsworth, 1971); trans. J. Jackson (3 vols, Loeb Classical Library, Cambridge, MA, 1931–37).
Tacitus, *Germania*, trans. M. Hutton, rev. E.H. Warmington (Loeb Classical Library, Cambridge, MA, 1970).
Tacitus, *Histories*, trans. C.H. Moore (2 vols, Loeb Classical Library, Cambridge, MA, 1925–31).
Terence, *Adelphoe*, trans. J. Sargeaunt, *The Brothers* (Loeb Classical Library, Cambridge, MA, 1912, pp. 213–323); ed. R.H. Martin (Cambridge, 1976).
Terence, *Andria*, trans. J. Barsby, *The Woman of Andros* (Loeb Classical Library, Cambridge, MA, 2001, pp. 51–169).
Terence, *The Eunuch*, trans. J. Sargeaunt (Loeb Classical Library, Cambridge, MA, 1912, pp. 231–351); trans. J. Barsby (Loeb Classical Library, Cambridge, MA, 2001, pp. 312–443).
Terence, *Hecyra*, trans. J. Barsby, *The Mother-in-Law* (Loeb Classical Library, Cambridge, MA, 2001, pp. 139–241).
Thegan, *Life of Louis the Pious*, trans. J.R. Ginsburg and D.L. Boutelle, rev. P.E. Dutton, in P.E. Dutton (ed.), *Carolingian Civilization: A Reader* (Ontario, 1993), pp. 141–55; ed. E. Tremp, *Gesta Hludowici Imperatoris* (*MGH Scriptores Rerum Germanicarum* 64, Hanover, 1995).
Thierry of Chartres, *Commentarius Super Libros De Inventione*, ed. K.M. Fredborg, *The Latin Rhetorical Commentaries by Thierry of Chartres* (Toronto, 1988).
Thietmar of Merseburg, *Chronicon*, trans. D.A. Warner, *Ottonian Germany* (Manchester, 2001); ed. R. Holtzmann (*MGH Scriptores Rerum Germanicarum*, Berlin, 1935).
Thomas Basin, *Libri Historiarum Rerum Gestarum Temporibus Karoli Septimi et Ludovici Eius Filii Regum Francorum* [*Historiae*], ed. and trans. C. Samaran, *Histoire de Charles VII* (2 vols, Paris, 1933–44), *Histoire de Louis XI* (3 vols, Paris, 1963–72).
Thomas Walsingham – see Walsingham.
Turgot, *Life of Margaret of Scotland*, trans. L.L. Huneycutt, in *Matilda of Scotland: A Study in Medieval Queenship* (Woodbridge, 2003), pp. 162–78.
Uguccione da Pisa – see Huguccio of Pisa.
Valerius Maximus, *Facta et Dicta Memorabilia*, trans. D.R. Shackleton Bailey, *Memorable Doings and Sayings* (2 vols, Loeb Classical Library, Cambridge, MA, 2000).
Valla – see Lorenzo Valla.
Venantius Fortunatus, *Poems*, trans. J. George, *Venantius Fortunatus: Personal and Political Poems* (Liverpool, 1995).
Vergil, *Aeneid*, trans. H.R. Fairclough, rev. G.P. Goold, *Virgil. Vol. I: Eclogues; Georgics; Aeneid 1–6* and *Virgil. Vol. II: Aeneid 7–12; Appendix Vergiliana* (Loeb Classical Library, Cambridge, MA, 2000).
Vergil, *Eclogues*, trans. H.R. Fairclough, rev. G.P. Goold, *Virgil. Vol. I: Eclogues; Georgics; Aeneid 1–6* (Loeb Classical Library, Cambridge, MA, 2000).
Vergil, *Georgics*, trans. H.R. Fairclough, rev. G.P. Goold, *Virgil. Vol. I: Eclogues; Georgics; Aeneid 1–6* (Loeb Classical Library, Cambridge, MA, 2000).
Vespasiano, *Memoirs*, trans. W. George and E. Waters, *Renaissance Princes, Popes and Prelates. The Vespasiano Memoirs: Lives of Illustrious Men of the XVth Century* (New York, 1963).

Vincent of Beauvais, *De Morali Principis Institutione*, ed. R.J. Schneider (*CCCM* 137, Turnhout, 1995).
Vincent of Beauvais, *Speculum Maius* [*Speculum Naturale, Speculum Doctrinale, Speculum Morale, Speculum Historiale*] (4 vols, Douai, 1624; reprinted Graz, 1964–65).
Wace, *Roman de Brut*, ed. and trans. J. Weiss, *Wace's Roman de Brut, A History of the British* (2nd edn, Exeter, 2002); trans. A.W. Glowka (Tempe, 2005).
Wace, *Roman de Rou*, trans. G.S. Burgess (Woodbridge, 2004).
Walsingham, *Chronica Maiora*, ed. and trans. J. Taylor, W.R. Childs and L. Watkiss (2 vols, Oxford, 2003–11).
Walter of Châtillon, *Alexandreis*, trans. D. Townsend (Philadelphia, 1996).
Walter Map, *De Nugis Curialium*, ed. and trans. M.L.R. James, rev. C.N.L. Brooke and R.A.B. Mynors (Oxford Medieval Texts, Oxford, 1983).
Wibald of Stavelot, *Letter* 147, trans. G. Ellspermann, in J.M. Miller, M.H. Prosser and T.W. Benson, *Readings in Medieval Rhetoric* (Bloomington, 1973), pp. 209–14; *PL* 189, cols 1249–57.
Widukind, *Res Gestae Saxonicae*, ed. and trans. E. Rotter and B. Schneidmüller (rev. edn, Stuttgart, 1992).
William FitzStephen, *Description of London*, trans. H.E. Butler, in F.M. Stenton, *Norman London: An Essay* (London, 1934), pp. 25–35.
William FitzStephen, *Vitae Sancti Thomae*, ed. J.C. Robertson, in J.C. Robertson and J.B. Sheppard (eds), *Materials for the History of Thomas Becket* (7 vols, Rolls Series, London, 1875–85), vol. III, pp. 1–154.
William of Jumièges, *Gesta Normannorum Ducum*, ed. and trans. E.M.C. van Houts (2 vols, Oxford Medieval Texts, Oxford, 1992–95).
William of Malmesbury, *Commentary on Lamentations*, ed. H. Farmer, in 'William of Malmesbury's Commentary on Lamentations', *Studia Monastica*, 4 (1962), pp. 283–311.
William of Malmesbury, *De Laudibus et Miraculis Sanctae Mariae*, ed. J.M. Canal, *El Libro De Laudibus et Miraculis Sanctae Mariae de Guillermo de Malmesbury* (2nd edn, Rome, 1968).
William of Malmesbury, *Gesta Pontificum Anglorum*, ed. and trans. M. Winterbottom and R.M. Thomson, *The History of the English Bishops* (Oxford Medieval Texts, Oxford, 2007).
William of Malmesbury, *Gesta Regum Anglorum*, ed. and trans. R.A.B. Mynors, R.M. Thomson and M. Winterbottom, *The History of the English Kings* (Oxford Medieval Texts, Oxford, 1999).
William of Malmesbury, *Historia Novella*, ed. and trans. K.R. Potter (London, 1955).
William of Malmesbury, *Polyhistor*, ed. H.T. Ouellette (Binghamton, 1982).
William of Malmesbury, *Vita Wulfstani*, ed. and trans. M. Winterbottom and R.M. Thomson, in *William of Malmesbury, Saints' Lives: Lives of SS. Wulfstan, Dunstan, Patrick, Benignus and Indract* (Oxford Medieval Texts, Oxford, 2002), pp. 8–155.
William of Newburgh, *The History of English Affairs*, books I, II, trans. P.G. Walsh and M.J. Kennedy (Warminster, 1988, 2007); ed. H.C. Hamilton (2 vols, London, 1856).
William of Poitiers, *Gesta Guillelmi*, ed. and trans. R.H.C. Davis and M. Chibnall (Oxford Medieval Texts, Oxford, 1998).
William of Tyre, *A History of Deeds Done Beyond the Sea*, trans. E.A. Babcock and A.C. Krey (New York, 1941); ed. R.B.C. Huygens (*CCCM* 63, Turnhout, 1986).
Wipo, *Deeds of Conrad*, trans. T.E. Mommsen and K.F. Morrison, in *Imperial Lives and Letters of the Eleventh Century* (New York, 1962; rev. edn 2000), pp. 52–100; ed. H. Bresslau, *Gesta Chuonradi* (3rd edn, *MGH Scriptores* 61, Hanover, 1915), pp. 1–62.

Secondary sources

Ainsworth, P.F., *Jean Froissart and the Fabric of History: Truth, Myth and Fiction in the Chroniques* (Oxford, 1990).
Ainsworth, P.F., 'Contemporary and "Eyewitness" History', in D.M. Deliyannis (ed.), *Historiography in the Middle Ages* (Leiden, 2003), pp. 249–76.
Ainsworth, P.F., 'Legendary History – *Historia* and *Fabula*', in D.M. Deliyannis (ed.), *Historiography in the Middle Ages* (Leiden, 2003), pp. 387–416.
Albu, E., 'Dudo of Saint-Quentin – The Heroic Past Imagined', *Haskins Society Journal*, 6 (1994), pp. 111–18.
Albu, E., *The Normans in Their Histories: Propaganda, Myth and Subversion* (Woodbridge, 2001).
Allen, M.I., 'Universal History 300–1100: Origins and Western Developments', in D.M. Deliyannis (ed.), *Historiography in the Middle Ages* (Leiden, 2003), pp. 17–42.
Allmand, C.T., *The Hundred Years War* (Cambridge, 1988).
Althoff, G., J. Fried and P.J. Geary (eds), *Medieval Concepts of the Past: Ritual, Memory, Historiography* (Cambridge, 2002).
Amidon, P.R., *The Church History of Rufinus of Aquileia: Books X and XI* (Oxford, 1997).
Ankersmit, F.R., 'Historiography and Postmodernism', *History and Theory*, 28 (1989), pp. 137–53.
Arbusow, L., *Liturgie und Geschichtsschreibung im Mittelalter* (Bonn, 1951).
Archambault, P., 'The Ages of Man and the Ages of the World – A Study of Two Traditions', *Revue des Études Augustiniennes*, 12 (1966), pp. 193–228.
Archambault, P., 'Sallust in France – Thomas Basin's Idea of History and of the Human Condition', *Papers on Language and Literature*, 4 (1968), pp. 227–57.
Archambault, P., 'Joinville – History as Chivalric Code', in P. Archambault, *Seven French Chroniclers: Witnesses to History* (New York, 1974), pp. 41–57.
Archambault, P., 'Thomas Basin – History *Cum Ira et Studio*', in P. Archambault, *Seven French Chroniclers: Witnesses to History* (New York, 1974), pp. 87–99.
Archambault, P., 'Commynes – History as Lost Innocence', in P. Archambault, *Seven French Chroniclers: Witnesses to History* (New York, 1974), pp. 101–15.
Arnaud-Lindet, M.-P., 'Introduction', in M.-P. Arnaud-Lindet (ed. and trans.), *Orose, Histoires (Contre les Païens)* (3 vols, Paris, 1990–91).
Arnold, D.W.H. and P. Bright (eds), *De Doctrina Christiana: A Classic of Western Culture* (Notre Dame, 1995).
Atherton, C., *Stoics on Ambiguity* (Cambridge, 1993).
Auerbach, E., *Mimesis: The Representation of Reality in Western Literature*, trans. W.R. Trask (Princeton, 1953).
Auerbach, E., 'Figura', in E. Auerbach, *Scenes from the Drama of European Literature* (New York, 1959), pp. 11–76.
Avril, F., *Manuscript Painting at the Court of France: The Fourteenth Century (1310–1380)* (London, 1978).
Bagge, S., 'Theodoricus Monachus – Clerical Historiography in Twelfth-Century Norway', *Scandinavian Journal of History*, 14 (1989), pp. 113–33.
Bagge, S., 'Ideas and Narrative in Otto of Freising's *Gesta Frederici*', *Journal of Medieval History*, 22 (1996), pp. 345–77.
Bagge, S., *Kings, Politics and the Right Order of the World in German Historiography c.950–1150* (Leiden, 2002).
Baldwin, C.S., *Medieval Rhetoric and Poetic (to 1400) Interpreted from Representative Works* (New York, 1928).

Barnes, H.E., *A History of Historical Writing* (New York, 1963).
Barnes, T.D., *Constantine and Eusebius* (Cambridge, MA, 1981).
Barrow, J.S., 'William of Malmesbury's Use of Charters', in R. Balzaretti and E.M. Tyler (eds), *Narrative and History in the Early Medieval West* (Turnhout, 2006), pp. 67–85.
Bartlett, R., *Gerald of Wales, 1146–1223* (Oxford, 1982).
Bartlett, R., *Trial by Fire and Water: The Medieval Judicial Ordeal* (Oxford, 1986).
Bartlett, R. (ed.), *History and Historians: Selected Papers of R.W. Southern* (Oxford, 2004).
Bartlett, R., 'Political Prophecy in Gerald of Wales', in M. Aurell (ed.), *Culture Politique des Plantagenêt (1154–1224)* (Poitiers, 2003), pp. 303–11.
Baswell, C., *Virgil in Medieval England: Figuring the Aeneid from the Twelfth Century to Chaucer* (Cambridge, 1995).
Bate, K., 'La Littérature Latine d'Imagination à la Cour d'Henri II d'Angleterre', *Cahiers de Civilisation Médiévale Xe–XIIe Siècles*, 34 (1991), pp. 3–26.
Bautier, R.H., 'L'Historiographie en France aux Xe et XIe Siècles', *Settimane di Studio*, 17 (1970), pp. 793–850.
Baxandall, M., *Giotto and the Orators: Humanist Observers of Painting in Italy and the Discovery of Pictorial Composition, 1350–1450* (Oxford, 1971).
Beer, J., *Narrative Conventions of Truth in the Middle Ages* (Geneva, 1981).
Bennett, B.S., 'The Significance of the *Rhetorimachia* of Anselm of Besate to the History of Rhetoric', *Rhetorica*, 5 (1987), pp. 231–50.
Bennett, J.A.W., 'History in Verse', in J.A.W. Bennett, *Middle English Literature* (Oxford, 1986), ch. 4.
Bennett, M., 'Poetry as History? The *Roman de Rou* of Wace as a Source for the Norman Conquest', *Anglo-Norman Studies*, 5 (1992), pp. 21–39.
Bennett, P.E., 'L'Épique dans l'Historiographie Anglo-Normande – Gaimar, Wace, Jordan Fantosme', in H. van Dijk and W. Noomen (eds), *Aspects de l'Épopée Romane: Mentalités, Idéologies, Intertextualités* (Groningen, 1995), pp. 321–30.
Benson, R.L. and G. Constable (eds), *Renaissance and Renewal in the Twelfth Century* (Oxford, 1982).
Berlioz, J. and M. Polo de Beaulieu (eds), *Les Exempla Médiévaux: Nouvelles Perspectives* (Paris, 1998).
Bernardo, A.S., 'The Selection of Letters in Petrarch's *Familiares*', *Speculum*, 35 (1960), pp. 280–8.
Beumann, H., *Widukind von Korvei: Untersuchungen zur Geschichtsschreibung Ideengeschichte des 10. Jahrhunderts* (Weimar, 1950).
Beumann, H., *Ideengeschichtliche Studien zu Einhard und anderen Geschichtsschreibern des früheren Mittelalters* (Darmstadt, 1962).
Beumann, H., 'Topos und Gedankengefüge bei Einhard', *Archiv für Kulturgeschichte*, 33 (1951), pp. 337–50.
Beumann, H., 'Historiographische Konzeption und politische Ziele Widukinds von Korvey', *Settimane di Studio*, 17 (1970), pp. 857–94.
Billanovich, G., *Lamperto di Hersfeld e Tito Livio* (Padua, 1945).
Billanovich, G., 'Petrarch and the Textual Tradition of Livy', *Journal of the Warburg and Courtauld Institutes*, 14 (1951), pp. 137–208.
Billanovich, G., 'Il Petrarca e Gli Storici Latini', in *Tra Latino e Volgare. Per C. Dionisotti* (Medioevo e Umanesimo 17, Padua, 1974), pp. 67–145.
Billanovich, G., *La Tradizione del Testo di Livio e le Origini dell'Umanesimo: Tradizione e Fortuna di Livio tra Medioevo e Umanesimo* (Padua, 1981).
Black, R., 'The New Laws of History', *Renaissance Studies*, 1 (1987), pp. 126–56.

Black, R., 'Humanism', in C.T. Allmand (ed.), *The New Cambridge Medieval History* (Cambridge, 1998), vol. VII, pp. 243–77.
Black, R., *Humanism and Education in Medieval and Renaissance Italy: Tradition and Innovation in Latin Schools from the Twelfth to the Fifteenth Century* (Cambridge, 2001).
Blacker, J., *The Faces of Time: Portrayal of the Past in Old French and Latin Historical Narrative of the Anglo-Norman Regnum* (Austin, 1994).
Blanchard, J., *Philippe de Commynes* (Paris, 2006).
Blatt, F. (ed.), *The Latin Josephus* (Copenhagen, 1958).
Bliese, J., 'The Study of Rhetoric in the Twelfth Century', *Quarterly Journal of Speech*, 63 (1977), pp. 364–83.
Bliese, J., 'Rhetoric and Morale – A Study of Battle Orations from the Central Middle Ages', *Journal of Medieval History*, 15 (1989), pp. 201–26.
Bliese, J., 'The Battle Rhetoric of Aelred of Rievaulx', *Haskins Society Journal*, 1 (1989), pp. 99–107.
Blythe, J.M., *Ideal Government and the Mixed Constitution in the Middle Ages* (Princeton, 1992).
Bonner, G., '*Quid imperatori cum ecclesia*? St. Augustine on History and Society', *Augustinian Studies*, 2 (1971), pp. 231–51.
Boskoff, P.S., 'Quintilian in the Late Middle Ages', *Speculum*, 27 (1952), pp. 71–8.
Boutet, D., *Formes Littéraires et Conscience Historique aux Origines de la Littérature Française 1100–1250* (Paris, 1999).
Brandes, P.D., *A History of Aristotle's Rhetoric with a Bibliography of Early Printings* (Metuchen, 1989).
Breisach, E. (ed.), *Classical Rhetoric and Medieval Historiography* (Kalamazoo, 1985).
Bremond, C., J. Le Goff and J.C. Schmitt, *L'Exemplum* (2nd edn, Typologie des Sources du Moyen Âge Occidental 40, Turnhout, 1996).
Bride, M., 'John of Salisbury's Theory of Rhetoric', *Studies in Medieval Culture*, 2 (1966), pp. 56–62.
Briscoe, M.G., *Artes Praedicandi* (Typologie des Sources du Moyen Âge Occidental 61, Turnhout, 1992).
Brooke, C.N.L., 'Geoffrey of Monmouth as Historian', in C.N.L. Brooke, D.E. Luscombe, G.H. Martin and D. Owen (eds), *Church and Government in the Middle Ages: Essays Presented to C.R. Cheney on His 70th Birthday* (Cambridge, 1976), pp. 77–91.
Brooks, N., *Bede and the English*, Jarrow Lecture (Jarrow, 2000).
Brown, E.A.R., '*Falsitas Pia Sive Reprehensibilis* – Medieval Forgers and Their Intentions', in *Fälschungen im Mittelalter* (6 vols, Hanover, 1988–90), vol. I, pp. 101–19.
Brown, P., *Augustine of Hippo: A Biography* (London, 1967).
Bruni, G., 'The *De Differentia Rhetoricae, Ethicae et Politicae* of Aegidius Romanus', *New Scholasticism*, 6 (1932), pp. 1–18.
Bullough, D.A., 'Games People Played – Drama and Ritual as Propaganda in Medieval Europe', *Transactions of the Royal Historical Society*, 24 (1974), pp. 97–122.
Burckhardt, J., *The Civilization of the Renaissance in Italy*, trans. S.G.C. Middlemore (London, 1878; reprinted Penguin Classics, Harmondsworth, 1990).
Burgess, R.W. 'The Dates and Editions of Eusebius' *Chronici Canones* and *Historia Ecclesiastica*', *Journal of Theological Studies*, 48 (1997), pp. 471–504.
Burke, P., *The Renaissance Sense of the Past* (London, 1969).
Burke, P., 'Tacitism', in T.A. Dorey (ed.), *Tacitus* (London, 1969), pp. 149–71.

Burrow, J.A., *The Ages of Man: A Study in Medieval Writing and Thought* (Oxford, 1986).
Busby, K., 'Narrative Genres', in S. Gaunt and S. Kay (eds), *The Cambridge Companion to Medieval French Literature* (Cambridge, 2008), pp. 139–52.
Callahan, T., 'The Making of a Monster – The Historical Image of William Rufus', *Journal of Medieval History*, 7 (1981), pp. 175–85.
Camargo, M., 'Toward a Comprehensive Art of Written Discourse – Geoffrey of Vinsauf and the *Ars Dictaminis*', *Rhetorica*, 6 (1988), pp. 167–94.
Camargo, M., *Ars Dictaminis, Ars Dictandi* (Typologie des Sources du Moyen Âge Occidental 60, Turnhout, 1991).
Camargo, M., 'Defining Medieval Rhetoric', in C.J. Mews, C.J. Nederman and R.M. Thomson (eds), *Rhetoric and Renewal in the Latin West 1100–1540: Essays in Honour of John O. Ward* (Turnhout, 2003), pp. 21–34.
Camille, M., 'Illuminating Thought – The Trivial Arts in British Library, Burney Ms.295', in P. Binski and W. Noel (eds), *New Offerings, Ancient Treasures: Studies in Medieval Art for George Henderson* (Stroud, 2001), pp. 343–66.
Campbell, W.S., P.S. Hawkins and B. Schildgen, *Medieval Readings of Romans* (London, 2007).
Canary, R.H., and H. Kozicki (eds), *The Writing of History: Literary Form and Historical Understanding* (Madison, 1978).
Caplan, H. 'The Four Senses of Scriptural Teaching and the Medieval Theory of Preaching', *Speculum*, 4 (1929), pp. 282–90.
Caplan, H., 'Classical Rhetoric and the Medieval Theory of Preaching', *Classical Philology*, 28 (1933), pp. 73–96.
Carruthers, M., *The Book of Memory: A Study of Memory in Medieval Culture* (Cambridge, 1990).
Cary, G. and D.J.A. Ross (eds), *The Medieval Alexander* (Cambridge, 1956).
Catalogus Translationum et Commentariorum: Medieval and Renaissance Latin Translations and Commentaries, ed. P.O. Kristeller, F.E. Cranz, V. Brown, *et al*. (Washington, DC, 1960–).
Celenza, C.S., 'Parallel Lives – Plutarch's Lives, Lapo da Castiglionchio the Younger (1405–1438) and the Art of Italian Renaissance Translation', *Illinois Classical Studies*, 22 (1997), pp. 121–55.
Celenza, C.S., *Renaissance Humanism and the Papal Curia: Lapo da Castiglionchio the Younger's De Curiae Commodis* (Ann Arbor, 1999).
Chadwick, H., *Boethius: The Consolations of Music, Logic, Theology and Philosophy* (Oxford, 1981).
Chaurand, J., 'La Conception de l'Histoire de Guibert de Nogent (1053–1124)', *Cahiers de Civilisation Médiévale*, 8 (1965), pp. 381–95.
Chazelle, C.M., 'Pictures, Books and the Illiterate – Pope Gregory I's Letters to Serenus of Marseilles', *Word and Image*, 6 (1990), pp. 138–53.
Chenu, M.D., 'Theology and the New Awareness of History', in M.D. Chenu, *Nature, Man and Society in the Twelfth Century: Essays on New Theological Perspectives in the Latin West* (Chicago, 1968), pp. 162–201.
Chesnut, G.F., *The First Christian Histories: Eusebius, Socrates, Sozomen, Theodoret and Evagrius* (Macon, 1986).
Chibnall, M., 'Charter and Chronicle – The Use of Archive Sources by Norman Historians', in C.N.L. Brooke, D.E. Luscombe, G.H. Martin and D. Owen (eds), *Church and Government in the Middle Ages: Essays Presented to C.R. Cheney on His 70th Birthday* (Cambridge, 1976), pp. 1–17.
Chibnall, M., 'Forgery in Narrative Charters', in *Fälschungen im Mittelalter* (6 vols, Hanover, 1988–90), vol. IV, pp. 331–46.

Christensen, T., *Rufinus of Aquileia and the Historia Ecclesiastica, Lib. VIII–IX of Eusebius* (Copenhagen, 1989).
Clanchy, M.T., 'Remembering the Past and the Good Old Law', *History*, 55 (1970), pp. 165–76.
Clanchy, M.T., *From Memory to Written Record: England 1066–1307* (2nd edn, Oxford, 1993).
Clark, J.G., *A Monastic Renaissance at St Albans: Thomas Walsingham and His Circle c.1350–1440* (Oxford, 2004).
Classen, P., '*Res Gestae*, Universal History, Apocalypse – Visions of Past and Future', in R.L. Benson and G. Constable (eds), *Renaissance and Renewal in the Twelfth Century* (Oxford, 1982), pp. 387–417.
Cochrane, E., *Historians and Historiography in the Italian Renaissance* (Chicago, 1981).
Coleman, J., *Ancient and Medieval Memories: Studies in the Reconstruction of the Past* (Cambridge, 1992).
Colish, M.L., 'The Stoic Theory of Verbal Signification and the Problem of Lies and False Statement from Antiquity to St. Anselm', in L. Brind'Amour and E. Vance (eds), *Archéologie du Signe* (Toronto, 1983), pp. 17–43.
Colish, M.L., *The Stoic Tradition from Antiquity to the Early Middle Ages* (2 vols, 2nd edn, Leiden, 1990).
Colish, M.L., 'Rethinking Lying in the Twelfth Century', in I. Bejczy and R. Newhauser (eds), *Virtue and Ethics in the Twelfth Century* (Leiden, 2005), pp. 155–73.
Comparetti, D., *Virgil in the Middle Ages*, trans. E.F.M. Benecke, intr. J.M. Ziolkowski (Princeton, 1997).
Conley, T.M., *Rhetoric in the European Tradition* (Chicago, 1994).
Constable, G., 'Forgery and Plagiarism in the Middle Ages', *Archiv für Diplomatik*, 29 (1983), pp. 1–41.
Constable, G., 'Past and Present in the Eleventh and Twelfth Centuries – Perceptions of Time and Change', in *L'Europa dei Secoli XI e XII fra Novità e Tradizione: Sviluppi di una Cultura* (Miscellanea del Centro di Studi Medioevali 12, Milan, 1989), pp. 135–70.
Cooper, A., '"The Feet of Those That Bark Shall Be Cut Off" – Timorous Historians on the Personality of Henry I', *Anglo-Norman Studies*, 23 (2001), pp. 47–67.
Cooper, S.A., *Marius Victorinus' Commentary on Galatians* (Oxford, 2005).
Courcelle, P., '*Nosce Teipsum* du Bas-Empire au Haut Moyen-Âge', *Settimane di Studio*, 9 (1962), pp. 265–95.
Cowdrey, H.E.J., 'Bede and the "English People"', *Journal of Religious Studies*, 11 (1981), pp. 501–23; reprinted in H.E.J. Cowdrey, *Popes, Monks and Crusaders* (London, 1984).
Cowdrey, H.E.J., *Popes, Monks and Crusaders* (London, 1984).
Cox, V., 'Ciceronian Rhetoric in Italy 1260–1350', *Rhetorica*, 17 (1999), pp. 239–88.
Cox, V., 'Machiavelli and the *Rhetorica ad Herennium* – Deliberative Rhetoric in *The Prince*', *Sixteenth Century Journal*, 28 (1997), pp. 1109–41.
Cox, V., 'Ciceronian Rhetorical Theory in the *Volgare* – A Fourteenth-Century Text and Its Fifteenth-Century Readers', in C.J. Mews, C.J. Nederman and R.M. Thomson (eds), *Rhetoric and Renewal in the Latin West 1100–1540: Essays in Honour of John O. Ward* (Turnhout, 2003), pp. 201–25.
Cranz, F.E., '*De Civitate Dei* XV.2 and Augustine's Idea of the Christian Society', *Speculum*, 25 (1950), pp. 215–25; reprinted in R.A. Markus (ed.), *Augustine: A Collection of Critical Essays* (New York, 1972).

Cranz, F.E., 'The Development of Augustine's Ideas on Society Before the Donatist Controversy', *Harvard Theological Review*, 47 (1954), pp. 255–316; reprinted in R.A. Markus (ed.), *Augustine: A Collection of Critical Essays* (New York, 1972).

Croke, B., 'The Origins of the Christian World Chronicle', in B. Croke and A.M. Emmett (eds), *History and Historians in Late Antiquity* (Sydney, 1983), pp. 116–31.

Croke, B., 'Latin Historiography and the Barbarian Kingdoms', in G. Marasco (ed), *Greek and Roman Historiography in Late Antiquity* (Brill, 2003), pp. 349–89.

Cubitt, C., 'Memory and Narrative in the Cult of Early Anglo-Saxon Saints', in Y. Hen and M. Innes (eds), *The Uses of the Past in the Early Middle Ages* (Cambridge, 2000), pp. 29–66.

Cubitt, G., *History and Memory* (Manchester, 2007).

Curtius, E.R., *European Literature and the Latin Middle Ages* (London, 1953).

D'Amico, J.F., *Renaissance Humanism in Papal Rome: Humanism and Churchmen on the Eve of the Reformation* (Baltimore, 1983).

Dale, S., A.W. Lewin and D.J. Osheim (eds), *Chronicling History: Chroniclers and Historians in Medieval and Renaissance Italy* (University Park, 2007).

Daly, S.R., 'Peter Comestor – Master of Histories', *Speculum*, 32 (1957), pp. 62–73.

Damian-Grint, P., *The New Historians of the Twelfth-Century Renaissance: Inventing Vernacular Authority* (Woodbridge, 1999).

Davenport, T., *Medieval Narrative: An Introduction* (Oxford, 2004).

Davidse, J., 'The Sense of History in the Works of the Venerable Bede', *Studi Medievali*, 23 (1982), pp. 647–95.

Davidse, J., 'On Bede as Christian Historian', in L.A.J.R. Houwen and A.A. MacDonald (eds), *Beda Venerabilis: Historian, Monk and Northumbrian* (Groningen, 1996), pp. 1–15.

Davis, C.T., *Dante and the Idea of Rome* (Oxford, 1957).

Davis, R.H.C. and J.M. Wallace-Hadrill (eds), *The Writing of History in the Middle Ages: Essays Presented to Richard William Southern* (Oxford, 1981).

De Jong, M., 'The Empire as *Ecclesia* – Hrabanus Maurus and Biblical *Historia* for Rulers', in Y. Hen and M. Innes (eds), *The Uses of the Past in the Early Middle Ages* (Cambridge, 2000), pp. 191–226.

De Jong, M., *The Penitential State: Authority and Atonement in the Age of Louis the Pious* (Cambridge, 2009).

Dean, R.J., 'The Earliest Known Commentary on Livy', *Medievalia et Humanistica*, 3 (1945), pp. 86–98.

Dean, R.J., 'Nicholas Trevet, Historian', in J.J.G. Alexander and M.T. Gibson (eds), *Medieval Learning and Literature: Essays Presented to Richard William Hunt* (Oxford, 1976), pp. 328–52.

Delhaye, P., 'Grammatica et Ethica au XIIe Siècle', *Recherches de Théologie Ancienne et Médiévale*, 25 (1958), pp. 59–110.

Deliyannis, D.M. (ed.), *Historiography in the Middle Ages* (Leiden, 2003).

de Lubac, H., *Medieval Exegesis: The Four Senses of Scripture*, trans. M. Sebanc (2 vols, Edinburgh, 1998).

Demandt, A., *Metaphern für Geschichte: Sprachbilder und Gleichnisse im historisch-politischen Denken* (Munich, 1978).

Dickey, M., 'Some Commentaries on the *De Inventione* and *Ad Herennium* of the Eleventh and Early Twelfth Centuries', *Medieval and Renaissance Studies*, 6 (1968), pp. 1–41.

Dorey, T.A. (ed.), *Livy* (London, 1971).

Dotson, J., 'The Genoese Civic Annals – Caffaro and His Continuators', in S. Dale, A.W. Lewin and D.J. Osheim (eds), *Chronicling History: Chroniclers and Historians in Medieval and Renaissance Italy* (University Park, 2007), pp. 55–85.

Dronke, P., *Fabula: Explorations into the Uses of Myth in Medieval Platonism* (Leiden, 1974).

Dronke, P., 'Peter of Blois and Poetry at the Court of Henry II', *Medieval Studies*, 28 (1976), pp. 185–235.

Dronke, P., *Verse with Prose from Petronius to Dante: The Art and Scope of the Mixed Form* (London, 1994).

Duggan, C. and A. Duggan, 'Ralph de Diceto, Henry II and Becket', in B. Tierney and P. Linehan (eds), *Authority and Power: Studies in Medieval Law and Government Presented to Walter Ullmann* (Cambridge, 1980), pp. 59–81.

Duggan, J.J., 'Medieval Epic as Popular Historiography – Appropriation of Historical Knowledge in the Vernacular Epic', in H.U. Gumbrecht, U. Link-Heer, P.-M. Spangenberg, *et al.* (eds), *La Littérature Historiographique des Origines à 1500: Grundriss der Romanischen Literaturen des Mittelalters* (Heidelberg, 1987), vol. XI, pp. 285–311.

Dumville, D., 'What Is a Chronicle?', in E. Kooper (ed.), *The Medieval Chronicle II: Proceedings of the International Conference on the Medieval Chronicle* (Amsterdam, 2002), pp. 1–27.

Dunbabin, J.H., 'The Maccabees as Exemplars in the Tenth and Eleventh Centuries', in K. Walsh and D. Wood (eds), *The Bible in the Medieval World: Essays in Memory of Beryl Smalley* (Oxford, 1985), pp. 31–41.

Eckenrode, T.R., 'Vincent of Beauvais – A Study on the Construction of a Didactic View of History', *The Historian*, 46 (1984), pp. 339–360.

Edbury, P.W., and J.G. Rowe, *William of Tyre: Historian of the Latin East* (Cambridge, 1988).

Edmondson, J., S. Mason and J. Rives (eds), *Flavius Josephus and Flavian Rome* (Oxford, 2005).

Ellspermann, G.L., *The Attitude of the Early Christian Latin Writers Toward Pagan Literature and Learning* (Catholic University of America Patristic Studies 82, Washington, DC, 1949).

Emerson, C., *Olivier de La Marche and the Rhetoric of Fifteenth-Century Historiography* (Woodbridge, 2004).

English, E.D. (ed.), *Reading and Wisdom: The De Doctrina Christiana of Augustine in the Middle Ages* (Notre Dame, 1995).

Evans, G. R., 'Hugh of St Victor on History and the Meaning of Things', *Studia Monastica*, 25 (1983), pp. 223–34.

Evans, G.R., *The Language and Logic of the Bible: The Earlier Middle Ages* (Cambridge, 1984).

Evans, G.R., 'Guibert of Nogent and Gregory the Great on Preaching and Exegesis', *The Thomist*, 49 (1985), pp. 534–50.

Fälschungen im Mittelalter (6 vols, Hanover, 1988–90).

Faral, E. (ed.), *Les Arts Poétiques du XIIe et du XIIIe Siècles: Recherches et Documents sur la Technique Littéraire du Moyen Age* (Paris, 1924).

Farmer, H., 'William of Malmesbury's Commentary on Lamentations', *Studia Monastica*, 4 (1962), pp. 283–311.

Feehan, T., 'Augustine on Lying and Deception', *Augustinian Studies*, 19 (1988), pp. 131–9.

Feehan, T., 'Augustine's Moral Evaluation of Lying', *Augustinian Studies*, 21 (1990), pp. 67–81.

Feehan, T., 'Augustine's Own Examples of Lying', *Augustinian Studies*, 22 (1991), pp. 165–90.
Fenster, T. and D.L. Smail (eds), *Fama: The Politics of Talk and Reputation in Medieval Europe* (London, 2003).
Fentress, J. and C. Wickham, *Social Memory* (Oxford, 1992).
Fleischman, S., 'On the Representation of History and Fiction in the Middle Ages', *History and Theory*, 22 (1983), pp. 278–310.
Flint, V.I.J., 'The Place and Purpose of the Works of Honorius Augustodunensis', *Revue Bénédictine*, 87 (1977), pp. 97–127.
Flint, V.I.J., 'The *Historia Regum Britanniae* of Geoffrey of Monmouth – Parody and Its Purpose. A Suggestion', *Speculum*, 54 (1979), pp. 447–68.
Flint, V.I.J., 'Honorius Augustodunensis *Imago Mundi*', *Archives d'Histoire Doctrinale et Littéraire du Moyen Âge*, 49 (1983), pp. 7–153.
Flint, V.I.J., 'World History in the Early Twelfth Century – The *Imago Mundi* of Honorius Augustodunensis', in R.H.C. Davis, J.M. Wallace-Hadrill, *et al.* (eds), *The Writing of History in the Middle Ages* (Oxford, 1981), pp. 211–38.
Fortin, E., 'Augustine and the Problem of Christian Rhetoric', *Augustinian Studies*, 5 (1974), pp. 85–100.
Foster, K., *Petrarch: Poet and Humanist* (Edinburgh, 1984).
Fowler, G.B., *The Intellectual Interests of Engelbert of Admont* (New York, 1947).
Franklin, C.V., 'Grammar and Exegesis – Bede's *Liber de Schematibus et Tropis*', in C.D. Lanham (ed.), *Latin Grammar and Rhetoric: From Classical Theory to Medieval Practice* (London, 2002), pp. 63–91.
Fredborg, K.M., 'Twelfth-Century Ciceronian Rhetoric – Its Doctrinal Development and Influences', in B. Vickers (ed.), *Rhetoric Revalued: Papers from the International Society for the History of Rhetoric* (New York, 1982), pp. 87–97.
Fredborg, K.M., *The Latin Rhetorical Commentaries by Thierry of Chartres* (Toronto, 1988).
Fredborg, K.M., 'The Scholastic Teaching of Rhetoric in the Middle Ages', *Cahiers de l'Institut du Moyen-Âge Grec et Latin*, 55 (1987), pp. 85–105.
Fredborg, K.M., 'Abelard on Rhetoric', in C.J. Mews, C.J. Nederman and R.M. Thomson (eds), *Rhetoric and Renewal in the Latin West 1100–1540: Essays in Honour of John O. Ward* (Turnhout, 2003), pp. 55–80.
Freeman, E., *Narratives of a New Order: Cistercian Historical Writing in England 1150–1220* (Turnhout, 2002).
Frend, W.H.C., 'Augustine and Orosius on the End of the Ancient World', *Augustinian Studies*, 20 (1989), pp. 1–38.
Friis-Jensen, K., '*Horatius Liricus et Ethicus* – Two Twelfth-century School Texts on Horace's Poems', *Cahiers de l'Institut du Moyen Âge Grec et Latin*, 57 (1988), pp. 81–147.
Friis-Jensen, K., 'The *Ars Poetica* in Twelfth-Century France – The Horace of Matthew of Vendôme, Geoffrey of Vinsauf, and John of Garland', *Cahiers de l'Institut du Moyen Âge Grec et Latin*, 60 (1990), pp. 319–88.
Fryde, E.B., 'Some Fifteenth-Century Translations of Ancient Greek Historians', in E.B. Fryde, *Humanism and Renaissance Historiography* (London, 1983), pp. 83–113.
Galbraith, V.H., *Historical Research in Medieval England* (London, 1951).
Galbraith, V.H., *Roger of Wendover and Matthew Paris* (Glasgow, 1944).
Galloway, A., 'Writing History in England', in D. Wallace (ed.), *The Cambridge History of Medieval English Literature* (Cambridge, 1999), pp. 255–83.
Ganz, D., *Corbie in the Carolingian Renaissance* (Sigmaringen, 1990).
Ganz, D., 'The *Epitaphium Arsenii* and Opposition to Louis the Pious', in P. Godman

and R. Collins (eds), *Charlemagne's Heir: New Perspectives on the Reign of Louis the Pious* (Oxford, 1990), pp. 537–550.

Ganz, D., 'The Preface to Einhard's *Vita Karoli*', in H. Schefers (ed.), *Einhard: Studien zu Leben und Werk* (Darmstadt, 1997), pp. 299–310.

Ganz, D., 'Einhard's Charlemagne – The Characterization of Greatness', in J. Story (ed.), *Charlemagne: Empire and Society* (Manchester, 2005), pp. 38–51.

Gardiner, F.C., *The Pilgrimage of Desire: A Study of Theme and Genre in Medieval Literature* (Leiden, 1971).

Garin, E., *Italian Humanism: Philosophy and the Civic Life in the Renaissance* (Oxford, 1965).

Garin, E., *Ritratti di Umanisti* (Florence, 1967).

Gaunt, S., 'Romance and Other Genres', in R.L. Krueger (ed.), *The Cambridge Companion to Medieval Romance* (Cambridge, 2000), pp. 45–59.

Geary, P.J., *Phantoms of Remembrance: Memory and Oblivion at the End of the First Millennium* (Princeton, 1994).

Geary, P.J., 'Oblivion Between Orality and Textuality in the Tenth Century', in G. Althoff, J. Fried and P.J. Geary (eds), *Medieval Concepts of the Past: Ritual, Memory, Historiography* (Cambridge, 2002), pp. 111–22.

Geary, P.J., *The Myth of Nations: The Medieval Origins of Europe* (Princeton, 2002).

Gehl, P.F., 'Preachers, Teachers and Translators – The Social Meaning of Language Study in Trecento Tuscany', *Viator*, 25 (1994), pp. 289–323.

Gibson, M.T. (ed.), *Boethius: His Life, Thought and Influence* (Oxford, 1981).

Gilbert, A.H., *Machiavelli's Prince and Its Forerunners: The Prince as a Typical Book De Regimine Principum* (2nd edn, New York, 1968).

Gilbert, F., *Machiavelli and Guicciardini: Politics and History in Sixteenth-Century Florence* (Princeton, 1965).

Gilbert, F., 'Machiavelli's *Istorie Fiorentine* – An Essay in Interpretation', in M.P. Gilmore (ed.), *Studies on Machiavelli* (Florence, 1972), pp. 73–99; reprinted in F. Gilbert, *History: Choice and Commitment* (Cambridge, MA, 1977), pp. 135–53.

Gillingham, J., 'The Context and Purposes of Geoffrey of Monmouth's *History of the Kings of Britain*', *Anglo-Norman Studies*, 13 (1990), pp. 99–118; reprinted in J. Gillingham, *The English in the Twelfth Century: Imperialism, National Identity and Political Values* (Woodbridge, 2000), pp. 19–39.

Gillingham, J., 'The Beginnings of English Imperialism', *Journal of Historical Sociology*, 5 (1992), pp. 392–409; reprinted in J. Gillingham, *The English in the Twelfth Century: Imperialism, National Identity and Political Values* (Woodbridge, 2000), pp. 3–18.

Gillingham, J., *The English in the Twelfth Century: Imperialism, National Identity and Political Values* (Woodbridge, 2000).

Gillingham, J., 'The Cultivation of History, Legend and Courtesy at the Court of Henry II', in R. Kennedy and S. Meecham-Jones (eds), *Writers of the Reign of Henry II: Twelve Essays* (New York, 2006), pp. 25–52.

Ginzburg, C., *History, Rhetoric and Proof* (Hanover, 1999).

Giovannini, G., 'The Connection Between Tragedy and History in Ancient Criticism', *Philological Quarterly*, 22 (1943), pp. 308–14.

Given-Wilson, C., *Chronicles: The Writing of History in Medieval England* (London, 2004).

Glenn, J., *Politics and History in the Tenth Century: The Work and World of Richer of Reims* (Cambridge, 2004).

Goetz, H.W., *Die Geschichtstheologie des Orosius* (Darmstadt, 1980).

Goetz, H.W., 'Geschichte als Argument – Historische Beweisführung und Geschichtsbewusstein in den Streitschriften des Investiturstreits', *Historische Zeitschrift*, 245 (1987), pp. 31–69.
Goetz, H.W., 'Fälschung und Verfälschung der Vergangenheit – zum Geschichtsbild der Streitschriften des Investiturstreits', in *Fälschungen im Mittelalter* (6 vols, Hanover, 1988–90), vol. I, pp. 165–88.
Goetz, H.W., *Geschichtsschreibung und Geschichtsbewusstsein im hohen Mittelalter* (Berlin, 1999).
Goffart, W., *The Narrators of Barbarian History* (Princeton, 1988).
Goffart, W., 'Bede's *Vera Lex Historiae* Explained', *Anglo-Saxon England*, 34 (2005), pp. 111–16.
Gombrich, E.H., 'The Style *all'Antica* – Imitation and Assimilation', in E.H. Gombrich, *Norm and Form: Studies in the Art of the Renaissance* (London, 1966), pp. 122–8.
Goodich, M., 'Biography 1000–1350', in D.M. Deliyannis (ed.), *Historiography in the Middle Ages* (Leiden, 2003), pp. 353–85.
Gorman, M.M., 'The Diffusion of the Manuscripts of Saint Augustine's *De Doctrina Christiana* in the Early Middle Ages', *Revue Bénédictine*, 95 (1985), pp. 11–24; reprinted in M.M. Gorman, *The Manuscript Traditions of the Works of St Augustine* (Florence, 2001), pp. 265–78.
Goullet, M., *Ecriture et Réécriture Hagiographiques. Essai sure les Réécritures de Vies des Saints dans l'Occident Latin Medieval VIII–XIIIe Siècle* (Turnhout, 2005).
Grafton, A., 'On the Scholarship of Politian and Its Context', *Journal of the Warburg and Courtauld Institutes*, 40 (1977), pp. 150–88.
Grafton, A., *Leon Battista Alberti: Master Builder of the Italian Renaissance* (London, 2001).
Grafton, A., *What Was History? The Art of History in Early Modern Europe* (Cambridge, 2007).
Grafton, A. and L. Jardine, 'Humanism and the School of Guarino – A Problem of Evaluation', *Past and Present*, 96 (1982), pp. 51–80.
Gransden, A., 'Realistic Observation in Twelfth-Century England', *Speculum*, 47 (1972), pp. 29–51; reprinted in A. Gransden, *Legends, Traditions and History in Medieval England* (London, 1992), pp. 175–97.
Gransden, A., *Historical Writing in England c.550–c.1307* (London, 1974).
Gransden, A., 'The Chronicles of Medieval England and Scotland', *Journal of Medieval History*, 16 (1990), pp. 129–50; 17 (1991), pp. 217–43; reprinted in A. Gransden, *Legends, Traditions and History in Medieval England* (London, 1992).
Gransden, A., 'Prologues in the Historiography of Twelfth-Century England', in D. Williams (ed.), *England in the Twelfth Century* (Woodbridge, 1990); reprinted in A. Gransden, *Legends, Traditions and History in Medieval England* (London, 1992), pp. 125–51.
Gransden, A., *Legends, Traditions and History in Medieval England* (London, 1992).
Grant, L., *Abbot Suger of St-Denis: Church and State in Early Twelfth-Century France* (Harlow, 1998).
Grant, R.M., *Eusebius as Church Historian* (Oxford, 1980).
Gray, H., 'Renaissance Humanism – The Pursuit of Eloquence', *Journal of the History of Ideas*, 24 (1963), pp. 497–514.
Green, D.H., *The Beginnings of Medieval Romance: Fact and Fiction 1150–1220* (Cambridge, 2002).
Green, L., *Chronicle into History: An Essay on the Interpretation of History in Florentine Fourteenth-Century Chronicles* (Cambridge, 1972).

Green, R.P.H., *Latin Epics of the New Testament: Juvencus, Sedulius, Arator* (Oxford, 2007).
Green, W.M., 'De Tribus Maximis Circumstantiis Gestorum', *Speculum*, 18 (1943), pp. 484–93.
Green, W.M., *Augustine on the Teaching of History* (University of California Publications in Classical Philology XII, Berkeley, 1944).
Green-Pedersen, N.J., *The Tradition of the Topics in the Middle Ages: The Commentaries on Aristotle's and Boethius' Topics* (Munich, 1984).
Greenway, D., 'Henry of Huntingdon and Bede', in J.-P. Genet (ed.), *L'Historiographie Médiévale en Europe* (Paris, 1991), pp. 43–50.
Greenway, D., 'Authority, Convention and Observation in Henry of Huntingdon's *Historia Anglorum*', *Anglo-Norman Studies*, 18 (1996), pp. 105–21.
Guenée, B., 'Histoires, Annales, Chroniques. Essai sur les Genres Historiques au Moyen Âge', *Annales*, 28 (1973), pp. 997–1016.
Guenée, B., 'Y a-t-il une Historiographie Médiévale?', *Revue Historique*, 258 (1977), pp. 261–75; reprinted in B. Guenée, *Politique et Histoire au Moyen Age: Recueil d'Articles sur l'Histoire Politique et l'Historiographie Médiévale 1956–1981* (Paris, 1981), pp. 205–19.
Guenée, B., *Histoire et Culture Historique dans l'Occident Medieval* (Paris, 1980).
Guenée, B., 'L'Histoire Entre l'Éloquence et la Science: Quelques Remarques sur le Prologue de Guillaume de Malmesbury à ses *Gesta Regum Anglorum*', *Comptes rendus de l'Académie des Inscriptions et Belles-Lettres* (1982), pp. 357–70.
Guenée, B., 'Histoire et Chronique. Nouvelles Réflexions sur les Genres Historiques au Moyen Age', in D. Poirion (ed.), *La Chronique et l'Histoire au Moyen Age* (Paris, 1984), pp. 3–12.
Guenée, B., *Between Church and State: The Lives of Four French Prelates in the Late Middle Ages* (Chicago, 1991).
Haahr, J.G., 'The Concept of Kingship in William of Malmesbury's *Gesta Regum* and *Historia Novella*', *Medieval Studies*, 38 (1976), pp. 351–71.
Haahr, J.G., 'William of Malmesbury's Roman Models: Suetonius and Lucan', in A.S. Bernardo and S. Levin (eds), *The Classics in the Middle Ages* (New York, 1990), pp. 165–73.
Hagendahl, H., *Latin Fathers and the Classics: A Study on the Apologists, Jerome and Other Christian Writers* (Gothenburg, 1958).
Hanawalt, E.A., 'Dudo of Saint-Quentin – The Heroic Past Imagined', *Haskins Society Journal*, 6 (1994), pp. 111–18.
Hannick, C., 'Liturgie und Geschichtsschreibung', in A. Scharer and G. Scheibelreiter (eds), *Historiographie im frühen Mittelalter* (Vienna, 1994), pp. 179–85.
Hanning, R.W., *The Vision of History in Early Britain: From Gildas to Geoffrey of Monmouth* (New York, 1966).
Häring, N.M., 'The Interaction Between Canon Law and Sacramental Theology in the Twelfth Century', in S. Kuttner (ed.), *Proceedings of the Fourth International Congress of Medieval Canon Law* (Rome, 1976), pp. 483–93.
Harrison, K., *The Framework of History to AD 900* (Cambridge, 1976).
Hathaway, N., 'Compilator – From Plagiarism to Compiling', *Viator*, 20 (1989), pp. 19–44.
Haug, W., *Vernacular Literary Theory in the Middle Ages: The German Tradition 800–1300 in Its European Context* (Cambridge, 1997).
Hay, D., 'Flavio Biondo and the Middle Ages', *Proceedings of the British Academy*, 45 (1960), pp. 97–128; reprinted in D. Hay, *Renaissance Essays* (London, 1988), pp. 35–63.

Hay, D., *Annalists and Historians: Western Historiography from the VIIIth to the XVIIIth Century* (London, 1977).
Head, T. (ed.), *Medieval Hagiography: An Anthology* (London, 2001).
Hedeman, A.D., 'Restructuring the Narrative – The Function of Ceremonial in Charles V's *Grandes Chroniques de France*', in H.L. Kessler and M.S. Simpson (eds), *Pictorial Narrative in Antiquity and the Middle Ages* (Hanover, 1985), pp. 171–81.
Heffernan, T.J., 'Christian Biography – Foundation and Maturity', in D.M. Deliyannis (ed.), *Historiography in the Middle Ages* (Leiden, 2003), pp. 115–54.
Heinzelmann, M., *Gregory of Tours: History and Society in the Sixth Century* (Cambridge, 2001).
Hexter, J.H., 'Seyssel, Machiavelli and Polybius VI – The Mystery of the Missing Translation', *Studies in the Renaissance*, 3 (1956), pp. 75–96.
Hissette, R., *Enquête sur les 219 Articles Condamnés à Paris le 7 Mars 1277* (Louvain, 1977)
Holford-Strevens, L., *Aulus Gellius: An Antonine Scholar and His Achievement* (rev. edn, Oxford, 2003).
Holtz, L., *Donat et la Tradition de l'Enseignement Grammatical* (Paris, 1981).
Huneycutt, L.L., 'The Idea of the Perfect Princess – The *Life of St Margaret* in the Reign of Matilda II (1100–1118)', *Anglo-Norman Studies*, 12 (1990), pp. 81–98.
Hunt, T., 'The Rhetorical Background to the Arthurian Prologue – Tradition and the Old French Vernacular Prologues', *Forum for Modern Language Studies*, 6 (1970), pp. 1–23.
Hunt, T., 'Tradition and Originality in the Prologues of Chrestien de Troyes', *Forum for Modern Language Studies*, 8 (1972), pp. 320–44.
Hunt, T., *Teaching and Learning Latin in Thirteenth-Century England* (3 vols, Cambridge, 1991).
Hutton, P.H., *History as an Art of Memory* (Hanover, 1993).
Ianziti, G., 'Leonardo Bruni – First Modern Historian?', *Parergon*, 14 (1997), pp. 85–99.
Ianziti, G., 'Bruni on Writing History', *Renaissance Quarterly*, 51 (1998), pp. 367–91.
Ianziti, G., 'Challenging Chronicles – Leonardo Bruni's History of the Florentine People', in S. Dale, A.W. Lewin and D.J. Osheim (eds), *Chronicling History: Chroniclers and Historians in Medieval and Renaissance Italy* (University Park, 2007), pp. 249–72.
Irvine, M., *The Making of Textual Culture: Grammatica and Literary Theory 350–1100* (Cambridge, 1994).
Jaeger, C.S., 'The Prologue to the *Historia Calamitatum* and the "Authenticity Question"', *Euphorion*, 74 (1980), pp. 1–15; reprinted in C.S. Jaeger, *Scholars and Courtiers: Intellectuals and Society in the Medieval West* (Aldershot, 2002).
Jaeger, C.S., 'Humanism and Ethics at the School of St. Victor in the Early Twelfth Century', *Mediaeval Studies*, 55 (1993), pp. 51–79; reprinted in C.S. Jaeger, *Scholars and Courtiers: Intellectuals and Society in the Medieval West* (Aldershot, 2002).
Jaeger, C.S., *The Envy of Angels: Cathedral Schools and Social Ideals in Medieval Europe 950–1200* (Philadelphia, 1994).
Jaffe, S., 'Antiquity and Innovation in Notker's *Nova Rhetorica*: The Doctrine of Invention', *Rhetorica*, 3 (1985), pp. 165–81.
Janik, L.G., 'Lorenzo Valla – The Primacy of Rhetoric and the De-moralization of History', *History and Theory*, 12 (1973), pp. 389–404.
Janson, T., *Latin Prose Prefaces: Studies in Literary Conventions* (Stockholm, 1964).

Jauss, H.R., 'Literary History as a Challenge to Literary Theory', *New Literary History* (1970), pp. 7–37; reprinted in H.R. Jauss, *Toward an Aesthetic of Reception* (Brighton, 1982), pp. 3–45.
Jauss, H.R., *Toward an Aesthetic of Reception* (Brighton, 1982).
John, E., 'The *Encomium Emmae Reginae* – A Riddle and a Solution', *Bulletin of the John Rylands Library*, 63 (1980), pp. 58–94.
Jones, C.W., *Saints' Lives and Chronicles in Early England* (Ithaca, 1947).
Jones, J.W., 'Allegorical Interpretation in Servius', *Classical Journal*, 56 (1961), pp. 218–22.
Jonsson, R., *Historia: Études sur la Genèse des Offices Versifiés* (Stockholm, 1968).
Jotischky, A., *The Carmelites and Antiquity: Mendicants and Their Pasts in the Middle Ages* (Oxford, 2002).
Kaiser, R., 'Die *Gesta Episcoporum* als Genus der Geschichtsschreibung', in A. Scharer and G. Scheibelreiter (eds), *Historiographie im frühen Mittelalter* (Vienna, 1994), pp. 459–80.
Kauffmann, M., 'The Image of St Louis', in A.J. Duggan (ed.), *Kings and Kingship in Medieval Europe* (London, 1993), pp. 265–86.
Kearney, R., 'Time, Evil and Narrative – Ricoeur on Augustine', in J.D. Caputo and M.J. Scanlon (eds), *Augustine and Post-Modernism: Confessions and Circumfession* (Bloomington, 2005), pp. 144–58.
Kelley, D.R., *Foundations of Modern Historical Scholarship: Language, Law and History in the French Renaissance* (New York, 1970).
Kelley, D.R., 'Clio and the Lawyers – Forms of Historical Consciousness in Medieval Jurisprudence', *Medievalia et Humanistica*, 5 (1974), pp. 25–49; reprinted in D.R. Kelley, *History, Law and the Human Sciences* (London, 1984).
Kelley, D.R., 'Tacitus Noster – The *Germania* in the Renaissance and Reformation', in T.J. Luce and A.J. Woodman (eds), *Tacitus and the Tacitean Tradition* (Princeton, 1993), pp. 152–7.
Kelly, D., 'Theory of Composition in Medieval Narrative Poetry and Geoffrey of Vinsauf's *Poetria Nova*', *Mediaeval Studies*, 31 (1969), pp. 117–48.
Kelly, D., *The Arts of Poetry and Prose* (Typologie des Sources du Moyen Âge Occidental 59, Turnhout, 1991).
Kelly, D., *The Conspiracy of Allusion: Disruption, Rewriting and Authorship from Macrobius to Medieval Romance* (Leiden, 1999).
Kelly, H. A., *Ideas and Forms of Tragedy from Aristotle to the Middle Ages* (Cambridge, 1993).
Kelly, J.N.D., *Jerome: His Life, Writings and Controversies* (London, 1975).
Kempshall, M.S., 'Some Ciceronian Models for Einhard's "Life" of Charlemagne', *Viator*, 26 (1995), pp. 11–37.
Kempshall, M.S., 'No Bishop, No King – The Ministerial Ideology of Kingship and Asser's *Res Gestae Aelfredi*', in R. Gameson and H. Leyser (eds), *Belief and Culture in the Middle Ages* (Oxford, 2001), pp. 106–27.
Kempshall, M.S., 'The Rhetoric of Giles of Rome's *De Regimine Principum*', in F. Lachaud and L. Scordia (eds), *Le Prince au Miroir de la Literature Politique de l'Antiquité aux Lumières* (Rouen, 2006), pp. 161–90.
Kennedy, G.A., 'The *Rhetorica* of Guillaume Fichet', *Rhetorica*, 5 (1987), pp. 411–18.
Kennedy, G.A., *Classical Rhetoric and Its Christian and Secular Tradition from Ancient to Modern Times* (2nd edn, Chapel Hill, 1999).
Kersken, N., 'High and Late Medieval National Historiography', in D.M. Deliyannis (ed.), *Historiography in the Middle Ages* (Leiden, 2003), pp. 181–215.
Kessler, E., *Theoretiker humanistischer Geschichtsschreibung* (Munich, 1971).

Kessler, H.L. and M.S. Simpson (eds), *Pictorial Narrative in Antiquity and the Middle Ages* (Washington, DC, 1985).
Kline, N.R., *Maps of Medieval Thought: The Hereford Paradigm* (Woodbridge, 2001).
Knape, J., 'Historia, Textuality and *Episteme*', in T.M.S. Lehtonen and P. Mehtonen (eds), *Historia: The Concept and Genres in the Middle Ages* (Helsinki, 2000), pp. 11–27.
Knappe, G., 'Classical Rhetoric in Anglo-Saxon England', *Anglo Saxon England*, 27 (1998), pp. 5–29.
Knox, R., 'Finding the Law – Developments in Canon Law During the Gregorian Reform', *Studi Gregoriani*, 9 (1972), pp. 419–66.
Kohl, B.G., 'Petrarch's Prefaces to *De Viris Illustribus*', *History and Theory*, 13 (1974), pp. 132–44.
Kraus, C.S. and A.J. Woodman, *Latin Historians* (Oxford, 1997).
Kretschmer, M.T., *Rewriting Roman History in the Middle Ages: The Historia Romana and the Manuscript Bamberg, Hist. 3* (Leiden, 2007).
Kristeller, P.O., 'Humanism and Scholasticism in the Italian Renaissance', in P.O. Kristeller, *Renaissance Thought and Its Sources* (New York, 1979), pp. 85–105.
Kristeller, P.O., F.E. Cranz, V. Brown, et al. (eds), *Catalogus Translationum et Commentariorum: Medieval and Renaissance Latin Translations and Commentaries* (Washington, DC, 1960–).
Krüger, K.H., *Die Universalchroniken* (Typologie des Sources du Moyen Âge Occidental 16, Turnhout, 1976).
Lachaud, F., 'Le *Liber de Principis Instructione* de Giraud de Barry', in F. Lachaud and L. Scordia (eds), *Le Prince au Miroir de la Literature Politique de l'Antiquité aux Lumières* (Rouen, 2006), pp. 113–42.
Lachaud, F. and L. Scordia (eds), *Le Prince au Miroir de la Literature Politique de l'Antiquité aux Lumières* (Rouen, 2006).
La Penna, A., 'Il Significato de Sallustio nella Storiografia e nel Pensiero Politico di Leonardo Bruni', in A. La Penna, *Sallustio e la 'Rivoluzione Romana'* (Milan, 1968), pp. 409–31.
La Storiografia Altomedievale: Settimane di Studio, 17 (1970).
Lacroix, B., *L'Historien au Moyen Âge* (Montreal, 1971).
Lacy, N.J. and J.T. Grimbart (eds), *A Companion to Chrétien de Troyes* (Cambridge, 2005).
Laistner, M.L.W., 'The Value and Influence of Cassiodorus' *Ecclesiastical History*', *Harvard Theological Review*, 41 (1948), pp. 51–67; reprinted in M.L.W. Laistner, *The Intellectual Heritage of the Early Middle Ages: Selected Essays* (Ithaca, 1957), pp. 22–39.
Lamarrigue, A.-M., *Bernard Gui (1261–1331): Un Historien et Sa Méthode* (Paris, 2000).
Lambert, D., 'The Uses of Decay – History in Salvian's *De Gubernatione Dei*', *Augustinian Studies*, 30 (1999), pp. 115–30.
Lampe, G.W.H. (ed.), *The Cambridge History of the Bible. Vol. II: The West from the Fathers to the Reformation* (Cambridge, 1969).
Lanham, C.D. (ed.), *Latin Grammar and Rhetoric: From Classical Theory to Medieval Practice* (London, 2002).
Lapidge, M., 'Gildas's Education and the Latin Culture of Sub-Roman Britain', in M. Lapidge and D. Dumville (eds), *Gildas: New Approaches* (Woodbridge, 1984), pp. 27–50.
Latouche, R., 'Un Imitateur de Salluste au Xe Siècle, l'Historien Richer', in R. Latouche, *Études Médiévales* (Paris, 1966), pp. 69–81.

Law, V., *Grammar and Grammarians in the Early Middle Ages* (London, 1997).
Lawler, T., 'The Two Versions of Geoffrey of Vinsauf's *Documentum*', in T. Lawler, *The Parisiana Poetria of John of Garland* (New Haven, 1974), pp. 327–32.
Leclercq, J., *The Love of Learning and the Desire for God: A Study of Monastic Culture* (3rd edn, New York, 1982).
Lehtonen, T.M.S., 'History, Tragedy and Fortune in Twelfth-Century Historiography with Special Reference to Otto of Freising's *Chronica*', in T.M.S. Lehtonen and P. Mehtonen (eds), *Historia: The Concept and Genres in the Middle Ages* (Helsinki, 2000), pp. 29–49.
Lehtonen, T.M.S. and P. Mehtonen (eds), *Historia: The Concept and Genres in the Middle Ages* (Helsinki, 2000).
Leigh, M., *Lucan: Spectacle and Engagement* (Oxford, 1997).
Leppin, H., 'The Church Historians – Socrates, Sozomenus and Theodoretus', in G. Marasco (ed.), *Greek and Roman Historiography in Late Antiquity: Fourth to Sixth Century AD* (Brill, 2003), pp. 219–54.
Levine, R., 'How to Read Walter Map', *Mittellateinisches Jahrbuch*, 23 (1988), pp. 91–105.
Lewis, S., *The Art of Matthew Paris in the Chronica Majora* (Aldershot, 1987).
Lewry, P.O., 'Rhetoric at Paris and Oxford in the Mid-Thirteenth Century', *Rhetorica*, 1 (1983), pp. 45–63.
Leyser, K., 'Liudprand of Cremona – Preacher and Homilist', in D. Wood and K. Walsh (eds), *The Bible in the Medieval World: Essays in Memory of Beryl Smalley* (Oxford, 1985), pp. 43–60; reprinted in K. Leyser, *Communications and Power in Medieval Europe: The Carolingian and Ottonian Centuries* (London, 1994), pp. 111–24.
Leyser, K., 'Ends and Means in Liudprand of Cremona', in K. Leyser, *Communications and Power in Medieval Europe: The Carolingian and Ottonian Centuries* (London, 1994), pp. 125–42.
Liebeschutz, H., 'John of Salisbury and Pseudo-Plutarch', *Journal of the Warburg and Courtauld Institutes*, 6 (1943), pp. 33–9.
Liebeschutz, H., *Medieval Humanism in the Life and Writings of John of Salisbury* (London, 1950).
Lifshitz, F., 'The *Encomium Emmae Reginae* – A "Political Pamphlet" of the Eleventh Century?', *Haskins Society Journal*, 1 (1989), pp. 39–50.
Ligota, C., 'Lucian on the Writing of History – Obsolescence Survived', in C. Ligota and L. Panizza (eds), *Lucian of Samosata Vivus et Redivivus* (London, 2007), pp. 45–70.
Linde, J., 'Die *Rethorici Colores* des Magisters Onulf von Speyer', *Mittellateinisches Jahrbuch*, 40 (2005), pp. 333–81.
Linehan, P., *History and the Historians of Medieval Spain* (Oxford, 1993).
Lohr, C.H., *Medieval Latin Aristotle Commentaries* (New York, 1964–74).
Loomis, L.H., 'Secular Dramatics in the Royal Palace, Paris, 1378, 1389 and Chaucer's "Tregetoures"', *Speculum*, 33 (1958), pp. 242–55.
Lorenz, C. (ed.), 'Comparative History – Problems and Perspectives', *History and Theory*, 38 (1999), pp. 25–99.
Loud, G.A., 'History Writing in the Twelfth-Century Kingdom of Sicily', in S. Dale, A.W. Lewin and D.J. Osheim (eds), *Chronicling History: Chroniclers and Historians in Medieval and Renaissance Italy* (University Park, 2007), pp. 29–54.
Lucas, R.H., 'Medieval French Translations of the Latin Classics to 1500', *Speculum*, 45 (1970), pp. 225–53.
Luce, T.J., *Livy: The Composition of His History* (Princeton, 1977).

Luce, T.J., 'Tacitus on "History's Highest Function" – *Praecipuum Munus Annalium*', *Aufstieg und Niedergang der römische Welt*, II.33.4 (1991), pp. 2904–27.
Luce, T.J. and A.J. Woodman (eds), *Tacitus and the Tacitean Tradition* (Princeton, 1993).
Luscombe, D.E., 'Peter Comestor', in K. Walsh and D. Wood (eds), *The Bible in the Medieval World: Essays in Memory of Beryl Smalley* (Oxford, 1985), pp. 109–29.
MacCormack, S.G., 'Latin Prose Panegyrics', in T.A. Dorey (ed.), *Empire and Aftermath: Silver Latin II* (London, 1975), pp. 143–205.
MacCormack, S.G., 'Latin Prose Panegyrics – Tradition and Discontinuity in the Later Roman Empire', *Revue des Etudes Augustiniennes*, 22 (1976), pp. 29–77.
MacCormack, S.G., *Art and Ceremony in Late Antiquity* (Berkeley, 1981).
MacKendrick, P., *The Philosophical Books of Cicero* (London, 1989).
Magdalino, P. (ed.), *The Perception of the Past in Twelfth-Century Europe* (London, 1992).
Mähl, S., *Quadriga Virtutum: Die Kardinaltugenden in der Geistesgeschichte der Karolingerzeit* (Cologne, 1969).
Marasco, G. (ed.), *Greek and Roman Historiography in Late Antiquity: Fourth to Sixth Century AD* (Brill, 2003).
Marenbon, J., *The Philosophy of Peter Abelard* (Cambridge, 1997).
Marenbon, J., *Boethius* (Oxford, 2003).
Markus, R.A., *Saeculum: History and Society in the Theology of Augustine* (Cambridge, 1970).
Markus, R.A. (ed.), *Augustine: A Collection of Critical Essays* (New York, 1972).
Markus, R.A., 'Church History and Early Church Historians', in D. Baker (ed.), *The Materials, Sources and Methods of Ecclesiastical History* (Oxford, 1975), pp. 1–17.
Markus, R.A., *Bede and the Tradition of Ecclesiastical Historiography*, Jarrow Lecture (Jarrow, 1975); reprinted in R.A. Markus, *From Augustine to Gregory the Great: History and Christianity in Late Antiquity* (London, 1983).
Markus, R.A., *Signs and Meanings: World and Text in Ancient Christianity* (Liverpool, 1996).
Marrou, H.I., 'Saint Augustin, Orose et l'Augustinisme Historique', *Settimane di Studio*, 17 (1970), pp. 59–87.
Marsh, D., *Lucian and the Latins: Humor and Humanism in the Early Renaissance* (Ann Arbor, 1998).
Martin, J., 'John of Salisbury as Classical Scholar', in M. Wilks (ed.), *The World of John of Salisbury* (Oxford, 1984), pp. 179–201.
Martin, R.H., *Tacitus* (London, 1981).
Maslakov, G., 'Valerius Maximus and Roman Historiography – A Study of the Exempla Tradition', *Aufstieg und Niedergang der römische Welt*, II.32.1 (1984), pp. 437–96.
Mayer, C. (ed.), *Augustinus-Lexikon* (Basel, 1986–).
Mayr-Harting, H., *The Venerable Bede, the Rule of St. Benedict, and Social Class*, Jarrow Lecture (Jarrow, 1976).
Mayr-Harting, H., 'Two Abbots in Politics – Wala of Corbie and Bernard of Clairvaux', *Transactions of the Royal Historical Society*, 40 (1990), pp. 217–37.
Mayr-Harting, H., 'Liudprand of Cremona's Account of His Legation to Constantinople (968) and Ottonian Imperial Strategy', *English Historical Review*, 116 (2001), pp. 539–56.
McCahill, E.M., 'Finding a Job as a Humanist – The Epistolary Collection of Lapo da Castiglionchio the Younger', *Renaissance Quarterly*, 57 (2004), pp. 1308–45.
McClure, J., 'Bede's Old Testament Kings', in P. Wormald, D. Bullough and R.

Collins (eds), *Ideal and Reality in Frankish and Anglo-Saxon Society: Studies Presented to J.M. Wallace-Hadrill* (Oxford, 1983), pp. 76–98.
McCormick, M., *Les Annales du Haut Moyen Âge* (Typologie des Sources du Moyen Âge Occidental 14, Turnhout, 1975).
McGinn, B., *Visions of the End: Apocalyptic Traditions in the Middle Ages* (rev. edn, New York, 1998).
McKeon, R., 'Rhetoric in the Middle Ages', *Speculum*, 17 (1942), pp. 1–32.
McKitterick, R., 'Political Ideology in Carolingian Historiography', in Y. Hen and M. Innes (eds), *The Uses of the Past in the Early Middle Ages* (Cambridge, 2000), pp. 162–74.
McKitterick, R., *History and Memory in the Carolingian World* (Cambridge, 2004).
McKitterick, R., *Charlemagne* (Cambridge, 2008).
Mégier, E., '*Fortuna* als Kategorie der Geschichtsdeutung im 12. Jahrhundert am Beispiel Ordericus' Vitalis und Ottos von Freising', *Mittellateinisches Jahrbuch*, 32 (1997), pp. 49–70.
Mehtonen, P., *Old Concepts and New Poetics: Historia, Argumentum and Fabula in the Twelfth- and Thirteenth-Century Latin Poetics of Fiction* (Helsinki, 1996).
Mehtonen, P., 'Scriptural Difficulty and the Obscurity of *Historia*', in T.M.S. Lehtonen and P. Mehtonen (eds), *Historia: The Concept and Genres in the Middle Ages* (Helsinki, 2000), pp. 51–67.
Mellor, R., *The Roman Historians* (London, 1999).
Mews, C., 'Peter Abelard on Dialectic, Rhetoric and the Principles of Argument', in C.J. Mews, C.J. Nederman and R.M. Thomson (eds), *Rhetoric and Renewal in the Latin West 1100–1540: Essays in Honour of John O. Ward* (Turnhout, 2003), pp. 37–53.
Mews, C.J., C.J. Nederman and R.M. Thomson (eds), *Rhetoric and Renewal in the Latin West 1100–1540: Essays in Honour of John O. Ward* (Turnhout, 2003).
Meyer, H. and R. Suntrup, *Lexikon der mittelalterlichen Zahlenbedeutungen* (Munich, 1987).
Meyvaert, P., *Bede and Gregory the Great*, Jarrow Lecture (Jarrow, 1964).
Michel, A. (ed.), *Rhétorique et Poétique au Moyen Âge* (Turnhout, 2002).
Miglio, M., 'Una Lettera di Lapo da Castiglionchio', in M. Miglio (ed.), *Storiografia Pontificia del Quattrocento* (Bologna, 1975), pp. 33–59.
Minnis, A.J., *Medieval Theory of Authorship: Scholastic Literary Attitudes in the Later Middle Ages* (2nd edn, Aldershot, 1988).
Minnis, A.J. and A.B. Scott (eds), with the assistance of D. Wallace, *Medieval Literary Theory and Criticism c.1100–c.1375: The Commentary Tradition* (Oxford, 1988).
Mollard, A., 'La Diffusion de l'*Institution Oratoire* au XIIe Siècle', *Moyen Âge*, 44 (1934), pp. 161–75; *Moyen Âge*, 45 (1935), pp. 1–9.
Momigliano, A., 'Pagan and Christian Historiography in the Fourth Century AD', in A. Momigliano (ed.), *The Conflict Between Paganism and Christianity in the Fourth Century* (Oxford, 1963), pp. 79–99; reprinted in A. Momigliano, *Essays in Ancient and Modern Historiography* (Oxford, 1977), pp. 107–26.
Momigliano, A., 'Polybius' Reappearance in Western Europe', in E. Gabba (ed.), *Polybe* (Geneva, 1974), pp. 345–72; reprinted in A. Momigliano, *Sesto Contributo alla Storia degli Studi Classici e del Mondo Antico* (2 vols, Rome, 1980), vol. I, pp. 103–23; and A. Momigliano, *Essays in Ancient and Modern Historiography* (Oxford, 1977), pp. 79–98.
Momigliano, A., 'Polybius Between the English and the Turks', in A. Momigliano, *Sesto Contributo alla Storia degli Studi Classici e del Mondo Antico* (2 vols, Rome, 1980), vol. I, pp. 125–41.

Momigliano, A., 'History Between Medicine and Rhetoric', in A. Momigliano, *Ottavo Contributo alla Storia degli Studi Classici e del Mondo Antico* (Rome, 1987), pp. 13–25.
Mommsen, T.E., 'Petrarch's Concept of the "Dark Ages"', *Speculum*, 17 (1942), pp. 226–42.
Mommsen, T.E., 'St. Augustine and the Christian Idea of Progress – The Background of the City of God', *Journal of the History of Ideas*, 12 (1951), pp. 346–74.
Mommsen, T.E., 'Orosius and Augustine', in T.E. Mommsen, *Medieval and Renaissance Studies* (Ithaca, 1959), pp. 325–48.
Monfasani, J., *George of Trebizond: A Biography and a Study of His Rhetoric and Logic* (Leiden, 1976).
Monfasani, J., 'Humanism and Rhetoric', in A. Rabil (ed.), *Renaissance Humanism: Foundations, Forms and Legacy* (3 vols, Philadelphia, 1988), vol. III, pp. 171–235.
Monfasani, J., 'Episodes of Anti-Quintilianism in the Italian Renaissance – Quarrels on the Orator as a *Vir Bonus* and Rhetoric as the *Scientia Bene Dicendi*', *Rhetorica*, 10 (1992), pp. 127–35.
Morris, C., *The Papal Monarchy: The Western Church from 1050 to 1250* (Oxford, 1989).
Morrison, K.F., *History as a Visual Art in the Twelfth-Century Renaissance* (Princeton, 1990).
Morse, R., *Truth and Convention in the Middle Ages: Rhetoric, Representation and Reality* (Cambridge, 1991).
Mortensen, L.B., 'The Texts and Contexts of Ancient Roman History in Twelfth-Century Western Scholarship', in P. Magdalino (ed.), *The Perception of the Past in Twelfth-Century Europe* (London, 1992), pp. 99–116.
Mortensen, L.B., 'Hugh of St. Victor on Secular History – A Preliminary Edition of Chapters From His *Chronica*', *Cahiers de l'Institut du Moyen-Âge Grec et Latin*, 62 (1992), pp. 3–30.
Mortensen, L.B., 'The Glorious Past: Entertainment, Example or History? Levels of Twelfth-Century Historical Culture', *Culture and History*, 13 (1994), pp. 57–71.
Mortensen, L.B., 'Change of Style and Content as an Aspect of the Copying Process – A Recent Trend in the Study of Medieval Latin Historiography', in J. Hamesse (ed.), *Bilan et Perspectives des Études Médiévales en Europe* (Louvain-la-Neuve, 1995), pp. 265–76.
Mortensen, L.B., 'Working with Ancient Roman History – A Comparison of Carolingian and Twelfth-Century Scholarly Endeavours', in C. Leonardi (ed.), *Gli Umanesimi Medievali* (Atti del II Congresso dell'Internationales Mittellateinerkomitee, Florence, 1998), pp. 411–20.
Mortensen, L.B., 'The Diffusion of Roman Histories in the Middle Ages: A List of Orosius, Eutropius, Paulus Diaconus and Landolfus Sagax Manuscripts', *Filologica Mediolatina*, 6–7 (1999–2000), pp. 101–200.
Mosshammer, A., *The Chronicle of Eusebius and Greek Chronographic Tradition* (Lewisburg, 1979).
Müller, C., 'Historia', in C. Mayer (ed.), *Augustinus-Lexikon* (Basel, 1986–), cols 366–77.
Munk Olsen, B., 'L'Humanisme de Jean de Salisbury, un Ciceronien au 12e Siècle', in M. Gandillac and E. Jeauneau (eds), *Entretiens sur la Renaissance du 12e Siècle* (Paris, 1968), pp. 53–69.
Munk Olsen, B., *L'Étude des Auteurs Classiques Latins au XIe et XIIe Siècles* (4 vols, Paris, 1982–89).
Munk Olsen, B., 'Virgile et la Renaissance du XIIe Siècle', in J.-Y. Tilliette (ed.),

Lectures Médiévale de Virgile: Actes du Colloque Organisé par l'Ecole Française de Rome (Rome, 1985), pp. 31–48.
Munk Olsen, B., *I Classici nel Canone Scolastico Altomedievale* (Spoleto, 1991).
Munk Olsen, B., 'La Diffusion et l'Étude des Historiens Antiques au XIIe Siècle', in A. Welkenhuysen, H. Braet and W. Verbeke (eds), *Mediaeval Antiquity* (Leuven, 1995), pp. 21–43.
Munk Olsen, B., 'Chronique des Manuscripts Classiques Latins (IXe–XIIe Siècles) I–III', *Revue d'Histoire des Textes*, 21 (1991), pp. 37–76; *Revue d'Histoire des Textes*, 24 (1994), pp. 199–249; *Revue d'Histoire des Textes*, 27 (1997), pp. 29–85.
Murphy, F.X., *Rufinus of Aquileia (345–411): His Life and Works* (Washington, DC, 1945).
Murphy, J.J., 'Saint Augustine and the Debate about a Christian Rhetoric', *Quarterly Journal of Speech*, 46 (1960), pp. 400–10.
Murphy, J.J., 'The Scholastic Condemnation of Rhetoric in the Commentary of Giles of Rome on the *Rhetoric* of Aristotle', in *Arts Libéraux et Philosophie au Moyen Age* (Actes du Quatrième Congrès International de Philosophie Médiévale, Montreal, 1969), pp. 833–41.
Murphy, J.J. (ed.), *Three Medieval Rhetorical Arts* (Berkeley, 1971).
Murphy, J.J., *Rhetoric in the Middle Ages: A History of Rhetorical Theory from St Augustine to the Renaissance* (Berkeley, 1974).
Murphy, J.J., *Medieval Eloquence: Studies in the Theory and Practice of Medieval Rhetoric* (Berkeley, 1978).
Murphy, J.J. and M. Davies, 'Rhetorical Incunabula – A Short-Title Catalogue of Texts Printed to the Year 1500', *Rhetorica*, 15 (1997), pp. 355–470.
Murphy, J.J., 'Rhetoric in the Fifteenth Century – From Manuscript to Print', in C.J. Mews, C.J. Nederman and R.M. Thomson (eds), *Rhetoric and Renewal in the Latin West 1100–1540: Essays in Honour of John O. Ward* (Turnhout, 2003), pp. 227–41.
Najemy, J.M., 'Machiavelli and the Medici – The Lessons of Florentine History', *Renaissance Quarterly*, 35 (1982), pp. 551–76.
Nederman, C.J., 'A Duty to Kill – John of Salisbury's Theory of Tyrannicide', *Review of Politics*, 50 (1988), pp. 365–89.
Nederman, C.J., 'The Union of Wisdom and Eloquence before the Renaissance – The Ciceronian Orator in Medieval Thought', *Journal of Medieval History*, 18 (1992), pp. 75–95.
Nelson, J.L., 'Public Histories and Private History in the Work of Nithard', *Speculum*, 60 (1985), pp. 251–93; reprinted in J.L. Nelson, *Politics and Ritual in Early Medieval Europe* (London, 1986), pp. 195–238.
Nelson, J.L., 'Reconstructing a Royal Family – Reflections on Alfred, from Asser Chapter 2', in I. Wood and N. Lund (eds), *People and Places in Northern Europe 500–1600* (Woodbridge, 1991), pp. 47–66.
Nelson, J.L., 'History-Writing at the Courts of Louis the Pious and Charles the Bald', in A. Scharer and G. Scheibelreiter (eds), *Historiographie im frühen Mittelalter* (Vienna, 1994), pp. 435–42.
Nelson, J.L., 'Kingship and Royal Government', in R. McKitterick (ed.), *The New Cambridge Medieval History. Vol. II: c.700–c.900* (Cambridge, 1995), pp. 383–430.
Nora, P., *Realms of Memory: Rethinking the French Past* (3 vols, New York, 1996–98).
Nykrog, P., 'The Rise of Literary Fiction', in R.L. Benson and G. Constable (eds), *Renaissance and Renewal in the Twelfth Century* (Oxford, 1982), pp. 593–612.
Oakley, F., *The Conciliarist Tradition: Constitutionalism in the Catholic Church 1300–1870* (Oxford, 2003).

O'Daly, G., *Augustine's City of God: A Reader's Guide* (Oxford, 1999).
O'Donnell, J.R., 'The Commentary of Giles of Rome on the *Rhetoric* of Aristotle', in T.A. Sandquist and M. Powicke (eds), *Essays in Medieval History Presented to Bertie Wilkinson* (Toronto, 1969), pp. 139–56.
O'Donovan, O., 'Augustine's *City of God* XIX and Western Political Thought', *Dionysius*, 11 (1987), pp. 89–110.
Olson, G., *Literature as Recreation in the Later Middle Ages* (Ithaca, 1982).
Oppel, J.W., 'Peace *vs* Liberty in the Quattrocento: Poggio, Guarino and the Scipio-Caesar Controversy', *Journal of Medieval and Renaissance Studies*, 4 (1974), pp. 221–65.
Orchard, A., 'The Literary Background to the *Encomium Emmae Reginae*', *Journal of Medieval Latin*, 11 (2001), pp. 156–83.
Osmond, P.J., '*Princeps Historiae Romanae* – Sallust in Renaissance Political Thought', *Memoirs of the American Academy in Rome*, 40 (1995), pp. 101–43.
Otter, M., *Inventiones: Fiction and Referentiality in Twelfth-Century English Historical Writing* (Chapel Hill, 1996).
Otter, M., 'Functions of Fiction in Historical Writing', in N. Partner (ed.), *Writing Medieval History* (London, 2005), pp. 109–30.
Oulton, J.E.L., 'Rufinus' Translation of the Church History of Eusebius', *Journal of Theological Studies*, 30 (1929), pp. 150–74.
Pade, M., *The Reception of Plutarch's Lives in Fifteenth-Century Italy* (2 vols, Copenhagen, 2007).
Palmer, J.J.N. (ed.), *Froissart: Historian* (Woodbridge, 1981).
Palmer, N., 'Exempla', in F.A.C. Mantello and A.G. Rigg (eds), *Medieval Latin: An Introduction and Bibliographical Guide* (Washington, DC, 1996), pp. 582–8.
Panofsky, E., *Renaissance and Renascences in Western Art* (Stockholm, 1960).
Partner, N., *Serious Entertainments: The Writing of History in Twelfth-Century England* (Chicago, 1977).
Partner, N., 'The New Cornificius – Medieval History and the Artifice of Words', in E. Breisach (ed.), *Classical Rhetoric and Medieval Historiography* (Kalamazoo, 1985), pp. 5–59.
Partner, N. (ed.), *Writing Medieval History* (London, 2005).
Phillips, M., *Francesco Guicciardini: The Historian's Craft* (Toronto, 1977).
Phillips, M., 'Machiavelli, Guicciardini and the Tradition of Vernacular Historiography in Florence', *American Historical Review*, 84 (1979), pp. 86–105.
Phillips, M., 'Representation and Argument in Florentine Historiography', *Storia della Storiografia*, 10 (1986), pp. 48–63.
Pizarro, J.M., *A Rhetoric of the Scene: Dramatic Narrative in the Early Middle Ages* (Toronto, 1989).
Pizarro, J.M., 'Ethnic and National History c.500–1000', in D.M. Deliyannis (ed.), *Historiography in the Middle Ages* (Leiden, 2003), pp. 43–87.
Plumer, E. (ed.), *Augustine's Commentary on Galatians* (Oxford, 2006).
Pollmann, K. and M. Vessey (eds), *Augustine and the Disciplines: From Cassiciacum to Confessions* (Oxford, 2005).
Poole, R.L., *Chronicles and Annals: A Brief Outline of Their Origin and Growth* (Oxford, 1926).
Quain, E.A., 'The Medieval *Accessus ad Auctores*', *Traditio*, 3 (1945), pp. 215–64.
Quillen, C.E., *Re-reading the Renaissance: Petrarch, Augustine and the Language of Humanism* (Ann Arbor, 1998).
Rajak, T., *Josephus: The Historian and His Society* (London, 1983).
Ray, R., 'Orderic Vitalis and His Readers', *Studia Monastica*, 14 (1972), pp. 16–33.

Ray, R., 'Medieval Historiography Through the Twelfth Century – Problems and Progress of Research', *Viator*, 5 (1974), pp. 33–59.
Ray, R., 'Orderic Vitalis on Henry I – Theocratic Ideology and Didactic Narrative', in G.H. Shriver (ed.), *Contemporary Reflections on the Medieval Christian Tradition: Essays in Honor of R.C. Petry* (Durham, 1974), pp. 119–34.
Ray, R., 'Bede, the Exegete, as Historian', in G. Bonner (ed.), *Famulus Christi: Essays in Commemoration of the Thirteenth Centenary of the Birth of the Venerable Bede* (London, 1976), pp. 125–40.
Ray, R., 'Bede's *Vera Lex Historiae*', *Speculum*, 55 (1980), pp. 1–21.
Ray, R., 'What Do We Know About Bede's Commentaries?', *Recherches de Théologie Ancienne et Médiévale*, 49 (1982), pp. 5–20.
Ray, R., 'Augustine's *De Consensu Evangelistarum* and the Historical Education of the Venerable Bede', *Studia Patristica*, 16 (1985), pp. 557–63.
Ray, R., 'Rhetorical Scepticism and Verisimilar Narrative in John of Salisbury's *Historia Pontificalis*', in E. Breisach (ed.), *Classical Rhetoric and Medieval Historiography* (Kalamazoo, 1985), pp. 61–102.
Ray, R., 'The Triumph of Greco-Roman Rhetorical Assumptions in Pre-Carolingian Historiography', in C. Holdsworth and T.P. Wiseman (eds), *The Inheritance of Historiography 350–900* (Exeter, 1986), pp. 67–84.
Ray, R., 'Bede and Cicero', *Anglo Saxon England*, 16 (1987), pp. 1–15.
Ray, R., 'Christian Conscience and Pagan Rhetoric – Augustine's Treatises on Lying', *Studia Patristica*, 22 (1989) [Papers Presented to the Tenth International Conference on Patristic Studies, 1987], pp. 321–5.
Ray, R., *Bede, Rhetoric and the Creation of Christian Latin Culture*, Jarrow Lecture (Jarrow, 1997).
Rebhorn, W.A., *Renaissance Debates on Rhetoric* (Ithaca, 2000).
Reeve, M.D., 'The Circulation of Classical Works on Rhetoric from the Twelfth to the Fourteenth Centuries', in C. Leonardi and E. Menestò (eds), *Retorica e Poetica tra i Secoli XII e XIV* (Florence, 1988), pp. 109–24.
Reeve, M.D., 'The Transmission of Florus, *Epitoma de Tito Livo* and the *Periochae*', *Classical Quarterly*, 38 (1988), pp. 477–91.
Regoliosi, M., '*Res Gestae Patriae e Res Gestae ex Universa Italia* – La Lettera di Lapo da Castiglionchio a Biondo Flavio', in C. Bastia and M. Bolognani (eds), *La Memoria e la Città: Scritture Storiche tra Medioevo ed Età Moderna* (Bologna, 1995), pp. 273–305.
Regoliosi, M., 'Riflessioni Umanistiche sullo "Scrivere Storia"', *Rinascimento*, 31 (1991), pp. 3–37.
Regoliosi, M., 'Lorenzo Valla e la Concezione della Storia', in *La Storiografia Umanistica* (Convegno Internazionale dell'Associazione per il Medioevo e l'Umanesimo Latini 1987, Messina, 1992), pp. 549–71.
Remensnyder, A.G., *Remembering Kings Past: Monastic Foundation Legends in Medieval Southern France* (Ithaca, 1995).
Remensnyder, A.G., 'Topographies of Memory – Center and Periphery in High Medieval France', in G. Althoff, J. Fried and P.J. Geary (eds), *Medieval Concepts of the Past: Ritual, Memory, Historiography* (Cambridge, 2002), pp. 193–214.
Reynolds, B., 'Bruni and Perotti Present a Greek Historian', *Bibliothèque d'Humanisme et Renaissance*, 16 (1954), pp. 108–18.
Reynolds, L.D. (ed.), *Texts and Transmission: A Survey of the Latin Classics* (Oxford, 1983).
Reynolds, S., 'Medieval *Origines Gentium* and the Community of the Realm', *History*, 68 (1983), pp. 375–90.

Reynolds, S., *Medieval Reading: Grammar, Rhetoric and the Classical Text* (Cambridge, 1996).
Richardson, B., 'Notes on Machiavelli's Sources and His Treatment of the Rhetorical Tradition', *Italian Studies*, 26 (1971), pp. 24–48.
Ricoeur, P., 'History and Rhetoric', in F. Bédarida (ed.), *The Social Responsibility of the Historian* (Providence, 1995), pp. 7–24.
Ricoeur, P., *Time and Narrative [Temps et Récit]* (3 vols, Chicago, 1984–88).
Ricoeur, P., 'L'Histoire Comme Récit', in D. Tiffenau (ed.), *La Narrativité* (Paris, 1980), pp. 3–24.
Rider, J., *God's Scribe: The Historiographical Art of Galbert of Bruges* (Washington, DC, 2001).
Rider, J. and A.V. Murray (eds), *Galbert of Bruges and the Historiography of Medieval Flanders* (Washington, DC, 2009).
Rigg, A.G., 'Henry of Huntingdon's Metrical Experiments', *Journal of Medieval Latin*, 1 (1991), pp. 60–72.
Rigg, A.G., *A History of Anglo-Latin Literature 1066–1422* (Cambridge, 1992).
Rist, J.M., *Augustine: Ancient Thought Baptized* (Cambridge, 1994).
Robert, S., 'Rhetoric and Dialectic According to the First Latin Commentary on the *Rhetoric* of Aristotle', *New Scholasticism*, 31 (1957), pp. 484–98.
Robinson, C., *Lucian and His Influence in Europe* (London, 1979).
Robinson, I.S., *Authority and Resistance in the Investiture Contest: The Polemical Literature of the Late Eleventh Century* (Manchester, 1978).
Robinson, I.S., *The Papacy 1073–1198* (Cambridge, 1990).
Robinson, I.S., *Henry IV of Germany 1056–1106* (Cambridge, 1999).
Roest, B., 'Medieval Historiography – About Generic Constraints and Scholarly Constructions', in B. Roest and H. Vanstiphout (eds), *Aspects of Genre and Type in Pre-Modern Literary Cultures* (Groningen, 1999), pp. 47–61.
Roest, B., 'Later Medieval Institutional History', in D.M. Deliyannis (ed.), *Historiography in the Middle Ages* (Leiden, 2003), pp. 277–315.
Rohrbacher, D., *The Historians of Late Antiquity* (London, 2002).
Rollinson, P., with P. Matsen, *Classical Theories of Allegory and Christian Culture* (Pittsburgh, 1981).
Rouse, M.A. and R.H. Rouse, 'The Medieval Circulation of Cicero's "Posterior Academics" and the *De Finibus Bonorum et Malorum*', in M.A. Rouse and R.H. Rouse, *Authentic Witnesses: Approaches to Medieval Texts and Manuscripts* (Notre Dame, 1991), pp. 61–98.
Rouse, R.H. and M.A. Rouse, 'John of Salisbury and the Doctrine of Tyrannicide', *Speculum*, 42 (1967), pp. 693–709.
Rubinstein, J., *Guibert of Nogent: Portrait of a Medieval Mind* (London, 2002).
Rummel, E., *The Humanist–Scholastic Debate in the Renaissance and Reformation* (Harvard, 1995).
Scharer, A. and G. Scheibelreiter (eds), *Historiographie im frühen Mittelalter* (Vienna, 1994).
Schellhase, K.C., *Tacitus in Renaissance Political Thought* (Chicago, 1976).
Schmale, F.-J., *Funktion und Formen mittelalterlicher Geschichtsschreibung: Eine Einführung* (Darmstadt, 1985).
Schmale, F.-J., 'Fälschungen in der Geschichtsschreibung', in *Fälschungen im Mittelalter* (6 vols, Hanover, 1988–90), vol. I, pp. 121–32.
Schneider, J., *Die Vita Heinrici IV und Sallust: Studien zu Stil und Imitatio in der mittellateinischen Prosa* (Berlin, 1965).
Schneider, J., 'Recherches sur une Encyclopédie du XIIIe Siècle: Le *Speculum*

Maius de Vincent de Beauvais', *Comptes Rendus de l'Académie des Inscriptions et Belles-Lettres* (1976), pp. 174–89.
Schneidmüller, B., 'Constructing the Past by Means of the Present – Historiographical Foundations of Medieval Institutions, Dynasties, Peoples and Communities', in G. Althoff, J. Fried and P.J. Geary (eds), *Medieval Concepts of the Past: Ritual, Memory, Historiography* (Cambridge, 2002), pp. 167–92.
Schreckenberg, H., *Die Flavius-Josephus-Tradition in Antike und Mittelalter* (2 vols, Leiden, 1972).
Schütt, M., 'The Literary Form of William of Malmesbury's *Gesta Regum*', *English Historical Review*, 46 (1931), pp. 255–60.
Schweyen, R., *Guarino Veronese* (Munich, 1973).
Searle, E., 'Fact and Pattern in Heroic History – Dudo of Saint-Quentin', *Viator*, 15 (1984), pp. 119–37.
Seigel, J., *Rhetoric and Philosophy in Renaissance Humanism: The Union of Eloquence and Wisdom, Petrarch to Valla* (Princeton, 1968).
Settimane di Studio del Centro Italiano di Studi Sull'Alto Medioevo 17 (1970) [*La Storiografia Altomedievale*].
Shopkow, L., *History and Community: Norman Historical Writing in the Eleventh and Twelfth Centuries* (Washington, DC, 1987).
Shopkow, L., 'Dynastic History', in D.M. Deliyannis (ed.), *Historiography in the Middle Ages* (Leiden, 2003), pp. 217–48.
Simon, G., 'Untersuchungen zur Topik der Widmungsbriefe mittelalterlicher Geschichtsschreiber bis zum Ende des 12. Jahrhunderts', *Archiv für Diplomatik*, 4 (1958), pp. 52–119; *Archiv für Diplomatik*, 5–6 (1959–60), pp. 73–153.
Simone, F., *The French Renaissance: Medieval Tradition and Italian Influence in Shaping the Renaissance in France* (London, 1969).
Siraisi, N.G., 'The *Expositio Problematum Aristotelis* of Peter of Abano', *Isis*, 61 (1970), pp. 321–39.
Skinner, Q., *Machiavelli* (Oxford, 1981).
Skinner, Q., 'Machiavelli's *Discorsi* and the Pre-Humanist Origins of Republican Ideas', in G. Bock, Q. Skinner and M. Viroli (eds), *Machiavelli and Republicanism* (Cambridge, 1990), pp. 121–41.
Skinner, Q., *Visions of Politics. Vol. I: Regarding Method* (Cambridge, 2002).
Small, G., *George Chastelain and the Shaping of Valois Burgundy: Political and Historical Culture at Court in the Fifteenth Century* (London, 1997).
Smalley, B., 'William of Middleton and Guibert de Nogent', *Recherches de Théologie Ancienne et Médiévale*, 16 (1949), pp. 281–91.
Smalley, B., *The Study of the Bible in the Middle Ages* (2nd edn, Oxford, 1952).
Smalley, B., *English Friars and Antiquity in the Early Fourteenth Century* (Oxford, 1960).
Smalley, B., 'Sallust in the Middle Ages', in R.R. Bolgar (ed.), *Classical Influences on European Culture AD 500–1500* (Cambridge, 1971), pp. 165–75.
Smalley, B., *Historians in the Middle Ages* (London, 1974).
Somerville, R. and B.C. Brasington, *Prefaces to Canon Law Books in Latin Christianity: Selected Translations 500–1245* (New Haven, 1998).
Sot, M., *Gesta Episcoporum, Gesta Abbatum* (Typologie des Sources du Moyen Âge Occidental 37, Turnhout, 1981).
Sot, M., *Un Historien et Son Église au Xe Siècle: Flodoard de Reims* (Paris, 1993).
Sot, M., 'Local and Institutional History 300–1000', in D.M. Deliyannis (ed.), *Historiography in the Middle Ages* (Leiden, 2003), pp. 89–114.
Southern, R.W., *St Anselm and His Biographer* (Cambridge, 1963).

Southern, R.W., 'Aspects of the European Tradition of Historical Writing I – The Classical Tradition from Einhard to Geoffrey of Monmouth', *Transactions of the Royal Historical Society*, 20 (1970), pp. 173–96; reprinted in R. Bartlett (ed.), *History and Historians: Selected Papers of R.W. Southern* (Oxford, 2004), pp. 11–29.

Southern, R.W., 'Aspects of the European Tradition of Historical Writing II – Hugh of St. Victor and the Idea of Historical Development', *Transactions of the Royal Historical Society*, 21 (1971), pp. 159–79; reprinted in R. Bartlett (ed.), *History and Historians: Selected Papers of R.W. Southern* (Oxford, 2004), pp. 30–47.

Southern, R.W., 'Aspects of the European Tradition of Historical Writing III – History as Prophecy', *Transactions of the Royal Historical Society*, 22 (1972), pp. 159–86; reprinted in R. Bartlett (ed.), *History and Historians: Selected Papers of R.W. Southern* (Oxford, 2004), pp. 48–65.

Southern, R.W., 'Aspects of the European Tradition of Historical Writing IV – The Sense of the Past', *Transactions of the Royal Historical Society*, 23 (1973), pp. 243–63; reprinted in R. Bartlett (ed.), *History and Historians: Selected Papers of R.W. Southern* (Oxford, 2004), pp. 66–83.

Spencer, J.R., '*Ut Rhetorica Pictura* – A Study in Quattrocento Theory of Painting', *Journal of the Warburg and Courtauld Institutes*, 20 (1957), pp. 26–44.

Spencer, M., *Thomas Basin: The History of Charles VII and Louis XI* (Nieuwkoop, 1997).

Spiegel, G.M., 'Political Utility in Medieval Historiography – A Sketch', *History and Theory*, 14 (1975), pp. 314–25.

Spiegel, G.M., 'Forging the Past – The Language of Historical Truth in the Middle Ages', *History Teacher*, 17 (1984), pp. 267–83.

Spiegel, G.M., 'History as Enlightenment: Suger and the *Mos Anagogicus*', in P. Gerson (ed.), *Abbot Suger and Saint-Denis* (New York, 1986), pp. 151–8; reprinted in G.M. Spiegel, *The Past as Text: The Theory and Practice of Medieval Historiography* (Baltimore, 1997), pp. 163–77.

Spiegel, G.M., 'History, Historicism and the Social Logic of the Text in the Middle Ages', *Speculum*, 65 (1990), pp. 59–86; reprinted in G.M. Spiegel, *The Past as Text: The Theory and Practice of Medieval Historiography* (Baltimore, 1997), pp. 3–28.

Spiegel, G.M., *Romancing the Past: The Rise of Vernacular Prose Historiography in Thirteenth-Century France* (Berkeley, 1993).

Spiegel, G.M., *The Past as Text: The Theory and Practice of Medieval Historiography* (Baltimore, 1997).

Spiegel, G.M. (ed.), *Practicing History: New Directions in Historical Writing After the Linguistic Turn* (London, 2005).

Stafford, P., *Queen Emma and Queen Edith: Queenship and Women's Power in Eleventh-Century England* (Oxford, 1997).

Stein, R.M., 'Signs and Things – The *Vita Heinrici IV Imperatoris* and the Crisis of Interpretation in Twelfth-Century History', *Traditio*, 43 (1987), pp. 105–19.

Stierle, K., 'L'Histoire Comme Exemple, l'Exemple Comme Histoire', *Poétique*, 10 (1972), pp. 176–98.

Stinger, C., *The Renaissance in Rome* (Bloomington, 1985).

Stones, E.L.G. and G.G. Simpson, *Edward I and the Throne of Scotland 1290–1296: An Edition of the Record Sources for the Great Cause* (2 vols, Oxford, 1978).

Struever, N., *The Language of History in the Renaissance: Rhetoric and Historical Consciousness in Florentine Humanism* (Princeton, 1970).

Swearingen, C.J., *Rhetoric and Irony: Western Literacy and Western Lies* (New York, 1991).

Syme, R., *Sallust* (Berkeley, 1964).

Taylor, J., *The Universal Chronicle of Ranulf Higden* (Oxford, 1966).
Thacker, A., 'Bede's Ideal of Reform', in P. Wormald, D. Bullough and R. Collins (eds), *Ideal and Reality in Frankish and Anglo-Saxon Society: Studies Presented to J.M. Wallace-Hadrill* (Oxford, 1983), pp. 130–53.
Thacker, A., *Bede and Augustine of Hippo: History and Figure in Sacred Text*, Jarrow Lecture (Jarrow, 2005).
Thélamon, F., 'L'Histoire de l'Église Comme Histoire Sainte', *Revue des Études Augustiniennes*, 25 (1979), pp. 184–91.
Thiry, C., *La Plainte Funèbre* (Typologie des Sources du Moyen Âge Occidental 30, Turnhout, 1978).
Thompson, J.W., *A History of Historical Writing* (New York, 1942).
Thomson, I., 'Manuel Chrysoloras and the Early Italian Renaissance', *Greek, Roman and Byzantine Studies*, 7 (1966), pp. 63–82.
Thomson, R.M., 'The Origins of Latin Satire in Twelfth-Century Europe', *Mittellateinisches Jahrbuch*, 13 (1978), pp. 73–83.
Thomson, R.M., *William of Malmesbury* (Woodbridge, 1987).
Thomson, R.M., 'Satire, Irony and Humour in William of Malmesbury', in C.J. Mews, C.J. Nederman and R.M. Thomson (eds), *Rhetoric and Renewal in the Latin West 1100–1540: Essays in Honour of John O. Ward* (Turnhout, 2003), pp. 115–27.
Tierney, B., '"Only the Truth Has Authority" – The Problem of Reception in the Decretists and in Johannes de Turrecremata', in B. Tierney, *Church, Law and Constitutional Thought in the Middle Ages* (London, 1979).
Tierney, B., *Foundations of the Conciliar Theory: The Contribution of the Medieval Canonists from Gratian to the Great Schism* (Cambridge, 1955; rev. edn, Leiden, 1998).
Tinkler, J.F., 'Praise and Advice – Rhetorical Approaches in More's *Utopia* and Machiavelli's *Prince*', *Sixteenth Century Journal*, 19 (1988), pp. 187–207.
Townend, G.B., 'Suetonius and His Influence', in T.A. Dorey (ed.), *Latin Biography* (London, 1967), pp. 79–111.
Trompf, G.W., *Early Christian Historiography: Narratives of Retribution* (London, 2000).
Tully, J. (ed.), *Meaning and Context: Quentin Skinner and His Critics* (Oxford, 1988).
Tyler, E.M., 'Fictions of Family – The *Encomium Emmae Reginae* and Vergil's *Aeneid*', *Viator*, 36 (2005), pp. 149–79.
Tyson, D.B., 'Patronage of French Vernacular History Writers in the Twelfth and Thirteenth Centuries', *Romania*, 100 (1979), pp. 180–222.
Ullman, B.L., 'Leonardo Bruni and Humanistic Historiography', *Medievalia et Humanistica*, 4 (1946), pp. 45–61; reprinted in B.L. Ullman, *Studies in the Italian Renaissance* (2nd edn, Rome, 1973), pp. 321–43.
Ullmann, W., 'Medieval Principles of Evidence', *Law Quarterly Review*, 62 (1946), pp. 77–87.
van den Boer, W., 'Some Remarks on the Beginnings of Christian Historiography', *Studia Patristica*, 4 (Texte und Untersuchungen 79, Berlin, 1961), pp. 348–62.
van Deun, P., 'The Church Historians After Eusebius', in G. Marasco (ed.), *Greek and Roman Historiography in Late Antiquity* (Brill, 2003), pp. 151–76.
Vasina, A., 'Medieval Urban Historiography in Western Europe 1100–1500', in D.M. Deliyannis (ed.), *Historiography in the Middle Ages* (Leiden, 2003), pp. 317–52.
Vasoli, C., 'Osservazioni sulle Teorie Umanistiche sulla Storiografia', *Nuova Rivista Storica*, 76 (1992), pp. 495–516.
Vaughan, R., *Chronicles of Matthew Paris: Monastic Life in the Thirteenth Century* (Gloucester, 1984).
Vaughan, R., 'The Past in the Middle Ages', *Journal of Medieval History*, 12 (1986), pp. 1–14.

Vaughan, R., *The Illustrated Chronicles of Matthew Paris* (Stroud, 1993).
Vesey, D.W.T.C., 'William of Tyre and the Art of Historiography', *Mediaeval Studies*, 35 (1973), pp. 435–45.
Viroli, M., *Machiavelli* (Oxford, 1998).
Vitale-Brovarone, A., 'Persuasione e Narrazione – *L'Exemplum* tra Due Retoriche (VI–XII Sec.)', *Rhétorique et Histoire: L'Exemplum et le Modèle de Comportement dans le Discourse Antique et Medieval*, Mélanges de l'École Française de Rome, 92 (1980), pp. 87–112.
Vitz, E.B., *Medieval Narrative and Modern Narratology: Subjects and Objects of Desire* (New York, 1989).
Vitz, E.B., *Orality and Performance in Early French Romance* (Woodbridge, 1999).
von den Brincken, A.-D., *Studien zur Lateinischen Weltchronistik bis in das Zeitalter Ottos von Freising* (Düsseldorf, 1957).
von Moos, P., *Consolatio: Studien zur mittellateinischen Trostliteratur über den Tod und zum Problem der christlichen Trauer* (4 vols, Munich, 1971–72).
von Moos, P., '*Poeta* und *Historicus* im Mittelalter – zum Mimesis-Problem am Beispiel einiger Urteile über Lucan', *Beiträge zur Geschichte der deutschen Sprache und Literatur*, 98 (1976), pp. 93–130.
von Moos, P., 'The Use of *Exempla* in the *Policraticus* of John of Salisbury', in M. Wilks (ed.), *The World of John of Salisbury* (Oxford, 1984), pp. 207–61.
von Moos, P., *Geschichte als Topik: Das rhetorische Exemplum von der Antike zur Neuzeit und die Historiae im Policraticus Johanns von Salisbury* (Hildesheim, 1988).
von Moos, P., 'Das argumentative Exemplum und die "wächserne Nase" der Autorität im Mittelalter', in W.J. Aerts and M. Gosman (eds), *Exemplum et Similitudo: Alexander the Great and Other Heroes as Points of Reference in Medieval Literature* (Groningen, 1988), pp. 55–84.
von Moos, P., 'Rhetorik, Dialektik und *Civilis Scientia* in Hochmittelalter', in J. Fried (ed.), *Dialektik und Rhetorik im früheren und hohen Mittelalter: Rezeption, Überlieferung und gesellschaftliche Wirkung antiker Gelehrsamkeit vornemlich im 9. und 12. Jahrhundert* (Munich, 1997), pp. 133–55.
von Moos, P., 'Literary Aesthetics in the Latin Middle Ages – The Rhetorical Theology of Peter Abelard', in C.J. Mews, C.J. Nederman and R.M. Thomson (eds), *Rhetoric and Renewal in the Latin West 1100–1540: Essays in Honour of John O. Ward* (Turnhout, 2003), pp. 81–97.
Walbank, F.W., 'History and Tragedy', *Historia: Zeitschrift für Altegeschichte*, 9 (1960), pp. 216–34.
Walbank, F.W., *Polybius* (Berkeley, 1972).
Walker, J., *Rhetoric and Poetics in Antiquity* (Oxford, 2000).
Wallace-Hadrill, J.M., 'The Franks and the English in the Ninth Century – Some Common Historical Interests', in J.M. Wallace-Hadrill, *Early Medieval History* (Oxford, 1975), pp. 201–16.
Walsh, P.G., *Livy: His Historical Aims and Methods* (Cambridge, 1961).
Ward, J.O., 'Classical Rhetoric and the Writing of History in Medieval and Renaissance Culture', in F. McGregor and N. Wright (eds), *European History and Its Historians* (Adelaide, 1977), pp. 1–10.
Ward, J.O., 'From Antiquity to the Renaissance – Glosses and Commentaries on Cicero's *Rhetorica*', in J.J. Murphy (ed.), *Medieval Eloquence* (Berkeley, 1978), pp. 25–67.
Ward, J.O., 'Some Principles of Rhetorical Historiography in the Twelfth Century', in E. Breisach (ed.), *Classical Rhetoric and Medieval Historiography* (Kalamazoo, 1985), pp. 103–65.

Ward, J.O., *Ciceronian Rhetoric in Treatise, Scholion and Commentary* (Typologie des Sources du Moyen Âge Occidental 58, Turnhout, 1995).
Ward, J.O., 'Quintilian and the Rhetorical Revolution of the Middle Ages', *Rhetorica*, 13 (1995), pp. 231–84.
Ward, J.O., 'Rhetoric in the Faculty of Arts (Paris and Oxford) – A Summary of the Evidence', in O. Weijers and L. Holtz (eds), *L'Enseignement des Disciplines à la Faculté des Arts, Paris et Oxford, XIIIe –XVe Siècles: Actes du Colloque International* (Paris, 1997), pp. 147–82.
Ward, J.O., '"Chronicle" and "History" – The Medieval Origins of Postmodern Historiographical Practice?', *Parergon*, 14 (1997), pp. 102–28.
Ward, J.O., 'The Monastic Historiographical Impulse c.1000–1260: A Reassessment', in T.M.S. Lehtonen and P. Mehtonen (eds), *Historia: The Concept and Genres in the Middle Ages* (Helsinki, 2000), pp. 71–100.
Ward, J.O. and V. Cox (eds), *The Rhetoric of Cicero in Its Medieval and Early Renaissance Commentary Tradition* (Leiden, 2006).
Wasselynck, R., 'Les *Moralia in Job* dans les Ouvrages de Morale du Haut Moyen Âge Latin', *Recherches de Théologie Ancienne et Médiévale*, 31 (1964), pp. 6–11.
Wasselynck, R., 'L'Influence de l'Exégèse de Saint Grégoire le Grand sur les Commentaires Bibliques Médiévaux (VIIe–XIIe Siècles)', *Recherches de Théologie Ancienne et Médiévale*, 32 (1965), pp. 157–204.
Weiler, B., 'Royal Virtue and Royal Justice in Walter Map's *De Nugis Curialium* and William of Malmesbury's *Historia Novella*', in I. Bejczy and R. Newhauser (eds), *Virtue and Ethics in the Twelfth Century* (Leiden, 2005), pp. 317–39.
Weiler, B., 'William of Malmesbury on Kingship', *History*, 90 (2005), pp. 3–22.
Wetherbee, W., 'The Function of Poetry in the *De Planctu Naturae* of Alain de Lille', *Traditio*, 25 (1969), pp. 87–125.
White, H., *The Content of the Form: Narrative Discourse and Historical Representation* (Baltimore, 1987).
White, H., 'The Value of Narrativity in the Representation of Reality', *Critical Inquiry*, 7 (1980), pp. 5–27; reprinted in H. White, *The Content of the Form: Narrative Discourse and Historical Representation* (Baltimore, 1987), pp. 1–25.
White, H., 'Rhetoric and History', in H. White and F.E. Manuel, *Theories of History* (Los Angeles, 1978), pp. 7–25.
White, H., 'The Fictions of Factual Representation', in A. Fletcher (ed.), *The Literature of Fact* (New York, 1976); reprinted in H. White, *Tropics of Discourse* (Baltimore, 1978).
Whitfield, J.H., 'Machiavelli's Use of Livy', in T.A. Dorey (ed.), *Livy* (London, 1971), pp. 73–96.
Whitman, J., *Allegory: The Dynamics of an Ancient and Medieval Technique* (Oxford, 1987).
Wieruszowski, H., 'Art and the Commune in the Time of Dante', *Speculum*, 19 (1944), pp. 14–33.
Wilcox, D.J., *The Development of Florentine Humanist Historiography in the Fifteenth Century* (Cambridge, MA, 1969).
Wilks, M. (ed.), *The World of John of Salisbury* (Oxford, 1984).
Williams, J.R., 'The Quest for the Author of the *Moralium Dogma Philosophorum*', *Speculum*, 32 (1957), pp. 736–47.
Williams, R., 'Politics and the Soul – A Reading of the City of God', *Milltown Studies*, 19–20 (1987), pp. 55–72.
Winterbottom, M., *Problems in Quintilian* (Bulletin of the Institute of Classical Studies, Supplement 25, 1970), pp. 3–7.

Wiseman, T.P., *Clio's Cosmetics: Three Studies in Greco-Roman Literature* (Leicester, 1979).
Witt, R.G., 'Salutati and Petrarch', in S. Bertelli and G. Ramakus (eds), *Essays Presented to Myron P. Gilmore* (2 vols, Florence, 1978), vol. I, pp. 335–46.
Witt, R.G., *Hercules at the Crossroads: The Life, Works and Thought of Coluccio Salutati* (Durham, 1983).
Witt, R.G., *'In the Footsteps of the Ancients': The Origins of Humanism from Lovato to Bruni* (Leiden, 2000).
Wogan-Browne, J., N. Watson, A. Taylor and R. Evans (eds), *The Idea of the Vernacular: An Anthology of Middle English Literary Theory 1280–1520* (Exeter, 1999).
Wolf, K.B., *Making History: The Normans and Their Historians in Eleventh-Century Italy* (Philadelphia, 1995).
Wolfram, H., 'Le Genre de l'*Origo Gentis*', *Revue Belge de Philologie et d'Histoire*, 68 (1990), pp. 789–801.
Woodman, A.J., '*Praecipuum Munus Annalium* – The Construction, Convention and Context of Tacitus, *Annals* III.65.1', *Museum Helveticum*, 52 (1995), pp. 111–26; reprinted in A.J. Woodman, *Tacitus Reviewed* (Oxford, 1998), pp. 86–103.
Woodman, A.J., *Rhetoric in Classical Historiography* (London, 1988).
Wright, N., 'Geoffrey of Monmouth and Gildas', *Arthurian Literature*, 2 (1982), pp. 1–40.
Wright, N., 'William of Malmesbury and Latin Poetry – Further Evidence for a Benedictine's Reading', *Revue Bénédictine*, 101 (1991), pp. 122–53.
Wright, N., '*Industriae Testimonium* – William of Malmesbury and Latin Poetry Revisited', *Revue Bénédictine*, 103 (1993), pp. 482–531.
Wright, N., 'Twelfth-Century Receptions of a Text – Anglo-Norman Historians and Hegesippus', *Anglo-Norman Studies*, 31 (2008), pp. 177–95.
Zagorin, P., 'Historiography and Postmodernism: Reconsiderations', *History and Theory*, 29 (1990), pp. 263–74.
Zanna, P., '*Descriptiones Urbium* and Elegy in Latin and Vernaculars in the Early Middle Ages', *Studi Medievali*, 32 (1991), pp. 523–96.
Zecchini, G., 'Latin Historiography – Jerome, Orosius and the Western Chronicles', in G. Marasco (ed.), *Greek and Roman Historiography in Late Antiquity* (Brill, 2003), pp. 317–45.
Zinn, G.A., 'The Influence of Hugh of St Victor's *Chronicon* on the *Abbreviationes Chronicorum* by Ralph of Diceto', *Speculum*, 52 (1977), pp. 38–61.
Ziolkowski, J.M. and M.C.J. Putnam, *The Virgilian Tradition: The First Fifteen Hundred Years* (New Haven, 2008).
Zumthor, P., *Essai de Poétique Médiévale* (Paris, 1972), trans. P. Bennett, *Toward a Medieval Poetics* (Minneapolis, 1992).

INDEX

Abelard 54n, 77n, 119, 127, 152, 154n, 178n, 308, 397n, 410–13
abscisio – *see* aposiopesis
Academy – *see* scepticism
Accessus ad Auctores 58n, 125, 126, 129n, 133n, 150, 177n, 361n, 413, 432, 466, 504, 529
accident 106, 109, 132, 179, 182, 271, 273, 282
  see also chance
account (*reddere rationem*) – *see* reason
accusation 10, 39n, 52, 77, 105, 116, 162, 171, 175, 176, 181, 195, 196, 200, 204–5, 206–7, 216, 217, 218, 226, 242, 329, 464, 537
  see also castigation; invective
actors 22, 287
  see also tableaux; theatre
Acts, Book of 54, 57, 58, 64, 91, 289, 383, 386, 392
  see also Luke
Adalhard 196–8, 202, 203, 206, 278
Adam of Bremen 307
Adam Usk 449
Adelheid, empress 215n, 251
admonition 54, 55, 66, 67, 68, 81, 162, 163, 164, 196, 279, 372, 412, 486, 537
adnominatio (word-play) 7, 109n, 117n, 311
advantage – *see* utility
Aeneas 77–8, 115, 131n, 149, 151, 176n, 183n, 213, 241, 334, 435
Aesop 187, 309, 364, 383, 385
aetiology 95, 107, 283, 444n, 445, 450, 511, 540
  see also causation
affidavit – *see* oaths

ages of the world – *see* world
Agnellus of Ravenna 25
Aidan 165, 311
Ailred of Rievaulx 341n, 366n
Aimoin of Fleury 258
Alan of Lille 13, 286n, 367–8, 406n, 435n, 500
Alberic of Monte Cassino 169
Alberti, Leon Battista 490, 495n, 505n
Albertus Magnus 467, 471, 544
Alcuin 10, 11n, 12, 81n, 140n, 168n, 196, 197n, 321n, 345n, 352n, 368n, 371n, 426, 435n
Aldhelm 173–4, 361n
Alexander III, pope 114
Alexander of Hales 379n
Alexander the Great 69, 72, 74, 76, 108–9, 132, 154n, 181, 256, 405, 472, 493
Alexios I Komnenos, emperor 238
Alfarabi 13
Alfonso V, king of Aragon, Sicily and Naples 497
Alfred, king of the West Saxons, 'the Great' 79, 250–1, 301
allegory (*permutatio*) 378, 379, 380, 383, 387, 390, 393, 396, 404, 406, 435, 444n, 541
Amatus of Monte Cassino 258
Amaury, king of Jerusalem 24
ambiguity 29, 187–9, 288, 311, 424
  see also doubt; equivocation
Ambrose of Milan 57, 128, 134n, 198, 378
Ammianus Marcellinus 35
amnesty 253
  see also forgetting

amplification 22, 263, 268, 305, 323, 330, 331, 363, 364
amplitudo 268
anachronism 296, 497, 503
anagogy 378, 393, 399, 403, 429, 430n
analogy 270, 325
anamnesis 374
anger 1, 32, 42, 43, 158, 170, 177, 195, 332
Anglo-Saxon Chronicle 88, 251, 258
animosity 183, 491, 518
  see also enmity; hatred; *invidia*
annals 24, 34, 35, 53, 64, 82, 84, 85, 88, 89–90, 117, 123, 280, 324, 351, 421, 441–6, 448, 449, 450, 451, 452, 454, 455–6, 457, 483, 495, 519, 526, 547–8
  definition of 123, 442, 445
  see also chronography
anniversaries 25, 146
anonymity 216–17, 401
Anselm of Besate 12
Anselm of Canterbury (Anselm of Bec) 226n, 239n, 246, 291, 403, 443
antapodosis 327, 328
apologia 1, 77n, 101, 455, 524
aposiopesis 29
apostrophe (direct address) 218, 247, 252, 336, 425
Appian 488, 509–10
appropriateness (*aptum, quid deceat*) 23, 267, 295–8, 299–301, 302–5, 310, 314–15, 322, 326, 348, 405, 412, 434, 467, 503, 515, 538, 549, 550–1
Aquinas, Thomas 95n, 154, 278n, 379n
archaeological record 72, 93, 496
argument 9, 19, 63, 182, 265, 266–8, 288, 337–8, 342, 347, 349, 350, 352, 411–12, 426, 428, 534, 538, 548, 550
  definitions of 123, 267, 316, 319, 338n, 412, 433, 541–2
  distinction between intrinsic and extrinsic 268, 284, 314, 426
  intrinsic 268–75, 281, 283, 284, 314, 406, 421, 426
  extrinsic 175, 182, 183, 187, 218, 219, 220, 224, 245, 268, 284–94, 314, 341, 406, 426
    see also testimony
  inductive – *see* induction
  see also invention; topics

Aristotle 13, 14, 16, 127, 170n, 231, 236n, 270n, 273, 274, 319n, 344, 355–6, 409, 413n, 418, 419, 420, 425n, 429, 441, 456–61, 462, 463, 464, 465, 466–7, 468–9, 470, 471, 473, 474, 475, 476, 477, 478, 479, 485, 489, 498, 499, 504, 517, 529, 530, 533, 534, 535, 543, 544, 545, 547
Arnold of Brescia 339n, 415
Arnulf of Orleans 133, 239n
arrangement – *see dispositio*
arrogance – *see* pride
ars dictaminis 14, 133–4, 169
ars historica 4, 136–7, 164, 478, 485, 489–91, 505, 531
ars praedicandi 14
  see also homilies; sermons
Arsenius 199–200
Asser 185, 218, 250–1
assertion 113, 128, 202, 219, 222
Assyria 94, 100, 105, 307n
'Astronomer' 115n, 200n, 240n
Athanasius 148n, 447n
Athens 43, 68, 150, 232n, 253, 532, 546
Atropos 74n
  see also Fates
attentiveness (*attentus*) 169, 170, 190, 191, 193, 197, 227–8, 312, 367, 491
attributes of events 178–9, 197, 222, 367, 428, 529
attributes of person 177, 179, 196–7, 367, 428, 529
audience 4, 9, 24, 33, 99, 154, 170, 208, 244, 283
  determines form and content of writing 17, 32–3, 99, 143, 170, 192, 204, 236, 245, 289, 302–3, 308–10, 311, 314–15, 320, 333, 348, 350–1, 353, 394, 405, 410, 412, 466, 467–8, 503, 538, 542, 551
  different levels within 32, 113–14, 119, 395, 396, 398, 406
  hostile or tired 158, 170, 192–3, 201–2, 209, 213, 215, 215–16, 227, 322, 405
  popular or less learned 236, 303–4, 309, 310, 314–15, 318, 338, 343, 355, 356, 387, 394–5, 396–7, 419, 426, 434, 462, 466, 467–8, 470–1, 475–6, 486, 492, 536, 542

INDEX

Augustine 5, 17–18, 47, 68n, 91–107, 108, 110, 111, 112, 113, 116, 119, 122, 140n, 168n, 178n, 179n, 205, 272, 275, 276, 278, 279–80, 281, 282, 286n, 294, 332n, 347n, 369–88, 389, 390, 391n, 399, 400, 403, 407, 409, 410, 411, 413, 419, 420, 424n, 426, 427, 429, 430, 433, 434, 436, 437n, 440, 444, 446, 447, 457, 465, 477n, 480, 482n, 484, 526, 529, 539–41, 547, 549, 551
Augustus – *see* Octavian
Aulus Gellius 30, 37n, 43n, 47, 82–3, 87, 349n, 442, 443, 484, 526, 547
authority 57, 100, 284, 423, 432, 458, 483
 of the Bible 53
 of events from the past 135, 243, 244–5, 285, 296–7, 324, 328
 of fables 338, 351, 387
 of the narrator 185, 190, 246, 336–7
 of testimony 174–5, 183, 186, 284, 285, 286, 320, 326, 417, 423, 500
 open to question 423, 477n
autopsy – *see* eyewitness
avarice 39, 40, 41, 42, 68, 75, 100, 101, 104, 182, 242, 254, 352, 472n, 518, 526
Averroes 13, 459n

Babylon 48, 55, 69–70, 71, 76, 102, 104, 105, 107, 108, 116, 205
 see also Persia
Baldwin IV, king of Jerusalem 24
Bartolomeo Facio 500, 501, 502
Battista Guarino 494n
battle scenes 38, 46, 49, 119, 132, 135, 261, 298, 304, 336, 341, 354
Bede 12, 25, 49, 56n, 69n, 79, 84–5, 87, 88, 94n, 102n, 111n, 160, 163, 164, 165, 184, 219, 240n, 252, 253, 257, 260, 289–90, 291, 294, 297, 306, 310–11, 335n, 345n, 362, 379n, 389–92, 393n, 394n, 401n, 410, 426, 429, 442, 451
Benedict of Nursia 204, 205
Benoît de Sainte-Maure 262
Bernard of Chartres 126
Bernard of Clairvaux 134n, 345n, 416

Bernardus Silvestris 43n, 74n, 99n, 126n, 130n, 151n, 155n, 183n, 190n, 212n, 241n, 271n, 283n, 301n, 360n, 361, 383n, 399n, 409n
Bible 4, 20, 25, 35, 52–9, 80, 86, 92, 95, 102, 106, 112, 127, 162, 279, 370, 377, 381, 387, 392, 410, 411, 412, 430, 453, 472, 497, 536
 see also Acts; Daniel; David; exegesis; Isaiah; Jeremiah; Luke; Maccabees; Moses; Paul; Revelation; Scripture; Solomon
biography 145, 157, 484
 as a combination of deeds and character 137, 156, 171, 176, 182, 265, 428, 537
 see also attributes of person; deeds (*res gestae*); *ethologia*; hagiography; judicial rhetoric; life; *passio*; vice; virtue
Bodin, Jean 530n
Boethius 8n, 9n, 11n, 14, 18, 19n, 74n, 75n, 79–80, 81, 109, 111, 115n, 127, 137n, 142n, 146, 156n, 161n, 177n, 178n, 180, 182n, 188n, 215n, 230n, 235n, 266, 267n, 269n, 270, 271n, 272–6, 281–3, 284, 285, 286n, 288n, 289n, 319, 326, 339n, 356n, 362, 366n, 371n, 374n, 398n, 408, 409, 411, 417, 418, 419, 420, 426, 444, 463, 482n, 526, 543
Bohemia 258
Bonaventure 53–4, 103n, 154, 249n, 379n, 444
Book of Life 148, 149
bravery 7, 24, 50, 56, 76, 139, 143, 144, 155, 164, 180, 237, 344
brevity 18, 47, 64, 73, 82, 90, 158, 162, 191, 197, 210, 287, 292n, 301, 317–18, 321, 327, 359, 483, 500, 501
British – *see* brutishness; Geoffrey of Monmouth; Gildas; Nennius
Brunetto Latini 14
Bruni, Leonardo 484, 486–7, 489, 495–6, 509, 516n, 521, 522, 523, 532, 545
Bruno of Merseburg 255
brutishness 42, 261, 351–2, 395
Burgundy 452, 477
Byrhtferth of Ramsey 12, 112n

604   ❦ INDEX ❦

Caffaro 255n
Calcidius 273n, 275n, 283n
calendar, calculation of (*computus*) 84, 85, 89, 113, 165, 307n, 444, 445
canon law – *see* law
Carmen de Hastingae Proelio 298n
Carthage 41, 47, 68, 69, 71, 72, 76, 238, 334, 487
  see also Dido; Hannibal; Punic Wars
Cassian, John 63n, 379n, 393n, 397, 447
Cassiodorus 10, 11n, 12, 48, 49n, 55, 57n, 78n, 257, 277–8, 345n, 370n, 411n, 443, 447
castigation 9, 21–2, 45, 51, 67n, 137, 138, 139, 140–1, 151, 161, 162, 163, 164, 166, 172, 176, 218, 227, 242, 262, 313–14, 358, 464, 472, 486, 499, 531, 536
  see also accusation
casuistry 116
  see also law; sophistry
casus – *see* accident; chance; event (occurrence)
Cato the Elder – *see Disticha Catonis*
Cato the Younger, 'Uticensis' 41, 131, 133, 180
causation 71, 95, 112, 114, 130, 131, 132, 137, 176, 177, 178, 180, 181, 208, 221–2, 269, 270–84, 302n, 314, 319, 321n, 346, 395n, 406, 421–2, 423, 428, 442, 443, 445–6, 450, 451, 452, 453, 455, 491, 492, 494, 511–12, 518, 519, 526, 528, 533, 534, 538, 540, 547
  antecedent 273, 283, 314
  efficient 127, 270–1, 272, 283, 314
  hidden or unknown 526
  multiple 46, 519, 526
  secondary 271, 283, 314
  see also accident; aetiology; chance; fate; fortune; intention; providence (divine)
chance (*casus*) 80, 132, 143, 272, 275, 281, 283, 284, 314, 421, 423.
  definitions of 273–4
  see also accident; event (occurrence); fortune
Chandos Herald – *see* Herald of John Chandos
changeability – *see* world, mutability of
Chanson de Roland 24
chansons de geste 27, 34, 450
character – *see* attributes of person; *ethologia*; judicial rhetoric; *mores*

Charlemagne 23, 157–8, 166, 250, 369, 472
Charles VII, king of France 452
Charles the Bald, king of the West Franks, emperor 168
Charles the Bold, duke of Burgundy 452, 455
Charles the Good, count of Flanders 221
charters 221, 224–7, 256
chastisement – *see* God; *plagae*
Chrétien de Troyes 192n, 436
chronicles 55, 83, 84, 88, 246, 361, 429, 442
  definition of 442, 443
  see also paralipomenon
  relationship to annals and histories 60, 89, 90, 441–56, 457, 547–8
chronography 35, 60, 81–91, 93–4, 113, 114, 226, 442, 445, 454, 479, 533, 536, 540
  see also annals
chronology 69, 74, 83, 87, 93, 94, 95, 96, 106, 113, 136, 224, 261, 443
  see also calendar; world, ages of
Chrysoloras, Manuel 531
Cicero 6, 8, 9, 11, 12, 14, 17, 18, 21, 22, 27, 28, 31, 44n, 82, 83, 87, 88, 99, 100, 125, 126, 128, 134, 136–7, 138–9, 139–40, 142, 143, 144, 165, 170, 172, 177–8, 179–80, 181–2, 187–8, 189, 192, 195, 197, 224, 229–31, 232–4, 235, 236, 237, 238, 240, 242–3, 245, 246, 262, 263, 266–71, 272, 273, 276, 277, 283, 284–5, 288, 295, 296, 302, 303, 304, 305, 312, 315–16, 317–18, 320, 321–3, 325–6, 329–30, 330–1, 332, 337, 338, 339, 345, 347–8, 351–2, 353, 355–6, 357, 358, 359, 360, 366–7, 368, 369, 371, 373, 374, 377, 388, 389, 398, 408, 409, 410, 411, 414, 418, 420, 426, 428, 436, 439, 445, 455, 457, 463, 464, 465, 476, 477, 480, 481–2, 483, 484, 485, 489, 492, 493, 494, 495, 498, 501, 502, 505, 508, 526, 536, 545
  transmission of works by 6, 12, 14, 15, 16n, 140, 373n, 481–2
  Academica 355, 373
  Brutus 14, 366–7, 504n
  De Amicitia 31n
  De Divinatione 283n

De Fato 273n
De Finibus 87, 398n
De Inventione 6, 8, 14, 15, 19, 125, 139, 140, 169, 171, 172, 173, 176, 177, 178, 179, 181, 182, 187, 188, 189, 190, 191, 193, 197n, 229, 230, 231, 232, 233, 234, 235, 245, 266, 267, 268, 276, 283, 286, 287, 288, 295, 305, 311, 315, 316, 317, 318, 319, 321, 322, 323, 325, 326, 329, 332, 338, 345n, 351, 352, 353, 366, 371, 377, 408, 435, 464, 465n
De Legibus 134, 136, 242, 357
De Natura Deorum 75n
De Officiis 99n, 125, 231, 234n, 237, 238, 366n, 369, 410, 420n, 508
De Optimo Genere Oratorum 9n
De Oratore 6, 8, 9, 14, 22, 82, 125, 128, 135, 136–7, 139–40, 142, 143, 144, 165, 172, 187, 189, 190, 235, 242, 243, 246, 263, 295, 297, 303, 304, 309n, 312, 317, 320, 321, 325, 329, 330, 345, 347n, 352n, 353, 355, 356, 357, 366n, 372n, 408, 414, 489, 492, 494, 500, 545
Letters 82n, 481, 482, 493
Orator 135, 172n, 179, 180, 243, 288, 302, 303, 308n, 330n, 353, 355, 356, 358, 409n, 418, 463
Partitiones Oratoriae 263n, 322
Pro Archia 481–2, 492, 493
Pro Milone 330n
Pro Sestio 162n
Topica 19, 139, 171, 180, 187, 190, 236, 266, 267, 269–70, 271, 272, 281, 283, 284, 285, 288, 317, 320, 326, 332, 339n
Tusculan Disputations 44n, 355, 374
circumstances 10, 33, 57, 86, 126–8, 142, 143, 177, 178, 222, 233–4, 236, 269, 270, 299, 300, 301, 302–3, 320, 330, 340, 346, 348, 390, 407, 412, 413, 417, 419, 423, 434, 457, 462, 493, 497, 499, 504, 505, 508, 514, 521, 525–6, 528, 529, 532, 533, 534, 537
   synonymous with secondary causes or fate 271
   see also description of place; occasion; opportunity
civic histories – *see* history-writing
civil war 29, 41, 68, 76, 130, 131, 132, 214, 253, 298, 522
clarity – *see* openness
classical tradition 4, 11–12, 17, 35–52, 99
Clio 23n, 151n
   see also glory; Muses
Clotho 74n
   see also Fates; weaving
Cnut, king of England 208, 209, 210, 213
collatio – *see* parallel
colours of rhetoric – *see* cosmetics; figures of speech; ornamentation; rhetoric; tropes
Coluccio Salutati – *see* Salutati
comedy 194, 316, 358, 364, 385, 403
   see also Plautus; Terence
commemoration 23, 25, 26, 50, 530, 531
   see also deeds (*res gestae*); *fama*; funeral speech; infamy; memorial; memory; posterity
commitment (*studium*) 1, 140, 177, 233, 400, 518
common law – *see* law
commonplace – *see* topic
Commynes, Philippe de 452–5, 456, 479, 527, 528, 533
comparative history 65, 66, 69–70, 76, 78, 79, 81, 108, 110, 328, 513–14, 550
comparison 29, 65, 76, 143, 166, 181, 213, 245–6, 250, 256, 269–70, 305, 325, 326–9, 332, 378, 404, 458
   see also example; likeness; parallel
compilation 35, 78n, 82, 83, 84, 85, 91, 119, 146, 251, 404, 442, 444, 445, 450, 451, 454, 479, 483
   see also annals; digest
computus – *see* calendar; chronology
concealment
   of artifice 28, 172, 190, 337, 447
   of meaning 29
   of truth 31–2, 383
   see also cosmetics; dissimulation; guile; *insinuatio*; integument; lies
conciliarism 477
conclusion (*peroratio*) 265, 296, 299, 331
confession 77n, 98, 99, 375, 398n, 399
conjecture 175, 180, 230
   see also opinion

Conrad II, emperor 159, 167, 397
Conrad of Hirsau 39n, 58, 126, 129n,
    130n, 131n, 133n, 190n, 267n,
    301, 316n, 348–9, 361, 363–4,
    368n, 379n, 434–5
consolation 77–8, 79, 103, 111, 113,
    152, 153n, 198, 200, 201, 242,
    278, 281, 328, 511, 513
Constantine I, emperor 61, 369
controversia (conflicting versions or
    opinions) 15, 177, 178, 179,
    180–1, 187, 220, 235, 246, 315,
    354, 392, 537
    see also debate
correctio 7–8
Cosmas of Prague 43n, 131n, 145n,
    212n, 237n, 238n, 241n, 258
cosmetics 83n, 115–16, 173, 174, 198,
    227, 447, 450, 490, 491, 493, 548
    see also rhetoric, colours of
counsel (*consilium*) 14, 41, 49, 53, 168,
    230, 237, 239, 242, 248, 249, 277,
    455, 465, 469–70, 475, 507, 511,
    512, 513, 527, 537
    see also deliberation; deliberative
    rhetoric; intention
courage – *see* bravery
covenant – *see* God
credence – *see fides*
credibility 47n, 136, 174, 175n, 189,
    191, 202, 203, 227, 246, 285, 289,
    290, 293, 295, 305, 309, 315, 319,
    320–1, 326, 331, 333, 358, 426–7,
    433, 459n, 461, 464, 470, 501,
    535, 538, 547
    see also fides; probability; verisimili-
    tude
criticism 165–6, 167, 228
    see also castigation; counsel
Crusades 24, 25, 56, 119, 145, 238,
    254, 256, 293, 308, 336, 392, 393,
    405, 415, 416, 422
cunning – *see* guile
cupidity – *see* avarice
curiosity 99, 117, 134, 483
Cuthbert 165n, 311, 297
cycles of history – *see* history
Cyprian 447
Cyriac of Ancona 496
Cyrus the Great, king of Persia 108

damnatio memoriae – *see* infamy
Daniel, Book of 56, 58, 69, 91, 108,
    112

Dante 71n
Dares Phrygius 129, 183
David 53, 55, 56, 103, 382, 472
Day of Judgment 56, 58, 67, 102, 104,
    107, 148
    see also eschatology
debate (*contentio, contio*) 22, 340, 392,
    465, 527
    see also controversia
deceit – *see* lies
dedicatory letters 109, 118, 159, 161,
    169, 209, 210, 211, 212, 213, 404,
    447
    see also prologue
deeds (*res gestae*) 42, 43, 60, 62, 82,
    118, 119, 137, 141, 143, 145,
    171, 196, 212, 241, 243, 244,
    249, 265, 305, 361, 364, 407,
    478, 537, 548
    as a guide to conduct (*res gerenda*)
    249, 397–8
    commemoration of, for posterity
    23–4, 42, 45, 50, 61, 73, 80, 87,
    117, 129, 132, 138, 145, 156, 165,
    167, 210, 537
    commemoration of, for imitation 23,
    44–5, 56, 117, 118, 150, 151, 156,
    157, 159–60, 201, 364
    commemoration of, for judgment
    148–9
    see also Book of Life
    commemoration in lead, stone or
    silver 147, 149, 150
    narrative of (*narratio rei gestae*) 123,
    141–2, 171, 181, 182, 224, 249,
    251, 262, 368, 433, 538, 539
    words and deeds (*dicta et facta*) 36,
    37, 89, 152, 155, 160, 515–16
    see also attributes of events; life
defence 10, 39n, 103, 116, 171, 175,
    176, 181–2, 192, 195, 196, 204,
    206–7, 215, 218, 226n, 249, 286,
    310, 329, 339, 346, 416, 464,
    537
    see also apologia; *purgatio*; *remotio
    criminis*
definition (etymology) 180, 187, 269,
    288, 304, 328
deliberation (*consilium*) 15, 82, 83, 137,
    176, 177, 181, 182, 221, 230, 234,
    237, 239, 242, 299, 451, 465, 470,
    486, 511, 526, 527, 528
    definitions of 177, 230, 237
    see also counsel; intention

INDEX

deliberative rhetoric 19, 137, 229–62, 263–4, 329, 340, 342, 344, 358, 392, 416, 423, 455, 465, 468–71, 473, 474, 476, 489, 507, 508, 518, 523, 534, 537–8
  goal of 230, 231, 240, 329, 507–8, 538
  relationship to demonstrative rhetoric 249, 469n
  relationship to judicial rhetoric 262
  role of historical events within 242–4, 245–6, 250, 469, 530
  see also counsel; *honestas*; mirror-for-princes; necessity; practicability; utility
delivery (*pronuntiatio*) 19, 21–6, 265, 319, 330
demonstrative rhetoric 19, 137, 138–71, 172, 227, 231, 263, 358, 464, 487, 489, 490, 518, 534, 536–7
  relationship to deliberative rhetoric 249, 469n
  see also castigation; *encomium*; mirror-for-princes; praise
Demosthenes 21, 484
Denmark 258
derhetoricization 3, 495, 534
descriptio (diatyposis) 330n
description of character – *see* attributes of person; *ethologia*; *mores*
description of place (*descriptio loci*) 39, 46, 50, 65, 132, 135, 137, 178, 305–7, 313, 333, 341, 490, 492, 493, 514–15, 516, 547
  see also circumstances
dialectic 9, 15–16, 267, 287, 288, 304, 309, 320, 352, 353, 408, 414, 417, 418, 439, 460, 465, 551
  relationship to rhetoric 419
  see also enthymeme; epicheireme; logic; syllogism; *trivium*
Dialogus de Scaccario 54, 86n, 129n, 148, 406n
dictamen – *see* ars dictaminis
Dido, queen of Carthage 76, 234, 334, 368n
digest 12, 36, 91, 240n, 371n, 443,452
digression (*excursus*) 49–50, 119, 132, 136, 256, 305, 313, 315, 354, 363, 496, 500, 514–15, 524
Diodorus of Sicily 531–2
Dionysius of Halicarnassus 49
discussion (*disceptatio*) 9, 161, 230

disorder 75, 80, 275, 375, 396, 521
dispositio (arrangement) 19, 265, 267, 299–300, 342, 457, 476, 483, 486
  see also order
dissimulation 46, 169, 192, 193, 195, 199, 210, 231, 234, 236, 342, 354, 382, 455, 519, 527, 534
  see also concealment; guile; lies
Disticha Catonis 155, 203, 416
distinctio – *see* redescription
divisio 265
documentation
  incorporation of 46, 56, 62, 113, 175n, 196, 214, 219–21, 221–2, 224, 226, 255, 392
  different interpretations of 187–9
  see also argument, extrinsic; charters; *controversia*; testimony, extrinsic
dolus – *see* guile
Dominicus Gundissalinus 11n, 19n, 123n, 345n, 347
Donation of Constantine 114, 497, 502, 545
Donatus 6n, 448
doubt 43, 113, 170, 171, 180, 182, 185n, 187, 193, 196, 197, 202n, 230, 234, 240, 267, 268, 270, 288, 289, 290n, 293, 295, 304, 308, 336, 350, 354, 412, 422, 423, 433, 461, 494, 525n, 538
  see also ambiguity; equivocation; God, inscrutability of; scepticism; uncertainty
dreams 49, 69, 212n, 248, 284, 331n, 341–2, 377
dubitatio 337
Dudo of Saint-Quentin 259, 306n, 362, 365n

Eadmer 81, 147n, 184n, 192n, 193n, 197n, 225–6, 239n, 248n, 278n, 291, 295n, 307n, 310n, 318n, 335, 336n, 395n, 401n
Eadric Streona 214, 237n
Easter tables 84, 444
Edward, king of England, 'the Confessor' 208, 210, 214, 323n, 362n
Edward I, king of England 246
Einhard 23, 38, 141n, 157–8, 159, 165–6, 168, 185, 193n, 218, 220–1, 246, 250, 293n, 298
elocutio – *see* style

eloquence 8, 9, 10, 11n, 20, 25, 87,
117, 120, 141, 145, 158, 174, 196,
197, 198, 223, 224, 288, 296, 341,
343, 351, 353, 355, 358, 360n,
361, 371, 431, 447
   and rhetoric 8, 371
   and wisdom 10, 16, 116, 130, 229,
246, 313, 352, 366, 371, 389, 409,
465, 480
   see also vir bonus dicendi peritus
   relationship between speaking and
writing 15, 128, 296
   of Creation (*eloquentia rerum*) 388
   absence of 63, 223, 447
   see also rusticity
Emma, queen of England 208, 209,
210, 213, 214
emotions 9, 21, 22, 23, 132, 152, 179,
263, 295, 299, 304, 309, 319, 322,
330, 331, 332, 333, 343, 354,
459n, 461, 466, 467, 475, 476,
480, 515, 539
   see also anger; fear; hatred; hope;
love; pity
emphasis – *see significatio*
empire (*imperium*)
   four world monarchies (Assyria,
Persia, Macedonia, Rome) 69, 71,
72, 92, 103, 108, 307n
   see also Carthage
   translatio imperii 69, 108
empiricism 460, 478, 479, 489, 498,
504, 517, 529, 530, 531, 534, 535,
544, 545, 546, 550
   see also induction
emulation (*aemulatio*) – *see* imitation
enargeia (*demonstratio, evidentia,
illustratio, repraesentatio*) 330–3,
337, 343, 348, 356, 459n, 504–5,
514, 516, 539, 546
   see also vividness
encomium (panegyric) 99, 105, 138,
139, 142, 143, 144, 151, 164, 167,
172, 195, 249, 365n, 464, 490,
493, 495, 500, 530, 533
   see also counsel; demonstrative
rhetoric; praise
Encomium Emmae Reginae 148n, 186–7,
196, 208–15, 218n, 237n, 336n
endoxa 461
   see also opinion, common or popular
Engelbert of Admont 71n, 476–7
enmity 200, 202, 228, 484
   see also animosity; hatred; *invidia*

Ennius 358
Ennodius 153n
entertainment – *see* pleasure
enthymeme (*commentum, commentatio*)
287–8, 304, 320, 352, 354, 458n,
461, 467, 471, 473, 544, 551
envy – *see invidia*
ephemera (*diarium*) 123, 251
epic 27, 34, 57, 58, 130, 358, 361, 365,
434, 481, 542
epicheireme 287–8, 304
epideictic – *see* demonstrative rhetoric
epitaphium – *see* funeral speech
Epitaphium Arsenii 110n, 131n, 148n,
151n, 166n, 185n, 198–208, 215,
283n, 355n, 391n, 400n
equity 10–11, 39, 144, 173, 180, 189,
232n, 352
   as the goal of judicial rhetoric 171
equivocation 311, 409
   see also ambiguity
Ermoldus Nigellus 334
error 115, 116, 165, 210, 290, 374,
407, 410, 418, 420
   scribal error 62, 93, 410
eschatology 84–5, 104
   see also Day of Judgment; last times;
Revelation
ethic of intention – *see* intention
ethnogenesis 257
   see also origin myth
ethnography 39, 46, 305–7, 313, 518
ethologia 15, 141–2, 182, 262
   see also description of character;
judicial rhetoric (*qualis est*)
etymology – *see* definition
Eugenius III, pope 415
Eugenius IV, pope 497
euhemerisation 101
Eusebius of Caesarea 18, 57, 59–64,
69, 72, 77, 79n, 80–1, 83, 84, 85,
86, 87, 91, 92, 94, 102, 103, 105,
106, 107, 113, 119, 123, 163, 183,
184, 219, 269n, 352n, 369, 389,
442, 451
Eutropius 36, 66, 91
event (occurrence) 44, 69, 109, 132,
137, 177
   sequence of (*series rerum, ordo rerum*)
388, 447
   significance of, distinct from
description 73
   prefigurative 67, 278, 391, 406
   see also sign; signification

INDEX 609

disorder of 75
fluctuation of 64–5
see also world, mutability of
see also deeds (*res gestae*)
event (outcome) 109, 137, 178, 208, 223, 271, 278, 403, 494, 518
evidence – *see* archaeological record; documentation; *enargeia*; eyewitness; *fama* (common report); hearsay; testimony
example (*exemplum*) 20, 36–7, 68, 89–90, 98, 99, 101, 106, 112, 117, 132, 136, 151, 152–5, 161, 165, 173, 183, 196, 214, 218, 228, 235, 243, 244, 245, 249, 250, 252, 259, 263, 269, 279, 289, 314, 324, 325, 326, 327–8, 334, 357, 360, 399, 401, 403, 404, 414, 416, 419, 431, 454, 457–8, 460, 464, 467, 471–3, 474, 475, 476, 478, 479, 482, 483–4, 485, 486, 492, 498, 506, 507, 523, 524–5, 528, 530, 533, 534, 536, 544, 545, 550
  definition of 270, 327
  as an argument from comparison 245, 269–70, 326–9, 457–8
  better than a precept 152–5, 246, 328, 414, 464
  see also induction; paradigm; parallel
excursus – *see* digression
exegesis 17, 94, 96, 282, 372, 378–9, 381, 389, 390, 392, 393, 396, 397, 403, 426, 429, 432, 439, 440, 444, 540
  see also Bible; *Glossa Ordinaria*; Scripture
exhortation 22, 135, 152, 278, 341n, 372, 530
exordium – *see* prologue
expediency – *see* utility
explanation – *see* causation; reason
eyewitness 50–1, 57, 62, 63, 93, 123, 126, 158, 174–5, 183–7, 201, 218, 219, 221, 284, 289, 290, 291, 294, 313, 314, 348, 373, 390, 392, 407, 417, 453, 539
  superiority of 183–5, 359
  see also enargeia; testimony, extrinsic

fable (*fabula*) 51, 76, 83, 115, 119, 122, 124, 126n, 132, 133, 179, 183n, 187, 192, 209, 212, 213, 245, 248, 279, 286, 293, 305, 309, 314, 320, 324, 325, 338–9, 341, 342, 347, 349, 351, 356, 357, 359, 364, 365, 366, 368, 380, 382, 383, 384, 386, 387, 408, 412–13, 426, 433, 434, 435, 436, 438, 440, 444, 448–9, 459n, 473, 476, 490, 496, 514, 540, 541, 546, 551
  definitions of 123, 316, 541–2
  differentiated from *historia* and *argumentum* 123
  old wives' tales (*aniles fabulae*) 87, 443, 445, 449, 515
  opposed to truth 203, 279
  as a vehicle of truth 212, 383, 541
  as testimony 285, 286, 338
  see also poetry
Fabricius 155
falsehood (*falsa*) 29n, 30, 43, 51, 76, 89, 136, 165, 175n, 183n, 206, 209, 210, 211, 212, 216, 217, 223, 238n, 286, 288, 304, 316, 319, 324, 325, 326, 336, 337, 339, 341, 342, 343, 344, 345, 346, 347, 349, 355, 358, 359, 364, 367, 368, 371–2, 374, 376, 379, 380, 385, 386, 387, 407, 408, 411, 415, 417, 424, 425, 436, 439, 440, 448, 458, 459n, 490, 493, 495, 502, 515, 516, 525, 535, 539, 540, 541, 542, 548, 551
false exposition (*falsa expositio*) 339, 340, 341–2, 347, 350
  see also 'fiction'; lies
fama (common report) 47, 174, 186, 212, 284, 285, 289, 290, 291, 294, 340, 353, 357, 436, 537
  see also opinion; rumour
fama (reputation) 24, 42, 43, 44, 45, 68, 80, 132, 135, 137, 138, 145–6, 150, 159, 165, 206, 232, 263, 285, 286, 291, 293, 334, 353, 402, 450, 517–18, 536
  dependent on history-writing 43–4, 146, 149, 151n
  immortality of 44, 156, 198, 493n, 511
  see also deeds, commemoration of; glory; infamy
fasti 64, 149–50
fate 77, 79, 109, 271, 272, 273, 274–5, 281, 282, 314, 334, 422, 423, 487
  definition of 275
  see also causation
Fates 74, 131, 132
  see also Atropos; Clotho; Lachesis

favour (*gratia*) 31, 51, 74, 136, 173, 175, 183, 184, 210, 219, 220, 286–7, 490, 494, 499, 516, 518
fear 41, 110, 118, 132, 150, 216, 309, 332, 416, 515, 517
   of speaking or writing the truth 29, 30, 32, 43, 45, 73, 183, 195, 199–200, 201, 203, 216–17, 224, 228–9, 446, 491, 499, 522
feast days 84, 146
Ferdinand I, king of Aragon and Sicily 497, 546
Ferdinand II, king of Aragon, Sicily and Naples 523
'fiction' (*ficta, fictio, fingere*) 30, 43, 51, 133, 176, 183, 184, 206, 209, 210, 212, 270, 286, 309, 315, 316, 323–5, 332, 336–48, 349, 350–1, 356–7, 359, 363, 365, 368, 369, 376, 380, 382, 384, 386, 387, 403, 407, 410, 424, 426, 432, 435–6, 535, 539, 541, 542–3
   figmentum 51, 216, 364, 365, 376, 412, 424–5
   poetic differentiated from rhetorical 351
   as verisimilar argument 338, 359
fides (belief, as a category of knowledge) 62, 63, 136, 179, 203, 267, 285, 288–9, 291, 315, 319, 324, 336, 348, 354, 357n, 366, 415, 418, 420, 421, 425–6, 440, 461, 470, 516–17, 535, 538, 543
   definition of 420
fides (credence, credibility, trustworthiness) 47, 51, 52, 76, 94, 97, 98, 99, 158, 174, 175n, 185, 189–90, 202, 203, 211, 218, 243, 246, 280, 284, 285, 290n, 293, 305, 308, 315, 407, 426, 464, 499, 516
   fides historiae 426, 551
   oculata fides 185, 218
figuration – *see* signification
figure – *see* sign
figures of speech 6–8, 29, 130, 135, 301, 311, 321, 331, 357, 363n, 370, 378, 382, 389, 500
   see also ornamentation; rhetoric, colours of; tropes
flattery 31, 51, 74, 105, 165, 168, 187, 365n, 446, 455, 490
Flavio Biondo 491, 495n, 496
Flodoard of Rheims 445

Florence 450, 451, 486, 487, 488, 491, 496, 522, 523, 526, 528, 531
Florus 36, 91
forensic rhetoric – *see* judicial rhetoric
foresight (*providentia*) – *see* providence
forgery 214, 226–7, 340, 497, 545
forgetting (*oblivio*) 63, 66, 109, 146, 158, 159, 168, 247, 249, 253, 257, 312, 342, 395, 401
   see also amnesty; silence
fortitude – *see* bravery
Fortunatianus 10–11, 12, 19n, 137n, 171n, 192n
fortune 39, 40, 43, 44, 48, 50, 80, 111, 129, 131, 132, 144, 177, 182, 197, 234, 271, 272, 273, 281–2, 283, 314, 316, 331, 421, 444, 452, 453, 469, 487, 488, 511, 512, 523, 524, 526
   personification of 272
   synonymous with unknown causes 271, 272
   synonymous with unintended consequences of other causes 273
Fourth Lateran Council (1215) 240n
Freculf of Lisieux 168
Frederick I, emperor, 'Barbarossa' 114, 115, 118
freedom of the will 276, 422, 423
friendship 31, 43, 51n, 142, 177, 195, 232, 287, 491, 512
   see also favour; love
Froissart 335n, 438, 450, 454
Frontinus 154n, 238n, 485n
Fulcher of Chartres 24, 186n, 256, 405, 407
Fulgentius 151n, 435
fullness – *see amplitudo*
funeral speech (*epitaphium*) 147, 172, 198, 201, 207, 215, 361, 362, 510–11

Gaimar 27n, 261
Galbert of Bruges 147n, 221–4, 336, 529
Gallus Anonymous 258
Gelasius I, pope 79
genealogy 62, 257, 261
Gennadius 151, 481
Genoa 255, 450
Geoffrey Malaterra 258
Geoffrey of Monmouth 49n, 261, 279n, 297, 306n, 365–6, 438, 544

INDEX

Geoffrey of Vinsauf 13, 29n, 166n, 283n, 285n, 287n, 301n, 330n, 340n, 360, 368n, 436, 542, 543
geographical description – *see* description of place
George of Trebizond 531
Gerald of Aurillac 148, 186, 195–6
Gerald of Wales (Giraldus Cambrensis) 2n, 7n, 24–5, 31–2, 37n, 45n, 75n, 129, 131n, 146n, 153, 159n, 184, 196, 238n, 241–2, 249, 253, 279, 280, 283n, 286n, 290n, 294, 302n, 311–14, 324n, 335n, 340n, 341, 352n, 359n, 361, 366n, 395–6, 415n, 451, 465n
Gerbert of Aurillac 293n, 360
Gervase of Canterbury 34n, 81n, 89–91, 113n, 153–4, 425n, 443–4, 446, 449, 453n, 547
Gervase of Tilbury 24n, 34n, 43n, 103n, 173n, 293n, 308n, 335n, 425n
Gesta Francorum 238n, 256
Gesta Regum Francorum 258
Gesta Romanorum 37
Gesta Stephani 110n, 282n, 299, 336n
Gilbert Crispin 437n
Gilbert of Mons 255n
Gilbert of Poitiers 308, 415
Gildas 81n, 161–3, 164, 218, 247, 260, 261n, 306n, 313, 366n, 389, 390, 391n
Giles of Rome (Aegidius Romanus) 16n, 460, 461–8, 470–6, 477–8, 530, 544, 551
Giovanni Aurispa 490
Glanvill 175n
glory 24, 42, 43, 44, 45, 51, 61, 68, 100, 101, 106, 142, 151, 159, 164, 167, 177, 207, 209, 213, 232, 235, 242, 401, 402, 405, 469, 483, 486, 487, 519, 521
   definition of 232
   see also fama (reputation)
Glossa Ordinaria 379n, 394n, 426n, 430n
   see also Bible; exegesis; Scripture
God 24, 58, 60, 61, 66, 69, 75, 79, 96, 102, 104, 116, 119, 157, 160, 187, 259, 276, 278, 279, 308, 375, 376, 393, 402, 403, 407, 412n, 420, 422, 472n
   chastisement by 66, 162, 163, 205, 247, 260, 314
   see also plagae

   covenant with 48–9, 55, 218, 247, 391
   inscrutability of 71, 97, 106, 109, 111, 112, 279–80, 422, 453, 526–7, 540
   judgment of 48, 67, 109, 111, 148, 173, 194, 218, 222, 252, 280, 453
   mercy of 65, 66, 70, 384
   providence of 65, 67, 69, 70, 79–80, 92, 94, 95n, 96–7, 98, 106, 109, 111, 118, 223, 272, 274–5, 277, 280, 281–2, 283–4, 314, 388, 390n, 403, 416–17, 420, 421, 422, 423, 431, 444, 452, 453, 526, 540
   punishment by 65, 66, 67, 71, 72, 79, 109, 163, 223, 225, 247, 252–3, 260, 314
   see also plagae
   retribution of 48, 55, 66, 79n, 194–5
Golden Legend 147
Gomorrah 67
goodwill (*benivolus, benevolentia*) 169, 170, 171, 190–1, 192–3, 210, 215, 227–8, 354, 367, 491
grammar 8, 15–16, 121, 122–3, 124, 316, 337, 339, 370, 408, 434, 448, 542
   definition of 8
   as moral instruction 125
   manuals of 6n, 122
   taught through poetry and historiography 121–6, 128, 360
   see also Donatus; Priscian
Grandes Chroniques 258, 335n
Gratian 175n, 381n, 416
   see also law, canon
greed – *see* avarice
Gregory I, pope, 'the Great' 7n, 17–18, 134n, 152, 168n, 249, 278n, 294, 305n, 333n, 335n, 347, 378–9, 382, 390n, 391, 394, 397, 399, 400–2, 403, 406, 429, 430, 465
Gregory VII, pope 216, 217
Gregory of Tours 43n, 49n, 58n, 60n, 68n, 72n, 78–9, 83–4, 103n, 163, 219, 224, 237, 247–8, 257, 260, 311, 334, 362, 391n, 394, 401
grief – *see* lamentation
Guarino da Verona 455–6, 488, 490, 492–4, 500
Guibert of Nogent 38, 56n, 145–6, 148, 184, 256, 280n, 285n, 336, 359n, 392–408, 414, 417

Guibert of Tournai 472n
Guicciardini 506, 520, 523–9, 530, 533, 534, 551
guile (*dolus*) 28, 214, 223, 231, 237–8, 241, 337, 368, 455
 see also dissimulation; strategy
Guillaume Peyrault 472n

Hadoard of Corbie 196
hagiography 34, 145, 146–7, 156, 278, 407
Haimo of Auxerre 278n
Hannibal 342, 515
harmony (*concordia*) 68, 80, 96, 104, 107
 see also order; peace
Harthacnut, king of England 208–9, 213, 214
hatred 29n, 30, 31, 42, 43, 51, 68, 75, 136, 175, 183, 203, 205, 206, 286, 332, 366n
 see also animosity; enmity; *invidia*
hearsay 64, 123, 185, 201, 288, 294, 359, 375, 376–7, 407, 453
 see also fama (common report); testimony, extrinsic
Hegesippus 49, 134n
 see also Josephus
Henry I, king of England 161, 226, 228–9, 252, 295, 363
Henry I, of Saxony 149, 244, 251
Henry II, king of England 20, 153, 249, 253, 299, 311, 415n, 443
Henry II, emperor 225, 251
Henry III, emperor 159, 166, 167
Henry IV, emperor 114, 115, 196, 215–18, 255
Henry V, emperor 173, 215, 218, 308
Henry of Andelys 16
Henry of Huntingdon 7n, 23n, 49n, 54n, 57n, 81, 101n, 109n, 112n, 146, 148n, 164, 185n, 229n, 238n, 240–1, 246, 249n, 252–3, 260–1, 280n, 283n, 291, 294n, 297, 299, 306, 307, 308n, 310, 322n, 323n, 336, 341, 362, 363, 366n, 401n, 485, 498
Henry Knighton 242n
Herald of John Chandos 438n, 450
Herbert of Bosham 446
hermeneutics – *see* Scripture, textual criticism of 5, 497
Herodotus 82, 134, 135, 357, 458, 509
Hesiod 309

'Hibernicus Exul' 24n
Hilary of Poitiers 278n, 413n, 446n
Histoire de Guillaume le Maréchal 438n
Historia Augusta 35, 36n, 44n, 87, 484
Historia Ecclesiastica Tripartita 78n
historians
 as judges, not advocates 369, 499
 as liars 367
 as medical doctors 277, 499
 as preachers 248
 as prophets 132, 162, 205, 276–80, 312, 453, 540
 lists of 53, 86, 134
 protestations of inadequacy by 28, 60, 116, 140–1, 158, 169, 191, 194, 201, 210
history
 as a series of calamities 64, 74, 107, 109, 112, 117, 152, 163
 as a cyclical process 64–5, 71, 75, 102, 520–1, 523
 as the literal sense of Scripture 86, 95–6, 98, 104, 378–9, 382, 426, 429–30
 see also time; world, ages of
history-writing
 definition of 123, 316, 337, 349, 433, 442, 445, 476, 538, 539, 541
 different categories of (ephemera or *diarium*; notes or *commentarii*; annals) 123
 breadth and fluidity of genre 32, 34–5, 432, 449–52, 455–6, 547–8
 and demonstrative rhetoric 502, 530, 533
 and judicial rhetoric 173, 502, 529–30
 and deliberative rhetoric 496, 502, 527, 528, 530, 533
 in monasteries 225–7, 256
 at courts 255
 civic histories 255, 450–1
 of nations or peoples 48, 257–9, 260
 see also ethnogenesis; origin myth
 of the world, universal history 34, 53–4, 65, 71, 80, 83n, 85, 92, 102, 105, 107, 226, 255, 280, 369, 376, 416, 444, 478, 482n, 513
 as accusation 171
 as castigation of vice 45, 160, 484
 as consolation 77–8, 81, 109, 485, 511
 as critique 45, 519

as defence (*apologia*) 64, 67, 77n, 171, 455, 524
as domestic politics and foreign war (*domus et militia*) 38–9, 487, 488, 510, 518, 522
as education for real life (*vera vita*) 510, 546
as entertainment or pleasure 76, 87, 116, 118, 161, 439, 490
as eyewitness account 50–1, 57, 123, 126, 183–4, 348–9, 442, 445, 455–6
as fruit-juice 135, 501
as hearsay 50, 63, 64, 175n, 183n, 294, 407
as judicial record 416
  see also judicial rhetoric
as juvenilia 2, 396
as lamentation 52, 77, 161
as legitimation 246–7, 251, 256–7, 258, 264, 477
as literature of rulers 23, 24, 53, 161, 244, 249, 252, 454, 470, 472
as liturgy 25–6, 35, 84, 146–9, 215n, 310
as moral instruction 44–5, 89–90, 101, 118, 152–3, 160, 164–5, 484, 485
  see also deeds, commemoration of; demonstrative rhetoric
as polemic 64, 67
as political counsel 67, 71, 73, 106, 118, 160, 163, 167–8, 229–62 *passim*, 328, 416, 439, 455, 469, 476, 479, 484, 485, 489, 510
  see also deeds, commemoration of; deliberative rhetoric
as prophecy 244, 245–6, 252, 485
as public service 42
as refreshment or relief (*recreatio*) 2, 478
as second-best to performing the deeds described 44, 45, 167
as storehouse, or treasury (*thesaurus*), of examples 136, 244, 454
as testimony 50, 244–5, 285
as warning 54, 61–2, 67, 117, 153, 162, 163, 247, 250, 252, 260, 278, 482
conditioned by national loyalties 115
conflicting accounts in 74, 113, 292, 354, 424, 425, 499
contempt for, or dismissal of 478

dangers of 29–30, 32, 43, 45, 73, 183, 195, 199–200, 201, 203, 216–17, 224, 228–9, 446, 491, 499, 519, 522
different motivations for 50, 73
differentiated from compiling annals 82, 85–6, 88, 89, 123, 351, 441–52
differentiated from oratory 135–6, 491, 501
differentiated from panegyric 173, 365n, 490, 493, 500, 530
difficulty of 30, 43, 45, 73, 88, 292, 312–13, 498, 499, 527, 533–4
law of (*lex historiae*) 52, 136, 289, 291, 294
limitations on 45–6, 62, 95–6, 106, 216, 218–19, 292, 427, 453, 528
more than just an intellectual exercise 76, 99, 483, 485
neglect of 431
neutrality of judgment in 46–7, 62, 114–15, 216, 219–20, 292, 294, 499
relationship to philosophy 164, 241, 363, 485, 498–9, 545, 546
relationship to poetry 116, 125, 126, 128, 129, 357–69, 434–5, 439, 458–9, 490, 492, 494, 498, 501, 505–6, 529, 533, 535, 542, 544, 546
rules of 136–7, 164, 489–91, 505
  see also ars historica
studied as part of grammar 121, 122–3, 124, 128, 434, 494n, 542
studied as part of rhetoric 121, 133–7, 439
style of 116, 119, 135, 501
suited to the laity 154, 396, 468
suited to the people 397
suited to the weak or slow in understanding 153–4, 397
suited to the young 23, 56, 58, 93, 125, 168, 396–7, 406n, 454, 472n, 542
trustworthiness of (*fides historiae*) 426, 551
truthfulness of 47, 51, 165, 173, 183, 293, 312, 313, 516
utility of 44, 51, 60, 61, 87, 94, 98, 99, 135, 149, 469, 478, 490, 498
vernacular 27, 37, 79, 255, 258, 432, 437, 450–1, 452
verse 361, 362, 432, 438
verse mixed with prose 362–3, 405, 435

Homer 129, 130n, 164, 183, 241, 277, 281, 300, 307n, 358, 359, 363, 484, 493, 498
homilies 26n, 372, 393, 399, 402
see also ars praedicandi; sermons
honestas (moral worth, dignitas, honestum)
synonymous with virtue 139, 181
paired with utility (honestum et utile) 230, 231, 232–3, 234, 235, 237, 240–1, 246, 252, 263, 329, 365n, 367, 415n, 425, 518, 538
differentiated from utility 164, 188, 190, 236, 239–40, 342, 487, 507–8
as the subject of demonstrative rhetoric 171, 173
Honorius of Autun (Honorius Augustodunensis) 19n, 34n, 81n, 133, 394n
hope 43, 45, 132, 144, 160, 277, 309, 499
Horace 14, 90, 116n, 125, 128, 155n, 163n, 167n, 212n, 216, 240n, 241, 297, 311, 335n, 347, 359, 360, 361, 363n, 385, 407, 435, 436, 483, 485, 493, 498
hostility – see animosity; enmity; hatred; *invidia*
Hrabanus Maurus 10, 11n, 54n, 124, 345n, 371n, 372n, 379n, 393n, 397, 426
Hugh of Fleury 87, 117, 443, 445
Hugh of St Victor 13, 20, 53n, 86, 88, 94n, 99n, 102n, 123n, 124, 134n, 153n, 233n, 240n, 249, 301n, 394n, 397–8, 399n, 409n, 417n, 420, 426, 430, 431, 481n, 543
Hugo Falcandus 258n
Huguccio of Pisa 174n, 316n, 338n, 353n, 442
humour 194, 385, 414
see also laughter
Hungary 308
see also Magyars
hyperbole 323
hypothesis 339, 347, 350, 387, 433, 440, 528, 542

image (*imago*) 44–5, 152, 197, 200, 326, 327, 331, 332, 333–4, 374, 375, 376, 377, 386–7, 420, 437, 457, 458, 483, 504, 550
differentiated from likeness (*similitudo*) 437
see also enargeia; painting; sculpture; tableaux

imitation (*imitatio*) 295–9, 313, 406, 481, 533
see also example
impersonation (*prosopopoeia*) 340
incredibility 51, 179, 186, 187, 191, 202, 324–5, 358, 367, 494, 515
induction 269, 270, 419, 441, 458, 461, 466, 476, 477, 544, 550, 551
see also empiricism
infamy 150
see also castigation; commemoration; *fama* (reputation); forgetting
Innocent II, pope 415
insinuatio (ephodos) 169, 170–1, 191–3, 196, 210, 213, 415–16
see also prologue
integument or *involucrum* 212, 383, 541
intellectio – see synecdoche
intention 82, 89, 175, 177–8, 181–2, 187, 188, 189, 233–4, 271, 300, 329, 330, 346, 347, 408, 410, 412, 422, 442, 451, 455, 492, 494, 511, 526, 528, 533, 537, 547
ethic of intention 178n
intercessory prayer 65, 147–8
introduction – see prologue
invective (*invectio*) 162, 205, 361, 517, 530, 546
see also castigation; polemic
invention (*inventio*) 19, 265, 266–315, 348, 538
definition of 266
see also argument
Investiture Conflict 114, 254–5, 308
invidia (envy, hostility, ill-will, spite) 30, 43, 51, 198, 201, 202, 288, 499
see also animosity; enmity; hatred
involucrum – see integument
irony 194
Isaiah 62, 67, 162, 402
Isidore of Seville 10, 11n, 12, 15n, 19n, 53, 55, 57n, 63n, 83, 102n, 112n, 122–3, 124n, 126, 133, 137n, 183, 190n, 218, 233n, 305n, 316n, 330, 344n, 345n, 356n, 361, 364n, 371n, 399n, 426, 539
Itinerarium Peregrinarum 150n, 183n, 185n
Ivo of Chartres 37n, 240
see also law, canon

Jacobus de Voragine – see *Golden Legend*

Janus 70, 276
Jeremiah 52, 93, 162, 201, 205, 215n
Jerome 44n, 47, 55, 57n, 58n, 62n, 69, 83, 85, 92, 94, 123, 151, 153n, 198, 269n, 289, 324n, 365, 380–1, 382, 410, 411, 426, 433, 446, 481, 493n, 540
Jerusalem 48, 55, 56, 71, 104, 105, 107, 205, 244, 391, 392, 393, 403n, 405, 406
John XII, pope 114, 196
John of Biclaro 185
John of Garland 13, 123n, 244n, 316n, 338, 360n, 361n, 383n, 396, 436
John of Salerno 67n, 141n, 146–7, 185n, 186, 401
John of Salisbury 8n, 13, 16, 28, 47, 56n, 87n, 124n, 126, 131n, 134n, 152–3, 155, 173n, 226, 253, 276n, 282n, 288n, 307n, 316n, 331, 352n, 354n, 355n, 359n, 363n, 395n, 398n, 408–26, 439, 462, 468n, 493n, 529, 543, 551
Joinville 24n, 254, 290n, 307, 472n
Jordan Fantosme 27n, 438n
Jordanes 257
Joseph of Exeter 183n
Josephus 18, 35, 38, 48–52, 56, 58, 60, 91, 129, 134n, 161, 183, 237–8, 239, 244, 298, 334, 369, 405
see also Hegisippus
judges – *see* audience; law
judicial rhetoric 19, 137, 171–229, 263, 329, 337, 340, 341, 344, 464, 465, 473, 497, 502, 504, 534, 537, 545
three questions (*an sit, quid sit, quale sit*) 179–80, 181, 268–9, 288, 325
what sort of person (*qualis est*) 141–2, 176–7, 181, 197, 201, 218, 497, 537
see also accusation; attributes of events; attributes of person; defence; equity; testimony; will (*testamentum*)
Judith, empress 168, 200, 250
Julianus Africanus 63
Julius Arator 58
Julius Caesar 35, 41, 63n, 66, 76, 130, 131, 177n, 298, 305–6, 313, 341, 405, 454, 472, 488
Julius Victor 10, 12
Junilius Africanus 277, 551

justice 7n, 26, 65, 106, 131, 139, 143, 144, 155, 163, 164, 167, 196, 205, 207, 216, 220, 222, 223, 232, 238, 254, 259, 343, 345, 352, 397, 414, 416, 531
see also equity; God; law; testimony
Justin 36, 37n, 65n, 87, 91, 240n, 494n
Justinian I, emperor 150n, 175n, 185, 369
Juvenal 125, 360, 399n, 522n
Juvencus 58

knowledge (*scientia*) 116, 174, 292, 375, 377, 478, 485, 535
degrees of 93, 98, 230, 270, 289, 293, 294, 295, 353, 354, 376, 412n, 418, 420, 421, 425–6, 427, 439–40, 460, 466–7, 476, 483, 535, 543, 547
differentiated from opinion 293, 320, 354, 355, 356, 373–4, 375, 376, 386, 417–19, 439, 535, 539, 549
limitations on 419–21, 451n
self-knowledge 375, 376, 398, 399, 400–1
'know thyself' 212n, 398n, 399
see also anamnesis; doubt; error; *fides* (belief); induction; opinion; probability; scepticism; sense experience; uncertainty

Lachesis 74n
Lambert of Ardres 255
lamentation 52, 77, 161, 198, 200–1, 206–7, 215
Lampert of Hersfeld 38, 255, 362n
language – *see* anachronism; appropriateness; audience; figures of speech; grammar; imitation; ornamentation; rhetoric; style; tropes; vernacular; vocabulary
Lapo da Castiglionchio 490, 491–2, 493, 494, 495, 496, 500
Last Judgment – *see* Day of Judgment
last times 65, 67
laughter 192
see also humour
Lavinia 213
law 10, 20, 46, 48, 70, 72, 83, 129, 131, 167, 170, 187, 189, 205, 207, 219, 223, 240, 242, 243, 289, 307n, 321, 351, 359, 424–5, 469, 470, 474, 494n, 532, 544

canon law 127–8, 175n, 185, 255n, 381n, 477n
  see also Fourth Lateran Council; Gratian; Ivo of Chartres
common law 175n
law courts 14, 19, 116, 137, 138, 223–4, 229, 465, 470
law of God 49, 51, 55, 155, 247, 248, 307n, 391, 417
  see also God, covenant with
law of history 52, 136, 164, 289, 291, 492, 515
law of poetry 364
law of truth 203
inquest (*inquisitio*) 222–3
judges 9, 97, 112, 116, 149, 167, 170, 171, 173, 191, 192, 193, 227, 228, 303, 309, 318, 322, 324, 325, 326, 328, 329–30, 331, 332, 343, 344, 346, 348, 350, 351, 369, 499
  see also audience
Roman law 150, 174, 175n, 185
  see also Justinian
and lies 344
and sophistry 474
  see also accusation; defence; equity; judicial rhetoric; testimony
legal rhetoric – see judicial rhetoric
letter writing – see ars dictaminis
Liber Eliensis 129n
Liber Pontificalis 148
liberal arts 5, 15, 121, 122, 448, 456
  see also dialectic; grammar; music; rhetoric; *trivium*
lies (*mendacium, mendacia*) 29n, 30, 31, 47n, 51, 74, 76, 99, 114, 115, 123, 173, 174, 185, 187, 200, 206, 211, 219, 223, 228, 231, 234, 236, 237, 291, 292, 339, 342–7, 350, 351, 364, 366–7, 367–8, 369, 374, 377, 379, 380, 381–6, 387, 407–8, 410–11, 417–18, 420, 424, 426, 436, 438, 439, 444, 446, 490, 502, 540–1, 542, 543, 548
  definition of 383–6, 411
  licence to lie (*licentia mentiendi*) 342, 344, 345, 351, 366
  see also fable; falsehood; 'fiction'; poetry
life (*vita*) 90, 142, 143, 145, 156, 157, 176, 196, 226n, 259, 537
  see also deeds (*res gestae*)
Life of Edward [the Confessor] 362n

Life of the Emperor Henry IV 7n, 38n, 42n, 215–18, 240, 280n, 299, 341
Life of Gregory [the Great] 25n
Life of Mathilda 251
likeness (*similitudo*) 29, 245, 326, 327, 328, 437
  see also comparison; example; image
liturgy 25, 82, 84, 146–7, 149, 215n, 310
Liutprand of Cremona 7n, 24, 74n, 81, 147n, 149n, 185, 193–5, 196, 237, 238n, 241n, 244, 251, 280n, 293n, 307n, 328–9, 334–5, 340n, 362
Livy 35, 36, 37, 38, 40n, 66, 87, 91, 100, 106, 123, 125, 129, 130n, 134, 136, 346, 354, 452, 482, 483, 484, 486, 487, 488, 499, 507, 509, 510, 517, 518–19, 532, 545, 546
logic 16, 370, 408–9, 417–18, 439
  definition of 16, 408–9
  see also dialectic
  demonstrative 417–18, 439, 543
  probable 417–18, 439–40, 543
Louis VI, king of France 25, 167, 302
Louis VII, king of France 167
Louis IX, king of France 254
Louis XI, king of France 452, 455
Louis the Pious, king of the Franks, emperor 115n, 166, 168, 198, 200, 221, 250, 334
Lovato Lovati 482
love 100, 104, 116, 177, 192, 195, 213, 410
  see also favour; friendship
Lucan 23, 90n, 119, 125, 129, 130–3, 146, 150n, 177n, 208, 209, 214, 217n, 220, 239, 240, 298–9, 301n, 357, 360, 494, 508–9
Lucian 4, 489, 490–1, 492, 493, 494, 498, 515, 517, 530–1, 532, 533, 545, 547
lucidity – see openness
Luke 57, 62, 63–4, 93, 184, 289, 294, 384, 499
  see also Acts, Book of

Maccabees 53, 56, 62n, 91, 145, 405
Macedonia 69, 71
  see also Alexander the Great; Philip of Macedon

INDEX

Machiavelli 346n, 506–9, 520–3, 524, 525, 528, 530, 533, 534
Macrobius 29n, 37n, 77, 78n, 82n, 130, 153n, 183n, 212n, 241n, 248, 276–7, 281–2, 287n, 293n, 300, 303n, 307n, 318n, 326, 330n, 347n, 368, 373n, 377, 383, 398n, 412–13, 424, 433, 435, 440, 447, 503, 541
Magyars 195, 329
maps 46
   mappae mundi 34
   see also description of place
Marianus Scotus 85, 88, 89
Marie de France 316n, 438n
Marius 42, 45
Marius Victorinus 11n, 15, 124, 127n, 173, 381n, 389, 408, 484
Martial 47
Martianus Capella 10, 12, 29n, 122, 134n, 173n, 190n, 266n, 267n, 305n, 306n, 330n, 337–8, 362, 367, 409
Martin of Tours 156–7
martyrologies 84, 146
marvels (*mirabilia*) 20, 294, 306, 312, 313, 356, 367
Mathilda, queen of Saxony 251
Matteo Palmieri 451
Matthew Paris 21, 449
Matthew of Vendôme 13, 177n, 359n
maxims 38, 56, 117, 119, 155, 159, 245, 262, 287, 314, 399, 467, 524
   see also sententiae
Medici 506, 521, 522, 523, 525, 528
medicine 129, 277, 499
Memmius 42
memorial (*monumentum*) 60, 61, 62, 72, 82, 123, 132, 135, 155, 163, 179, 200, 242, 248, 324, 334
memory 24, 26, 73, 110, 145, 156, 159, 163, 179, 198, 265, 317, 331, 342, 375, 387, 398, 407, 456–7, 539
   as memorisation, mnemonic technique 19–21, 23, 331, 375
   as commemoration (*memoria posteritatis*) 40, 56, 61, 87, 123, 135, 137, 138, 145–6, 149–51, 165, 167, 201, 222, 223, 235, 243, 247, 248, 263–4, 335, 400–1, 537
   as part of prudence, a means of comprehension, reminiscence 98, 276–7, 375–7, 403, 456–7, 539
   as a storehouse or treasury (*thesaurus*) of sense experience 20, 53, 375, 420, 457
   see also deeds, commemoration of; forgetting; memorial; sense experience
Menander 358
mercy 7n, 65, 66, 70, 259, 384
Merlin 279
metaphor (*translatio*) 269, 326, 327, 378, 387, 458
Metellus 42
metonymy 117n
Minos 149
miracles 90, 112, 294, 336, 367
   see also marvels
mirror 155n, 159, 161, 162, 164, 166, 168, 250, 403, 491
mirror-for-princes (*speculum principis*) 153, 168, 249, 464, 471–2, 475, 476, 478, 508n, 530, 537, 544
moral worth – *see honestas*; virtue
Moralium Dogma Philosophorum 7n, 37n, 43n, 99n, 155, 168, 234, 238n, 239–40, 241n, 277n, 366n, 369n
mores (character, conduct) 10, 41, 90, 142n, 143, 151, 190, 197, 200, 259, 265, 321
   see also attributes of person; *ethologia*
Moses 48, 51, 53, 164, 499
motive – *see* intention
Muses 23, 150
   see also Clio
music 22, 23, 122
Mussato, Albertino 482
mutability – *see* world

Naples 497, 505, 526, 546
narrative 4, 9, 21, 22, 32, 86, 88, 94, 95, 123, 135, 141, 181, 265, 299, 315–48, 473, 549
   definition of 315, 320, 321n, 323, 338, 367
   three categories of (*historia, argumentum, fabula*) 316–17, 337–8, 349, 433–4, 449, 456, 541–2
   three virtues of (brevity, openness, credibility) 18, 197, 317, 321, 333, 380, 428, 538
   of events 315–16, 325, 333, 349
   see also deeds, narrative of
   of persons 315–16
   order of (natural *vs* artificial) 299, 300–2, 312, 319, 322

Nature 92, 96, 123, 139, 144, 177, 197, 224, 271, 276n, 285, 312, 319, 320, 325, 326, 333, 337, 338n, 348, 350, 353, 368n, 418, 423, 426, 440, 520, 538, 543
necessity 80, 127, 179, 182, 233, 234, 240, 271, 273, 275, 284, 299, 329, 417, 439, 458, 459, 508, 543
Neckham, Alexander 125, 126, 390n, 422n
necrologies 84, 146, 147, 444
negligence 7n, 218, 323, 431
  see also sloth
Nennius 102n, 306n
Neoplatonism 272, 274, 280, 383, 440, 541
Nero 97, 180
Niccolò Perotti 509, 515, 532
Nicholas V, pope 509, 531
Ninus, king of Assyria 37, 65
Nithard 204n
Normandy 259
Norway 258
notes (*commentarii*) 63, 123, 490
Notker Labeo 12
number, significance of (numerology) 59, 69–70, 97, 112n, 274, 280

oaths 175, 186, 187, 202
  see also testimony, extrinsic
oblivion – *see* forgetting
occasion (*occasio*) 178, 211, 233–4, 237, 299, 407, 413, 512
  see also circumstances; opportunity
occultatio – *see praeteritio*
Octavian (Augustus) 70, 76, 213, 221, 369, 484, 488, 518
Odilo of Cluny 215
Odo of Cheriton 316n
Odo of Cluny 141n, 147, 148, 185, 186, 195–6, 401, 551n
Odo of Deuil 149
omens 49
  see also portents
Onulf of Speyer 12–13
openness 18, 23, 197, 296, 317, 318–19, 331–2, 359, 483, 501
opinion
  as a category of knowledge 46, 113, 128, 291, 293, 294, 336, 354, 355–6, 369, 372–4, 410, 411–12, 417, 418, 420–1, 422, 433, 439, 461, 539, 543, 551

common or popular 284–5, 286, 288, 289, 293, 308–9, 314, 325, 392, 410, 461, 496, 537
  see also fama (common report); *fides* (belief)
opportunity (*opportunitas*) 178, 233n, 319, 320
oratory 8, 99, 133, 135, 136, 172, 224, 351, 353, 501
  see also eloquence
order (*ordo rerum*) 19, 53–4, 60, 65, 71, 74, 75, 80, 82, 88, 93, 94, 95, 96, 97, 102, 108, 111, 112, 114, 117, 130, 136, 143, 146n, 243, 272, 273n, 274, 275, 280, 281, 284, 299–302, 305, 306, 319, 322, 359, 388, 442, 444, 485, 521, 539
  see also disorder; *dispositio*; harmony
Orderic Vitalis 24n, 25, 37, 38n, 49, 81n, 86, 103n, 129n, 134n, 194n, 226, 229n, 252n, 259, 279n, 280, 292n, 341n, 364n, 390n, 403–4, 444
Origen 102, 378
origin myth 257, 496
  see also ethnogenesis
ornamentation 51, 63, 82, 90n, 116, 135, 172, 209, 210, 215, 223, 262, 263, 267, 268, 287, 296, 303, 321, 327, 328, 330, 351, 357, 358, 360, 368, 371, 404, 405, 407, 447, 448, 456, 500
  see also figures of speech; rhetoric; tropes
Orosius 18, 34n, 47, 64–78, 81, 83, 85, 88, 91–2, 101n, 107, 108, 109, 110, 113, 120, 130n, 133, 134n, 181, 222, 239n, 247, 260, 281, 306, 328, 334, 340–1, 369, 389, 453, 514
Osbern of Gloucester 442n
Otto I, emperor 114, 145, 147, 193, 196, 251
Otto II, emperor 225, 251
Otto of Freising 47n, 48, 53n, 56n, 58n, 68n, 69n, 70n, 71n, 74n, 75n, 86n, 107–20, 128, 133n, 147, 149, 155n, 183–4, 193n, 194n, 196n, 241, 255n, 282, 297–8, 308, 318n, 325n, 335, 336, 339n, 341n, 352n, 394n, 411n, 451, 484n
Ovid 26n, 125, 435

Padua 255, 478, 482

painting 34, 126n, 197, 200–1, 216, 311–12, 333–5, 343, 359, 367–8, 422, 470, 491, 492, 493, 504–5
  see also image; rhetoric, colours of; Zeuxis
panegyric (*laudatio*) – *see* encomium
Paolo Cortesi 505n
parable 347, 384, 385, 387, 477
  see also parallel
paradigm 245, 461, 471, 472, 473, 551
  see also example
paradyastole – *see* redescription
paralipomenon 55, 442n
  see also chronicles
parallel (*collatio, parabole*) 326–7, 458, 550
parataxis 444, 445, 452, 548
Paris, schools and university of 16, 126, 311, 408, 440, 453, 478
parrhesia (*licentia*) 195
partiality – *see* favour
particularism – *see* empiricism
Paschasius Radbertus 110n, 131n, 148n, 149n, 151, 166, 185n, 196–208, 215, 240n, 278, 280n, 283n, 317n, 336n, 355n, 391n, 400n, 529
passio 222
Paul, apostle 57, 63, 378, 380, 381, 382, 386, 390, 394, 400, 540
Paul the Deacon 23, 36, 58n, 148, 219, 247n, 258, 306, 334, 336, 362
peace 26, 39, 66, 104, 106, 107, 132, 167, 181, 205, 207, 213, 216, 223, 235, 248, 259, 453, 469, 488, 518, 522
  pax Augusta 70–1
Persia 69, 100, 307n
  see also Babylon
Persius 360
personification (*conformatio*) 340–1
persuasion 8, 10, 23, 63, 99, 170, 179, 192, 197, 230, 239, 242, 244, 245, 246, 248, 251, 263, 287, 308, 320, 323, 326, 329, 331, 338, 352, 371, 379, 387, 412, 414, 419, 459n, 461, 466, 470, 471, 473, 475, 480, 484, 540, 544
Peter of Abano 478
Peter of Blois 133–4, 415n
Peter Damian 448–9
Peter Lombard 278n
Peter of Spain 458n
Peter Tudebode 256

Peter the Venerable 431
Petrarch 16, 151, 318n, 480–4, 486, 487, 489, 492, 496, 503, 545
Petrus Comestor 430n, 438–9
Petrus Helias 408
Philip IV, king of France 254
Philip of Macedon 68, 74, 76
philology 430, 496–7, 502, 503–4, 505, 529, 531, 534, 545
Pier Candido Decembrio 509–10
Pier Paolo Vergerio 485n
pity 22, 43, 283, 330, 331, 332, 514
plagae 58, 67, 81, 92, 109, 163, 252–3, 260
  see also God, chastisement by; God, punishment by
Plato 93, 273n, 274, 276n, 307, 345, 366, 373, 374, 446–7
  see also Neoplatonism
plausibility – *see* credibility; verisimilitude
Plautus 364
pleasure 9, 23, 37n, 78, 87, 118, 119, 125, 129, 143, 161, 164, 172, 194, 201, 203, 227, 228, 243, 263, 287, 297, 304, 305, 307, 308, 309, 315, 321, 347, 348, 353–4, 355, 357, 358, 363, 371, 380, 385, 414, 477, 483, 485–6, 490, 501, 513, 541
  combined with utility 87, 88, 311, 483, 490, 492, 498, 506, 514–15, 522, 545, 546
pleonasm 186
Pliny the Elder 150, 306, 313, 460
Pliny the Younger 306n, 501
Plutarch 481, 484, 487n, 492n, 495, 545
poetics 360n
poetry 14, 22, 23–4, 57, 122, 165, 292, 324, 337, 340, 347, 357–61, 363–5, 385, 432, 434, 435, 448, 458–9, 479, 482, 490, 493, 532
  as lies 364, 368, 434–5, 439
  as moral instruction 125–6, 129, 133, 481, 482
  as painting 335, 359
  as pleasure 357, 358, 359, 532
  as prophecy 23, 132
    see also vates
  different types of 209, 361
  mixed with prose (*prosimetrum*) 56, 117, 435
  relationship to history-writing 124, 126, 128, 129, 133, 311, 360, 434

relationship to philosophy 383, 458–9, 498, 541, 546
relationship to rhetoric 22, 324, 357–60, 434–5
studied as part of grammar 122, 124, 128, 360, 434
suited to children 126, 362
utility of 359–60, 481–2
see also comedy; epic; fable; satire, tragedy; verse
poets 25, 76, 124, 125, 126, 129n, 130, 133, 165, 271, 285, 286, 287, 296, 324, 338, 340, 357–8, 360, 361, 362n, 363, 364, 386n, 444, 450, 458, 494, 498, 499, 500, 516, 542, 544, 548
see also Homer; Horace; Lucan; Ovid; Statius; *vates*; Vergil
Poggio Bracciolini 486, 488, 489n, 490, 502, 521, 522, 523
Poland 258
polemic 64, 67, 101, 105, 134, 254, 488
see also invective
Politian (Poliziano) 503
Polybius 35, 150, 509–17, 519, 520, 526, 532–3, 534, 546–7
Pompeius Trogus 36, 37, 65n, 66, 69, 87, 91, 125, 134n, 515
Pompey (Pomeius Magnus) 130, 131, 177n, 239, 240
Pontano, Giovanni 505–6, 529
Porphyry 99, 105, 127
portents 49, 72, 90, 132, 284
see also omens
posterity 24, 31, 43, 45, 50, 68, 117, 132, 135, 150, 151, 156, 158, 159, 160, 165, 196, 198, 207, 210, 249, 263, 291, 292, 364, 446, 485, 491, 501, 517–18
remembrance by (*memoria posteritatis*) 61, 87, 135, 138, 145, 151, 167, 222, 235, 243, 247, 248, 263–4, 537
postmodernism 33n, 549n
practicability 233, 236, 237, 240, 455, 508, 521, 533
see also utility
praeteritio (*occultatio*) 7, 117n, 206
praise 9, 23, 24, 44, 51, 74, 76, 115, 137, 138, 140–1, 143, 144, 151, 156, 165, 166, 172, 198, 203, 209, 227, 242, 249, 262, 305, 308, 402, 454, 464, 472, 483, 490, 493, 499, 536
see also demonstrative rhetoric; *encomium*; flattery

preaching – *see ars praedicandi*; sermons; homilies
preface – *see* prologue
pride 39, 41, 42, 45, 68, 70, 101, 104, 105, 194, 205, 248, 400, 401, 448
Priscian 7n, 138n, 142n, 287n, 316n, 333n, 337–8, 340n
probability 325, 417–19, 439
see also credibility; opinion; verisimilitude
proemium – *see* prologue
prolepsis (*praeoccupatio*) 494
prolixity 5, 211, 318, 501
prologue (*exordium*) 28, 50, 60, 62, 108, 112, 114, 118, 119, 156, 157, 160, 161, 164, 185, 190, 192n, 209, 227, 246, 265, 295–6, 299, 300, 538
guidelines for composition of 140–1, 168–71
three goals of (attentiveness; goodwill; teachability) 169, 190–1
different types of 39n
proemium differentiated from *insinuatio* 169, 191–2, 196, 304, 415–16
pronuntiatio – *see* delivery
proof (*probatio, confirmatio*) 9, 135, 175n, 265, 288, 289, 320, 428, 460, 500
see also argument; evidence; testimony
prophecy 49, 56, 57–8, 62, 91, 98n, 105, 132, 162, 205, 276–80, 312, 365, 383n, 386, 421, 540
see also dreams; providence, foresight
prophets 23, 50, 54, 55, 97, 162–3, 277–8, 314, 363, 399, 444, 453
see also Isaiah; Jeremiah; *vates*
propositions condemned in 1277 440
proverbs – *see* maxims; *sententiae*
providence (*providentia*)
definitions of 276
divine 65, 67, 69, 70, 79–80, 92, 94, 95n, 96–7, 98, 106, 109, 111, 118, 223, 272, 274–5, 277, 280, 281–2, 283–4, 314, 388, 390n, 403, 416–17, 420, 421, 422, 423, 431, 444, 452, 453, 526, 540
active differentiated from permissive 92, 96–7, 111, 280, 282, 431, 540
foresight 244, 248, 271, 276–7, 278, 279, 377
see also prophecy; prudence

prudence 243–4, 276–7, 278, 344,
    377, 419, 420–1, 457, 494n, 499,
    518, 520
  see also knowledge; memory;
    providence, foresight; virtue;
    wisdom
pseudo-Augustine 171n, 197n
pseudo-Cicero – *see Rhetorica ad
    Herennium*
Punic Wars 40, 41, 68, 97, 509, 516n
  see also Carthage; Hannibal; Scipio
    Africanus
punishment – *see* God
purgatio 182–3
  see also defence; *remotio criminis*

Quintilian 6, 7, 8, 9–10, 11, 12, 14,
    17, 18, 19, 20, 21, 22, 23, 27, 28,
    29, 39, 47, 87n, 124, 125–6, 128,
    130, 134–5, 135–6, 138, 139, 142,
    143–4, 151, 154–5, 169, 170, 171,
    172, 173, 176, 177, 178, 179–80,
    182, 183, 186, 187, 188, 189–91,
    195, 229, 230, 234, 236, 242, 243,
    244, 245–6, 249, 262–3, 266, 269,
    270–1, 284, 286–7, 288–9, 295–6,
    296–7, 299, 300–1, 302–3, 303–4,
    305, 308–9, 315, 316, 317, 318,
    319, 320, 321–2, 323–4, 327, 330,
    331, 332–3, 337, 339, 340, 341,
    342–7, 348, 350, 351, 353, 354,
    356, 358–9, 360–1, 366, 368, 369,
    371, 384, 388, 408, 409, 414, 426,
    428, 439, 446n, 458, 476, 489,
    492, 499, 501, 502, 505, 532, 536
  transmission of 6, 12, 14, 502n
  Institutio Oratoria 6, 7, 8, 9–10, 12,
    14, 17, 18, 19, 20, 21, 22, 23, 27,
    28, 29, 39n, 47, 87n, 124, 125,
    126, 128, 130, 134, 135, 136, 138,
    139, 142, 143, 144, 151, 154, 155,
    169, 170, 171, 172, 173, 176, 177,
    178, 179, 180, 182, 183, 186, 187,
    188, 189, 190, 191, 195, 229, 230,
    234, 236, 242, 243, 244, 245, 246,
    249, 262, 263, 266, 269, 270, 271,
    284, 286, 287, 288, 289, 295, 296,
    297, 299, 300, 301, 302, 303, 304,
    305, 308, 309, 315, 316, 317, 318,
    319, 320, 321, 322, 323, 324, 327,
    330, 331, 332, 333, 337, 339, 340,
    341, 342, 343, 344, 345, 346, 347,
    348, 350, 351, 353, 354, 356, 358,
    360, 361, 366, 368, 369, 371, 384,
    388, 408, 409, 414, 426, 428, 439,
    446n, 458, 476, 489, 492, 499,
    501, 502, 505, 532, 536
Quintus Curtius 125, 134n

Rahewin 24n, 38, 41n, 43n, 49, 50n,
    52n, 116n, 150, 186n, 219–20,
    234n, 238n, 298, 304–5, 335,
    426–7
Rainald of Dassel 109, 115, 118
Ralph de Diceto 20, 39n, 55n, 87, 89,
    134n, 160n, 161n, 240n, 279n,
    306n, 307, 313n, 317n, 318n,
    443, 445
Ranulf Higden 307, 325n, 425n, 449
Rationes Dictandi 169, 217n, 301
Raymond of Aguilers 256
reason (*ratio*) 75, 82, 95, 112, 114,
    177, 189, 195, 216, 221, 245, 267,
    273n, 274, 319, 346, 395n, 397,
    413n, 421, 446n, 451, 468, 511,
    512, 515, 518, 524, 525, 528, 534,
    540
  account (*reddere rationem*) 112, 114,
    148, 150
  see also causation; intention; order
redescription (paradyastole, *distinctio*)
    7, 72, 131, 180–1, 206–7, 323, 344
refutatio 265, 500
Reginald of Canterbury 365
Regino of Prüm 29n, 445–6
Regulus (Marcus Attilius) 110, 155
relief (*recreatio*) 109n, 194, 305, 307,
    358
remembrance – *see* memory
reminiscence – *see* memory
remotio criminis (displacement of
    accusation) 181, 218, 323
  see also defence; *purgatio*
'Renaissance' 429, 441, 442, 479–80,
    481, 495, 497, 503, 506, 547
  sense of the past 503–5
re-presentation – *see enargeia*
reputation – *see fama*
res gestae – *see* deeds
res publica ('republic') 40, 41, 42, 44,
    82, 100, 115, 130, 176, 181, 191,
    229, 231, 243, 248, 255, 298, 307,
    321, 488, 506, 507, 508, 519, 520,
    521, 522, 523
  definitions of 100
retribution – *see* God
Revelation, Book of 54, 57–8, 69, 85,
    91

revolution 282
see also world, mutability of
rhetoric
  definitions of 6, 8, 9–11
  three functions of (*docere, movere, delectare*) 1, 8–9, 143, 151, 295, 304, 353–4, 371–2, 480–1, 483, 506, 536
  three categories of (demonstrative, judicial, deliberative) 19, 137–8, 484, 536, 545
  five aspects of (*inventio, dispositio, elocutio, memoria, pronuntiatio*) 19, 265, 367
  six parts of (*exordium, narratio, divisio* or *partitio, confirmatio, confutatio* or *refutatio, conclusio* or *peroratio*) 265
  colours of 13n, 116, 187, 223, 263, 311, 366, 367, 368n, 447, 493, 500
  comprehensive scope of 8, 9–11, 243, 321, 414
  flowers of 88, 169n, 311
  manuals of 4, 10–11, 21, 28, 140, 169, 172, 239, 263, 295, 314, 317, 349, 350, 357, 366, 456, 457, 507, 538, 541
  utility of 350–1
  as an art 8, 9, 355–6
  as the mother of history (*mater historiae*) 500
  relationship to grammar 6n, 8, 15–16, 121, 434
  relationship to dialectic 9, 15–16, 460–3, 465, 474–5, 478
  relationship to poetry 22, 324, 357–60, 434–5
  relationship to political thought 229, 414, 461, 462
  practised through writing 27, 296
  schoolroom exercises 14–15, 296, 315, 340, 358
  concealment of artifice 28, 172, 190, 337, 447
  dangers of 344–5, 366, 371–2, 447–9, 479
  and the Bible 370–2, 381
  see also eloquence; language; oratory; ornamentation; wisdom
Rhetorica ad Herennium 6, 7, 8, 14, 15, 17, 19, 20, 22, 28, 29, 125, 138, 139, 140, 141, 142, 143, 166, 169, 170, 171, 172, 176, 182–3, 187, 189, 191, 192, 193, 195, 215n, 230, 231, 232, 234–5, 237, 243, 244, 245, 262, 266, 267, 285–6, 287, 300, 303, 305, 315–17, 318, 319, 321, 324, 326–8, 330, 331, 332, 335, 339, 340, 358, 360, 369, 378, 408, 428, 435, 458, 464, 476, 489, 500, 508n, 509n, 536
  transmission of 6
Richard of Devizes 78n, 81n, 109n, 128, 279, 299, 365, 386n, 435n
Richard FitzNigel – *see Dialogus de Scaccario*
Richer of Rheims 28n, 37, 306n, 360, 445
Robert of Basevorn 154, 305n, 345n, 394n, 395n
Robert the Monk 53n, 256
Robert of Torigni 240n, 259
Roger of Howden 279n
Roger of Wendover 449
romance 432, 436, 437, 449
Rome 39, 40, 44, 64, 68, 69, 71, 72, 76, 92, 94, 100, 101, 108, 115, 131, 150, 155, 180, 217, 232, 243, 328, 412, 484, 487, 488, 496, 509, 515, 518, 520, 523, 524, 525, 532, 546
  providential role of 69, 70, 79
  sack of (410) 64, 66, 67, 70, 103, 496
Rufinus [of Antioch] 357n
Rufinus [of Aquileia] 59, 77, 109n
Rufinus [of Bologna] 352n
rumour 185n, 203, 206, 212, 218, 285–6, 288, 293, 314, 353, 354, 453, 519
  see also fama (common report)
Rupert of Deutz 47n
rusticity 28n, 115n, 116, 193, 297, 309, 394
  see also style

saga 27, 450
Saint-Denis, abbey of 25, 258
saints' days 84
  see also feast days
saints' lives – *see* hagiography
Salimbene 134n
Sallust 3, 18, 35, 37–8, 38–47, 49, 50, 62, 65, 66, 68, 87, 91, 100, 111, 123, 124–5, 126, 129, 130, 132, 134, 135, 152, 155n, 166, 167n, 168n, 180, 209, 210, 212, 216, 219, 237, 248, 261, 292, 298, 305, 307, 318, 336, 364n, 369, 395,

452, 453, 483, 487, 488, 499, 501,
    509, 517, 518–19, 545, 546
Salutati, Coluccio 151, 154n, 372n,
    463, 484–6, 487, 489, 492, 498,
    532, 545
Salvian of Marseille 447–8
sapientia – *see* wisdom
Sarapis 276
satire 125, 129, 361, 415n, 500, 533
    see also Horace; Juvenal; Persius
Saxo Grammaticus 258
scepticism 354–5, 372–4, 387, 422–4,
    528, 551
schema – *see* figures of speech
Scipio Africanus 238, 481, 488
Scotland 246, 257
scourge – *see* God, chastisement by;
    plagae
Scripture 83, 107, 112, 127, 160, 163,
    279, 362, 363, 369, 371, 377,
    380–1
    four senses of (history, tropology,
        anagogy, allegory) 378–9, 393,
        399, 403, 429, 430
    textual criticism of 5, 93–4, 127,
        390, 410, 497
    see also Bible; exegesis; *Glossa
        Ordinaria*
sculpture 34, 150, 248, 359, 491, 504
    see also image
Sedulius 58
Sedulius Scottus 393n
selectivity 64, 89, 149, 167, 301–2,
    318, 322–3
    see also brevity; digest; silence;
        summary
self-knowledge – *see* knowledge
Seneca the Elder 15, 168, 169n, 345,
    367n, 482n
Seneca (Lucius Annaeus) 47n, 77,
    99n, 124n, 155, 201, 202, 204,
    239, 273n, 312, 367, 412n, 481,
    482n
    see also Disticha Catonis; Stoicism
sense experience 373, 374, 375, 376,
    386–7, 418, 420, 460, 539
    past sensibles 374, 421, 539
    see also eyewitness; hearsay
sententiae 30, 46, 78, 117, 125, 132,
    287, 288, 358, 453, 471, 501, 518,
    524, 533
    see also maxims
sermocinatio 339–40, 341, 516
    see also speeches

sermons 14, 372, 393, 394, 399, 402
    see also ars praedicandi; homilies
Servius 78n, 130, 133, 212n, 338n,
    349n, 435, 456
Sicily 76, 258
Sidonius Apollinaris 29n, 125, 168,
    293n
Sigebert of Gembloux 47n, 85, 134n,
    416
sign (*figura*) 58, 67, 85, 92, 95, 96, 104,
    180, 182, 215n, 288, 289, 325,
    370, 374, 380
    see also event (occurrence), pre-
        figurative
significatio (emphasis) 29
signification 59, 66, 67, 69, 70, 71,
    77, 81n, 95, 106, 114, 132, 249,
    328, 339, 347, 378, 379, 380, 382,
    384–5, 386, 387–8, 390, 391, 397,
    406, 421, 429, 430, 477, 539, 540,
    541
    see also allegory; anagogy; tropology
silence 31, 42, 43, 118, 145, 146, 149,
    158, 186, 187, 199, 203, 211, 216,
    248, 300, 323, 446, 517
    see also forgetting (*oblivio*)
simile 326, 458
    see also example; metaphor
similitudo – *see* likeness
simplicitas 7n, 323
Sinon 212n, 238n
sixth age – *see* world, ages of
sloth 39, 41, 44, 45, 62, 68, 191, 194,
    197, 203, 248, 363, 401, 431
    see also negligence
Snorri Sturluson 165, 218–19
Sodom 48, 67
solace – *see* consolation
Solinus 47n, 125, 306n, 447
Solomon 53, 55, 56, 472
soothsaying (*haruspices*) 72, 94,
    279–80
sophistry 116, 368, 372, 417–18, 439,
    465, 474, 543, 551
    see also law; logic
Spain (Iberian peninsula) 258n
speculum principis – *see* mirror-for-
    princes
speeches 38, 40, 42, 46, 49, 87, 119,
    132, 135, 167, 305, 322, 340, 341,
    354, 392, 487, 491, 492, 497, 499,
    500, 515, 518, 527, 547
    see also sermocinatio
spite – *see invidia*

Statius 57n, 125, 129, 130n, 299, 360, 364
statues – *see* sculpture
Stephen, king of England 252, 253, 341
Stoicism 132, 271, 272, 273n, 346, 385n
  see also Seneca (Lucius Annaeus)
strategy 238, 455
  see also counsel; guile
studium – *see* commitment
style (*elocutio*) 6–7, 19, 90–1, 116, 119, 135, 199, 265, 295–8, 303, 312–13, 316, 319, 337, 340, 359, 371, 404–5, 470, 486, 491, 504
  plain or straightforward 119, 211, 295, 297–8, 365, 394, 396, 404
  mixed or intermediate 199, 295–6
  grand 295, 298, 365
  see also rusticity
Suetonius 35, 37, 38, 66, 91, 125, 134n, 221, 298, 452
Suger of Saint-Denis 25–6, 38, 146n, 147n, 148, 167, 185n, 233n, 241n, 278n, 279n, 302, 308, 310, 318n, 335, 336, 341, 397n
Sulpicius Severus 115n, 156–7, 157–8, 193n, 209, 212, 362, 447
summary 46, 55, 60, 84n, 86, 317, 318n, 322, 331, 443, 446
  see also brevity; digest
Svein, king of England 209, 213
syllogism 270, 287, 304, 352, 419, 458n, 461, 467, 468, 551
  see also dialectic; enthymeme
synecdoche (*intellectio*) 7, 117n, 183, 194

tableaux 34, 334, 335n
  see also image; painting; theatre
Tacitus 29n, 35, 66, 87, 134n, 150, 180–1, 509, 517–20, 526, 533
teachability (*docilis*) 169, 170, 190, 191, 197, 227–8, 367, 491
temperance 39, 139, 143, 155, 164, 241
Temple of Jerusalem 48, 55, 56, 61, 391
Terence 31, 155n, 194n, 201, 347, 358, 360, 364
testimony 50, 60, 67, 94, 136, 148, 172, 174–5, 182–4, 196, 202, 242, 244–5, 284–7, 314, 324, 335, 428, 458, 473, 476, 486, 499, 500, 537, 538
  extrinsic 175, 182–93, 406
  intrinsic 406, 268–71
  see also causation
  human 175, 182–7, 218–19, 284
  documentary 175, 182, 187–9, 219, 284, 289, 291–2
  see also argument; documentation; eyewitness; hearsay; oaths
textual criticism 93–4, 126–7
  see also Accessus ad Auctores; Scripture
theatre 22, 68
  see also actors; tableaux
Thegan 200n
Theodoricus Monachus 258
Theodosius I, emperor 23n, 79, 105, 199–200
Thierry of Chartres 15n, 338, 408, 433, 436
Thietmar of Merseburg 7, 26n, 39n, 81n, 145, 147–8, 148–9, 163–4, 167n, 178n, 184n, 185, 186n, 187, 195n, 196n, 224–5, 237, 238n, 241n, 247n, 251, 260, 280n, 282, 293n, 294n, 299, 307, 311n, 322n, 341n, 398n, 551
Thomas Basin 43n, 168n, 452
Thucydides 35, 82, 134, 491, 498, 501, 509, 510, 532, 533, 546, 547
time 94, 98, 178–9, 182, 276, 375–6, 422, 549
  sequence of 53, 83, 94, 101, 136, 280, 388, 442, 444, 478, 539
  past, present and future 98, 110, 276, 353, 375–6
  see also calendar; chronography; chronology; history; world, ages of
Titus 50, 71, 256, 334, 405
topics 266, 267–8, 314, 320, 348, 409
  common topics ('commonplaces') 268, 281, 283, 314, 329, 348, 368, 538
  see also argument; invention
topography – *see* description of place
torpor – *see* sloth
tragedy 52, 109, 110n, 118, 129, 194n, 316, 361, 403, 500, 514, 515–16, 517, 546
Trajan 424, 472, 520
transitio 244n
translatio imperii – *see* empire
Trevet, Nicholas 482n

trivium (grammar, rhetoric, dialectic) 5, 15–16
  see also liberal arts
tropes 6–8, 29, 116n, 117, 311, 363n, 389, 500
  see also figures of speech; ornamentation; rhetoric, colours of
tropology 249, 378, 393, 394, 397–8, 429, 430
Troy 57n, 183, 256, 257, 334, 405
truth 9, 29n, 30, 31, 43, 47, 51, 52, 62, 76, 87, 89, 90, 96, 112, 114, 115, 116, 133, 136, 146n, 158, 163, 170, 175n, 185, 195, 197, 202, 203, 207, 210, 219, 220, 222, 223, 288, 293, 294, 301, 316, 325, 331, 349, 353, 355, 368, 371–2, 387, 390, 415, 425, 435, 540–1, 543, 551
  necessary 288, 417–18, 439, 543
  degrees of 46, 93, 98, 172, 230, 270, 287, 288, 289, 293, 294, 295, 353, 354, 376, 412n, 418, 420, 421, 425–6, 427, 439–40, 460, 466–7, 476, 483, 535, 543, 547
  likeness of (*similitudo veri*) – *see* verisimilitude
  differentiated from opinion 411–12, 417–18, 439
  incredibility of 186, 324n
  dangers of 29, 30, 32, 43, 45, 73, 183, 195, 199–200, 201, 203, 216–17, 224, 228–9, 446, 491, 499, 519, 522
  laws of 31, 203
  light of (*lux veritatis*) 149, 174, 242, 312, 499
  faces of 551
  multiplication of 96, 390
  and eloquence 447
  and history-writing 51, 165, 173, 183, 293, 312, 313
  and justice 205–6, 304
    see also prophecy
  veiled or covered 212, 383, 541
  mixed with falsehood 31, 211, 212, 217, 359, 364, 425
  the daughter of time 30
  the mother of hatred 30–1
Turgot 187
tyranny 29, 42, 50, 61, 80, 97, 101, 131, 162, 180, 205, 210, 217, 218, 253, 255, 259, 346, 423, 470, 519, 520

uncertainty 113, 283, 293, 354, 421, 529, 551
  see also doubt; God, inscrutability of; knowledge, degrees of; opinion; scepticism; truth, degrees of
universal history – *see* history-writing
utility (advantage, expediency, *utilitas*, *utile*) 10, 20, 44, 45, 61, 96, 98, 99, 127, 133, 153, 162, 215, 230–2, 234, 239–40, 241, 250, 323, 351–2, 370, 381, 414, 415, 447–8, 455, 464, 469, 484, 490, 491, 492, 493, 495, 498, 506, 509, 512, 516, 519, 520, 531, 532, 533, 534, 540
  definition of 230
  paired with moral worth (*honestum et utile*) 230, 231, 232–3, 234, 235, 237, 240–1, 246, 252, 263, 329, 365n, 367, 415n, 425, 507–8
  differentiated from moral worth 236, 239–40, 342, 508
  paired with pleasure 87, 88, 311, 483, 490, 492, 498, 506, 514–15, 522, 545, 546
  see also counsel; dissimulation; guile; lies; necessity; practicability; strategy

Valerius Maximus 7n, 9n, 23, 36–7, 40n, 44n, 47n, 109n, 130n, 141n, 150, 150–1, 152, 155n, 173n, 232, 234, 238, 253, 271n, 282n, 331n, 333–4, 426, 452, 482, 494n, 533
Valla, Lorenzo 495n, 496–502, 503, 504, 505, 509, 529, 532, 533, 545–6, 551
vates 23, 132, 277, 279
  see also poets; prophets
Varro 99–100
Venantius Fortunatus 168n, 362
Vergerio – *see* Pier Paolo Vergerio
Vergil 7n, 23, 39n, 46n, 57n, 71, 76, 77–8, 88, 90, 99–100, 115, 119, 125, 129, 130, 131n, 149, 150, 151–2, 183, 186n, 209, 212, 213, 216, 230n, 234, 237n, 238n, 241, 257, 277, 281, 293, 301n, 307n, 318n, 334, 340, 346, 347, 357n, 360, 361, 364, 368, 383n, 434–5, 451, 481, 484, 494
verisimilitude 19, 188, 292, 315, 316, 317, 319–21, 324, 325, 329, 332, 333, 336, 344, 345, 348–9, 350, 373–4, 424, 432, 433, 436–7, 439,

440, 449, 456, 459, 500, 502, 515, 516, 529, 534, 535, 538, 540, 542–3, 544, 546, 548, 550
definitions of 412n
synonymous with probable or plausible argument 19, 63, 265, 266, 268, 315, 316–17, 319, 324, 337–8, 339, 349, 352, 356, 369, 426, 433, 436, 495, 548
see also hypothesis
vernacular 14, 27, 37, 79, 192n, 209, 251, 255, 258, 261–2, 432, 437, 450, 451, 452, 463, 467, 486, 506n
see also chansons de geste; romance; saga
verse 14, 22, 58, 146, 159, 193, 203, 296, 316, 358, 360, 447, 458, 501, 542
and prose (*prosimetrum*) 296, 358, 360
and history-writing 27, 34, 117, 129–30, 132, 261–2, 361–3, 405, 432, 438, 439, 450
see also poetry
Vespasian 50, 71, 256
Vespasiano da Bisticci 492n
vice 7, 9, 40, 41, 45, 50, 125, 129, 139–43, 151, 161, 163, 164–5, 170, 175, 193, 200, 205, 242, 260, 263, 344, 358, 361n, 363, 395, 397, 400, 414, 423, 464, 483, 484, 485, 486, 494n
see also avarice; Babylon; castigation; curiosity; Gomorrah; infamy; negligence; pride; sloth; Sodom; theatre; tyranny
Villani, Giovanni 130n, 450, 486
Vincent of Beauvais 11n, 19n, 88, 124n, 242n, 276n, 315n, 316n, 317n, 345n, 472n, 478
vir bonus dicendi peritus 10, 344–5, 347, 465, 481
virtue 7, 41, 42, 43, 44, 45, 50, 56, 68, 72, 100, 101, 110, 118, 125, 129, 131, 138–40, 140–5, 149, 150, 151, 156, 159–61, 163, 164–5, 170, 175, 190, 191, 193, 198, 201, 206, 207, 230, 231, 232, 236, 237, 239, 240, 241, 242, 243, 246, 263, 284, 288, 308, 344, 345, 359, 361n, 366n, 397, 401, 402, 414, 423, 464–5, 466, 467, 468, 469, 470, 475, 483, 484, 485–6, 487,
488, 493, 498, 508, 510, 511, 517–19, 521, 522, 524, 531, 545
definition of 139
four cardinal (wisdom or prudence, bravery, justice, temperance) 133, 139, 143, 155, 164, 230, 239, 241, 252, 469
different categories of 144–5
commemoration of 483
see also honestas; praise; redescription
vividness 38, 327, 328, 329–30
see also enargeia
vocabulary 19, 296, 297, 312, 357, 358, 359, 445, 501, 503–4
see also language; style

Wace 27n, 262
Wala 196, 198–208
Walsingham, Thomas 449
Walter of Châtillon 72n, 74n, 152n, 334n, 493n
Walter Map 7n, 90n, 149n, 153n, 238n, 307n, 349n, 359n, 373n, 376n, 386n, 415n, 431n, 493n
wealth – *see* avarice
weaving 31, 70, 74–5, 108, 111, 117, 120, 135–6, 143, 198, 211, 212n, 243, 267, 273, 275, 283, 302, 349n, 368, 449
see also Clotho
Wibald of Stavelot 345n
Widukind of Corvey 37, 38, 113n, 131n, 141n, 147, 193n, 238n, 241, 258, 292n, 294n, 307n, 310n
will (*testamentum*) 134, 187, 189, 220–1, 251, 284, 329–30, 497, 504, 537, 545
will (*voluntas*) – *see* freedom of the will; intention
William I, king of England, 'the Conqueror' 176, 227–8, 259, 298, 341, 364, 365, 403, 404, 414n
William II, king of England, 'Rufus' 38n, 228–9, 298
William of Apulia 258
William of Conches 338n
William FitzStephen 306–7
William of Jumièges 25n, 29n, 90n, 259, 290n, 306n, 365n
William of Malmesbury 2n, 7n, 29–30, 37, 38, 39n, 46n, 47n, 49n, 56n, 75n, 78n, 81n, 88–9, 128n, 131n, 146n, 147n, 152, 161, 169n, 173, 187, 202n, 226–9, 246, 252, 256,

282, 290–1, 291–4, 297, 298, 299n, 301–2, 308, 310, 318n, 322n, 323n, 335–6, 341n, 344n, 345n, 354n, 361n, 368, 384n, 405n
William of Newburgh 2, 57n, 283n, 365–6, 438, 543
William of Poitiers 38, 63n, 176n, 259, 298, 341, 364–5
William of Tyre 24, 30–1, 88n, 148n, 256, 335
Wipo 7, 24n, 37, 44n, 53, 71n, 159–60, 166–7, 168, 184n, 240, 244, 246, 248, 318n, 341n, 397
wisdom (*sapientia*) 10, 194, 238
   and eloquence 10, 16, 116, 130, 229, 246, 313, 344–5, 352, 366, 371, 389, 409, 465, 480
   see also vir bonus dicendi peritus
   see also knowledge; prudence; truth
wit (*facetia*) 193, 194
witness (*index, testis*) – *see* testimony, human
word-play – *see adnominatio*
world (*mundus, saeculum*)
   ages of 102–3, 307n, 369
     sixth age of (old age, *senectus mundi*) 85, 104, 110, 200, 444, 540
   mutability of 70, 80, 107, 108, 109, 111, 114, 117, 118, 132, 182, 233, 275, 277, 281, 282, 283, 316, 375, 420, 521
   contempt for 109, 111
   monarchies – *see* empire
   history of – *see* history-writing

youth 23, 58, 125, 126, 168, 383, 466, 467, 468, 516, 542

Zeuxis 197, 201, 205, 311